Financial Risk Management

An End User Perspective

Financial
Risk
Management

An End User Perspective

Don M. Chance
Louisiana State University, USA

World Scientific

NEW JERSEY · LONDON · SINGAPORE · BEIJING · SHANGHAI · HONG KONG · TAIPEI · CHENNAI · TOKYO

Published by

World Scientific Publishing Co. Pte. Ltd.

5 Toh Tuck Link, Singapore 596224

USA office: 27 Warren Street, Suite 401-402, Hackensack, NJ 07601

UK office: 57 Shelton Street, Covent Garden, London WC2H 9HE

Library of Congress Cataloging-in-Publication Data

Names: Chance, Don M., author.

Title: Financial risk management : an end user perspective / Don M. Chance
   (Louisiana State University, USA).

Description: New Jersey : World Scientific, [2019] | Includes bibliographical references and index.

Identifiers: LCCN 2019018769| ISBN 9789811201837 | ISBN 9789811202674 (pbk.)

Subjects: LCSH: Financial risk. | Financial risk management.

Classification: LCC HB615 .C528 2019 | DDC 658.15/5--dc23

LC record available at https://lccn.loc.gov/2019018769

British Library Cataloguing-in-Publication Data

A catalogue record for this book is available from the British Library.

For any available supplementary material, please visit
https://www.worldscientific.com/worldscibooks/10.1142/11321#t=suppl

Desk Editor: Shreya Gopi

Typeset by Stallion Press
Email: enquiries@stallionpress.com

Printed in Singapore

Preface

The origins of this book go back to somewhere in the mid-1990s, when I was teaching at Virginia Tech and had been offering courses in derivatives pricing. I began to realize that the typical finance student was not going to become a financial engineer. I sensed that what was missing in graduate education in finance was a book written for the end user, or buy side, which is the entity that would purchase risk management services from a bank or dealer, which is the sell side. There was really no course or textbook that I could find that would meet this need. So, I created a course, which was based on a practitioner book called *Managing Financial Risk* by Charles Smithson. *MFR* is really an excellent book but it is oriented toward the practitioner and not the student. I used the book for many years, through at least one revision and then it began to get a bit outdated, so with some sadness, I dropped it and taught the course from my own notes. Well, as is often the case, notes morph into a book, and this book is the result of that evolution.

I class-tested the book in manuscript form for several years and then approached World Scientific about publishing it. WSP publishes many books on derivatives and risk management, but I believe this book is unique in its focus on the end user. I appreciate WSP's foresight to see the potential.

Many people deserve far more than a note of thanks but a note is about all I can give them. I would like to thank my graduate students at LSU for putting up with the manuscript form of this book and for their comments and suggestions. In particular, I would like to thank Brandt Green for many helpful comments and corrections and for doing the index.

I would also like to thank Bob Brooks, with whom I have collaborated on another book and several articles. He assisted me with some final edits. I would also like to thank my wife, Jan, for her help in editing. Finally, I appreciate the work of my editor, Shreya Gopi of World Scientific, for seeing the potential of this book and for her careful edits and excellent coordination during the process.

I accept responsibility for all errors. Please email me with any corrections, or comments in general, at dchance@lsu.edu.

Don Chance, PhD, CFA
Louisiana State University
Baton Rouge, LA, USA

Contents

Symbols Used in this Book

Letter/Symbol	Definition	Chapters
A		
A_0, A_T	value of a company's assets at time 0 and time T	11
α	percentage of wealth allocated to risky asset	3
α_p	alpha of portfolio p	14
a_j	number of units of asset j held in portfolio	3
B	price of bond	6, 7, 8, 9
B_{CTD}	price of cheapest-to-deliver bond	8
$B_0, B_1, \ldots$	price of floating-rate bond component of vanilla interest rate swap	9
B_j	value of bond j in a portfolio of J bonds	8
$BASIS_t, BASIS_{t^*}, BASIS_T$	basis of hedge at times t, t^*, and T	8
β_j	beta of asset j	3
β_p	beta of portfolio p	8, 14
β_p^T	target beta of portfolio p	8
β_S	beta of stock component of portfolio	8
β_f	beta of stock index futures	8

Letter/Symbol	Definition	Chapters
$b_0, b_1, \ldots, b_M$	coefficients of stock return sensitivity equation	7
$Bflt_0$, $Bflt^*$	value of floating-rate bond component, including notional, of vanilla interest rate swap, at times 0 and t^*, respectively; may be subscripted with d for domestic and f for foreign	9
$Bfix_0$, $Bfix_{t^*}$	value of fixed-rate bond component, including notional, of vanilla interest-rate swap, at times 0 and t^*, respectively; may be subscripted with d for domestic and f for foreign	9

C

Letter/Symbol	Definition	Chapters
CF	conversion factor of deliverable bond	8
cf_t	cash flow paid out by generic asset at time t	3, 8
$\widehat{\mathrm{cov}}_{ji}$	sample estimate of covariance of returns of assets j and i	3
cov_{ij}	covariance of variables i and j	3, 7
cov_{Sf}	covariance of spot and futures prices	8
c_t	price of European call at time t (may be $t+1$ or $t-1$)	7
χ	risk-adjustment factor in Value-at-Risk formula	7
c_b	coupon rate on bond	7
CDS_{PV}	present value of series of payments on CDS	11
$CDSq$	Quarterly CDS payment	11
$CDSbpa$	CDS premium in basis points per annum	11
$CFaR$	cash-flow-at-risk	7
CF	conversion factor for bond on delivery of bond futures contract	8
$c_0(X,T)$, $C_0(X,T)$	price at time 0 of European and American calls with exercise price X and expiration T	4, 10

Letter/Symbol	Definition	Chapters
$c_T(X,T)$, $C_T(X,T)$	value at expiration of European and American calls with exercise price X and expiration T	10
$c_0(X,T_m)$, $C_0(X,T_m)$	price at time 0 of European and American interest rate calls with exercise price X and expiration T_m	10
c_0	value of a call option (omitting arguments)	10, 11
c_1, c_2	value of two calls, identified as 1 and 2, in delta-gamma hedge	10
c, c_u, c_d, c_{uu}, c_{ud}, c_{dd}	prices of calls in binomial process (with upper case C for American options)	10
D		
D_0	value of a zero coupon bond that is subject to default	11
$D_1, D_2, \ldots, D_N$	dividends paid on stock during life of derivative	8
d	one plus return if asset goes down in binomial model	3, 10
d	subscript to denote domestic LIBOR, swap fixed rate, or bond price	9
d_1, d_2	calculated parameters of the Black-Scholes-Merton model	10, 11
ΔVaR_p	change in VaR of portfolio	7
Δw_j	change in weight of asset j	7
Δ_c	delta or price change of European call	7, 10
Δ_1, Δ_2	deltas of options 1 and 2 in delta-gamma hedge	10
Δ_p	delta of European put	10
ΔS	change in value of underlying	10
DUR	duration of bond	7
DUR_m	modified duration of bond	7, 8, 9
DUR_{mf}	modified duration of futures	7, 8
DUR_{mj}	modified duration of bond j in portfolio of J bonds	8

Letter/Symbol	Definition	Chapters
DUR_{mp}	modified duration of bond portfolio p	8
DUR_{mp}^{T}	target modified duration of bond portfolio p	8
DUR_T, DUR_B, DUR_S	duration of target, bond portfolio, and swap	9
δ	discrete dividend yield on stock	8
δ_c	continuous dividend yield on stock	8
E	generic variable E	3
EVA	economic value added	14
η, η_u, η_d (eta)	hedge ratio in binomial model	10
$E(\cdot)$	expected value of argument in parentheses	3
$E(V_p)$	expected value of portfolio	7
$E(R_j)$	expected return of asset j	3
$E(R)$	expected return (may be subscripted with V for VTI or B for BND ETFs)	3, 7
$E(R_{ji})$	expected return of a portfolio consisting of assets j and i	3
$E(R_p)$	expected return of portfolio p	3, 4, 7
$E(R_m)$	expected return on market portfolio	3
$E(R_c)$	expected return on European call	7
$E(H)$	expected value of H (cash flow)	7
$E(U(W))$	expected utility of wealth, W	3
F	generic variable F or forward price	3, 7
ϕ_1, ϕ_2	prices of pure securities in states 1 and 2	3
FV	future value of an amount of money	7
f	subscript to denote foreign LIBOR, swap fixed rate, or bond price	9
$f_0(T)$	futures price at time 0 for contract expiring at time T	7, 8, 10
$f_t(T)$, $f_{t^*}(T)$	futures price at times t and t^* for contract expiring at time T	8

Letter/Symbol	Definition	Chapters
f_0	generic futures price at time 0	8
$F(0,T)$	forward price established at time 0 for contract expiring at time T	4, 8
$F(t^*,T)$	forward price established at time t^* for contract expiring at time T	8
$FVCF(0,T)$	future value of cash flows paid by asset over period 0 to T	8
$FVSC(0,T)$	future value of storage costs incurred on asset over period 0 to T	8
$FVCC(0,T)$	future value of cost of carry on asset over period 0 to T	8, 9
$FVRP(0,T)$	future value of risk premium on asset over period 0 to T	8
$FVCY(0,T)$	future value of convenience yield on asset over period 0 to T	8
$FS(0,T_m)$	fixed rate on swap set at time 0 maturing at time T_m	9, 10
$FS_c(0,T_m)$	fixed rate on commodity swap set at time 0 maturing at time T_m	9
$FS_d(0,T_m)$	fixed rate on domestic leg of swap set at time 0 maturing at time T_m	9
$FS_f(0,T_m)$	fixed rate on foreign leg of swap set at time 0 maturing at time T_m	9
G	Number of total assets when more than one asset is used	3
g	$g = 1, \ldots, G$ (counter for double summation in portfolio variance)	3
Γ_c, Γ_p	gammas of calls and puts	10
Γ_1, Γ_2	gammas of calls 1 and 2 in delta-gamma hedge	10
γ	percentage of wealth invested in risky asset	3
H	company cash flow	7
H_L	critical value of cash flow to avert liquidity crisis	7

Letter/Symbol	Definition	Chapters
h	number of days to maturity in zero coupon bond or underlying Eurodollar in FRA, swap	7, 8, 9, 10
I		
J	Number of total assets or bonds in a portfolio	3, 8
j	$j = 1, \ldots, J$; identifier for multiple assets	3, 7, 8
K	Total number of ex ante outcomes	3
k	$k = 1, \ldots, K$ (multiple ex ante outcomes)	3
L	generic LIBOR	8, 9, 10
L_0, L_1, L_2, L_3	generic LIBOR for floating rate note with annual payments	9
LC	Identifier for levered company	6
$L_0(T_m)$	LIBOR at time 0 for LIBOR loan maturing at time T_m	8
$L_0(T_m + h)$	LIBOR at time 0 for LIBOR loan maturing at time $T_m + h$	8
$L_0(h)$	LIBOR at time 0 for LIBOR loan maturing at time h	9
$L_{0,d}(h), L_{0,f}(h)$	Domestic and foreign LIBORs at time 0 for LIBOR loan maturing at time h	9
$L_{t^*}(T_m - t^*)$	LIBOR at time t^* for LIBOR loan maturing at time $T_m - t^*$	8
$L_{t^*}(T_m + h - t^*)$	LIBOR at time t^* for LIBOR loan maturing at time $T_m + h - t^*$	8
$L_{t^*}(T_u), L_{t^*}(T_{u+1}), \ldots, L_{t^*}(T_m)$	LIBOR term structure at time t^* with upcoming payment at time T_u	9
$L_{T_m}(h)$	LIBOR at time T_m for h-day LIBOR loan	8

Letter/Symbol	Definition	Chapters
$L_{T_{u-1}}(h), L_{T_u}(h)$	h-day LIBOR observed on days $T_{u-1}, T_u, \ldots$ between payments $u-1$ and u	9
λ	coefficient of risk aversion in power utility function	3
M	maximum number of variables in stock return sensitivity equation	7
m	total number of swap payments	9
μ	general expected return of a distribution	7
μ_A	expected rate of return on a company's assets	11
$MVaR_p$	marginal *VaR* of portfolio	7
$MVaR_j$	marginal VaR with respect to asset j	7
N	number of dividends paid on stock over life of derivative	8
NPV	net present value	14
N_f	number of futures contracts in duration-based hedge	7, 8
n	number of binomial time periods	10
$N(d_1), N(d_2)$	normal probabilities in the Black-Scholes-Merton model	10
O		
ω	number of units of underlying for delta hedge	10
$\omega_u, \omega_1, \omega_2$	number of units of underlying and options 1 and 2 in delta-gamma hedge	10
P	notional of swap	9
π	risk-neutral probability of up move in binomial model	3, 10
Ψ	parameter used in determining optimal asset allocation	3
$PVCF(0, T)$	present value of cash flows paid by asset over period 0 to T	8
$PVSC(0, T)$	present value of storage costs incurred on asset over period 0 to T	8

Letter/Symbol	Definition	Chapters
$PVCY(0,T)$	present value of convenience yield over period 0 to T	10
$PVD(0,T)$	present value of dividends over period of 0 to T	10
$\prod_{t,t^*},\ \prod_{t,T}$	profit from strategy started at time t and terminating at times t^* and T	8
$PVF(0,T_1), PVF(0,T_2),\dots,$ $PVF(0,T_m)$	present value factors on LIBOR swap from time 0 through time T_m with interim periods $T_1, T_2,\dots$; may be subscripted with f for foreign and d for domestic	9, 10
$p_0(X,T),\ P_0(X,T)$	price at time 0 of European and American puts with exercise price X and expiration T	4, 10
$p_T(X,T),\ P_T(X,T)$	value at expiration of European and American puts with exercise price X and expiration T	10
$p_0(X,T_m),\ P_0(X,T_m)$	price at time 0 of European and American interest rate puts with exercise price X and expiration T_m	10
p_0	value of a put option (omitting arguments)	10, 11
$p,\ p_u,\ p_{uu},\ p_{ud}$	prices of puts in binomial process (with upper case P for American options)	
Q	number of forward contracts in quantity hedge	7
q_k	probability of ex ante outcome k	3
q	probability of up move in binomial model	3

Letter/Symbol	Definition	Chapters
R	return on generic asset in arbitrary state at arbitrary time	3
R^*	return on portfolio that defines *VaR*	7
$RAROC$	risk-adjusted return on capital	14
R_k	return on generic asset or portfolio in state k	3
R_j	return on asset j	3
R_{jk}	return on asset j in state k	3
R_m	return on market portfolio	3, 14
R_t	return on asset at time t	3, 7
R_p	return on portfolio p at any time	14
$\bar{R}$	sample estimate of average return (may be subscripted with V for VTI or B for BND ETFs)	3, 7
$R(\pounds)$	return on British pound	3
$R(\euro)$	return on euro	3
R^*	value of portfolio that would bring the current level down to the *VaR* for the mean-adjusted *VaR*	7
R_c	return on European call	7
R_s	return on asset S	7
$R(T_m, h)$	rate established at time 0 for FRA maturing at time T_m with underlying of h-day LIBOR	8, 9
$\hat{\rho}_{ji}$	sample estimate of correlation of returns between assets j and i	3
ρ_{ij}	ex ante correlation of returns between assets i and j (may be subscripted with V for VTI or B for BND ETFs)	3, 7
r	annually compounded risk-free rate	3, 6, 8, 9, 10, 14
r_b	binomial risk-free rate for an annual rate of r	10
r_f	foreign risk-free rate	8
r_d	domestic risk-free rate	8

Letter/Symbol	Definition	Chapters
r_D	discount rate on zero coupon bond	7
r_A	add-on rate on zero coupon bond	7
r_c	continuously compounded risk-free rate	8, 10, 11
S	price of underlying in binomial model	10
SR_p	Sharpe ratio of portfolio p	14
SC_t	storage cost paid at time t	9
S_j	price of asset j	3
S_t	price of asset at time t (may be t-1, t+1, etc.)	3, 7
S_T	spot price or exchange rate at expiration of derivative contracts at time T	4, 5, 7, 8, 10, 11
S_0	spot price of asset at time 0	4, 8, 10
$S_0, S_1, \ldots, S_T$	spot exchange rate or commodity price at times $0, 1, 2, \ldots, T$	9
$S_0, S_{T_1}, S_{T_1}, \ldots, S_{T_m}$	sequence of stock prices in equity swap or commodity prices in a commodity swap	9
$S1_0, S1_{T_1}, S1_{T_1}, \ldots, S1_{T_m};$ $S2_0, S2_{T_1}, S2_{T_1}, \ldots, S2_{T_m}$	sequence of prices of stock 1 and 2, respectively, in equity swap	9
σ_A	volatility of a company's assets	11
$\hat{\sigma}$	sample of estimate of volatility of return	3
σ_m^2	variance of the return on the market portfolio	3
σ	volatility of return (generic) (may be subscripted with V for VTI or B for BND ETFs)	3, 7, 10, 11
σ_j	volatility of asset j	3

Letter/Symbol	Definition	Chapters
σ_{ji}	volatility of return of portfolio consisting of assets j and i	3
σ_p	volatility of return on portfolio p	3, 4, 7, 14
σ_c^2	variance of return on call	7
σ_H	volatility of H	7
σ_s^2	variance of spot price	8
σ_f^2	variance of futures price	8
σ_b^2	variance of basis	8
$\sigma_{S,f}^2$	variance of value of portfolio of spot and futures (other subscripts may be used for different assets and derivatives)	7, 8
T	time to expiration of derivative or a future point in time or maturity of debt	4, 7, 8, 9, 10, 11
T_S, T_L	time to expiration for shorter- and longer-term options	10
T_s	total number of observations in a sample	3
T_S, T_L	shorter and longer times to expiration of two derivatives	10
T_{m+h}	days to maturity of LIBOR loan underlying FRA	8
T_m	days to maturity of FRA or a LIBOR loan	8, 10
$T_1, T_2, \ldots, T_m$	time in days to each respective swap payment date	4, 9
T_{u-1}, T_u	last swap payment date and next swap payment date, respectively	9
t	time indicator, $t = 1, \ldots, T$; also sometimes expressed as $t-1$, $t+1$, etc.	3, 7, 8, 9, 10
t^*	arbitrary point of valuation	9, 10
τ	time to maturity of bond in years	7
τ_C	corporate tax rate	6
U		
$U(t+1)$	utility of wealth at future time $t+1$	3
UC	identifier for unlevered company	6

Letter/Symbol	Definition	Chapters
U_L, U_H	lower and upper limits of uniform distribution	7
$U(W)$	utility of wealth W	3
u	one plus return if asset goes up in binomial model	3, 10
V	generic portfolio value and value of binomial hedge portfolio	8, 10
VaR	value at risk	7
VaR_p	value at risk of a portfolio in currency units	7
VaR_r	value at risk in terms of rate of return	7
$V_p \chi \sigma_p$	mean-adjusted VaR	7
V_U	value of unlevered firm	6
V_L	value of levered firm	6
V_j	value of asset j	3
V_p	value of portfolio p	3, 7, 8
V_{pf}	value of portfolio p and futures contract	8
V_p^*	value of portfolio p that defines the level of VaR	7
v_f	value of futures	8
$v_1, v_2, \ldots, v_M$	variables in stock return sensitivity equation	7
$V_{t^*}(F(0,T)),$	value at time t^* of forward contract established at time 0 expiring at T	8
$V_T(F(0,T))$	value at time T (expiration) of forward contract established with price $F(0,T)$ expiring at T	8
$V_t(F(0,T))$	value at time t of forward contract at price $F(0,T)$ expiring at T	8
$V_0(T_m, h)$	value at time 0 of FRA expiring at time T_m on h-day LIBOR	8
$V_{T_m}(T_m, h)$	value at time T_m of FRA expiring at time T_m on h-day LIBOR	8

Letter/Symbol	Definition	Chapters
$V_{t^*}(T_m, h)$	value at time t^* of FRA expiring at time T_m on h-day LIBOR	8
v_f	value of futures contract	8
$VS_0(T_m, h)$	value at time 0 of vanilla interest rate swap on h-day LIBOR expiring at T_m	9
$VS_{t^*}(T_m, h)$	value at time t^* of vanilla interest rate swap on h-day LIBOR expiring at T_m	9
V, V_u, V_d	value of hedge portfolio in binomial model	10
$VPSW_{T_m}(T_m, h)$	value of payer swaption at expiration T_m	10
$VRSW_{T_m}(T_m, h)$	value of receiver swaption at expiration T_m	10
W	wealth for generic outcome	2, 3
$W(t)$	wealth at time t	3
w_i, w_j	weights (relative market values) of assets i and j in a portfolio; (may be subscripted with V for VTI or B for BND ETFs)	3, 7
X	exercise price or rate of option	3, 4, 5, 10, 11
X_L, X_H	lower and higher exercise prices	10
X_c, X_p	exercise rates of interest rate calls and puts	10
x	generic variable x	4, 7
x_t	generic variable x at time t	4
x_1, x_2	calculated parameters of BSM model applied to valuing stock as an option on the assets	11
x_{1A}, x_{2A}	calculated parameters of BSM model applied to valuing stock as an option on the assets that assumes growth at the cost of capital rate	11

Letter/Symbol	Definition	Chapters
Y		3
y	yield on bond	7, 8, 9
y_s	continuously compounded yield spread on bond	11
y_c	continuously compounded yield on bond	11
Z	face value of zero coupon bond	11
z	standard normal random variable; may be subscripted with 1 and 2 to distinguish two variables.	7, 8

About the Author

Don M. Chance, Ph.D., CFA, holds the James C. Flores Endowed Chair of MBA Studies and is Professor of Finance at the E. J. Ourso College of Business, Louisiana State University (LSU). He previously held the William H. Wright, Jr. Endowed Chair for Financial Services at LSU, and the First Union Professorship in Financial Risk Management at Virginia Tech. Prior to his academic career, he worked for a large southeastern bank.

Professor Chance has had numerous articles published in academic and practitioner journals and has authored three books: *An Introduction to Derivatives and Risk Management* (10th ed.) co-authored with Robert Brooks, *Essays in Derivatives: Risk Transfer Tools and Topics Made Easy* (2nd ed.), and *Analysis of Derivatives* for the CFA Program. His recent research examines a variety of topics in risk management and finance.

He is often quoted in the media on matters related to derivatives and risk management as well as financial markets and the economy in general. He has extensive experience conducting professional training programs, and his consulting practice (Omega Risk Advisors, LLC) serves companies, organizations, and law firms. He is also involved in the development and writing of the derivatives curriculum in the CFA Program.

Part I

Introductory Concepts

Chapter 1

Introduction and Overview

(G)enuine risk management makes a neutral, well-informed assessment of the risk the business entails. It looks for ways to shed or mitigate the unwanted risks and to retain and manage only the risks that are necessary or desirable to take.

Dan Borge
Risk magazine, June 2009, p. 56

We begin this book with a fictionalized story. Bob Doyle has just been promoted to treasurer of a Fortune 1000 company. With Bob's new salary, stock options, and bonus potential, he begins thinking that the sedan he drives is not quite the appropriate vehicle for a person of his new status. After all, Bob will now have his own parking space in the company lot. Bob's wife Kathy agrees, and the two of them drive the sedan to a local upscale car dealership. After informing the salesman that they are looking for a new vehicle appropriate for a corporate executive, he proceeds to show them several models. The salesman, clearly interested in selling the Doyles the most expensive car he has, is pushing them toward a very nice and sophisticated sporty car. The following conversation ensues:

> Salesman: Let me tell you a few things about this fine machine. And it is indeed a fine machine, worthy of being owned by such an intelligent and clearly successful couple as you two. It has a 429 horsepower 4.7-liter V-8 twin turbo engine of diecast alloy block and heads. Its rapid multispark ignition can fire up to four times a millisecond. It has a net torque of 516 pound-feet at 1,800 to 3,500 rpms and a compression ratio of 1.5-to-1. Its final drive ratio is 2.65-to-1 and it accelerates from zero to 60 in 4.5 seconds with a coefficient of drag of 0.29. Its four-wheel disc brakes include perforated and internally ventilated front discs with four-piston calipers. It even has an adaptive damping system. Can you believe that? I'll tell you folks. It just doesn't get any better than this.

Bob: (Pretending to know what the salesman is talking about). Yes, it does sound interesting.

Kathy: Don't you just need a nicer car than what you had? And this "machine" is pretty expensive.

Bob: Yes, but quality matters and this new wave technology is important too.

Salesman: You said it Bob. This little superb piece of technology is not just fast and pretty but safe. There are so many safety features in here, you're getting your money's worth just on that factor. Why don't you folks take it for a spin? I promise you'll love it.

(Back in the showroom 30 minutes later after test driving)

Bob: That was great, wasn't it Kathy?

Kathy: I have to admit, it looks, rides, and feels good. But I'm still a little uneasy about the cost. I know we can afford it, but we don't have to blow everything on a car just because you're now some hotshot executive financial person, whatever that means. Geez, I'm a surgeon and I'm fine with my Subaru.

Salesman: And absolutely don't worry about the cost. I'm sure we can make you a deal that will make you feel like you're not even paying for it. We have financing terms that a corporate treasurer wishes he could get for his company.

What transpired here undoubtedly happens every day in the car buying business. In spite of Bob and Kathy's best efforts, the salesman has convinced them that the latest, most complex, and most expensive technology is what they need. Bob and Kathy thought they were smart shoppers, but they do not realize that as much as they know, they do not know as much as the salesman. All of the technical jargon sounds impressive but are these features really important? Is this car really what they need?

Now let's take a look at an incident that occurs a few months later in Bob's professional life. The company he works for does a substantial amount of business in Europe and is exposed to the risk of the euro exchange rate. Bob is meeting today with Steve Robeson, the salesman for MDM Bank, the primary bank for Bob's company. Steve is accompanied by Nigel Doring, the chief financial engineer of the Financial Strategies Group of MDM.

Steve: Bob, it's great to see you again. I hear you bought a fine new automobile.

Bob: Yes, how'd you know?

Steve: Well, actually I saw it in that parking spot outside that has your name on it. That's a great vehicle and a bargain for the money. Obviously you're a man who spends his money carefully and gets great value. Anyway, let's get down to business. First, let me introduce my colleague Nigel Doring. Nigel is our new technical guru. Excuse me, Nigel, I mean our chief quant. Nigel is from London, got his bachelor's degree at Oxford, and came over here to take a masters and PhD at MIT, and has been in the business for 14 years.

(Bob and Nigel greet one another.)

Steve: Anyway, Bob, I know you guys have considerable exposure to the euro. You have sales offices in Europe and generate a ton of cash in that currency. That exposure has got to leave you uneasy.

Bob: Yes, I know the company has been tolerating exchange rate volatility for a long time, but with this new promotion, it is *my* problem now. We've got to do something about it.

Steve: Well, our risk management group can construct some very effective strategies to help you do just that.

Bob: What kinds of strategies?

Steve: Let me let Nigel take that one.

Nigel: First we'll need to calibrate your exposure. My guess is that you're net long the euro with a delta one, though if you guys have any contingent exposure, the delta's attenuated a bit. We can easily deal with that if so. We could start you off with some vanilla European puts, but the timing of your cash flows could make it worthwhile to use American puts. I know you are concerned with cost, so we might want to look at some up-and-out barrier options. Maybe even a stochastic barrier. This could keep your premium low, while offering solid protection that dies only in stochastically infinitesimal circumstances. I also hear that you borrow floating at LIBOR + 300 bips but hold large cash balances invested primarily in T-bills. That means you have latent exposure that could benefit from a basis swap, with maybe even a cap to keep the cost down. Another possibility is some credit derivatives, because that basis exposure derives from systemic credit risk. We're working on some new credit default swaps that pay off based on market-wide credit risk with an interesting twist. They're ideal for companies in your situation. I wish I could tell you about them right now, but they're currently in the R&D phase.

Steve: Anyway you look at it, Bob, we can buy that exposure from you for a reasonable price.

Bob: That sounds interesting. But tell me, what do you guys do with all of this exposure I get rid of?

Nigel: We reallocate the risk by delta-hedging in external markets. We monitor our gammas and occasionally put on a hedge using other options. There is some vega risk but we've got an effective volatility swaps desk that has really saved us in a few critical circumstances. In fact, they might be able to help you all if you have a vomma problem. But the point is, and trust me on this, we're experts. We buy risk and manage it on a routine basis.

Bob: *(Wondering if he has a vomma problem, but afraid to ask.)* Doesn't all of this cost you a lot of money, which ultimately costs me a lot of money?

Steve: Yes, it does cost, but we're so large and do so much of this business that we keep the costs down. Bob, you guys have been great clients. We're here to serve you. Just in the last two years, our bank has invested $100 million in personnel, hardware, and software to give companies like yours the latest in risk management products. You can trust us on this.

Bob: I need to think about this some and talk to my staff, as well as my superiors. But I must say, it sounds like you could really help us.

Steve: That's great Bob. Go ahead and get it approved internally. In the meantime, I'll talk to our legal group and draw up an ISDA master agreement with a credit support annex. It'll all be ready and we can put this deal to bed in no time flat. Then we'll celebrate with the juiciest steaks you've ever seen, on us, of course.

In both cases, Bob is buying something relatively technical without the benefit of knowing much about what he's buying. In contrast, the seller has considerable technical knowledge. The car and the options sound pretty sophisticated, but Bob knows that all successful corporate treasurers drive fine automobiles and most use derivatives to manage their financial risk. While Bob will read a few articles about derivatives, he mostly just reads the contract to see if anything looks fishy. But Bob's problem is, he doesn't know what's fishy and what's not. He knows, however, that exchange rate risk is hurting his company, keeping him awake at night, and could significantly erode his year-end bonus, a portion of which he just spent on that car. And Bob trusts MDM Bank. He cannot see how they would recommend something that he would later regret. So, Bob plans to have his company buy the knock-out options and enter into a basis swap. Or whatever Nigel and his quant team think is best.

MDM bank goes to great lengths to describe the strategies to Bob, and it requires that Bob sign a document stating that he realizes that MDM is not an advisor and is not recommending the strategy. MDM emphasizes that it is offering these products only in its capacity as a counterparty. Before banks added these formal statements to their contracts, many companies thought that the bank was advising them in much the same way that an investment manager advises a client, that is, as a fiduciary. And although Bob is aware that he acknowledged the bank's impartiality, he does not fully appreciate what it means, nor does he completely understand why the bank does this kind of work or how it makes money. He's afraid to ask, however, because he does not want to reveal his ignorance.

While the car and the derivatives might work out, Bob will be lucky if over the long run the things that he buys always work out. Much like the car, Bob may purchase derivatives that are far more sophisticated and costly than necessary to do what he wants to do. Bob may also pay far more than a fair price for the derivatives. These derivatives may roughly achieve their objectives of transferring risk, but any initial success could tempt Bob to take on even more sophisticated and costly derivatives. Bob may eventually cross the line between eliminating the exposure he does not want and taking on some new exposure he should not have in the first place.

Bob's tendency to be impressed by those with technical skills and his limited training in risk management has put him into this situation. As finance specialists, you may someday find yourself in the same scenario. This book is designed to help you to intelligently deal with those situations. It will not make you a financial risk manager any more than a surgery book will make you a surgeon. But before taking any action that could do damage, like making an incision, a future surgeon must sit down and read what his craft is all about. So like the future surgeon, the future financial manager should read this book on financial risk management.

1.1 What is Financial Risk Management?

Financial risk management is a process that describes the practice of identifying, measuring, and controlling the financial risk carried by an organization. Note that we describe financial risk management as a both a *process* and a *practice*. A process is an ongoing activity. One cannot simply set a process in motion and let it go. There is no autopilot setting in financial risk management and in most other processes. Financial risk must be actively and continually managed. Financial risk management is also a practice. Professionals such as physicians, dentists, and attorneys are said to *practice* their professions. This characterization recognizes and implies that perfection is never achieved, but that serious professionals are constantly honing their skills by facing different scenarios that require their knowledge, judgment, and experience.[1] This is indeed what good financial risk management entails.

Notice also that we described financial risk management in terms of three activities:

- Identifying risk
- Measuring risk
- Controlling risk

These actions combine to form the process of *managing* risk. First, we can hardly manage risk if we do not know what risks we have. Hence, we must identify the risks. But identifying risk does not mean one knows how much risk there is. For example, a person with a family history of colon cancer would probably know that he has a greater than average risk of contracting the disease. But how much greater than average is this person's risk? On average one out of every 20 people will get colon cancer in their lifetimes. Is this person's risk two out of 20? Three out of 20? Good risk management in health and in finance requires knowing how much risk there is. And knowing what the risk is and how much risk there is does not mean controlling it. The person with the high risk of colon cancer could choose to eat a low fat diet and get frequent examinations as a means of controlling this risk. Or, as all too many do, he could hope that the bad luck will bypass him, a poor risk management strategy indeed with a very costly penalty if an adverse outcome occurs.

Identifying, measuring, and controlling financial risk are the primary top-down activities of financial risk management. There are other activities, some that come before, some that come after, and some that come in between. In this course we will study these activities in great detail later in this book.

---

[1]Note that in some activities, practice can lead to perfection. A musician can practice a song until she has mastered the ability to play it repeatedly without mistake. Music, though often thought of as an art, is actually a precise science consisting of a sequence of tonal frequencies with mathematical specifications that describe exactly how a piece is played. A piece can be practiced until the sequence of tonal frequencies can be delivered with perfection. Though a string musician might occasionally break a string, there are few elements of uncertainty. If a piece is played the same way two times, it will sound the same. In contrast, medicine, law, and financial risk management are rarely, if ever, practiced to perfection because of the element of uncertainty. The same such activity done twice will not necessarily deliver the same results.

1.2 Why We Call It Financial Risk Management

Notice that our focus has been stated as financial risk. Most all risks, even health risks, ultimately have financial consequences. This point is particularly true in a business, government, or non-profit organization. But some risks are typically viewed as financial risks and others as non-financial risks. For example, for a manufacturing firm, the risk of factory accidents is typically viewed as a non-financial risk. The risk of a product recall is usually viewed as a non-financial risk. But both of these events have enormous financial impacts. Financial risks, however, are normally thought of as risks that are associated with movements in interest rates, exchange rates, stock prices, and commodity prices, along with the risk of credit loss.

In addition, there are some other risks related to activities closely tied to these sources of risk that typically come under the umbrella of financial risk management. For example, the banking industry is required by regulators to manage its operational risk, which is the risk of hazards such as terrorism, losses caused by nature, computer viruses and hackers, fraud, etc. There are also risks associated with processing transactions and risks associated with liquidity where markets can dry up and almost cease to function at the very time when an entity needs to sell an asset.

There are also risks associated with legal, accounting, tax, and regulatory matters that would not, in a strict sense, be viewed as financial risks. But the current state of knowledge of managing all of these types of risks has benefited greatly from the body of knowledge of the management of traditional financial risks such as interest rate risk, exchange rate risk, and credit risk. Much of what we now know about managing risk has evolved from research on managing financial risk. As noted earlier, the banking industry is the leading provider of financial risk management products and has led the way to understanding the management of these other types of risks.

With that in mind, it is tempting to just call this activity *risk management*. *Risk management* is a term that has been used for many years to describe the insurance business. In fact, there are a number of insurance textbooks already that use the term *risk management* in the title.[2] Risk management is certainly a more general and accurate term for what you are going to learn, but using it increases the risk (no pun intended) that people would assume this is a book on insurance. Hence, we will stick with the

---

[2]The term *risk management* is also used in the safety engineering industry. It is popular phrase and probably a bit overused. It certainly sounds good. No one would get anything but kudos for practicing *risk management*.

term *financial risk management.* There is little harm in using the term *risk management,* however, within the book, and we will do so on occasion.

1.3   What is a Financial Risk Manager?

As you might have guessed, a financial risk manager is a professional who practices financial risk management. Such a person would have extensive knowledge of how to identify, measure, and control risk. At the present time, one cannot typically major in financial risk management in undergraduate programs, what more get a full degree in the subject at that level. There are, however, master's degrees in the subject and a considerable number of courses available, both in degree programs and in continuing education. A person holding the position of financial risk manager will have normally had extensive experience in financial markets and securities, and perhaps taken some specialized university, continuing education, or professional development courses. She could be a member of professional organizations and have completed certification programs on financial risk management. But the title of *financial risk manager* is typically found only in large financial institutions, such as banks, who offer financial risk management products and services to their customers.

Nonetheless, it is important to understand that you can practice financial risk management without *being* a financial risk manager. Just as in your personal life, you can and hopefully will manage your own personal risks without being a trained risk manager. In fact, most corporations, governments, and non-profits cannot afford an extensive investment in financial risk management personnel or technology. In organizations other than large financial institutions, financial risk management must typically be practiced by financial managers, who have other responsibilities as well. As in our example of Bob Doyle, our fictional Fortune 1000 treasurer, a typical financial manager will not have the knowledge to compete on an even keel with the specialized expertise of financial institutions who are offering their financial risk management products for sale. The pressure to buy products and manage risk in the manner recommended by the financial institution puts most corporations at a severe disadvantage, often resulting in the purchase of snazzy sports car-like products when simpler and less expensive ones will do the job.

As noted earlier, this book will not make you a financial risk manager. But it will teach you something about financial risk management. And you will be better able to practice financial risk management and decide which products and services your organization needs.

1.4 How Financial Risk Management Relates to Corporate Finance

Most finance programs (whether undergraduate, MBA, or Master of Science) are centered around the subject of corporate finance. Corporate finance is the study of how corporations acquire and allocate their financial resources. Usually the first course one takes in a finance program is called Corporate Finance, Financial Management, or Principles of Finance. Regardless of what it is called, the course is pretty much the same. Even if your employer is a nonprofit organization, the study of financial principles that are important in running a business provides valuable knowledge that is usually directly transferable to the nonprofit setting. From there, a student interested in a career as a financial manager would typically go down a route that includes courses in advanced corporate finance/financial management and perhaps international finance, working capital management, and corporate governance. Other students will pursue an investments track and take courses in investments, financial markets, and portfolio management.

The sub-title of this book emphasizes that the point of view of this book is from the perspective of the financial manager of a corporation who is said to be an end user of risk management products. A course based on this book would follow quite well after a course in corporate finance, regardless of what that course is called. The principles learned here will be directly applicable to dealing with problems faced in corporate finance. From reading other books on risk management instruments such as books on options, one might obtain the impression that there are more appropriate sophisticated techniques for managing the risk of portfolios than we will see in this book. Indeed, the risk management of portfolios is an important subject, but our focus is more from the point of view of the corporate financial manager. We will occasionally talk about risk in a portfolio context. Corporations, after all, are just portfolios of assets, funded by some borrowing and some equity investments. Also, corporations sometimes hold securities and often have pension funds, which are typically rather large portfolios of securities.

1.5 Why Financial Risk Management is Important to Financial Managers

Financial managers make decisions about how to acquire and allocate an organization's financial resources. These decisions are traditionally thought of as involving the analysis of long-term assets (typically called capital budgeting), short-term assets (cash and working capital management), and decisions about how much debt financing relative to equity financing to use (the capital structure decision), as well as how much to pay in dividends (the dividend decision). Financial managers also make decision about mergers and acquisitions, executive and employee compensation, the sale of securities through investment bankers, the arrangement of bank loans and issuance of commercial paper, international financial management problems, and operational planning and forecasting. Virtually all of these decisions are made facing considerable risk. But it has not been until recent years that risk has come to be viewed not simply as a factor that guides these decisions but as something to be actively managed. The closest financial managers have typically come to this view of financial risk management is in dealing with exchange rate fluctuations. The new approach is to view risk as a subject in itself, worthy of study and analysis in the context of financial management.

To many financial managers, risk may seem like the proverbial 800-pound gorilla, a dangerous beast that must be harnessed and controlled in order that financial decisions can be correctly made. But in fact, risk can never be mastered, harnessed, or completely controlled.[3] In fact, managing risk is somewhat like shooting at a moving target. Not only is there risk itself, but the risk can even change, something one might call the *risk of risk*. But that does not mean one can do nothing about risk. Like shooting at a moving target, steadiness and a feel for how the target moves can improve one's aim. Building the knowledge and skills to manage risk will, therefore, make it much easier for a financial manager to make good decisions about capital budgets, working capital, and other such matters.

But having invested all of this time and energy into learning financial risk management, one must wonder whether it will really be worth it. Because you have probably had a previous finance course, you have likely learned that financial markets are pretty competitive. No one can predict what will happen in the financial world. In that case, why is it worthwhile to do something such as hedge the risk of adverse movements in exchange rates? Does it really matter? No one can foresee where exchange rates are going. If one eliminates the risk, isn't it as likely that a favorable move will occur as an unfavorable one? Is protecting against risk really worthwhile?

As you will learn in this book, financial risk management can add value. Exactly how it adds value, however, is a somewhat controversial topic. Some economists claim that it can enable an organization to improve its credit rating, stabilize its cash flows, and, if it pays taxes, to reduce its

---

[3]Again, that is why risk management is *practiced*, realizing that perfection is unachievable.

taxes. The controversy lies in whether these conceptual ideas provide clear measurable benefits. We will discuss this point in more detail in Chapter 6. But more than anything else, financial risk management can enable an organization to bear the risks it wants to bear and should be bearing and avoid those it should not bear. Does it not make sense that an organization should assume risks in areas where it has expertise and avoid risks where it does not?

For example, airlines face many risks but the primary one is uncertainty in the price of jet fuel. Airlines are not energy companies; they are simply big consumers of energy. They have no competitive advantage in the energy market, at least not in the way an energy company might. Airlines have a competitive advantage in the market for the services — the demand for and supply of passengers and transportation of cargo. One does not have to look hard to see that successful airlines, such as Southwest Airlines, have an extensive program of hedging their fuel costs on a fairly regular basis, while unsuccessful airlines hedge only sporadically or only a portion of their needs.[4] Successful global pharmaceutical companies like Merck, Phizer, and Eli Lilly have extensive exchange rate hedging programs that protect the value of their foreign currency cash flows, which provide the funds to support their research and development of new drugs. They actively take risks in the markets for their products, but they avoid risks in exchange rate markets, where they have no competitive advantage in forecasting the future. In doing so, they add value for their shareholders. And adding value is what good financial decision making is all about.

When Greeting Card Companies Go Wild

In 1991, Gibson Greetings, a small greeting card company in Cincinnati, Ohio entered into various derivative transactions to attempt to lower the cost on a $50 million fixed-rate loan. The trades involved the use of interest rate swaps, which were positioned to lower Gibson's cost of financing provided interest rates fell. For a while rates did fall and Gibson was looking very smart for having done the deals. But Gibson tried some additional transactions, which were more complex and leveraged so that if Gibson's expectations were correct, it would benefit more rapidly.

---

[4]Sporadic or partial hedging even suggests that these other airlines believe they know where fuel costs are going, so they are essentially speculating. They hedge when they fear rising costs and do not hedge when they wish to speculate that costs will decline.

Gibson's transactions had crossed the line between controlling a risk and betting on a market in which it had no expertise. Unfortunately, if its expectations were wrong, it would take substantial losses. And that is just what happened. This small company, whose expertise was in greeting cards and not interest rates, had bet on the latter and lost. The cost: $23 million. Although legal action against the dealer counterparty, Bankers Trust, ultimately resulted in a loss of only about $6 million, Gibson suffered considerable embarrassment. And Bankers Trust was fined $10 million by the Securities and Exchange Commission (SEC) for unlawful actions.

Source: J. Overdahl and B . Schachter (1995).

Postscript: Although not directly related to this incident, neither company exists today. In 1999, Bankers Trust was purchased by Deutsche Bank, and Gibson Greetings was acquired by American Greetings.

Making good financial decisions is, however, a two-part process. Deciding what to do is one thing and doing it is another. Managing a risk by purchasing a risk management product from a financial institution puts the financial manager in a disadvantaged position relative to the financial institution, with its greater knowledge and information. As in the example of our Fortune 1000 treasurer, the financial manager needs to be a smart shopper of risk management services. This book will put you, the potential future financial manager, on the right course to smarter shopping for risk management services.

1.6 The Tools You Need to Study Financial Risk Management

If you are reading this book, you are probably taking a graduate or advanced undergraduate elective course in finance.[5] Many of you will be MBA students concentrating in finance, but some of you will probably be from other fields like economics, accounting, agricultural economics, and the sciences. Some

---

[5]It is possible that some of you are taking a continuing education course in financial risk management. This book will suit your needs as well. And some of you may be reading this in a bookstore or at home, maybe electronically, having purchased the book. Do not stop reading. You will benefit as well. Most of a person's knowledge does not occur in formal coursework but through experience and self-study. This book is a good self-study book.

of you may be working on a specialized master's degree in finance or even financial risk management.

Financial risk management is not nuclear physics but it is not a freshman-level subject either. This book will assume you have had some exposure to finance so that you understand a little about financial markets, and know what stocks, bonds, and currencies are. It assumes you understand present value and future value, and the basic statistical concepts of expected value, standard deviation, and correlation.[6] It also assumes some elementary knowledge of accounting, to the extent that one understands how a balance sheet consists of various asset accounts, liability accounts, and owners' equity, and how an income statement reflects the firm's revenues minus its expenses. Some understanding of how cash flow and income differ would also be helpful.

Typically business students are most uncomfortable when encountering concepts from calculus. Even though virtually all business students are exposed to elementary calculus, they often do not use it. Retention of math knowledge is not easy when the tools are rarely used. In this course, we will encounter a few elementary calculus concepts. If you are uncomfortable with the formality of calculus, but understand the notion of a rate of change, meaning one thing changing when something else changes, you will have no problems.

Most business students have also had some exposure to economics. While we will rarely require much direct material from economics courses, the principles learned in economics are extremely valuable in studying financial risk management. Economics teaches people to think rationally and not emotionally about how to acquire resources and how to allocate them. Many risk management mistakes have been made because of emotional thinking. Economics also tells us a lot about how markets work and how decisions should be made.

Complementing the rational thinking brought from economics is good judgment, intuition, and a strong sense of ethical standards. No book or course can teach you these things, but one should not think they are innate characteristics that one is either born with or not. Good judgment arises from learning from one's mistakes. Intuition comes from trusting the instincts we all have and is far more than just common sense. It is listening to our inner selves. For example, if something does not seem quite right, it probably isn't. Many financial risk management mistakes have been made by not noticing that something just didn't seem right. And high ethical standards come

---

[6]Some basic review of these statistical concepts will be done in Chapter 3.

from applying the classic golden rule of treating others as we would want to be treated. If we engage in ethical lapses, we are implicitly saying that we have no problem with others acting unethically toward us. Being ethical is a conscious decision to do the right thing by treating others fairly and how you would want to be treated. None of these factors is purely innate. They are learned through observation, experience and the development of a moral compass.

Finally, we should add that this book can be beneficial to MBA students not in finance. Most all business students study about making business decisions in the presence of risk. Finance is the business function that devotes the most effort toward understanding risk. MBA students not in finance will still benefit from this book. As long as you have had at least one course in finance (and hopefully you kept your book for reference), you are quite qualified.

1.7 Why this Book?

The objective of this book is both modest and ambitious. It is modest in the sense that it is not intended to turn its reader into a financial risk management specialist and in particular into a derivatives pricing expert. It is ambitious in that it endeavors to teach corporate end users who come from traditional graduate business programs how to manage risk. The world of risk management is a highly technical one in which the corporate end user, like Bob the treasurer, is at a severe disadvantage. The greatest body of knowledge on risk management has been developed and advanced in the banking industry and that is not going to ever change, nor should it. Banks are natural providers of risk management products, they need to be on the cutting edge of what is known, and they need to be constantly developing new financial products. Yet, their largest body of customers is their corporate clients whose knowledge of these products is a level or two below that of the banks. The history of risk management is littered with sad stories of how the sellers of these products — the banks — took advantage of the buyers of these products — the corporations, non-profits, and governments. And even when banks do nothing illegal, unethical or wrong at all, the corporate end user is at a clear disadvantage when searching for risk management solutions. Just like Bob and the sports car.

As you now know, shopping for risk management products is not much different from shopping for any very technical product, such as an automobile. Most likely you will be at a severe disadvantage when negotiating a purchase with a counterparty that really knows what he is talking about. Yet, risk management products, many of which are classified as derivatives, are simply tools to be used in managing risk. But to use these tools properly, end users need to know whether they even need them and if so, which tools they should buy. You might buy a hacksaw when what you really need is a miter saw, but you can probably return it if you quickly realize that you bought the wrong product. And even if you cannot return it, it is not a total loss. That hacksaw will be waiting for you to use it the first time you have to cut a piece of metal and it probably will not do any damage while it patiently waits. But if you buy a double barrier swap when all you really need is a plain vanilla swap, you are liable for any losses you might incur if the barrier feature is triggered.

There are probably more books written about risk management products than there are about any other topic in the world of finance. Many of these books are highly technical. In some you might encounter integral equations as early as the first page. These are the books for the sell-side people, meaning the banks who create and sell these products. The book you are reading is for the buy-side people, the corporate, non-profit, institutional, and government end users who need to know how to shop intelligently for risk management products so as not be disadvantaged by the more knowledgeable and technical experts on the sell side. Those experts might even deride this book for its simplicity. But simplicity has enormous benefits. It breaks down complexity into its relevant parts so that the proverbial forest can be seen through the trees.

This book is heavily oriented toward graduate business students. In finance, graduate business students are those students typically working on MBAs and MS degrees in finance. While some may have a technical background, they are not being bred to become the technical experts that work on the sell side. The sell-side people, sometimes called financial engineers or quants, are on the opposite side of the table of the people who should be reading this book. Graduate business students in finance, however, are far too often erroneously groomed to be derivatives pricing experts. A typical elective course that a graduate business student might take may be called "Derivatives," "Risk Management," "Financial Risk Management," or some variation thereof, but such a course almost invariably is a course in derivative pricing. Why? Professors enjoy teaching the subject, and there are many great books on it. There are few academic specialists in this field who do not enjoy demonstrating the derivation of the Black-Scholes-Merton partial differential equation and then showing how the Nobel Prize-winning formula solves the equation. Your author is no exception. But those are poor reasons to teach a course. A course exists for the students and not for the professors. While I am not saying that deriving the Black-Scholes-Merton formula is a waste of time, it is unlikely that such a course also addresses the organization and human barriers that stand in the way of effective risk management in a corporate end user. Far more risk management problems have been created by not understanding these issues than by misusing a derivative pricing formula.

Moreover, teaching such a course fails to acknowledge that derivatives pricing experts do not typically come from the ranks of graduate students in finance. They come from math and physics and/or they may hold a masters in quantitative finance or financial engineering, programs often taught outside of business schools. It takes a lot more knowledge than one can garner in a second-year business school elective to know how to create risk management products and manage risk in a bank. A graduate business student taking such an elective gets just a sip of what the process is and almost invariably gets a slightly lighter version of it. A graduate business student completing a course in derivatives or risk management has learned a lot but much of what he learned is not helpful in managing risk by end users, meaning the very types of companies and jobs he or she is likely to go into after graduation.

This books seeks to fill that gap. As noted, it has modest but ambitious goals, the foundations of which can best be summarized as follows:

- Graduate business students are more likely to become corporate end users than sell-side derivatives experts.
- Corporate end users are at a clear disadvantage to sell-side experts when shopping for risk management solutions.
- Corporate end users require a different type of training and a different approach than sell-side experts.

It may appear that we are coming down hard on the sell side. Not too many years ago, the sell side deserved to be hammered. The last approximately thirty years of financial history is filled with stories of end users that bought derivatives for which they had no need. Until some well-defined legal interpretations, end users believed that they had a fiduciary relationship with their bank, meaning that they were placing their trust in the bank. The typical end user had experienced many years of a satisfying business relationship with its bank, so it probably rightfully had a reason to believe that the bank would not take advantage of it. Sadly, that was not the case. Loans and risk management products are quite different. Banks extend credit and earn a return. Borrowers take the funds and use them productively, or at least that is how it is supposed to work.

Risk management products, however, are a zero-sum game. If a bank enters into a swap with a corporation, any gain or loss by one party is the corresponding mirror-image loss or gain to the other. Banks offer these products to end users but do not earn a profit from timing the direction of the market. Banks profit from making a market in the product. That is, they offer the product, absorb the risk transferred from the end user, and hedge that risk by transferring the risk to another market at a more favorable price. In this manner, banks are intermediaries of risk transfer services. Thus, the bank has laid off the risk of that loss or gain, and the end user presumably has employed the risk management product to achieve an objective, which is normally to hedge some other risk it faces.[7]

That description sounds symbiotic, a type of economic-ecological harmony whereby both parties benefit. But when banks first began offering these products, low barriers to entry in these markets made the industry more competitive and reduced profit margins. Banks began looking for ways to increase profits and found two ways to do this.

First, they could increase their selling efforts. But, there are limits to increased selling efforts, however, and after all, every bank was increasing their selling efforts. Second, however, they could create higher-margin products, meaning typically more complex customized products. The limits to creating more complex, customized products are less restrictive and confined only by human creativity. It was at this time that banks discovered

---

[7]One might ask the obvious question of why the end user does not lay off the risk in the same way the bank does, thereby avoiding the bank as intermediary. That is a good question, but its answer lies in simply understanding the nature of the middleman in an economy. It is not practical to buy cars from Toyota, so we buy them from Toyota dealers who are intermediaries that can deliver and service the cars more efficiently. When banks lay off risk, it is not simply a matter of transferring that risk and ignoring it. Banks typically engage in dynamic risk management, meaning that they must manage their risk transfer transactions on an ongoing basis, which is not a simple task. A company that manufactures products does not typically have the technical expertise to dynamically manage financial risk. While large companies could, of course, acquire that expertise, it would probably not be worth it. By exploiting economies of scale, however, and their natural positions as financial intermediaries, banks can dynamically manage financial risk far more efficiently than can their clients.

that the foundational knowledge of risk management products they used lay in mathematics and physics.

The universities of the world have rarely had a shortage of PhD graduates in mathematics and physics, but employment possibilities have been somewhat weak for all but a rare few. The lengthy post-doc process and the tremendous competition for grant money oftentimes relegates many very talented people to underemployed positions, when their best talents lie in research. Moreover, with the fall of the Soviet Union and the reduction in the arms race, many scientists from Eastern Europe now needed private sector jobs. Banks stepped right up to the plate and hired these "rocket scientists," as they were often euphemistically called, offering salaries previously unheard of. Mathematics and physics departments of universities began teaching courses in how to use their disciplines in finance.

These people soon became known as financial engineers and sometimes quants.[8] They created an explosion (no pun intended) in the number of risk management products available. They literally launched (no pun intended again) a new industry. The complexity of these products spawned the term *exotic derivatives*, which then necessitated a counter-term for derivatives that were not exotic: *plain vanilla derivatives* or sometimes just *vanilla derivatives*.[9]

These new complex financial products were more difficult and costly to create and manage, and as such, the banks were able to extract larger profit margins. Moreover, the banks gained a tremendous advantage over their end user clients. While a typical corporate end user can usually understand a simple risk management product such as a vanilla swap, an exotic version of a swap, such as one that has barriers or pays off based on how long an interest rate stays within a given range, is much harder to understand. So, at that point, the bank has a tremendous advantage over the end user, and we get a situation like Bob Doyle is facing.

Having such an advantage does not mean that the bank exploits the end user. A car salesman has a tremendous advantage in knowing the technical features of a car, but he does not automatically exploit the customer. After

---

[8]For a great reading on one of the first such quants, see Derman (2004). See also Patterson (2010).

[9]The term "vanilla" or "plain vanilla" came about because vanilla is considered the most basic form of ice cream. Other corresponding terms for these risk management products were first-generation derivatives (vanilla) and second-generation derivatives (exotics).

all, he wants the customer to recommend him and to return. So what is the problem? Do banks not want their customers to be satisfied?

Of course they do. But many banks got very caught up in the high profitability of selling complex customized risk management products. Moreover, the banks believed that *there was no fiduciary relationship*. The banks understood that the end user was responsible for its own decisions. If the end user wanted to speculate in complex derivatives, it ought to have that right. The end user, however, believed that *there was a fiduciary relationship*. Accountants, lawyers and doctors *are* fiduciaries: they are required to put their clients' needs before their own. End users often believe their bankers were fiduciaries and for some banking services, they are.[10] The famous P&G — Bankers Trust Case established that there was no fiduciary relationship.[11]

From that point forward, banks began writing explicit language into the contracts governing these products and requiring the end users to acknowledge that the bank was merely a counterparty, not a fiduciary. Not surprisingly, the number of disastrous risk management experiences fell substantially, but it did not go away. And while much progress continues to be made, there is much more to go. End users need to constantly strive to improve their knowledge of risk management, and in particular, the risk management products offered by banks.

This book is a no-nonsense approach to financial risk management. Unlike virtually all other books on financial risk management, it is not a derivatives pricing book. We need another one of those like we need another global financial crisis. This book is designed to create smart shoppers in the world of risk management products, shoppers who will not be awed by the technical jargon and plethora of complex products offered by the sell side people. The primary target is the graduate business student.

1.8 What You Will Learn From this Book

This book is divided into 14 chapters that compose four main parts. Part I, Introductory Concepts, consisting of this chapter and Chapters 2 and 3, covers introductory concepts. Part II, consisting of Chapters 4–6, lays out the foundations of financial risk management. Part III, containing

---

[10]For example, a bank might manage the pension fund of a corporation.
[11]See Marthinsen (2009).

Chapters 7–10, describes the tools and techniques of financial risk management. Part IV, Chapters 11 and 12, covers non-market risks. Part V, Chapters 13 and 14, is a treatment of organization issues and concerns. We now take a quick stroll through the contents of each chapter.

Chapter 2: Understanding the Nature of Risk is all about risk in general, with very little about risk encountered in the business world. The purpose of the chapter is to get you to thinking about risk in more familiar settings. It uses examples that deal with risk in health, law, and public policy. It asks questions like what really is risk? How do people respond to risk? What does risk mean for you? How do you react to risk? The chapter then gives a light treatment of some basic concepts in finance that we need to know to study risk.

Chapter 3: Principles of Risk, Return, and Financial Decision Making contains a great deal of material that you may have encountered in previous finance courses, such as rates of return, probability distributions, and ex ante and ex post measures of return and risk. We then endeavor to understand how people make decisions in light of risk, which uses the notion of expected utility. We next look at equilibrium models that tell us how much additional return we should get for the risk taken. Other topics we examine include arbitrage, stochastic dominance, and state preference theory. This material is largely covered in other courses, so you may be able to use it only as review material. In other words, if you have encountered this material before, completing skipping this chapter would not be a problem.

Part II, called *Foundations of Financial Risk Management*, consists of Chapter 4–6. *Chapter 4: Basic Concepts of Financial Risk Management* is our first real look at financial risk. A great deal of this material will already be familiar to students of finance. We take an introductory look at the long-run historical behavior of interest rates, exchange rates, and energy prices and begin to think about the impact these factors have on an organization. We discuss some well-known alternatives for managing this risk, such as forecasting and insurance. We then introduce a primary theme of this book — that derivatives are excellent tools for managing financial risk. We give light definitions and examples of the various types of derivatives and discuss the attractions of derivatives as well as the criticisms of them. The chapter concludes with diagrams that illustrate how the basic process of risk management works.

Chapter 5: The Financial Risk Management Environment describes the financial risk management industry. We encounter the exchange-listed and over-the-counter derivative markets and describe the institutions that operate in these markets. Considerable emphasis is placed on distinguishing dealers from end users, with this book oriented toward the latter. The chapter also provides charts using data from the Bank for International Settlements that illustrate the size and growth in the over-the-counter derivatives industry. It concludes with reference material on professional associations and sources of information on financial risk management.

Chapter 6: The Value of Financial Risk Management. This chapter is an important one, not so much for the practical tools it teaches, but because it answers the question of why we care about financial risk management. Reaffirming that the ultimate goal of a company is maximizing shareholder value, it first establishes that risk management in perfect financial markets is of little use to shareholders. If perfect markets preclude any value to risk management, the justification must come from market imperfections. The chapter goes on to describe the various imperfections that give rise to financial risk management value. One notable feature of this chapter is that these arguments are presented and evidence is cited that either supports or refutes the justification. While the chapter is largely conceptual, it also presents practical support for risk management, such as how risk management helps companies plan more easily. It concludes with a reminder that hedging, so often epitomized as the virtuous side of risk management, is really just making a bet that a bad event will occur. Therefore, hedging is a form of speculating.

Part III is called *Managing Market Risk*. Market risk refers to the risk of interest rates, exchange rates, commodity prices, and stock prices. In other words, market risks are driven by uncertainty in prices and rates as these values fluctuate in their respective markets. This unit consists of Chapters 7, 8, 9, and 10 and describes the techniques for managing risk in these markets. *Chapter 7: Measuring Market Risk* introduces several important tools for measuring financial market risk, the primary one of which is Value-at-Risk (*VaR*). An extensive treatment of *VaR* is provided, with due regard for keeping the mathematics to a minimum. This book is not designed to turn out an expert on topics like *VaR*, but to put you in a position to have a foundation-level grasp of the topic. In addition to *VaR*, the chapter covers cash flow risk, with an emphasis on quantity risk, and also beta and equity risk and duration and interest rate risk. And if you are one of the critics of *VaR*, do not worry. We will provide the warning signs.

Qantas Airlines: Ahead of Its Time

One of the most progressive corporations in the practice of risk management is Qantas Airlines, the primary carrier in Australia. Until 1995, Qantas was owned by the Australian government. In 1994, in anticipation of its conversion to a publicly-owned company, Qantas did an extensive examination of its risk management system. Even at that time, Qantas was well ahead of the game, using such techniques as Value-at-Risk, stress testing, and implementing the best known recommendations and practices, all of which you will study in this course. But at that time, and to a great extent even today, these measures were employed primarily by dealers and not end users like Qantas. Qantas also recognized that its front office, the people who engage in its risk management transactions, and its back office, the people who do the paperwork for the its risk management transactions, were not separated. As we shall learn, this is one of the foremost mistakes in risk management systems and is much like having the dogs guard the meat. It then made extensive changes in its organization structure to separate these activities. Qantas was actively managing the risk of its fuel costs, interest rates, and exchange rates. Qantas admittedly takes some risks when doing these risk management trades, but risk management is not just about reducing risk. Occasionally risk must be increased. But Qantas measures the risk-return tradeoff carefully to ensure that it knows the risk it is taking and that the risk it takes is the risk it wants.

Source: Nusbaum (1996).

Chapter 8: Managing Market Risk with Forward and Futures Contracts has two main parts, forwards and futures. These instruments are quite similar but have some distinctions. Each chapter component carefully describes and illustrates the contracts. The section on forward contracts works through the principles that lead to the pricing and valuation of foreign currency and interest rate forward contracts. Examples are given of how these contracts are used. The futures material does not devote much space to pricing. The general principles are presented but at this level of the material, the reader does not need to get into the more complex matters of how prices are related to the daily settling of futures contracts and the choices parties have regarding when, where, and how to deliver the underlying asset. We will treat futures prices as being equivalent to forward prices, with due regard for the credit risk difference. Also, most corporations use over-the-counter instruments where the pricing is more opaque. With futures, prices are determined by open outcry in a competitive and fairly transparent market. Therefore, obtaining good futures prices is fairly easy in practice.

Chapter 9: Managing Market Risk with Swaps deals with the most widely employed derivative by corporate end users. We describe the characteristics of plain vanilla swaps, with a light treatment of variations such as basis swaps and forward swaps. We discuss the success of the swaps market and show applications in managing interest rate, currency risk, equity, and commodity risk. Remembering that prices and values of over-the-counter instruments are not transparent, full coverage is provided of these topics, which is so critical to using these instruments effectively.

Chapter 10: Managing Market Risk with Options deals with options, which typically form the nucleus, if not much of the full content, of most derivatives books. This is because options take more time to cover and for most technically oriented people, options are the most interesting derivative. Our treatment of options is fairly basic. We explain the characteristics of options with an understanding that the pricing must proceed in a methodical manner. After introducing the instruments, this chapter covers the fundamental principles of option valuation, plus the binomial and Black-Scholes-Merton models at a basic level. The chapter also covers options on futures, interest rate options, currency options, and swaptions. Where possible, and without getting too involved, pricing of these instruments is presented. But the emphasis in the chapter is on applications for typical end users. End users usually purchase or sell options that are tailored to eliminate a specific risk, but the dealers, on the other side of the transaction, are absorbing that risk. It is useful for end users to see how dealers manage that risk. Hence, the chapter gives a light treatment of how dealers hedge options.

Part IV is called *Managing Non-Market Risks* and consists of Chapters 11 and 12. It deals with risks other than those driven by market prices and rates. *Chapter 11: Managing Credit Risk* begins a two-chapter unit that moves past traditional market risk management. The chapter begins by explaining how default is an option itself and shows how option pricing models can be used to help understand credit risk. The chapter covers the credit risk of various financial instruments and how credit risk is measured and managed, with an increasingly popular class of instruments known as credit derivatives.

Chapter 12: Operational and Other Risks deals with some of the more subtle risks, most of which would not be strictly called financial risk. It is a relatively non-quantitative chapter because most of these risks are difficult to measure and even when measurable, they are more difficult to capture in a model. But business decision makers need to understand the basics of these risks, particularly given that banks, their counterparties in most derivatives transactions, are starting to focus heavily on managing these risks.

Part V is called *Accounting, Disclosure, and Governance in Risk Management*, and consists of Chapters 13 and 14. *Chapter 13: Accounting and Disclosure in Financial Risk Management Activity* is a somewhat unique chapter. With a few exceptions, most textbooks on derivatives do not cover accounting and disclosure issues. But these matters are extremely important to end users. Using derivatives can lead to some very challenging issues in these areas. Although this material is not intended to cover all of the bases in accounting, taxation, and disclosure rules, it should give any reader a sound introductory treatment of the principles. An added feature will be examples from corporate annual reports of the concepts being illustrated here.

Chapter 14: Organizational Structure, Corporate Governance, and Financial Risk Management is our concluding chapter. With the passage of the Sarbanes-Oxley Act in the United States, the subject of corporate governance has become a huge concern, if not an industry in itself. Risk management was not the primary reason why the federal government mandated rules to force better behavior on the part of corporate boards, but risk management is an important responsibility of corporate boards. This chapter focuses on how corporations can practice effective risk management so that they are acting in the best interests of their shareholders, thereby engaging in good corporate governance. We will take a good look at how several well-known companies do it.

1.9   What You Will Not Learn from this Book

To reiterate a point made previously but worth emphasizing, most advanced undergraduate and graduate level courses that might call themselves risk management or financial risk management are typically not courses in risk management. They are courses far more focused on the instruments themselves, in particular, options.[12] Option pricing theory provides a rich reservoir of knowledge about managing risk. And, unlike a lot of theories, option pricing theory is actually applied in the financial world. In fact, there is probably no theory more applied in all of economics and finance. But pricing options is a very specialized and advanced topic and is part of the related but separate discipline called *financial engineering* or *quantitative finance*.

---

[12]In fact, most often such courses are called *Options*, *Derivatives*, or some combination of these terms.

Financial engineering is an activity that involves the creation of financial products for the purpose of managing a variety of risks. Oftentimes these risks are complex, unusual, and unique to a specific organization. Financial engineering is more likely to be practiced by the financial institutions that are dealers in these financial products. These institutions, which are mostly banks, can usually justify the large investments in personnel and technology to support the research and marketing of a broad range of risk management products. The skills required to build models to capture these complex risks require specialized and highly technical knowledge. Hence, these institutions tend to employ financial engineers, who usually hold advanced degrees in subjects such as finance, economics, mathematics, physics, and statistics. These people are often called *quants*. The process of creating these financial products leads to the development of models for pricing these products and managing the risk created when these products are traded. Thus, clearly risk management plays a role in financial engineering. But financial risk management is not itself financial engineering. Financial risk management is a process practiced by dealers and their clients, the end users, while financial engineering is an activity normally practiced only by dealers. Financial engineering is the R&D of financial institutions.

An introductory graduate-level course in options and/or derivatives will usually give you some of the foundations necessary to understanding option pricing and financial engineering. Such a course will typically be one of the most challenging courses one could possibly take in a traditional graduate business program. But in spite of that somewhat frightening fact, the course will actually be nothing more than an elementary treatment of the subject. It will attempt to teach you financial engineering but it will not make you a financial engineer, because it will just barely scratch the surface of this complex subject. A typical MBA student concentrating in finance probably aspires to become a financial officer of a corporation. Some may work in banks. Others may want to become entrepreneurs. None should want to become financial engineers and option pricing specialists. If they do, they are pursuing the wrong degree.

This book is oriented toward the graduate student in finance. It will expose that student to what he or she needs to know about financial risk management. While it is primarily aimed at MBA and MS students, those from other disciplines including financial engineering can benefit from this book. You will get a light treatment of the fundamentals of pricing options and other derivatives and some of the elementary principles that underlie how dealers create these products and manage the risk assumed when their customers buy the products. But the material will be presented in a straightforward manner, and the degree of difficulty will be carefully controlled. The primary focus of the book is on the end user — the corporations, governments, and non-profits that purchase financial risk management products from dealers. By reading this book and taking such a course, end users will become better consumers of financial risk management products.

And yes, we have made this point more than once in this chapter — but it is a critical one.

Risk Management a Long Time Ago

There is plenty of evidence that formal risk management practices were present in business many years ago. For example, the Code of Hammurabi, which was written around 1800 BC, describes a type of loan used to finance a ship's voyage where the loan principal does not have to be repaid if the ship is lost. Similar loans have resurfaced in recent years, where the loan principal does not have to be repaid if some event occurs. For example, the Roman Emperor Claudius (10 BC–AD 54) assumed losses for Roman commercial ships lost in storms.

Even William Shakespeare mentions a risk management technique in his most business-oriented play, "The Merchant of Venice", written between 1596 and 1598:

> "My ventures are not in one bottom trusted
> Nor to one place; nor is my whole estate
> Upon the fortune of this present year
> Therefore, my merchandise makes me not sad"

(Act I, Scene I)

Of course, Shakespeare is talking about one of the oldest, simplest, and most reliable risk management techniques of all: diversification.*

*It is interesting to note that in *The Tragedy of Pudd'nhead Wilson* (1894), American writer Mark Twain wrote virtually the opposite: "Behold, the fool saith, "Put not all thine eggs in the one basket" — which is but a manner of saying, "Scatter your money and your attention"; but the wise man saith, "Put all your eggs in the one basket and — watch that basket!"

Source: P. L. Bernstein, *Against the Gods: The Remarkable Story of Risk*. New York: John Wiley (1996).

1.10   Chapter Summary

This chapter is just an introduction and overview of the book. It does not contain much to learn and remember. Its primary purpose is to give you a preview of the remainder of this book. Hopefully it will have piqued your curiosity, if not fully stimulated your interest, and make you want to read on not just because you have to, but because you want to.

1.11   Questions and Problems

1. Identify the three primary activities involved in managing financial risk.
2. Why is financial risk management referred to as a practice?
3. Why is financial risk management important in the process of financial management?
4. To whom is this book primarily oriented? Why does this orientation differ from that of most other books on financial risk management?
5. Why are the dealer and end user not in a fiduciary relationship?
6. Why is this book not about financial engineering or quantitative finance?

Chapter 2

Understanding the Nature of Risk

In order to understand risk, we must first define risk.

> George Costanza (fictional
> television character)
> *Seinfeld*
> Episode: "The Fatigues"
> October 31, 1996

The study of finance and in fact much of the broader field of economics is frequently based on the assumption that people act consistently and rationally. Rational behavior leads to statements, models, and theories that describe how asset prices, interest rates, and exchange rates are generated in financial markets. Knowing how prices and rates are determined is instrumental and in fact critical to making effective financial decisions and practicing good financial risk management. But in reality, people often act inconsistently and irrationally. Such behavior is nearly always sub-optimal and frequently leads to poor performance over the long haul. In fact, there are investment managers whose central trading philosophy is based on the notion that many investors can be counted on to be consistently wrong and irrational and that it is possible to take advantage of the errors these investors make.[1]

---

[1]For example, one type of investment strategy called *contrarianism* is based on the notion that the majority of investors are wrong, so the optimal strategy would be to do the opposite. In more recent years, some investment managers have come to follow behavioralist models of investing in which irrationality, sentiment, and human mistakes play a formal role in the pricing of securities, and in which these behavioral biases can be exploited.

Practicing good financial risk management requires understanding financial risk. In turn, understanding financial risk requires, among other things, understanding how people perceive risk, meaning how individuals evaluate risk and how they respond to risk. The objective in this chapter is for you to draw on your own observations and experiences with the risk you are exposed to in life and to think about what risk really is and how you and others go about dealing with it. This chapter is not a formal treatment of behavioral biases, but it will cover many of these biases. Perhaps you will observe some of your own biases, which hopefully will encourage you to take corrective action. When you have an understanding of how you and others perceive risk, we can then move into a more formal and focused treatment of managing financial risk, the subject of the rest of this book.

2.1 What is Risk?

Just as *Seinfeld*'s George Constanza told us, we first need a good definition of risk. For the moment, however, we need only a reasonable working definition and not a formal definition that meets demanding statistical and economic requirements. As a general and very simplistic definition, let us try the following:

> *Risk is the potential that the outcome of an event will be one of many possible outcomes, and we do not know which event will occur.*

For example, consider the event to be your performance on a financial risk management exam. Assuming your instructor grades on a 100-point scale and awards no fractional points, there are 101 outcomes: $0, 1, \ldots, 99, 100$. The possible outcomes are known, but you do not know which outcome will occur. Of course, you do have a great deal of control over the matter. You can study hard, relax, and get a good night's sleep.[2] But other than perhaps knowing that the exam covers certain material and excludes other material, you have almost complete uncertainty over what questions will be on the exam. In this example, the possible outcomes are known, but in many cases, the outcomes are not known. For example, suppose you are not married and the event in question is "Given that you do eventually marry, who will your spouse be?" It may well be a person you know, or it might be a person you have not yet met. While there are not an infinite number of possibilities, there certainly are quite a few.

---

[2]And by all means, let's rule out cheating.

In facing an event such as an exam, it is possible that you have an expectation of what might happen. Indeed, it is quite likely that you have an expectation. You may feel highly confident, cautiously confident, or outright terrified about the exam. Assuming you are cautiously confident, when asked what grade you think you might make, let us say you guess an 85. Realistically 85 is just an average of the possible outcomes weighted by their probabilities of occurrence. Your chance of actually making precisely 85 may be fairly low. In the second risky situation mentioned above, you might also expect to marry a particular person you already know, perhaps someone you have just started dating and you have begun to observe that the relationship is going well. But the actual outcome could differ from what you expect. Risk captures the notion of unexpected outcomes, defined as those that occur that were not expected.

In some cases, we might know that an unexpected outcome is the most likely result. This is usually the case when the possible outcomes are extremely large if not infinite in number. For example, say you witness a crime and are asked to give a description of the criminal. Assume you got only a partial look and notice that the man is wearing a heavy coat. Among other characteristics, you may be asked to estimate the person's weight. Assuming it is an adult male, most estimates would be between 120 and 300 pounds (about 54 to 136 kg). Assuming an integer guess is sufficient, there are 181 possible integers between 120 and 300 (including the end points). Guessing the exact weight is unlikely, given so many possibilities. Of course, some possibilities can be virtually eliminated. Assuming the person appeared to be fairly average in weight, you might be able to narrow it down to a range of 170 to 200 pounds. You are in effect assigning probabilities such that the more extreme values are less likely. Nonetheless, it is a virtual certainty that the man is not precisely the same weight you guessed.

In some cases, the average value is not even possible. For example, a roll of a six-sided die could produce a result of 1, 2, 3, 4, 5, or 6. If you engaged in a large number of rolls and averaged the outcomes, it would come to 3.5, the unweighted average of the six numbers. Thus, 3.5 is the average value, but clearly a roll of 3.5 cannot occur. In short, the actual outcome is often not likely to equal the expected outcome.[3]

---

[3]Of course, that statement does not mean that the actual outcome can *never* equal the expected outcome in general. If the event in question is whether one will make an A in the financial risk management course, clearly an A is possible. Even expressed in the form of "what grade will you make in the course?" it is possible to make the expected grade.

Some events have outcomes that are both desirable and undesirable. Sometimes this phenomenon is called *good risk* and *bad risk*. But some events have only bad outcomes and a few have only good outcomes. For example, suppose your supervisor has told you that due to financial difficulties in the company, your job will either be terminated or you will have a salary reduction, to be determined later. There are no truly good outcomes here, but *good* is a relative notion: one outcome is clearly better than the other.

Some events have highly skewed outcomes. For example, let us say you go on a trip by automobile. As so often occurs, a friend wishes you to "Have a safe trip." Now consider the event to be the question of whether you return safely. Returning safely is clearly the good outcome. Returning unsafely encompasses a wide range of outcomes, some of which are only moderately bad and some of which are terrible. Notice that the outcomes are quite skewed. Regardless of the likelihood of occurrence, there is a tremendous downside but little if any upside. As we shall cover later in this book, extending credit is this same type of event. A creditor either pays you back the amount promised or defaults and pays back a lesser amount that ranges from a little less than the full amount owed right down to zero.

It is even possible to identify events in which there are no outcomes that are particularly undesirable. For example, suppose you enter a photograph in a contest. The worst outcome is that you lose, but there is really not much pain in losing. While one might occasionally have some interest in such events, they are not really of much interest to us in studying financial risk management.[4]

What They Said About Risk

In addition to George Costanza, many famous (and real) people have commented about the nature of risk. Here is a small collection of some interesting quotes:

> *It is part of a good man to do great and noble deeds, though he risk everything.*
> Plutarch, Greek Philosopher, 45AD–120AD

---

[4]There may actually be a slight downside in the photography contest. In order to enter the contest, you would probably be required to give your name, address, telephone number, and email address whereupon that information would go into a data base that may be sold to companies offering photographic products and services. In this day and age, the loss of privacy is a subtle downside to many seemingly harmless activities.

Risk isn't a word in my vocabulary. It's my very existence.
Slash (Saul Hudson), rock guitarist, 1965-

He who observes the wind will not sow, and he who observes the clouds will not reap.
(Ecclesiastes 11:4)

It seems to be a law of nature, inflexible and inexorable, that those who will not risk cannot win.
John Paul Jones, Scottish-American naval officer, 1747–1792

Take calculated risks. That is quite different from being rash.
George S. Patton, American army general, 1885–1945

If you risk nothing, then you risk everything.
Geena Davis, American actress, 1956-

Only those who will risk going too far can possibly find out how far one can go.
T. S. Eliot, American writer, 1888–1965

He is no wise man that will quit a certainty for an uncertainty.
Samuel Johnson, British writer, 1709–1784

The biggest risk is not taking any risk... In a world that is changing really quickly, the only strategy that is guaranteed to fail is not taking risks.
Mark Zuckerberg, American entrepreneur, 1984-

It is not in giving life but in risking life that man is raised above the animal.
Simone de Beauvoir, French writer, 1908–1986

Great deeds are usually wrought at great risks.
Herodotus, Greek historian, 484BC–425BC

We might quibble with some of these statements, but clearly these people, all highly successful, have thought about risks and the potential rewards.

The most important factor of interest to us in all risky scenarios is that there is at least one undesirable outcome, with undesirability defined on a relative basis. That statement means that there is at least one outcome that is desirable or less undesirable than at least one other outcome. So let us redefine risk with a definition that better suits our purposes:

Risk is the exposure to an event in which the outcomes are uncertain and at least one of the outcomes is undesirable relative to at least one other outcome.

Now let us more carefully examine the elements of this definition of risk.

2.2   Elements of a Definition of Risk

Our definition of risk contains two important elements: exposure to an event and uncertain outcomes. We now discuss each in turn.

2.2.1   *Exposure to an Event*

Starting a new business, investing in the financial markets, taking a drive in an automobile, going out on a date with someone you do not know very well. These are all somewhat risky events. Life in general is a sequence of risky events. And while some people pay a lot of money for the services of psychics and read their daily horoscopes, the truth is that we probably would not want to live a life without risk. A life without risk would include knowledge of when we are going to die and other bad things that we will face before death.

Hence, life is a sequence of risk exposures. But some exposures can be avoided, so the event is not a source of risk. The risk of dying in an airplane crash is essentially zero if the person chooses not to fly.[5] The risk of losing money at the race track is zero if we never place a bet. The risk of drowning in a swimming pool is zero if we never go near a pool. But of course, there are opportunity losses from not taking risks. We might never lose money in the stock market if we keep our money in bank deposits, but we will lose the opportunity to make money from the market and we assume the risk of losing purchasing power due to inflation. We would never enjoy the refreshing feeling of a splash in a pool on a hot summer day if we avoid the pool. In general, we would never enjoy the good things in life if we do not take some risks and engage in these activities.

Exposure exists in degrees. Though everyone who rides in an automobile is at some risk of being in an automobile accident, individuals who commute to work are at far greater risk of being in an automobile accident than those who take the train to work and drive their cars only occasionally. People who work and play around water are in far greater danger of drowning than are people who never go near the water.

In addition, for exposure to exist, the outcomes must have an undesirable element. Holton (2004) argues that a test for whether exposure exists is the simple question of whether a person would care if the outcome occurs. Thus, in order to know if there really is an exposure, we will ultimately be forced

---

[5]We are disregarding the infinitesimal probability of being killed on the ground in a plane crash.

to address the question of how a person feels about the risk. This topic is extremely important and we cover it later in this chapter.

The element of exposure we have been discussing is direct exposure. There is also indirect exposure. Take, for example, the risk of drowning. If you never go near a body of water large enough to drown you, your direct exposure is essentially zero and, thus, your risk of dying by drowning is virtually zero. But this fact does not mean that drowning could never affect you. Someone you love may have high exposure. If that person drowns, you do sustain an indirect loss from drowning. We are still correct in saying that you have essentially no risk from drowning, but we are not saying that the risk of drowning has no effect on you.

To summarize this point, though exposure does not have to be large, the existence of risk requires exposure to an event. As long as there is some possibility of an undesirable outcome, the required element of exposure in our definition of risk is present. Exposure can be direct or indirect.

2.2.2 *Uncertain Outcomes*

There is no risk if either the outcome is known or, equivalently, if all possible outcomes are the same. If a suicidal person fires a loaded gun at his head, the event of whether he will be hurt is not a risky event.[6] The extent of the damage is certainly a risky event, but damage of some form is certain. In the financial world, we often describe investments as having outcomes defined as *states of nature*, *states of the world*, or sometimes just *states*. The stock market increasing 10% or decreasing 10% in a year would be examples of two possible states.

What about the return on a zero coupon government bond, which is a riskless event, at least in terms of nominal returns?[7] Regardless of the state of the world, the holder of a zero coupon government bond receives the same amount at maturity. A government bond does not imply that risk does not exist, because there are still multiple states of the world. It simply implies that the security itself does not expose the holder to risk. But in one sense, even a government bond is not riskless. The investor who holds a government bond will find his return falling below the returns on risky securities in some states of the world. Such a loss is a type of opportunity cost, such as earning 3% on the bond when the stock market went up 10%. We will see this notion

---

[6]We are assuming the gun cannot misfire, nor can the person aim at his head and miss.

[7]A nominal return means that we are not considering how inflation can consume some of the purchasing power of the wealth generated by the return.

later in this book when we learn how to eliminate or reduce risk by a strategy called hedging. We will see that hedging is equivalent to taking a position that something bad will happen. On occasion, nothing bad will happen and the hedger will regret having taken such a position. In short, we can never really eliminate risk, provided that regret is still an uncomfortable feeling.

But getting back to our definition of risk, let us recall that at least one of the outcomes must be undesirable relative to at least one other outcome. We acknowledged that it is possible to have all good outcomes, but such an event is not of much interest to us in studying financial risk management. We are worried about adverse outcomes, because they make us feel bad. We will discuss what those feelings mean later.

2.3   Probability as a Useful but (Sometimes) Confusing, if not Misleading, Measure of Risk

Risk is oftentimes associated with probability. Peter Bernstein in his fascinating book *Against the Gods: The Remarkable Story of Risk* (1996) gives us an excellent history of the philosophical and mathematical foundations of risk as a subject of scholarly and practical interest. The ancient Greeks were extraordinarily skilled in mathematics but failed to develop any notions of randomness. The Greeks focused on deriving rules and descriptions of order and precision through the development of theorems and proofs, mostly related to geometry. Geometry, like many branches of mathematics, is largely based on certainty. The formula for the area of a circle, the square of π times the radius, is definitively the area. Given the radius, there is no uncertainty over what the area is. Randomness, although observed throughout life, was totally contradictory to their philosophical interests. Their observations on randomness were explained away as being determined by Zeus and the many other their gods. This apathy toward exploring the mathematical laws of probability by ancient civilizations is quite remarkable, given we know that gambling is frequently mentioned in ancient texts, including the Bible.[8]

The dawn of Christianity led to a belief that what was perceived as randomness was simply God's will. It was not until the middle of the

---

[8]Gambling is often referred to as "casting lots." At the crucifixion the Roman soldiers wanted Jesus' robe as a souvenir and planned to divide it at the seams and distribute the parts among themselves, but it had no seams so rather than cut it, they gambled for it (*John* 19: 23–24) with winner take all.

16th century that probability was explored in a formal manner.[9] Bernstein tells us that Girolamo Cardano of Italy was probably the first person to develop the idea of probability. An enthusiastic gambler, Cardano was motivated to quantify and better understand the notion of randomness. Interestingly, Cardano believed that his work was more theoretical than practical. Little did he know that the ideas he developed would become widely used in nearly all areas of life, particularly in business.

While mathematicians have much more formal definitions, probability is somewhat casually defined as *a measure of the likelihood of occurrence of the outcome of an event.* This definition does not help us much, because we then have to backtrack and define *likelihood.* So let us redefine probability as *the relative frequency with which the outcomes of an event occur.* This definition replaces the term *likelihood* with the notion of relative frequency, which is a much more intuitive idea. People typically understand this concept as representing the number of times an outcome occurs divided by the total number of possible outcomes. A 5% probability of an outcome occurring on a daily basis means that the outcome would be expected to occur once every 20 days. Looking back over a large number of days, we would count the number of days in which the outcome occurred relative to the total number of days. If this ratio is not relatively close to 5%, then 5% is probably not the correct probability.[10]

Probability is, however, just a means of quantifying risk. It is not the risk itself. One does not have to know the probability for the risk to exist, a point we take up in more detail later. For example, do you know the probability that your car will break down the next time you go for a drive? Probably not, but there is still almost surely a possibility that this event will occur. In fact, most of the time when faced with risk, we do not know the probabilities.

Probability can be a helpful but misleading way to quantify risk, and research shows that people are not very good at processing probability information. We will now take a look at several examples of how even very intelligent people are often unable to correctly interpret probability.

---

[9]Interestingly, double-entry bookkeeping, the basis for modern accounting, was developed in 1494 before the theory of probability came around (Bernstein (1996)). Thus, recording the outcomes of random events was established well before consideration was given to the likelihood of these events.

[10]Statisticians would, of course, tell us that there are more rigorous procedures that would have to be followed in order to reject the notion that 5% is the true probability.

2.3.1 *The Monty Hall Problem*

In 1963, the game show *Let's Make a Deal* premiered on American television. Monty Hall was the emcee of the show, and one particular gamble he offered became quite famous. It involved wagering the amount the contestant had won to that point on the show on the possibility of winning a more valuable prize that would be behind one of three doors. The setup is shown in Exhibit 2-1. The contestant sees three doors.

Monty asks the contestant to choose a door. Let us say the contestant chooses Door #3. Monty knows what is behind each door, and on that basis, he opens either Door #1 or Door #2, making sure that the one he opens does not contain the valuable prize. Let's say Monty opens up Door #1 to reveal a worthless prize. Now the contestant faces the situation in Exhibit 2-2.

Contestant chooses Door #3. Monty opens Door #1 to reveal a worthless prize. Monty then asks the contestant if she would like to change her decision from Door #3 to Door #2. Here is where the game becomes seemingly complicated.

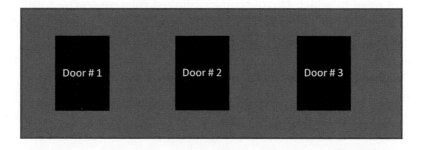

Exhibit 2-1. The Monty Hall Problem: The Possibilities

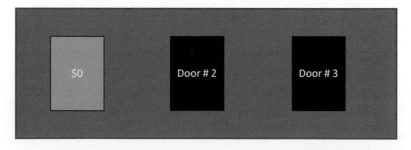

Exhibit 2-2. The Monty Hall Problem: Contestant Chooses Door, Monty Opens Another Door

Most people seem to believe that there is a 50-50 chance that the valuable prize is under either Door #3 or Door #2. Thus, with equal probabilities, most people feel that switching to Door #2 does not matter. They assume that the valuable prize is as likely to be under the door they chose (#3) as it is behind the door to which they could switch (#2).

In 1990, *Parade Magazine* columnist Marilyn Vos Savant, reportedly one of the most intelligent people on earth, received a reader inquiry about the most appropriate strategy for winning the game. Marilyn replied that switching is the better strategy, because it doubles the chance of winning from 1/3 to 2/3. She then proceeded to receive more than 10,000 responses, including more than 1,000 from people with PhDs. She stated that over 90% of the general public disagreed with her answer and about two-thirds of the academics opposed her answer. To prove that she was correct, Marilyn invited schools to play the game and submit their results along with whichever strategy was pursued. The results agreed with her answer: switching wins about twice as often.[11] I predict you do not see why, so take a look at Exhibit 2-3.

As the exhibit shows, in order to win by not switching we have to choose the winning door from the start. The probability of that happening is 1/3. But if we switch, the only way we lose is if we choose the winning door

---

Fact:

     Probability of winning + Probability of losing = 1

Fact:

     Probability of Winning by Not Switching = 1/3
     (To win, you would have to have picked the right door from the start)

Therefore,

     Probability of Losing by Switching = 1/3

Therefore, using the first fact above,

     Probability of Winning by Switching = 1 − 1/3 = 2/3

Exhibit 2-3. The Monty Hall Problem: Why Switching is the Better Strategy

---

[11]Vos Savant, http://marilynvossavant.com/game-show-problem/.

Prize is Under Door #	Contestant Chooses	Monty Opens	Contestant Switches to	Outcome
1	1	2 or 3	3 or 2	Loses
	2	3	1	Wins
	3	2	1	Wins
2	1	3	2	Wins
	2	1 or 3	3 or 1	Loses
	3	1	2	Wins
3	1	2	3	Wins
	2	1	3	Wins
	3	1 or 2	2 or 1	Loses

Exhibit 2-4. The Monty Hall Problem: All Possible Outcomes

from the start. So the probability of losing by switching is also 1/3. So the probability of winning by switching must be the complement, 2/3.

Alas. Most people still do not see the answer, and you may be one of the doubters. Exhibit 2-4 shows all nine of the possible equally likely outcomes. The switching strategy wins six out of nine times.

So what do we learn from the Monty Hall problem? We learn that sometimes even very smart people cannot grasp simple notions of probability. The PhD mathematicians who told Marilyn she was wrong should have known she was right. Perhaps the human brain is simply not conditioned to understand certain simple concepts without considerable effort. Perhaps our brains are simply fooled, in much the same way as in an optical illusion.

2.3.2 *Jeopardy and Risk*

Jeopardy is one of the most popular game shows of all time. It tells us a lot about risk. In fact, the word "jeopardy" actually means "risk." In the last segment of the program, which is called "Final Jeopardy," the three contestants have an opportunity to wager any portion up to all of the money they have won to that point on one final question.[12] If the response is correct,

---

[12]Well, technically it is not a question. In *Jeopardy* you are given the answer, and you must supply the question.

the wager amount is added to the contestant's money. If it is incorrect, the wager amount is deducted. The contestant with the most money at the end of this round wins and keeps all of his money, and the losers get only consolation prizes that are usually worth less than the money they have won. The contestants are told the category of the question and then must wager before they get the question.

Consider three contestants A, B, and C, who have won money to that point. Assume A has won $5000, B has won $2000, and C has won $1000. A knows that B can wager no more than $2000 so victory is assured for A if he wagers less than $1000. Of course A might be daring and a bit greedy and wager more than $1000 if he feels particularly confident of his knowledge in this category. B can count on A only to make a larger bet than necessary and also miss the question. Sometimes A is particularly lacking in confidence and wagers little if anything.

An Economist Looks at *Jeopardy*

Harvard economist Andrew Metrick (1995) collected data from *Jeopardy* during the period 1989–1992 to study the decisions made by about 1,000 contestants during the Final Jeopardy round. The data revealed that the person with the most money going into Final Jeopardy got the final answer correct 57% of the time, the person with the second-most money was correct 51% of the time, and the third place person was correct 46% of the time. The bet in which the person in first place wagers just enough to ensure that the person in second place cannot win even if both answer the question correctly is called the shut-out bet, and it occurs in almost half of the games. Perhaps more interesting is the fact that it does not occur more often, as it assures victory. Metrick analyzes a number of strategies that would appear to be rational and surprisingly finds that the players do not always follow these strategies. He finds that many contestants overestimate their abilities. Another interesting finding is that the players seem to behave as if they are not risk averse but are neutral toward risk. This finding may arise from the fact that the game does not expose the person's wealth to risk, other than what he has won on the show that day. Also, as has been shown in many other studies related to gambling, people enjoy the participative aspects of playing and will take risks they might not otherwise take because they are having fun. This characteristic can give the appearance that they are less averse to risk than they really are.

Source: Metrick (1995)

Now let us change the figures and let A have only $3500. A knows that B can wager $2000 and end up with $4000. Therefore A will probably have to wager at least $500. Sometimes A makes a wager like $501, reflecting his fear of missing the question. And on a few occasions, we find people who in spite of passing the tests necessary to get selected for the program, are unable to do the arithmetic to determine the necessary wagers to give them a possibility of winning. Of course, we have not exhausted all of the strategic considerations in *Jeopardy*, and there are many more game shows that have similar relevance to understanding risk. But the next time you watch a game show, think about it in terms of how contestants evaluate the risk and make their decisions. Are they behaving rationally? Would they make the same decisions if the wealth they had before going on the show were at stake?

2.3.3   *The Risk of Cancer*

In his book *Calculated Risks* (2002), Professor Gerd Gigerenzer of Germany illustrates how some very intelligent professionals fail to grasp the notion of probability. Let us look at a slightly modified example from the book.

> *One out of 100 forty-year-old women has breast cancer. Mammography is used to detect the presence of suspicious tissue. A positive mammogram usually leads to a biopsy. But mammography is not perfect. It will detect 90% of breast cancers but will indicate a problem 9% of the time in women who do not have breast cancer. These problems are usually benign tumors, cysts, and in some cases, simply random illusions that appear on the image.*
>
> *Now suppose that a 40-year-old woman gets a positive mammogram. What is the probability she has breast cancer? Gigerenzer gave 48 German physicians with an average of 14 years of experience this scenario and asked them this question. The estimates ranged between 1 and 90%. The median estimate was 70%. A third estimated more than 90%. Only four came close to the correct answer. What is the correct answer?*

This example is an excellent study in how probabilities are misunderstood. In this case, there is the risk of a false positive, a positive mammogram that leads a woman to believe that she is likely to have breast cancer. Exhibit 2-5 explains how to organize the information to determine the answer.

As the figure shows, consider 10,000 forty-year-old women, of whom 100 (1%) have breast cancer. Of these 100 women, 90 (90%) will have a positive mammogram. Of the 9,900 who do not have breast cancer, 891 (9%) will also have positive mammograms. Therefore, $90 + 891 = 981$ women will have a positive mammogram, but only 90 have breast cancer. Therefore, the probability that the woman has breast cancer is only $90/891 = .092$, or 9.2%.

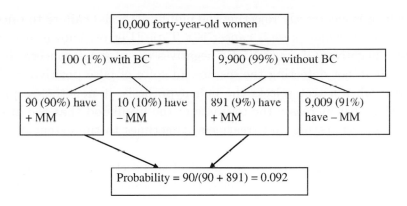

Exhibit 2-5. Analyzing the Risk from a Positive Mammogram

Of course, without having the mammogram, she might assume that she has a 1% chance of having cancer. With the positive mammogram, her likelihood is about nine times higher, and that is an important piece of information. Thus, the mammogram does provide information. But the probability of cancer is nowhere near the typical estimates of the true probability made by physicians and others. Obviously each case is different and other factors such as family history can also affect these odds. Interestingly, when the facts were presented in terms of numbers instead of probabilities, the physicians were better able to estimate the true likelihood of cancer.

The false positive rate is a serious issue in many forms of medical testing. For example, the PSA (prostate-specific antigen) test is a simple blood test primarily used in middle-aged and elderly men to examine the possibility of prostate cancer. A false positive PSA result can arise from so many innocuous conditions that the false positive rate has been estimated at as high as 75% in the U.S. False positives, however, lead to many unnecessary biopsies that can have negative consequences, not to mention a tremendous amount of anxiety by patients. It is estimated that as many as 1,000 men must take the test to save one life (National Cancer Institute (2012)).

False positives are an example of a statistical problem known as a Type I error. In statistical testing, you specify a hypothesis in the form of an initial presumption such as "The patient does not have cancer." This is called the null hypothesis. A medical test then generates a statistic that allows you to draw a conclusion that will have less than 100% confidence. Rejecting the null hypothesis would occur when a medical test indicates a reasonable possibility of cancer. If there is in fact no cancer, the error is called a Type I error, which is incorrectly rejecting the null hypothesis. Failure to reject the null hypothesis when there is cancer is a Type II error, known in medicine as a false negative. Of course, false negatives are of great concern, because they result in not detecting the disease. In spite of false positives and false negatives, when a test rejects the null hypothesis, it nonetheless provides information that increases the estimate of the likelihood that the disease is present. Further testing and treatment sometimes to the extent of surgery usually follows.

Statisticians will recognize the point of this section as an application of the notion of conditional probability. Having some information is certainly better than having none, but it is important not to over-state or under-state the true probability.

2.3.4   *Using Risk to Sell a Product*

Gigerenzer gives another interesting example that shows how probability is sometimes misused in the business world in an attempt to make a product more marketable.

> *A cholesterol-lowering drug is advertised as giving a 22% reduction in heart attacks for people with high cholesterol. What does this mean? Most people think that of 1,000 people with high cholesterol, 220 will not die if they take the drug, making the drug sound relatively effective. What it really means is quite different.*
>
> *One thousand people with high cholesterol were given the drug and another 1,000 people with high cholesterol were given a placebo. Of the group taking the drug, 32 died from a heart attack. Of the group given the placebo, 41 died from a heart attack. The 22% figure comes from the ratio 9/41 = 0.22.*

What is the correct interpretation? Exhibit 2-6 illustrates how to analyze this problem.

We see that 32 of 1,000 people had heart attacks while taking the drug and 41 of 1,000 had heart attacks when taking a placebo. The difference between 32 and 41 is indeed a 22% reduction, so the information used in marketing the drug is not wrong. But assuming the drug is effective, nine people lived who would have died had they not taken the drug. Thus, only 0.9% (9 out of 1,000) benefited from the drug. That means it would require 111 people (1/(.009)) taking the drug for one life to be saved. Now the drug does not sound so effective. Imagine marketing a drug in which you promote

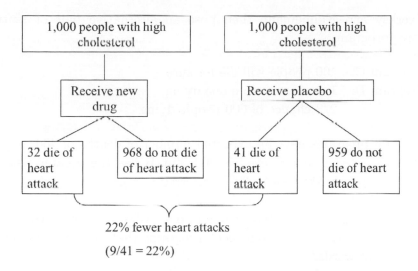

Exhibit 2-6. Using Risk to Market a Product

the fact that 1 of every 111 people who take the drug will be saved. What are the odds it would be you? (Well, 1 in 111.)

2.3.5 *Misunderstanding Expectations*

Tversky and Kahnemann (1981) have shown that many people are not even able to compare *identical* risks. They propose the following situation. A country is facing an outbreak of a dangerous disease. If the government does nothing, 600 people will die. It is considering the following mutually exclusive alternatives of two treatment programs.

Program A: 200 people will be saved for sure
Program B: 1/3 chance of 600 people being saved
             2/3 chance of none being saved

Both programs have the same expected value. The number saved is expected to be 200 and the number of deaths is expected to be 400, but B has greater risk. In a sample of 200 people, 72% preferred A over B. This result makes sense. Given equivalent expected values, the alternative with the lower risk should be preferred. Of course, that still leaves the disconcerting result that 28% of the people could not identify that program B produced the same expected result with greater risk.

Tverksy and Kahnemann then pose an alternative pair of mutually exclusive programs:

Program C: 400 people will die for sure

Program D: 1/3 chance of no one dying

2/3 chance of 600 people dying

Again, both programs have an expected number of deaths of 400, implying that the expected number saved is 200, but B has the greater risk. In a different sample of 200 people, 22% preferred C over D. But notice that C and A are the same program, and B and D are the same program. Yet, A is preferred to C by more than three-to-one. Why is there a tremendous difference in preference for equivalent programs that are simply explained using different words?

Tversky and Kahnemann argue that the way the problem is framed leads to the answer. Programs A and B are framed in terms of the number of people saved, while Programs C and D are framed in terms of the number of people who die. When framed in terms of survivors, the alternative of a sure number saved prevails. When framed in terms of deaths, a total of 400 certain deaths seems inferior to a one-in-three chance of no one dying.

The examples in this section illustrate that human beings have a difficult time processing information on probability and risk. Sometimes these mistakes seem like reasonable errors that people might make analyzing complex problems. Yet the examples here are not complex problems and when explained to them, many people still fail to grasp the explanations. Perhaps it is human nature to misunderstand probability. If those who use probability regularly in their work fail to understand it, there is potential for serious risk management mistakes.

2.4   Unconditional, Conditional, and Joint Notions of Risk

The breast cancer example above illustrates the notion of conditional risk compared to unconditional risk. Even though the probability of having cancer if a woman has a positive mammogram is much smaller than most people expect, she nonetheless has a much greater probability of breast cancer than a woman without a positive mammography. In this section we take a look at several more examples of how probability is misleading.

2.4.1 *The O. J. Simpson Case*

Here is another interesting story from Gigerenzer that very clearly identifies the notion of conditional probability:

> *The celebrated O. J. Simpson trial in 1995 brought out the best and worst in the legal process. Little known is the fact that it brought out the worst in the use of risk information, which probably contributed to the acquittal. The prosecution argued that Simpson's history of spousal abuse constituted a pattern and a motive, increasing the likelihood that he was the killer. Famous criminal defense attorney and Harvard law professor Alan Dershowitz argued against this claim by noting several facts. As many as four million women are battered annually by husbands and boyfriends in the U.S. In 1992 the FBI reported that 913 women were killed by husbands and 519 by boyfriends. So, Dershowitz claims that of four million incidents, only 1,432 ended in homicides. Therefore, only about 1 in 2,500 incidents of abuse ends in murder.*

It was compelling evidence for the jury, and the prosecution was unable to show the fallacy of this argument. Exhibit 2-7 shows how to determine the true probability that O. J. did it.

The defense's line of reasoning ignored the fact that *two events occurred*: Nicole Simpson had been battered *and* murdered. That simple fact requires a different analysis. If 1 in 2,500 abused women is murdered, we would expect about 40 murders in every 100,000 battered women. We need to know the numbered of battered women killed each year by someone other than a

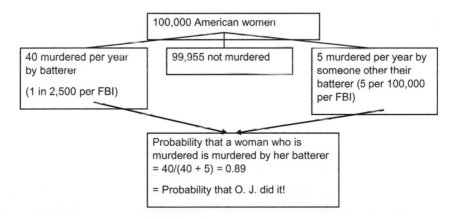

Exhibit 2-7. The Probability that O. J. Committed the Murder

husband or boyfriend. Assuming this ratio is the same as for the general population, statistics show that it is about five out of 100,000. So consider 100,000 battered women. We would expect 40 (1 in 2,500) to be murdered by their batterers and five to be murdered by someone else. Thus, *if a woman is murdered, the probability she was murdered by her batterer is 40/45 = 0.89, about 89%.*

The relevant probability concept is that of conditional probability. Given the condition that she was battered and murdered, what is the probability that she was murdered by her batterer? Clearly in this case it is much higher than the unconditional probability.

2.4.2   *A Nobel Experiment*

The research of Tversky and Kahneman exposed many elements of human irrationality with respect to making decisions under risk. Consider their example of a hypothetical woman named Linda,[13] who

- Is 31 years old
- Is single
- Is outspoken
- Is very bright
- Majored in philosophy
- As a student, was deeply concerned with issues of discrimination and social justice and participated in anti-nuclear demonstrations.

So now you probably have a good idea what kind of person Linda is like. Think you do? Take a guess as to which of the following statements is *more* likely.

A. Linda is a bank teller.
B. Linda is a bank teller and a feminist.

More than 85% of the people who were asked this question said "B." Yet the correct answer is A. Look at Exhibit 2-8. The left circle represents the women who are feminists, and the right circle is those who are bank tellers. The intersection of the two circles is those who are both. Clearly the intersection is much smaller than either circle. Even if the number of feminist bank tellers is quite large, it cannot be more than the number of bank tellers in total or

---

[13]Tversky and Kahnemann (1983).

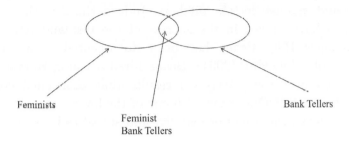

Feminists

Bank Tellers

Feminist
Bank Tellers

Exhibit 2-8. Bank Tellers and Feminists

the number of feminists in total. Therefore, it cannot be true that Linda is more likely to be both than to be either a feminist or a bank teller.

2.4.3 *Risk in Sports*

Sports are a great source of probability and risk information. Watching a baseball game in particular inundates us with probabilities in the form of batting averages and earned run averages. Suppose a particular batter steps up to the plate and we are told that his average is 0.250. Most fans will know that this statistic means the batter has gotten a hit about one time in every four official at-bats. On occasion we might be told, however, that his average against this pitcher is much higher at 0.300. In other words, even though he is hitting only 0.250 against all pitchers, he is hitting 0.300 against this pitcher. We now know that, at least historically, he has been a much better hitter against this pitcher and he has gotten hits three times in every ten official at-bats against this pitcher. If the historical batting average is a good measure of the probability of getting a hit, we can interpret his batting average against every pitcher as an unconditional probability and his batting average against this pitcher as a conditional probability. The condition is that he is batting against a particular pitcher, not just against any pitcher selected at random.[14]

If used properly, probability can be very helpful. As the manager of a baseball team, it is important to know how a hitter is performing. Such information provides the basis for predicting how he will do in

---

[14]Baseball experts should resist the temptation to cry "foul." Yes, indeed the author knows that the probability of getting a hit is not the batting average, because there are at-bats that do not count in the total of official at-bats. In addition, there are other ways of getting on base that are as valuable as getting a hit. Rather than get into these complexities, let's go with batting average.

the future and against certain pitchers. Indeed the role that probability and statistics have played in the success of the Oakland Athletics under general manager Billy Beane has been documented in Michael Lewis' bestselling book *Moneyball* (2004). Beane hired a young Harvard graduate who uncovered numerous statistical results that challenged conventional thinking in baseball.[15] Operating with one of the lowest payrolls in baseball, Beane has parlayed the use of probability and statistics into one of the most successful franchises in sports.

Likewise, the financial risk manager will want to know something about the probability that a large exchange rate move will significantly impair his company's foreign cash flows. That manager will want to take into account all conditions that could affect his company's outcomes, such as how exchange rate volatility could change if the Federal Reserve tightens interest rates. When appropriately used, probability theory is a valuable tool, but biases, conventional wisdom, and gut feelings are dangerous, as we will discuss later in this chapter.

Probability can be misleading, however, especially when we confuse conditional and unconditional probabilities. Probability can be misleading when we measure it badly. Used correctly, probability can give a company a valuable competitive edge. We will use probability concepts frequently in this book, but we will be very careful and try not to misuse them.

2.5   Risk vs. Uncertainty

Almost 100 years ago, economist Frank Knight made a distinction between risk and uncertainty. He argues that risk is when the probabilities are known, and uncertainty is when the probabilities are not known. In reality, nearly all situations fall under his classification of uncertainty. We rarely know the probabilities. Even when we have a lot of statistical data, such as the probability of breast cancer in a 40-year-old woman, we do not know how special circumstances affect that probability. She might have a family history of breast cancer, but she exercises regularly, is not overweight, and has other low-risk characteristics. In a few cases, we might know the true probabilities

---

[15]For example, Beane learned that statistically the stolen base is one of the most overrated feats in baseball, and he has practically prohibited his players from stealing. He also found that the conventional wisdom of bunting late in the game with his team one run behind and a runner on first base with no outs is statistically less successful than swinging as normal.

such as drawing an ace out of full deck, but most of these situations are not particularly important in life and in particular, in the world of finance.

But ultimately we often need estimates of probabilities. We usually just make educated guesses and then proceed to use these probabilities, sometimes without much regard for the notion of Knightian uncertainty. Knight argues that this is how business decisions are typically made: through observations of historical patterns and the assessment of subjective probabilities based on those patterns. Thus, there is a distinction between objective probabilities, such as would occur with a coin toss, and subjective probabilities, which are more often the case in real life.

A related notion is the fact that probabilities can change randomly. We might know the probabilities today, but they might change tomorrow. For example in a casino, we might know the odds on the first hand of a blackjack game. After some cards are played, the odds then change. While it is technically possible for a brilliant person to "count cards," it is still extremely difficulty for most people. In the financial world, the volatility of the stock market can be greater today than it was yesterday, which changes the probabilities. We have now established another characteristic of risk: risk is risky. In finance, this is oftentimes called the volatility of volatility.[16]

On June 6, 2002 United States Secretary of Defense Donald Rumsfeld gave a press conference at NATO headquarters in Brussels in which he made the following quote:

> *There are things we know that we know. There are known unknowns. That is to say there are things that we now know we don't know. But there are also unknown unknowns. There are things we don't know we don't know. So when we do the best we can and we pull all this information together, and we then say well that's basically what we see as the situation, that is really only the known knowns and the known unknowns. And each year, we discover a few more of those unknown unknowns.*

Because this statement made little sense to the average person and to most reporters, Rumsfeld was the butt of many jokes. Yet, in fact, Rumsfeld had explained in a very accurate and concise manner that there were known facts and unknown risks and that over time some of the unknowns became known, but many more unknowns remain. Indeed, risk changes. The types of risks change, their likelihood changes, the exposures change, and new risks emerge.

---

[16]Experts in volatility call this *stochastic volatility*. "Stochastic" is simply a word that means random.

2.6 Processing Risk

Risk is only half of the picture. We must also deal with how we feel about risk and how we react to it. One person might stress over a financial loss of $100 to the point of requiring anti-depressive medication, while another might regard it as a risk worth taking that just did not happen to work out this time. In order to understand risk, we must understand the extent to which an individual tolerates risk. Economists explain this notion using a concept called utility.

2.6.1 *Utility*

Utility is a measure of satisfaction. Satisfaction comes in a variety of forms such as consumption of goods and services, love and companionship of family and friends, art, literature, music, sports, and pride from success. Our concern in this book is in the utility that derives from the consumption of goods and services. Ultimately this utility comes from financial wealth. We equate wealth maximization to utility maximization, because the more wealth we have, the more we can consume, and therefore the more utility we receive.

We explore the basic idea behind utility with a famous story. In the eighteenth century, Swiss mathematician Nicholas Bernoulli asked his cousin, the mathematician Daniel Bernoulli, a puzzling question. Suppose Peter tosses a coin and continues tossing until it comes up heads. He offers to give Paul one ducat if it lands on heads the first time, two if it lands on heads the second time, four if it lands on the heads the third time and so on.[17] In other words, the payoff doubles each time the coin fails to land on heads. The game continues until the player wins.

First we should determine Paul's expected payoff. Then we might want to know how much Paul would be willing to pay Peter to play the game. This problem is called the Petersburg paradox because it had been introduced at a meeting of mathematicians in Petersburg, Russia (today, St. Petersburg). And as we shall see, it does indeed appear to be a paradox.[18]

We expect to earn one ducat on the first toss with probability one-half, two on the second toss with probability $(1/2)^2$ and so on. The expected

---

[17]A ducat was a gold coin used in Europe until around the early 20th century that weighed about 3.5 grams, about an eighth of an ounce, of nearly pure gold. Thus, if gold costs $1,000 an ounce, the value of a ducat would be about $125.

[18]Details are provided in Bernoulli (1954), a translation of the original paper that first appeared in 1738.

payoff is thus,

$$2^0 \left(\frac{1}{2}\right) + 2^1 \left(\frac{1}{2}\right)^2 + 2^2 \left(\frac{1}{2}\right)^3 + \cdots = \frac{1}{2} + \frac{1}{2} + \frac{1}{2} + \cdots = \infty.$$

Because it is, however remotely, possible that heads will never come up, this expression will contain an infinite number of positive terms each with a value of 1/2. Thus, the expected payoff is infinite.

But would Paul pay an infinite amount to play? Or more interestingly, would *you* pay an infinite amount to play? Most people would not. Suppose you were willing to pay one ducat. Would a counterparty accept a ducat as a reasonable price? Probably not. The probability of earning more than one ducat is 0.5. Would you pay eight ducats? The probability of a payoff of more than eight ducats is only one-sixteenth.[19] Nonetheless, the average or expected payoff is infinite.

Daniel Bernoulli proposed a solution to this problem by applying a new theory of risk based on how people feel about risk: the expected utility paradigm. He proposed that we evaluate risky propositions not in terms of their expected values but in terms of the utility they provide. To do that, however, requires that we specify a mathematical function that converts wealth to utility. He proposed the logarithmic, or log, function to represent the utility of an amount of money. Let w be the wealth. Then $\ln(w)$ is the utility where "ln" refers to the natural logarithm.[20] The log function always increases with wealth, so more wealth will always give us more utility. In other words, we will always like more wealth. But utility increases at a decreasing rate, which is what economists call *diminishing marginal utility*. It turns out that risk will account for this diminishing marginal utility and make the gamble less desirable for more wealth. As Daniel argued, an additional unit of wealth at a high level of wealth brings less satisfaction than

---

[19]The probability of a payoff of one ducat is 0.5, two ducats is 0.25, four ducats is 0.125, and eight ducats is 0.0625. Thus, $0.5 + 0.25 + 0.125 + 0.0625 = 0.9375$, the probability of a payoff of eight ducats or less. Thus, the probability of a payoff of more than eight ducats is $1 - 0.9375 = 0.0625 = 1/16$.

[20]The natural logarithm or natural log of a number x is the power to which you raise the constant e, which is $2.71828\ldots$, to obtain x. Natural logs are widely used in finance because they reflect the accrual of wealth at a continuous rate, which is a good approximation of reality. Sometimes the natural log function is written as $\ln x$, sometimes as $\log_e(x)$, and sometimes as $\log(x)$, although the latter can easily be mistaken for the common log where the base is 10. In this book, we will use the $\ln(x)$ notation. Also, we will occasionally write it as $\ln x$, which is commonly done but does run the "ln" and the "x" together a bit tightly.

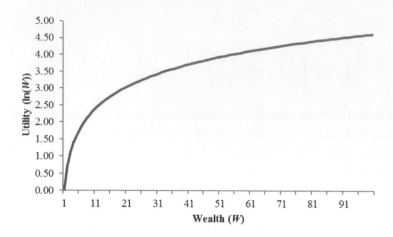

Exhibit 2-9. Bernoulli's Log Utility Function

an additional unit of wealth at a low level of wealth. The risk associated with trying to achieve greater wealth will reduce the marginal value of the wealth. An example of Bernoulli's log utility function is shown in Exhibit 2-9.

On the horizontal axis, we plot the money or wealth (W) of the individual, here ranging from 1 to 100, while on the vertical axis we plot the utility, $\ln(W)$. Notice that utility always increases with wealth — more money is always preferred to less — but notice also that the decreasing slope means that there is less and less additional utility as wealth increases, the principal of diminishing marginal utility, and it simply means that while we want more money, the additional benefit of each increment of money is less and less. In addition, we sometimes describe the curve as being concave, meaning arched downward.

Bernoulli's utility concept facilitates a resolution of the Petersburg paradox. Bernoulli rationalized that if utility, not money, is what we ultimately want, then we should attempt to maximize expected utility when making decisions under risk. Expected utility is a weighted average of the utility of all possible outcomes in which the weights are the probabilities of the respective outcomes. The expected utility of the Petersburg paradox problem is

$$\ln(2^0)\left(\frac{1}{2}\right) + \ln(2^1)\left(\frac{1}{2}\right)^2 + \ln(2^2)\left(\frac{1}{2}\right)^3 + \cdots$$

$$= 1\left(\frac{1}{2}\right) + 0.6931\left(\frac{1}{2}\right)^2 + 1.0836 + \left(\frac{1}{2}\right)^3 + \cdots$$

Solving this problem looks difficult, but it makes use of a known formula for an infinite sum. Ultimately, the above calculation reduces to $\ln(2) = 0.6931$.

But what does this mean? Do we know anything useful by knowing that engaging in this bet achieves expected utility of 0.6931? Well, what it tells us is that if we gave up two units of currency, we would forfeit utility of 0.6931. Hence, two is the maximum we should pay to engage in this bet.

The Petersburg Paradox, the Doubling Strategy, the Gambler's Ruin, and the Fall of Barings Bank

In 1995, the venerable and conservative 200-year-old Barings Bank was financially ruined by a 28-year-old clerk in its Singapore office. Nick Leeson had been sent to Singapore by Barings' London office to straighten out a paperwork backlog. Leeson began trading derivatives and started hiding losses in a special account that was not easily detectable. As the losses mounted, Leeson attempt to recover his losses with a strategy based somewhat loosely on the Petersburg paradox and known in gambling as the *doubling strategy*. For every unit of currency bet and lost, one doubles the gamble. Although the expected payoff is infinite, the likelihood is generally quite high that the investor will have all of his resources depleted before earning the big payoff necessary to recover all previous losses. This point is known as the *gambler's ruin*. Ultimately, Leeson lost about \$1.2 billion for the bank, which had capital of only about \$500 million. The Bernoullis probably would have said "We told you so."

Source: Leeson (1996)

The log utility function, however, has one very limiting characteristic: it is the same for everyone. But people are quite different. They vary considerably in how they feel about risk. There are, however, other utility functions that are more complex but can accommodate how people vary in their feelings toward risk. We will say a little more about utility in the next chapter.

The modern view of financial markets is that competition forces markets to reward higher returns with the higher risks that are required to earn those returns. If it were any other way, the most attractive financial opportunities would be bid up in price until they were less attractive. Utility reflects both return and risk, the benefits of the former and the costs of the latter. Two investments of equal expected return but unequal risk will not be viewed equivalently. The one with the lower risk will be taken and the other will be ignored, after which its price will fall and make it more competitively attractive. In equilibrium all assets must offer the same expected return per unit of risk.

The feelings people have about return and risk are usually characterized by the two concepts of *non-satiation* and *risk aversion*. Non-satiation means that a person is never satisfied with the amount of money he has. He always wants more. Thus, more money always gives us more utility. In Exhibit 2-9, that means the curve always increases. Risk aversion means that a person dislikes risk. Risk aversion is the property that creates diminishing marginal utility, the characteristic that while the curve always increases with additional money, it does so at a lower rate.[21]

People who are risk averse will not take on risk without the expectation of a reward, which we call a *risk premium*. For example, suppose one can invest money in a government-insured bank deposit and earn 1%. What would it take for someone to forgo that 1% return for certain and invest the money in a mutual fund the return on which is risky? The mutual fund must offer an expected return that exceeds 1%. Nonetheless, regardless of the return the mutual fund produces, it is risky. If the mutual fund offers an average return of 8%, we think of it as offering a 7% risk premium. That return is expected to be earned on average over a long period of time, but the return in any one period can be positive and high or quite negative and low.

A major limitation of the use of utility is that it is very difficult to measure utility. One can use a particular utility function, but it is just a guess as to whether that function correctly captures how the person feels about risk. In particular, as noted above, the log utility function treats everyone the same. Other functions exist, but to use them correctly, you have to estimate a measure of each person's feelings about risk.

In the world of finance, determining fair prices for risky investments involves incorporating expected returns, risk, and risk preferences or how people feel about risk. In the world of risk management, however, we shall

---

[21]It may not be visually apparent why the curve in Exhibit 2-9 implies risk aversion. Consider an investment that offers wealth of 10 with absolute certainty. Its utility is $\ln(10) = 2.30$. Now consider a risky investment that offers a 50% chance of wealth of 5 and a 50% chance of wealth of 15. The expected wealth is 10 obtained as $0.5 \times 5 + 0.5 \times 15$, but it is not as satisfying as the safe investment of 10. The expected utility of the risky investment is $0.5 \times \ln 5 + 0.5 \times \ln 15 = 2.16$, so the risky investment has less utility. The risky investment would, however, be equivalent to a safe investment that offers wealth of $\exp(2.16) = 8.67$.

benefit from the ability to price risk management instruments such as financial derivatives without resorting to the use of risk premiums. If we hold a stock and assume the risk of the stock, a derivative contract that insures against loss on the stock will cost an amount that is a function of the risk of the stock and a few other factors, but not the risk of the derivative. The derivative is merely a tool that alters the stockholder's risk, but it is not a source of risk itself. The derivative will allow one to transfer the risk but does not create any risk that did not already exist in the first place. Hence, we can think of derivatives as a form of insurance that enable us to transfer risks from those who do not want them to those willing to bear them. The price of this insurance is a function of the amount of risk being transferred, which is determined by the amount of underlying risk and the amount of this risk that the risk taker is willing to bear. As a result, we will be able to treat people as though they are risk neutral, when in fact, they are risk averse. Their risk aversion manifests in the prices and volatilities of the underlying sources of risk, but not in the derivative contracts used to transfer that risk. By treating people as though they are risk neutral, we simplify the pricing. But remember that above all, *we are not assuming that people are risk neutral*. We are just safely disregarding their risk aversion, which we can do, because their risk aversion is captured in the price of the underlying source of risk such as a stock price, a bond price, or interest rate. While this material may seem complex, being able to ignore risk preferences when pricing derivatives will actually make it much simpler. Of course, we will cover this material later in more detail, and slowly and carefully so that you will fully understand it. There is no risk in that statement. It is safely guaranteed.

Having said all of that, we must emphasize that risk aversion, while not a factor in the pricing of derivative instruments, does play an important role in risk management. It determines how much risk a party is willing to take. High risk-averse people tend to take low amounts of risk and low risk-averse people tend to take high amounts of risk. An important complementary expression for risk aversion is *risk tolerance*. A high risk-averse person has a low degree of risk tolerance, while a low risk-averse person has a high degree of risk tolerance.

Before we leave this section on utility theory, we must acknowledge that a methodology called *prospect theory* as proposed by Kahnemann and Tversky (1979) may be a better specification of how people make risky decisions. In utility theory, people make decisions based on what wealth they will have after the outcome is revealed. In prospect theory, people care more about the *change* in their wealth and more accurately, the rate of change. For example, two people with similar risk aversion might make quite reasonable but opposite decisions based on the potential absolute change from a risky decision. A gamble with a $100 expected payoff might be of little interest to a wealthy person but might be of much interest to someone who is not wealthy. In other words, the relative change is what matters. Prospect theory is quite consistent with the typical way in which we believe financial decisions are made: rates of return matter more than prices. Prospect theory still incorporates risk aversion in that a loss of $x\%$ hurts more than a gain of $x\%$.

2.6.2 *Determinants of Risk Tolerance*

It is a fact that some people tolerate risk more than others. In this section, we will take a look at the factors that determine risk tolerance.

Risk tolerance is an innate characteristic, so deeply imbedded in the elementary composition of living beings that we even observe it in animals. Most wild animals have a low degree of risk tolerance. The snake that sees or hears a hiker will tend to quickly slither away, because it realizes that the hiker is a source of only downside risk. The hiker is not likely to feed the snake, so there is no reward to justify the risk of an encounter with a human. Some wild animals, however, have a low degree of risk tolerance. Dolphins, for example, are naturally drawn to humans, possibly because they have an effective system of risk controls — they are strong, fast, can defend themselves, and if necessary, they can swim away quite rapidly. Humans may present a curiosity in which the possibility of reward justifies the risk. Domesticated animals vary widely in their degree of risk tolerance. Surely everyone knows someone's dog that treats you like a suspicious stranger every time it sees you, even though it has a long history of encounters with you that have led to no harm and the pleasure of frequent petting. And you almost surely have encountered a dog you have never met that is the epitome of friendliness and affection even though it has no experience with you. The fly that buzzes annoyingly around your head has a high degree of risk tolerance, bad information, and poor risk controls. There is no possible reward and only risk. Not surprisingly, flies have a very short life span, perhaps because they are poor managers of risk.

Indeed, risk tolerance is innate. While risk tolerance may vary from person to person, within a single person in different situations and across time, an important element of risk tolerance is imbedded in our genes.

Perhaps the most fundamental determinant of risk tolerance is gender (Byrnes *et al.*, 1999). Males are generally far more risk tolerant than females, but the primary driver of this effect is not simple whether one is male or female: it is the hormone testosterone. Women do have a small amount of testosterone and women who have more of it take more risks in comparison to women who have less. Likewise men who have less testosterone take fewer risks than men who have more testosterone (Sapienza *et al.*, 2009).

Financial risk taking is a special type of risk taking in which an individual is willing to forgo money for the possibility of a larger gain but with the risk of a loss. An extensive history of laboratory experiments confirms that males and the testosterone factor are more risk tolerant, but these studies have serious limitations. Posing a hypothetical situation, such as "would you be willing to invest $10 for a gamble with a 50% chance of making $20 and a 50% chance of making $5" does not measure the person's risk tolerance very well, because it is not real. There is no risk. Even if you gave the person $10 on the spot, there is no assurance that the person would make the same decision in comparison to having the person reach into his pocket and come up with his own $10 to gamble. People exhibit a characteristic called the *endowment effect*, which we discuss in more detail later, that means that they value the $10 out of their own pocket more than the $10 handed to them, even though choosing not to gamble would mean they could keep the $10. There have, however, been a number of studies that examine actual financial traders, and these studies have confirmed that males take more risks than females and that testosterone is the primary driver of risk. We can be pretty confident of that fact.

Other factors that affect risk tolerance are age and wealth. Age, however, is largely a correlate with experience and can have direct or opposite effects. For example, a young person who has not been exposed to many negative outcomes may have higher risk tolerance simply because he has not seen the many bad things that can happen. A young person may be emboldened by what merely amounts to lack of information. This characteristic was used by the allied armies in the D-Day invasion. World War II historian Stephen Ambrose (1995) relays the fact that the first soldiers who came off of the landing boats and onto the heavy gunfire of the Normandy beaches were relatively inexperienced. The generals who planned the invasion knew that experienced soldiers would anticipate the horrors they would face and might have their courage dominated by their fears. With regard to financial risk, however, a young person with a long future ahead of him may feel he can take more risks now, because there will be many opportunities to recover from bad outcomes. On the other hand, a young person with a lot of responsibility, such as a growing family, is likely to have less risk tolerance.

Wealth is also a correlate with risk tolerance. A person with more wealth can afford to take more risk. Nonetheless, the relationship is not clear and consistent. More wealth is often associated with more age and experience, and it is not clear which is the more dominant factor. Other factors include marital status, current job, and education (Grable (2000)).

The age and wealth factors also imply that a person can exhibit different degrees of risk tolerance as his age and wealth change. Interestingly, a person can also exhibit situational risk tolerance, meaning that his risk tolerance can vary in different scenarios. This inconsistency of risk tolerance is a well-known human characteristic. The same people who buy insurance and yet engage in lotteries and gamble in casinos, neither of which offer risk premiums, are good examples of these inconsistencies (Friedman and Savage (1948)). In the following sections, we examine some human traits in which risk tolerance is inconsistent or irrational.

Risk Tolerance and Your Fingers

As we discussed, testosterone is the primary determinant of risk tolerance. One can measure testosterone with a blood test and roughly but somewhat less effectively with a saliva sample. Another simple albeit less effective measure can be done quite easily with your fingers.

The index finger, called the second digit (2D) and the ring finger, called the fourth digit (4D), combine to produce a sexually dimorphic property, meaning that they are distinct between males and females. The relationship between the sizes of these two fingers also varies within the male and female sexes.

Specifically, the ratio of the length of the second finger to the fourth finger is a measure of exposure to testosterone in the mother's uterus. This ratio, known as 2D:4D, is affected by the male hormones in the mother. All women have male hormones to varying degrees, and a fetus is exposed to all chemicals in the mother's body. Some fetuses, however, are exposed to more male hormones in the uterus than others. These hormones are not determinants of the sex of the fetus. That factor is, of course, determined by the 23rd pair of chromosomes. These additional male hormones cause the fourth finger to grow longer. As a result of the longer fourth finger, males are generally able to do some physical activities better than females, such as grip a large object like a basketball.

Take out a ruler and measure your second and fourth fingers (suggestion: do it with a photocopy of your hand). If a finger has ever been broken, do not use that hand. Measure the distance from the crease at the base of the finger to the tip of the finger. Divide the second finger length by the fourth finger length and that is your 2D:4D measure. The average for males is about 0.947. The average for females is about 0.965. (The author's ratio is about 0.952).

Studies have shown that the 2D:4D ratio is correlated with risk tolerance, though it does not correlate as well as an actual measure of active testosterone. Testosterone varies over one's life and even during a given day, so a more dynamic measure is better. Nonetheless, the static measure of the 2D:4D ratio is a moderately effective indicator of risk tolerance.

Source: Sapienza *et al.* (2009)

2.6.3 *Irrationalities, Peculiarities, and Inconsistencies in Risk Tolerance*

Many of the models used in financial decision making are based on the concept of *homo economicus*, which refers to the notion that human beings are rational and act in their own best interests. Yet, research and casual observation has led to the contrary idea that people are not necessarily rational, nor always self-interested. In this section we examine some of irrationalities that people exhibit when they make decisions under risk.

People have a difficult time separating what has happened in the past from what might happen in the future. Hindsight is 20-20. The Latin terms *ex post* (after the fact) and *ex ante* (before the fact) are frequently used in the financial world in particular with respect to how risk is described. With ex post, however, there is no risk. The event has already happened. Risk exists only in an ex ante sense. Ex post analyses of the outcomes of events can be potentially useful, however, in evaluating the risk going forward, but only if the risk remains constant. Investment managers are acutely aware of this distinction, because they are frequently required to remind their clients and prospective clients that "past performance does not guarantee future results." Yet, investment managers always look into the past and use it to make predictions of the future. Investment professionals often develop models based on data extracted over historical periods and use those models over future periods without regard to whether conditions have changed, a process called *backfitting* that can lead to good historical models but poor future models. Investment professionals often assume that just because an event has never occurred, it is excluded from the set of possible future events, a risk that has come to be known as Black Swan risk.[22]

In sports this effect is often called *Monday morning quarterbacking,* a concept from American football. It reflects the fact that in American football the quarterback is such a critical player and is constantly required to make critical decisions, often with little information or within a nanosecond of receiving information. When the outcomes are not favorable, fans often question the decisions on Monday morning.[23] Of course, questioning a decision after the fact is easy to do since the outcome is known. People in general have a very difficult time separating ex post from ex ante. To do so requires forgetting much of the past. While we might collect data from the past, we must forget that the actual outcome, while known today, would not have been known in the past. Hence, the decision maker cannot be held to as high a standard as do the Monday morning quarterbacks.

Failure to appreciate this point has brought much criticism to some people. Whenever there is a terrible shooting by a mentally disturbed person, society seems to be amazed that no one could see it coming. In reality, the emotional profiles of shooters match that of thousands of other mentally ill people who are no danger to anyone but themselves. Many people wonder why economists did not see through the charades of Enron and Bernie Madoff, but on the surface Enron and Bernie Madoff looked pretty good to most people.[24]

People often think that if good outcomes occur, it is because of their foresight, whereas bad outcomes are often seen as simply bad luck. Let us say that you buy a stock and watch it go up. Then you might be tempted to think how skilled you are. Suppose you sell a stock and watch it go down. Once again, you think you are pretty smart for having staved off an undesirable event. Unfortunately, this kind of thinking has led to numerous risk management mistakes, some of which have destroyed organizations.

---

[22]The concept of the Black Swan is one we will take up in Chapter 14. Impatient readers can refer to Taleb (2007).

[23]The games are primarily played on the weekend. Hence, fans discuss them at work on Monday morning.

[24]A small number of people apparently did see through Enron and Madoff, but their voices were unheard, because the possibility of fraud seemed so small.

Consider this hypothetical experiment. One million people go to an Internet site where each person pays $1 and gets to predict the outcome of a coin toss. At a designated time, the coin is tossed (perhaps with illustrative graphics of coins floating through the air). Those who call the toss correctly continue playing. The losers have to quit. After 10 coin tosses, those who have called all 10 tosses correctly split the $1 million. How many people would you expect to call all 10 tosses correctly?

The probability of one person calling 10 consecutive coin tosses correctly is $0.5^{10} = 0.00097656$. Assuming the calls are independent, we would expect $1,000,000(0.00097656) = 976.56$ people to call all 10 tosses correct. Let us just round that number to 1,000. So 1,000 people would each receive $1,000. Would this be skill? Would National Football League teams line up to hire these people, enlisting their aid in helping to call the coin toss at the beginning of the game? Of course not. These people merely got lucky. There are so many of them only because a small amount of luck exists in any random outcome. With so many participants, it is easy to find a lot of lucky players. Indeed there is reason to doubt the investment skill displayed by so many successful investors. If every highly successful investor could be identified, they would probably be just a small sample of the entire universe of investors over the entire history of financial markets.

In the financial world, you should never forget what an enduring element of luck there is to the day-to-day movements in the markets. The humility of knowing that you are not as smart as you are tempted to think is a useful watchdog that should guide the decisions of good risk managers.

True skill is a difficult quality to measure and can require an extraordinary amount of experience to provide a statistically reliable result. Some experts have calculated that demonstrating true investment skill would require more years of trading than in a normal human life span. In spite of this fact, we find that the investment management business typically pays bonuses to portfolio managers based on annual performance. Consider an investment manager who in her 40-year career earns an average annual return of 7% and a standard deviation of return of 25%, both reasonable numbers. Suppose the risk-free rate is 3%. It sounds like she did well, beating the risk-free rate on average by 4%. Yet, statistically, it is not possible to acknowledge that the return is greater than the risk-free rate. The t-statistic is $(7\% - 3\%)/(20\%\sqrt{40}) = 1.26$, which is not large enough to eliminate the possibility that the result could have been earned randomly. It would take approximately 100 years of annual returns for this result to be statistically upheld. No investment manager manages a portfolio that long.[25] Taleb (2001) has written an entire book on this idea, that people are misled by the randomness of life and that nowhere is this more obvious than in the financial world.

People often perceive the risk to be greater when they have less information about the probabilities. As noted earlier, knowledge of true probabilities is rare but sometimes we have less information than at other times. Initial public offerings are an excellent example of risky situations in which the amount of information is often quite small. Casino gambling is an example of a risky situation in which the risk is fairly well-defined and the probabilities are more or less known (see Rosenthal (2006, especially Chapters 3 and 4)). Government-sponsored lotteries nearly always quote the odds. Perhaps this partially explains why casino gambling and lotteries are so popular.

Risk and information about the risk are not the same thing. The risk is not necessarily greater when there is less information about the probabilities, nor is it less when there is more probability information. Such an attitude assumes that no information is bad information. Nonetheless, there is some usefulness to this view, even if it is not totally correct. If people are risk averse, a loss of x dollars is more painful than the positive feeling from a gain of x dollars. Thus, assuming that we know less penalizes outcomes with little information and makes us less risk tolerant, which can be a reasonable approach: that is, when you know less, take risk conservatively.

People will take sometimes extraordinary measures to avoid loss or generate gains. For example, some women with a family history of breast cancer have chosen to have prophylactic mastectomies to virtually eliminate any possibility of having the disease. With great advances in methods of detection and treatment and mounting statistical evidence, there is growing controversy on whether prophylactic mastectomies are justified (Lagnado (2015)). In the financial world, investors who generate significant losses will oftentimes engage in speculative behavior to attempt to recover their losses. In many cases, they will take far greater risks to recover losses than they took to generate the losses.

---

[25]The numerator of the formula is the risk premium earned. The denominator is the standard deviation of the average return, which is the standard deviation of the return divided by the square root of the sample size. A sample size of 100 would produce a t-statistic of about 2.00, which is sufficient to reject the null hypothesis that the performance is random, accepting a 5% possibility of a wrong conclusion.

People fear risk less if information about the risk is thought to be more trustworthy. When we think we have good information about the risk, we seem more willing to take it. For some reason, people tend to trust the government more than private industry in providing information about risk, though there is no reason to believe that the government is better able to accurately measure risk. In the financial world, a tremendous amount of trust is placed in the ratings assigned to debt by bond rating agencies such as Moody's, Standard and Poor's, and Fitch's, even though they change their ratings much more slowly than the response of bondholders to changes in companies' creditworthiness, and their ratings greatly understated the risk of many entities in the credit crunch of 2007–2009.

The author can relate a personal example of this phenomenon. The United States government provides a taxpayer-subsidized flood insurance program offering relatively inexpensive policies that cost about $35 a month for $250,000 of coverage for the building and $100,000 for its contents. Purchase of a policy is optional unless the house is in a 100-year flood plain, a government classification that the house has at least a 1% chance of being flooded in a year. If the house is in a 100-year flood plain, the lender of any mortgage on the house requires that it be covered by flood insurance. The author heard a neighbor state that she was not going to buy flood insurance unless the government classified her house into the 100-year flood plain, meaning that she would not buy this extremely inexpensive insurance unless the government essentially forced her to do so. Even though she was aware that an adjacent neighborhood was in the 100-year flood plain, she was allowing the government to make an important risk management decision. The author, aware of the nearby neighborhood's classification, the possibility of errors in government flood plain classifications, the potential for large loss, and the low cost of the insurance, purchased a policy.

Surprising Facts about Certain Risks

David Ropeik and George Gray of the Harvard Center for Risk Analysis have devoted much of their careers to the study of the risks we face in life. As they show, there are a number of ways to measure the magnitude and probability of certain adverse events. There is the likelihood of exposure as well as the consequences, which reflect the severity of damage and the number of victims. In their fascinating look at the risks around us, we learn some most unusual facts.

Radiation exposure and its potential for causing cancer is probably one of the most feared of all risks. Scientists have studied the approximately 90,000 survivors of the atomic bombs of Hiroshima and Nagasaki in 1945. In a population of that size, about 17,000 cancer deaths would be expected over their lifetimes. At the time of publication of their book, there had been only about 8,000, but of course many of these people are still alive and may still contract cancer. Of the 8,000 people who have died of cancer, comparisons have enabled scientists to conclude that about 500 can be attributed to radiation.

The Environmental Protection Agency estimates that someone living near a hazardous waste site and drinking well water has a chance of contracting a health hazard of no more than 1 in 10,000.

The number of cases of mild to severe food poisoning in the United States in one year is over 70 million, or about one in four people. About 5,000 people die. Food poisoning is identified by Ropiek and Gray as one our greatest but surely least recognized risks.

Your odds of drowning in a bathtub are about the same as winning a pick-four lottery.

Source: Ropiek and Gray (2002).

Many people are less afraid of risk the further back in history an adverse outcome occurs. Fear of terrorist attacks, plane crashes, and large drops in the stock market seem to fade from people's minds the further away they get from the date of an event. This phenomenon, sometimes called "letting your guard down," is a dangerous thing, for it tends to underestimate the likelihood of adverse events. Extreme events that occur few and far between are, by definition, rare. It is these events that are of the greatest concern when managing risk. While the frequency may be low, the consequences are high and being on guard is of the utmost importance.

Many people are more afraid of risks that affect them more directly than those that affect them less directly and affect others more directly. For example, many white collar workers have less fear of the risk of a weakening economy than blue collar workers because it affects white collar workers less directly, since blue collar workers tend to get the first layoffs. Nonsmokers have less fear of lung cancer, in spite of the fact that there is considerable risk from second-hand smoke and pollutants. Banks that do not engage in risky, speculative lending or trading are not immune from some risks that arise from that type of trading, because the banks may have credit extended to parties that do have direct exposure. These risks are almost hidden from view, but they should not be forgotten.

Some people weigh the risk of less probable events with severe consequences more than more probable events with less severe consequences. As a result of this characteristic, sometimes certain people take strange precautions against highly unlikely events. For example, many people worry far more about being killed in a plane crash than being killed in an automobile accident.[26] Once again, people often fail to distinguish conditional from unconditional probability. The unconditional probability of being killed in a car accident is far more than that of being killed in a plane crash. If you are involved in a plane crash, however, the probability of being killed is far greater than if you are involved in an automobile accident. Conditional probability only becomes relevant once the condition is certain. That is, given that you are in a plane crash, you are more likely to be killed than if you are in an automobile accident. But unless you are reading this on a plane going down, the conditioning event has not occurred, and the unconditional probability is the relevant one. This irrationality often manifests in strange precautions. For example, for a few months following the terrorist attacks of September 11, 2001, many people refused to fly and a lot of organizations made their employees travel by car rather than fly. Gigerenzer (2002) estimates that more people died (350) as a result of automobile travel taken to avoid flying than were killed flying in the September 11 attacks (266).

As a corollary to this risk, people sometimes mistakenly evaluate risks with equal consequences but unequal probabilities. For example, gun control advocates often use the emotional argument that guns around a house are dangerous for children. But Levitt and Dubner (2005) note that the number of children accidentally killed in a house that has a swimming pool but not a gun is 100 times more than the number killed in a house that has a gun but not a swimming pool. People can get extremely emotional about certain risks, but far too often, they are unaware of the true extent of the risks, which are often quite different from what they think.

The media plays an important role in conveying risk information, a role that is sometimes unhelpful, misleading, and incorrect. Media stories of the increased risk of a particular malady from taking a certain pharmaceutical

---

[26]We are not understating the potential severity of an auto accident but simply saying that the expected loss from being in an auto accident is far less than the expected loss from being in a plane crash.

designed to treat another malady are often misleading. Suppose 1,000 women take a new drug designed for hormone replacement therapy and 1,000 other women take nothing. Of the women who take the existing nothing, 12 contract breast cancer. Of the women who take the drug, 24 get breast cancer. Otherwise, the new drug is almost completely effective in treating the problem for which it was designed. The media says that this new drug designed to treat post-menopausal symptoms doubles the risk of ovarian cancer. Is this helpful information? Perhaps. But the details are never reported. Twelve women out of 1,000 may have contracted breast cancer from this drug. Would you take a drug designed to address a problem that has near 100% effectiveness but with which one in 83 will get breast cancer? Stated another way, would you take a drug that is virtually guaranteed to solve a severe problem if there is a 1.2% chance of developing cancer? You might not do so, and there may be other risks and benefits to the drug that would ultimately help you decide. Nonetheless, some people certainly would take the drug, particularly if they were given all of the information. But negative publicity may well kill the drug.

FoxBusiness journalist John Stossel (2004) offers this interesting story. Suppose the media reports that a new form of energy had been developed. Large companies would be given licenses to pump this energy into our homes. It would burn cleanly, be in large supply, and would be relatively inexpensive. But it would be expected to kill 200 Americans a year. Would this energy likely win praise from the media and government approval? Probably not. But then, it would not need to win approval. We already use it. It is called natural gas.

If automobiles were introduced today would the media and many people see the risk as worth the reward? In the United States, over 30,000 people a year are killed in automobile crashes. It is hard to imagine that automobiles might not be approved by our government, because they are such an ingrained part of our lives. But it is also hard to imagine in this day and age that any new product that would be involved in 30,000 deaths a year would be approved by the government.

People often believe they are more skilled than they really are. This trait is extremely common in investment professionals. Everyone knows some people who are excessively overconfident. This trait is frequently seen in sports. A baseball pitcher struggling through a game gets a visit to the mound by the manager who asks him, "How do you feel?" The pitcher replies, "I'm fine." The manager says, "You don't look so fine. You look tired. Your pitches are off. I think it's time for you to sit down." The pitcher says, "I'll be fine.

I can get the next guy out." Business executives and financial decision makers seldom admit that they no longer have the ability to perform at the level necessary to deliver superior performance.

Overconfidence is sometimes referred to as the Lake Wobegon effect. Lake Wobegon is a fictional town in Minnesota created by American humorist Garrison Keillor for his radio program *A Prairie Home Companion*. Keillor jokingly describes Lake Wobegon as a place where "all the women are strong, all the men are good looking, and all the children are above average." The Lake Wobegon effect appears to be believed by quite a few people. For example, in a study of how people rate their driving skills, 93% of Americans and 69% of Swedes believe they are better drivers than the median driver (Svenson (1981)).

Overconfidence is a trait of highly risk-tolerant people but is not to be confused with high risk tolerance. High risk tolerance is a characteristic that simply means that a person does not have much regret when a risky decision turns out badly.[27] Overconfidence is a trait in which one believes that one has significant ability to forecast and/or control the future. This characteristic seems to exist even in light of evidence that the person cannot predict the future beyond what might be obtained completely at random.

Some people invariably believe that others are responsible for bad outcomes while they themselves are responsible for good outcomes. Some people are arrogant and selfish, preferring to seize the credit for successes that arise from the work of others or a team effort, and they blame others when their own failures occur. This trait is particularly dangerous in business, for it fails to acknowledge the problem and thereby prevents corrective action. It is closely related to a point made earlier that some people cannot distinguish luck from skill. Amazingly some people who have this trait are able to be very successful in their professional careers.

Some people believe they can influence the outcome of a largely random event. The illusion of control is much like a superstition. Finding a four-leaf clover, the number seven in western countries and eight in eastern countries, and a rabbit's foot are symbols of good luck that many people believe in. Athletes who will not change clothes while performing well and blowing on the dice before a roll are other signs that people somehow believe they can influence the outcomes by doing things that make no sense.

---

[27]There is famous adage that goes, "If at first you don't succeed, try, try again." Unless failure has extremely low costs and consequences, that adage is likely a characterization of a highly risk tolerant person.

Most people seem to believe that a good (bad) outcome means that a good (bad) decision was made. It is important to distinguish between the quality of a decision and the quality of the outcome. A good (or bad) outcome does not automatically mean that a good (bad) decision was made. For example, a health-conscious person may choose not to smoke, to drink alcohol in moderation, to eat healthy foods, and to exercise vigorously and regularly. And yet that person may die before his life expectancy. Likewise a person with an unhealthy lifestyle may live a long time. We know that the lifestyle choices we make greatly influence life expectancy, but we should also know that they are not the sole determinant of life expectancy. Seeing a friend take good care of himself but die before reaching old age should not influence one's decision to live a healthy lifestyle. A decision to lead a healthy lifestyle is generally agreed to be a good decision but is certainly not one that will always work out well. Part of risk management is about tilting the odds in your favor, but there are certainly no guarantees.

Yet, all too commonly, a bad outcome is equated to a bad decision. Many times we have heard people say "If I had only done it the other way." This view is not the correct way to evaluate risky decisions. A story from the history of the global soft drink company Coca-Cola makes this point quite well.

In 1983, Coca-Cola was losing market share to Pepsi and consumers who had stated that they preferred Coca-Cola tended to prefer Pepsi in blind taste tests. Pepsi is considered a sweeter product, so Coca-Cola concluded that its customers preferred the taste of Pepsi. Thus, Coca-Cola decided to change its product, removing the 100-year old standard Coca-Cola product from the market and replacing it with a sweeter version, referred to simply as Coke, only to see its customers get irate. After about a year, the company was forced to bring back its product, renamed Coca-Cola Classic, and the new Coke eventually died. Many people think the replacement of the original Coca-Cola with a version that was more similar to the competitor's product was a bad decision, but it was probably a good decision. While losing market share and faced with information that customers prefer another product, most of the time the correct decision is to take action. It is virtually inconceivable that the best course of action would be to ignore that information. And yet on occasion, the outcome will not be favorable. Nonetheless, the company effectively learned that liking a soft drink product and liking the taste of it were not the same concept. Its customers had a loyal attachment to the product that was separate from the taste. This concept of attachment has spawned the marketing concept of branding, whereby a product is valued for more than its consumption value. Expensive brands do not necessarily perform better or last longer than inexpensive ones, but customers effectively "buy the brand" rather the "buy the product." It is not difficult to ultimately conclude that not only was the company's decision probably the right decision but that it enabled the company to learn a lot about its customers from observing how they responded when their product was taken away.

All too often people fail to compare reward against risk. Some people take incredible risks for very little reward. For example, in my city, a person hired three young men to kill his ex-wife for a total payment of $10,000. I repeat, $10,000 *in total,* not $10,000 each. So, for a payment of $3,333 each, three people committed murder, and they were caught just a few weeks later. The reward seems incredibly small for the risk of facing life imprisonment or death by capital punishment. Of course, the utility of $3,333 is probably much higher for the three criminals than for anyone reading this book, but a simple analysis of their future earning power would suggest that they would earn more than that amount staying out of jail. To justify the crime, they would have needed certainty of not being caught. Many crimes seem to be committed for rewards that are relatively minor in comparison to the risk of severe punishment. The insider trading that television personality and businesswoman Martha Stewart engaged in, that generated a profit of only $75,000 for a person worth hundreds of millions of dollars, seems a small gain with tremendous risk.

There may be some other factors that explain such behavior. Perhaps the hired murderers were in desperate need of a few thousand dollars to avoid eviction or repossession, or perhaps they were addicted to drugs. In some cases, a person may simply get a thrill out of engaging in something with high risk and little return, such as the proverbial joker whose last words were "Hey guys. Watch this!" And in the case of celebrities and some politicians, there may simply be a feeling that they are above the law.

Many people fail to determine the cost of risk reduction, thereby often failing to eliminate low-reward risks that could be easily removed. Seat belts are a classic example of this point. Conditional on an accident occurring, seat beats substantially reduce the risk of severe injury or death at very low cost. Since all vehicles are generally equipped with seat belts, the first and highest cost is already paid when the car is acquired. The second cost is the cost of buckling the belt, which would seem to be extremely small. A seat belt places virtually no restrictions on a user and is not generally uncomfortable. Yet, an incredible percentage of drivers fail to use seat belts, even in light of mandatory legal requirements. In the United States, seat belt usage is in the range of 85–90%, but seat belts in some form for certain ages are required in all 50 states.[28]

Perhaps one of the reasons why so many people fail to use seat belts is that they assess unconditional risk rather than conditional risk. The probability of being in a potentially fatal automobile accident is fairly small. The U.S. National Highway Traffic Safety Administration (2016) estimates that there are 1.18 fatalities per 100 million vehicle miles traveled. Thus, if you travel 12,000 miles a year, a rough average for U.S. drivers, the probability of being killed is 0.014%. Or roughly one in every $1/0.00014 =$ 7062 people who drive 12,000 miles per year will be killed.[29] For a seat belt to save a life or prevent an injury, we require an accident. Non-seat belt users simply believe that the overall probability of being killed or seriously injured is too small to justify their use. Indeed, the probability is small, but the cost of substantially reducing that probability is extremely small. In short, there seems to be little benefit of not wearing seat belts and low cost of wearing them. Hence, the cost of reducing the risk is quite low in relation to the benefit. But anywhere from 10–15% of the U.S. population does not wear them.

We all too often expect our leaders to always make the decision that turns out well. It is easy to criticize decision makers. They place themselves in highly visible positions and make very difficult decisions without knowing what will happen in response. In particular, we criticize our politicians and government leaders and often vote on the basis on a single bad decision. Truthfully, no one can be expected to make the right decision all of the time. It is easy to criticize after the fact, a behavior we previously referred to as Monday morning quarterbacking, but in reality, decisions made under risk are fraught with uncertainty and cannot be expected to be always right. Unless we expect our decision makers to be clairvoyant, adverse outcomes will occur, perhaps even quite often.

---

[28]The National Highway Transportation Safety Administration estimates that in 2016, seat belts saved almost 15,000 lives. Given that there were about 37,000 deaths from car crashes in 2016 in the U.S., the reduction is about 29%, an incredible benefit in light of the cost. (https://www.nhtsa.gov/risky-driving/seat-belts). Add estimates of injury reduction and the rate of overall risk reduction is considerably higher.

[29]With 1.18 fatalities per 100 million miles, the probability of a fatality per mile is $1.18/100,000,000 = 0.00000001$. So, driving 12,000 miles would produce a probability of $12,000 \times 0.00000001 = 0.00014$.

Compare, for example, two important political/military decisions in history. In June 1944, the allied governments vested in the hands of the Supreme Commander of the Allied Expeditionary Forces, General Dwight D. Eisenhower, the power to decide when the Allied Armies would invade Europe. General Eisenhower, along with his advisors and fellow generals from the U.S., British, and Canadian armies, struggled tremendously with the timing. There was considerable uncertainty regarding the strength of the German defenses and the skill and bravery the Allied soldiers would show when faced with relentless horror. Moreover, weather was a major issue. Because a full moon was needed for extra light, only a narrow window of opportunity presented itself in early June 1944. Bad weather was forecast for June 5, and the invasion was postponed one day. Conditions on June 6 were not ideal, but Eisenhower gave the go-ahead. In preparation he wrote two speeches, one if victory occurred and one accepting personal responsibility for defeat. As we know, victory occurred, and Eisenhower went on to serve two terms as President of the United States.

Contrastingly, in 2003 President George W. Bush made the decision to invade Iraq, a decision that would haunt his legacy forever. Five different countries confirmed that Iraq possessed weapons of mass destruction (WMD) and Iraq had ignored U.N. resolutions. Moreover, Iraq had previously used WMD against the Kurds in 1991. Thus, the information available to President Bush pointed heavily toward the possibility that Iraq had WMD. And we all know that while the invasion was successful, and Saddam Hussein was deposed and eventually executed by the Iraqis, but there were no WMD.

Historical examples of this point are numerous. Eisenhower. Bush. John Kennedy's fateful decision to invade Cuba in the Bay of Pigs incident in 1962 that ended disastrously. U.S. Army General George Meade's decision not to pursue the Confederate Army of General Robert E. Lee following the U.S. victory at Gettysburg in 1863, a decision that almost surely prolonged the war. Stranded in Antarctica in 1916, Ernest Shackleton's decision to divide his men and lead one group in a small boat on a dangerous 700-plus nautical mile voyage on the open sea for South Georgia Island where help could be secured. Napoleon's decision to invade Russia in 1812, stretching his 500,000-man army the furthest it had ever gotten from its home base. These were major decisions made under enormous risk, some of which worked out well and some of which did not. We invariably praise those with good endings and criticize those with bad endings, as if the decision makers should be right every time.

Politicians are constantly hounded by their opponents who argue that they did the wrong thing. For example, Senator Obama's criticism of the Iraq war that he did not support no doubt gained him some political ground, while his opponent, Senator McCain, criticized Senator Obama for not supporting the troop surge that turned out to be extremely successful. Critics of decision makers who are forced to make such difficult decisions impose a higher standard on decision makers than they would impose on themselves. They are guilty of failing to understand that decisions made under risk cannot be correct all of the time. But for a slight twist of fate, all of these decisions might well have turned out another way.

In reality, we can rarely assess after the fact whether a decision was right or wrong, because often the decision affects the course of events and we cannot go back and replay history under the condition that the opposite decision was made. When the decision does not affect the course of events we can replay history. For example, if we bought a stock and it performed poorly, we can reasonably assume that it would have performed the same had we not bought the stock. But we cannot assume that the course of events would have ensued the same way had most major political and military decisions been the opposite. In that case, a different course of events would have doubtlessly ensued. Many of the decisions in life cannot be analyzed in that manner.

Forecasts are overrated. Billions of dollars are spent every year on forecasting. We forecast markets, fashions, weather, sports, and a variety of other random events of which there might be some value to having advance knowledge. Forecasts vary in their accuracy, but for the most part, they seem to be quite inaccurate except over very short intervals. Perhaps this record is because of the fact that anything worth forecasting is probably difficult to forecast, as it is so highly influenced by unpredictable factors that influence the outcome.

Even weather forecasts, based as they are on scientific principles, are notoriously inaccurate except over very short periods of time. Moreover, weather forecasts are hedged bets, because they are often associated with probabilities. The Weather Channel even sometimes biases its probability upward so that people are more likely to appreciate it when the prediction is correct and not care when it is not.[30] In fact, it is not even clear what the "Probability of Precipitation" concept means. The U.S. National Weather Service (NWS) says that the Probability of Precipitation (PoP) is a measure

---

[30]See Silver (2012, Chapter 4).

derived as the product of its confidence that some part of the area will receive measurable precipitation (at least 0.01 inches) times the percentage of the area in which measureable precipitation will occur. If the NWS is 80% confident that measurable precipitation will occur in 50% of the area, the PoP is 80% × 50% = 40%. The Weather Channel and Accuweather define PoP as the probability that measurable (>0.01 inches) precipitation will occur in the area covered by the forecast. These are different definitions. The NWS definition is a statement of the confidence of the forecaster times the fraction of the area likely to experience precipitation. The Weather Channel and Accuweather definitions are statements that suggest that under the assumed meteorological conditions, there is measureable precipitation that percentage of the time over the collective area (Bialik (2008)). The author recently heard a local television weathercaster state yet another definition: "The probability of rain is 10% so expect 10% of the area to get rain."[31]

In any case, is such precision necessary? Would our plans change if the number were 40% instead of 50%, assuming we even knew what the number means? Economic forecasts are even worse. The average GDP growth estimate of a group of economists is no more likely to be the actual GDP growth than any other wild guess that lies within a reasonable range.

In spite of the inaccuracy, predictions may well exhibit the quality of unbiasedness, meaning that on average the prediction is correct. Unbiasedness is a desirable quality, but it has only minor value, as it does not mean that a prediction is very close to the actual outcome.

Interestingly, some people think that crowd predictions are better, believing that somehow the collective wisdom of a crowd is supposed to result in a correct prediction. Suppose the following question is asked of a television game show participant: Who was the 38th Vice President of the United States? The choices are (a) Richard Nixon, (b) Lyndon Johnson, (c) Hubert Humphrey, (d) Spiro Agnew. Even though all of these men are well-known 20th century figures, this is a difficult question. The number of the Vice President does not correspond to the number of the President, though it is relatively close. Not many Presidents and even fewer Vice Presidents are known by their numbers. If we ask an individual, the odds are pretty

---

[31]Interestingly, it has been shown that many people believe that a 40% probability of rain means that 40% of meteorologists believe it will rain. Paulos (1988) even tells the story of a local television weathercaster who reported that the chance of rain on Saturday was 50% and the chance of rain on Sunday was 50%, so the chance of rain on the weekend was 100%. LOL.

high that this person will not know the answer. Ask a large group of people, however, and the odds are pretty high that the most common answer is the correct answer, but it is not for the reason you may think.

The correct answer is likely to emerge as the most common answer, because the group of people is comprised of two sub-groups: those who know the answer and those who do not. Those who know the answer will choose it. Those who do not know the answer will guess and their answers will be distributed among the four choices. Those who guess correctly will add to the total for the correct answer, and those who guess incorrectly will have their answers disbursed among the wrong answers, thus reducing the likelihood that one of the wrong answers will emerge. So the right answer is likely to be the one with the most votes. And the right answer is ....[32]

Forecasts of key economic figures are often made of a large number of economists, perhaps mistakenly believing in this fallacy of the wisdom of the crowd. And in this case, the crowd is allegedly experts. The game show result in which the crowd is correct does not work here. No economist knows what the figure will be. All of their predictions simply average out to a single figure that provides no more information than just guessing (Sherden (1999)). Forecasts are useful for giving us an expected value, but as we discussed from the very start: risk is the expectation that the outcome will deviate from the expected value. The variation around the expected value is a lot more important than the expected value itself.

Some people seem to do something simply because everyone else does it: the lemming effect. Lemmings are small arctic rodents that have come to be known for a habit of following each other off of a cliff and thereby committing mass suicide. The lemming effect has become recognized as following a group without questioning whether what the group is doing makes any sense. People often exhibit this characteristic when they "jump on the bandwagon" or "go along with the crowd," to quote a couple of euphemisms. Financial crashes and crises are often a result of this effect. For example, on October 19, 1987, the Dow Jones Industrial Average fell about 23% in a single day. On that day, there was no news of a substantial drop in corporate profits sufficient to trigger a massive sell-off. A modest sell-off started, followed by a great deal of apparent panic, whereupon a large number of other investors were then motivated to sell simply because everyone was doing so and not because of any significant economic information. There was in fact no major news that day about a decline in the economy. In the course of history, mass

---

[32] Hubert Humphrey.

hysteria over economic matters has led to bubbles and panics of this sort, some lasting for an extraordinary length of time.[33]

Urban legends, old wives' tales, and superstitions are examples of the lemming effect. The fact that something can be repeated so many times that it becomes virtually the truth is a dangerous impediment to making decisions under risk.[34]

Many people value something they own far more than they value the same thing if they do not own it. To repeat, this is the endowment effect. Tversky and Kahnemann (1981) pose the following question to a group of subjects:

> Imagine that you want to see a play in which the ticket costs $10. You buy the ticket in advance. As you arrive at the theater you discover that you have lost the ticket. Would you pay $10 for another ticket?

Forty-six percent of respondents said "yes." To a different set of people, they pose the following:

> Imagine that you pass a theater and notice a play that you are interested in seeing. Admission is $10 per ticket. Would you buy the ticket?

Eighty-eight percent of respondents said "yes."

Both problems are the same: in each case you are at the theater, are interested in seeing the show, but you have no ticket. The only difference is that in the first case, you thought you had one and you realized that you bought one but lost it or left it at home. But in both cases, you either pay $10 at the theater and see the play or you go home. Yet less than half the respondents would pay the $10 when the ticket had been lost. These people clearly value the ticket they lost at more than $10 or the ticket they do not own at less than $10. If these people were rational, their reasoning would be as follows. When they arrive at the theater, they would decide if they wanted to pay $10 for a ticket. They might well opt out of paying $10 because maybe they are not feeling well, maybe they read a review of the play that said it was not very good, or maybe they now realize they have something better to do with their time. Whether the play is worth $10 is a risky decision, but it should not be influenced by whether they have already lost $10.

---

[33]See the classic *Extraordinary Popular Delusions and the Madness of Crowds* by Mackay (1841).

[34]The quote "If you tell a lie big enough and keep repeating it, people will eventually come to believe it," is attributed to Nazi propagandist Joseph Goebbels who used it to spread Nazi propaganda. Goebbels added that "the truth is the greatest enemy of the state." One might also add that the truth is certainly an enemy of bad risk management.

As noted, this characteristic is called the endowment effect, as it refers to the notion of an endowment, something you own. The endowment effect is a variation of the effect of *sunk costs*. Money expended in the past is gone. It may be possible to earn money that can cover the loss and result in an overall profit, but whether one takes a risk to do so should be unrelated to any money already spent. Thaler (1980) gives the hypothetical example of a man who pays $300 for an annual membership in a tennis club, but then develops a very painful injury yet continues to play because he does not want to waste the $300.[35]

The endowment effect and the bias from sunk costs get in the way of good risk management. Decisions should always be made in light of the information currently available and only in regard to the future — never the past.

When you observe only successful people, you obtain a biased view of the risk. This phenomenon is called survivor bias and is a common problem that interferes with good decision making as well as accurate interpretation of past events and what might happen in the future. It is a particularly common bias in the economic world where historical data tend to include only surviving investors and businesses. Survivor bias is, however, common anywhere in which we attempt to judge success and failure over a long period of time. For example, we observe many great professional athletes, but we have few observations on those who pursued such a career but were not successful. Consider the National Basketball Association and the progression of an athlete from high school to the NBA. There are 30 NBA teams with each team allowed to dress 13 players for a game. Thus, at any given time there are 390 players in uniform. In 2018, the NCAA, the governing body for university-level competitive sports in the U.S., estimated that about 3.4% of high school basketball players would go on to play at the university level and that about 1.2% would go on from the university-level competition to play in the NBA. These statistics combine to mean that about 0.0401% of high

---

[35]On the other hand, there is some contrasting evidence to the sunk cost effect. Gym memberships accelerate in the first few weeks of the year, a result of overeating during the holidays followed by a New Year's resolutions to get fit. Statistics show that about 80% of new gym memberships are unused by the second week of February. There is, however, an additional cost to the membership in the form of the effort required to go to the gym plus the effort required to exercise. So when someone stops going to the gym, maybe that person considers the cost of further effort in excess of the benefit and does not consider the sunk costs.

school basketball players will eventually play in the NBA.[36] Clearly the sport is extremely competitive and virtually everyone who takes up basketball will not be able to make a career of it. For a young person to allow for the fact that he observes nearly 400 people earning a living playing in the NBA to motivate him to give up the better years of his life pursuing a goal that is virtually impossible to attain is probably bad decision making under risk. He sees only the successes and little of the failures. Although statistics on actors and musicians are hard to come by, they are likely to mirror those of athletes and to give the unsuspecting a false sense of the odds of being successful. Nonetheless, clearly some people pursue such careers and are successful and that is certainly a good thing.[37]

Famous investor Warren Buffett attempts to use survivor bias to make a point that fundamental security analysis as developed by Benjamin Graham and David Dodd is the best approach to investing (Buffett (1984)). He uses a variation of the well-known example of having every person in the United States compete in a coin-tossing experiment, an example used earlier in this chapter. Each person predicts heads or tails. If that person is correct, he continues on to the next round for another coin toss. If he loses, he drops out. So Buffett proposes that the 240 million Americans, roughly the U.S. adult population at that time, put in $1 each, forming a winner's pool of $240 million. After 10 tosses, the pool is distributed to the winners. By the laws of probability, we should observe $240,000,000(0.5)^{10}$, or about 234,000 people who have called all 10 tosses correctly. Each person would win a little more than $1,000. Buffett argues that we would call that result nothing but luck, except that if we found they all had something in common we might start to wonder if that common factor provided the explanation. Buffett then goes on to tell the story of eight successful investors who learned their skill studying under Benjamin Graham and David Dodd. Buffett argues that this number is too many to be coincidental.

---

[36] See National Collegiate Athletic Association Research (2018). The comparable figures in other sports are 0.03% for women's basketball, 0.11% for (American) football, 0.67% for baseball, 0.76% for men's hockey, and 0.08% for men's soccer.

[37] Entertainment is an even more difficult field in which to be successful. In sports, performance is unambiguous. A quarterback can throw accurate passes, a basketball player can accurately shoot field goals, a baseball player can hit for a reasonably high average. In entertainment, success if far more subjective. Many of the most famous singers do not have as a good of a voice as you might even have. Yet, they have something you do not, though it is hard to tell what it is.

The problem with this argument is that it suffers from survivor bias. These eight successful investors are but a sample and probably a small one from all of the people who were taught by Graham and Dodd. Graham was only a part-time professor, but he undoubtedly taught a large number of students and took many others under his wing in the professional world. Dodd taught security analysis at Columbia, one of the oldest and largest business schools, for almost 40 years. Their books undoubtedly led to numerous other followers who adopted their techniques, though maybe never actually studying under Graham and Dodd themselves. Graham and Dodd lived long lives, with Graham dying at 84 and Dodd at 93. They undoubtedly influenced a tremendous number of securities analysts in their lengthy and distinguished careers. To be sure that these nine investors, counting Buffett, were truly outstanding as a result of their tutelage under Graham and Dodd, we would need to know how many students studied under Graham and Dodd and engaged in active investment management. Even simple statistical measures such as the probability of an error in which we conclude that the manager has ability and that the result is not random, indicate that the likelihood of a false conclusion of this sort would occur once every 20 investment managers. Thus, a small sample of 160 pupils of Graham and Dodd would be expected to have nine showing outstanding results. Thus, if we could find 160 followers of Graham and Dodd and verify that eight of them were outstanding, the results would be explainable by sheer luck.

Survivor bias is a subtle form of error. Even the brilliance of Warren Buffett did not see that the other pupils of Graham and Dodd would have to be analyzed to determine if these eight investors could be deemed to be abnormal as a result of their training.

Some risk takers often misestimate the odds based on recent outcomes. Many gamblers who encounter a string of bad luck believe that good luck must start eventually. This belief is presumably based on how the gambler mistakenly thinks probability must play out. Assume for example that in a dice game a gambler has a streak of bad luck, losing repeatedly over several trials. In order to break even he must have a streak of good luck, winning repeatedly over several trials. The gambler believes that in the long run, the bad luck and good luck must cancel out, with the bad luck slightly exceeding the good luck to give the casino a small edge. He simply does not believe that he will have a streak of bad luck that is not followed by a streak of good luck to offset. In reality, the bad luck of losing multiple times is simply an extreme outcome that would be expected to occur on some rare occasions. Good luck is no more likely to follow than is more bad luck.

To illustrate, I (electronically) rolled a single die 1,000 times and obtained the following outcomes.

Outcome	Number
1	149
2	169
3	182
4	157
5	176
6	167
Total	1,000

Exhibit 2-10. Outcomes from 1,000 Rolls of a Die

With a probability of 1/6, we should expect to see about 166 to 167 of each. Notice, however, that we obtained as few as 149 of #1 and as many as 182 of #3. Assuming the die is not biased, would these results suggest that in future rolls, we would tend to see more 1s and fewer 3s? In fact, they suggest nothing of the sort. The outcomes are quite normal. The probability of each number on the next roll is still 1/6.

Let us create a simple gambling game in which you place a bet on a roll of a single die. The gambler wins if the die comes up on the number on which he bet. The gambler should expect to win 1/6 of the time, regardless of whether he bets on different numbers or changes the number on which he bets. Suppose he has yet to win in 10 tries. Since the gambler should win once every six times, he believes he is almost certain to win on the next two rolls, as the likelihood of losing 12 straight times seems too low. This logic is, however, misguided.

The probability of the gambler losing 10 times is 16% (that is, $(5/6)^{10}$). The gambler believes that he is likely to win both of the next two, or if he recognizes that the outcomes will not conform perfectly to expected outcomes, he might think he is sure to win at least once in the next two rolls. In fact, his probability of winning each of the next two times is $(1/6)^2 = 1/36$. His probability of winning at least once in the next two tries is $1 - (5/6)^2 = 31\%$. Interestingly, his greatest probability on the next two outcomes is losing twice, $(5/6)^2 = 69\%$. The gambler does not realize that the probability of losing 12 straight times is (perhaps) amazingly high at 11% ($(5/6)^{12}$). For example, suppose in a class of say 18 students you play the game 12 times. We would expect two people to lose all 12 times.

These extreme outcomes occur surprisingly often. A run of such outcomes does not alter the probability of future outcomes. Gambler's bias is a belief of just the opposite. It is, quite simply, a failure to recognize that under completely normal circumstances, extreme outcomes do occur from time to time. Future outcomes do not have to balance these extreme past outcomes.

It is human nature to associate change with risk. Keeping the status quo provides a measure of certainty. As an example, suppose you current hold a job with which you are generally pleased. You work for a large firm, are paid a satisfactory salary, generally enjoy the job and your co-workers, and you like your supervisor. One day you are contacted by a search firm and made aware of a job at another company. This company is a younger and smaller company. You go for an interview and determine that the company and the job have great potential for growth. You would be one of a small number of employees with specialized skills. The starting pay is only slightly higher than your current salary, but there is more room for bonuses and salary growth in the future. You receive an offer. What do you do?

Of course, there is no right or wrong answer. The decision is a risky one. Your current job offers a path of relatively low risk. You are not likely to lose your job or encounter any major surprises in the future. A modest rate of salary growth is likely and there is some long term potential, but you are low in seniority and there are many talented people working for this large company. The new job has considerably more risk. There is great potential for moving up in this younger and smaller company and having substantial increases in salary and responsibility. On the other hand, this company is not well established. Its future success is not just a function of you, but of a handful of other people. Thus, there are substantial risks over which you have little control.

This example is a case in which there is considerable risk of change. But not all change involves greater risk. In the reverse situation, working for the smaller younger company when the opportunity comes to go to a larger more established company, the risk of change is less.

People often associate change with risk simply because change is often associated with more uncertainty. As such, there is often a fear of change. Doing things the old way, however ineffective, is often viewed by some as the right path. This type of thinking can lead to poor decision making, because opportunity is the potential for improvement.

People often believe that when a hypothesis is confirmed by a single observation, the hypothesis is correct. Similarly, people are often fixated on a hypothesis because the facts are consistent with the hypothesis. Suppose you believe that the respiratory infection commonly seen in winter and referred to as a "cold" is due to cold weather. This hypothesis is certainly a common belief. Colds and other respiratory viruses are indeed more common in the winter. The weather is cold in the winter. Therefore, cold weather must be the source of these illnesses. Right? Indeed, it is probably not surprising that a family of similar illnesses is often referred to collectively as "colds." The truth is quite different: cold weather is only indirectly the problem, but it is not the cold itself. It is how we respond to cold weather. First, we spend more time indoors, and within confined space we spread more germs because we are in closer contact with each other. We also touch more indoor objects and leave our germs awaiting the next person who touches them. Second, to keep us warm we use indoor heat. But indoor heat dries out the air, producing dangerously low levels of humidity. Humidity provides a vital ingredient that keeps our immune systems activated. That is why cool mist vaporizers can improve our ability to fight off viruses and bacterial infections well before these illnesses take hold. Nonetheless, a belief that cold weather causes such infections is confirmed from year to year, leading to the mistaken view that cold temperatures are the source of these infections. As such, we often fail to take the proper precautions and the illnesses can linger longer than necessary.

A more extreme version of confirmation bias is called *tunneling*. Tunneling is a behavior in which one is obsessed with a particular cause-and-effect relationship to the degree that contradictory evidence is ignored. Tunneling is a common problem in the medical profession, as described in Groopman (2008). Dr. Groopman, a hematologist and oncologist at the Harvard Medical School, writes about this issue from personal and professional experience. Almost every combination of symptoms is consistent with numerous illnesses. Medical science is mixture of science and educated guesswork. A doctor observes a set of symptoms and makes a diagnosis based on the most common disease associated with those symptoms. Groopman observes from his own struggles with an illness he had that was difficult to identify. When doctors make a diagnosis, prescribe a course of treatment, and observe results that do not lead to a cure, many of them are unable to reconsider the diagnosis. Continued efforts with the same or only slightly different lines of treatment still yield no results, and yet many doctors are unable to accept the fact that their initial diagnoses are not correct. After years of frustration, Groopman sought an alternative opinion, which led to success in treating his illness. Hence, as we are always advised: when in doubt, get a second opinion.

Tunneling is virtually the same problem as being unable to admit that one is wrong. The facts align perfectly with the original opinion, thereby providing a form of confirmation bias. And even when the facts do not line up with the original opinion, some people still refuse to admit that they were wrong. Clearly these issues interfere with good decision making under risk.

Many people think of one risk as fairly high and another as relatively lower when in fact, the truth may be quite the opposite. As mentioned earlier, many people became afraid of flying following the September 11 attacks and resorted to automobile travel, resulting in an increase in automobile deaths. While terrorists might well have successfully launched another attack, it is virtually indisputable that the probability of dying in a terrorist attack in the few months following September 11 was much smaller than the probability of dying in an automobile accident.

Yet, people often exhibit an irrational fear or lack thereof for particular risks. As an example, firearms are often implicated in deaths, but in fact water is much more dangerous. Consider that in the U.S., arguably one of the countries in which guns are most prevalent, in 2015, 489 people died from accidental discharge of firearms, whereas 3,602 died from drowning and submersion (Center for Disease Control and Prevention (2017)). Think about that. Roughly 10 people per day die from drowning in the U.S.

Many of the routine and sometimes fun activities we engage in seem relatively harmless, while certain others appear quite risky. Yet the risk is often not at all what it appears. The U.S. Consumer Product Safety Commission compiles data on emergency room visits. For 2017 (US Consumer Product Safety Commission, 2017), there were 457,266 visits involved bicycling accidents, while 898,485 visits were made for accidents involving beds, mattresses, and pillows. Think about that for a moment: Beds appear to be more dangerous than bicycles. There were 669,992 visits involving chairs, and 355,821 involving tables. These figures continue to challenge our imagination. While bicycles do appear to have an element of danger, over 1.9 million emergency room visits were made for accidents involving beds, chairs, and tables. It stretches the imagination. Also, beware: 51,260 emergency room visits involved injuries related to television sets and stands. And the next time you wash your hands, your body, or your clothes, remember that 61,416 visits involved soap or detergent. Of course, everyone respects the dangers of lawn mowers, which resulted in 89,608 visits, but this total seems quite small compared to the 417,306 injuries involving clothing.

The data on these types of events, however, are driven by not only the risk but also by the exposure and the precautionary measures taken. For example, the large number of visits related to beds is likely to be primarily due to the tremendous amount of time spent in bed. For a person averaging eight hours of sleep a night, one-third of that person's life is spent in bed, which is a tremendous amount of exposure. By comparison, there were fewer visits for injuries involving lawn mowers (89,608) than those involving grooming devices (e.g., hair dryers) and razors (101,626). There is little question that grooming devices and razors are less dangerous than a lawn mower and yet they lead to a somewhat greater number of emergency room visits. Why? Exposure might account for some of the difference. More people engage in shaving and grooming than use lawn mowers. But why are lawn mowers seemingly far more dangerous and yet statistically no more dangerous? Undoubtedly, it is the appearance of greater risk and the precautionary measures taken with lawn mowers. Shavers and groomers do not seem very dangerous and beds seem almost completely innocuous. There lies the greater risk: thinking something is not very risky when it is combined with a great deal of exposure. But it is still quite costly to think something has high risk when in fact the risk is quite low.[38]

Bad outcomes stick in our memory while ordinary outcomes fade. Patrons of Walmart know this experience well. You are ready to check-out and have numerous cashier lines from which you can choose. Have you not felt that whichever line you chose, it always turned out to be the slowest line? In reality, there is no way the line you choose could consistently be the slowest. Nor can the lane you choose to drive your car in on the highway consistently be the slowest. Yet you remember the bad results, because they impart a significant amount of negative utility. When you choose a check-out line or a highway lane that turns out to be fast, the positive utility is short-lived. Hence, anything other than fast service or steady moving traffic in your lane is memorable, while the opposite is a memory that fades quickly because it simply met your expectation. Restaurant service is similar. You tend to remember bad service a lot more than good service, because you expect the latter. You may even be likely to view a single episode of bad service as sufficient reason not to return to a restaurant.

---

[38]The author cannot resist telling the story of the rustic lodge he checked into on a lake in upstate New York that had no locks on the doors, purportedly because it trusted that no one who would harm someone who would be staying there and no previous incidents had ever occurred. Yet, while someone could break into someone's room and steal or harm them, the lodge itself provided coat hangers that were permanently attached to the crossbar in the closet. Thus, you could steal someone's property or inflict personal damage on them in their room, but you could not steal the lodge's coat hangers.

The problem with this issue is that making decisions in this manner is like drawing a sample of one observation and concluding that what you find generalizes broadly. There should be no correlation between Walmart lines or highway lanes and your decision, and few restaurants consistently give bad service. If they did, they would quickly go out of business. Hence, good decision making does not just mean remembering the bad outcomes, but it also requires keeping a mental tally of bad outcomes *and* good outcomes to determine how well they balance.

2.6.4 *Information Asymmetry, Adverse Selection, and Moral Hazard*

Many models of financial markets assume that the buyer and seller have access to the same set of information. But often this is not the case, especially in markets that are not financial. One of the most common risky scenarios involves two parties who are considering engaging in a transaction with each other. We could be referring to something as simple as a person buying a car from a complete stranger. Or it could be a more complex transaction, such as an investor purchasing shares of an initial public offering. Quite often this type of scenario is characterized by *information asymmetry*, meaning that one party has a great deal more information or better quality information than the other. For the car purchase, the seller/owner of the car has a tremendous amount of information about the history and performance of the car. The buyer has little such information. In fact, almost all of the information the buyer has, such as Blue Book value, can be obtained by the seller. In such a situation, the seller starts off with a tremendous advantage. A rational buyer should view the asymmetry as another form of risk and should take it into account in deciding how much to pay. In the end, the seller may get a lower price even when selling a high quality product simply because the buyer perceives some risk arising from the information asymmetry. The more open and efficient markets are, however, the more likely the price will accurately reflect the quality of the asset being sold. Of course, not all buyers recognize the effect that information asymmetry has on the risk. Some are confused about the relationship of the seller to the buyer. In car transactions, often the seller will present himself as more concerned about the buyer's welfare than that of his employer. In doing so, the seller gains the confidence of the buyer and the buyer is then more willing to do what the seller recommends.

Information asymmetry has two important variations. One is information asymmetry when information is absent, such as any case in which a non-technical buyer is interested in purchasing a technical product, and the other is information asymmetry when information is present but the decision maker does not know how to process the information. In the latter case, suppose you are wondering what a bond is worth. You are given the dates of the interest payments, the amounts of the interest payments, the maturity date, and the rate required by investors to purchase the bond. An expert on financial markets or even just a student having completed one finance course would know how to determine the value of the bond. A person who has not been exposed to time value of money and the pricing of bonds would find that information of little use. This example makes a good case for getting an education: a good justification for reading this book.

Information asymmetry can also lead to another problem called *adverse selection*. Sometimes a buyer or seller has reason to fear that the other party will engage in transactions that are favorable to the counterparty and unfavorable to it. For example, dealers in financial instruments worry that parties that come to them for trades know something about the instrument being traded that the dealer does not know. Hence, the dealer will recognize the possibility that it will be forced to bear more risk than is apparent. The dealer would then factor this effect into the price at which it is willing to trade. One common example of adverse selection is where insurance companies fear that customers that want insurance the most are the ones with the highest risk. Customers that the insurer would prefer to insure are those that least need the insurance. Consequently, it should be easy to see that adverse selection can be a critical problem in risk management. If a company has reason to fear a particular risk, such as an increase in the price of oil, it might pass that risk on to a dealer in financial instruments, who might then fear that the company had private information that made it want to dispose of this risk. Because of this reason, most dealers dispose of risk they have taken on from their customers.

Moral hazard is the condition in which the allocation of risk creates an incentive for a party to engage in unethical behavior. An example would be when a party has a considerable amount of insurance coverage and either fails to take sufficient precautions against the risk or actually engages in behavior that causes the risky outcome to occur. Burning down one's own insured building is an extreme case. Insurance contracts usually guard against this damage by forcing the insured to bear some of the risk.

Government support programs are classic examples of moral hazard. When the government provides a strong safety net, people can benefit but they can also lose the incentive to take care of themselves. But this risk is not confined to indigent individuals. The savings and loan (S&L) collapse in the U.S. in the 1980s was a classic case of moral hazard. Federally-provided insurance meant that the taxpayers ultimately bore most of the risk of failure, so many S&L's took few precautions and engaged in extremely risky behavior that led to very adverse and costly consequences for the taxpayers. The Financial Crisis of 2008–2009 also was a case in which the U.S. government was willing to support the very risky sub-prime mortgage market, thereby providing incentives for private borrowers to take on very high risk loans.

2.6.5 *Risk and Competitive Games*

Some risky situations involve competition in which there is no human opponent. For example, games like golf and bowling are competitive sports but there is no human attempting to influence the outcome. Although the physical requirements to be successful in these sports are difficult to master, the sports themselves are less complex to play because there is no element of human interaction. On the other hand, sports like tennis and racquetball pit one human against another. The physical requirements of these sports are every bit as difficult to master, but the sports themselves are more complex because they involve human interaction. If you play these sports, you must take into account that your opponent is attempting to influence your behavior and responds to your actions so as to maximize the likelihood of his winning. In both types of sports there are risky decisions to be made, but the human interaction game has considerably more risk because you do not know how your opponent will react in the presence of risk.

Game theory is a branch of mathematics and economics that examines how parties behave in competitive situations, such as games. From our perspective in this book, game theory gives us additional insights into decision-making under risk. One of the most famous examples of game theory is the *Prisoner's Dilemma*. Suppose two people are arrested for the same crime. The police do not have enough evidence to convict either. The two prisoners are placed in separate rooms and interrogated. Each is offered the opportunity to testify against the other, for which he will be granted his freedom. If one testifies, he will receive his freedom and the other will be severely punished. If both testify, they will both be given a light sentence. If neither testifies, both are likely to still be punished. Both prisoners are in a risky scenario and neither knows what the other will do.

Let us define the degrees of outcomes in order of severity (negative utility) as freedom, light punishment, punishment, and severe punishment. Now let us arrange the outcomes as shown in Exhibit 2-11:

		Prisoner B	
		Cooperate	Do not cooperate
Prisoner A	Cooperate	A: light punishment B: light punishment	A: freedom B: severe punishment
	Do not cooperate	A: severe punishment B: freedom	A: punishment B: punishment

Exhibit 2-11. The Prisoner's Dilemma

What is the optimal strategy? Assume you are Prisoner A and that you have no reason to believe that Prisoner B is more likely to cooperate or not. If you cooperate, you are equally likely to receive either light punishment or freedom. If you do not cooperate, you are equally likely to receive either severe punishment or punishment. Since freedom is preferred to punishment and light punishment is preferred to severe punishment, your optimal strategy is to cooperate. Prisoner B would draw the same conclusion. In the Prisoner's Dilemma, optimal strategies are easily determined by both parties, because cooperation results in light punishment in the worst case, whereas non-cooperation results in punishment in the best case. That is, the worst outcome of one strategy is better than the best outcome of the other strategy. The result of this game is what we call an equilibrium solution. Note, however, that for the prisoners as a whole the outcome is less than ideal. They both are punished instead of at least one of them going free. Of course, in reality, prisoners may not act in the optimal manner.

The Prisoner's Dilemma is a simple and easily resolvable game but other games are far more complex. Much of the research on game theory has been developed after World War II and has been widely used in studying military strategy, economics, and business decision-making. Finance and investment are classic examples of game theoretic situations. Participants in financial markets compete with each other and face uncertainty about what other participants will do.[39] In fact, financial market competition is even

---

[39]For readers interested in the application of game theory to finance, see Shafer and Vovk (2001).

more complex, because markets are a collective expression of the actions of a multitude of participants. Moreover, rules for optimal strategies do not always work, because not all participants act rationally. For example, if investors continue to buy a stock on which the potential earnings of the company do not look good, one might wonder if the other investors in the market are irrational. Indeed, that is precisely what happens during bubbles such as the Internet Bubble, sometimes called the Dot Com Bubble, that lasted from roughly 1997 through 2000. During that time the stock of virtually any company with a ".com" attached to its name did well, even though many of these companies generated little cash flow and had poor prospects and tremendous competition. Likewise during panics and crashes, investors sell stocks in massive quantities in spite of the absence of any fundamental information about the companies that looks pessimistic.

The renowned economist John Maynard Keynes is noted for describing the stock market as like a beauty contest in which participants are required to select the face most likely to be selected by everyone else. Keynes believed that successful investing was not as much about selecting the stocks of companies that would be the most successful but rather like selecting the stocks of companies that others believe would be most successful. In Keynes' mind, whether those companies were actually successful was of secondary consideration relative to whether people continues to buy those stocks and push up their prices. Keynes' view of the stock market is not correct on the whole. Nonetheless, markets do exhibit irrationality and mindlessness at times, because they are driven by the actions of people, and people do not always behave rationally.

Renewed interest in game theory was heightened by the awarding of the 1994 Nobel Prize in Economics to mathematician John Nash and by the 2002 Oscar-winning movie about Nash called *A Beautiful Mind*.[40] In a few more pages we shall return to a game-theoretic situation that drew the attention of the entire world in 2003, a President's dilemma.

2.7   Risk and Arbitrage

One of the most important concepts in studying risk management and indeed all of finance is *arbitrage*. Arbitrage is a market condition in which it is possible to earn a return with no risk and no investment of funds.

---

[40]Due credit should go to Sylvia Nasar for her biography *A Beautiful Mind* (2001).

Indeed, arbitrage is sometimes described as a money tree, implying that large amounts of money can be created at no cost. Investors who exploit arbitrage opportunities are called *arbitrageurs*, and sometimes the slangy expression, *arbs*.

An arbitrage opportunity will be quickly eradicated by the combined pressure of those that exploit it. Consider the following simple example. Suppose you have an opportunity to play a game in which you earn $100 if a coin toss comes up heads and $0 if it comes up tails. If it costs nothing to play this game, you would clearly play. Even though half the time, you would walk away with no gain or loss, the other half of the time you would walk away with a gain. Since there is no cost, there is no possibility of a loss and some possibility of a gain. Such an example, while theoretically possible, is not realistic. If the opportunity existed, anyone offering the game would be besieged and would quickly go bankrupt.

Now consider a variation of this game. Suppose Game 1 offers a return of $100 if a coin toss comes up heads and $0 if a coin toss comes up tails. Game 2 offers a return of $50 if the same coin toss comes up heads and $0 if it comes up tails. Now assume you have to pay money to play both games. If the two games are offered at the same price, either the first is underpriced or the second is overpriced relative to the other. Let us say it costs $35 to play either game. What would you do? You would pay $35 to play the first game and offer the second game for $35. You would receive $35 and pay $35, netting nothing. But if heads comes up, you receive $100 and pay $50 for a net gain of $50. If tails comes up, you net nothing. You have everything to gain and nothing to lose by playing. Everyone would take this action and the price of the first game would have to rise and/or the price of the second fall. Eventually the first game would have to cost twice the second.

Let us now look at a more realistic possibility, such as an asset or combination of assets selling for two different prices. Later in the course we shall see that one combination of assets and derivatives on the asset might sell for a different price than another combination of assets and derivatives that produces the same results. If this price discrepancy exists, investors will buy the cheaper combination and sell the more expensive one, thereby eliminating the risk and earning the difference in prices. The combined effects of a large number of investors engaging in this type of trading will force the price of the more expensive combination down and the price of the cheaper combination up until the prices are equal and no further gains can be made by trading. Ultimately there can be only one price. This principle is sometimes called the *law of one price*.

Another type of arbitrage opportunity could occur if the component securities of an exchange-traded fund (ETF) are not equal in value to the price at which the ETF is trading in the market. If the securities add up to more than the ETF price, you can buy the ETF, present it to the institution that created the ETF and receive the securities, which you can presumably then sell for more than you paid for the ETF. If the securities cost less than the price of the ETF, a party can create a new ETF, buying up the securities and selling the ETF for a higher price. Ultimately, the price of the ETF must equal the prices of the component securities, hence reaffirming the law of one price.

When situations can be analyzed using arbitrage as a basis, there is no need to worry about a person's risk aversion. Every person, whether risk averse or not, would take advantage of arbitrage opportunities. It turns out that managing risk can be nearly always be analyzed this way. Hence, treating people as though they are risk averse but willing to engage in arbitrage opportunities is perfectly acceptable and does not mean they are *not* risk averse. We will return to this topic in later chapters.[41]

2.8   Risk and Financial Market Efficiency

We oftentimes talk about financial markets being *efficient*. Sometimes we say markets are a *random walk*, essentially meaning that prices are unpredictable but more precisely meaning that the returns on securities are independent and identically distributed. Independence essentially means that tomorrow's return is completely unrelated to today's return, so you cannot use today's return to predict tomorrow's return. Being identically distributed essentially means that the probability distribution of today's return is the same as that of tomorrow's return. This characteristic does not contradict the first point — that returns are unpredictable — but it does imply that the distribution is stable from day to day. In other words, the statistical characteristics of average and volatility among other things remain constant, but this point is not the same as saying that the outcomes are constant. The outcomes in fact are quite volatile.

Efficient markets are markets in which participants expect to earn returns that are commensurate with the risks taken. Risk-free investments should earn the risk-free rate. Risky investments expect to earn a risk premium, as described above. In an inefficient market, an investor earns a greater return than is justified given the risk. Arbitrage would be a case in

---

[41]For a more through treatment of arbitrage, see Billingsley (2006).

which a risk-free investment earns more than the risk-free rate and is clearly a violation of the notion of an efficient market. Since funds can theoretically be borrowed at the risk-free rate or perhaps a little higher, the transaction requires no commitment of funds. Arbitrage is the easiest violation to observe in the market, because we do not have to know what the risk premium is. If no money is invested and there is no risk, one should earn no return. That does not mean that arbitrage opportunities occur frequently. In fact, arbitrage opportunities are the least frequent violations of the rule of market efficiency. For risky investments, we have to know what risk premium was expected to know if the return is truly in excess of what would be normal for the level of risk.

The notion of earning an abnormal return, sometimes loosely referred to as "beating the market," is, however, a long-run concept. Just earning an occasional abnormal return is not sufficient proof that markets are inefficient. As I write this at approximately the closing hour of the New York Stock Exchange, two stocks have increased more than 10% today, a day in which the market as a whole was slightly down. Almost 100 stocks increased by more than 2% on this day. Such gains would clearly exceed any notion of a reasonable return given the risk. These short-run unusual returns are common, but in an efficient market, these returns are spread out among investors. No one can consistently capture them over the long run in an efficient market.

Are markets truly efficient? We do not know. But we should operate with the belief that they are highly competitive and probably close to efficient. The benefit of market efficiency is that the prices of assets and derivatives should be fair. But we must not take this idea so seriously that we assume markets are *always* efficient. If everyone did this, then they would stop processing information rapidly and markets would become inefficient. Thus, *markets can be efficient only if a sufficient number of people are skeptical about whether they are efficient.*

Risk is an important element of efficient markets. When markets are efficient, risk is the means by which wealth is allocated. In efficient markets, risk takers are rewarded over the long run with greater wealth. But during the interim, investors that take more risk will suffer more ups and downs.

2.9   Risk and the Law

Risk comes into play in the legal profession often, if not almost always. We already saw the example in the trial of football star O. J. Simpson, which we

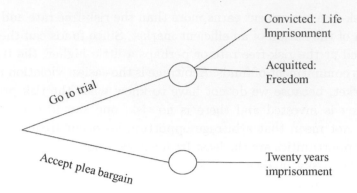

Exhibit 2-12. The Accused's Decision

used earlier to describe how conditional probability affects the interpretation of statistical results.

In criminal cases, the prosecution brings charges against the accused person, who is allowed to use legal counsel for a defense. Prior to the trial, the opposing attorneys often engage in discussions that can lead to a plea bargain. For example, a person accused of an offense that can be punishable by life in prison might be offered a plea bargain in which he accepts a 20-year sentence. The defendant is faced with a risky decision as illustrated in Exhibit 2-12.

A plea bargain is an example of risk concept called a *certainty equivalent*. Accepting a plea bargain resolves the uncertainty and results in a 20-year sentence. The alternative of facing the risk of a trial could result in complete acquittal and freedom, a much better outcome, or a much worse outcome of a conviction and a life sentence. Whether the defendant will accept the plea bargain depends on his feelings about the risk of the trial, the disutility of the possible punishments, and the probability of securing an acquittal. The defendant may even offer a more agreeable alternative such as 10 years' imprisonment, which the prosecution may or may not take. The prosecution's decision is less personal, however, as it wants a conviction but will not suffer personally other than possible loss of reputation for failing to secure a conviction.

In civil trials, one party brings suit against another for a monetary claim. The attorneys may propose a settlement that avoids a trial. For example, if Party A is suing Party B for $20 million, Party B may offer a settlement of $5 million to avoid the trial. If $5 million is the minimum amount that Party

A will take to avoid the trial, then \$5 million is the certainty equivalent. If Party A requires a greater amount, possibly because it believes it has a better chance of winning, then Party A may make a counteroffer of say \$7.5 million. If the parties eventually agree, then the settlement amount is the certainty equivalent.

In general, a certainty equivalent is an amount paid or accepted to avoid the risk. Certainty equivalents play an important role in risk management. When parties engage in hedging they accept an amount, the certainty equivalent, in lieu of facing the risk.

The law is also used to regulate risk-taking behavior. Society often prohibits or restricts activities that endanger people. It is certainly common and widely accepted that society can enact laws to regulate risk-taking behavior that endangers people other than or in addition to the risk-taker, such as the case of speed laws. But society also routinely enacts laws primarily designed to protect people from their own risky behavior, such as seat-belt and motorcycle helmet laws. Sometimes, however, these laws are far more costly and save far fewer lives than we realize. For example, Levitt and Dubner (2005) show that child-resistant packaging saves only 50 lives per year, flame-retardant pajamas save only 10 lives per year, and safety drawstrings on children's clothing save only two lives per year. These numbers probably seem surprisingly low.

2.10 Risk, Government, Politics, and Policy

Without trying to take a political position, let us think about President Bush's decision in 2003 to invade Iraq. In fact, we will examine it in the context of a game theory scenario. As leader of the United States, President Bush bore responsibility for the safety and security of its citizens and arguably many other countries of the world, particularly Israel. The information available was that Iraq had used weapons of mass destruction (WMD) against the Kurds following the Gulf War of 1991, a fact documented by the United Nations (U.N.). Also, intelligence provided by the CIA, Great Britain, Russia, and several middle-eastern nations indicated that Iraqi leader Saddam Hussein currently had WMD. U.N. resolutions requesting permission to give inspectors free rein in Iraq and to allow private interviews with Iraqi scientists were denied by Saddam. All of this information pointed to the likelihood that WMD were in Iraq.

Consider the decision matrix in Exhibit 2-13.

Decision	Outcome	
	Saddam has WMDs	Saddam has no WMDs
Attack	Likely capture and stop WMDs	Severe political fallout
Do not attack	Saddam may use WMDs	Nothing

Exhibit 2-13. A President's Dilemma

Obviously we have simplified the decision somewhat, because there are certainly other consequences and benefits of attacking or not attacking. For now, we are focusing only on the WMD issue.

From a risk-reward perspective, how should this decision be analyzed? Given the information that Saddam likely has WMDs, the ex ante probability is highly tilted toward there being WMD. The consequences of not attacking are that Saddam uses these weapons. The gain if there are no WMDs is nothing. The consequences of attacking are that Saddam has no WMDs and President Bush and all those involved in the decision suffer severe political fallout, possibly leading to loss of the 2004 election. The gain if there are WMDs is stopping them. Clearly there is no simple equilibrium. The decision maker has to weigh the rewards against the costs. As we know, the decision was made to attack. Whether this was the right or wrong decision *after the fact* is not important in understanding the risk. What matters is whether it was the right or wrong decision *before the fact.* Of course, it is not possible to definitively answer that question. The decision maker's personal views on risk determine the decision. But we can gain some insights into how and why the decision was made.

Naturally, we all know what happened and how much has been analyzed about this decision ex post. Criticism from the media and many individuals have nearly dominated political discussions since that time. But a decision is correct ex post if that same decision would be made in the same ex ante circumstances with the same information. It is difficult to imagine being faced with that decision again and being able to forget this ex post result, but all risky decisions should be analyzed under their own unique circumstances, making proper use but not abuse of historical information. Ex post decision analysis is of little use, except in how it can be used to improve the quality of information available for future decision making. Therein lies the only real legitimate concern: that substantial amounts of corroborative information were inaccurate. Even then we must realize that decisions are rarely made in the presence of perfect information. If so, there is no risk and the decision is an easy one. A computer could be programmed to make that decision. If President Bush knew for absolute certain that there were no WMD, he probably would not have attacked. If he knew for absolute certain that there were WMD, he obviously would have attacked.

Ex post analysis of decision makers also ignores the element of responsibility. When citizens were asked before the invasion "Should the U.S. invade?", the most common answers were "yes" and "no." The only real correct answer was "I don't know." If a citizen believes we should not go to war, but Saddam has WMD and uses them, no one will hold that citizen responsible. Likewise, a citizen who believes we should go to war is not held responsible when we do go to war and no WMD are found. The decision maker bears the greatest risk, because that person has the responsibility. In almost all cases, the decision maker has access to the full set of information, however imperfect or misleading it might be. Only the decision maker who holds responsibility can make the decision. Others can analyze, re-analyze, and over-analyze ad infinitum ex ante and contribute very little to understanding why a decision was made and whether it was a correct one.

Noted American pediatric neurosurgeon and 2016 Presidential candidate Dr. Ben Carson (2009) explained his rules for risky decision making as follows. He asks himself: (1) What is the best thing that can happen if I do this? (2) What is the worst thing that can happen if I do this? (3) What is the best thing that can happen if I do not do this? (4) What is the worst thing that can happen if I do not do this? Carson then examines the ratio of best to worst and uses that factor to make a decision. Although this rule focuses somewhat on the extreme outcomes, it does provide a heuristic for decision making under risk and is likely to be essentially the rule that was followed in the Iraq decision.

In recent years, it seems that society has grown far more intolerant of risk, in particular the randomness that occurs in life. In particular our government decision makers are held responsible for their decisions that were made under conditions of extreme uncertainty and highly imperfect information. When adverse outcomes occur, we criticize the decision makers and oftentimes file litigation against them or their organizations. Power discusses this point quite effectively in his essay "The Risk Management of Everything," (2004). When we view risk this way, we find that those responsible oftentimes are more interested in managing their own risks.[42] So instead of using good judgment and taking prudent and sensible risks, decision makers must take extraordinary precautions to protect their own exposures. In particular, government regulators impose heavy and costly regulations because they have a "not-on-my-watch" mentality. Random outcomes are rarely viewed as truly random: it always seems to be someone's fault, either for causing the outcome or not having taken steps to prevent it.

There are so many risks in life that we can hardly begin to manage all of them, nor should we blame every adverse outcome on a particular decision maker. Many of these risks seem almost invisible. Ross (1999), for examples, notes that 140,000 Americans a year are injured by zippers, buttons, and articles of clothing. Is anyone to blame for these accidents? Are zippers, buttons, and articles of clothing so loaded with latent dangers that someone must pay when we misuse them? When that happens we end up with toy Superman capes that contain warnings such as "This cape does not enable user to fly" and hair dryers with statements such as "Do not use hair dryer in bathtub." Even when others are not held responsible for accidents, the precautions we must take are wasteful and costly.

The intelligence business, sports, corporate decision making, and life are sequences of risky decisions. We must not confuse the past with the future. As former baseball player and social philosopher Yogi Berra allegedly once said "Predicting is very hard, especially when it involves the future," we might add, "Predicting is very easy when it involves the past." In government or business, we select leaders to make decisions under risk. We must keep in mind what is reasonable to expect of decision makers, for as business students we are likely to become corporate decision makers some day and will have to make decisions in the presence of imperfect information.

2.11   What Managing Risk Means for Businesses and Nonprofits

The focus in this book is on how organizations manage risk. All organizations face risk; indeed risk taking is what life in general is all about. Without risk

---

[42]When fiduciary parties place their own needs before those of the parties they represent, we refer to this as *agency costs*. The agent, operating on behalf of the principal, will generate costs borne by the principal. The topic of agency costs in risk management is discussed later in this book.

taking, no one could expect much success. Managing risk is the process of defining the risk an organization wants, measuring the risk it has, and ensuring that the former equals the latter. Managing risk sometimes means adjusting the risk upward, and sometimes it means adjusting the risk downward, a process usually called hedging. The focus of this course, and indeed most of the risk management process, is about hedging.

Stating this point more formally, managing risk is about taking actions that alter the likelihood of undesirable outcomes. There are three general ways in which risk is managed.

- Diversifying a portfolio by spreading out the risk that undesirable events associated with one component of the portfolio will not have a significant effect on the overall wealth of the holder of the portfolio.
- Purchasing a contract that passes on the risk to another party. This arrangement is equivalent to insurance, but in our world of financial risk, this strategy will usually take the form of options.
- Forgoing the opportunity to benefit from favorable outcomes in return for protection against unfavorable outcomes. This form of risk management characterizes forward contracts, futures contracts, and swaps.

We will not spend much time on diversification, because it is well-covered in investments courses, and also because it is a very simple and inexpensive way to manage risk. Our primary focus is on the use of forwards, futures, swaps, and options. But before we can begin examining these instruments, we have to study more about what risk means to an organization.

2.12 Chapter Summary

This chapter has provided an introduction to the concept of risk. The chapter is quite different from most introductory treatments of risk. There are no formulas and no analysis of data. Instead it focuses on descriptive characteristics of risk and how people process and respond to risk. A major takeaway is that the human mind does not do a particularly good job processing risk information. Human biases often get in the way. While these biases are numerous and cannot be completely controlled, what more eliminated, knowledge of them brings an awareness of the limitations of decision making under risk.

2.13   Questions and Problems

1. Identify the three key elements in the definition of risk.
2. What is the concept of conditional probability and why is it relevant in decision making under risk?
3. What do Tversky and Kahnemann say about how a survey question is framed and its impact on a person's answer?
4. What is Monday morning quarterbacking? What is its relevance in terms of risk in finance and business?
5. What is the risk of risk?
6. What is the concept of expected utility, why is it the optimal method for making decisions, and what are its limitations?
7. What is a risk premium and what is its relevance for risk averse people?
8. What is risk tolerance, and how does it relate to risk aversion?
9. Name some factors that determine a person's risk aversion.
10. How do human biases interfere with optimal decision making under risk?
11. What is information asymmetry, adverse selection, and moral hazard?
12. What is arbitrage?
13. What is the concept of financial market efficiency? Why does an efficient market require that enough investors do not believe the market is efficient?
14. How are plea bargains and settlements related to risk?
15. What are the three general ways of managing risk?

Chapter 3

Principles of Risk, Return, and Financial Decision Making

I learned to admire risk takers and entrepreneurs, be they farmers or small merchants, who went to work and took risks to build something for themselves and their children, pushing at the boundaries of their lives to make them better.

Ronald Reagan
An American Life
Gallery Books (1990)

In the previous chapters we explored some basic concepts related to how people feel about risk, how they react to risk, and how they manage risk at a very fundamental level. Most of these ideas were examined in a broader or more societal context than that of a business or non-profit organization. Now it is time to gear up toward managing risk within the framework of an organization. As we shall see throughout this course, there are a variety of sources of risks, but the ones that occupy center stage for much of this book are market risks, i.e., those that arise from changes in interest rates, exchange rates, commodity prices, and stock prices. The examples we will begin to see, starting with this chapter, mostly represent risks derived from these sources of uncertainty. There are other sources of risk, and they will be covered in detail in Chapters 11 and 12.

The material in this chapter also introduces the first quantitative notions of risk. Much of the information in this chapter is standard material in investments books and in most books on financial management. If the reader has sufficient foundational knowledge from courses on these subjects, this chapter can probably be omitted, but it is provided here for several possible purposes. It can be covered in the standard manner. Alternatively, it can be covered in class and assigned as supporting reading. Finally, it can serve as a source of reference for later in the book when some of these concepts resurface.

The chapter begins by introducing the notions of long and short positions. It then examines the concept of a rate or return on an asset and its characterization in an ex ante sense, meaning before the uncertainty is resolved. We then look at what happens to returns when assets are combined into portfolios or as companies, which are just combinations of assets. Then we turn to an examination of returns in an ex post or historical context, meaning after the uncertainty is resolved.

Equipped with this information, we can then begin looking at how individuals feel about the returns and risks to which they are exposed. We look at the characteristics of individual preferences by examining how utility functions provide models to capture these feelings. Recall that we introduced the concept of a utility function in the previous chapter to help resolve the St. Petersburg paradox. We show how the optimal amount of risk to be taken is determined and how this result leads to models that relate return to risk, meaning how much additional return we should expect for the risk we have assumed.

We end the chapter with three alternative but nonetheless complementary views of the relationship between risk and return. One is through the mechanism of arbitrage, which will play a critical role throughout this book. Of course, arbitrage was briefly mentioned in Chapter 2. The second view is through stochastic dominance, and the third is called state preference theory.

We emphasize that this chapter provides only a basic treatment of these topics for this course. The study of risk management involves the determination of how to best align the risk an organization is taking with the risk it desires. But determining the desired risk is a very complex process, and as such, we cover it only at a fundamental level. And ultimately, the desire to accept risk is a personal trait. A manager accepts an amount of risk for his organization to take that is commensurate with the goals he is trying to achieve for the organization and himself and the unease he is willing to bear when those goals are not achieved. Fully understanding this tradeoff is a deeply human inquiry that we cannot hope to make here.

So let us now move into an examination of these basic topics. If some of this material seems too simple or too much of a review, it means that you are very well-prepared to study financial risk management. If it seems a bit hard, take your time.

3.1 Long and Short

In the financial world, we frequently describe the position or exposure that a party has to a particular price or rate as being *long* or *short*. A typical characterization of a long position held by a party is that the party owns something. *Going long* is said to be the same as buying, owning, or holding something. But there are some exceptions. Hence, a better definition is as follows:

> *A long position is one in which the party suffers an adverse outcome if the price or rate associated with the underlying source of risk decreases, and incurs a beneficial outcome if the price or rate associated with the underlying source of risk increases.*

It should be obvious that if a party owns something, an adverse outcome occurs when the price falls. For example, one might own a stock or a bond whose price falls. One might convert her local currency to a foreign currency and see the foreign currency value fall relative to her local currency. A homeowner might find the price of his house fall due to a decline in the housing market. In contrast to actually owning something, however, a long position can also exist by implication, such as when a person anticipates selling something he does not own. The classic example of this form of being long is a company planning to issue new bonds or stock. If the price of the bond or stock falls, the party suffers an adverse outcome. Whenever an adverse outcome is implied by a fall in the price or an exchange rate, the party is said to be long or to have long exposure. We even sometimes refer to the party with the long position as simply *the long*, using the word as a noun instead of an adjective.

In the examples that follow, we will assume that the asset has a linear payoff. For example, a stock, bond, currency, or commodity has a linear payoff. A linear payoff means that the profit changes one-for-one with the price. If I buy something for ¥1,000 and it decreases by ¥10, I have made a loss of ¥10. If I am committed to selling something later that is currently worth ¥1,000 and it decreases in value by ¥10, I have made a loss of ¥10. Options do not have linear payoffs, however, a point we will introduce in the next chapter, so at this time, we are not talking about options. Forwards, futures, and swaps do have linear payoffs, but at this point, it would be best to think of the long position as being in an ordinary asset, such as a stock, bond, currency, or commodity.

Exhibit 3-1 shows the perspective of a party with a long position in a linear asset. The gain or loss, meaning the profit, is on the vertical axis,

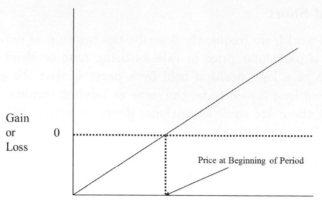

Exhibit 3-1. The Peformance of a Long Position in a Linear Asset

while the value of the asset is on the horizontal axis. Note that the party has unlimited gains on the upside as there is no limit to the price. On the downside, the loss is large but limited to the price paid for the asset, as the asset value cannot go below zero. Otherwise, it is not an asset.

Now let us define the notion of being short:

> *A short position is one in which the party suffers an adverse outcome if the price or rate associated with the underlying source of risk increases, and incurs a gain if the price or rate associated with the underlying source of risk decreases.*

An example of a short position is when a party plans to buy something at a later date. For example, you might be planning to purchase a new car upon graduation. If this plan is a relatively firm commitment, you will suffer an adverse outcome if the price of the car increases before you make the purchase. Hence, you can be viewed as short the car. If a German company will need to acquire Japanese yen to pay for some purchases from a Japanese company at a later date, it will suffer an adverse outcome if the yen increases in value, because that would mean that more of the German currency, the euro, is required to purchase a fixed amount of yen.

In the financial world, however, one of the most common instances of being in a short position is to borrow an asset, sell it to someone else and then plan to buy it back later and return it to the original owner. On a personal level, you would certainly not borrow your friend's car and sell it to someone else, but in the financial world, the borrowing of securities is done on a routine basis. The people who do it are called *short sellers*. Sometimes such a party is just called the *short*, using the word as a noun instead of an adjective. These parties are said to be *shorting, going short, selling short,* or *short selling.* There are some finance professionals that even specialize in short selling. They scour the financial markets looking for companies they believe are overvalued, and in some cases companies that they believe are even likely to fail. They sell the shares short and try to profit from a subsequent decrease in the price of the stock. Some investors try to anticipate takeovers, shorting the acquiring firm, whose stock typically falls, and going long the target firm, whose stock typically rises. Other short sellers are merely attempting to achieve balance in a portfolio, being long some securities and short others, so as to spread out the risk and achieve a more desirable position.

Exhibit 3-2 shows the profit position of the short seller for a linear asset, such as a stock, bond, currency, or commodity. Note the unlimited loss if the price rates. If the price falls, the potential gain is limited to the full original price, which would occur if the asset value falls to zero.

To emphasize, Exhibits 3-1 and 3-2 show the potential gains and losses of the holders of the long and short positions for traditional assets such as securities, currencies, and commodities. As we shall see later in this book, these images do not generally depict the long and short positions of *all* assets. Options in particular have quite different graphs. They are, as we said, non-linear assets, and for one type of option, known as a put, a long position would benefit from a decrease in the source of risk.

Now we take a look at how to measure financial performance with the concept of a rate of return.

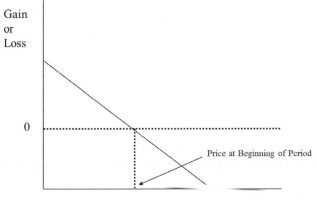

Exhibit 3-2. The Performance of Short Position in a Linear Asset

3.2   Rates of Return

Probably the most fundamentally important concept in the financial world is that of a rate of return. The rate of return is the change in price plus any cash payments received or costs incurred over a period of time relative to the original price. While that definition is acceptable for starters, we shall need a formal definition more suitable for computational purposes.

First let us define a time point t and a previous time point $t-1$. Let S_t and S_{t-1} be the prices at times t and $t-1$, respectively. Let cf_t be the net of cash payments received and costs incurred in holding an asset from $t-1$ to t. If cash payments received exceed (are less than) costs, cf_t is positive (negative). The rate of return is then formally defined as

$$R_t = \frac{S_t - S_{t-1} + cf_t}{S_{t-1}}. \tag{3.1}$$

Note that the numerator contains the change in price, $S_t - S_{t-1}$, from the time point $t-1$ to t, plus the net cash payments. The denominator can be thought of as the base value. Hence, the rate of return is the percentage gain or loss from holding one unit of the asset over the period ending at t. By the way, when we refer to a rate of return, we always mean the return to a long position. If we say the return was 10%, we always mean that the long earned 10%. It is simply customary and more intuitive to imply the long position when we are speaking of returns in general.

A stock pays dividends and incurs little if any costs of holding. Hence, for stocks cf_t would be any dividends. A bond pays interest and incurs little if any costs of holding. Hence, for bonds cf_t would be the interest. A commodity such as gold or oil makes no cash payments but incurs significant costs of holding. Hence, cf_t would likely be negative.[1] In all cases, however, there is one subtle factor that we must consider: *these cash flows need not occur precisely at time t.* Depending on the length of time spanned by $t-1$ to t, these cash flows could easily occur anywhere in that time interval and could be relatively far apart. For example, if the length of the interval is one year and there are four dividend payments, the dividends will occur three months apart. Thus, for annual returns, we might simply aggregate the dividends, thereby ignoring the time value of money, or we might compound them to the

---

[1]There are theories that argue that certain commodities such as oil or gold offer non-pecuniary benefits that should be included in cf_t. We shall ignore these for now, but they will be discussed in Chapter 8.

end of the year. Or perhaps, better, we might decide that quarterly returns are better.

In some cases, cf_t is either zero or ignored. Stocks that pay no dividends or bonds that pay no interest during the interval of $t-1$ to t have cf_t of zero. The costs of holding some commodities is certainly not zero but is sometimes considered a transaction cost, which is often ignored or treated in a separate context.

For examples of the computation of rates or return, consider the following:

You purchase a stock for $15. At the end of three months, the company pays a dividend of $0.50 and the stock is at $16. What is the rate of return for the three-month period?

$$R_t = \frac{\$16.00 - \$15.00 + \$0.50}{\$15.00} = 0.10, \text{ or } 10\%.$$

A zero-coupon bond is worth $925.52. One year later, it is worth $975.50. What is the rate of return over the one-year period?

$$R_t = \frac{\$975.50 - \$925.52 + \$0.0}{\$925.52} = 0.054, \text{ or } 5.4\%$$

The price of oil is $48 a barrel. One month later, it is $44 a barrel and it costs $0.60 to store a barrel for one month. What is the rate of return for one month?

$$R_t = \frac{\$44.00 - \$48.00 - \$0.60}{\$48.00} = -0.0958, \text{ or } -9.58\%.$$

In these examples, all we did was to take the change in value plus any cash flows and divide by the original value.[2]

Of course, as we see in the oil example, a rate of return can be negative. Now, let us consider these problems from the point of view of the short position. The computation of the rate of return is simple. We just reverse the sign. Hence, in the first problem, someone with a short position in stock would have a rate of return of -10%. In the second problem, a party that is short the zero coupon bond would have a rate of return of -5.4%. In the third problem, someone shorting the oil would have a rate of return of $+9.58\%$. In all cases, the rate of return tells us the percentage gain or loss

---

[2]From a purely computational standpoint, it is easier and much faster to calculate the rate of return by dividing the ending value by the beginning value and then subtracting 1. Try it. Calculate $16 - 15 + 0.50$ divided by 15. Then calculate $16 + 0.50$ divided by 15 and subtract 1. There is one fewer keystroke with the latter approach.

of the party. It is important to understand, however, that a short position is not a commitment of funds up front. Thus, the notion of a rate of return to a short position is somewhat ambiguous. In general, we tend to prefer to express rates of return from the perspective of the party who is long. Hence, we need not define a short rate of return, and Equation (3.1) will suffice as a general specification of a return. When we are interested in the rate of return to a short position, we will simply reverse the sign and note that it is a short position.

Finally, let us add that sometimes the term *rate of return* is often abbreviated to *return*. That expression is the term we shall primarily use.[3]

3.3   Ex Ante Concepts of Return and Risk

In the three examples in the previous section, we calculated returns based on price changes and cash flows incurred while holding the asset. But suppose we are positioned at time $t - 1$. We would not know the return, R_t. Given that the central theme of this book is managing risk, it seems reasonable to think that we might want to use as much information as we have available at $t-1$ to try and predict the return R_t. What we are doing is examining the ex ante characteristics of the return. To do that, we must begin by identifying the possible returns and their probabilities. We shall start with a simple example.

Consider an asset, which we shall refer to as asset j. The distribution of possible returns and the probabilities are given in Exhibit 3-3.

We see that our return might be as high as 20% or as low as -15%. The most likely return is 5%, because there is a 60% chance of it happening.[4]

Outcome	Return	Probability
1	20%	0.30
2	5%	0.60
3	-15%	0.10

Exhibit 3-3.   The Ex Ante Distribution of Returns on Asset j

---

[3]In a few other books, you may seem the terms *holding period return* or *price relative*, though these terms typically refer to the final price plus any cash earned or paid divided by the original price. They indicate the amount of money one has at t per unit of money that one had at $t - 1$. Subtracting 1 gives the rate of return.

[4]Statisticians refer to the most likely outcome as the mode.

If we had to forecast the return based on this information, what would our forecast be?

3.3.1   *The (Ex Ante) Expected Return*

The *expected return* is generally considered to be the best forecast of the return, because it is the return that would be incurred on average over a large number of trials. It is an ex ante concept by definition, so we can call it the ex ante expected return, with some redundancy, or we can just call it the expected return. The word "expected" automatically implies that it is an ex ante concept. It is found by calculating a weighted average of each outcome, where the weights are the probabilities of occurrence of the respective outcomes. Let the outcomes be indexed by the letter k, where k is either $1, 2, \ldots, K$. In our example of asset $j, K = 3$. Let the returns be denoted as R_k and the probabilities be q_k.[5] Given n possible outcomes, the expected return is defined as

$$E(R) = \sum_{k=1}^{K} q_k R_k. \tag{3.2}$$

Thus, for asset j,

$$E(R) = \sum_{k=1}^{K} q_k R_k$$

$$= 0.30(0.20) + 0.60(0.05) + 0.10(-0.15)$$

$$= 0.075.$$

So our forecast of the return would be 7.5%, the expected return. If these are the correct outcomes and probabilities, then over the long run we would earn an average return of 7.5% if we faced this situation many times, provided the information in Exhibit 3-3 is correct.

Of course, no single outcome will ever equal 7.5%. At least one outcome is much more and one outcome is much less. When managing risk, we are concerned about how much risk there is. So we need a measure of the risk, which turns out to be the ex ante volatility.

---

[5] We are going to avoid using the obvious choice, p_i, because p will be used in later chapters to represent the price of a put option.

3.3.2 *The Ex Ante Volatility*

Risk is reflected in the deviations around the expected value. If, however, we just average the deviations from the expected value, the positive and negative deviations will tend to cancel and there will not appear to be much risk. While we could compute a probability-weighted average of the absolute values of the deviations from the expected values, the most commonly used measure of risk is the volatility, which is roughly the probability-weighted average squared deviation from the expected value. By squaring the deviations, we convert them to positive numbers. The greater the average of the squared deviations, the more variability there is in the numbers. We can then infer that there is more risk.

Most statistics books present this concept in the form of the *variance*, which is the average squared deviation. The square root of the variance is called the *standard deviation*. Here we shall use the term that is most commonly used in the financial world: the *volatility*.[6] The volatility is the standard deviation and is commonly denoted with the Greek letter σ (sigma). It is computed as follows:

$$\sigma = \sqrt{\sum_{k=1}^{K} q_k (R_k - E(R))^2}. \tag{3.3}$$

Of course, inside the square root is the variance, σ^2. An alternative, equivalent, and occasionally more convenient formula is

$$\sigma = \sqrt{\sum_{k=1}^{K} q_k (R_k)^2 - (E(R))^2} \tag{3.4}$$

$$= \sqrt{E(R^2) - (E(R))^2}.$$

In other words, the volatility is the square root of the expected value of the return squared minus the square of the expected value of the return, with the outcomes weighted by their probabilities.

Volatility is a much easier measure to use than variance because it is expressed in the same units as the original data. In our example, with the data in the form of percentages, the volatility will be expressed as a percentage, as we will see in our example a few paragraphs away. If we used

---

[6]In fact, financial traders often just call it *vol*.

variance, the computed value would be the square of a percentage, which is not a very intuitive concept.

Now let us see how to implement these formulas. In our example, we can obtain the volatility using either Equation (3.3) or (3.4),

$$\sigma = \sqrt{\sum_{k=1}^{K} q_k (R_k - E(R))^2}$$

$$= \sqrt{0.30(0.20 - 0.075)^2 + 0.60(0.05 - 0.075)^2 + 0.10(-0.15 - .075)^2}$$

$$= 0.1006$$

or,

$$\sigma = \sqrt{E(R^2) - (E(R))^2}$$

$$= \sqrt{(0.30(0.20)^2 + 0.60(0.05)^2 + 0.10(-0.15)^2) - (0.075)^2}$$

$$= 0.1006.$$

So the volatility is 10.06%. Note that volatility of return is in the same units as the original data. We will see later how to interpret this number.

3.3.3 *The Ex Ante Covariance and Correlation*

In the examples above, we had only a single asset, but in practice we are nearly always concerned with more than one asset at a time. When our risk is driven by more than one asset, we must consider the relationships between the two assets. One of the most useful measures of how two assets are related is the coefficient of correlation, sometimes just called the *correlation*. It is a measure of the linear relationship between two random variables.

Exhibit 3-4 shows the relationship between two hypothetical variables E and F, neither of which is necessarily a financial variable. The heavy curved line is F as it relates to E. The dotted line is an imaginary straight line fit through the points denoted by F. As we can see F does seem to be linearly related to E. This requirement is met by the fact that a line can be fit reasonably well through the points, and that line has a positive slope. F is not perfectly linearly related to E, however, as all of the points of the curve line are not on the straight line. But modeling the curved line with the straight line is not a bad approximation. Perfect linearity is not required to characterize something as being linear, however, and there are statistical measures that show how well the line fits the curve.

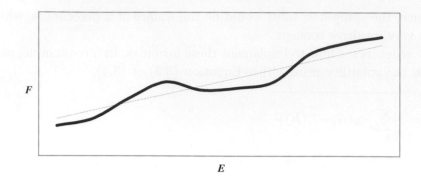

Exhibit 3-4. F Linearly Related to E

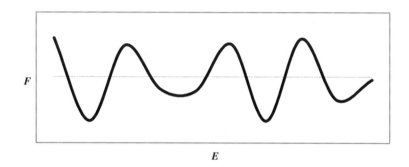

Exhibit 3-5. F Non-Linearly Related to E

If F is positively related to E, we say that it has positive correlation. If the line were downward sloping, we would say that it has negative correlation. But it is important to understand that correlation reflects only a linear relationship between F and E. In Exhibit 3-5, F and E are essentially uncorrelated because you cannot fit an upward or downward sloping line through the points. But in fact, F and E are highly related because F is what is called a sine wave and is the simple function $F = \sin(E)$. In other words, if you knew the value of E, you would easily know that the value of F is $\sin(E)$. Clearly, F and E are related. In fact, they are perfectly related, but they are not linearly related.

Appreciating this point is a valuable lesson in risk management, because many relationships among risky variables are nonlinear. Correlation is a useful tool in measuring linear risks but not nonlinear risks. We will run into some nonlinear risks later in this book. But for now, let us focus only on linear relationships, which are captured by the correlation.

Correlation is a numerical measure of the strength of the linear relationship between two random variables. The correlation between two variables, E and F, will be denoted in this book as ρ_{EF}, which is the Greek letter *rho* subscripted with E and F. By the manner in which it is constructed, correlation is limited to a range of -1 to $+1$. A correlation of -1 indicates perfect negative correlation, which would arise when the variables move opposite to each other in a perfectly linear manner. A graph would show a negatively sloped line with all of the points of F falling right on the line. A correlation of $+1$ indicates perfect positive correlation, which would arise when the variables move directly with each other in a perfectly linear manner. A graph would show a positively sloped line with all of the points of F falling right on the line. A correlation of precisely zero would rarely occur, but would represent two variables that are completely unrelated to each other in a linear manner. Correlations between 0 and 1 are referred to as positive correlation and represent cases where a line through the points is upward sloping but all of the points are not on the line. Correlations between -1 and 0 are referred to as negative correlation and represent cases where a line through the points is downward sloping but all of the points are not on the line.[7]

Understanding this point is an important prelude to understanding the concept of independence. Correlation is the notion of a linearly dependent relationship. Two random variables that are completely independent of each other will have zero correlation, and there will also be no non-linear relationship between them. As we saw with the sine function, you can have virtually zero correlation but still not be independent.

It is also important to understand that correlation does not imply causality. If E and F are highly correlated, it does not mean that the relationship occurs because F is responding to E or E is responding to F. That is, there is not necessarily causality. One does not *cause* the other. For example, there are more sales of heavy coats during the winter than during the summer. There are also more respiratory illnesses during the winter. These two variables may be highly correlated, but it hardly means that buying a coat increases your chance of a respiratory illness, nor does it mean that having a respiratory illness increases your chance of buying a coat. There is a common factor driving the correlation, however, and that is the season.

---

[7]The graph of the sine function in Exhibit 3-4 has a correlation of -0.14. Thus, in the sine function Y and X have a weak negative correlation.

To obtain the correlation, we first calculate a measure called the *covariance*. For E and F, the covariance would be denoted as cov_{EF}. Now we turn these variable into the returns on assets j and i. First, let R_{j_k} and R_{i_k} be the returns on assets j and i, respectively, for outcome k. Now, taking into account that there are multiple events identified as $k = 1, 2, \ldots, K$, the covariance between the returns on assets i and j is defined as follows:

$$\text{cov}_{ji} = \sum_{k=1}^{K} q_k (R_{j_k} - E(R_j))(R_{i_k} - E(R_i)). \tag{3.5}$$

An alternative and sometimes preferable formula is

$$\text{cov}_{ji} = \sum_{k=1}^{K} q_k R_{j_k} R_{i_k} - E(R_i)E(R_j), \tag{3.6}$$

which is equivalent to $E(R_j R_i) - E(R_j)E(R_i)$. That is, we take the expected value of the product of the two returns, R_i and R_j, and subtract the product of the expected values of the two returns.

The formula for the correlation between two random variables representing the rates of return of two assets is the covariance divided by the product of the standard deviations of the two variables:

$$\rho_{ji} = \frac{\text{cov}_{ji}}{\sigma_j \sigma_i}. \tag{3.7}$$

Later in this book, we find ourselves concerned with how corporate cash flows vary with different sources of risk. For example, suppose an airline wants to know how its cash flows are related to the price of energy. In that case, it might want to calculate the covariance and correlation of its cash flows with either the prices or percentage changes of a representative measure of its energy costs. When working with prices, we use the same formulas as when working with returns but we use price instead of return as the random variable. Thus, for prices S_j and S_i we have the expected prices and standard deviations of the price and also the covariance and correlation of prices S_j and S_i given as

$$E(S_j) = \sum_{k=1}^{K} q_k S_{j_k},$$

$$\sigma_j = \sqrt{\sum_{k=1}^{K} q_k \left(S_{j_k}\right)^2 - (E(S_j))^2}, \quad = \sqrt{E(S_j^2) - (E(S_j))^2}$$

$$E(S_i) = \sum_{k=1}^{K} q_k S_{i_k},$$

$$\sigma_i = \sqrt{\sum_{k=1}^{K} q_k (S_{i_k})^2 - (E(S_i))^2}, \quad = \sqrt{E(S_i^2) - (F(S_i))^2}$$

$$\text{cov}_{ji} = \sum_{k=1}^{K} q_k S_{j_k} S_{i_k} - E(S_j)E(S_i), \quad \rho_{ik} = \frac{\text{cov}_{ij}}{\sigma_j \sigma_i}.$$

Exhibit 3-6 provides information on the probabilities of various prices for two energy assets, crude oil and natural gas, and also the cash flows sufficient to calculate the returns on crude oil, natural gas, and the cash flow of a hypothetical airline we shall call Easy Air. The expected prices and volatilities are shown and have been computed using the above variations of formulas (3.2) and (3.3).

Now let us calculate the covariances. Note that we replace j and i with *oil* and *gas*, respectively. We also introduce a third asset, *EA*, representing the return on Easy Air.

$$\text{cov}_{oil,gas} = 0.40(40 - 48)(5.50 - 6.30) + 0.40(50 - 48)(6.00 \quad 6.30)$$

$$+ 0.20(60 - 48)(8.50 - 6.30)$$

$$= 7.60.$$

| | | Return on | | |
Outcome	Probability	Crude Oil (*oil*)	Natural Gas (*gas*)	Easy Air Cash Flow (*EA*)
1	0.40	$40	$5.50	$400
2	0.40	$50	$6.00	$200
3	0.20	$60	$8.50	$100
Expected Value		$48	$6.30	$260
Volatility		$7.48	$1.12	$120

Note: Crude oil price is per barrel, natural gas price is in 10,000 million BTUs, Easy Air cash flow is in millions.

Exhibit 3-6. The Ex Ante Distribution of Returns on Oil and Natural Gas and the Cash Flow of Easy Air

$$\text{cov}_{oil,EA} = 0.40(40-48)(400-260) + 0.40(50-48)(200-260)$$
$$+ 0.20(60-48)(100-260)$$
$$= -880.00$$
$$\text{cov}_{gas,EA} = 0.40(5.50-6.30)(400-260)$$
$$+ 0.40(6.00-6.30)(200-260)$$
$$+ 0.20(8.50-6.30)(100-260)$$
$$= -108.00$$

The correlations are, therefore,

$$\rho_{oil,gas} = \frac{7.60}{(7.48)(1.12)} = 0.9048$$

$$\rho_{oil,EA} = \frac{-880.00}{(7.48)(120)} = -0.9800$$

$$\rho_{gas,EA} = \frac{-108.00}{(1.12)(120)} = -0.8018.$$

Note that as we might expect, crude oil and natural gas are highly correlated at 0.9048, and Easy Air's cash flow is highly negatively correlated to oil at −0.98. Another interesting point is revealed by the correlation between natural gas and Easy Air's cash flow. In all likelihood, Easy Air uses substantial amounts of oil but little natural gas. The strong negative correlation between oil and cash flow probably reflects causality: higher oil prices reduce cash flow. But note that cash flow is also highly negatively correlated with natural gas. This correlation does not, however, imply causality. Easy Air's cash flow is not materially affected by the price of natural gas. The high correlation is merely a reflection of an indirect effect whereby higher natural gas prices occur when oil prices are higher and Easy Air's cash flow is lower. This example illustrates the fact that correlation and causality are not the same concept.

Now that we have introduced a second variable, we can begin to look at how to combine assets. In the language used in investments, such combinations are typically called portfolios, but we do not always have to be situated in an investment context. Companies are themselves merely combinations of assets, and it is the management of the risk of these combinations of assets that is our principal concern.

3.3.4 *Ex Ante Concepts for Combinations of Assets*

To understand how to manage the risk of combinations of assets, we must understand how the returns on such combinations behave. In most finance books and courses, this knowledge is gained by studying how securities are combined into portfolios. Consider a company that owns two individual assets. These assets could represent broad classes of assets, such as portfolios, or they could be individual assets. The only requirement is that we know the expected returns and standard deviations of the two assets and the correlation between them. Earlier in this chapter we looked at a single asset that we called asset j. Now we shall add asset i. Let us say that we have their Expected Returns ($E(R_j)$, $E(R_i)$), their volatilities (σ_j and σ_i), and the correlation between the returns on assets j and i (ρ_{ji}). There are many ways that assets j and i can be combined. For example, we could have 60% of our wealth invested in asset j and 40% in asset i, or we could have 75% of our wealth invested in j and 25% in asset i.[8] The percentages of assets made up of j and i will be denoted as w_j and w_i, respectively. These measures are often referred to as the weights associated with the assets. Clearly w_j and w_i must sum to 1.

Now we can show the formula for the expected returns on the combination of assets A and B:

$$E(R_{ji}) = w_j E(R_j) + w_i E(R_i). \tag{3.8}$$

This formula means that the expected return on the combined position of j and i is a weighted average of the expected returns on assets j and i where the weights are the relative investments in the two assets.

The volatility of a combination of j and i is not, however, just a simple weighted average of the volatilities of assets j and i. The volatility of a combination of assets must take into account the relationships between the returns on assets: in other words, it must account for the correlation between assets j and i. The formula for the volatility of the combination of j and i is

$$\sigma_{ji} = \sqrt{w_j^2 \sigma_j^2 + w_i^2 \sigma_i^2 + 2 w_j w_i \rho_{ji} \sigma_j \sigma_i}. \tag{3.9}$$

Under the square root sign is a set of terms, $w_j^2 \sigma_j^2 + w_i^2 \sigma_i^2$. These are the squares of the weights times the respective variances. The other term,

---

[8]We will not get into short selling here, but if short selling were possible, we would have a negative weight in the short asset and the weight in the other asset would exceed one. The weights have to add to 1.

$2w_j w_i \rho_{ji} \sigma_j \sigma_i$, is a weighted combination of twice the covariance. That is, $\rho_{ji} \sigma_j \sigma_i$ represents the covariance between j and i. There are two sets of these values because the covariance can be viewed as two relationships: the covariance between j and i and the covariance between i and j. These two covariances are the same values, but the formula requires that the value appear twice. The remaining terms are the weights w_j and w_i. The logic of the formula arises from the fact that the risk of a combination of assets does not just arise from the sums of the risks of the individual assets but reflects also their interrelationships. These interrelationships typically provide a great benefit commonly known as diversification. As long as the two assets are less than perfectly correlated, diversification will reduce the risk. Diversification is the primary method of how insurance companies manage risk, a point we will take up later.

Let us now do one simple example showing the calculations to obtain the expected return and risk of the combined portfolios. Recall that we previously had $E(R_j) = 0.075$ and $\sigma_j = 0.1006$ for asset j. Let us assume that for i, $E(R_i) = 0.0890$, $\sigma_i = 0.1299$ and that the correlation between j and i is 0.3757. Let the weights be $w_j = 0.60$ and $w_i = 0.40$. In other words, we have 60% of our money in j and 40% in i. Then the expected return and volatility for this combination of j and i are

$$E(R_{ji}) = 0.6(0.075) + 0.4(0.0890) = 0.0806$$

$$\sigma_{ji} = \sqrt{\begin{array}{c} (0.6)^2(0.1006)^2 + (0.4)^2(0.1299)^2 \\ + 2(0.6)(0.4)(0.1006)(0.1299)(0.3757) \end{array}}$$

$$= 0.0933.$$

Note the beneficial effect of adding asset i to asset j. If we owned only asset j, we would have an expected return of 7.5% and a volatility of 10.06%. By allocating 40% of our wealth to asset i, our expected return is higher at 8.06%, a relative increase of +7.5%. The volatility goes down from 10.06% to 9.33%, a relative decrease of 7.3%. So the expected return is higher and the volatility lower. Had we all had all of our money in i and then allocated 60% of it to j, the expected return would go from 8.90% to 8.06%, a decrease of 9.4%, while the volatility would go from 12.99% to 9.33%, a decrease of 28%. The expected return is lower but the volatility is even lower. This effect is the benefit of diversification due to the correlation between assets j and i being fairly low at 0.3757. As long as the correlation is not a perfect 1.0, the allocation of money from one asset to more than one asset will be beneficial.

In other finance courses, you may study portfolio management where you would learn that the weights used here might not be the best way to combine assets j and i. There are weights that achieve the greatest return for a given amount of risk. We will not concern ourselves with this much detail at the moment, but we will return to the subject later in this chapter. For our purposes in understanding risk management, a basic knowledge of how the risk of combinations of assets is influenced by the way in which they are combined is the important point at this time.

To generalize our results for the case of $j = 1, 2, \ldots, J$ assets, the formulas for expected return and volatility of portfolio are

$$E(R_p) = \sum_{j=1}^{J} w_j E(R_j)$$

$$\sigma_p = \sqrt{\sum_{j=1}^{J} w_j^2 \sigma_j^2 + 2 \sum_{\substack{j=1 \\ j \neq g}}^{J} \sum_{g=1}^{G} w_j w_g \sigma_j \sigma_g \rho_{jg}}.$$

(3.10)

While the volatility formula looks more complicated than formula (3.9), it continues to be nothing more than a combination of the squared weights times the variances of the component assets and twice all pairwise covariances.

In some applications in risk management, we will measure performance not in terms of returns but in terms of currency units. Then we would want the expected value of a position and the volatility of that value. The weights would be the number of units of each asset held. For example, let a_j be the number of units of asset j. Letting V_j be the value of asset j and V_p be the value of the overall position, the expected value and volatility formulas would be

$$E(V_p) = \sum_{j=1}^{J} a_j E(S_j)$$

$$\sigma_p = \sqrt{\sum_{j=1}^{J} a_j^2 \sigma_j^2 + 2 \sum_{\substack{j=1 \\ j \neq g}}^{J} \sum_{g=1}^{G} a_j a_g \sigma_j \sigma_g \rho_{jg}},$$

(3.11)

where the variances and the correlation are measured in currency units and not rates of return. For example, reconsider Exhibit 3-5 where we looked at crude oil and natural gas, along with the cash flow of Easy Air. Suppose we have 100 units of crude oil and 500 units of natural gas in our inventory. Recall that their expected values and volatilities are $E(V_{\text{oil}}) = \$48, \sigma_{\text{oil}} = \$7.48, E(V_{\text{gas}}) = \$6.30, \sigma_{\text{gas}} = \$1.12$, and the correlation is $\rho_{\text{oil,gas}} = 0.9048$. The expected value and volatility of a combination of 100 units of crude oil and 500 units of natural gas are, therefore,

$$E(V_p) = 100(\$48) + 500(\$6.30) = \$7,950$$

$$\sigma_p = \sqrt{\begin{array}{l} (100)^2(\$7.48)^2 + (500)^2(\$1.12)^2 \\ + 2(100)(500)(\$7.48)(\$1.12)(0.9048) \end{array}}$$

$$= \$1,278.67.$$

So far we have looked only at ex ante return and risk. As discussed in Chapter 2, it is seldom the case that we actually know the probabilities. We typically gather data from the past and estimate various statistical measures to estimate the probabilities. In the next section, we shall look at how risk parameters are estimated using ex post data.

3.4   Ex Post Measures of Return and Risk

Now we shall take a look at how data representing past movements in a source of risk can be used to quantify the risk. Of course, we must keep in mind that the characteristics of the past might not repeat themselves, but it is the only source of data we have, so the past is where we typically start. Let us pretend that we are a currency trader for a large U.S. financial institution. Assume that we have a position of €35 million (euros) and £72 million (British pounds). Assuming these currencies are in the form of interest-bearing accounts in foreign banks, they will pay interest, but we shall concentrate only on the risk associated with their respective exchange rates, which are effectively the prices of these currencies in dollars. The risk associated with variability in the interest payments will be quite low compared to the risk of the exchange rates.

Exhibit 3-7 shows the monthly exchange rates for the pound and euro in dollars for the two-year period of 2016–2017.

We see that both currencies have appeared to have moved in sync. But how would a position exposed to these currencies have performed? Exhibit 3-8 shows the monthly rates of return on those currencies that would be implied by the exchange rates depicted in Exhibit 3-7.

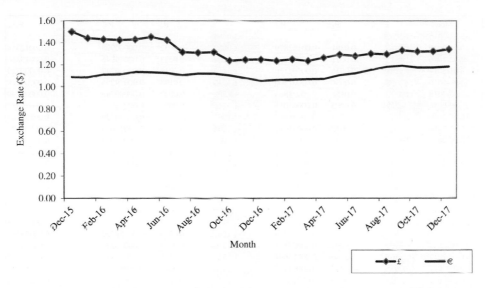

Exhibit 3-7.   British Pound and Euro Monthly Exchange Rate vs. U.S. Dollar, 2016–2017

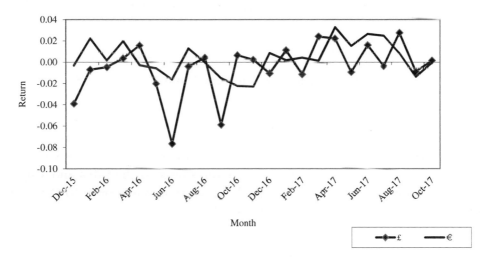

Exhibit 3-8.   Monthly Rates of Return on British Pound and Euro vs. U.S. Dollar, 2016–2017

Given these figures, we might be even further convinced that the two currencies are highly correlated. But let us look at the actual data and determine how they performed and the relationship between the currencies. Exhibit 3-9 is a table containing the rates and various calculations that we will explain.

Month	£	$R_£$	$R_£^2$	€	$R_€$	$R_€^2$	$R_£R_€$
31-12-2015	1.5002			1.0894			
31-01-2016	1.4415	-0.0391	0.00152879	1.0859	-0.0032	0.00000998	0.00012354
29-02-2016	1.4313	-0.0071	0.00005034	1.1102	0.0223	0.00049943	-0.00015856
31-03-2016	1.4247	-0.0046	0.00002150	1.1119	0.0016	0.00000247	-0.00000729
30-04-2016	1.4298	0.0036	0.00001300	1.1340	0.0198	0.00039296	0.00007148
31-05-2016	1.4523	0.0158	0.00024863	1.1309	-0.0027	0.00000743	-0.00004299
30-06-2016	1.4229	-0.0203	0.00041011	1.1245	-0.0057	0.00003214	0.00011480
31-07-2016	1.3140	-0.0765	0.00585597	1.1061	-0.0163	0.00026729	0.00125109
31-08-2016	1.3088	-0.0040	0.00001616	1.1204	0.0129	0.00016633	-0.00005185
30-09-2016	1.3143	0.0042	0.00001802	1.1203	-0.0001	0.00000000	-0.00000024
31-10-2016	1.2369	-0.0589	0.00347002	1.1034	-0.0151	0.00022803	0.00088953
30-11-2016	1.2449	0.0065	0.00004241	1.0786	-0.0224	0.00050308	-0.00014607
31-12-2016	1.2478	0.0023	0.00000515	1.0538	-0.0230	0.00052796	-0.00005215
31-01-2017	1.2346	-0.0105	0.00011104	1.0629	0.0086	0.00007420	-0.00009077
28-02-2017	1.2484	0.0112	0.00012445	1.0649	0.0019	0.00000343	0.00002067
31-03-2017	1.2341	-0.0114	0.00013079	1.0695	0.0043	0.00001868	-0.00004942
30-04-2017	1.2638	0.0241	0.00058040	1.0709	0.0013	0.00000169	0.00003133
31-05-2017	1.2920	0.0223	0.00049714	1.1061	0.0329	0.00108229	0.00073351
30-06-2017	1.2799	-0.0094	0.00008757	1.1230	0.0152	0.00023231	-0.00014263
31-07-2017	1.3005	0.0160	0.00025694	1.1529	0.0266	0.00070889	0.00042678
31-08-2017	1.2956	-0.0038	0.00001415	1.1816	0.0249	0.00062137	-0.00009375
30-09-2017	1.3313	0.0276	0.00076204	1.1912	0.0082	0.00006657	0.00022524
31-10-2017	1.3196	-0.0088	0.00007798	1.1749	-0.0137	0.00018746	0.00012090
30-11-2017	1.3215	0.0015	0.00000213	1.1745	-0.0003	0.00000012	-0.00000051
31-12-2017	1.3404	0.0143	0.00020416	1.1845	0.0085	0.00007255	0.00012170
	Sum	-0.10512995	0.01452889	Sum	0.08658963	0.00570665	0.00329434
	count	24		count	24		
	Average	-0.00438041		Average	0.00360790		Covariance 0.00015972
	Variance	0.00061167		Variance	0.00023453		Correlation 0.4217
	Stdev	0.02473194		Stdev	0.01531445		

Exhibit 3-9. Monthly Data for British Pound and Euro vs. U.S. Dollar for 2016–2017

We see that the pound varied between a low of \$1.2341 and a high of \$1.5002, while the euro varied between a low of \$1.0538 and a high of \$1.1912. The returns are found in the columns next to the rates and are, by definition, the percentage changes in the rates from one month to the next. For example, the first pair of returns is calculated as

$$R(\pounds) = \frac{\$1.4415}{\$1.5002} - 1 = -0.0391,$$

$$R(\text{€}) = \frac{\$1.0859}{\$1.0894} - 1 = -0.0032.$$

To calculate an average return, we use the traditional formula for an average: the sum of the values in the sample divided by the number of values in the sample. As a general formula for a sample of T_s returns, each return denoted as R_t, where t is an integer from 1 to T_s, the average is found as:

$$\bar{R} = \frac{\sum_{t=1}^{T_s} R_t}{T_S}. \tag{3.12}$$

The standard deviation is, of course, the square root of the variance and is found as follows:

$$\hat{\sigma} = \sqrt{\frac{\sum_{t=1}^{T_s} (R_t - \bar{R})^2}{T_s - 1}}. \tag{3.13}$$

We put a caret above the sigma to distinguish this sample or ex post estimate of the standard deviation from the ex ante standard deviation discussed earlier in the chapter. Ultimately we will drop the caret and just use the sigma sign, but we should take care to remember whether it is an ex post or ex ante volatility.

And alternative formula that is sometimes easier to use is

$$\hat{\sigma} = \sqrt{\frac{\sum_{t=1}^{T_s} R_t^2 - \frac{\left(\sum_{t=1}^{T_s} R_t\right)^2}{T_s}}{T_s - 1}}. \tag{3.14}$$

Now let us apply these formulas to the pound and the euro. Using the summations in Exhibit 3-9, we obtain the following values:

For the £:

$$\sum_{t=1}^{T_s} R_t = -0.10512995; \quad \bar{R} = \frac{-0.10512995}{24} = -0.00438041$$

$$\sum_{t=1}^{T_s} R_t^2 = 0.01452889; \quad \hat{\sigma} = \sqrt{\frac{0.01452889 - \frac{(-0.10512995)^2}{24}}{23}}$$

$$= 0.02473194$$

For the €:

$$\sum_{t=1}^{T_s} R_t = 0.08658963; \quad \bar{R} = \frac{0.08658963}{24} = 0.00360790$$

$$\sum_{t=1}^{T_s} R_t^2 = 0.00570665; \quad \hat{\sigma} = \sqrt{\frac{0.00570665 - \frac{(0.08658963)^2}{24}}{23}}$$

$$= 0.01531445.$$

To obtain the correlation, we first estimate the covariance. The formulas for correlation and covariance of ex post data for assets j and i are

$$\widehat{cov}_{ji} = \sqrt{\frac{\sum_{t=1}^{T_s} R_{tj} R_{ti} - \frac{\left(\sum_{t=1}^{T_s} R_{jt}\right)\left(\sum_{t=1}^{T_s} R_{it}\right)}{T_s}}{T_s - 1}}$$

$$\widehat{\rho}_{ji} = \frac{\widehat{cov}_{ji}}{\widehat{\sigma}_j \widehat{\sigma}_i}.$$

(3.15)

Using the sum of the last column in Exhibit 3-9, we obtain an estimate of the covariance and correlation for the pound and euro as

$$\widehat{cov}_{\pounds,\text{\euro}} = \sqrt{\frac{0.00329434 - \frac{(-0.10512995)(0.08658963)}{24}}{23}} = 0.00015972$$

$$\widehat{\rho}_{\pounds,\text{\euro}} = \frac{0.00015972}{(0.02473194)(0.01531445)} = 0.4217.$$

Thus, the correlation between the pound and the euro with respect to the dollar was fairly positive at about 0.42 during the years 2016–2017.

Chaos and Financial Markets

Someone who has observed the frenzied trading in stock and derivatives markets, whether on the floor of an exchange or the trading floor of a financial institution could get the sense that there is no order. People are often running, yelling, and throwing paper. But in fact, the process is very organized. It is the rapid flow of information and the need to quickly react to that information that gives the chaotic appearance.

Appearing chaotic is one thing. *Being* chaotic is another. In recent years, scientists have begun to describe biological systems with a new theory: the theory of chaos. A biological system is a complex web of interacting organisms. Chaos theory predicts that small disturbances in factors that affect one component of the system can have effects that ripple through the system and accumulate into much greater effects. For example, suppose a new factory is built in an area. The factory dumps its purified waste into a local river. Studies have shown that the purified waste contains no pollutants that harm flora or fauna, but unknown to local scientists, the waste matter slightly raises the temperature level over a period of years. This increased temperature level stunts the growth of trout that live in the river. Over time, the river, which was once a major source of tourism because of its attractive fishing, gradually becomes known as one where the trout are abnormally small. Fishermen and tourists find new locations, economic activity decreases, and local government tax revenues decline. Jobs are lost and funding cuts strain the local school system. The quality of life and economic opportunities are reduced for the next generation of residents. All of these effects occur because of a slight increase in water temperature from the dumping of non-toxic waste.

This made-up example also shows how biological and economic systems interact. Economic and financial systems are often viewed as complex webs of potentially chaotic interacting factors. The random fluctuations of stock prices, commodity prices, interest rates, and exchange rates are not, in and of themselves, evidence of chaos. Information is, after all, random. No one can predict the future. So random fluctuations should be observed in financial variables. But chaotic economic systems go beyond the randomness and find evidence of irrationality, such as over- and under-reactions. Perhaps arbitrage opportunities themselves are manifestations of chaos. Chaos theory does not help predict prices, but it can help in managing risk by making us more aware of the subtle but complex ways in which prices react to small disturbances in systems.

For an entertaining look at how chaos theory explains how small disturbances in biological systems have significant consequences, see the book or movie *Jurassic Park* and of course, all of its sequels.

In the study of financial markets, historical data can be a good starting point, but as we cautioned in Chapter 2, history has a way of not repeating itself. Any chosen historical time period can be a poor representation of the upcoming period. One must use historical data with a great deal of caution. On the other hand, if we had no historical data, getting good estimates of ex ante risk would be almost impossible. We would have a hard time even coming up with a starting point for a wild guess. We will have much more to say about this problem when we examine the use of historical data in estimating Value-at-Risk, an important risk management tool.

3.5 Statistical Distributions of Returns

Characterizing returns in terms of only the expected return and standard deviation is an implicit assumption that the returns are normally

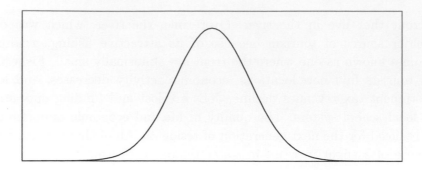

Exhibit 3-10. Normal Probability Distribution

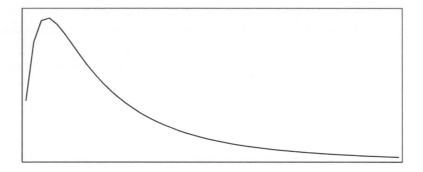

Exhibit 3-11. Lognormal Probability Distribution

distributed. A normal distribution, the familiar bell-shaped curve depicted in Exhibit 3-10, is often used to describe data in finance, economics, the social sciences, and the physical sciences. A normal distribution is a symmetric distribution centered on the expected value. That is, the peak of the normal distribution is at the expected value and half of the distribution lies to the left and the other half to the right. A normal distribution has the convenient property that all of the information about the distribution is contained in only two values: the expected value and the standard deviation.

In contrast to a normal distribution, there are distributions that are asymmetric, such as the lognormal distribution, pictured in Exhibit 3-11.

If a variable is lognormally distributed, its distribution is skewed as shown in Exhibit 3-11, but the distribution of the logarithm of the variable is normal as in Exhibit 3-10. Non-normal distributions usually have skewness or asymmetry or kurtosis, meaning unusually peaked or flat.

For convenience and simplicity, normal distributions are widely used to describe real phenomena but are seldom encountered in real life. The

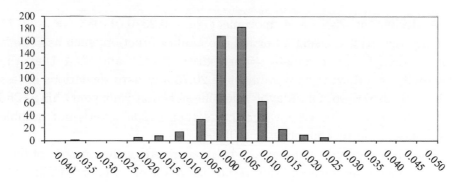

Exhibit 3-12. Distribution of Daily Returns on S&P 500, 2016–2017

performance of investments, such as in the stock market, is often described with a normal distribution. Consider, for example, Exhibit 3-12, which shows the distribution of daily returns on the S&P 500 index for the years 2016–2017.

Does this picture look like a normal distribution? No, not exactly. But if we drew an imaginary curve over the tops of the bars, it would not be completely symmetric, but it would not be too far off. In fact, it would not take a tremendous stretch of imagination to see a normal distribution in the above data. We must be careful, however, in that we have simply drawn two years of daily data for a particular stock index. In accordance with most of the principles of finance, we will lean heavily on the normal distribution, but we will be mindful of the implications for risk management when the actual outcomes depart notably from normality.

Who You Callin' Normal?

Are blue-chip stocks normally distributed? One way we can address that question is to look at extreme outcomes and see if they defy the characteristics of a normal distribution.

First, let us assume that the performance of the stocks in the Dow Jones Industrial Average (DJIA) is normally distributed. Taking the daily prices for the DJIA from finance.yahoo.com for every day from December 31, 1924 through December 31, 2017, we can estimate the daily volatility. Doing so, we obtain 1.0996%. The average daily return is 0.0277%.

Now let us roll the clock back to October 19, 1987, a day on which the DJIA fell about 23%. Yes, that is a 23% decline in a single day! It seems fairly obvious that this was an abnormal event. But how abnormal was it?

A decline of 23% is a movement of $-0.23/0.011086 = -20.75$ standard deviations. Using a normal probability function, such as Excel's "=normsdist()", we calculate =normsdist(-20.75) and find that the probability of a downward movement of 20.75 standard deviations or less is about 6.12957E-96. Ok. Maybe scientific notation isn't your thing. The number is 0.000 ...(96 zeroes in all) and then 612957. Let's not quibble over fractions, so just round it to 6.0E-96.

The inverse of that number can be interpreted as the number of days it would take to see such an event occur just one time, which is 1.67E+95. If you want it written out, move the decimal point 95 places to the right. That is how many trading days you would expect in order that this event happens once — if the DJIA is normally distributed.

Scientists estimate that the earth is about 4.5 billion years old, which is equivalent to about 1.1 trillion trading days, loosely assuming that there is some notion of "trading days" that far back. The number 1.1 trillion expressed in scientific notation is 1.0E+12. So, if a normal distribution is correct, it would take about 1.48E+83 earth life-times for the event to occur. And of course, there would have to be trading all these gazillions of days.

Now consider from 1926 through 2017, the DJIA has experienced only three days of losses in excess of 10%. It has experienced seven days of gains in excess of 10%. A 10% move is $0.10/0.010996 = 9.09$, or roughly nine standard deviations. A move downward of at least nine standard deviations has a probability of 1.2859E-19, the inverse of which is roughly 8.86063E+18. That is, such a move would occur only once every 8.86063E+18 days. There have been about 24,000 trading days since 1926 and such a move has occurred three times. On the upside, a similar conclusion would be drawn. In short, the extreme outcomes observed in practice go far beyond those predicted by a normal distribution. Even if the 23% decline on October 19, 1987 had never occurred, the data would still be inconsistent with the normal distribution on the basis of extreme returns.

So, while the distribution of returns might look a lot like the normal distribution, we have to be very mindful of extreme outcomes. They are the ones that will get a company or organization into the most trouble.

In spite of its obvious flaws, we still tend to use the normal distribution more often than any other distribution. A trade-off is typically made between the costs of going to a more complex distribution, meaning one requiring more information than just the mean and standard deviation, and the benefits of using a normal distribution, with due regard given to the fact that there could be some inaccuracies. Emphasis is on that last point: *normal distributions tend to understate the frequency of rare events*, such as the crash of 1987 and other days of rather large return. If we keep the limitations of the normal distribution in mind, we can gain a great deal of understanding from it and still be on guard for its shortcomings.

3.6 Expected Utility: Quantifying the Value of Returns and Wealth

In Chapter 2 we introduced the notion of utility theory in the context of the St. Petersburg paradox, which is essentially the origin of utility theory. We learned that Daniel Bernoulli proposed utility theory as way of measuring the value people obtained from risky ventures. The notion of utility enables us to better understand how people feel about the economic consequences of various risky financial situations. As we noted in Chapter 2, utility is a measure of how satisfied we are with something.

For example, suppose your favorite dessert is a slice of apple pie. Your second favorite dessert is rocky road ice cream. Although you cannot say how much more you like the pie over the ice cream, you are certain that the pie is preferred to the ice cream. Now say you are at a restaurant, these two items are on the menu, and both cost the same. There are no other items on the dessert menu that you want. We will also assume you are aware of the sizes of the two desserts and one is not disproportionately larger than the other. Given equal costs, you are certain that you prefer the pie over the ice cream. In making that statement we have used the notion of *ordinal utility*, the simple idea that one thing is preferred to the other without saying how much the one is preferred to the other or how many units of the less preferred item is equivalent to a unit of the preferred item.

Of course, with the pie and ice cream decision, there is no significant uncertainty. While it is possible that the chef does a better job preparing one versus the other, in all likelihood, there is no risk that you will be disappointed. You know what the pie and the ice cream will taste like. But if confronted with risk, it might not be clear which alternative is preferred. For example, you can be certain that you would prefer $100 over $50. But would you prefer a 50–50 gamble on $100 or $50 for certain. The notion of utility will tell us how, in all likelihood, you would prefer the $50 for certain. We will shortly see why.

    While ordinal utility is a simple ranking of risky endeavors according to preferences, cardinal utility assigns numeric values to the utility. Henceforth in this chapter, we will be referring to cardinal utility.

    The quantification of utility is done in the form of a mathematical function that measures the satisfaction received from units of wealth. This function is called, appropriately, a utility function. A utility function is an algebraic relationship that translates a quantity of money into satisfaction, which is defined in units of satisfaction that are called *utils*. There are a number of different utility functions, but for a while we shall focus on the log utility function that we introduced in Chapter 2 with the St. Petersburg paradox. The log utility function is written as

$$U(W) = \ln(W), \tag{3.16}$$

where W represents the amount of wealth or just money, $\ln(.)$ is the natural log function, and $U(W)$ is the resulting value of utility in utils. Exhibit 3-13 illustrates the log utility function for different degrees of wealth ranging from \$100 to \$2,000.

    Notice that the function increases because more money is always preferred to less, which is a universal trait. But the function increases at a decreasing rate, because the additional utility from more money is less and less, a concept called *diminishing marginal utility*. This characteristic of how people feel about money will have a critical impact on how people view the risk associated with most decisions.

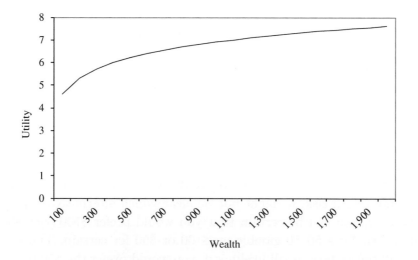

Exhibit 3-13. Log Utility

Economists have established that an appropriate rule for evaluating risky decisions is to maximize expected utility. Thus, given all of the possible ways in which a person could invest her money, she would choose the one that gives the maximum expected utility. Expected utility is determined in the same way as any expected value: by weighting all possible outcomes by the probabilities of their occurrence. Thus, expected utility is found as

$$E(U(W)) = \sum_{k-1}^{K} q_k U(W_k).\tag{3.17}$$

Note the similarity between Equation (3.17) and Equation (3.2). They both provide expected values, but Equation (3.17) encompasses a great deal more. It takes into account how the person *feels* about the return, not just the return itself. For example, a return of 4% is clearly twice a return of 2%, but a person does not necessarily feel twice as happy about 4% as about 2%.

Now let us apply this rule to evaluating a risky decision. Recall the data in Exhibit 3-3 dealing with asset A, which is repeated here as Exhibit 3-14 with two additional columns. Assume that the decision maker's utility is defined by the log utility function. Now, we also define the outcomes in terms of the amount of money to be received. Let us just assume that the returns are applied to a base value of $1,000.

The expected utility is calculated as

$$E(U(W)) = 0.30(7.0901) + 0.60(6.9565) + 0.10(6.7452) = 6.9755.$$

So this investment offers expected utility of 6.9755. But what does this tell us? Well, for one it tells us that any other mutually exclusive investment offering less expected utility would not be preferred. But in addition, it can also tell us something about how much one would be willing to pay to enter into this investment. Recall that the expected return is 7.5%, so the expected wealth is $1,075. Would someone pay $1,075? Well, think about it. Paying $1,075 means forgoing utility of ln(1,075) = 6.9801 utils and getting only

Outcome	Return	Wealth	Probability	Utility
1	20%	$1,200	0.30	ln($1,200) = 7.0901
2	5%	$1,050	0.60	ln($1,050) = 6.9565
3	−15%	$850	0.10	ln($850) = 6.7452

Exhibit 3-14. **The Ex Ante Distribution of Returns on Asset j, Your Wealth and Your Utility**

expected utility of 6.9755 utils. So, presumably no one would be willing to pay \$1,075.

One of the attractive features of the log utility function is that we can invert it to obtain the level of wealth we would be willing to give up to take this risk. We simply use the inverse of the log function, which is the exponential function: e^x. So, we simply calculate $e^{6.9755} = \$1,070$. In other words, \$1,070 has the same satisfaction to us as does this risky gamble with three outcomes and an expected value of \$1,075. The difference between \$1,075 and \$1,070 is \$5. This amount is called the *risk premium*, a concept we shall cover in more detail in this chapter and which will surface again later in this book. In short, the risk premium is the additional return we demand in order to take a risk. So, here we would be willing to pay only \$1,070 for an investment with an expected outcome of \$1,075.

Utility functions that have this property of diminishing marginal utility assure us that investors will demand risk premiums to assume risk. The notion of a risk premium is one of the most important concepts in finance, and critical to understanding risk management. While we do not require an understanding of utility functions to accept the fact that investors require risk premiums, understanding utility enhances our understanding of the bigger picture of how people want as much return for as little risk as possible.

The notion of a risk premium is a characteristic of investors who are said to be *risk averse*. Risk averse investors dislike risk and will not assume risk unless they expect to be compensated with additional expected return. In contrast, there are two other types of investors: those who are *risk lovers* and those who are *risk neutral*. Risk lovers are compensated *by* the risk they take. A risk lover will pay more than the expected value of \$1,075 to try this investment. While the notion of a risk lover is an interesting theoretical construction, we virtually never assume that anyone is a risk lover in the financial world.[9]

Another type of investor is said to be *risk neutral*. Such an investor does not consider the risk and will pay the expected value, here \$1,075. We do

---

[9]People who engage in organized betting can be thought of as risk lovers. As we know, they willingly enter into games in which the amount they pay to play is more than the expected outcome. We can rationalize this behavior by noting that the enjoyment of playing provides them with a certain non-monetary utility. Risk lovers are not of much use to us in studying risk management. We must believe that shareholders, boards of directors, and the people they entrust to manage the company do not engage in risky activities simply because they enjoy the risk.

not believe people are risk neutral, but as we shall see in a later section of this chapter and in later chapters, the prices of financial derivatives can be obtained by acting as though people are risk neutral, a point we hinted at in Chapter 2. This point will surely seem vague right now, but it will become clear and simple later.

Let us summarize and contrast the three types of people with respect to their feelings about risk in a very simple risky scenario, a coin toss paying $10 if called correctly and $5 if called incorrectly. A risk neutral person would be willing to pay the expected value of $7.50. Each time he wins, the risk neutral person wins $2.50, and each time he loses, he loses $2.50. Suppose he plays the game two times, winning once and losing once.[10] He will feel the same after playing and breaking even as he would by not playing. Suppose a risk averse person could be convinced to pay $7.50 to play. After playing twice, winning once and losing once, he would find that the discomfort of losing $2.50 more than offsets the pleasure of winning $2.50, so on the whole he would regret playing. It should be easy to see why we do not believe investors are risk lovers. Only by paying less than $7.50 so that he wins more than he loses on average will he be glad that he played. The risk lover will also not be satisfied. He would rather lose more than win. So, he will pay more than $7.50 to play. A risk averse person who plays two times with one win and one loss will not view the results as offsetting. He will have more regret from the loss than the happiness of the gain, so he will regret having played. To induce him to play a game in which he expects the wins and losses to offset, he has to pay less than $7.50. As noted, we assume that no one is a risk lover.

The log utility function is a particularly simple and convenient way to quantify how people feel about risk and serves as a good generalization of the characteristics of a risk averse investor. It has the disadvantage, however, that it cannot be personalized. Two investors with log utility would have equivalent feelings about an investment. In reality, there are a variety of feelings that investors have about risk. As such there are other utility functions that allow preferences to vary across individuals. For example, the log utility function is a special case of a family of utility functions called

---

[10]We know that he might not experience one win and one loss in two tries, but we let the example of two tries represent the expected outcome in a large number of tries. In other words, we make the reasonable assumption that the number of wins balances the number of losses.

power utility that are of the following form:

$$U(W) = -\frac{W^{1-\lambda} - 1}{1 - \lambda},$$

where the value λ varies from one individual to another and reflects the how risk averse a person is. The log utility function is the special case where λ is 1.[11] There are other utility functions that have a variety of desirable characteristics but there is no perfect, one-size-fits-all utility function. For now, all we need to know is that individuals make decisions based on their desire to achieve the highest possible expected utility and that in doing so, they exhibit the characteristic of risk aversion.

It is important to understand that a risk averse person will not completely avoid risk. For example, Kahneman (2011) gives a variation of the following example.

> Suppose a friend offers you an opportunity to gamble at no cost on a coin toss in which you make $200 if a head comes up and lose $100 if a tail comes up. Would you take the offer?

Many people would not take the offer for fear that a tail would come up and they would lose $100. Yet it is apparent that if you could repeat the gamble a large number of times, you would make $50 on average. For example, if you could do it 100 times, you would almost surely make around $5,000. How does one justify a willingness to repeatedly engage in a risky activity, but not to do so only once? Clearly risk aversion comes into play on any single gamble. But risk aversion also implies that when subjected to repeated trials, the benefits of gains can more than outweigh the costs of losing. Just as an investor knows that he may lose money on any single investment, the average expected return can be sufficiently large so as to justify the taking of risk. Thus, we can assume that risk averse investors evaluate opportunities based not on a single exposure but on multiple exposures.

3.7 A Simple Example to Determine the Optimal Amount of Risk

Let us see how expected utility can tell us the optimal amount of risk that an individual would take. Consider someone with $100 to put into a market that consists of a single stock priced at $1 and a risk-free bond that pays 7%

---

[11]Some operations using limits and the application of L'Hôpital's rule are required to make the general power utility function converge to the log function.

interest. This person will make a decision about how much money to invest in the asset and how much to put into the risk-free bond. Then the stock will move to a new price. Assume that the stock can increase to $1.50, a 50% return, with probability 0.65, or decrease to $0.60, a 40% loss, with probability 0.35. Thus, the expected return and standard deviation of the stock are

$$E(R) = 0.65(0.50) + 0.35(-0.40) = 0.185$$

$$\sigma = \sqrt{(0.65)^2(0.50 - 0.185)^2 + (0.35)^2(-0.40 - 0.185)^2} = 0.2896.$$

Let us start by naively assuming that the investor allocates his wealth 50% to the stock and 50% to risk-free bonds. Then he will buy 50 units of the stock at $1 each and invest $50 in risk-free bonds. After one period, his stock will be worth $(1.50/1)\$50 = \$75$, and his bonds will be worth $\$50(1.07) = \$53.50$ for a total of $128.50 if the stock goes up, and $(0.60/1)\$50+\$50(1.07) = \$83.50$ if the stock goes down. The expected utility is, therefore,

$$0.65 \ln(128.50) + 0.35 \ln(83.50) = 4.7051.$$

Of course, at this point we have no way of knowing if this allocation is optimal. Let us try another asset allocation: 75% to asset and 25% to bonds. The portfolio would then be worth $(1.50/1)\$75 + \$25(1.07) - \$139.25$ if the asset moves up and $(0.60/1)\$75 + \$25(1.07) = \$71.75$ if the asset moves down. The expected utility is

$$0.65 \ln(139.25) + 0.35 \ln(71.75) = 4.7042.$$

This is slightly less utility, so a 75% allocation to the asset is worse than 50%.

Exhibit 3-15 shows the expected utility for various allocations.

A visual inspection of this graph suggests that the optimum is around 60% invested in the asset. Omitting the mathematical details, which are available in the chapter appendix, it can be shown that the optimum is given by a specific formula. Let $u =$ one plus the return if the asset goes up (here, $u = 1.5$), $d =$ one plus the return if the asset goes down (here, $d = 0.60$), $q =$ the probability of an up move (here, 0.65), $r =$ the risk-free rate (here, 0.07), and π be the value $(1 + r - d)/(u - d)$. The optimal asset allocation is

$$\gamma = \frac{1 + r - \Psi(1 + r)}{\Psi d - \Psi(1 + r) - u + 1 + r},$$

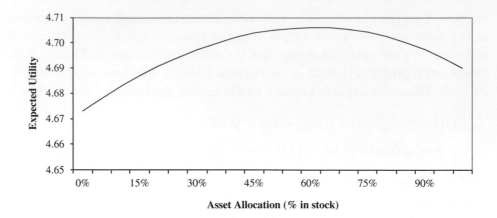

Exhibit 3-15. Expected Utility for Various Asset Allocations

where

$$\Psi = \left(\frac{(1-q)\pi}{q(1-\pi)} \right)^{-1}.$$

In our example, the values of π and γ are

$$\pi = \frac{1.07 - 0.60}{1.50 - 0.60} = 0.5222$$

$$\Psi = \left(\frac{(1-0.65)(0.5222)}{0.65(1-0.5222)} \right)^{-1} = 1.6991,$$

and the optimal allocation is

$$\gamma = \frac{1.07 - 1.6991(1.07)}{1.6991(0.60) - 1.6991(1.07) - 1.50 + 1.07} = 0.6089.$$

Indeed, as the graph shows, the answer is close to 60%. Thus, in this problem, maximum utility is achieved by allocating 60.89% of one's wealth to stock.[12] When we study options, this value π will resurface and be referred to as the *risk-neutral probability* and sometimes the *quasi probability*.

---

[12] Again, if you are curious about how these formulas are derived, the details are provided in the chapter appendix.

If this result is the optimal asset allocation, it will also tell us how much risk the person is willing to take. Earlier in the chapter we looked at the expected return and risk of a two-asset portfolio where the assets were called j and i. These values were defined by Equations (3.8) and (3.9). In the current problem, let us view the asset as asset j and the risk-free bond as asset i. Of course, the risk-free bond has zero standard deviation, and the correlation between any risky asset and a risk-free asset is zero.[13] Thus, the expected return and risk of the investor's optimally allocated portfolio is

$$E(R_{ji}) = w_j E(R_j) + w_i E(R_i)$$

$$= 0.6089(0.185) + 0.3911(.07) = 0.14$$

$$\sigma_{ji} = \sqrt{\begin{matrix} (0.6089)^2(0.2896)^2 + (1 - 0.6089)^2(0)^2 \\ + 2(0.6089)(1 - 0.6089)(0)(0.2896)(0) \end{matrix}}$$

$$= 0.1763.$$

So the optimal asset allocation implies that the volatility will be 17.63% and that the expected return is 14%.

Note that we are not making a claim that investors actually plug numbers into these formulas. These models and in fact the whole notion of expected utility are concepts designed to model decision making under risk. In a situation like this, we would expect investors with similar views on risk to allocate their portfolios with about 61% in the asset and 39% in risk-free bonds. But regardless of how investors allocate their portfolios, the risk they are taking is determined by their own preferences for return in light of the risk that must be assumed.

If investors act in this manner, it is possible to make statements about the returns and risks of assets in the market as a whole.

3.8 The Relationship between Risk and Return in a Competitive Financial Market

One of the most important findings in the body of knowledge on how financial markets work is the Capital Asset Pricing Model, or CAPM. The CAPM describes the relationship between risk and expected return of a risky asset if market participants behave in a rational manner and if a number of other

---

[13] Any risk-free asset has zero correlation with a risky asset, because there must be a non-zero volatility for both assets in order for two assets to be correlated.

assumptions are consistent with the actual operations of markets. In reality, we know that these assumptions are not strictly met and investors do not always act rationally. Nonetheless, most financial economists believe that even if it does not provide the absolute truth, the CAPM is a useful model. Hence, it is worthwhile to review its basic characteristics.

3.8.1 *Risk and Return: The Capital Asset Pricing Model*

In a market that fully incorporates all information, the return that one should expect to justify investing in a risky asset j is

$$E(R_j) = r + [E(R_m) - r]\beta_j, \tag{3.18}$$

where r is the risk-free rate of interest, $E(R_m)$ is the expected return on a portfolio consisting of all risky assets in the market, called the market portfolio, and β_j is the measure of risk of the asset and is referred to as the beta. Notice that even though we call this model a "pricing model," it does not specify the actual price of the asset. Any risky asset is a function of the stream of expected future cash flows emanating from it and the rate at which one would discount those cash flows. The CAPM gives us the discount rate. It does not tell us how to forecast cash flows from a risky asset. It merely tells us at what rate to discount these cash flows so that the investor pays a price that is fair, given the risk assumed.

This risk measure β_j is defined as

$$\beta_j = \frac{\text{cov}_{jm}}{\sigma_m^2}. \tag{3.19}$$

The CAPM implies that all investors hold broadly diversified portfolios. Consequently, the risk of the performance of any asset is relatively minor. What matters is the collective performance of all of the assets in a portfolio. The beta measures the contribution of the risk of the individual asset to the risk of the most broadly diversified portfolio of assets, the market portfolio. It is sometimes called the systematic risk, market risk, or non-diversifiable risk and measures the risk relative to the market portfolio.

Beta is a relative, rather than an absolute, measure of risk. The beta of the market portfolio is 1, which represents the average beta of all risky assets. Assets with betas more (less) than 1 contribute more (less) than the average asset to the risk of a diversified portfolio. The overall beta of a portfolio is a weighted average of the betas of the individual components of the portfolio. The weights represent the relative amounts invested in the respective assets in the same manner in which the weights are used to find the portfolio standard deviation.

But if beta is the risk measure, what happens to the standard deviation as a risk measure? Does it not also measure risk? The capital asset pricing model tells us that beta is the proper risk measure and not standard deviation, because the latter reflects risk that can be eliminated at no cost by merely diversifying. Hence, the standard deviation is considered to overstate the risk. Such a conclusion is somewhat controversial in practice. In particular, for companies, which hold concentrated and not diversified portfolios of assets, standard deviation would be an appropriate measure of risk.

Risk Goes with Return

One of the best-known failures of risk management was the case of Orange County, California. In 1995 the Orange County Treasurer's Office lost about $2 billion with a series of highly leveraged financial transactions, resulting in a shocking declaration of bankruptcy by one of the wealthiest counties in the United States. These decisions were made by its 69-year old elected treasurer Robert Citron.

The fund was a vehicle for Orange County and other localities in California to invest their excess cash into short-term low risk investments. Citron took some of these low-risk securities in the fund and pledged them as collateral for a series of transactions called repurchase agreements, which are essentially loans backed by other assets. Citron could then use the proceeds from the loans to invest in more of the same types of securities. All in all Citron was able to turn a $7.5 billion fund into one holding $20 billion of securities, supported of course with loans for the difference. When interest rates rose, the values of these securities fell sharply but the loans were still due. Hence, the collateral was insufficient to cover the loans.

How did this activity manage to escape the watchful eyes of the county's governing body, its auditors, and the public? After all, government finance is heavily scrutinized. The answer is quite simple. Until interest rates rose sharply in late 1995, the fund had generated extraordinary returns. For the previous several years, the fund had beaten the average returns of a benchmark of money market funds by about 2% annually. In other words, *the fund was thought to be investing in essentially risk-free securities but earning about 2% more than the risk-free rate.* If high return must be accompanied by high risk, it would be impossible to consistently earn returns that far above the risk-free rate without taking risks. On top of that, Orange County had no risk controls. It simply had not measured how much risk it was taking.

The Orange County story is but one of many famous risk management disasters. A common theme is a belief that high returns can be earned without taking high risks. Perhaps the reason for this belief is hubris, the excessive self-confidence that comes with periodically and temporarily showing outstanding performance. Large gains are seen as skill, while large losses are viewed as bad luck and avoidable the next time. Risk managers and those responsible for risk managers should never forget the oldest lesson in the financial world:

You cannot get something for nothing. High returns are accompanied by high risk.

Source: Jorion (1995).

P.S. Why must high returns be accompanied by high risk? Because if they were not, everyone would invest in the high earning-low risk investments, which would increase demand for these investments and push up their prices without affecting their future payoffs. The increased prices would lower the expected returns until the excess demand goes away.

Earlier in this chapter, we reviewed how to estimate the standard deviation. If we wish to use the beta, we will also need to estimate it. To do that, we would need to collect some historical data on the return on the risky asset and the return on a broadly diversified portfolio of risky assets. While there is no universally accepted definition of such a portfolio, the S&P 500 is a widely-used proxy. Having collected this data, we would then run a statistical technique called linear regression, or ordinary least squares, that provides an estimate of the slope of a line fit between the points. Alternatively, we could estimate Equation (3.19) using the formulas for estimating the covariance (Equation (3.15)) and standard deviation (Equation (3.4)).

For your purposes in understanding risk management, the beta measure is a useful figure for capturing the risk of a diversified portfolio. It will come in handy later when we take a look at how to manage the risk in stock portfolios.

It is also important to be aware that other factors can contribute to risk. In particular, the Arbitrage Pricing Theory proposes that a variety of other unidentified factors can drive performance and lead to higher expected returns. Some of these factors might be interest rates, credit risk, and the price of energy. Other models, stimulated by empirical research, suggest that measures such as a company's size and its market value relative to its book value are determinants of expected returns. These ideas are important, but they do not play a major role in the remaining material in this book, so we will omit them here.

3.8.2 *The Linkage between Modern Portfolio Analysis and Financial Risk Management*

The CAPM is often said to be the culminating result of a body of knowledge called Modern Portfolio Analysis, sometimes Modern Portfolio Theory. One of the interim results, or assumptions, if you prefer, is that investors optimize. They choose the absolute best portfolios, and those are the ones that offer the highest excepted returns for any given level of risk. That is, one should choose any level of risk as defined by volatility. Then, a rational investor will choose the portfolio that has the highest expected return for the level of risk the investor chooses. In this manner, the investor is maximizing expected utility.

Of course, some investors are highly risk averse. They will tend to set their desired levels of risk fairly low. Others will be less risk averse and, therefore, more tolerant of risk and will choose to take relatively high levels of risk. In any case, given whatever level of risk chosen by the investor, the appropriate portfolio is the one with the maximum expected return. Since we are talking about an expected return, we must realize that there is no guarantee that the portfolio will produce a realized return equal to the expected return. That is the nature of risk.

In modern portfolio analysis, investors choose their desired levels of risk by deciding how much to borrow or lend of the risk-free asset. Every investor holds the fully diversified market portfolio. Those investors with higher than average risk aversion hold a combination of the market portfolio and the risk-free asset, while those with above average risk aversion borrow money by issuing risk-free securities and use the borrowed funds to buy more of the market portfolio. These investors are said to be using leverage, and thereby taking more risk than the average investor.

The CAPM rests on this foundation and means that investors can identify how much risk they are willing to take, as specified by an acceptable volatility of their portfolio return. Then they choose the appropriate portfolio, the one that maximizes expected return for the chosen level of risk. Right here there is a connection with the process of risk management: risk management means that the chosen level of risk is correct, as it satisfies the investor's tolerance for risk and indeed is the optimum degree of risk to be taken. The actual practice of risk management should, therefore, focus on making sure the risk that the entity is taking is the risk that it desires. That is very different from avoiding risk or bad outcomes. By its very nature, any risk taken will at times result in adverse outcomes. The realized frequency of adverse outcomes should align with the expected number. Choosing a desired level of risk does not happen automatically. It must be implemented and managed, and that is where financial risk management comes in.

In very simple terms, if an investor wants a standard deviation of 0.30, then the realized outcomes should produce a standard deviation of 0.30, or at least one that is statistically close to 0.30. If the realized standard deviation is much higher than 0.30, then the investor is not practicing good risk management. He has more risk than desired. If the realized standard deviation is far less than 0.30, that too is an example of poor risk management. The investor wanted a given level of risk and ended up taking too little.

So, risk management is all about making sure the risk taken is the desired level of risk. In the world of modern portfolio analysis and the CAPM, the ability to do that is considered automatic. In the real world, one has to actually practice risk management to make it happen.

3.9   Stochastic Dominance as a Risk-Taking Criterion

Suppose you are offered the following mutually exclusive opportunities. A coin will be tossed. If it lands on heads, you will receive $10; if it lands on tails, $5. The alternative is a draw from an urn containing 100 red balls and 100 green balls. If you receive a red ball, you get $15; a green one pays $5. You can choose to play only one game. Which game is preferable? Ignoring the cost of playing, the second game is clearly better, because you have a better opportunity of earning more than $5. The preferred alternative is said to stochastically dominate the other one. Of course, stochastically dominant alternatives will cost more.

This example was simple. For more complex examples, stochastic dominance is more difficult to apply. To do so, we must examine the cumulative probabilities for all levels of wealth. Exhibit 3-16 illustrates two risky alternatives, which we shall call i and j.

Outcome	Outcome j Probability	Outcome i Probability
$200	0.30	0.40
$400	0.40	0.30
$600	0.30	0.30

Exhibit 3-16. Two Risky Alternatives, j and i

Outcome	Alternative j Probability	Cumulative Probability	Alternative i Probability	Cumulative Probability
$200	0.30	0.30	0.40	0.40
$400	0.40	0.70	0.30	0.70
$600	0.30	1.00	0.30	1.00

Exhibit 3-17. Two Risky Alternatives j and i in which One Dominates the Other by First-Order Stochastic Dominance

First, note that the probability of the worst outcome, a payoff of $200, is greater for i than for j. Based on just this one outcome alone, j would seem to be preferred to i. Note also that the probability of making $400 or less is 70% for j and 70% for i. Equivalently, the probability of earning more than $400 is the same for i as for j. These comparisons show that j is preferred to i. It has a lower probability of the lowest outcome and higher probabilities of higher outcomes. Alternative j is said to be preferred over Alternative i by *first-order stochastic dominance*. Alternative j dominates Alternative i in that it is not possible at any outcome to say that i is better than j in a probability sense.

We reached this conclusion somewhat heuristically. We can reach it more analytically by comparing the cumulative probabilities. Exhibit 3-17 extends Exhibit 3-16 with the cumulative probabilities calculated.

As we noted above, j has a lower chance than i of the worst outcome of $200. Alternatives j and i both have the same chance of a payoff of the middle outcome of $400 or worse. And j and i both have a 100% chance of a payoff of $600 or less. We say that an alternative j is first-order stochastically dominant over an alternative i if the cumulative probability for every level of wealth for j is never more than that for i and is less for at least one level

| | Alternative j | | Alternative i | |
Outcome	Probability	Cumulative Probability	Probability	Cumulative Probability
$200	0.30	0.30	0.40	0.40
$400	0.40	0.70	0.25	0.65
$600	0.30	1.00	0.35	1.00

Exhibit 3-18. Two Risky Alternatives j and i in which Neither Dominates the Other by First-Order Stochastic Dominance

of wealth. In other words, j would be preferred to i regardless of anyone's risk aversion.

Unfortunately, it is not always possible to find a clear preference of one alternative over the other using first-order stochastic dominance. Exhibit 3-18 is an example of two risky alternatives in which neither dominates the other by first-order stochastic dominance.

Here we note that at a level of $200, j is preferred to i, but i has a great chance of producing wealth of more than $400. First-order stochastic dominance fails in this situation, because we cannot say that the cumulative probability for j is equal to that of i for some outcomes and less for at least one outcome. In some cases like this, it is possible to obtain a preference by resorting to *second-order stochastic dominance*. Second-order stochastic dominance takes into account the risk preferences of the individuals by assuming that people are risk averse. It makes no assumption about the type of utility function. It assumes only that the marginal utility of wealth decreases with increasing wealth. As we noted earlier, that feature is a characteristic of risk aversion. With second-order stochastic dominance, we examine the differences in the cumulative probabilities of the alternatives. Alternative j is preferred to i if the differences in cumulative probabilities (the cumulative probability of j minus the cumulative probability of i) are always non-negative and positive for at least one case. Exhibit 3-19 resolves the example in Exhibit 3-18 by using second-order stochastic dominance.

The sixth column is the information required for first-order stochastic dominance, structured here with the cumulative probability of j subtracted from the cumulative probability for i. If that difference is never negative and positive at least once, j dominates i. If it is never positive and negative at least once, i dominates j. Of course, in this problem, it is positive once, negative once, and zero once, so the problem cannot be resolved. To resolve the problem with first-order stochastic dominance, it must be negative or

Outcome	Alternative j		Alternative i		Difference in Cumulative Probabilities (i minus j)	Sum of Differences in Cumulative Probabilities
	Probability	Cumulative Probability	Probability	Cumulative Probability		
$200	0.30	0.30	0.40	0.40	0.10	0.10
$400	0.40	0.70	0.25	0.65	−0.05	0.05
$600	0.30	1.00	0.35	1.00	0.00	0.05

Exhibit 3-19. Two Risky Alternatives j and i in which One Dominates the Other by Second-Order Stochastic Dominance

zero but not positive, or positive or zero but not negative. The final column simply sums the sixth column. As long as that sum is never negative and positive at least once, j dominates i. If it is never positive and negative at least once, i dominates j. Here we see that j indeed dominates i. The logical explanation for this is that the higher probability i has of achieving a level of wealth of \$600 is partially offset by the diminishing marginal utility of this high level of wealth.

Not all risky alternatives can be compared by second-order stochastic dominance. In that case, rules for decision making under third- and higher-order stochastic dominance can be used.

Stochastic dominance is an appealing decision rule, as it makes no assumptions about the utility function of the decision maker. Its value is in its simplicity. Regardless of the specific utility function, stochastic dominance can sometimes be used to evaluate the decision. The disadvantage, however, is that it requires very accurate information on the entire probability distribution. Also, there are no guarantees that every comparison can be ranked with simple rules, such as first- and second-order stochastic dominance. Also, stochastic dominance simply ranks alternatives. It does not take into account the fact that a stochastically dominant alternative will cost more, and it does not tell us what we should pay for a risky investment. Finally, we should note that stochastic dominance is a criterion for ranking only mutually exclusive decisions.

3.10 States and Preferences

Another approach to evaluating the pricing of assets and derivatives is called *state-preference theory*.[14] It is very closely related to the no-arbitrage approach.[15] Consider an asset priced at \$50 that can move up to \$60 or down to \$40. The probabilities are not necessarily equal, nor do we need to know the probabilities. We do need to know the risk-free rate, however, which we shall assume is 3%.

It is common in evaluating risky alternatives to refer to outcomes as *states* and sometimes *states of nature*. The outcome in which the asset moves up to \$60 will be called the "plus-state" and the other outcome where it moves to \$40 will be the "minus-state." State preference theory tells us that

---

[14]In some books, you may hear this method referred to as *time-state-preference theory*, acknowledging that time, along with risk, is a determinant of market prices.

[15]All decision rules must be consistent with the no-arbitrage approach, because all market participants would exploit arbitrage opportunities.

all risky assets are combinations of fundamental assets, which are sometimes called *pure assets*. These assets can be thought of as the atoms upon which other assets, like molecules, are built. Let us make the assumption that a pure security exists for each state and pays $1 if that state occurs and $0 otherwise. So, our asset consists of 60 plus-state pure assets and 40 minus-state pure assets. Viewing the asset this way is like looking at it under a microscope, where we see its underlying components: certain combinations of pure assets. Of course, we cannot truly buy these securities, but when we buy another other security, we are assuming that we are buying a combination of state securities.

Because the future value of the asset consists of 60 plus-state assets and 40 minus-state assets, the current value of the asset, $50, must also consist of the current value of 60 plus-state securities and 40 minus-state securities. Denoting the values of these pure assets as ϕ_1 and ϕ_2, we can break down the $50 current price in the following manner:

$$60\phi_1 + 40\phi_2 = 50.$$

Now suppose an investor purchases one unit of each pure asset. In that case, he will be guaranteed an outcome of $1 for sure. In other words, if the plus-state occurs, he gets $1 from one security and none from the other, and if the minus-state occurs, he gets $1 from the other security and none from the first. Thus, a combination of all pure assets is risk-free. Hence, it should have a value equal to the present value of $1. Thus,

$$\phi_1 + \phi_2 = \frac{1}{1 + 0.03}.$$

From this second equation, we know that

$$\phi_2 = \frac{1}{1 + 0.03} - \phi_1.$$

Substituting this result into the first equation tells us that

$$60\phi_1 + 40\left(\frac{1}{1.03} - \phi_1\right) = 50.$$

Solving gives

$$\phi_1 = 0.5583$$
$$\phi_2 = 0.4126.$$

Notice the sum of the prices of the two pure assets, $0.5583 + $0.4126 = $0.9709 is the present value of $1. That is $1/(1.03) = $0.9709, subject to rounding.

The price of this asset that pays $60 in the plus-state and $40 in the minus-state implies that it costs $0.5583 to obtain an asset that pays $1 in the plus-state and $0.4126 to obtain an asset that pays $1 in the minus-state. That is, when you are purchasing this asset for $50, you are implicitly purchasing 60 units of a plus-state pure asset at $0.5583 and 40 units of a minus-state pure asset at $0.4126.

But how will this help us? Suppose we purchase the asset and wanted to ensure that the value of our investment does not fall below its current value of $50. We could simply purchase 10 units of the minus-state pure security, which would cost 10($0.4126) = $4.1260. If the minus-state occurs, the asset would lose $10, but the 10 units of the pure security would pay us $10. If the plus-state occurs, the asset would be worth $60 and the minus-state pure security would pay nothing.

Later in this book, we will see that the 10 units of the minus-state we purchased is equivalent to a put option with an exercise price of $50. It will allow us to sell the asset at $50 if its value falls below $50. We will see, using this same example, that the put option will cost $4.1260. In other words, if the price falls to $40, we can sell the asset for $40 and collect $10 from the pure asset. Likewise, an option that enables us to buy the asset at $50 is equivalent to 10 units of the plus-state pure security, so it would cost 10($0.5583) = $5.5830. Later we will see that this transaction is like a call option with an exercise price of $50. In other words, if the price rises to $60, we will receive $10 from the pure asset that will partially compensate for having to pay $60 for the asset. Options are thus like pure securities in that they pay off in certain states and not in others.

How would we create a completely hedged position? If we bought the asset at $50 and wanted it to be completely hedged, it should earn a risk-free return of 3%. Thus, if we invested $50 risk-free, it ought to be worth $50(1.03) = $51.5 one period later. To accomplish this hedge we could sell 8.5 of the plus-state securities and buy 11.5 of the minus-state securities. The short position in the 8.5 plus state securities would generate cash of 8.5($0.5583) = $4.75 at the start and require that we pay $8.5 if the asset goes to $60, thereby reducing our wealth to $60 − $8.5 = $51.5. The long position in the 11.5 minus state securities would cost 11.5($0.4126) = $4.75 and would pay us $11.50 if the minus state occurs, thereby increasing our wealth from $40 to $51.50. The money received at the start from selling the plus-state securities offsets the money paid for the minus-state securities, so we can effectively hedge at no up-front cash cost. What we have just created is the equivalent of a forward contract, which we will cover in great length in this book.

The state preference approach to pricing risky assets is just another way of looking at the no-arbitrage approach to pricing, but one that breaks down prices into their more fundamental components. Its role in the theory of financial economics has been diminished somewhat by the overwhelming emphasis on arbitrage as a pricing mechanism, which arose out of the body of knowledge on how to price risk management instruments. Hence, state-preference theory is not seen much in contemporary writing on asset pricing. Nonetheless, it is helpful to be able to see that assets merely represent combinations of claims that pay off in certain states. The management of the risk associated with these state payoffs is the central theme of risk management.

H. G. Wells and Arbitrage

H. G. Wells' classic novel *The Time Machine*, written in 1895, has been one of the most popular of all science fiction novels. Wells writes vividly about many details of a future he sees and takes the reader on a journey with a time-defying device. But evidently it never occurred to Wells that the financial world could exploit his machine to a mind-boggling degree. In an article in *The Journal of Portfolio Management* in 1986, finance professor Marc Reinganum proposed that arbitrage provides a straightforward proof of the impossibility of time travel.

Let us assume that a time machine is built and we are able to use it to go backward and forward in time. Now suppose that we fill our pockets with $100 bills and enter the machine. We set the machine for a destination well back in the past but in an era in which banking and investment exist. We reach this distant time point with the money in our pocket. Of course, we are, in the context of that time period, a very wealthy person but we shall need nothing to live on in that period, because we are going to return to the present pretty quickly. But before doing so, we place that money in a risk-free investment in a bank that we know has survived all of these years. We then re-enter the time machine and return to our modern time, whereupon we retrieve the money from the bank account. After accruing interest for all of these years, the balance will be tremendous. But of course, this is only the start. We again load up with as much money as we can possibly carry and repeat the process. We continue to do this until we own the vast majority of all of the wealth in the world in our current era.

The opportunity to transport money without interest across time is an arbitrage opportunity. After all, money has a cost — interest — and a time machine would enable the owner to avoid this cost. He would simply hop into the machine and transport the money at no cost. He would then invest it at an earlier date and return to the current time, retrieving the money from the bank account. Alternatively, he could invest some money in a bank today, go into the future and retrieve the money, put it in his pocket and return on the time machine. He would then have more money at no risk in the present than he started off with.

Yet another clever way to exploit the time machine is by using it to learn which risky investments will perform well. Imagine today looking at a number of young startup companies. Then you go into the future and see which ones have done well. You then return to the present and use that knowledge, buying the successful ones and shorting the ones that eventually fail.

So, not only can a time machine beat the so-called time value of money rule, it can also beat the requirement that to earn higher returns you must take higher risk. And what conclusion can we draw from this? Time travel is impossible. If it were possible, someone could use it to amass enormous wealth, far more than the rest of the world combined.

3.11 Practical Considerations in Deciding How Much Risk to Take

This chapter has talked a lot about taking risk and the implications for financial markets. With the exception of when we use utility curves, we have not been able to nail down just exactly how one decides how much risk to take. In fact, even with utility theory, we still have the problem of trying to identify our own utility functions. Utility theory is a helpful guide in understanding how risky decisions are made, but it is difficult to put into practice. Ultimately, a decision maker can decide how much risk to take only by incorporating his feelings about risk.

This book is about risk management for organizations. Deciding how much risk an organization should take is typically a decision made at the highest levels, i.e., directors and/or trustees, in consultation with management and risk experts. We will return to the issue in Chapter 14, but from this point forward, we will accept that the decision has been made. As a placeholder, let us assume that an organization chooses to take risks only in the areas in which it believes it has expertise and a competitive advantage. It avoids risks in areas in which it has no expertise or competitive advantage. As an example, an airline faces a number of broad classes of risks. One of the primary ones is jet fuel risk. Another is currency and interest rate risk. Yet another is the business risk of its industry, meaning the uncertainties airlines face in delivering their services. Good risk management for an airline would involve eliminating jet fuel risk, interest rate risk, and currency risk for sure. Airlines have no expertise in predicting the future in these areas. Airlines do have expertise in delivering people and cargo safely and on time. These risks are the ones they should take. Of course, what a company *should* do and what it does are not necessarily the same thing, but that is another story for another time.

3.12   Chapter Summary

This chapter provides a summary and overview of some of the basic principles related to financial risk. The objective is to give you an idea of how people make decisions about how much financial risk to take. We first reviewed the basic concepts of long and short exposures. We then looked at how risk is quantified in the form of outcomes and probabilities. We considered the risk of a single asset and then examined how multiple exposures interact, through correlation, to determine the overall risk. We next looked at how information on past performance is quantified to arrive at estimates of the risk faced in the future.

We then examined the subject of utility theory, an economic treatment of how people feel about risk. We looked at utility functions and how they characterize risk aversion. We showed that risky decisions should be analyzed by choosing the alternative that maximizes expected utility. We introduced the notion of a risk premium, which is an expected return that would be required by any risk averse investor before undertaking a risky endeavor. We illustrated an example of how a decision is made in allocating funds between a risky asset and a safe asset. We reviewed the basic elements of the Capital Asset Pricing Model, which relates expected return to risk if certain assumptions are met.

We introduced the notion of arbitrage and noted that it will reappear many times in this book as a dominant theme in the pricing of risk management instruments. We concluded the chapter with a brief look at two alternative schemes for risky decision making, stochastic dominance and state preference theory, the latter of which we showed is just a more fundamental and microscopic method of looking at risk.

3.13   Appendix: The Optimal Asset Allocation in a World with Two Assets and Two Outcomes

The application discussed in the body of this chapter and here in the appendix is an adaptation of Merton's (1969, 1971) continuous time model of capital asset pricing. Assume we are positioned at time t and the next time period is $t + 1$. The probabilities of the two outcomes are q and $1 - q$. Let the rate of return if the asset goes up be $u - 1$ and the rate of return if the asset goes down be $d - 1$. The risk-free rate is r. The expected utility at time $t + 1$ is written as $E(U(t + 1))$. Let the percentage of wealth invested in the risky asset be γ. The wealth at time $t + 1$ is

$$W(t)(\gamma u + (1 - \gamma)(1 + r)) \text{ with probability } q$$

$$W(t)(\gamma d + (1 - \gamma)(1 + r)) \text{ with probability } 1 - q.$$

The objective is to maximize the expected utility by the appropriate choice of α:

$$\max_{\alpha} E(U(t + 1)).$$

Although we will ultimately use the log utility function, we will start with the more general case of the power utility function mentioned in the chapter, which takes the form $U(W) = W^{1-\lambda}/(1 - \lambda)$. The reason we prefer to start with the power utility function is that when we differentiate with respect to α in the log utility function, there are no α terms left, which complicates the solution. So we will start with the power utility function and then take the limit of our end result to get to the log utility function.

To maximize the expected utility, we take the derivative of the expected utility with respect to α:

$$\frac{\partial EU(W(t + 1))}{\partial \gamma}$$

$$= \frac{\partial}{\partial \gamma} \left(q \frac{W(t + 1, u)^{1-\lambda}}{1 - \lambda} + (1 - q) \frac{W(t + 1, d)^{1-\lambda}}{1 - \lambda} \right),$$

where we denote our wealth in the two outcomes as $W(t+1,u)$ and $W(t+1,d)$, respectively. Now, doing the math:

$$\frac{\partial}{\partial \gamma}\left(q\frac{W(t+1,u)^{1-\lambda}-1}{1-\lambda}+(1-q)\frac{W(t+1,d)^{1-\lambda}-1}{1-\lambda}\right)$$

$$=\frac{\partial}{\partial \gamma}\left(\begin{array}{c}q\dfrac{(W(t)(\gamma u+(1-\gamma)(1+r))^{1-\lambda}-1}{1-\lambda}\\[2mm]+(1-q)\dfrac{W(t)(\gamma d+(1-\gamma)(1+r)^{1-\lambda}-1}{1-\lambda}\end{array}\right)$$

$$=q\left(W(t)(\alpha u+(1-\alpha)r)\right)^{-\lambda}W(t)(u-(1+r))$$
$$+(1-q)\left(W(t)(\alpha d+(1-\alpha)(1+r))\right)^{-\lambda}W(t)(d-(1+r)).$$

Now specify the following parameter:

$$\pi=\frac{(1+r)-d}{u-d}.$$

This parameter will play a major role in this book, but we will get to that point later. Using this result, we have $d-(1+r)=-\pi(u-d)$ and $u-(1+r)=(1-\pi)(u-d)$. Substituting and setting the derivative to zero gives:

$$q(1-\pi)(u-d)W(t)(\gamma u+(1-\gamma)(1+r))^{-\lambda}W(t)$$
$$+(1-q)(-\pi)(u-d)(\gamma d+(1-\gamma)(1+r))^{-\lambda}W(t)$$
$$=0.$$

Now define the variable:

$$\Psi=\left(\frac{(1-q)\pi}{q(1-\pi)}\right)^{-1/\lambda}.$$

Substituting this value and solving for α gives the solution, which is the optimal asset allocation.

$$\gamma=\frac{(1+r)-\Psi(1+r)}{\Psi(d-(1+r))-u+(1+r)}.$$

To verify that this result gives the maximum expected utility and not the minimum, we take the second derivative,

$$\frac{\partial^2 E(U(W))}{\partial \gamma}$$

$$= -q(1-\pi)(u-d)\lambda(W(t)(\gamma u + (1-\gamma)(1+r))^{-\lambda} W(t)^2 (u-(1+r))$$

$$- (1-q)\pi(u-d)\lambda(W(t)(\gamma d + (1-\gamma)(1+r))^{-\lambda} W(t)^2 ((1+r)-d).$$

A close examination of each term and the signs reveals that the overall sign is positive.

In the special case of log utility, $\lambda = 1$. That means that

$$\Psi = \left(\frac{(1-q)\pi}{q(1-\pi)}\right)^{-1}.$$

The example in the text uses these formulas with log utility.

3.14   Questions and Problems

1. Define the concept of the rate of return on an investment.
2. What is the difference in the ex ante and ex post concepts of returns?
3. Given the following information, calculate the ex ante expected returns, volatilities, and the correlation for the two assets, AA and BB, indicated.

Outcome	Probability	Return on Asset AA	Return on Asset BB
1	0.28	0.15	0.12
2	0.40	0.04	0.06
3	0.32	−0.08	−0.02

4. Asset MM and asset JJ have expected returns, volatilities, and a correlation as follows. Determine the expected return and volatility of a combination in which 47% of the funds are invested in asset MM and 53% are in asset JJ.

$$E(R_{MM}) = 0.12, \sigma_{MM} = 0.25$$

$$E(R_{JJ}) = 0.08, \sigma_{JJ} = 0.18$$

$$\rho_{JJMM} = 0.32$$

5. Explain the difference in and relationship between the concepts of correlation, causality, and independence.
6. Calculate the average return, volatility, and correlation for the two assets *HH* and *CC* below, based on this historical sample of prices. Ignore dividends or any other cash flows that might have been paid by the assets.

Time Period	Price of Asset *HH*	Price of Asset *CC*
1	20.00	110.00
2	21.52	101.55
3	19.01	108.90
4	22.25	111.15
5	23.09	114.48

7. What is the attraction of using a normal distribution in comparison to a non-normal distribution?
8. What is a major disadvantage of the normal distribution in finance?
9. Use the data below and determine which of the two investments, *GG* and *LL*, has the greater expected log utility, and, therefore, would be preferred if they were mutually exclusive. Assume that the investment is made with $1,000.

Outcome	Probability	Return on Asset *GG*	Return on Asset *LL*
1	0.38	0.21	0.15
2	0.40	0.02	0.04
3	0.22	−0.10	−0.20

10. Use the data in the above problem and determine the implied risk premium using log utility for assets *GG* and *LL*.
11. Explain the limitation of the log utility function and how the power utility function comprises the log utility function as well as other utility functions.
12. Explain the differences in the characteristics of investors who are risk averse, risk loving, and risk neutral.

13. Assume an asset priced at 80 that can go up by 25% with probability 0.62 or down to 25% with probability 0.38. The risk-free rate is 2%. Determine the optimal asset allocation.

14. In a world of fully diversified investors, explain why the beta is the appropriate measure of risk, as opposed to the volatility.

15. Explain how financial risk management nests within the primary results of modern portfolio analysis.

16. Explain why stochastic dominance can serve as a decision criterion under risk even if we do not know the utility function of the decision maker.

17. Use stochastic dominance to determine the preferred alternative from among the two alternatives below, QQ and RR. Identify if first-order stochastic dominance is sufficient, and if not, apply second-order stochastic dominance. If first-order stochastic dominance does provide a solution, show that second-order stochastic dominance is in agreement.

Return	Probability for Alternative QQ	Probability for Alternative RR
−0.20	0.10	0.08
−0.10	0.15	0.17
0.00	0.35	0.40
0.12	0.30	0.28
0.22	0.10	0.07

18. Consider an asset priced at 40 that can go up to 45 or down to 37.5 with probabilities 0.56 and 0.44, respectively. The risk-free rate is 2.5%. Find the following:

   a. The prices of the two pure securities that pay 1 unit of the asset in each of the two states.

   b. The price of an asset that will assure that you can buy the asset at a price of 40.

   c. The price of an asset that will assure you that you can sell the asset at a price of 40.

Part II

Foundations of Financial Risk Management

Chapter 4

Basic Concepts of Financial Risk Management

Creativity requires risk. So do exploration and innovation. Anyone who thinks outside the box is taking a risk. Leadership brings many risks. Courage is exercised in the face of risk. Investments involve risk. Decision-making always means a certain degree of risk.

> Dr. Benjamin S. Carson
> *Take the Risk: Learning to*
> *Identify, Choose, and Live with*
> *Acceptable Risk*
> New York: Zondervan (2009), p. 120

This book examines how organizations manage risk. These organizations are primarily shareholder-oriented companies, but the principles are applicable in non-profits as well. Both types of entities are expected to be good stewards of the capital entrusted to them. Both must raise and allocate capital and do their best to, first, survive, and, second, achieve their objectives. Both types of entities reflect an appetite for risk and are damaged by adverse outcomes, while benefitting from favorable outcomes. While there can be considerable variation in the types of risks faced by organizations, the fundamental principles of risk management are common to all.

In this book, we address three basic types of risks that are faced by virtually all organizations. The first is called *market risk*, the second is referred to as *credit risk* and sometimes *default risk*, and the third is a catch-all category rather loosely referred to as *other risks*. The concept of market risk refers to the risks arising from four general sources: interest rates, exchange rates, commodity prices, and stock prices. The concept of credit risk refers to the risk associated with the possibility that a party that owes money to another party will not pay. The catch-all category, other risks, encompasses a wide range of risks but as an example of one in particular, there is the risk associated with an entity's operations, such as the consequences if a company is forced to shut down or curtail operations.

In this chapter we start Part II, which lays the foundations for the study of financial risk management. Chapter 4 examines certain basic concepts of financial risk management. Chapter 5 looks at the financial risk management environment, meaning the markets, institutions, and participants. Chapter 6 examines the question of whether financial risk management adds value.

If you have previously studied finance, you have become familiar with certain classifications of risk. In the study of corporate finance, you become familiar with the concepts of business risk and financial risk. When you study portfolio management, you learn about the concepts of systematic and unsystematic risk. We will start this chapter with a description of these classifications of risk, so that you can see and place them in perspective with the other classifications of risk that we shall use. Then we shall take an introductory look at market and credit risk. Our objective is to acquire a sense of how this risk changes over time and to understand some basic tools for managing these risks. Operational and other risks are so different from market and credit risk that we will defer our treatment of them until Chapter 12.

4.1 Basic Concepts and Classifications of Risk in Finance

As mentioned earlier, there are two general classifications of risk that are encountered in other finance courses, books, and treatments. Let us take a look at each.

4.1.1 *Business Risk and Financial Risk*

In the study of corporate finance, we distinguish the concepts of *business risk* and *financial risk*. Business risk is defined as the risk of an entity's assets. For a business it reflects the pure risk of the business, hence the name, "business risk." These risks are those related to creating and selling their products and services, as well as the risks arising from regulatory, political, and competitive factors. In its simplest form, think of business risk as the risk of an entity's assets.

Business risk is heavily influenced by the ratio of assets with fixed costs to assets with variable costs. This ratio is captured by the concept of *operating leverage*. Companies with a high ratio of fixed cost assets to variable cost assets have relatively more operating leverage. As a result, the financial performance of their assets is more volatile. If sales revenue increases, the use of more fixed assets generates a higher return on assets. If sales revenue decreases, however, the use of more fixed assets leverages downward, resulting in a lower return on assets. As an example, consider two U.S. companies, A and B, with assets of $1,000. Both companies generate $100 of revenue by selling 100 units at $1 apiece. Company A's costs consists of fixed costs of $50 and variable costs of $0.10 per unit. Company B's costs consist of fixed costs of $40 and variable costs of $0.20 per unit. Thus, both companies have $60 in total costs. For both companies, with revenue of $100 and costs of $60, the profit is $40 and the return on assets (ROA) is 4%.

Now suppose each company experiences a 20% increase in sales. Thus, both companies sell 120 units at $1 apiece for revenue of $120. Company A's costs comprise fixed costs of $50 and variable costs of 120($0.10) = $12 for a total of $62. Its profit is, therefore, $120 − $62 = $58 and its ROA is 5.8%, an increase of 45% over its previous ROA of 4%. Company B's costs comprise fixed costs of $40 and variable costs of 120($0.20) = $24, for a total of $64. Its profit is, therefore, $120 − $64 = $56, an ROA of 5.6% and an increase in the ROA of 40%. By using more fixed assets, Company A's improved asset performance is amplified over that of Company B. Operating leverage is a double-edged sword, however, in that a decrease in sales is also amplified. Try to see that point yourself. Let both companies experience a 20% decrease in sales and see how Company A's ROA goes down 45%, while Company B's ROA goes down 40%.

A company's business risk is partially determined by its operating leverage, which to a great extent reflects the nature of the industry the company is in. Some industries such as energy require a large investment in fixed assets. Others such as retailing are more dependent on variable cost inputs. And as noted above, the competitive nature of the industry, as well as the political and regulatory environment, combine to influence a company's business risk.

As we will discuss in the next few major sections, business risk is partially driven by market risk as well as credit risk, operational risk, and a variety of other risks. We will cover the basic ideas behind these concepts in this chapter and the details in much of the remainder of this book.

Financial risk is not a contrasting concept in relation to business risk but rather is an enhancing concept. It refers to the risk arising from the use of debt in relation to equity to finance the assets. Thus, it captures the notion of financial leverage. Consider for example two companies L and U, both of which have $1,000 in assets. Company L uses financial leverage and finances the assets using $400 of debt at a rate of 4% and $600 of equity. Company U uses no financial leverage, so it has no debt and $1,000 of equity. Suppose both companies generate $100 of net operating income (NOI). Company L must pay $16 in interest, so its net income is $84 and its return on equity (ROE) is 14% ($84/$600). Company U pays no interest so it has a net income of $100, and its ROE is 10% ($100/$1,000).

Now suppose both companies experience a 20% increase in NOI, which grows to $120. Company L must still pay $16 in interest so its net income is $104 and its ROE is 17.33% ($104/$600). Company L pays no interest, so its net income is $120 and its ROE increases to 12% ($120/$1,000). Here the use of financial leverage benefitted company L, as its ROE increased by 23.81% (14% to 17.33%). Company U has no financial leverage, so its ROE increased by the same percentage increase as its NOI, 20% (10% to 12%). Now try a 20% decrease in NOI. You should be able to determine that Company L's new ROE is 10.67%, a reduction of 38.46% (14% to 10.67%), and Company U's new ROE is 8%, a reduction of 20% (10% to 8%). Indeed, financial leverage magnifies improvements and deteriorations in performance.

Financial leverage is one of the most important topics in corporate finance. Indeed, determining the optimal amount of debt to use in relation to equity is a major decision that companies make. The more debt a company uses, the riskier is the overall company. Unlike business risk, which is affected by many external factors, financial risk is primarily influenced by internal decisions, the main one being how much debt to use.[1] Financial risk is also heavily affected by market risk, credit risk, and risks related to tax policy and regulations. We will get into these points later in this chapter and in much of the remainder of the book.

Before we leave this section, we must issue a warning. As noted, the term "financial risk" as described in this sub-section refers to the risk created by the use of financial leverage. This notion is the idea behind this concept in the study of corporate finance, — the choice of debt versus equity. But in the last 20 years or so, the term has come to mean virtually any type of risk that an entity faces. Hence, the term "financial risk management" is used synonymously with the term "risk management." In effect, adding the word "financial" as a modifier means virtually nothing in informal use.

---

[1]A secondary decision is how much to pay in dividends. The dividend decision is a type of contra-financing decision, since the payment of dividends returns equity capital to shareholders. In addition, the repurchase of shares has the same effect of returning capital to shareholders and is an internal decision.

Thus, even though you have perhaps studied financial risk as it relates to the use of leverage in other courses, you will need to use the term as the more inclusive notion of all types of risks.

4.1.2 *Systematic and Unsystematic Risk*

In studying portfolio management, you may have encountered the concepts of systematic and unsystematic risk. In fact, we talked about these types of risks in Chapter 3. *Systematic risk* is the risk arising from movements in an overall market. Conceptually, the notion of an overall market can refer to the ups and downs of an economy, but more often it refers to volatility in an asset market, such as the stock market. For example, the stock market goes up and down, creating a systematic risk effect. Likewise, interest rates, exchange rates, and commodity prices go up and down and impart their effects on companies, governments, and non-profits. These effects are driven by the individual entities that operate within the market, and they combine to produce an overall or systematic effect.

Unsystematic or nonsystematic risk is the risk associated with an individual entity. For example, if a corporation finds that it has a problem with a product that will necessitate a recall, the effect is unsystematic. Not all products in the economy or even within an industry experience the problem. In other words, the problem is unique to the company. This type of risk is often called *idiosyncratic* or *specific* risk. For investors holding well-diversified portfolios, the effects of random positive and negative factors on their holdings are diversified. Hence, the risk is also called *diversifiable risk*, which leads to the fact that systematic risk is often called *non-diversifiable risk*.

One can make a good argument that to diversified shareholders, nonsystematic risks do not matter. Such a case would beg the obvious question of whether managing financial risk matters. Many of these risks are nonsystematic. Good question. We will take up this issue in Chapter 6.

Finally, we should note that systematic risk is sometimes called *market risk*, but this terminology clashes somewhat with the standard use of the term "market risk" in financial risk management. As noted above, market risk in financial risk management refers to the risk of interest rates, exchange rates, commodity prices, and stock prices, without making a distinction between the diversifiable and non-diversifiable components. Let us now take a look at what market and credit risk mean in the context of financial risk management.

4.2   A First Look at Market and Credit Risk

As mentioned above, market risk is the risk associated with interest rates, exchange rates, commodity prices, and stock prices, while credit risk is the risk associated with loss from non-payment of an amount owed by one party to another. We will first take a look at market risk.

4.2.1   *Market Risk*

In simple terms, it is the risk associated with the volatility of prices and rates in financial markets. Not all entities are exposed to each of these four sources of market risks, but the sources do generally encompass all types of market risks. We will now take a first look at these sources of risk. There may be some surprises about which markets are the riskiest and which are the least risky.

4.2.1.1   *Interest Rates*

Interest rates represent the cost of borrowing money. Because so many organizations borrow money, interest rate risk is undoubtedly the most common risk faced in economic life. A given interest rate has three components. One is the *time value of money*, sometimes referred to as the price of waiting, the second is an additional amount, called a premium, for *expected inflation*, and the third is an additional amount, also a premium but often called a *spread*, for the potential that the borrower will not repay the loan, which reflects the *credit risk*. Thus, an interest rate consists of the time value of money plus premiums for bearing the risk of inflation and the risk of credit losses.

As an example, if a lender extends a loan to a borrower in the amount of €1,000 for one year, the lender foregoes consumption for one year. The lender could consume goods and services worth €1,000 now and will clearly be unable to do so if it makes the loan. By engaging in the loan, however, the lender can charge interest and be able to consume more than €1,000 a year later. The rate of interest reflects the price of waiting and is the concept referred to by the phrase, "the time value of money." This rate is also called the *real rate of interest*, for a reason that will become clear in the next paragraph. Let us assume that the real rate is 3%. Thus, the lender makes a loan of €1,000, thereby forgoing consumption of €1,000 of goods and services today, and a year later expects to be repaid €1,030, with which he can then buy €1,030 of goods and services.

In addition, the lender should recognize the possibility that an increase in the level of prices of goods and services can erode his purchasing power. As noted, a one-year, 3% loan of €1,000 would be expected to return €1,030 one year later. If the price level has risen 1%, however, the €1,000 of goods and services that could be purchased at the time of the loan will cost €1,010 one year later. Incorporating the loss of purchasing power, the lender would earn a return of only €1,030/€1,010 − 1 = 0.0198, meaning only 1.98%. A rational lender will, however, build this factor into the rate he charges. Thus, if he expects 1% inflation, he would charge 1.03 × 1.01 − 1 = 0.0403, or 4.03%. Then, the lender would expect to receive €1,040.30 from repayment of the loan and would be able to buy goods and services worth €1,040.30/1.01 = €1,030. The rate the lender charges that reflects the expectation of inflation is called the *nominal rate*. The rate earned after inflation is the real rate. In other words, the nominal rate is the quoted rate, while the real rate reflects the rate you actually earn in terms of constant purchasing power.[2]

It is possible, however, that the borrower will fail to pay back some, if not all, of the loan. The lender will anticipate this possibility and embed an additional rate into the interest rate to reflect the possibility of non-payment. If the borrower does repay the loan, the lender will therefore earn an additional return that compensates him for the worry of bearing the credit risk. If the borrower defaults, the aggregate amount charged for the credit risk over all of the loans he makes is designed to compensate the lender for the loss from default on some of the loans.

---

[2]The description here of nominal and real rates is a very light overview. As mentioned, the lender anticipates a certain inflation rate and incorporates a premium for this expected inflation. After the fact, the actual inflation is likely to be different, given that, not surprisingly, inflation itself is volatile and unpredictable. Higher (lower) than expected inflation benefits borrowers (lenders) because they pay back their loans in cheaper (more expensive) units of currency. In practice, the relationship between the nominal and real rates is usually expressed additively. In this example, the nominal rate would be 4%, which is obtained as the real rate of 3% plus the expected inflation rate of 1%, an approximation that is off slightly by the product of the two rates (3% × 1% = 0.03%). In other words, this factor (0.03%) plus the sum of the real and expected inflation rates is 4.03%. One final consideration is that an overall expected inflation rate does not necessarily reflect the inflation rate on the specific goods and services that the lender would buy with the money. It tends to be a more general estimate based on a large number of goods and services. Thus, it may not necessarily be applicable for a given individual with a need or interest in purchasing specific goods and services.

What is an Interest Rate? Really

Most adults could probably give a fairly accurate definition of an interest rate: it is the cost of borrowing money. And since most everyone saves money from time to time, they should also know that interest is also the return from lending money, the mirror image of borrowing. But finance professionals need a better understanding of what an interest rate really is.

Let us say you borrow $100 and pay back $104 one year later. If asked to identify the interest rate, most people would say 4%. But in fact, there are many possible answers. If the interest were compounded semiannually, the rate would be the solution to the equation: $104 = 100(1 + r)^2$, the answer of which is $r = 0.0198$, which if compounded every six months, is equivalent to $(1.0198)^2 - 1 = 0.0399$, rounded up to 4%. That is, $100 could compound at 1.98% for six months, equaling $101.98, which could then compound at 1.98% for another six months to equal $104. If interest were compounded daily, the answer would be the solution to the problem $104 = 100(1 + r)^{365}$, which is $r = 0.000107$. In that case, $100 compounds one day to a value of $100 \times (1 + 0.000107)$, which compounds another day to $100 \times (1 + 0.000107)^2$, and this continues for 363 more days, to eventually equal $104, subject to a bit of round-off error. The daily rate of 0.0107% is equivalent to an annual rate of $(1.000107)^{365} - 1 = 0.0398$, or 3.98%. As we will see later in this book, the LIBOR method of interest is of the form, $104 = 100(1 + r(\text{days}/360))$ where days is the number of days in the loan and 360 is always the denominator.

The point here is that there are many mathematical relationships that connect the present value of $100 to the future value of $104. An interest rate is simply a mathematical specification that converts the present value to the future value. Of course, there are some mathematical specifications that work but do not make much sense. For example, we can say $104 = $100 + c$, and $c = 4. That specification tells us how much interest there is, but it does not tell us the rate. A specification of the form $FV = PV(1 + r)^n$ tells us that a given periodic rate, r, compounded for n periods will precisely convert the present value, PV, to the future value, FV. The equation $FV = PV(1 + r)^n$ is a single equation with two unknowns $(r$ and $n)$, which implies that there are an infinite number of specifications that work. Thus, there are an infinite number of rates and compounding periods that can convert a present value to a future value. So, there are truly many possible answers to the question "What is the rate on a loan?"

In the financial world, there is one such combination that we use often, which is called *continuous compounding*. Suppose we write the equation as $FV = PV(1 + r/n)^n$ and let n be very large. Mathematically, we write $n \to \infty$ and say it as "n approaches infinity." Then, as it turns out, $FV = PVe^r$ where r is called the continuously compounded rate, and e is the base of the natural log system and is approximately equal to 2.71828. We use this concept often in derivatives, in particular to convert a continuously compounded rate to its annual equivalent and to take a future value and a present value and infer a continuously compounded return. So that is one more way to relate present to future value.

In short, there is no unique interest rate.

Interest rates fluctuate based on the supply of and demand for money, which is influenced heavily by a combination of government policies and central bank market activities, with the latter having a more direct effect. Thus, when we hear of the U.S. Federal Reserve tightening its monetary policy, we know that it is bidding aggressively to sell bonds to banks so as to remove money from the banking system and thereby raise interest rates. Similar activities occur in central banks in virtually every major country. In addition, the state of the economy generates a demand for and supply of money from the private sector as well. Changes in the all of these factors lead to changes in interest rates.

Of course, there are thousands of different interest rates in the market and coverage of many of these rates is the focus of a course on financial markets and instruments. In this book, the rate we will focus on is LIBOR, which stands for the *London Interbank Offer Rate*. Banks with excess cash commonly lend it to other banks in need of cash. In London, this market is called the London Interbank Market. The average offer rate, which is the rate that banks are offering to pay when they borrow from other banks, is called LIBOR. This rate is compiled by a derivatives exchange called Intercontinental Exchange, known as ICE. When the word "LIBOR" is used, it usually means dollar LIBOR, the rate at which London banks borrow dollars from other London banks. There are, however, LIBORs for different currencies. Thus, in addition to dollar LIBOR, there are euro LIBOR, yen LIBOR, sterling LIBOR, etc.[3]

---

[3]Euro LIBOR is created in London. On the European continent, there is another similar rate called Euribor.

Dollar LIBOR is also sometimes referred to as the *Eurodollar* rate or just, the Eurodollar. "Eurodollar" is a term for a dollar that is borrowed and lent in the London interbank market. More generally, a Eurodollar is a dollar trading outside of the United States, but the concept is mostly used in reference to the London LIBOR market. In addition, there are Euroyen, Eurosterling, and even Euroeuro, all in reference to loans in those currencies trading outside of their home domain.

Dollar LIBOR is the basis for many loans and derivative contracts. The majority of business loans have rates that periodically adjust to market conditions. These loans, which are called floating rate loans, are commonly tied to dollar LIBOR and have many possible maturities. There are rates based on 30-day LIBOR, 60-day LIBOR, 90-day LIBOR, and other such periods. These rates are, thus, based off of the rates on interbank loans corresponding to these maturity periods. For example, suppose a small company borrows from its local bank for 90 days. The bank might charge a rate of LIBOR plus 3%, adjustable monthly, with the 3% added to cover the credit risk and contribute to the profit of the bank. Let us say LIBOR is 1% starting off, so the rate the company pays is then 4% for the first month. At the end of the first month, the rate is adjusted to the new 30-day LIBOR, plus 3%. The rate continues to adjust each month. Interest for each month is calculated based on that month's rate, adjusted for either the number of days in the month or an assumption of 30 days.

So, LIBOR is a very important interest rate in the market and its volatility is a source of risk to many borrowers and lenders. Exhibit 4-1 illustrates a history of dollar LIBOR for 90-day loans and reflects the monthly average of the daily rates from 1971 through the end of 2017.[4]

During this time, LIBOR has been as high as about 19.5% and as low as $1/4$%. The very high levels occurred from around 1978–1982, a period of very high inflation. Thus, these high levels reflected the premiums charged by lenders for the expected erosion of their purchasing power, a point mentioned earlier in the chapter. LIBOR has, however, been below 1% from around the middle of 2009 through the end of 2016, a reflection of low expected inflation and the U.S. Federal Reserve's policy, often referred to as *Quantitative Easing*, which is a strategy designed to keep interest rates low to help stimulate economic activity.

It is common to show the level of a rate or price series, and the visual in Exhibit 4-1 does project a general idea of the up and down movements.

---

[4]Henceforth, dollar LIBOR will be referred to as simply "LIBOR."

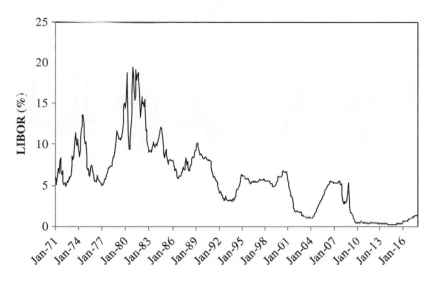

Exhibit 4-1. Monthly 90-day LIBOR

Nonetheless, the *level* of a rate or price is not as important as *movements* in the rate or price. Whether LIBOR is 10% or 2%, the risk lies in whether it moves up or down and by how much. Thus, a better measure of the risk can be found by quantifying the movements in LIBOR. While we could convert Exhibit 4-1 into the changes from one observation to another, a better measure is percentage changes. For example, if LIBOR is 6% and moves up to 6.1%, we could express it as a change of 0.1%, but a better measure is the percentage change, $0.061/0.06 - 1 = 0.0167$, or 1.67%.[5] As we will see, by using percentage changes we can more easily compare the relative risk of different markets.

---

[5] When dealing with interest rates, the terminology we use must be selected with great care. For example, a change from 6% to 6.1% can be expressed as a change of 0.1% or a percentage change of 1.67%. Since the variable of interest is also a percentage, there can be confusion. We find ourselves saying that 6% changed by 0.1% or 6% changed by 1.67%, the former being additive and the latter multiplicative. The financial world has invented a term called a *basis point* that helps avoid confusion. A basis point is one one-hundredth of a percent. For example, 6% is 600 basis points. A change to 6.1% is a change of 10 basis points. A basis point is effectively the fourth decimal in a percentage expression of the rate. For example, 6.15% can be expressed as 0.0615. An increase to 0.0616 (6.16%) is an increase of one basis point. A decrease from 6% to 5% is a decrease of 100 basis points. Another expression for a basis point is a *bip*, which comes from the symbol *bp* used to represent a basis point. Thus, 100 basis points is 100 *bips*. When studying finance, it is important to understand this lingo.

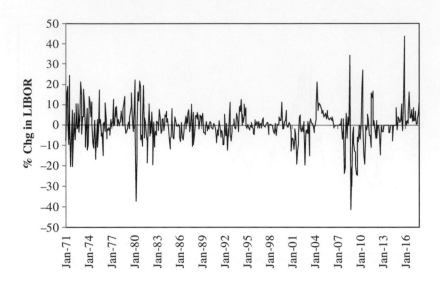

Exhibit 4-2. Monthly Percentage Changes in 90-day LIBOR

Exhibit 4-2 presents the monthly percentage changes in the LIBOR series depicted above. This graph gives a much better picture of the fluctuations in LIBOR from month to month. We can easily see the large changes that occurred in the 1979–1980 period, a period in which the U.S. Federal Reserve altered its approach to monetary policy, and also in 2007–2009, a period referred to as the Financial Crisis.

Another way to look at risk is to directly measure the volatility. In Chapter 3, we mentioned that the most common way of doing so is by the concept of the standard deviation, sometimes referred to as the *volatility*. As a quick review, assume we are interested in a random variable called x. We observe its value at point t and refer to that value as x_t. Thus, x_t might mean the value of LIBOR in month t, where t is, say, December of 2013. Given a sample of T_s observations, we estimate the standard deviation, σ, as follows:

$$\sigma = \sqrt{\frac{\sum_{t=1}^{T_s}(x_t - \bar{x})^2}{T_s - 1}},$$

where $\bar{x}$ is the average value of x over all T_s observations, found by summing x and dividing by T_s.

A good measure of risk for LIBOR is the volatility of the percentage change in LIBOR. Thus, x_t would represent the percentage change in LIBOR. As the previous exhibits show, there are about 40 years of

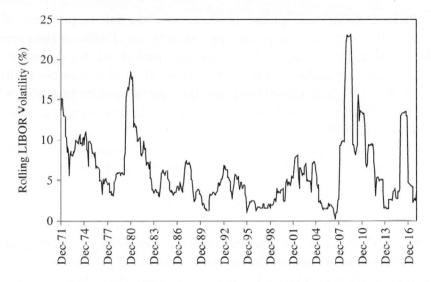

Exhibit 4-3. Rolling Volatility of Percentage Changes in LIBOR

monthly observations. We could use them all to estimate a single volatility. Alternatively, we could parcel the data into segments, say years, and get a volatility number for each year. We will implement a third alternative of estimating, which is called a *rolling volatility*. We will use the first twelve percentage changes to estimate the volatility for the twelfth month of the first 12 observations. We will then drop the oldest month and add the next month and estimate a new volatility using the 12 observations that reflect dropping the first month and adding the thirteenth. We continue to follow that procedure one month at a time. The resulting series is referred to as a rolling volatility. It appears in Exhibit 4-3.

A rolling volatility gives a good impression of how the volatility is changing. It smooths out large monthly changes that may or may not reflect true volatility changes. As we see once again, the rolling volatility is high in the 1979–1980 period as well as in 2007–2009. The maximum is about 23% per month with the minimum less than a quarter of a percent per month. The average rolling volatility is about 6.1%.

4.2.1.2 *Exchange Rates*

An exchange rate is the rate at which one currency is converted into another. For example, the cost of a euro in dollars might be expressed as $1.10. Tradition in foreign exchange markets is that five currencies (the euro, the British pound, the Canadian dollar, the Australian dollar, and the

New Zealand dollar) are quoted in terms of U.S. dollars per unit of the currency. Most other currencies are quoted in terms of units of the currency per U.S. dollar. For example, if the exchange rate of yen for dollars is 130, it means that one dollar converts into ¥130. It is also possible to invert the exchange rate and thereby express the cost of dollars in euros, which would be 1/$1.10 = €0.9091, or the cost of yen in dollars, which would be 1/¥130 = $0.007692.[6]

Exchange rates fluctuate based on changes in demand and supply for a given currency in relation to another currency. In principle, if U.S. citizens begin to buy more European-made goods and services in relation to European citizens' purchases of U.S.-made goods and services, the euro would start to increase in relation to the dollar. Central banks of various countries often trade in the markets, however, and exert enormous pressure on their currencies, sometimes to the point of artificially inflating or deflating the values of their currencies in relation to what they should be. And of course, foreign exchange traders engage in transactions as they attempt to anticipate what will happen in the market. Their expectations, whether ultimately right or wrong, will, thus, be a major determinant of foreign exchange rates.

These changes in exchange rates obviously affect any organization that buys or sells its products or services internationally, as well as those that buy raw materials internationally. In addition, there is a subtle form of exchange rate risk that affects organizations that may appear to do no direct international business. Such a business may be affected by how exchange rates render foreign competition and foreign-made substitute products less or more expensive. Thus, exchange rate fluctuations can have a significant impact on an entity even if its business is completely domestic.

In Exhibit 4-4, we look at the history of one particular exchange rate, the euro in relation to the dollar through 2017. The euro was introduced in 1999, so the history is not particularly long.

---

[6]It is also possible to express the price of any asset in this inverted manner. For example, a Coca-Cola that costs $2.50 could be expressed in terms of the cost of a dollar with respect to a Coca-Cola. Thus, $1 would be worth 1/$2.50 = 0.40 Coca-Colas. A share of Siemens stock selling for €97 could be expressed as the cost of a euro in terms of Siemens shares, which is 1/€97 = 0.010309. That is, one euro is worth 0.010309 shares of Siemens. While exchange rates are easily interpreted in the reverse manner, it is considerably less intuitive to interpret the prices of securities and ordinary goods this way. Imagine shopping on the Internet and seeing that a Sony PlayStation on the U.S. site of Amazon costs 0.004545: That is, 1/0.004545 = $220.

Exhibit 4-4. Monthly Value of the Euro in Dollars

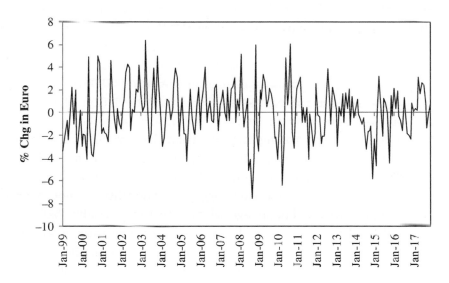

Exhibit 4-5. Monthly Percentage Changes in the Euro

As of this writing, the euro has been as high as $1.58, which occurred in the summer of 2008, and as low as $0.85, which occurred in the summer of 2001. As we previously noted, a better impression of the changes can be obtained by observing the relative changes. Exhibit 4-5 shows the monthly percentage changes in the euro.

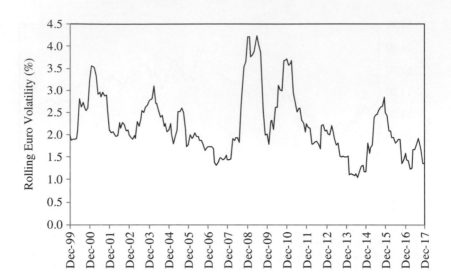

Exhibit 4-6. Rolling Volatility of Monthly Percentage Changes in Euro

We see that these percentage changes have fluctuated around a value of zero. Indeed that result makes sense. Over the long run, no currency should trend upward against another, as this pattern would imply that the weaker currency would eventually be worth almost nothing compared to the stronger currency. The average percentage change in the euro is 0.06%.

Finally, we see the rolling monthly standard deviation of the euro in Exhibit 4-6. We note that the euro is not nearly as volatile as LIBOR. We mentioned that the rolling LIBOR volatility averages around 6.1%. The average rolling euro volatility is around 2.2% with a maximum of about 4.2% and a minimum of around 1%. This observation suggests that it is worth pointing out that exchange rate volatility is not nearly as high one might expect. The image of the currency trader battling the unpredictable and massive ups and downs of exchange rates is an illusion. Exchange rate volatility is one of the lowest volatilities in the market. Let us keep that fact in mind as we now look at oil as a source of commodity price risk.

4.2.1.3 *Commodity Prices*

Commodities are assets that typically have various practical applications but are used for investment purposes. The class of instruments known as commodities includes (1) fossil fuels, such as oil, coal, and natural gas,

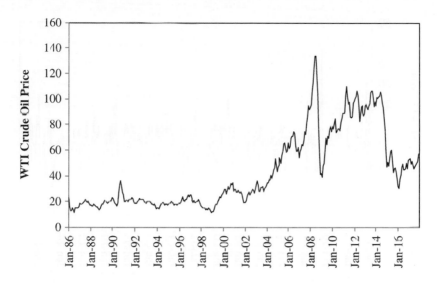

Exhibit 4-7.   Monthly West Texas Intermediate Crude Oil

(2) precious metals such as gold, silver, and platinum, and (3) agricultural products, such as corn, soybeans, and wheat. In this section, we will take a look at oil, specifically West Texas Intermediate crude oil, referred to as WTI. WTI is but one form of crude oil, which is of course but one form of fossil fuel, though a very important one and one that is closely observed by market participants. Clearly energy is a driving force behind the global economy, and energy prices exert pressure on every entity on the planet.

Exhibit 4-7 shows the historical monthly price of WTI through 2017. It has ranged from a high of almost $134 a barrel in the summer of 2008 to a low of nearly $11 a barrel in December of 1998.

Exhibit 4-8 shows the monthly percentage changes in WTI, which clearly illustrate several periods with sharp spikes. We notice that large increases occurred in 1990, in particular in August when the price increased by more than 48%. Large price decreases occurred in 2008 when the market began adjusting to the global recession.

Finally, Exhibit 4-9 shows the rolling 12-month volatility of the percentage changes in WTI. We see that some periods of oil volatility have been extremely high, with an average of about 7.7%, a maximum of about 19.7% and a minimum of about 3.3%. This notion of fluctuating volatility gives rise to the concept of the risk of risk that we mentioned in Chapter 2 and to which we will return later.

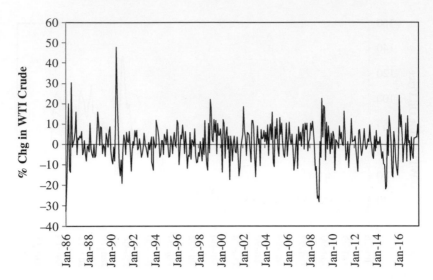

Exhibit 4-8. Monthly Percentage Changes in West Texas Intermediate Crude Oil

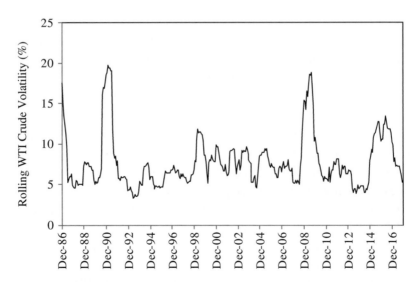

Exhibit 4-9. Rolling Volatility of Monthly Percentage Changes in West Texas Intermediate Crude Oil

4.2.1.4 *Stock Prices*

Of course, stock prices are widely followed by investors in the global economy. The performance of the stock market may well be one of the most watched indicators of economic activity and is a major item provided by all news services. Oddly enough, however, stock price risk is not necessarily a direct concern of most corporations. Naturally, publicly traded companies do care about their own market values, but a company's stock price is a broad reflection of investors' views of all of the company's expected future performance. Companies do not manage risk, however, by managing their own stock price. They manage risk by managing the risks that affect their operations. Most businesses do not invest heavily in the stock market: they invest in the assets they need to produce their products and services. Thus, the stock market is not a direct source of risk for most companies. A business might well have a pension fund that invests in the market, so it is not completely immune from the market, but the pension fund is not its primary business. The point is that the assets of most businesses are exposed to interest rates and some to exchange rates and commodity prices but not directly to stock prices. Inasmuch as the stock market is a barometer of the expected overall economy, businesses may be sensitive to movements in the stock market, but this sensitivity is indirect. It is the overall economy to which they are fundamentally sensitive.

Clearly these points do not apply to entities that manage equity portfolios. This class of organizations, called asset management firms, includes mutual funds, hedge funds, endowments, and pensions.

Nonetheless, it is useful to take a look at the level and risk of the stock market. Exhibit 4-10 shows the S&P 500, a measure of roughly the 500 largest companies in the U.S. from 1950 through 2017.[7]

We see that much of the growth of the index has occurred in the last 30 years, though some dips have been quite sharp. Exhibit 4-11 shows the monthly percentage changes.

Notice the sharp fluctuations in 1987. In October of 1987 the S&P 500 fell more than 21%, reflecting a decline of slightly more than 20% on a single day, October 19. In spite of that precipitous drop, the S&P 500 was up for that year about 2%. We also see that large drops occurred in August of 1998, about −14.5%, and in October 2008, almost −17%.

Exhibit 4-12 shows the rolling monthly volatility of the S&P 500.

Here we see that there have been several volatility spikes, meaning periods of very high volatility, since 1950. These occurred in 1974, 1987,

---

[7]The S&P 500 was not actually created until 1957, but it has been constructed backwards in time by determining its value had it been created earlier than it was.

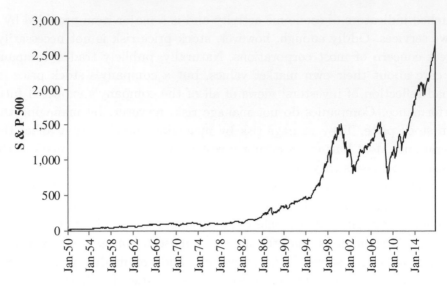

Exhibit 4-10.   Monthly Level of S&P 500

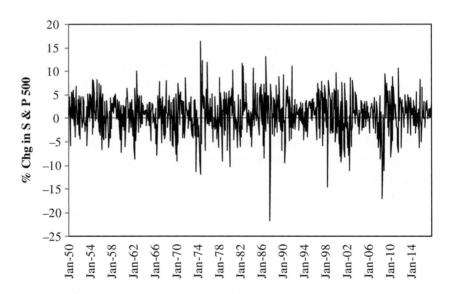

Exhibit 4-11.   Monthly Percentage Changes in S&P 500

and 2009, reaching a maximum of around 9% a month. The minimum has been around 1.1% a month, and the average rolling volatility is around 3.8%. Stock market volatility has indeed fluctuated quite a lot over time, again giving rise to the notion that volatility is volatile.

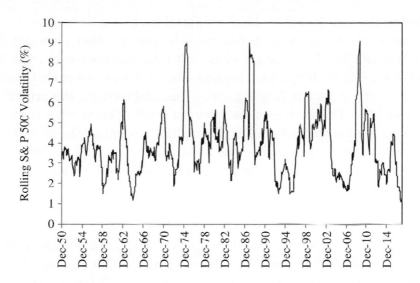

Exhibit 4-12. Rolling Monthly Volatility of Percentage Changes in S&P 500

4.2.2 *Credit Risk*

The direct source of credit risk is the default by a party on an amount it owes to another party. A default could occur on a loan or bond or it could occur on a lease, which is a type of contract in which one party agrees to lend another the use of an asset in return for a series of agreed-upon payments. Failure to make a required lease payment is a default. The required loan or bond payments could be interest, principal, or sinking fund payments on certain bonds. Note that we said that the *direct* source of credit risk is the potential for default. There are also several indirect sources. One is the *potential* for default. Suppose for example that party A owes money to bank B, but the next payment is not due for a year. Party A, however, gets into serious financial trouble. Even though the loan payment is not due for a year, the potential for default becomes much higher, and the bank would need to seriously consider the possibility that it will not get paid at this later date. When situations like this arise, banks will sometimes take a charge against earnings to reflect the increased potential for default.

There is yet one other indirect source of credit risk, and that is the risk that the defaults of other parties will have an effect on parties not engaged in the specific loans that defaulted. The financial crisis of 2008 is a good example. The tremendous number of defaults and the increased potential for default resulted in a substantial loss of stock market value and a weakening of the economy that affected almost everyone.

Bonds that are issued by large corporations and governments trade in a market in which holders of bonds can sell them to other investors. Bond prices fluctuate based on changes in interest rates and also on changes in the potential for default. If you were holding a bond of a borrower that suddenly announced that it was undergoing severe financial distress, the price of that bond would fall. This decline in the price is a result of an increase in the yield or expected return on the bond, as the creditor recognizes the increased risk that interest and/or principal on the bond will not be paid in the future.

A major factor that drives the prices of bonds is credit ratings, sometimes called bond ratings, provided by certain companies that specialize in evaluating the creditworthiness of bonds. Standard and Poor's (S&P) and Moody's are the two most well-known such companies. S&P ratings are classified into the following broad categories: AAA, AA, A, BBB, BB, B, CCC, CC, C, R, SD, D, and NR. The categories of AA through CCC can also be modified with a plus (+) or a minus (−). Bonds in the highest category, AAA, referred to as "triple-A," are believed to essentially have no risk of default. The category R means that the company, often a bank, is under regulatory supervision. The SD rating means that the company has selectively defaulted on some obligations. The rating D means that the company has defaulted and it is believed that it will do so on remaining obligations. NR means that the bond issue is not rated. Moody's has a similar set of ratings but uses upper and lower case letters as well as numbers. It appends 1, 2, or 3 to each category from Aa through Caa. The S&P category AA+ is equivalent to Moody's category Aa1.

The ratings companies evaluate the likelihood of default and assign a rating at the time the bond is issued. They follow the companies and change the ratings when they believe the issuer has a higher or lower chance of default. Bonds rated BBB or above are referred to as *investment grade*, while bonds below BBB are referred to as *speculative*. Obviously these terms are extremely subjective, but they are so commonly used that you should be familiar with them.

Exhibit 4-13 shows the historical default rates for investment grade, speculative, and overall bonds since 1981 through 2016.[8]

The overall historical default rate over that period averages about 1.46%. The average for speculative grade bonds is 4.08%, while the average for investment grade bonds is 0.09%. It is easy to see how the rate for speculative grade bonds rises during weaker economies. It was as high as 11.05% in 1991.

---

[8]http://www.spratings.com

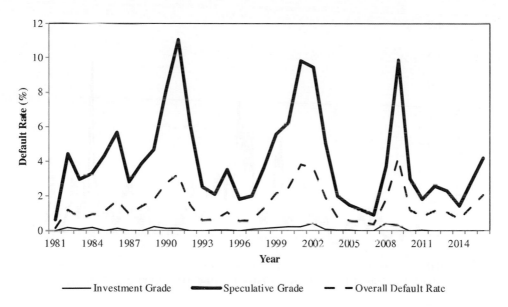

Exhibit 4-13. Historical Default Rates for Investment Grade, Speculative, and Overall Bonds

Exhibit 4-14 shows the monthly yield differential between the Moody's Aaa-rated bonds and Baa rated bonds since 1950 through 2017. Having higher credit risk, the Baa-rated bonds have a higher yield. Thus, the series that is graphed is the Baa yield minus the Aaa yield.

The spread averages 0.96%, with a maximum of 3.38% in December 2008 and a minimum of 0.32% in January of 1966.

While these exhibits give a picture of the default rates and potential for large corporate borrowers to default, they do not tell us anything about small borrowers. Exhibit 4-15 shows the rates from 1985 through 2017 that banks charge for defaults, referred to here as delinquencies, and for charge-offs, which reflect when banks write down loans against their earnings because they believe the loans will not be repaid. This data also includes leases provided by the banks.

The historical average delinquency rate is a little under 1%, with a maximum of 3.14% in the fourth quarter of 2009 and a minimum of 0.34% in the first quarter of 2006. The historical average charge-off rate is 3.56%, with a maximum of 7.50% in the first quarter of 2010 and a minimum of 1.45% in the second quarter of 2006.

These graphs give a general picture of the magnitude and variability in credit risk. We will study credit risk in much more detail in Chapter 11. Let us now take a first look at how organizations deal with risk.

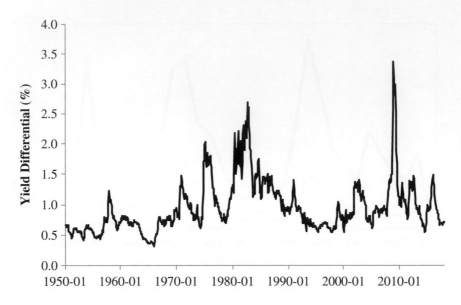

Exhibit 4-14. Yield Spread between Aaa- and Baa-Rated Bonds

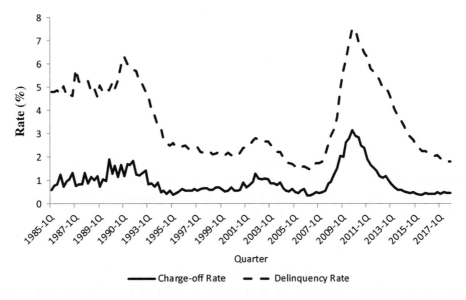

Exhibit 4-15. Historical Quarterly Charge-Off and Delinquency Rates of U.S. Banks

4.3 How Organizations Deal with Risk

There are five primary ways in which an entity can manage risk: forecasting, diversification, coercive transfer, deceptive transfer, and cooperative transfer.

The process of cooperative transfer takes several forms: spot market transactions, insurance, and derivative market transactions.[9] We now take a light look at each of these practices.

4.3.1 *Forecasting*

Forecasting is a process in which an entity makes a statement about what will happen in the future, in other words, a prediction. The prediction may be definitive, such as "it will rain," "the economy will shrink at a rate of 0.5%," or "Duke will win the NCAA basketball tournament." Or, the prediction may be given within some element of probability, as in "the chance of rain is 30%," "there is a 25% chance of a recession," or "Duke is a 2-to-1 favorite to win the NCAA basketball tournament."

In statistical terms, a prediction is often called the expected value. It is important, however, to distinguish between the true statistical expected value and the one offered by a forecaster or group of forecasters. For example, as I write this paragraph in the middle of the summer, I am looking at five forecasts of the high temperature in Los Angeles tomorrow. Accuweather predicts 83 degrees (all Fahrenheit), the Weather Channel predicts 86, Intellicast predicts a high of 83, Weather Underground predicts 80, and the U.S. National Weather Service predicts 83. A consensus estimate might be the average of 83. The long run historical average for this day according to Intellicast's historical data base is 84. Clearly tomorrow's weather is expected to be about normal. The forecasters do not provide much information other than affirm that tomorrow's weather is about normal. For Chicago, however, the long run average for that day is 85, but the weather service forecasts range from 90 to 94, an average of 93. Clearly Chicago is expected to be abnormally hot. Weather forecasters incorporate current information and projections of climatic patterns over the next 24 hours, and in all likelihood improve the forecast. If forecasters are trying to predict something that is relatively scientific and in which the past is correlated with the future, they can provide value.

[Incidentally, while the predicted high for that day in Chicago was around 93, a day later it was revealed that the actual high as recorded by Intellicast was 89.8. The predicted high for Los Angeles was about 83. The actual high was 87.2]

---

[9]See Kolb (2011b) for an excellent discussion of several of these forms of risk transfer and the costs to society.

As we described in Chapter 2, forecasts are nothing more than opinions. They may be educated opinions, but they are often biased ones. In particular, forecasters often tilt their forecasts so that they warn us of impending negative outcomes more often than they predict positive outcomes. For every financial crisis or just simply every market dip, there are those who claim to have seen it coming. Such a fact should be not surprising. At any given time, there are many people making forecasts. At any time, there are almost always people who predict falling markets, in fact sometimes predicting sharply falling markets. Every significant market drop seems to spawn a new market guru who "saw it coming." There is no evidence that any one such person can consistently call the major turns in markets, what more the future in general.[10]

Companies spend a great deal of money on forecasts and apparently take actions based on those forecasts. An argument can be made that such forecasts are useful in quantifying an expected value, from which one can then begin to gauge the possible unexpected outcomes that might be encountered. It is after all not possible to conceptualize the unexpected without an expected outcome as a benchmark. Herein lies probably the only significant value of forecasting. Yet, a lot of money is spent on obtaining these forecasts, which could often be constructed simply by historical estimates. Although it is easy to criticize using history as a benchmark, we must remember that we are not betting that the expected historical average will occur: in fact, we are pretty sure that it will not and we simply use that average as a gauge of how far off we might be.

Short-term weather predictions notwithstanding, predicting is a very difficult and inaccurate process, certainly for risk management. For example, suppose you are asked to predict tomorrow's closing value of the Dow Jones Industrial Average. You must submit your prediction at the close of business today. What is the first thing you would do? Let us hope that at the close of

---

[10]Many people give Nostradamus and Jules Verne too much credit for making predictions that came true. Nostradamus made many predictions of tragedies and the rise of dictators and powerful monarchs, which hardly seems remarkable. Up to that point, history had a long litany of tragedies and dictators. Had he named names, such as Hitler and Napoleon, and identified years, the predictions would have been a bit more impressive. Jules Verne is widely credited with predicting space travel, but in his time, humans had already begun to travel in balloons, so extrapolating that feat into a highly technical machine that could go high in the air might seem incredibly imaginative but is actually fairly unimpressive. His most famous novel, *Twenty Thousand Leagues under the Sea*, published in 1870, may have seemed to predict submarines, but early versions of submarines had appeared more than 100 years prior.

business you would determine today's closing Dow Jones Industrial Average. After all, it would probably get you somewhere within a reasonable range. If you did not know that number, you would have to rely on your memory of what you think is a reasonably close value to the current average. But why do that when you can look it up and be more accurate? Now, you must realize that just getting somewhere near the current value is not sufficient. Anyone can do that. You are trying to predict the daily return. Since the end of 1950 through 2017, the average daily return has been 0.0321%. How accurate do you think you can be? You might as well predict zero. And yet zero implies an annual expected return of 0.00%, while 0.0321% implies an annual return (multiply by 250) of 8.04%, a pretty large difference.

Go back and review Exhibits 3-2, 3-5, 3-8, and 3-11, which show the sequence of percentage changes of LIBOR, the euro, oil, and the S&P 500. If you truly believe anyone can predict such a series, this book will not do you any good. When it comes to financial markets, predicting is a poor substitute for risk management. It denies the virtual certainty that actual outcomes will not equal predicted outcomes. Perhaps worse is that it expends a great deal of money and effort on finding out just how wrong you can be by relying on predicting.

4.3.2 *Diversification*

One of the most important principles of financial risk management and indeed in all of the discipline of finance is that of diversification. The principle has apparently been known for a long time, and is the origin of the idiom *don't put all of your eggs in one basket*. Although some very successful people have parodied the expression by saying that it seems to be appropriate to put all of your eggs in one basket if you watch that basket very closely, it is easy to argue after the achievement of success that putting all of your risk in the same place was a good strategy. We never hear from the losers who put all of their eggs in one basket and dropped the basket.

The principle of financial diversification is a solidly grounded result that relies on an assumption of less-than-perfect correlation between assets. Finance courses and books often illustrate how the addition of an asset with less than perfect correlation to a portfolio reduces risk. Indeed, we showed how this happens in Chapter 3. This type of thinking is common but not always correct. The addition of a less than perfectly correlated asset to a portfolio does not always reduce the risk. In addition, it can also reduce the return by considerably more. Here is an example.

Consider a broadly diversified portfolio with an expected return of 10% and a standard deviation of 20%. These numbers are reasonably close to the long-run expected return and volatility of the S&P 500. Now consider reallocating just 5% of that portfolio to a new stock that has an expected return of 8% and a standard deviation of 40%. Let the correlation of that stock with the portfolio be 0.75. The expected return and standard deviation of the new portfolio are

$$E(R_p) = 0.95(0.10) + (0.05)0.08 = 0.0990$$

$$\sigma_p^2 = (0.95)^2(0.20)^2 + (0.05)^2(0.40)^2$$

$$+ (0.95)(0.05)(0.75)(0.20)(0.40) = 0.0422$$

$$\sigma_p = \sqrt{0.0422} = 0.2054.$$

The expected return is 1% lower, the variance is 5.5% higher, and the standard deviation is 2.71% higher, all from just re-allocating 5% to the new stock.

Other examples can also be created. One can reduce the risk but reduce the expected return by a greater percentage, thereby reducing the risk-reward tradeoff. In the above example, if the expected return on the new asset were 4%, the reallocation would result in the overall expected return falling from 10% to 9.7%, a 3% drop, while the variance would fall from 0.04 to 0.0395, a reduction of 1.15%, and the standard deviation would fall from 0.2 to 0.1988, a reduction of −0.58%.

Therefore, in spite of what you have heard, the addition of securities does not reduce risk and improve the risk-return tradeoff in every single situation. For it to do so, certain things have to be true. In particular, if the new asset has very high correlation with the existing portfolio, it is much harder for the new asset to spread out the risk.

As a general rule, diversification is thought to be a type of free risk reduction. Indeed, it can be and often is for investment managers holding very large portfolios. The marginal impact of any one asset on the expected return is fairly small and the effect is linear. Note the equation for expected return, as in the calculation directly above. The new asset affects the expected return in a linear manner. The effect on risk, however, is non-linear. The risk reduction if it occurs can therefore be proportionately greater than the effect on return. But, as we see here, risk reduction must occur, and that is not always the case.

As we will see in Section 4.3.7, the insurance profession relies almost entirely on the principle of diversification. As a risk management tool, most organizations use insurance in some form for certain types of risk, thereby expecting the insurer to pool risks. As a direct risk management tool, however, diversification is of very limited value for two reasons.

One is that most companies do not have such a large pool of low-correlated assets that they can diversify effectively, improving their risk-reward tradeoffs. Second, diversification at the corporate level is unlikely to benefit shareholders, because those shareholders could presumably buy and sell shares of stock that would enable them to gain or reduce exposure to whatever diversifying line of business the company is adding. In fact, there is some evidence that diversified companies sell at a discount that is attributable to the diversification. Nonetheless, many companies do manage risk this way by engaging in diversification by asset acquisitions and mergers. For example, if an oil company decides to reallocate some of its assets into a new line of business, say the filming and distribution of movies, it is engaging in diversification. If the oil company decides to buy a movie film and distribution company, it is also engaging in diversification.

Nonetheless, we have to conclude that for most entities, diversification is not a practical means of managing risk. The exception is certainly for asset management companies, but even then, they must be particularly careful about whether the reallocation truly improves the tradeoff of risk to return.

4.3.3 *Coercive Transfer*

Coercive transfer occurs when one party exercises power over the other and forces the other to accept the risk. A good example of this is universal health care. A society without universal health care usually has a large number of uninsured people. It is reasonable to presume that a large number of these people are low income and somewhat unhealthy. A mandatory health insurance program uses government fiat to transfer the risk to young and healthy individuals. Coercive risk transfers almost always occur with government. Another example is that government guarantees for too-big-to-fail financial institutions transfer the risk to all of society, as do deposit insurance and insurance programs for pensions. Coercive risk transfer certainly exists, but it is not a practical means of risk management for most organizations. It is, however, a common means of risk management for societies through their governments.

4.3.4 *Deceptive Transfer*

Another form of risk transfer is through deception. For example, a person who buys life insurance but engages in a high risk lifestyle without the insurance company knowing has transferred some of the risk. Of course, he has not transferred all of the risk, since he will presumably lose utility if he dies or is injured. A person who sells his house or car to another person but does not tell that person about an extremely latent or hidden problem has transferred the risk deceptively. Any seller of any product that is aware of problems but does not reveal them has transferred the risk deceptively. It goes without saying that we can hardly recommend this strategy as a risk management method. Moreover, even if we were morally depraved, there would be tremendous limits to whether we could manage risk in this manner. Other organizations tend to closely scrutinize assets they are considering for purchase.

4.3.5 *Cooperative Transfer*

Cooperative transfer refers to the type of risk transfer in which each party is aware of the risk and agrees to the terms. We are not saying that each party is in complete agreement on the risks. We simply mean that each party enters into the transaction willingly. For example, if a company were selling a division to another company, the seller apparently considers the risk-reward tradeoff unacceptable. The buyer apparently considers it acceptable. The two parties simply have different opinions. We cannot rule out deceit in all practical situations, but we will assume there is none. There are three forms of cooperative transfer: spot market transactions, insurance, and derivative market transactions.

4.3.6 *Spot Market Transactions*

As previously described, the spot market is the market where transactions are done immediately, as opposed to the derivatives market where transactions are arranged and agreed upon but consummated at a later date. The term *spot market* is derived from the expression *on the spot*, meaning something done immediately. One very simple and straightforward method of managing financial risk is to engage in spot market transactions. In so doing, the entity transfers the risk to a willing party. As an example, suppose the corporate treasurer of a U.S. company knows that he will need to borrow $10 million six months from now with the rate set when the loan begins.

He realizes that he is exposed to the risk of interest rates over the next six months. One option is to do nothing right now, but that choice leaves him vulnerable to the risk that interest rates will increase during the next six months. If that happens, when he eventually borrows the money, he will have to pay more interest. Another alternative is to go ahead and borrow the money now, but in that case, he pays interest for six months on money he does not currently need. Or suppose he is not absolutely certain that he needs the loan in six months. Borrowing now is a commitment for money he may not need and a waste of money on the interest.

Consider another scenario in which a Belgian investment manager has a portfolio consisting of €30 million invested in a European stock index exchange-traded fund (ETF) and €20 million in a European bond index ETF. The manager currently has an allocation of 60% to stock and 40% to bonds, and this allocation is his desired long run allocation. A year later, the stock index ETF has risen to a value of €34.5 million and the bond index ETF has fallen to €19.75. Now the allocation is 63.6% to stock and 36.4% to bonds. The policy is to rebalance at least annually or whenever the actual allocation moves away from the desired allocation by at least 3% on an absolute basis. Since 63.6% is slightly more than 3% absolute from the desired allocation of 60%, a reallocation is required. The portfolio value is €34.5 + €19.75 = €54.25, so to return to the desired allocation, the equity ETF would need to have a value of €54.25 × 0.6 = €32.55 and the bond ETF would require a value of €54.25 × 0.4 = €21.70. Thus, the manager would need to sell €34.5 − €32.55 = €1.95 million of the equity ETF and buy the same amount of the bond ETF. The manager could do these trades directly in the spot market, selling the stock ETF and buying the equivalent amount of the bond ETF. Alternatively, he could do the trade in the derivatives market, which has considerable advantages, as we will begin to discuss in Section 4.4.

4.3.7 *Insurance*

Insurance is one of the oldest forms of risk management known to mankind. Although its origins are difficult to identify, a variation of insurance is referred to in the Code of Hammurabi, around 1754 BC. The first person to construct a mortality table was either John Graunt, an English statistician, in 1662, or it may have been Edmund Halley, noted for the famous comet, in 1693. It is often unclear as to who was really first. But in any case, data of this sort formed the basis for the business of life insurance, which began in London early in the 18th century.

One of the early and most successful uses of insurance was in the management of the risks of shipping. Until modern times, shipping was extremely dangerous. Weather, shipwrecks, and piracy were major risks faced in shipping. When the owners of a ship sent it out, they never knew if it was coming back. Insurance contracts developed to provide compensation to the owners if the ship was destroyed. The owner would pay a premium before sending the ship out. The seller of the insurance contract, called the underwriter, would use historical statistical data to estimate expected losses and would determine the premium in such a manner that expected losses would be covered, a margin of error would be provided, and the insurer would earn a profit.

Of course, as we know today, insurance is widely used to cover the risk of loss from casualty damages, health expenses, and loss of life itself. The concept of insurance is based on the aforementioned principle of diversification of risks. An insurer collects statistical data on the frequency of the risk it is insuring and calculates the premium to provide sufficient funds to cover losses to a margin of error and earn a profit. As long as the insurer diversifies the risks, the realized amount of loss claims will not vary greatly from the expected amount. If the risks are not diversified, however, the realized amount of claims can greatly exceed the premiums collected. For example, if the insurer sells too many policies that cover weather damage in a given area, a severe storm can result in an unexpectedly large number of claims. This example is a clear case of too high of a correlation between assets.

To control the problem of having undiversified risks, the insurance industry has developed a system called reinsurance in which insurers can sell risks to other insurers. For example, consider a company that has written a substantial amount of property insurance on the U.S. Gulf Coast where there is significant risk of catastrophic loss from hurricanes. No insurer wants to turn down customers, but no insurer can afford to absorb too much concentrated risk. Thus, these insurers with concentrated hurricane risk can sell some of the coverage to other insurers who bear different risks. For example, in the central Midwest part of the U.S., there is a high degree of tornado risk, and in California there is a great deal of earthquake risk. Insurers with heavy concentrations of risk in these areas can sell some of that risk to insurers of property in the U.S. Gulf Coast, who can sell some of their risk to insurers in the Midwest and California.

AIG, Diversification, and Credit Derivatives

The American International Group (AIG) is a New York-based global insurance company that originated in Shanghai, China in 1919 under the name American Asiatic Underwriters. Incorporated under its current name in 1967, AIG had been an extremely successful insurance company until the financial crisis of 2008, for which some people claim was largely due to AIG's reckless engagement in high risk transactions.

Over its history, AIG has offered a broad variety of traditional insurance services. Growing substantially due to its international operations (hence, the "I" in its name), AIG ultimately became a leading insurer for consumers as well. Early in the 21st century, AIG began to get into the business of insuring against default in the form of credit default swaps. A credit default swap or CDS is an arrangement in which one party, the risk seller, agrees to make a series of periodic fixed payments to another party, the risk buyer, who agrees to indemnify the risk seller in the event of a credit loss. Though there are many more details of these arrangements and we will study them in Chapter 11, the essential idea is that the risk seller pays a sum of money and the risk buyer agrees to cover losses if they occur during the life of the contract. Thus, a CDS is like an insurance policy against default, though it is not called *insurance*, because in the U.S., insurance is regulated at the state level and has extensive and quite onerous requirements that must be met by risk buyers. By not referring to the product as insurance, CDS sellers can effectively provide insurance as though it were just another derivative. In fact, by calling it a swap, the arrangement gave the illusion that credit default swaps were just slight variations of simple interest rate and currency swaps, which had operated for many years without any problems.

As a traditional insurer, AIG relied on the ability to diversify its risk. AIG would not insure too many adjacent houses against fire. It would either not sell the policies or it would sell the policies and then sell the risk to other insurers in the reinsurance market. When AIG went into the CDS market, it attempted to operate in much the same way. It felt that credit, like all other risks, was diversifiable. AIG hired a well-known professor to build models that would help it manage the risk. It stated repeatedly that it did not have excessive risk. But it did.

When the financial crisis of 2008 occurred, AIG fell into deep trouble. The crisis was rooted in the subprime mortgage market, which arose from the easy, cheap, and excessive mortgage lending that occurred as part of the U.S. government's program to make home ownership affordable for everyone. We hardly have the space here to cover the Financial Crisis, but suffice it to say that mortgage loans were available to people who had no jobs or assets. When house prices turned downward, the loans exceeded the collateral values for millions of individuals and as a result, defaults and the threat of defaults ensued.

AIG had insured billions of dollars of portfolios of these mortgages and began to reel from pressure placed on it to provide more collateral to cover its future potential obligations. Ironically, this insurer of credit losses became a high risk party itself. Eventually AIG reached a point at which it no longer had the resources to meet these collateral demands. Because the failure of AIG would have placed tremendous stress on the financial system and would nullify millions of consumer insurance policies, the U.S. government and the Federal Reserve bailed out AIG by injecting over $180 billion to keep the company alive. And it was a good investment. AIG eventually paid back a little over $200 billion.

The lesson to be learned from AIG is that financial models are never perfect and diversification sometimes sounds better than it is. In spite of the enormous confidence placed in them by quantitative analysts, financial models are models of human behavior that are often required to be credible in stressful market environments. AIG never expected credit defaults and the threat of more defaults to be so widespread, but credit risk is not diversifiable the way life and property risk are. Recessions can cut deeply into the core of an economy, and there is no way to diversify that risk.

Sources: Kolb (2011a) and Mollenkamp *et al.* (2008)

In some respects, insurance is one of the easiest of all businesses. Underwriters have a considerable amount of data on the risks and expected losses. Determining an insurance premium is fairly simple, particularly for life insurance. Statistical data will tell insurers what percentage of the population of newborn babies will die within five years, 10 years, 15 years, etc. The average age of death is the life expectancy of a person. For babies born in the U.S., the life expectancy as of 2014 as reported by the Center for Disease Control for a white, non-Hispanic female is 81.3 years. Given the distribution of how many people will die at various ages of their lives, the insurer can calculate the required premium, which will take into account its ability to invest the premium and earn additional returns. Some insurance policies also provide a return to the insured and some can serve as collateral for loans. Again, insurers have sufficient data to enable them to calculate the necessary premiums given these conditions. Insurers also adjust premiums for known conditions that can tilt the risk in one direction or another. For example, holders of college degrees typically get lower rates on auto and life insurance as they have slightly less risk. Non-smokers may get better rates on health insurance for obvious reasons.

Because insurers have such accurate data on their overall risk and because they diversify these risks, they are not particularly concerned about the risk of any one insured party. The greatest risk to an insurance company is in its investment portfolio. An insurer may factor in a certain rate of return expected to be earned on premiums collected, but the actual return may be less.

Most organizations, both companies and non-profits, manage some of their risk through insurance policies. Insurance is not, however, an effective mechanism for managing many of the financial risks faced by an entity. A primary reason for this problem is in the regulatory structure of the insurance business. Governments traditionally view insurance as a consumer product that is widely used across income brackets. In a desire to protect consumers, the insurance industry is heavily regulated. In the U.S. for example, insurance is regulated at the state level. Thus, there are 50 insurance regulators. If an insurer wants to do business in all 50 states, it must deal with 50 different regulators. Thus, insurance can be a costly and cumbersome product to offer to manage financial risks. As we will see shortly, there are similar but much more efficient products that can be used to manage financial risks. That said, these financial products are not as well-suited to manage the risks of property, casualty, life, and health risks as are traditional insurance policies.

Interestingly, the expression *risk management* has been widely used in the insurance business for far longer than it has been used in its current form, the management of financial risk of a company or non-profit. The notion of insurance has been synonymous with the notion of risk management, and the terms are historically interchangeable. Yet, in the last 30 years, the term has come to mean far more than insurance, and that is the subject of this book.

4.3.8 Derivative Market Transactions

To understand derivatives and derivatives market transactions, we must first understand the concept of the *spot market*, sometimes called the *cash market*. Of course, we covered this concept in Section 4.3.6. A spot market is simply a market for a transaction that is done immediately. If this notion causes confusion, it is likely because you have not done a transaction in the derivatives market. In a spot transaction, the buyer and seller meet and agree to engage in a transaction at that time. Buying or selling a stock is a spot transaction, as is buying and selling a car, a house, your groceries or most other consumer goods. In contrast, a derivative transaction is one in which the two parties agree on a transaction that will occur at a later date.[11] The two parties establish all of the terms of the transaction, in particular the price, but they do not engage in the transaction until a later date. During the intervening period, the item that is to be delivered by the seller and purchased by the buyer can experience fluctuations in value, making the derivative contract beneficial to one party and harmful to the other.

Derivatives can provide the two parties the mutual obligation to engage in the future transaction, or to one party, the right but not the obligation to engage in the future transaction. They can also provide for a single future transaction or multiple future transactions. Derivatives are such an important part of the practice of risk management that we will take them up in more detail in Part III and in even more detail throughout the rest of this book.

There is actually one final method of managing risk that we should mention: doing nothing. Ignoring risk is one of the most dangerous things organizations can do, however, and most have come to learn that doing nothing, while possibly a reasonable strategy for the risks it is consciously willing to take, is an extremely naïve and dangerous strategy for most risks. And besides, there are so many ways to manage risk that doing nothing is just the lazy way. In the next section let us take our first look at derivatives, just below the surface.

4.4 Derivative Tools for Managing Risk

In 2009, the International Swaps and Derivatives Association conducted a survey of the 500 largest companies in the world, covering 32 countries.

---

[11]Some spot transactions do have an element of delayed consummation. For example, when two parties agree to buy and sell a house, there is generally a period of time over which the paperwork is done, the financing is arranged, and inspections of the property are made. All of the terms are agreed to, but the transaction itself occurs somewhat later. Nonetheless, this type of transaction is still considered a spot transaction even though as we will see later, it has the characteristics of a derivative transaction. Similar comments might apply for buying a car, even though the period from the time the parties agree on the transaction to the time the transaction is actually done is considerably shorter.

It found that 94% of these companies use derivatives. So derivatives must be important. Let us get to know them a little here, in preparation for what we will learn in later chapters.

First, let us state a formal definition of a derivative.

A derivative is a contract between two parties that provides for a payoff at a future date that will be determined by the value of an underlying asset, rate, other derivative, or risk factor.

Let us take the elements of that definition one-by-one. First, we see that it is a contract between two parties. Being a contract, it is a legal agreement engaged in by the two parties. These two parties are referred to as the *buyer* and the *seller*. In financial transactions, the party referred to as the buyer is said to be the owner of the contract and is described as being *long* or having a *long position*. A buyer of a derivative is sometimes simply referred to as *the long*. In financial transactions, the seller is said to be *short* and is sometimes referred to as *the short* or having a *short position*. Parties that are long benefit from increases in the underlying and parties that are short benefit from decreases in the underlying. For further review of the long-short concept, see Chapter 3.

Continuing with this definition of a derivative, we see that a derivative provides for a payoff at a future date that will be determined by the value of an underlying asset, rate, other derivative, or risk factor. In other words, at a future date, a derivative will make a payoff from one of the parties to the other. This payoff is based on the value of an underlying asset, rate, other derivative, or a risk factor. Assets are easy to identify. Derivatives can be based on stocks, bonds, commodities, or anything that might be called an asset. A derivative, however, can also make its payoff based on a rate, such as LIBOR or the euro exchange rate, as we examined earlier in this chapter. A derivative can also have its payoff based on another derivative, which of course has its payoff based on an underlying asset, rate, other derivative, or risk factor. Note that we have referenced the somewhat opaque expression, *risk factor*. A risk factor can be anything that represents a source of risk not already encompassed by assets, rates, or derivatives. An example would be weather, inflation, the cost of shipping, or electricity. None of these factors are assets but all can be a source of risk to many entities.

The notion of an underlying asset, rate, other derivative, or risk factor can be a difficult concept to grasp when first trying to understand what a derivative is. First note that the word *underlying* applies to all of these words. The derivative is based on an underlying asset, underlying rate, underlying other derivative, or underlying risk factor. As such, the derivatives industry has taken to referring to the underlying asset, rate, other derivative, or risk factor as simply *the underlying*. Thus, derivatives are said to be based on an underlying. As awkward as that expression sounds, it greatly facilitates the terminology and conveys the meaning with considerable clarity.

On the English Word *Underlying*

In the definition of a derivative, we refer to an underlying asset, rate, other derivative, or risk factor. The payoff of a derivative is based on this asset, rate, other derivative, or risk factor. A derivative is said to *derive* its value from something else. A derivative can be based on an underlying asset, such as a stock, bond, or commodity. Or a derivative can be based on a rate, such as an interest rate or an exchange rate. An exchange rate is actually not so much a rate as it is the price of an asset — the foreign currency. Nonetheless, we typically refer to the price of a foreign currency as a rate, specifically an exchange rate. A derivative can be based on another derivative. Later in this book, we will become quite familiar with a derivative called a swaption, which is an option based on a swap. Thus, a swaption is one derivative based on another derivative. Finally, there are derivatives that are based on rather vague sources of risk known as risk factors. A risk factor is a catch-all category that can accommodate such derivatives on the weather, inflation, the cost of shipping, or electricity. Most any other underlying that financial institutions have come up with in the past or will do so in the future will fall into one of these categories.

But we cannot say that a derivative is based on an underlying asset, when it may be on an underlying rate, underlying other derivative, or underlying risk factor. We cannot use any one of these categories and cover all of the others. Thus, to keep from having to always refer to an underlying asset, rate, other derivative, or risk factor, the industry has adopted a rather generic term, *the underlying*.

English is the language of global finance and is an extremely flexible language. New words are constantly being added, and there is no oversight entity so sometimes these words violate well-established rules. In this case, *underlying* is a violation of the structure of English. The word *underlying* is a participle, which is an adjective constructed out of a verb. In this case the verb is *to underlie,* meaning to *lie below* so as to form the foundation of something. Under the traditional rules of English, we would not say "the underlying," as this expression should be prompted with a response of "the underlying what?" *Underlying* is a participle, so it acts like an adjective, so it must be modifying something, right? Yet, when *underlying* is used in the context of derivatives, it is used as a noun. One need not say "the underlying asset" or "the underlying rate," for example. One can just say, "the underlying."

So in spite of violating the rules of English, the use of the word *underlying* serves an extremely useful purpose in the world of derivatives. We can even shorten the definition of a derivative to the following:

A derivative is a contract between two parties that provides for a payoff at a future date that will be determined by the value of an underlying.

There are two primary classes of derivatives. One is called *forward commitments* and the other, *contingent claims*. Forward commitments are derivative contracts that require that the two parties engage in the future transaction. When a forward commitment is created, one party agrees to buy the underlying from the other at a future date at a price they agree on now. In addition to the price, the two parties agree on all other terms and conditions of the contract, including what the specific underlying is, how many units of the underlying will be exchanged, when the transaction will occur in the future, and how payment will be settled.[12] A forward commitment is exactly what it says, a commitment. Neither party can legally back out of the obligation, although bankruptcy is possible. The family of forward commitments includes forward contracts, futures contracts, and swaps. We will discuss each type of forward commitment in detail in later chapters.

Contingent claims include a class of derivatives called options. An option is a derivative contract in which one party pays a sum of money today to the other, and obtains the right to buy or sell the underlying at a later date, at the price agreed on today. As indicated, the buyer of an option acquires *the right* to buy or sell the underlying at a later date *but not the obligation* to do so. Using that right is referred to as *exercising* the option. If the value of the underlying at the later date is not favorable, the option buyer will choose not to exercise the option, thereby allowing it to expire. As mentioned, an option can provide the right to buy the underlying or the right to sell the underlying, but it does not provide both rights at the same time. An option

---

[12]Derivative contracts can be settled by actual delivery of the underlying or an equivalent cash settlement. We will explain this distinction later.

to buy is referred to as a *call option* or just a *call*, and an option to sell is referred to as a *put option* or just a *put*.

This family of derivatives that is referred to as contingent claims is largely comprised of options, but there are so many varieties of options that we sort of need a broader term, hence the words *contingent claims*. For example, a few paragraphs above, we mentioned that there are options on swaps. While these instruments are technically options, they are not called options. Instead they are called swaptions. In addition, callable and convertible bonds contain options embedded within them, but they are not called options. Many instruments contain elements of spot transactions or other derivatives combined with options.

We will be covering these instruments in much detail in later chapters. For now, let us take a brief introduction to derivatives. In order to facilitate our initial explanation of derivatives, we are going to position ourselves in a scenario. First we introduce the notion of time. Today will be referred to as time 0. The derivative expires at time T. You could as easily think of 0 as today's date and T as a date in the future. It will eventually be beneficial to obtain a measure of how much time exists between today (0) and T. Thus, we will later let $T = $ days/365, wherein T will represent the number of years until the expiration. Do not let this notion of "number of years" confuse you into thinking that a derivative must exist for more than one year. We can have fractions of a year. So, if the derivative expires in 30 days, $T = 30/365 = 0.0822$.

Let the price of the underlying today be S_0. This value is known because we can look into the spot market and observe it right now. The value of the underlying when the derivative expires at T is denoted as S_T. This value is not known today, but it will be known when time T arrives. The setup we have described is illustrated in Exhibit 4-16.

This depiction will be very useful in understanding how derivatives work.

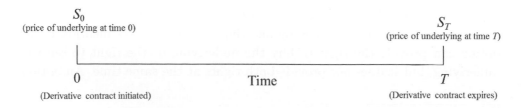

S_0
(price of underlying at time 0)

S_T
(price of underlying at time T)

0
(Derivative contract initiated)

Time

T
(Derivative contract expires)

Exhibit 4-16. Basic Setup for a Derivative Contract

4.4.1   *Forward Contracts*

As described, forward contracts are derivatives in which two parties agree to engage in a future transaction in the underlying at a price they agree on today. Thus, at time 0, they agree that one party, the buyer or long, will purchase the underlying from the other party, the seller or short, at time T at a price they agree on at time 0. In a later chapter we will explain in detail the procedure for determining the price they agree on. For right now, we will denote this price as $F(0, T)$, which represents the price agreed on at time 0 for a forward contract expiring at time T.[13] In other words, at time 0 the two parties agree that at time T, the seller will deliver the underlying to the buyer who will pay the seller $F(0, T)$.

When time T arrives, the value of the underlying is S_T. The buyer of the forward contract pays the amount $F(0, T)$ to the seller, who in turn delivers the underlying, which is worth S_T. The buyer, thus, pays $F(0, T)$ and receives an asset worth S_T, thereby netting a profit of $S_T - F(0, T)$. If the underlying is worth more than the amount paid, $S_T - F(0, T) > 0$, there is a profit or net gain to the buyer; otherwise, there is a loss to the buyer and a gain to the seller. The prospective outcomes are illustrated in the profit diagram in Exhibit 4-17.[14]

Notice that the buyer breaks even if the underlying price at expiration of the forward contract equals the agreed-upon forward price, $F(0, T)$. If the underlying price exceeds the forward price, the buyer makes a profit; otherwise, he incurs a loss. Observe how the profit potential of the buyer is unlimited, inasmuch as the underlying has no upper limit. The loss, however, is limited to $F(0, T)$ and occurs if the underlying value goes to zero.

The position of the seller is the mirror image. If the underlying is worth more than the amount paid, $S_T > F(0, T) > 0$, there is a loss to the seller; otherwise, there is a gain to the seller. Exhibit 4-18 illustrates the profit diagram for the seller, which is simply the mirror image of that of the buyer. It has unlimited loss potential and large but limited gain potential.

Forward contracts are customized transactions, meaning that the buyer and seller agree on whatever terms they so desire as long as these terms

---

[13]In this book, we will follow a general pattern that a subscript such as in S_0 or S_T indicates a time point that can change, whereas an argument indicated in parenthesis is a fixed value.

[14]We have made no assumption about how the current value of the underlying, S_0 is related to $F(0, T)$. Indeed, we will take up in Chapter 8 how the latter is derived from the former.

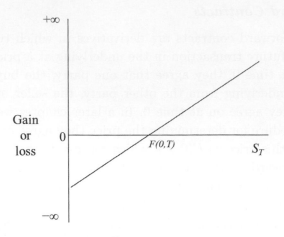

Exhibit 4-17. Profit Diagram for Buyer of Forward Contract

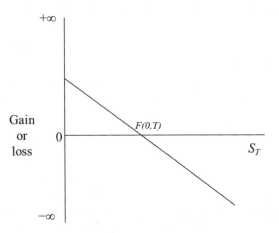

Exhibit 4-18. Profit Diagram for Seller of Forward Contract

are permitted within the laws of the country in which the transaction is made.[15] These contracts are created in a market called the *over-the-counter market*, a concept we will discuss in detail in the next chapter. We next move to futures contracts, which are similar to forward contracts, but they have some special differences.

---

[15] For example, a forward contract for an illegal substance would not be legal.

4.4.2 *Futures Contracts*

Futures contracts are standardized versions of forward contracts that trade on an organized entity called a *futures exchange*. The concept of standardization of derivatives is the notion that only certain contracts with specific terms and conditions are allowed to be traded. That is, while forward contracts can be created on virtually any underlying, futures contracts exist only on certain underlyings that have been determined by the derivatives exchange and approved by regulatory authorities. While forward contracts can have any expiration, futures contracts expire only on certain dates. In addition, while forward contracts are generally designed to be held until expiration, futures contracts can be bought and sold before expiration.[16] In essence, futures contracts can be traded much like stocks and bonds.

The gains and losses of futures contracts are settled every day, so that the profits and losses accumulated since the previous day are converted to cash as they are incurred. This system, to be covered in Chapter 5, helps assure each party that it does not have to worry about default of the other. Forward contracts are not generally conducted in this manner, though they can be operated with a similar procedure that we will cover later.

We will not illustrate the profits and losses on futures contracts, as they are essentially like those of forward contracts, as shown in Exhibits 4-17 and 4-18.

4.4.3 *Swaps*

While a forward contract is a derivative that specifies a single transaction that will be done at a future date, a swap is a derivative that specifies that the parties will engage in a series of future transactions at prices agreed upon today. Hence, the diagram in Exhibit 4-16 would apply to each of a sequence of dates, say $T_1, T_2, \ldots, T_m$ on which the parties would consummate pre-arranged transactions in the underlying at the price or rate agreed on at time 0. In essence, a swap is like a portfolio of forward contracts that expire on a series of dates in the future. Swaps are the most common form of derivative, owing to the ease and popularity of using interest rate swaps in converting floating rate loans to fixed rate loans. We will not illustrate the payoffs of swaps here, because given the multiple dates on which swaps

---

[16]While forward contracts are not typically bought and sold prior to expiration like futures contracts, it is possible to terminate them early. We will cover this point in Chapter 8.

make payments, it would be virtually impossible to do so. The payoff of any one payment is essentially the same as in Exhibits 4-17 and 4-18.

4.4.4 *Options*

As described above, an option is a derivative that grants the buyer the right but not the obligation to buy the underlying from the seller or sell the underlying to the seller. As noted, if the option is used to buy or sell the underlying, the action is referred to as *exercising the option*. Whether the option is exercised depends on whether the underlying value is above or below the fixed price the parties agreed upon at the start. This fixed price is called (alternatively) the *exercise price*, the *strike price*, the *strike*, or the *striking price*. We will more typically use the term *exercise price* and the symbol X.

As previously mentioned, an option to buy the underlying is referred to as a call option or just a call, and an option to sell the underlying is referred to as a put option or just a put. The call (put) buyer pays a premium to the call (put) seller at the start that we will denote as $c_0(X, T)(p_0(X, T))$. The subscript 0 indicates that the value reflects the information available at time 0, and that this value could change as time elapses and other information is realized. The exercise price, X, and the expiration, T, are fixed. Similarly for a put, the premium is denoted as $p_0(X, T)$.

At expiration, the buyer of a call makes a decision on whether to exercise it. If the value of the underlying is greater than the exercise price, the call is worth exercising, because the call buyer acquires the underlying that is worth S_T by paying the exercise price X, which is lower. If the value of the underlying is less than the exercise price, the call buyer will simply let the call expire unexercised.[17] The profit diagram for a call option buyer is illustrated in Exhibit 4-19.

Notice that the profit line has two distinct segments. The horizontal segment covers the range in which S_T is between 0 and X, the exercise price. If the underlying value at expiration is in this range, the option is not worth exercising at expiration. As such, the option simply expires and the call buyer generates a loss of the amount paid for the option, $c_0(X, T)$.

---

[17]We have made no assumptions about where the current value of the underlying, S_0, is in relation to the exercise price, X. The exercise price is a chosen value so it can bear any relation to the current value of the underlying as the parties desire, but how high or low it is plays a role in determining the value of the option. We will cover this topic in Chapter 10.

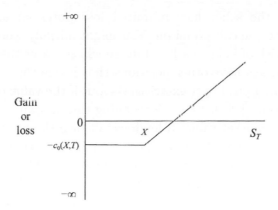

Exhibit 4-19. Profit Diagram for Buyer of Call Option

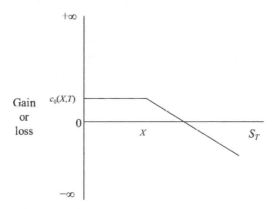

Exhibit 4-20. Profit Diagram for Seller of Call Option

The upward sloping segment of the profit diagram occurs over the range in which $S_T > X$. Over this range for the value of the underlying at expiration, the call buyer would exercise the option, thereby acquiring the underlying that is worth S_T for a price of X and netting a benefit of $S_T - X$ and a profit of $S_T - X - c_0(X, T)$. The profit figure rises directly with S_T and has no upper limit, because there is no upper limit on S_T.[18]

The profit diagram of the seller is the mirror image of that of the buyer. We illustrate the seller's position in Exhibit 4-20.

---

[18]We have not specifically mentioned the case in which $S_T = X$. This point intersects both segments of the line and can be thought of as the case in which the option could be exercised but would produce a value of zero. A similar comment will apply to puts.

Notice that the seller has unlimited loss potential and limited gain potential equal to the call premium. You might initially wonder why anyone would bear the risk of being a seller, but we will see later that knowledgeable sellers almost always have other positions that hedge the risk.

At expiration, a put buyer exercises the put if the value of the underlying is below the exercise price, $S_T < X$, meaning that he can sell the underlying for more than its market value. If he does not own the underlying, he either acquires it in the market for its price S_T, or if short selling is possible, he borrows it and sells it for X by exercising the option. If the underlying value at expiration is greater than the exercise price, $S_T > X$, the put buyer simply lets the option expire. If he needs to sell the underlying, he can get more for it by selling it at its market price, S_T, than by exercising the option. The profit diagram for a put buyer is shown in Exhibit 4-21.

Note that for values of the underlying in excess of the exercise price, X, the put is not exercised and the put buyer ends up losing the premium paid, $p_0(X,T)$. This outcome is the horizontal segment of the profit graph above. For values of the underlying below the exercise price, the put buyer exercises for a gain of $X - S_T$ and makes a profit of $X - S_T - p_0(X,T)$. This outcome is represented by the downward sloping segment above. The direction of the line segment is downward because the lower the price of the underlying at expiration, the higher the profit. There is a limited loss, though the gain is not limited and occurs if the underlying value is at zero at expiration. The put seller has the mirror image position of the put buyer, as shown in Exhibit 4-22.

These profit diagrams are commonly used to illustrate the characteristics of derivative contracts, but come with a word of caution. Profit diagrams do

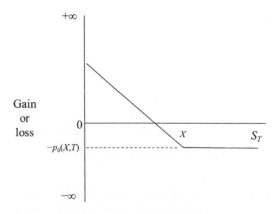

Exhibit 4-21. Profit Diagram for Buyer of Put Option

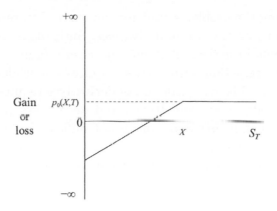

Exhibit 4-22. Profit Diagram for Seller of Put Option

not indicate the relative likelihood that a particular outcome will occur. If anything, they might even suggest that all outcomes over the range depicted are equally likely. As an example, the unlimited gain potential for the buyer of a call option, and corresponding unlimited loss potential for a seller of a call option, are extreme values that would not be expected to occur but on very rare occasions.

Another type of option is the credit default swap, which is used as insurance against credit loss. Yes, it sounds strange to refer to it as a swap. There is reason for that, but we will address it later. We will in fact cover credit default swaps in much detail in Chapter 11.

4.4.5 *Other Instruments*

There are a variety of other derivative-like instruments, but all contain a derivative embedded within them. Some of them are even referred to as hybrids, inasmuch as they combine elements of derivative and non-derivative instruments. The risk management world is an extremely creative one with literally thousands of types of instruments, but all of them generally fall into the category of having an element of a forward commitment or a contingent claim or both.

4.5 Benefits and Controversies of Derivatives

Derivatives are extremely beneficial to the markets, but they are not without controversy. In particular, when markets fall rapidly and/or when the economy nosedives, derivatives are often found in the portfolios of institutions that either fail or nearly fail. In that case, derivatives are often blamed for causing the problems, and governments often respond by putting greater restrictions on the use of derivatives. Such blame is misdirected. If a swimmer drowns in a river, it is not the river's fault. A river is clearly dangerous. Safe interaction with a river requires a considerable amount of knowledge and care. Likewise, safe use of derivatives requires a considerable amount of knowledge and care. Rivers and derivatives provide enormous benefits, but they can be misused if one is not sufficiently careful. By reading this book, you are taking the first step toward learning how to use derivatives properly. It is not time to dive into the water, but that time will come later, provided you learn this material.

4.5.1 *The Positives of Derivatives*

Let us first take a look at the benefits of derivatives. Many of these benefits are related in that some occur because of others.

4.5.1.1 *Enable the Transfer of Risk at a Fair Price*

Perhaps the most important benefit of derivatives is in their ability to enable effective risk management at a fair price. Parties wishing to eliminate or add risk can do so quite easily by taking positions in derivatives. The highly competitive nature of derivative markets means that the prices of derivatives can be expected to be fair and reflective of an economically appropriate cost of risk transfer. We will see later more specifically what this concept means, but as a first pass at it, it means that neither party can generally take advantage of the other by engaging in arbitrage at the counterparty's expense. As such, the cost of risk transfer is fair and reasonable to all market participants.

4.5.1.2 *Provide Greater Liquidity than the Spot Market*

Because derivatives require considerably less capital than do transactions in the underlying, there is much more liquidity in the derivatives market than in the underlying spot market. As a result, it is much easier to trade derivatives and thereby transfer risk using derivatives than by using the spot market. As such, derivatives markets can even reflect new information faster than can the spot markets.

4.5.1.3 *Are Easier to Benefit from Price Declines in the Underlying*

If an entity believes that the value of an underlying will decrease and the entity does not own the underlying, in the absence of derivatives the only way to profit from a price decline in the underlying is to borrow it and sell it short. Short selling can be done for most securities, but there are some burdensome costs and regulatory requirements. By taking short positions in forwards, futures, calls, or by buying puts, a party can position itself to profit if its expectation turns out to be correct. Taking these positions is generally much easier than selling short the underlying. In fact, for some underlyings, it is extremely difficult to sell short. For example, if an agricultural expert believes that the price of coffee will decrease sharply over the next six months, it would be virtually impossible to borrow coffee and sell it short. But coffee derivatives can be obtained quite easily. In short (pun intended), derivatives make it easy to go short and thereby profit from a declining price of the underlying.

4.5.1.4 *Provide More Exposure for Lower Cost*

Suppose an energy company wants to speculate on the price of oil and considers the possibility of buying 10 million barrels of oil. At its current price of around $60 a barrel, the total cost of 10 million barrels would be $600 million. A futures contract could be obtained at no significant up-front cost except the posting of a margin deposit of about $40 million, well under 10% of the cost of the oil. The futures position would enable the firm to effectively control a position in 10 million barrels of oil at but a fraction of the cost of the oil.

4.5.1.5 *Reveal the Cost of Risk Reduction*

Because derivatives are designed for risk transfer, they must provide information on the cost of risk transfer. For example, as I write this chapter, the spot price of WTI oil is around $60 a barrel, and the price of a six month futures is about $62 a barrel (both rounded prices). Thus, if an entity were planning to purchase oil six months later, it could go ahead and lock in a price of $62 a barrel. At a premium of $2 over the current spot price, the cost of locking in certainty is $2 a barrel. Later we will cover exactly how the futures price is determined, but for now you should think of it as a reflection of the cost net of benefits of engaging in a contract for delivery later in relation to acquiring the oil now and having to store it. By doing a futures contract rather than buying the oil, any costs net of benefits during the six-month period are avoided, but most importantly, the risk is eliminated.

4.5.1.6 *Reveal Information on the Price of the Underlying*

Some assets on which derivatives trade do not have a centralized market that provides an easily obtainable single price for the asset. This characteristic is typical of agricultural products. For example, wheat is an extremely vital product in U.S. food production. Wheat is grown in many parts of the U.S., and because of this fact, there is no single market for wheat. Wheat is generally sold close to where it is produced. Determining the so-called "price of wheat" is difficult. The Chicago Mercantile Exchange's wheat futures contract allows for eight different variations of wheat to be delivered in settlement of the contract, and delivery can be made in over 20 locations, all in the U.S. Midwest. Since all grades and locations are not equal, the final price is adjusted to reflect these differentials. If one wanted an estimate of the spot price of wheat, the best estimate would be the price of a soon-to-expire futures contract. Usually this contract would have less than 60 days to expiration. Thus, futures contracts can provide information on the spot market that cannot be provided by the spot market itself, since there is no unique spot market. This characteristic of futures markets is called *price discovery*.

Now let us consider a financial asset. The value of the underlying for a futures contract on the exchange rate of the U.S. dollar for the euro would seem easy to determine. You just look up the current exchange rate. But is it really that simple? There may be a posted current exchange rate, but an exchange rate exists anywhere currency is exchanged. Thus, there is no single market for exchange rates. Nonetheless, the foreign exchange industry is sufficiently well-organized to provide a single quote that is accessible on Bloomberg, Reuters, and the Internet, and which should reflect a reasonable average of current trades and quoted rates. The price discovery characteristic of futures is valuable in markets that are not sufficiently well-organized to produce a single number representing the current spot price. That is the case for agricultural products, but the reason is not simply the lack of effort on the part of the industry. It is that there is tremendous variation across the prices of physical assets that are costly to move and store. This problem is not a factor in foreign currency futures, since money can be transferred almost instantaneously at very low cost. In fact, one does not even need money at a local facility. It can be at a bank far away and be just as accessible. For underlyings that do not have this characteristic, futures markets have a keen ability to sense when and where delivery will occur and exactly what variation of the underlying will be delivered. That information then ultimately formulates the so-called spot price.

4.5.1.7 *Reveal Information on the Volatility of the Underlying*

Option prices are determined by the value of the underlying, the exercise price, the time to expiration of the option, the risk-free rate of interest, any benefits paid by the underlying, and the volatility of the underlying. The first five items are fairly easily observable inputs, but the volatility of the underlying is not. Parties that trade options agree on a price, however, and that price can reveal their estimates of the volatility of the underlying. We will cover this point in much detail later, but to keep it simple for now, you should understand that these six factors go into a formula that produces the option price. Given that we do not know one of the factors, the volatility, we can insert the price observed in the market and the other factors into the formula and back into the volatility. This volatility that we infer is called the *implied volatility*. Thus, options provide valuable information on how investors feel about the volatility of the market. As we will see later, measures of the overall market volatility are quoted and provided to the public as a measure of the concern investors have about the stability of the market.

4.5.1.8 *Make the Underlying Spot Market More Fair and Competitive*

Last but not least, the final benefit of options that we discuss is that they make the spot market a better marketplace by making it more fair and efficient. As we will discuss in detail later, derivatives markets are linked to their respective spot markets via the arbitrage mechanism. We described earlier how derivatives markets react quickly to new information. Because derivatives markets operate so efficiently to exploit and quickly eliminate arbitrage opportunities, the information will be transmitted quickly to the spot market. The end result is that spot market prices will be constantly and quickly moving to fair and competitive levels.

Derivatives have not, however, been without controversy. In the next section, we will take a look at some of the alleged costs and criticisms of derivatives, in short, the negatives.

4.5.2   *The (Alleged) Negatives of Derivatives*

Clearly the position taken in this book emphasizes the positive role of derivatives in helping entities to manage risk. Nonetheless, derivatives have been the subject of much criticism, particularly when markets fall steeply and when economic recessions occur. These criticisms are somewhat understandable but misguided. Nonetheless, it is important to address these points that the critics are making.

4.5.2.1   *Contribute to Speculation*

As previously noted, trading derivatives requires very little capital. As such, they can be used quite easily to speculate. Indeed, they are widely used by sophisticated speculative investors such as hedge funds, but they are also used by many unsophisticated investors to speculate.

The foundation of this argument, however, is that speculation has little value. Indeed, speculators are often viewed as evil in that they might seem to profit off of the misfortunes of others. Sharp increases in the price of oil are habitually blamed on speculators pushing up the price of oil. This argument might be reasonable if speculators were also credited for sharp decreases in the price of oil, but alas, they are not. Selling oil futures can push the price of oil down as easily as buying them can push the price up, and speculators are no more averse to going short than to going long.

It is important to understand that speculation and those who practice it, the speculators, play an extremely important role in the market. They are vital for effective risk management. Speculators take on the risk that others want to transfer. It would be virtually impossible to successfully practice good risk management in the absence of speculators.[19] How would hedgers be able to eliminate risk if no one were there to take the risk?

4.5.2.2   *Destabilize the Spot Market*

Derivatives have suffered the criticism that they destabilize the spot market. This criticism is again based on the notion that people use them to speculate

---

[19]There is one exception to this statement. Let us say a party is exposed to an increase in the price of an asset. If that party could find another party that is exposed to a decrease in the price of the asset, it is possible the two parties could engage in a direct transaction that would benefit them both. The problem with successfully doing this type of transaction, however, is that (1) the sizes of the exposures are not likely to match, (2) the timing of the exposures is not likely to match, and (3) the two parties would probably have a difficult time finding each other. Thus, a dealer market could be created that would accept both risks and hedge any net difference with a speculator. In the end, a speculator almost always ends up holding risk that other parties wish to eliminate.

and that speculating is destabilizing. There is potentially some truth to this criticism in that derivatives are often used by unsophisticated investors. These investors are believed to have such little information that they trade at prices that are unfavorable to them. Such trades can add a great deal of additional volatility in the market in the form of volatility that largely reflects rumors and inaccurate information rather than economic fundamentals. These types of traders are even called *noise traders* and this form of trading is called *noise trading*. The problem with this argument is that even though there are far more noise traders than there were many years ago, noise traders are unlikely to make up the majority of investors in the market. The internet has played a role in making it possible for unsophisticated investors to receive information quickly and trade at low cost, but ultimately, most of the volatility in the market is driven by sophisticated investors who have so much more capital at stake.

As noted earlier, the oil markets have experienced wide fluctuations. Indeed, of the four markets we examined earlier (LIBOR, the euro, oil, and the S&P 500), the oil market was the most volatile. Sharp increases in energy prices are frequently blamed on speculators. This argument is completely false, however, because, as noted earlier, if speculators drove prices up, then they should be credited with driving prices down, but they are not. There is no question that speculation can fuel speculation, but speculators that trade at unrealistic prices would be quickly driven out of business. Speculation is an extremely competitive business, and speculators must trade at relatively rational prices to survive and be successful.

4.5.2.3 *Are a Form of Legalized Gambling*

Derivatives have been criticized as being nothing more than a way to gamble. There is certainly an element of speculation. Even to a hedger, reducing the risk is a gamble that the adverse event will not happen. A hedger may regret having hedged if that happens. But this view of derivatives vis-à-vis gambling fails to compare the benefits. Gambling is an industry that caters strictly to speculation. The gambling industry depends on having each participant believe it can be the rare winner. Gambling is well known to have a negative expected value to all but the parties that provide the gambling service. Thus, gamblers are motivated by a combination of naiveté and the sheer enjoyment of the games themselves, irrespective of money won or lost. Gambling has limited benefits to society as a whole. It is a viable industry and certainly employs a lot of people in Las Vegas, the Mississippi Gulf Coast, Macao, Monte Carlo, and Atlantic City, but the contribution of gambling to society as a whole is quite limited. It is simply one of hundreds of industries. Derivatives, on the other hand, bring numerous benefits to financial markets, as discussed in Section 4.1. Hence, the reach of derivatives is far greater than the reach of gambling.

Warren Buffett on Derivatives

Warren Buffet, the legendary investor and chairman of Berkshire Hathaway, has made some extremely candid statements about the dangers of derivatives. In his 2002 Chairman's letter to the Berkshire shareholders, Buffett states that "We (Buffett and Vice Chairman Charlie Munger) view them as time bombs, both for the parties that deal in them and for the economic system." He goes on to say that "In our view, derivatives are financial weapons of mass destruction, carrying dangers that, while now latent, are potentially lethal." Yet, he goes on to say that "Indeed at Berkshire, I sometimes engage in large-scale derivatives transactions in order to facilitate certain investment strategies." So, Buffett is both a critic and a user of derivatives.

Buffett does make a distinction, however, between collateralized exchange-traded derivatives and privately negotiated non-collateralized over-the-counter derivatives. His primary beef is with the latter. Putting the comments in context, Buffett had just recently acquired General Re, an insurance company that had attached to it a derivatives subsidiary called General Re Securities that Buffett did not want but was forced to take to acquire the parent firm, which he did want. This derivatives business was shut down in 2010.

In what seems to be a contradiction, however, Buffett states the following in the 2014 Annual Report. "Some years ago, we became a party to certain derivative contracts that we believed were significantly mispriced and that had only minor collateral requirements. These have proved to be quite profitable." With the introduction of the Dodd-Frank Act, most OTC contracts now require collateralization. Buffett goes on to add that "Recently, however, newly-written derivative contracts have required full collateralization. And that ended our interest in derivatives, regardless of what profit potential they might offer. We have not, for some years, written these contracts, except for a few needed for operational purposes at our utility business."

So, where does Warren Buffett stand on derivatives? Hard to tell.

4.6 An Overview of the Risk Management Process

Although this book focuses on the risk management process and covers many topics in detail, here we will take a light overview of that process. Exhibit 4-23 shows a diagram centered around the organization, which can be a company, a non-profit, or a government entity. We see that the organization is hit from both sides by risks, some non-financial and some financial. The financial risks include market risk and credit risk, which we have discussed. We also identify a variation of market risk called liquidity risk, which is the risk that a market is not sufficiently liquid to engage in a transaction without the transaction moving the price by a large amount. Among the non-financial risks, we see a broad variety that are related to accounting, tax, legal, regulatory, settlements, model and operational factors. We will discuss each of these risks later in this book.

The process of managing risk is illustrated in Exhibit 4-24. Again, we see that the organization is hit by financial and non-financial risks. But a paramount part of the process is defining the organization's risk tolerance — its appetite for risk. Once that is done, it is necessary to set policies and procedures that reflect that risk tolerance, to identify the relevant risks, to measure these risks, and to calibrate the risks, meaning to bring the risk taken in line with the desired risk. We see that the financial and non-financial risks generate information and data that are used in this process. We also see that calibrating risks means to identify appropriate transactions, assess the cost of those transactions, and execute the transactions. The process then loops around, thereby forming a continuous stream of measurement and calibration of the risk.

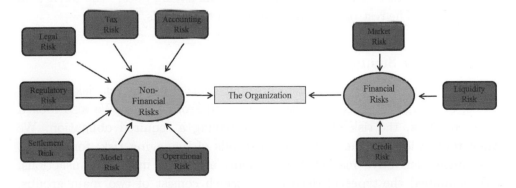

Exhibit 4-23. The Risks Faced by an Organization

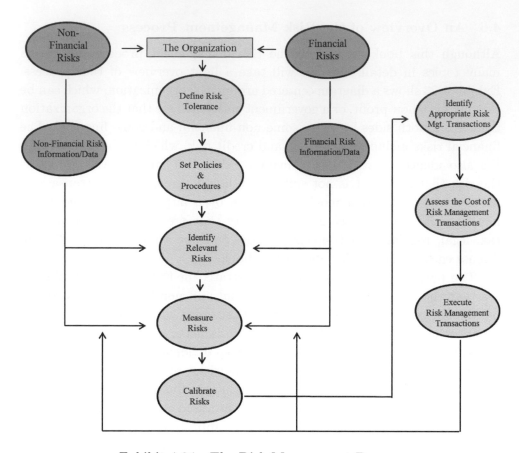

Exhibit 4-24. The Risk Management Process

If everything were as easy as flow charts imply, the process would be simple. In the case of risk management, as the saying goes, "the devil is in the details." The rest of this book gives you the details.

4.7   Chapter Summary

In this chapter, we see that there are four sources of market risk: interest rates, exchange rates, commodity prices, and stock prices. We also looked at credit risk, the risk of someone not paying a required obligation. We then took a look at the four basic methods of managing risk: forecasting, insurance, derivative market transactions, and spot market transactions. We examined the types of derivatives, which consist of two main groups: forward commitments and contingent claims. Within the category of forward commitments, we learned that there are forward contracts, futures contracts, and swaps. The category of contingent claims consists of options and other instruments that contain options embedded within them. In addition, there are a variety of other derivatives that combine features of different types of derivatives.

We then examined the positives and negatives of derivatives. Obviously, this book favors the positive side, but it is important to understand the negatives. Derivatives are powerful tools, but they can be dangerous if misused. There are, however, many powerful forces in life that can be dangerous, such as water, electricity, and chemicals. If used improperly, these forces can be lethal. Yet we use them routinely without problems, because we understand them and respect their power. Derivatives are the same way. But unfortunately, users of derivatives will always have to defend them against critics.

4.8   Questions and Problems

1. Distinguish the concepts of business risk and financial risk as they are traditionally taught in finance courses.
2. Distinguish the concepts of systematic and unsystematic risk as they are traditionally taught in finance courses.
3. How do operating leverage and financial leverage contribute to the risk of an entity?
4. Define market risk by identifying its four sources.
5. What does LIBOR stand for and why is it an important interest rate in the financial markets, and in particular, the derivative markets? What other term is used to refer to LIBOR?
6. What is the relationship of a nominal rate to a real rate of interest on a loan?
7. What determines the direct and indirect sources of credit risk?
8. How are bond ratings supposed to reflect credit risk?
9. What role does forecasting play in risk management?
10. How does diversification work in managing risk, and why is it of fairly limited value for companies?
11. Explain the concepts of coercive transfer and deceptive transfer and how they relate to risk management.
12. Identify and briefly explain the three forms of cooperative transfer in risk management.

13. What are the two main classifications of derivative contracts and what types of derivatives are encompassed within each classification?
14. Explain how the payoffs of forwards, futures, and swaps, collectively, are different from the payoffs of options.
15. Identify the eight benefits of derivatives.
16. Identify the three criticisms of derivatives.

Chapter 5

The Financial Risk Management Environment

This industry has reinvented itself more in the last 30 years than Madonna.

Richard Sandor
Futures magazine
Fall, 2005 special issue, p. 8

Before we begin to look at the details of how to manage financial risk, we need to set the story in its proper perspective. So let us next take a look at the environment in which risk management is practiced. Of course, that environment can be viewed as the entire global economy and in particular, the global financial and commodity markets. Inasmuch as the practice of risk management relies heavily on the use of derivatives, we need to examine the basic structure and special characteristics of the derivatives markets.

Derivatives are created in two types of markets, the *exchange-traded derivatives market* and the *over-the-counter derivatives market*. We will take each one in order, but it is important to get a general perspective on both. So, let us start by explaining that the exchange-traded derivatives market is the market comprised of derivatives exchanges. These exchanges are entities that provide an organized marketplace for the trading of standardized derivatives contracts. In contrast, the over-the-counter market refers to any types of derivative contracts that are created between any two parties. Thus, you and your friend could create an option, and it would technically be created in the over-the-counter market. In general, when we refer to the over-the-counter market, however, we mean transactions between large entities and derivatives dealers, who are largely the banks that offer to take either side of the transaction. These cursory descriptions clearly do not do full justice to these concepts, but it is important in understanding one market to have a general idea of what the other does. We will now dive into the two types of markets in more detail.

5.1 The Exchange-Traded Derivatives Market

As noted, the exchange-traded derivatives market is comprised of derivatives exchanges, which are organizations that create a specialized market for derivatives. In order to get a better understanding of this type of market structure, we will relate an interesting historical story of how derivatives exchanges got started.

The origins of futures and options are difficult to identify. There is some evidence that futures contracts were traded in medieval times, and that instruments similar to futures on rice were traded in Japan in the 17th century. Options are known to have existed in the U.S. in the 19th century and possibly quite earlier. The only definitive origins we have of a derivatives exchange go back to the mid-19th century in the American Midwest.

In the 1840s, the city of Chicago was, as it still is today, a major U.S. city for business. At that time, Chicago's favorable location in the Midwest with its connections to the Great Lakes made it an important agricultural market. Midwestern farmers would bring their grain to Chicago, where it would be sold to companies that used it in the creation of their products. The seasonal nature of grain production, however, caused a great deal of price volatility. Most of the grains were harvested and brought to Chicago in the fall, at which time prices would drop steeply. In addition, grain storage facilities were inadequate to accommodate the large supply. It has been said that some farmers who could not sell or store their crops in Chicago found it less costly to dump the crops in the Chicago River rather than take them back to the cornfields of Illinois and Iowa. Shortly before the harvest, prices would be steep as demand exceeded current supply by a wide margin. These rising and falling prices gave some businessmen an idea to create a type of contract that would enable a farmer to lock in a price for delivery of the grain at a future date. Thus, a farmer could harvest the grain in September and sell it at a fixed price for delivery in March. During the intervening time, he would store the grain at his farm or a local facility near his farm.

These arrangements were called *to-arrive contracts*. With these contracts, a farmer could actually sell his crop before he had planted it, though that would have been quite risky, since crop production is highly uncertain. The farmer would not know how much of the commodity his farm would produce. A safer alternative would be to determine the size of the crop and sell it for later delivery with a to-arrive contract. So let us say that in September, a farmer sells 50,000 bushels of corn for delivery on a specific day in March. In October, another farmer sells 50,000 bushels for delivery on that same day in March. During the September to October period, new information arrives, so the second price is not likely to be the same as the first. That new information will reflect revised expectations of the size of the season's crop and the expected future demand for the crop. If the farmer who sells his crop in September for March delivery gets, say, $1 a bushel, and the farmer who sells his crop in October for March delivery gets $1.05 a bushel, the first farmer's position loses value because he has locked in a price of $1. When the delivery day in March arrives, a new contract for immediate delivery will be worth the spot price at that time. If the price rises from September to March, a farmer who sold his crop in September will lose but will have locked in the price back in September. A speculator who bought the contract in September will profit.

These fluctuating prices soon came to draw much interest from speculators who had no real need for the crop, but felt they were astute traders who could process information and use it to trade profitably. Such a trader could in effect buy (sell) a contract for March delivery and sell it (buy it back) before March, thereby reaping a profit if the price rises (falls). The trader need not take or make delivery of the crop.

In 1848 a group of these traders organized an exchange for trading these contracts, and they named the exchange the Chicago Board of Trade. Eventually these to-arrive contracts became known as *futures contracts*. In 1898 another exchange, the Chicago Butter and Egg Board, was formed and it eventually became the Chicago Mercantile Exchange (CME).[1] The CME eventually formed a parent company called the CME Group and now owns the Chicago Board of Trade, the Chicago Mercantile Exchange, and two exchanges in New York, COMEX and NYMEX. In 1973 the first options exchange was created out of the Chicago Board of Trade. It was named the Chicago Board Options Exchange and is sometimes called the CBOE. Numerous other exchanges exist around the world.

The Contribution of the Chicago Board of Trade in the United States Civil War

From April 12, 1861 through April 9, 1865, the 36 United States fought one of the bloodiest wars in history. Eleven southern states withdrew from the United States, formed their own country called the Confederate States of America, and initiated war to compel the U.S. government to remove

---

[1] For an interesting novel that describes life in the futures trading environment of Chicago at the turn of the century, I recommend Frank Norris' *The Pit: A Story of Chicago* (1903).

its armies and influence from the Confederacy. The southern states were well-known to be heavily reliant on slave labor, and hence, the war was fought largely over the issue of slavery. Because Americans were fighting Americans, the roughly 750,000 Americans who died exceeded the total of the four deadliest wars fought by the United States since that time: World War II, World War I, the Vietnam War, and the Korean War. More than two-thirds of the deaths in the Civil War did not happen in combat but rather occurred as a result of the state of medical knowledge of how to treat wounds and fight diseases.

When the war started, the Chicago Board of Trade had been in existence for 13 years and had achieved a high degree of success. About 15 months after the start of the war, President Lincoln sent out a call for volunteers to join the Army and fight for the preservation of the Union and provide financial support. The Chicago Board of Trade raised about $15,000 and 180 men and mustered the unit into what became known as the Chicago Board of Trade Battery. A battery is an artillery unit with between six and 12 cannons or mortars. The Board of Trade Battery had six guns called James rifled six-pounders, meaning that they fired shells weighing six pounds through a grooved barrel. Shortly after mustering, they exchanged some of their rifled cannons for smooth bore guns. The unit was assigned to the Army of the Ohio (in reference to the Ohio River) of Major General Don Carlos Buell.

The Battery was originally organized as a unit of field artillery, which means it was assigned to provide artillery support to the infantry. The unit's first combat was at the Battle of Stone's River, near Murfreesboro, Tennessee, on the last day of December, 1862. In mid-1863, the unit was converted to horse artillery, which means that it then operated to support cavalry units, being now assigned to the Army of the Cumberland. The Battery supported General William T. Sherman's march and siege on Atlanta in 1864 and after the capture of the city, it was assigned to General James Wilson's army as it pursued the city of Nashville. It subsequently fought in Alabama, and when the war ended, it was in Macon, Georgia. Suffering only light casualties, with but 19 killed, the Battery distinguished itself and was mustered out in July of 1865.

A monument to the Chicago Board of Trade Battery was erected in 1901 in Chicago's Rosehill Cemetery.

Source: http://crossedsabers.blogspot.com/2008/10/chicago-board-of-tra de-battery.html

As we will discuss in more detail later, derivatives exchanges offer certain types of derivative contracts for trading. Some offer futures, some offer options, and some offer both. Some also offer trading in securities. Many of today's exchanges, however, are holding companies that own various other exchanges. Hence, fair comparisons of exchange size are quite difficult. In addition, the exchanges determine the sizes of their contracts, and comparisons of exchanges by size are based on trading volume. With different size contracts, there can be quite large differences in exchange sizes solely due to the sizes of the contracts that trade on a given exchange. For example, one of the CME's most active contracts is its crude oil futures contract traded on its NYMEX subsidiary. Each contract covers 1,000 barrels of crude oil. The Multi-Commodity Exchange of India has a nearly identical contract, but its size is 100 barrels. Thus, one unit of volume on both exchanges does not mean the same.

Comparisons involving futures against options are also difficult. The CME's S&P 500 futures contract covers 250 units of the S&P 500. Across town, the CBOE's S&P 500 option contract covers 100 units of the S&P 500. Hence, for a given amount of exposure, one exchange might have many times the volume of another exchange strictly based on the design of the contract.

In spite of these concerns, the derivatives exchanges compete heavily, and each aspires to rise in the list of exchanges by size. Let us take a look at this list. In 2018, *MarketVoice* magazine identified 54 derivatives exchanges around the world. Exhibit 5-1 lists the 10 largest derivatives exchanges ranked by trading volume in 2017.

From the notes in the Exhibit, you can see that indeed many exchanges are essentially holding companies of other exchanges. Not too many years ago, many of these subsidiary exchanges were distinct entities themselves. Global competition has stimulated a number of these mergers and acquisitions, as the various exchanges scramble to compete with one another.

Exhibit 5-2 presents a time series of global futures and options volume from 2002. It shows futures volume as one series, options volume as another, and then an overall total for both futures and options. The latest figures, 2017, have futures volume at about 14.8 billion contracts and options volume at about 10.4 billion contracts, for total volume of about 25.2 billion contracts.

We have given a general overview of the exchanges that operate in the exchange-traded derivatives market. Let us now take a more specific look at how the contracts are structured and the manner in which trading takes place. It is the specification of the contracts and how they are traded that

Exchange	2017 Volume (# of contracts traded)
CME Group (Chicago, USA)[a]	4,088,910,011
National Stock Exchange of India	2,465,333,505
Intercontinental Exchange[b]	2,125,404,062
CBOE Holdings[c]	1,810,195,197
B3 (Brazil)	1,809,358,955
Nasdaq[d]	1,676,626,292
Eurex	1,675,896,310
Moscow Exchange	1,584,632,965
Shanghai Futures Exchange	1,364,243,528
Dalian Commodity Exchange (China)	1,101,280,152

[a]Includes Chicago Mercantile Exchange, Chicago Board of Trade, New York Mercantile Exchange, & Commodity Exchange (COMEX); [b]Includes ICE Futures Europe, NYSE Arca, ICE Futures U.S., NYSE Amex, ICE Futures Canada, ICE Futures Singapore; [c]Includes Chicago Board Options Exchange, BATS Exchange, C2 Exchange, CBOE Futures Exchange, EDGX Options Exchange; [d]Includes Nasdaq PHLX, Nasdaq Options Market, International Securities Exchange, International Securities Exchange Gemini, Nasdaq Exchanges Nordic Markets, International Securities Exchanges Mercury, Nasdaq Commodities, Nasdaq NLX.

Source: *MarketVoice* magazine, March 2018, available at marketvoicefia.org

Exhibit 5-1. Largest Global Derivatives Exchanges by Trading Volume, 2017

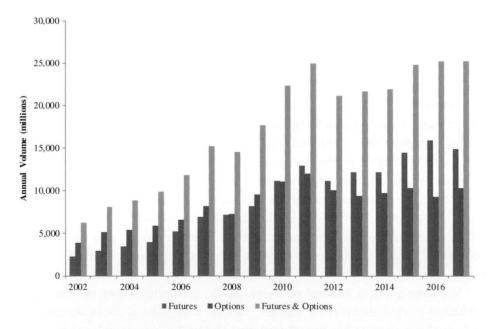

Exhibit 5-2. Global Futures and Options Volume Since 2002

Source Data: *MarketVoice* magazine, http://marketvoicemag.org (March issue of each year provides annual volume data.)

gives the exchange-traded derivatives market its uniqueness. We begin by examining what it means when we refer to a standardized contract.

Until the early 2000s or so, it has been customary that exchanges were owned by members, who had trading privileges called *seats* or *memberships*. These seat-holders were the only ones allowed to trade on the exchanges. Seats could be bought and sold. These seat-holders still exist today, but many exchanges are now profit-making corporations with shareholders. Some of them are publicly traded themselves. In fact, some even have options available on their stock. Thus, a "CBOE option" could refer to an option trading on the CBOE on some underlying or it could be an option in which the underlying is the CBOE's stock, which itself trades on Nasdaq.

5.1.1 *Standardized Contracts*

A number of times we have mentioned the standardization of contracts. Let us describe more precisely what this concept means. If you were in the market to buy a house, there are three ways you could do it. One is to buy a house that someone already owns and is offering for sale. Another way is to arrange for a specialist called a builder to construct the house according to your desires. A third way is to buy a newly built house from a builder.[2]

A standardized derivatives contract is like the third type of house. The house is completed and offered for sale by the builder. You, the buyer, more or less have to accept the house as it is, as there are rarely any significant changes that can be made. The price, however, is negotiated between you and the builder, who is the seller. If you were in the market for this type of house, you would have to accept whatever houses are available. Likewise, with a standardized derivatives contract, a buyer or seller would have to accept whatever contracts are available in the market. In Section 5.1.3, we will discuss how a contract is offset and how that arrangement is like buying a house on the secondary market, wherein all of the specifications are customized. In Section 5.2 we will discuss how an over-the-counter contract is like the case of having your home build to your requirements.

A derivatives exchange decides which contracts it will offer. In doing so, it attempts to offer contracts in which it believes there will be trading interest. It makes this assessment by determining what underlyings have sufficient hedging and speculative interest. For example, as underlyings, major government bonds, stock indexes, currencies, and commodities are almost always available for trading in the form of derivatives.

---

[2]In the U.S., this type of house is commonly referred to as a *spec house*, referring to the fact that the builder is speculating by building the house without a buyer lined up.

Given a particular underlying, the exchange must decide which, if any, variations of the underlying are eligible for delivery. For many commodities, such as wheat or corn, there are a number of slightly different varieties. Contract provisions usually allow for delivery of multiple grades of the commodity with an appropriate adjustment to the price paid by the buyer to the seller for variations in quality. At the CME, for example, the 10-year Treasury Note futures contract allows for the delivery of any U.S. government Treasury Note with a maturity of between $6^1/2$ and 10 years on the first day of the expiration month. An adjustment factor is applied to account for the differences in maturity.

Given a particular underlying, the exchanges must decide on a minimum of four contract specifications for futures and an additional three more for options. We take a look at these now.

5.1.1.1 *Futures Contract Specifications*

The exchange must first decide on the *settlement procedure* of the contract, as this procedure determines some of the other specifications. Contracts can be settled by physical delivery or cash settlement. At the expiration of a physical delivery contract, the parties holding short positions must deliver the underlying to the holders of long positions. For a large physical commodity such as wheat or oil, delivery can usually be made at one of several locations. For financial underlyings, delivery is usually made by an electronic transfer. For certain underlyings, physical delivery is not particularly practical. For example, the CME's Eurodollar futures contract is based off of LIBOR as set in London, but the contract cannot require physical delivery of a Eurodollar loan, as these loans are made only by one bank to another bank and are not transferable. The Eurodollar contract merely trades off the LIBOR rate. As such, the contract is settled in cash. Under physical delivery, the S&P 500 futures contract would require that the short deliver to the long a portfolio equivalent to the S&P 500 index. But the S&P 500 index is a hypothetical portfolio of 500 common stocks combined according to their market value weights.[3] Delivery of a 500-stock portfolio

---

[3]Weighting by market value means the following. Suppose we have two stocks, A and B, combined into an index. Assume that the market value of company A is $100 billion and the market value of company B is $150 billion. A market-value weighted index consisting of stock A and stock B would be weighted such that A would make up $100/($100 + $150) = 0.40, or 40% of the index and B would be 60%. A physical delivery futures contract would, therefore, require delivery of a portfolio with 40% of the money in stock A and 60% in stock B.

with the specified weights would be quite impractical. Thus, the contract is cash settled. In both cases, cash settlement works in a very simple manner. If the long owes the short $100,000 for delivery of the underlying and the spot price or rate on the underlying is equivalent to a value of the underlying of $110,000, the short simply pays the long the difference of $10,000. The exchange decides when it creates the contract whether a contract is physical delivery or cash settlement. The parties do not have the right to decide for themselves on whether the contract is physical delivery or cash settlement.[4]

All futures contracts have a given *size*. For a physical delivery contract, the exchange decides on how many units or how much of the underlying each contract covers. For example, the CME's crude oil futures contract covers 1,000 barrels. Its Treasury bond futures contract covers $100,000 face value of U.S. Treasury bonds. Its euro futures contract covers 125,000 euros. For physical delivery contracts, the full price is the quoted price times the specified number of units that determine the contract size. The size of a cash settlement contract is a simple multiplier. For example, the CME's S&P 500 futures contract has a multiplier of $250. So if the contract price is 1,800, the total price of a single contract is 1,800($250) = $450,000. Thus, for all contracts the full price is the quoted price times the contract size.[5]

The futures exchanges also must decide the *price quotation unit*. For example, the CME's U.S. Treasury Note futures contract price is 1/32, the same as the quotation unit for the spot market for U.S. Treasury notes. Combined with the contract size of $100,000, 1/32 of $100,000 is $3,125. Thus, a Treasury note futures might have a price quote that looks like 122-28, which means 122 28/32. Since 28/32 is 0.875, the price quote is 122.875. For a contract size of $100,000, the price is, thus, $122,875. The crude oil contract is quoted in dollars per barrel, and the euro contract is quoted in dollars per euro. Closely related to the quotation unit is the *minimum tick size*.[6] The exchanges specify a minimum price change. This notion does not

---

[4]Some physical delivery contracts do allow the parties to agree on an alternative delivery procedure called *exchange-for-physicals*, also known as *against actuals*. The parties might agree that a grade of the commodity or a different delivery location other than those specified by the exchange as acceptable can be delivered. The exchange permits this procedure if the parties agree on it.

[5]If this point seems confusing, think of it like the price of a share of stock in comparison to the value of an order to buy 100 shares. If the stock is at $20 a share, we might quote the price at 20 but the full cost of 100 shares is $2,000. All futures contracts are quoted on a per unit basis, such as 1,800 for the S&P 500 futures, but the total price is $450,000.

[6]In the financial world, a tick is a price change from one trade to another. The minimum tick size is the smallest allowable price change.

mean that each transaction must result in a price change, but rather that if the price changes it must change by a certain minimum. The Treasury note contract has a minimum price change of 1/64. The crude oil contract has a minimum price change of $0.01 per barrel. The euro contract has a minimum price change of $0.0001.

One of the most important specifications is the *expiration*. Most futures contracts are identified by an expiration month. Thus, for example, a Treasury note futures contract might be referred to as the September contract, meaning that it expires in September. The exchanges also specify the exact expiration date, such as the third Friday in September but the contract is referred to only as the September contract. Futures contracts typically have expirations only once per month. Thus, you would not likely see two contracts expiring on different dates in September. Some contracts expire on a quarterly cycle, such as the January cycle (January, April, July, October), the February cycle (February, May, August, November), and the March cycle (March, June, September, December). Some contracts also have monthly cycles, meaning that there is a contract expiring each month usually for the next few months. Given a particular contract expiration and expiration day, the exchanges also specify the last trading day, which may or may not be the expiration day or the last trading day of the month. In addition, the exchange specifies the trading hours, which are usually coordinated with the customary trading hours in the spot market.

The exchange may also specify a limit on the number of contracts a given party can hold, referred to as *position limits*. For some contracts there may also be *price limits*, which are restrictions on how high or how low the price can go in a given day. These limits are done to facilitate the collection of funds through the exchange's clearing house. In addition, the exchange specifies margin requirements, which reflect the amount of money the parties must deposit at the start of a contract and on a daily basis while the position is open. We will discuss how the margining and clearing system works in Section 5.1.2.3.

5.1.1.2 *Options Contract Specifications*

All of the features described above for futures are also relevant for the exchange-listed options markets and are specified by the exchanges. In addition, options require the specification of one major additional feature, the exercise price.

Recall that futures contracts are obligations for two parties to engage in a transaction at a future date. In contrast, options contracts grant the buyer the *right* to buy the underlying from the seller if the option is a call, or the right to *sell* the underlying to the seller if the option is a put at a later date but *not the obligation*. A call buyer has the right to buy the underlying from the call seller at a fixed price that we referred to as the exercise price. A put buyer has the right to sell the underlying to the put seller at a fixed price that we referred to as the exercise price. The exchanges specify that options with certain exercise prices are available for trading. Usually the exercise prices will be near the price of the underlying. Of course, over time the underlying may move substantially and as that happens, the exchanges will typically add options with new exercise prices for trading. The exchanges also have to specify the interval between exercise prices. For the CBOE S&P 500 index option, the interval is around 25 points. Putting that into perspective, if the S&P 500 were at 1,800, the exercise prices might be 1800, 1825, 1850 etc. as well as 1775, 1750, etc. For options on common stocks, the CBOE uses intervals of $2^{1}/_{2}$ points for stocks between $5 and $25, 5 points for stocks between $25 and $200, and 10 points for stocks over $200.

Options also have an important variation concerning the timing of exercise. Certain options can be exercised at any time up to expiration. These options are referred to as *American options* or *American-style exercise*. Other options can be exercised only at expiration. These options are referred to as *European options* or *European-style exercise*. These terms have nothing to do with where the options are traded. Both types of options are traded on both continents, as well as in many other markets around the world. As we cover later, American-style options are far more complex than European-style options (but see the boxed item below).

Origins of the Terms "European Option" and "American Option"

S. A. Nelson (1904) describes the origins of the terms European and American option in his description of the options markets in the early 20th century. At that time, options traded in London and in New York. He states (footnote on p. 12)

In Wall Street the option is so written that its owner can exercise the rights therein contained "on one day's notice except the last day, when notice is not required." This distinguishes the New York option from that of London, where the rights can only be exercised on a specified future date.

He goes on to compare the London option trader with the New York option trader, and the comparison is a bit "interesting."

(p. 14)

The London buyer of options is accustomed to "trade against his options" to a much greater extent than the New Yorker, and trading of this character calls for quite complicated calculations that would puzzle and confuse the average American stock speculator who wants a simple, rather than a complicated proposition, and who preferably always demands a quick, rather than a slow decision.

So, in other words, Nelson believes that London investors are more sophisticated and have longer-term horizons and that the European-style option is more complex and would not be easily understandable to an American investor who has a shorter horizon.

Little does Nelson know that American options are far more complex than European options. We will take up this point later in this book.

Source: S. A. Nelson (1904).

An American-style option is essentially equivalent to a European-style option with the additional rights to exercise at any time prior to expiration. These additional rights can have significant value under some circumstances. Under other circumstances, they may have no value.

As noted in the previous section, exchanges specify position limits, which are applicable to futures and options. For options, the exchanges may also specify *exercise limits*, which are restrictions on the number of options that can be exercised on a given day or series of days.

We should note that the cash settlement feature mentioned in the previous section for futures is also applicable to the exercise of options. Exercise of a physical delivery call option contract would result in the long paying the exercise price to the short and receiving the underlying from the short. Exercise of a physical delivery put option contract would result in the long delivering the underlying to the short and receiving the exercise price from the short. For cash settlement, an example works best. Suppose the long has a cash-settled call option with an exercise price of €25. The value of the underlying at the time of exercise is €28. Exercise of the call would result in the short paying the long €3. If the long has a cash-settled put option with an exercise price of €30 and the underlying is at €28, the short pays the long €2. Of course, both of these payoffs are multiplied by the contract size.

It is common terminology in the exchange-listed options market to refer to an option by its month and exercise price. Thus, one might see a somewhat strange reference like the *September 35 call*. As much as this appears to be a call expiring on the non-existent date of September 35, it actually refers to a call expiring in September with an exercise price of 35. Thus, if you see something like a September 20 call, you must remember that the 20 is the exercise price and not the date. In addition, it is common terminology to refer to an option with an exercise price such as 20 as the *20-strike* call or put.

5.1.2 *Trading*

Derivatives trading has two forms: *floor trading*, which is sometimes called *pit trading* and sometimes *open outcry*, and *electronic trading*. In floor trading, people who hold memberships on the exchanges physically go to a location in the exchange's building, called the trading floor. The trading floor is divided into areas known as pits. The traders stand in the pits and trade with each other. Floor trading is the original form of trading, but in 1992 the CME introduced the first electronic trading system, which was called GLOBEX. In an electronic trading system, trades are executed through a computer. Instead of the two parties actually standing to face to face with each other, they see an electronic screen with information on what buyers and sellers are in the market at that time and at what prices they are interested in trading. With the development of derivatives exchanges around the world and the tremendous degree to which each new generation is comfortable doing just about everything electronically, floor trading began to lose volume to electronic trading. Floor trading has always been mostly a U.S. phenomenon, and today's markets are almost exclusively electronic. What little floor trading remains is mostly at the Chicago exchanges and appears to be an endangered species.

5.1.2.1 *Types of Traders*

Whether there is floor trading or electronic trading, a derivatives market is generally made up of three types of traders: *dealers*, *brokers*, and *speculators*. The dealer, also called a *specialist* or *market maker*, is a person who creates a market by being willing to take either side of a transaction. The dealer quotes a price at which he is willing to buy, called the *bid* or *bid price*, and the price at which he is willing to sell, called the *ask* or *ask price*, also sometimes called the *offer price*. The ask is higher than the bid, and the difference is called the *bid-ask spread*, which is how the dealer earns a profit. A dealer does not speculate on the derivative going up or down. When he takes a position, he tries to offset that position with another derivative or perhaps even a position in the underlying. He may have to adjust his bid-ask spread. Lowering the spread brings down the ask in relation to the bid or brings up the bid in relation to the ask and will attract someone to trade with him. A system of multiple competitive dealers as is used by most exchanges makes a market tend to have the lowest possible spreads, which is a positive for other market participants.

The Bid-Ask Spread as a Transaction Cost

Transaction costs are a major factor in virtually any investment. For investors that are not members of exchanges, there is always a commission. A commission is a fee paid to a broker to execute trades on behalf of other investors. In addition, however, the most important transaction is the one that is the least obvious: the bid-ask spread.

Suppose you wanted to buy a security or derivative. Unless you happen to know someone who wants to do the exact opposite transaction at the same time for the same volume, you will need to transact with the dealer. The dealer quotes the bid as the price he is willing to pay to buy it and the ask as the price he is asking to sell it. Thus, from your perspective you will pay the ask if buying and receive the bid if selling.

Suppose the quote is a bid of 10.50 and an ask of 10.75. These quotes imply a spread of 0.25. Now, let us see how the spread is a transaction cost. Suppose you buy the security or derivative at 10.75, but immediately you realize that you made a mistake. To unwind that mistake, you need to immediately sell it. You would have to sell it at 10.50 and would thereby incur a cost of 0.25. Thus, the spread is a transaction cost.

Alternatively, let us say that you buy it and hold it in anticipation of a price increase. How much does the price need to increase to make a profit? Let us hold the spread constant at 0.25. Remember that you will be selling at the bid. Keeping the spread constant, suppose the bid and ask increase by 0.10 to 10.60 and 10.85. You would now sell at 10.60 and would lose 0.15. It should be obvious that the bid and ask have to increase by the spread of 0.25. That is, if the bid went to at least 11.00 and the ask to at least 10.75, you would make at least break even.

You can think of what is happening as there being an equilibrium price at the center of the spread. This price is usually called the midpoint, and it is the average of the bid and ask prices. With the bid at 10.50 and the ask at 10.75, the midpoint is 10.625. To make a profit the midpoint must rise by one-half the spread to 10.75.

Of course, the spread can change. Suppose the midpoint is at 10.625 and the bid and ask are at 10.50 and 10.75 respectively. You buy at 10.75. Now suppose the spread widens to 0.30. Where does the midpoint need to go? We know that the bid has to get to 10.75 for you to profit. With a spread of 0.30, the midpoint has to get to 10.90, giving an ask of 11.05. Thus, the midpoint must rise by one-half the current bid ask spread of (0.125 as one-half of 0.25) plus one-half of the new bid-ask spread (0.15 as one-half of 0.30) for a total of 0.275. Thus, the midpoint rises from 10.625 to 10.625 + 0.275 = 10.90 to result in a profit. The original trade is still profitable, however, if the new bid is at least equal to the original ask. That is all that is required. So indeed, the bid-ask spread is a transaction cost. You can think of this cost as half the spread on the buy transaction and half the spread on the sell transaction. By trading at the bid or ask instead of the midpoint, you effectively pay half the spread.

Sometimes, the bid-ask spread is expressed as a percentage of the midpoint. With a constant spread, the percentage bid-ask spread is lower at higher midpoints.

Of course, you should never think of the bid-ask spread as a deadweight cost. It is what you pay for the price of immediacy, the ability to do a trade right now.

A broker, sometimes referred to in the futures markets as a *futures commission merchant* or *FCM*, is a trader that executes transactions for someone else. For example, many major financial institutions offer futures and options trading to the general public. These firms usually have a broker on the floor or at an electronic terminal to execute customer orders. The broker and/or his firm earns a profit from a commission on each trade.

Finally, there are speculators, sometimes called *locals*, that are simply exchange members who represent either themselves or their employers. Speculators engage in a variety of types of trades including pure speculation and arbitrage. They take risks in the pursuit of profit.

Finally, it should be mentioned that some derivatives exchanges employ traders whose objective is to help clear the market. For example, the CBOE has a trader called the *order book official* who keeps the limit orders placed by the public and facilitates their execution. We will discuss limit orders in a few paragraphs.

The descriptions in the previous few paragraphs refer to direct market participants, meaning those that engage directly in transactions with one another. Naturally there are indirect market participants. Individual investors, companies, banks, and institutional investors such as mutual funds, pension funds, and hedge funds that also engage in exchange-traded derivatives transactions, but many do so using brokers.[7] Many major banks and institutional investors have their own memberships on derivatives exchanges, thus bypassing the broker and saving money.

5.1.2.2 *Types of Orders*

On most securities markets you can place any of a variety of types of orders to buy or sell securities. Generally, these same kinds of orders can be placed on derivatives exchanges. The three most popular types of orders are *market orders*, *limit orders*, and *stop orders*. A market order is an order to buy at whatever is the current price in the market. There will be, of course, a number of bids and offers by competing market makers. The best bid and offer establishes the current market quote, but a bid and ask price are relevant only for a specified quantity. Thus, a market order need not get filled at the best bid and offer quote for the entire order.[8] The important point about a market order is that it makes no restriction on the price. It is filled as quickly as possible.

A limit order places a limit on the price. Thus, one might offer to buy an option at a limit of $4.25, which means that the buyer will not pay more than $4.25. If the lowest ask price is above $4.25 the order will not be filled at this time. In fact, the order may not be filled for a long time, if at all. Similar if one wants to sell an option at a limit of $3.50, meaning that the seller will not accept less than $3.50 and the best bid is $3.45, the order will not be filled immediately and possibly never. Limit orders are filled as expeditiously as possible when the relevant bid or ask price is on the required side of the limit order price.

A stop order is an order designed to sell or buy if the relevant bid or ask price reaches a specified level. Whereas a limit order places a condition under which an order will not be executed, a stop order places a condition under which an order is activated. A stop order is usually applied to a position

---

[7]Certain specialized brokers that service large institutional investors such as hedge funds are called *prime brokers*.

[8]It is possible to place a restriction on an offer to fill the entire order at the same price. In that case, it is possible that an order might have to wait until a single price is quoted by a dealer that will fill the entire order.

already in place that needs to be closed out. A stop order is often placed to reduce a possible loss. For example, a holder of a long position might place a stop order to sell, which is sometimes called a *stop-loss order*, at a price lower than the current price. If the best bid price reaches the stop order level, the stop order turns into a market order. While it may not always be possible for the trade to be executed at that price, it would generally be executed at close to that price. In a similar manner, holders of short positions are worried about the price going up, so they may execute a stop order to buy at a higher price than the current price.

How fast an order is executed and how close the order is executed to the desired price is determined by how liquid the market is. Derivatives exchanges authorize a certain number of dealers who are charged with making markets. There can be some restrictions on the bid-ask spread by an exchange, but generally speaking, the dealers are free to set the bid and ask prices at whatever levels they want. The dealers are competing with each other, however, and they have an incentive to offer the smallest bid-ask spreads. If there is not much trading on the part of the public, one might think that small bid-ask spreads would induce trading, but in fact, the bid-ask spreads are likely to be large when there is not much trading. Dealers that open positions want to offset their positions with the opposite transaction fairly quickly so that they do not have exposure. If there is not much interest in the derivative on the part of other traders and investors, dealers are likely to quote higher bid-ask spreads and the market will not be very liquid.

Market liquidity is, however, a complex issue and is influenced by the degree of to which the dealer is concerned about whether he has as much knowledge of the security or derivative as the investor. This situation, referred to as *asymmetric information* and *adverse selection*, will cause a dealer to widen the spread.[9] A more volatile underlying will also lead to a wider spread and generally less liquidity. We will return to the issue of liquidity in Chapter 12 as we discuss liquidity risk.

---

[9]Adverse selection is a consequence of a problem called *asymmetric information* and effectively means that a one party in possession of significant and reasonably accurate information will trade a position to another party. Selling a car that has a problem you are aware of, to someone else who is not aware of the problem just so they will have to deal with it, is a case of adverse selection. As we mentioned in Chapter 4, it is also an example of deceptive risk transfer.

5.1.2.3 *Clearing*

There are two major distinguishing features of derivatives exchanges in contrast to OTC markets. One is, as we discussed, the standardization of contracts and the other is the *clearing* process. Clearing refers to the procedure in which a buy order is matched up to a sell order and recorded in the accounting system of the exchange, whereupon the buyer's funds are then transferred to the appropriate party. All derivatives exchanges operate with or in relationship to an entity called a *clearinghouse*. In some cases, the clearinghouse is a legal part of the exchange and in some cases the clearinghouse is a completely separate entity. The objective of the clearinghouse is to match up each buyer with a seller, to collect and disburse money, and to execute cash settlement or delivery procedures that terminate derivatives contracts. The most important role played by a derivatives clearinghouse is to provide a guarantee that any party that makes a profit off of a transaction will get paid. If the losing party does not pay, the clearinghouse pays.

Let us start by explaining the role of the clearinghouse when two parties execute a transaction. First, we need to introduce the concept of *margin requirements*. In the securities markets, investors can borrow money to buy securities. The amount borrowed is called the margin and the remaining amount is a loan from a broker to a customer. The transaction is called a margin trade and is done to provide leverage, which amplifies losses as well as gains. As an example, suppose an investor buys a stock selling at €100 and finances it by borrowing €25 and investing €75 of his money. Now suppose the stock moves up to €102. If the investor had invested the full €100 from his own money, he would have earned a return of 2%. By investing only €75, however, he earns a return of 2.7% ($€2/€75 - 1$). If the stock falls to €98, an investor who invests €100 will lose 2%, while an investor who invests only €75 will lose 2.7%. Leverage, thus, magnifies gains and losses. Investors who have strong feelings about the direction of the stock and are comfortable with the risk may choose to do a margin trade in a security.

A similar concept applies in derivatives, but there are several major differences. Let us start with futures contracts. The derivatives clearinghouse imposes certain margin requirements in the form of minimum initial and maintenance margins. The *initial margin* requirement is expressed as a fixed amount that usually is less than 5% of the price of the futures contracts. Thus, a futures contract might have a price of €100 and the initial margin might be around €4. The clearinghouse also specifies a maintenance margin, which is less than the initial margin. In this case, let us assume that the maintenance margin is €2.50. Of course, the contract size as discussed above applies, so a contract covering 1,000 units effectively has an initial margin of 1,000(€4) = €4,000 and a maintenance margin of 1,000(€2.50) = €2,500 per contract. It should be noted that the margin process for a futures transaction, unlike that of a securities transaction, does not involve the extension of credit. In other words, there is no loan. For that reason, futures margins are best thought of as either down payments or good faith deposits. The CME actually uses the term *performance bonds* instead of margins, reflecting the fact that the money is more of a good faith deposit.

When a transaction is executed, both the long and the short have to deposit the initial margin in an account at the clearinghouse.[10] The process is illustrated in Exhibit 5-3. The key institutions — the exchange, the

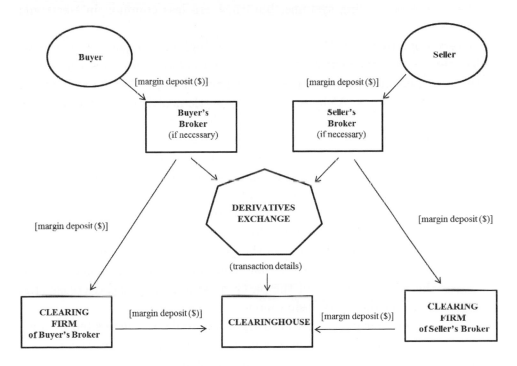

Exhibit 5-3. A Futures Trade on a Derivatives Exchange

---

[10]In reality, there is often a chain of parties. The trader creating the position may have a broker. Thus, the trader deposits the money with the broker who deposits the money with the clearinghouse. Most clearinghouses use clearing firms, which are companies that have accounts at the clearinghouses. Each direct and indirect market trader must have an account at a clearing firm or have an account at a broker that has an account at a clearing firm. The deposits pass through all of these entities but ultimately the money comes from the trader and ends up at the clearing firm account at the clearinghouse.

clearinghouse, and the clearing firms — are in bold and all caps. Note that both the buyer and the seller have to deposit margin money. The clearinghouse, thus, holds a balanced set of records. All long positions are matched with corresponding short positions.

Notice that the derivatives exchange passes information on each trade to the clearinghouse. The clearinghouse in turn expects to receive a matching amount of margin money from the clearing firms of both the buyer and the seller. At the end of each trading day, the clearinghouse engages in this matching process. Given either a buy or sell order, if it does not receive a matching order, the trade is classified as an *out-trade*. The clearinghouse then contacts the two parties and requires that they work out any difference before either can trade the next day. Out-trades are fairly common but quickly resolved in floor trading systems, but they are less common in electronic trading.

Every day after a trade is done, the clearinghouse engages in a process called the *daily settlement* or *marking to market* that updates the values of the positions of both parties based on price changes that have occurred since the previous day. Although the daily settlement is done at the end of the day, it is not necessarily based on the final price of the day, which is typically called the closing price. Most exchanges designate an average of the last few trades of the day as the *settlement price*. The exchange then marks each account value to a new value based on the settlement price. If the settlement price increases over the previous day, the long has generated a gain and the short has incurred a corresponding loss. If the settlement price decreases over the previous day, the long has incurred a loss and the short has generated a gain. The amount of the gain or loss is transferred from the party that lost money to the party that made money. This transfer of funds increases the margin balance of the party making money and decreases the margin balance of the party losing money.

As mentioned earlier, the initial margin requirement is deposited by both parties on the day of the transaction. Each subsequent day, the margin balance must be no less than the maintenance margin requirement. If the margin balance falls below the maintenance margin requirement, the trader must deposit sufficient funds to bring the margin account balance *up to the initial margin requirement*, not the maintenance margin requirement. So, the initial margin requirement must be met on the day on which a position is opened and when a margin call is made.

Exhibit 5-4 presents an example of a daily settlement. On the first day, Day 0, the trader goes long 50 contracts at a price of $150. The contract

Day	Opening Balance	Initial Margin Deposited	Settlement Price	Mark-to-Market Amount	Margin Balance	Adequate Margin?	Additional Margin Deposited	Ending Margin Balance
[1]	[2]	[3]	[4]	[5]	[6]	[7]	[8]	[9]
0	$0.00	$312.50	$151.00	$50.00	$362.50	yes	$0.00	$362.50
1	$362.50	$0.00	$152.75	$87.50	$450.00	yes	$0.00	$450.00
2	$450.00	$0.00	$148.20	−$227.50	$222.50	no	$90.00	$312.50
3	$312.50	$0.00	$149.65	$72.50	$385.00	yes	$0.00	$385.00
4	$385.00	$0.00	$146.15	−$175.00	$210.00	no	$102.50	$312.50
5	$312.50	$0.00	$147.55	$70.00	$382.50	yes	$0.00	$382.50

Exhibit 5-4. Daily Settlement Example for a Long Futures Position

has an initial margin requirement of $6.25 per contract and a maintenance margin requirement of $4.50 per contract. Thus, on the first day of the trade, Day 0, the trader must deposit 50($6.25) = $312.50. On each day thereafter he must maintain a balance of 50($4.50) = $225.00. If, however, his maintenance margin balance falls below $225.00, he must deposit sufficient funds to bring the balance back up to $312.50. Let us walk through Exhibit 5-4.

On Day 0, he purchased 50 contracts at $150, so he must make an initial deposit of $312.50, which appears in column 3. The position will be marked-to-market at the end of the day. The settlement price at the end of Day 0 is $151, so his account is marked to market and $50 is added (column 5). The $50 reflects a price increase of $1 applied to 50 contracts. The margin balance (column 6) at the end of Day 0 is, thus, $312.50 + $50 = $362.50. Column 7 checks to see if this balance exceeds the initial margin requirement on Day 0 of $312.50. If it did not, he would have to deposit additional funds. Thus, column 8, the additional margin deposited, contains $0, and the ending balance for the day is $362.50.

The ending balance for Day 0 is carried forward to the opening balance of Day 1. Column 3, initial margin deposited, will be zero the rest of the days, as it reflects only the initial margin. The settlement price at the end of Day 1 is $152.75, column 4, which is an increase of $1.75 over the previous day settlement price. Thus, the account is credited $1.75(50) = $87.50 as shown in column 5. The balance is now $362.50 + $87.50 and exceeds the maintenance margin requirement of $225.00, so no additional funds must be deposited.

On the next day, however, there is a large price decrease, from $152.75 to $148.20, a decline of $4.55. Multiplied by 50 contracts, the result is a charge to the account for $4.55(50) = $227.50, bringing the balance down to $222.50. This amount is less than the maintenance margin of $225.00, so he must deposit $90. Remember that a margin call requires that the trader bring the balance up to the initial margin requirement, not the maintenance margin requirement. Upon depositing the funds, the balance is now at $312.50. On the following day there is a price increase, and the balance goes to $385.00. On Day 4, however, there is a substantial price decrease that brings the balance down to $210.000, which is below the maintenance margin requirement. He must then deposit $102.50 to bring the balance back up to the initial margin deposit. We carry the example forward to the end of Day 5, at which time the balance is $382.50. To that point, he has deposited the initial margin of $312.50 and made additional deposits of $90 and $102.50, for a total amount contributed of $505.00. With a final balance of $382.50, the long has lost $122.50, which is the net of the charges and credits to his account from the daily settlement. These charges and credits are sometimes referred to as *variation margin*.

If the position had been a short transaction, the trader would have had to deposit the same initial amount and would have the same maintenance margin, but he would have profited from price decreases and lost from price increases. Exhibit 5-5 shows the result for a short trader doing the same trade as our long example.

Notice that the mark-to-market gains and losses, column 5, are the opposite in sign to that of the long position. But with regard to margin

Day	Opening Balance	Initial Margin Deposited	Settlement Price	Mark-to-Market Amount	Margin Balance	Adequate Margin?	Additional Margin Deposited	Ending Margin Balance
[1]	[2]	[3]	[4]	[5]	[6]	[7]	[8]	[9]
0	$0.00	$312.50	$151.00	−$50.00	$262.50	no	$50.00	$312.50
1	$312.50	$0.00	$152.75	−$87.50	$225.00	no	$87.50	$312.50
2	$312.50	$0.00	$148.20	$227.50	$540.00	yes	$0.00	$540.00
3	$540.00	$0.00	$149.65	−$72.50	$467.50	yes	$0.00	$467.50
4	$467.50	$0.00	$146.15	$175.00	$642.50	yes	$0.00	$642.50
5	$642.50	$0.00	$147.55	−$70.00	$572.50	yes	$0.00	$572.50

Exhibit 5-5. Daily Settlement Example for a Short Position

calls, do not think that when the long gets a margin call, the short does not and when the short gets a margin call, the long does not. Each party can have sufficient margin. It is not possible, however, that both can get a margin call. Assuming that both parties are above the minimum at the beginning of the day, one party will be marked with a gain and the other with a loss. The party with a gain clearly will not get a margin call, while the party with the loss might. We noted that the long deposited $505 and ended up with $385, which is a loss of $122.50. The short deposited $312.50 on the first day and made margin call deposits of $50 and $87.50 on Days 0 and 1 for a total deposited of $450. The short ends up with $572.50, a gain of $122.50, which came from the long.

There are a few other details to mention. Margin deposits can be made in cash or often with certain low-risk interest-bearing securities. Margin accounts may or may not pay interest on cash deposited. On a given day if the trader receives a margin call, which is made after the market closes but before it opens the next day, he can choose not to deposit the additional funds and can instruct the clearing firm to close out the position when the market opens. The trader is then responsible for any additional losses that might occur before the closing trade can be done. We should also note that margin balances in excess of the initial margin requirement can usually be withdrawn, though we have not done that in this example. Finally, we should note that the clearinghouse has the authority to mark an account to market during a trading day, thereby requesting additional funds before the market closes. This practice is sometimes done during very fast moving markets. In addition, certain futures transactions that have offsetting positions, such as being long a contract with one expiration and short a contract with a different expiration but the same underlying, are eligible for lower margin requirements, because of the somewhat offsetting nature of these positions, resulting in lower risk.

The objective of the daily settlement is to quickly and regularly collect funds from traders that incur losses and pass them on to traders with gains. As such, the process facilitates the guarantee against credit losses. The clearinghouse collects the funds from the clearing firm, which collects the funds from the broker, which collects the funds from the trader. The clearinghouse is the ultimate guarantor, and it maintains a large reserve to cover such contingencies. If the clearinghouse failed, it would be a major financial disaster for a country. In the entire history of clearinghouses, however, no trader has ever generated a profit that was not realized in cash. Thus, the process has worked effectively and in fact, no clearinghouse has

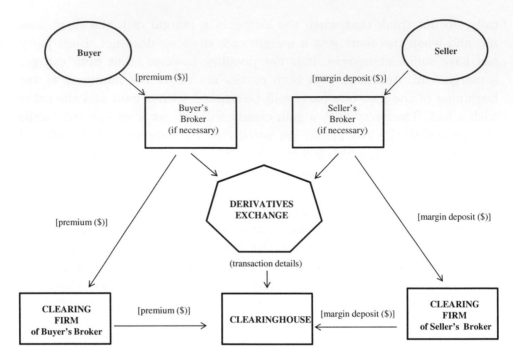

Exhibit 5-6. An Option Trade on a Derivatives Exchange

ever been seriously in danger, even during periods of high market stress accompanied by failures of parties that lose money.

To this point, we have been discussing the clearing process for futures. Now let us take a look at the process for options. Exhibit 5-6 illustrates the clearing process for an option traded on a derivatives exchange.

The only difference in Exhibit 5-5 for options and the corresponding exhibit, 5-4 for futures, is that the option buyer deposits the premium through the chain of entities ultimately to the clearinghouse. Recall that the buyer of an option pays the price of the option, called the premium, to the seller. The premium, however, remains in the clearinghouse and is never returned to the buyer. Of course, the buyer may later receive a payoff or possession of the underlying if the option is exercised. And, because the seller may have to deliver the asset if the option is a call or come up with the funds to buy the asset if the option is a put, the seller must deposit margin.

Because the buyer of an option does not have to ever do anything with the option, long option positions are typically not subject to the same daily settlement as are futures. The buyer pays for the option and can exercise it later or let it expire. The seller, however, is subject to daily margin calls if the amount deposited is not above a minimum. The seller's margin account balance is the sum of the seller's margin deposit, plus the premium deposited by the buyer, plus an additional amount the seller has to come up with if the option is in-the-money or minus an additional amount if the option is out-of-the-money. Certain contracts that have offsetting positions are eligible for reduced margin requirements.[11]

In Section 5.2, we will discuss over-the-counter option trading wherein we will note OTC transactions may or may not be subject to clearing. The clearing we have described is called *bilateral clearing*, as the process clears each transaction with a matching transaction. In the OTC market there is another form of clearing, and we will get to that in Section 5.2.

5.1.3 *Offsetting*

Recall how we described that buying or selling a house in the secondary market is like offsetting a derivatives contract. In this section, we will describe this process in more detail.

One of the attractive features of derivatives exchanges is that they create a market to buy and sell derivative contracts. This market is created by having the exchange authorize dealers to operate in making a market. The dealers stand ready to buy or sell. Thus, a party that desires either a long position or a short position can engage in a transaction, with the dealer willingly taking the opposite side. Because of the availability of these dealers and the standardization of the contracts, a previously established long position can always be offset by going short the same contract. Likewise, a previously established short position can always be offset by going long the same contract.

Recalling how the clearinghouse operates, each long position is matched with a short position. Let us say that you, party A, previously went long 50 contracts, which was matched by someone else, party B, going short 50 contracts. Now at a later time but before expiration, let us suppose you want to offset the 50 contracts. In very simple terms, you previously bought 50 contracts, and now you want to close out your position by selling the

---

[11]The specific margin requirements can vary substantially from exchange to exchange and product to product. At the CBOE, the margin for sellers is a percentage of the market value of the underlying and is normally 15% for index options and 20% for options on stocks.

50 contracts.[12] You do not have to offset with the same party with whom you originally traded. You simply need to find a party or a combination of parties who will go long 50 contracts. Assuming that transaction is now done with a single party called party C, the clearinghouse now shows that there are 50 long contracts held by party C and 50 short contracts held by party B. You, party A, have no positions open.

Now let us add a twist. Suppose party B, holder of 50 short contracts, wants to offset 30 of those contracts but remains short 20 contracts. Suppose party C does not want to change his position. Now suppose party B buys 30 contracts to offset from party D, leaving him with 20 short contracts. Now what do the open positions look like? Have you followed this?

Party B has 20 contracts short, and party D has 30 contracts short. Remember that party C did not want to change his position so he has 50 contracts long. Once again, the shorts match the longs.

These transactions may seem complex, but it is really quite simple if you just remember that each long position is offset by a corresponding short position held by a different party. If a single party goes long a certain number of contracts and later short a different number contracts, his net position is the number of long contracts minus the number of short contracts. Whether that position is net long or short, depends on which number of contracts is greater. Each trade has a long for every short, so the longs and shorts will balance.

At this point, we introduce the concept of *open interest*. Open interest is the number of contracts open at the clearinghouse. The open interest total counts only the long or short number of contracts, not both. Thus, when C went long 50 contracts and B short 50 contracts, the open interest is 50, not counting any other traders of course. After B offsets 30 contracts with D, open interest does not change, because D created new positions. If two parties that already own positions mutually offset, then open interest will decline.

Derivatives exchanges report their open interest as rough indication of the liquidity of the market. You should take this number with a grain of salt, however, as not all open positions will eventually be closed, as we shall see in the next section.

---

[12]It is tempting to say that what you want to do is to capture your profit or loss, but in fact, the daily settlement procedure means that you have already realized your profit or loss. If this transaction were a long position in a security or option, you would not have realized your profit or loss, so closing it by selling would capture it.

5.1.4 *Expiration Settlement and Delivery*

While many derivative positions will be offset before expiration, there will generally be some remaining positions that must be settled. For contracts with physical delivery, the exchanges specify certain delivery procedures that must be followed. In many cases, there are multiple variations of the underlying that can be delivered. The contract specifications describe what can be delivered, where it can be delivered, and when it must be delivered. The most important point to remember is that the short essentially delivers the underlying to the long, so the long has realized a gain or loss based on the difference in the spot price and the previous day's settlement price, and the short realizes the opposite.

If a contract has the cash settlement feature, it will be terminated by a cash payment. A cash-settled futures contract is terminated quite easily. The exchange simply sets the final settlement price on the expiration day to the spot price. The long and short accounts are then marked to market one final time and all positions are officially terminated with no further transactions.

For a physical delivery call, if the underlying is at S_T and the exercise price is X, the call holder determines if S_T is greater than X. If so, he exercises the call, thereby paying X and receiving an asset worth S_T. If S_T is not more than X, the call holder simply lets the call expire. If the call is cash settled, the exchange determines the value $\text{Max}(0, S_T - X)$, meaning the greater of $S_T - X$ or zero. The call seller then pays $S_T - X$ if this value is positive and if not, the option simply expires. In short, the amount of the payoff of the option is the same with physical delivery or cash settlement, though the costs of handling the underlying would clearly come into effect for a physical delivery contract.

For a physical delivery put, the holder would deliver the underlying worth S_T and receive X if S_T is greater than X and lets the option expire otherwise. Thus, if $S_T < X$, the cash settlement procedure simply requires that the short pay the long $X - S_T$. If S_T is not less than X, the option simply expires with no payment.

This section completes our discussion of the exchange-listed derivatives market. We now turn to the over-the-counter or OTC market.

5.2 The Over-the-Counter Derivatives Market

Recall that we described how having a house built for you is like an OTC transaction. In this section, we will explain that process in more detail.

At one time there were many distinguishing features of the OTC market in comparison to the exchange-traded market. Over recent years, those distinctions have become more blurred. The primary remaining difference is that OTC contracts are customized, whereas exchange-traded contracts are standardized. Customized contracts are created between two parties who design the contract to fit their needs. The foundation of the OTC market is the set of dealers who are willing to trade virtually any type of contract so desired by their end user customers. The OTC dealers are generally large banks and financial institutions that have invested considerable sums of money into their derivatives operations.[13] They compete with each other for customer business. At one time, these dealers were regulated only to the extent of ordinary banking and securities laws. The Financial Crisis of 2008 changed all of that. In the U.S., the Dodd-Frank Act of 2010 brought more regulation of the OTC market under the U.S. federal government. This is not to say, however, that the same degree of regulation exists in the OTC market as in the exchange-traded market. OTC dealers are still basically free to offer customized derivatives without receiving regulatory permission. We will return to this topic in Section 5.3 when we discuss the regulatory structure of the derivatives industry.

First, however, let us take a look at the size of the OTC market. Many people express great concern about how large this market is, but some of this concern arises over confusion between the concepts used to measure the size of the market.

Recall that for the exchange-traded market, we typically measure its size in terms of volume.[14] We saw that volume is not a perfect measure in that the same contract trading on two different exchanges can have different sizes. Thus, for a transaction executed by a particular party with a given exposure, volume on the market with the smaller size contract would exceed volume on the other. We also saw that the volume of an option is not necessarily comparable to the volume of a futures on the same underlying. In addition, a given volume on a derivative on a commodity such as gold is not comparable to volume on financial asset, say the S&P 500. Thus, no real

---

[13]For example, The National Futures Association maintains a registry of swap dealers operating in U.S. markets at the web site https://www.nfa.futures.org/ NFA-swaps-information/regulatory-info-sd-and-msp/SD-MSP-registry.HTML. Most of these swap dealers also make markets in other derivatives.

[14]Occasionally open interest is used, but volume is a more common measure.

market measure of exchange-traded derivatives gives a completely accurate picture of market size.

Likewise, for the OTC market, there is no single completely accurate measure. Volume is not even recorded as there is no standard size contract. The two measures most commonly used are *notional* and *market value*. The concept of notional, sometimes called *notional principal* or *notional value*, reflects the size of the contract. It is an artificial amount of money or units of an asset on which payments will be made. For example, a swap requiring that one party make a series of payments at a fixed rate and another make a series of payments at a floating rate will require the specification of a notional. The notional is the amount on which the payments are based. Most importantly, the notional is never actually paid. The parties pay only the net of one interest payment over the other applied to the notional. We will see more precisely how that works in Chapter 9, but for now just think of it as the amount on which interest payments are made.[15] Nonetheless, this principal amount is never paid itself on interest rate swaps.[16] For options, the notional is the value of the underlying in terms of exercise price. Thus, an option on say 20,000 units of the SPDR (pronounced "spider"), which is the exchange-traded fund (ETF) based on the S&P 500, would have a notional of 20,000 times the exercise price. But remember, the notional is not paid. The payoff is based on the difference in the underlying value and the exercise price factored up by the size of the contract. In the case of the SPDR options, the payoff is $20,000\text{Max}(0, S_T - X)$ where S_T is the value of the underlying at expiration and X is the exercise price.

Exhibit 5-7 gives the history from 1998–2015 of the size of the OTC market in terms of notional, for all derivatives combined and by the two largest categories, interest rate and foreign exchange derivatives. This information comes from the surveys conducted by the Bank for International Settlements (BIS), located in Basel, Switzerland. The BIS is a cooperative global banking association that facilitates the payments of funds between banks and attempts to provide coordination of banking regulation. Twice a year the BIS engages in surveys of banks on their OTC transactions. The graph reports only the year-end figure.

Without fully appreciating the point of the previous paragraph, the numbers might seem to be staggering. The most recent number is about

---

[15]The point is equally applicable to forwards.

[16]On some currency swaps, the notional amount is paid. We will see that type of instrument in Chapter 9.

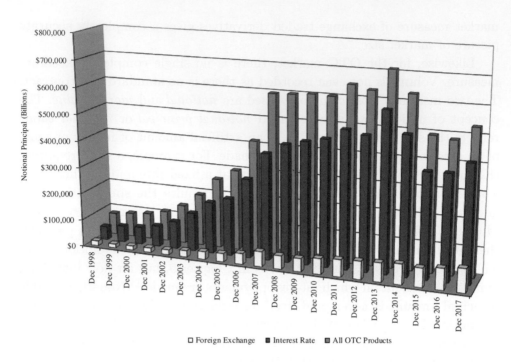

Exhibit 5-7. Notional of the Global OTC Derivatives Market Since 1998

$531 trillion, and it reached a peak at about $710 trillion in 2013. Currently, interest rate derivatives account for about $426 trillion, about 80% of the total, and currency derivatives are about $87 trillion, 16% of the total.

$531 trillion in all! Let us put that number in perspective. There are 31,536,000 seconds in a 365-day year. Doing the math, it would take about 31,710 years for a trillion seconds to elapse. And of course, as I write this chapter, the U.S. debt is at about $21.2 trillion. There are about 25.4 millimeters on an inch, and 384 billion millimeters to the moon, which means that it would take about $2\frac{1}{2}$ trips to the moon to cover a trillion millimeters.[17]

But wait. As we said earlier, the notional amount is just the amount on which the payments are based. A more accurate measure of the size of a derivative contract is its market value. Banks estimate the market values

---

[17] Amazingly, the word "Kardashian" returned only 302 million Google hits, or only about 0.03% of a trillion. The author found that number surprisingly low, but he is relieved to know that it is not higher.

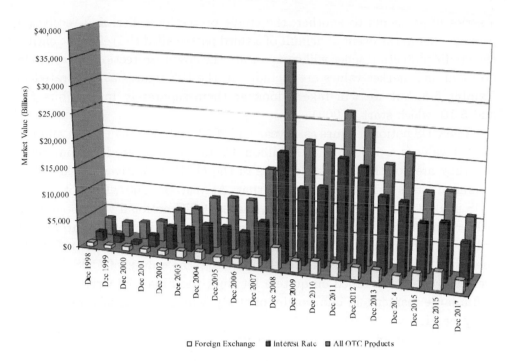

Exhibit 5-8. Market Value of the Global OTC Derivatives Market Since 1998

of their derivatives, netting their long and short positions and report these figures to the BIS.[18] Exhibit 5-8 shows the corresponding market values.

Now we get a more reasonable number of the amount of money involved. At the end of 2017, the total was about $11 trillion, with interest rate derivatives at around $7.6 trillion and foreign currency derivatives at around $2.3 trillion. Putting it in perspective, for the market as a whole, the market value is about 2.1% of the notional.

Worries about the size of the derivatives market are invariably worries about default. The Financial Crisis of 2008 in particular brought worries about systemic default to a lot of ordinary people who had never paid much attention to financial markets. One derivative instrument that received a great deal of attention in the Financial Crisis was the credit default swap or CDS, which we briefly mentioned in Chapter 4. Basically, a CDS is a derivative contract in which one party, the credit protection buyer, makes

---

[18]There is some cause for concern over double counting, wherein two banks report the same transaction. The BIS states that it adjusts for double counting, but you should probably take this point with a grain of salt.

a series of payments to another, the credit protection seller, and receives a promise that in the event of default of a third party called the reference entity, the credit protection seller will compensate the credit protection buyer. CDS notional and market values are included in the BIS figures as illustrated in Exhibit 5-8, but we will take a look at them separately in Exhibits 5-9 and 5-10, which start in 2004.

The CDS notional figure as of year-end 2017 is about $9.4 trillion and the market value is a little over $304 billion. Certainly these are large numbers, but they are not the largest elements of the OTC derivatives market. The Financial Crisis of 2008 took care of that. At year-end 2007, the notional of CDS peaked at around $58 trillion, while the OTC notional was about $600 trillion. Market value of credit default swaps peaked a year later at around $5 trillion, while overall OTC market value was at around $35 trillion. Clearly the effect of a credit crunch greatly increases the values of CDS. As you see, CDS usage has tailed off quite a lot since the Financial Crisis, but it is still a large market and one worthy of study, which we will take up later in Chapter 11.

As measures of market size, both notional and market value, however, have their advantages and disadvantages. Notional is a far more accurate number in one sense: it is written into the contract by the two parties.

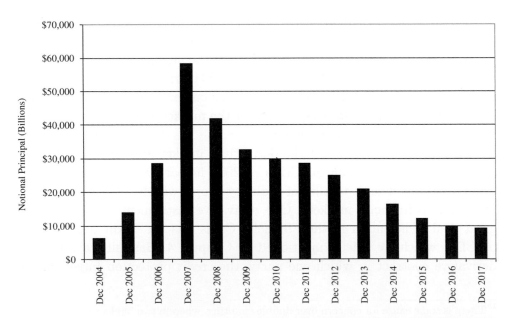

Exhibit 5-9. Notional Value of Global Credit Default Swaps Market Since 2004

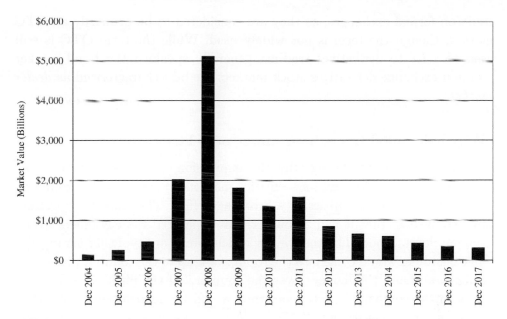

Exhibit 5-10. **Market Value of Global Credit Default Swaps Market Since 2004**

A notional of $100 million on a particular derivative is unambiguous. The two parties agreed on it, wrote the number into the contract, and the payments are based on it. Yet, as we saw, it overstates the amount of money being paid. As such, it tends to give an unnecessarily alarming picture of the risk. Market value, on the other hand, gives a better image of the amount of money involved. Yet, market value must be estimated. We will learn how to do that later in this book, and you will see that for options at least, it can require a great deal of judgment. Two parties could be far apart in their estimates of the market value.

5.2.1 *Trading*

The concept of OTC derivatives trading essentially refers to any type of derivative created on any market anywhere. For example, you could create a derivative with your friend, and it would be an OTC derivatives contract. The reference to the term "OTC" aligns the derivatives market with the OTC stock market. In the U.S., the OTC stock market is Nasdaq, but given the slow demise of floor trading in favor of electronic trading, the distinction between Nasdaq and the formal exchanges that trade stocks, such as the New York Stock Exchange, is also becoming blurred. Bonds do not traditionally trade on formal exchanges, so they are considered to be primarily an OTC market, though the term is not widely used. While the term OTC is still used to refer to derivatives trading, generally speaking the bond market and non-exchange derivatives stock markets are best characterized as *dealer markets*.

Why is it called Over-the-Counter or OTC?

In case you are wondering why the expression "over-the-counter" has been used to describe certain securities markets, it refers to the common practice of buying securities in a brokerage office. The office floor would be arranged so that it had a counter that separated the customers from the employees, much like the way in which banks are typically arranged. The customer would come into the room, walk up to the counter, place the order, and hand the money "over the counter." If the physical securities were in the company's possession, they would be handed back "over the counter" to the customer. If the broker did not have the securities on hand, it would have to acquire them and that would take a few days. Only certain securities, usually small companies, traded in this type of market.

As the market became better organized, an association of U.S. firms organized themselves into the National Association of Securities Dealers or NASD. It specialized in small company stocks and was generally viewed as where a stock traded when it first became a public company. As the NASD began to automate its system of price quotations, the trading system became known as the National Association of Securities Dealers Automated Quotations, or NASDAQ. You may notice, however, that the entire organization is now known as Nasdaq, that is, without the all capital letters. In English usage, the practice of using all caps applies to an acronym, which is an abbreviation. But Nasdaq is no longer an abbreviation. Over time people began referring to the entire organization as NASDAQ, when in fact NASDAQ was at one time only the quotation system. The organization eventually conceded that its name had been changed by usage from NASD to NASDAQ. While being highly automated, the organization no longer refers to the automated system within its name. Thus, it formally changed its name from NASDAQ to Nasdaq. In other words, its name is no longer an acronym.

As noted, Nasdaq has typically been the home of trading in small company stocks. As these companies develop into larger companies, they usually aspired to being listed on the New York Stock Exchange, sometimes called *The Big Board*. But companies like Microsoft, Apple, Google, and many other famous high-tech companies have stayed on Nasdaq. These powerful tech companies determined that they did not need the NYSE. In effect, they realized that they were so large that they themselves were more powerful than the NYSE.

So, in the U.S., Nasdaq simply refers to a stock exchange that does not have a physical trading floor where buyers and sellers meet. All trading is done electronically. The term OTC has been extended to refer to any form of informal trading between two parties. Thus, in the derivatives world, even though exchanges have electronic trading systems that replaced their floor trading, they are referred to as the exchange-listed market, while derivatives that are created by any two parties and customized to the parties' needs are referred to as the OTC market.

The dealers are the foundation of the OTC market. They offer a wide variety of types of derivative contracts. A dealer essentially provides a quote indicating that it stands ready to take a long or a short position opposite the customer. The derivatives contracts they offer are generally divided into two types: vanilla and exotic. *Vanilla derivatives*, occasionally referred to as *plain vanilla*, are the most common types of derivatives, such as simple options, forwards, and swaps. We have not gotten sufficiently far into these instruments to appreciate the fact that more complex versions of them are available. These instruments are often called *exotic derivatives* or sometimes just *exotics*.[19] For example, one can buy an option that expires prematurely if the underlying reaches a certain level. One could buy a swap that pays off only if the underlying stays within a certain range. Exotic derivatives usually involve the attachment of certain features or conditions to vanilla derivatives. As this is a book primarily for end users, you should do a careful watch for these complex instruments. They are useful to end users only in extremely specialized situations. Most dealers have readily available quotes for their bid and offer prices of vanilla derivatives. The exotic instruments usually require highly customized transactions.

As mentioned, the customers are the end users, and they are corporations and institutional investors such as pension funds, endowments, mutual funds,

---

[19]They are also sometimes called second- and third-generation derivatives, implying that vanilla derivatives are first generation derivatives.

hedge funds, and at times, local governments. On occasion, wealthy individuals may engage in customized derivatives, but you can generally think of most end users as corporations, institutional investors, and some local governments. End users come to dealers and request quotes, either through direct contact or through electronic trading systems that the dealers offer or participate in. In many cases, however, dealers call on end users and try to convince them to use derivatives.[20] The history of derivatives has shown evidence of strong pressure for end users to employ complex derivatives often to the detriment of the end user.

The derivatives dealer business is highly competitive. There are many derivatives dealers, which are mostly the largest global banks and other financial institutions. The profit margins on vanilla products are relatively small, but they are much larger on exotic products. Hence, there is pressure on banks to increase profits by getting end users to employ exotic derivatives.

Now let us take a look at how dealers profit off of derivatives. As noted, they quote a bid and ask price. For example, consider an option on a stock index trading at around 100. Given the terms of the option, the dealer determines that an appropriate price is around 5. The dealer might then quote an ask of 5.25 and a bid of 4.75. These numbers mean that the dealer is willing to sell the option for a price (premium) of 5.25 or buy it for 4.75. If an end user wants to buy the option, it pays 5.25, and if the end user wants to sell the option, it will receive 4.75. Let us assume that the end user buys the option at 5.25. The dealer then holds a short position in the option and will be hurt if the underlying strengthens. Although we will cover what the dealer does in more detail later, for now just understand that the dealer does not bear this risk for long. Almost immediately the dealer searches for a way to profit from an upward move in the underlying that will offset the loss on the contract entered into with the end user. As examples, the dealer might buy the underlying, or it might buy a futures, an option on a futures, a forward, a swap, or it might sell a put. In other words, the dealer will hedge the risk from the original contract by engaging in one of these other transactions. There is not necessarily a one-to-one correspondence between the risk of the original transaction and the hedge transaction. The dealer usually has to do some balancing, whereby say two positions in the original derivative might need to be offset by three positions in the hedging instruments. Most

---

[20]Remember the opening story in Chapter 1 in which Bob, the newly appointed CFO, is approached by a bank salesman and his quantitative colleague.

importantly, the dealer has the ability to do this hedge at a lower cost than the original position, thus, netting a profit.

The point is that the dealer hedges away the risk. Of course, this fact begs the obvious question: why could the end user not do the hedge and bypass the dealer? In some cases, the end users might be large enough and have enough knowledgeable personnel to be able to do the hedge. But hedging derivatives is a complex activity. Most end users specialize in providing non-financial products and services. They do not have the expertise to do derivatives hedging. Even if they acquired the knowledge, their need for it may not be sufficiently large that they can justify the investment in personnel and systems. In short, derivatives dealers like any other intermediaries have specialized knowledge and economies of scale that enable them to efficiently provide these services to end users.

The previous sentence does not, however, mean that end users get the most attractive and competitive prices. Like any other party in a two-way transaction, each participant tries to extract the most favorable terms from the other. End users are always free to turn to other dealers, just as you can always shop around when buying a car or just about anything else.

While exchange-traded contracts can be executed almost immediately, OTC contracts can take a little longer. For the former, we know that there is a standard set of terms, and there is no variation from transaction to transaction, other than the price. In an OTC transaction, however, virtually all of the terms are subject to negotiation. In the early days of the OTC derivatives market, basically in the 1980s, a contract could take several weeks to finalize. The main delay was due to attorneys having to read the contracts and approve them. This procedure has now become streamlined through an organization called ISDA, the International Swaps and Derivatives Markets.[21] ISDA created a standardized document called the ISDA Master Agreement, which is essentially a template that can accommodate virtually every derivatives transaction.[22] ISDA also created a second type of document called the ISDA Credit Support Annex or CSA that plays a role in managing the credit risk of OTC transactions, a topic we will take up in the next section and in detail in Chapter 11.

---

[21] ISDA was originally known as the International Swap Dealers Association. ISDA later wanted to expand the implication of its coverage to all derivatives. Although swaps are derivatives, ISDA decided it was best to retain the acronym and separate swaps and derivatives even though the latter include the former.

[22] The ISDA Master Agreement can even be adapted to work outside the derivatives arena. The author has seen standard loans documented using the ISDA Master Agreement.

The two parties to an OTC derivatives transaction are commonly referred to as *counterparties*, meaning that they are opposite (counter) to each other. Their relationship gives rise to a concept referred to as *counterparty risk* or *counterparty credit risk*, which we will take up in the next section.

The actual execution of an OTC contract has been traditionally done by informal negotiation, making wide use of telephonic, fax, and electronic communication such as email. In the last 10 years, however, the industry has developed trading systems that are commonly called *swap execution facilities* or SEFs. These systems are electronic services that provide for the posting of bids and offers and the consummation of transactions between parties who agree to terms.

5.2.2 *Offsetting an OTC Transaction*

The exchange-listed derivatives market is often described as having considerable liquidity, which is thought to be advantageous over the OTC market. The truth, however, is that the liquidity in the exchange-listed market can vary considerably from highly liquid to relatively illiquid. Liquidity is guaranteed by the exchange, but liquidity means only that there will always be a dealer offering a bid and an ask. But the bid-ask spread can be quite wide, meaning that if you want to do a trade you will have to buy at a relatively higher price or sell at a relatively lower price than you would if liquidity were better.

One of the illusions of liquidity that has occurred in the exchange-listed market is the visual image of the derivatives trading floor. There are hundreds, perhaps a thousand or more people running around busily doing their jobs. This image gives the impression of liquidity. Thus, in a loose sense, you think you can *see* the liquidity. Because the OTC market has no central market place where people gather, there is no way to create a similar image. You can show the trading desks of a financial institution where there certainly appears to be a lot of activity, but that image pales in comparison to the trading floor of an exchange. There simply are not as many people running doing their jobs. Yet, the OTC market is highly liquid. You just cannot capture it visually. People tend to believe virtually all of what they can see and far less of what they hear of or read about.

OTC contracts are often described as primarily created for the purpose of holding them until they expire. This characterization is almost but not completely true. While a party that holds an exchange-listed derivatives contract can offset that contract before expiration, it is also true that a party holding an OTC contract can do the same. Let us take a simple example. Suppose a U.S. company called M enters into a forward contract with bank N to buy 10 million euros in six months at a rate of $1.12. These terms mean that in six months, M will pay the bank $11.2 million (10 million times $1.12), and the bank will deliver the 10 million euros to M. For reference, let us note that the spot rate for euros at the time the transaction is initiated is $1.10.

M may have entered into the contract for a variety of reasons, but in all likelihood it anticipated the need for 10 million euros in six months. Let us say that two months later, M determines that it no longer needs the 10 million euros in four months. Perhaps the project it needed them for has been canceled. Now M has a pure speculative position in the euros. Not being inclined to speculate in the currency market, it would like to close the position. Let us see how it could do that.

First, let us look into the currency market and see what the spot and forward rates are for euros. Let the spot rate be $1.118 and the forward rate be $1.125. At this point M is long 10 million euros with an expiration in four months. One thing M could do is to enter the market and request a new forward contract to go short 10 million euros in four months. Assuming the $1.125 quote is a bid rate, M can enter into a new contract to deliver 10 million euros in four months at $1.125. Let us assume that M enters into this new contract with bank R. Now M's position is that it is committed to buy 10 million euros, paying $1.12 in four months on the first contract with bank N, and deliver 10 million euros and receive $1.125 in four months on the second contract, which is with bank R. Because in four months M will buy the euros at $1.12 and immediately deliver them for $1.125, M is now hedged against any further move in the euro. Nonetheless, M is not hedged against credit risk, because of the possibility that one party might default. For example, when M executes the first contract, bank N might be unable to deliver the euros. Or, when M delivers the euros to bank R, bank R might be unable to pay for them. Moreover, if M does not receive the euros from bank N, it cannot use that as an excuse to not deliver the euros to bank R.

As an alternative way to offset the risk, M could go back to bank N and ask for an offset. Bank N would calculate the market value of the contract and one party would pay the other. The market value is easily seen as the difference between $1.125 and $1.12 times 10 million, discounted four months. In other words, M will pay $1.12 and receive $1.125 on 10 million euros in four months. Assuming M's annual interest rate is 1%, the value is ($1.125 − $1.12)(10 million)$(1.01)^{-4/12}$, which equals around $49,834.

M's position is a positive value of $49,834, while N's position is a negative value of $49,834. So M and N could settle the contract by having N pay M $49,834. The contract is now terminated, and there is no further risk of any form. This type of offsetting settlement is allowed for in the ISDA Master Agreement, and while most contracts are intended to be held to expiration, occasionally circumstances arise that necessitate an early settlement of this sort.

So, M can offset the risk by entering into the opposite transaction with a different dealer, or M can return to the same bank and enter into an offsetting settlement. For a forward or a swap, the dealer will determine that one party owes the other the greater amount and will arrange a simple settlement, which could be paid from dealer to end user or end user to dealer. If the transaction is an option, option values are always non-negative to the long, so the dealer will determine the value of the option and will pay it to the end user. For a short position in an option, the end user will pay the dealer.[23]

5.2.3 *The Credit Risk of OTC Contracts*

From its inception, one of the distinguishing characteristics of OTC contracts in comparison to exchange-listed contracts is in the credit risk. OTC contracts have the potential for one party to default to the other, whereas exchange-listed contracts are executed through a clearinghouse that guarantees against default. As we saw, the clearinghouse uses margins and daily settlements to manage the credit risk, and all of the clearinghouses of the world have to this point been completely successful in eliminating the possibility that a party that makes money will not get paid.

But as we said, OTC contracts have potential credit risk. In today's markets, that potential is being mitigated by the increasing use of clearing OTC contracts. For right now, however, let us look at how credit risk arises in an OTC contract.

Consider an arrangement in which party C enters into a forward contract with dealer D in which C agrees to buy $10 million par value of U.S. Treasury bonds at a price of 125. Now, let us move to the expiration date and assume

---

[23]There is yet one other but uncommon way to settle. One party could arrange for a third party to take over its position, subject to approval of the original counterparty, a process called *novation*. This type of settlement would tend to be used in mergers, where one party merges or takes over another party, or in bankruptcy, which often involves mergers or possibly the federal government taking over the obligations of a bankrupt entity.

that the Treasury bonds are selling for 127. Dealer D is obligated to deliver bonds worth 127 and is due to receive 125 from counterparty C. Thus, dealer D effectively owes party C $20 million ($2 per bond times 10 million par value of bonds). Now, suppose dealer D is bankrupt. That means that C becomes a creditor in the bankruptcy of D.[24] If the price fell below 125 and D is bankrupt, C owes D the greater amount, and C would still be obligated to pay. The standard ISDA Master Agreement requires that the two parties net the amounts they owe. And neither party can abrogate its obligations to the other. Hence, only one party owes money to the other at a given time.

The same principle in the above paragraph applies to swaps, but their values are a little harder to determine and we will defer the details until Chapter 9. You should just realize that a swap is a series of payments owed by the two parties to each other with only the net being paid. Thus, a swap is like a portfolio of forward contracts. We will illustrate that point also in Chapter 9.

For an option, let us say that C buys a call option on $10 million of Treasury bonds from dealer D with an exercise price of 120. Now at expiration let us say the bond is worth 124. Thus, D owes C an effective amount of $40 million ($4 times 10 million par value of bonds). If D defaults, once again C becomes a creditor of D. With an option, however, default can be only one way. C, as the holder of the option can never owe D once it has made the initial premium payment.

As we see, credit risk exists in OTC derivatives. While we will cover credit risk in more detail in Chapter 11, let us take a brief look at how parties to OTC derivative contracts can mitigate this risk. One way is to require that margin be posted with a third party. Because of the bilateral nature of the contract, at any given time the value is positive to one party and negative to the other. The parties can agree that the party with the negative position can post margin equal to the value of the position or some other amount of margin with a third party. The party holding the positive position may also be required to post a modest amount of margin just as a precaution against possible fast moves in the price.

One of the most universal techniques for counterparty risk management is called *netting*. There are two forms of netting: *payment netting* and *cross-product netting*. Payment netting is applicable to swaps and forwards,

---

[24]We shall see in Chapter 11 that derivative claims in bankruptcy receive accelerated treatment, due to the fact that their values can vary tremendously before the bankruptcy is settled.

because each party owes something to the other. The amounts owed are netted, resulting in only one party owing the net difference to the other. By reducing the separate flows of money owed, some of the credit risk is reduced. Payment netting is not applicable to options, because only the short owes money to the long.

Cross-product netting carries this process a step further. Suppose company A has derivative contracts with counterparty Dealer B. Naturally company A and Dealer B engage in payment netting. In all likelihood, they also engage in cross product netting, as this feature is provided under the ISDA Master Agreement. Cross-product netting means that in the event of a bankruptcy of one of the parties, the two parties agree to net all payments owed between them. As an example, consider the following scenario in which A declares bankruptcy:

> *Company A owes Dealer B $10.5 million in market value for a swap*
> *Dealer B owes Company A $2.25 million in market value for an option*
> *Company A owes Dealer B, which is also a bank, $4.25 million in a loan*

Thus, A owes B $14.75 for the swap and the loan, but B owes A $2.25 million for the swap. With cross-product netting, A owes B $14.75 million −$2.25 million = $12.50 million. Cross-product netting greatly simplifies the complexity of the bankruptcy process, and it significantly reduces the flow of money.

Another form of credit control is limiting the amount of exposure to any one party. This method tends to diversify the credit risk, but as was seen in the Financial Crisis of 2008, credit risk can be systemic, so this technique can be quite limited.

In addition, OTC transactions can require the use of collateral, which is essentially margins. Accounts can be marked-to-market, with the party owing the greater amount having to post either the market value it owes or a percentage of the market value. We will have more to say about this technique momentarily.

Finally, the party with exposure can use credit derivatives. As noted, we will cover credit risk management in Chapter 11, where credit derivatives and the other techniques of credit risk management will be discussed in more detail.

In spite of great efforts to control credit risk, losses do occur, and they can be quite large, particularly if they are systemic. During the Financial Crisis of 2008, the U.S. government either bailed out or played a substantial role in protecting AIG, Fannie Mae, Freddie Mac, Merrill Lynch, Citi, GMAC, and many other large institutions that were considered systemically important. As a result of these actions, in 2010 the U.S. government passed the Wall Street Reform and Consumer Protection Act, known more commonly as the Dodd-Frank Act. Many other countries passed similar legislation. One of the recommendations of the act was that OTC contracts would be cleared through multilateral clearinghouses. We have looked at bilateral clearing, which is the form of clearing used by derivatives exchanges. Now let us look at multilateral clearing and the somewhat unusual notion of clearing and settling OTC contracts.

5.2.4 *Clearing of OTC Contracts*

As you now know, one of the most important differences between exchange-listed and OTC contracts is that the former are standardized and the latter are customized. For many years, the exchanges have taken advantage of how standardization facilitates bilateral netting and enables the exchanges to essentially eliminate credit risk. It has been largely assumed that without standardization, the use of clearinghouses is not feasible. But the notional of multilateral clearing developed, and it embodies the element of clearing non-standardized products. With multilateral clearing, there can be a virtually infinite number of derivatives with very diverse characteristics.

Exhibit 5-11 illustrates multilateral clearing using three entities and a clearinghouse. Look at Panel A where you will see that Party C owes Party D $50, while Party D owes Party E $30, and Party E owes Party C $15. The contracts each party has with the other need not be the same types. In the absence of a formal clearinghouse, Party C would pay Party D $50, Party D would pay Party E $30, and Party E would pay Party A $15. The problem here is that there is a lot of money flowing, and the credit risk is potentially quite high. For example, if E cannot pay the $15 it owes to C, then C might not be able to pay the full amount of $50 it owes to D. Of course D owes E, so it might not be able to pay E. In other words, there is a chain of obligations that in practice involves many more entities.

Now look at Panel B where we introduce a multilateral clearinghouse. Each party clears its contracts with the clearinghouse. Notice in Panel A that Party C owes $50 and is owed $15, so on net, it owes $35. Party D owes $30 and is owed $50 so on net it is owed $20. Party E owes $15 and is owed $30 so on net it is owed $15. The clearinghouse makes and receives those precise payments. It receives $35 from C and disburses $20 to D and $15 to E.

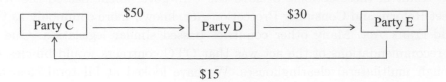

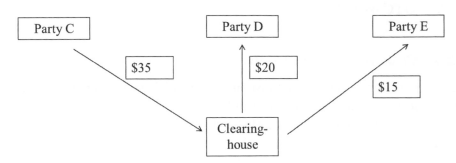

Exhibit 5-11. How a Multilateral Clearinghouse Reduces Credit Risk

The above process illustrates only how payments are netted. It does not address how the clearinghouse manages the risk. If the clearinghouse does not get paid by a party owing money, it has to have a way of making payments to parties that are due money. It maintains its integrity with the use of margin accounts and a daily clearing and settlement process.

Although the OTC market is not completely to the point to having all contracts cleared, it is moving in that direction. Virtually all credit default swaps and interest rate swaps are cleared, and other types of OTC derivatives are increasingly being cleared.

Multilateral clearinghouses are thought by some to be the most important step the markets can take to control risk. Yet, there is always a cost to every obvious benefit. Multilateral clearinghouses work very much like airport hubs: they concentrate the risk. When everything works well at the hub, the system is very reliable. But if the airport hub shuts down due to bad weather, the entire system is affected and more so than if there were no hub. Similarly, because so much risk is concentrated at the clearinghouse, if the clearinghouse runs into problems, the entire system experiences a major breakdown. In some sense, clearinghouses are the opposite of diversification. They concentrate the risk, but when they work well, they are far more efficient and the overall system is safer. And the historical record to date is that they have worked extraordinarily well.

5.3 The Regulatory Structure of the Derivatives Industry

The objective of regulation is to insure fair markets, meaning to provide that accurate information is accessible to everyone and to prevent market manipulation, which is an unethical and illegal action whereby a single market participant or small group of participants attempts to drive the price to an artificially high or low level. How these objectives are carried out varies widely from country to country and type of derivative.

Until the enactment of the Dodd-Frank Act in 2010, the OTC market was considered unregulated, both in the United States and in most other countries. The characterization of the industry as essentially unregulated means that the derivatives they offer do not have to be approved by regulators. OTC dealers are, however, almost always banks, and their activities are regulated under banking laws. Banking in fact is a highly regulated industry in all countries, so the derivatives activities of banks have always been watched very closely. Regulators examine the financial statements of banks and endeavor to be alert for signs of trouble.

In contrast, the exchange-traded derivatives industry is highly regulated. In the United States, the origins of this regulation are in the Grain Futures Act of 1922 and the Commodity Exchange Act of 1936. Because futures trading in the U.S. at that time was exclusively in agricultural futures, regulatory authority was vested in the United States Department of Commerce. This structure was replaced when the Commodity Futures Trading Act of 1974 was passed, authorizing creation of a separate agency called the Commodity Futures Trading Commission or CFTC. The CFTC exists within the Executive Branch of the U.S. Government but is not within a particular department. Among its authority is the requirement that all futures and options on futures contracts must be approved and regulated by the CFTC. This authority does not mean each transaction but rather, each contract. Thus, as a hypothetical example, if the CME decides to start a futures contract on mobile phone rates, it would have to get the contract approved by the CFTC. Once approved, all trading on that contract can proceed without further approval.

In addition, the CFTC monitors the futures market for fairness and may take action, including civil action and legal prosecution through the Department of Justice for such actions as market manipulation or insider trading. The CFTC also is required to approve the creation of new futures exchanges. Moreover, the Dodd-Frank Act granted the CFTC many additional powers, including the regulation of swaps. Based on the definition of swaps in the Act and the apparent trends in the last few years, the CFTC has essentially obtained full authority over the OTC market. That authority does not, however, mean that the CFTC must approve OTC contracts, but the act does give the CFTC additional oversight.

The regulatory structure in the U.S. is somewhat unique in that there are two primary regulatory agencies. As noted, there is the CFTC, but in addition, there is the Securities and Exchange Commission, or SEC, that was created in 1934. The SEC's authority is primarily over securities exchanges and trading, but it also covers the exchange-traded options market. Exchange-traded options were introduced in 1973 with the creation of the Chicago Board Options Exchange. At that time, the CFTC did not exist and authority seemed naturally to flow to the SEC.

This two-agency structure contrasts with the system used in most countries in which there is a single regulatory agency. There have been extensive discussions in the U.S. over the need to merge agencies. The two agencies each tend to have their own supporters in the U.S. Congress, and CFTC supporters have fought any such merger. The SEC is a larger agency, and some experts believe that the CFTC would lose its power if absorbed within the SEC. So far, the two agencies remain independent.

As noted, the regulatory structure within most countries is with a single regulator. In fact, the European Union, which includes almost 30 countries, regulates the OTC market with a single law called the European Market Infrastructure Regulation (EMIR).[25] That law is undergoing final revisions, but some of its provisions are already in place. Each country regulates its markets with its own agency. In France, it is the Autorité des Marchés des Financiers (Financial Markets Authority), and in Germany, it is the Bundesanstalt für Finanzdienstleistungsaufsicht (Federal Financial Supervisory Authority). In other countries as well, there is usually a single regulator, such as the Financial Services Agency of Japan, the Financial Services Authority (FSA) of the U. K., and the Australian Securities and Investments Commission.

---

[25]The European Union is not synonymous with the euro. Some countries in the Union do not use the euro, such as Sweden, Denmark, the Czech Republic, Croatia, Bulgaria, Hungary, Poland, and Romania.

In addition, banking regulators in various countries maintain a role in the derivatives markets through their regulation of banking activities. Moreover, there are many industry self-regulatory agencies, such as the Financial Industry Regulatory Authority (FINRA) in the U.S. At the global level, there are associations of regulatory agencies, such as the International Organization of Securities Commissions (IOSCO) and the Basel Committee on Banking Supervision, a division of the aforementioned Bank for International Settlements (BIS).[26]

5.4 Professional Associations in Risk Management

There are two primary professional organizations dedicated to risk management: GARP, the Global Association of Investment Professionals (www.garp.org), and PRMIA, the Professional Risk Managers International Association (www.prmia.org). Both organizations offer certification exams.

GARP's Financial Risk Manager (FRM) program consists of two four-hour exams. The first exam covers foundations of risk management, quantitative analysis, financial markets and products, and valuation and risk models. The second covers market risk measurement and management, credit risk measurement and management, operational and integrated risk management, risk management and investment management, and current issues in financial markets. GARP also offers two other examination programs, the International Certificate in Banking Risk and Regulation (ICBRR), and the Energy Risk Professional Certificate (ERP).

PRMIA's exam is called the PRM (Professional Risk Manager) and consists of four separate exams on financial theory/instruments/markets (two hours), mathematical tools (two hours), risk management practices (three hours), and case studies/standards of practice/conduct and ethics/PRMIA bylaws (one hour). The exams are offered during four three-week testing periods each year, and they must be passed within a two-year period. PRMIA also offers two other certifications called the Associate PRM Certificate, which is designed for risk management staffers, and the Operational Risk Manager Certificate, which is designed for specialists in operational risk management, a topic we will cover in Chapter 12.

There is one other organization devoted to risk management, called the International Association of Financial Engineers (IAFE). In addition, many

---

[26]A list of all regulatory agencies and associations is found at http://www.world-stock-exchanges.net/regulators.html.

other finance associations, such as the CFA Institute, play an active role in the risk management profession.

5.5 Chapter Summary

In this chapter we looked at the distinctions between the exchange-traded derivatives markets and the over-the-counter derivatives markets. The primary difference is that the former covers standardized contracts and the latter covers customized contracts. We examined how the contracts are traded, who the market participants are, how the contracts are cleared, how the contracts are settled, and how they are terminated when they expire. We also discussed the regulatory structure of the industry, and we identified the two professional associations in the risk management industry, GARP and PRMIA.

5.6 Questions and Problems

1. In what city and in what decade did exchange-traded derivatives markets begin and what was the name of the first derivatives exchange?
2. How did futures contracts solve the problem of too much or too little supply of certain agricultural products at a particular time of the year?
3. Why is volume a misleading measure of the size of a futures exchange?
4. What is the objective of standardized derivatives contracts and what terms are fixed and not fixed when a contract is standardized?
5. Explain what would happen for each party under physical delivery and under cash settlement for a futures contract for each of the following outcomes at expiration with A as the buyer and B as the seller. The settlement price the day before expiration was $55.

   a. The contract expires with the settlement price at expiration at $56.
   b. The contract expires with the settlement price at expiration at $53.

6. Explain what would happen for each party under physical delivery and under cash settlement for a call option for each of the following outcomes at expiration with B as the buyer and S as the seller. The exercise price is $55.

   a. The contract expires with the settlement price at expiration at $56.
   b. The contract expires with the settlement price at expiration at $53.

7. Briefly explain the two forms of trading on derivatives exchanges. Which is the more dominant form?

8. Identify and briefly describe the different types of traders and state how each makes a profit.

9. Identify and briefly describe the three primary types of orders on derivatives exchanges.

10. Explain how the clearing process works by using margins and daily settlements.

11. Fill in the following table to determine the variation margin and margin deposits for a futures transaction, given the sequence of settlement prices as indicated. Take the perspective of the buyer who goes long 10 futures contracts at a price of $80. The initial margin requirement is $5 and the maintenance margin requirement is $3.50. The settlement prices on days 0, 1, 2, and 3 are $82, $83.25, $76, and $77.25, respectively. Determine the cumulative profit or loss.

Day	Opening Balance	Initial Margin Deposited	Settlement Price	Mark-to Market Amount	Margin Balance	Adequate Margin?	Additional Margin Deposited	Ending Margin Balance
[1]	[2]	[3]	[4]	[5]	[6]	[7]	[8]	[9]
0								
1								
2								
3								

12. Explain how an exchange-traded derivative can be terminated.

13. What are the two primary measures of activity in the OTC derivatives market and what are the advantages and disadvantages of each?

14. Why are some OTC derivatives called vanilla or plain vanilla, while others are called exotic?

15. What is counterparty risk in an OTC derivative? What are the ways in which this risk is managed?

16. How can OTC contracts be effectively offset in a manner similar to that of exchange-traded contracts, and yet with an important difference?

17. How does the U.S. derivatives regulatory structure differ from that in most other countries?

Chapter 6

The Value of Risk Management and Hedging

What is a cynic? A man who knows the price of everything and the value of nothing.

Oscar Wilde
Lady Windermere's Fan
1892

We have completed five chapters on the subject of risk management, but we have yet to ask a very important question: *is risk management worth the effort?* Specifically, *does risk management add value? Does it do something for shareholders that they could not do for themselves?* This question is not an easy one to answer. In fact, it is an extremely difficult one. There are many possible benefits of risk management, but not all of them necessarily make legitimate contributions to the welfare of the owners of the company. We did not raise this question until now because there were some things you needed to know about risk management before we got into this subject. Now that you have the foundations in place, let us dive into this issue.

Before we got going, however, we need to remind ourselves of the distinction between risk management and hedging and what they have in common. As we covered earlier, risk management in very simple terms is the process of identifying an entity's risk tolerance, measuring the risk the entity is currently taking, and then aligning the risk being taken with the risk tolerance. In other words, it means that the risks the entity takes are the risks it wants to take. We also emphasized that risk management does not universally mean hedging. Hedging is one form of risk management, which is specifically related to the action of reducing risk. On occasion, however, risk management can entail increasing risk. But as a practical matter, risk management is largely synonymous with hedging. In essence, risk management amounts to getting rid of, or at least minimizing, risks

269

that the entity does not want, leaving only those risks that the entity does want. From time to time, an organization will need to make a decision to increase risk, but for the most part, risk management is far more related to reducing or eliminating risks that the organization does not want to take. Much of the discussion in this chapter will be about hedging, but let us keep in mind that hedging is but a part of risk management, although a very critical part.

To fully appreciate the issues of this chapter, we have to understand what hedging really is. We can seemingly describe hedging as reducing if not eliminating risk, but we need to understand the fact that a decision to reduce or eliminate risk is a conscious design to speculate that an adverse event will occur. For example, consider an airline that chooses to hedge jet fuel. In doing so, it is taking the position that that there is a reasonable possibility that the price of jet fuel will increase and that the consequences of such an increase are sufficiently adverse to the company that a reduction of this risk is warranted. In short, the airline is making a bet, a bet that could turn out to be wrong, that the price of jet fuel might increase. But what if the price of jet fuel decreases? In that case, the airline will wish it had not hedged. When you buy insurance, you are making a bet that there is a reasonable possibility that an adverse event will occur and that if it does occur, the consequences are sufficiently negative for you that you feel you must reduce this risk. When you buy insurance, you are hedging. Thus, hedging is a form of speculation. Specifically, it is speculation on the occurrence of an adverse event in which the hedger would otherwise bear a significant cost.

Interestingly, many entities are praised for being hedgers. Society tends to view hedging as a virtuous activity. Hedgers are lauded for their conservatism. On the other hand, speculators are traditionally vilified. The same person who might praise a hedger might criticize a speculator. Yet the speculator is simply an entity that assumes the risk transferred from a hedger. Speculators and hedgers are co-dependent, and they play an important role in maintaining a well-functioning market.

Moreover, the argument that hedging is virtuous holds only from a very limited perspective. For example, if the airline hedges and the price of jet fuel increases, the airline looks smart and its cash flow is protected. In particular, it will look very good in comparison to airlines that did not hedge, who will find that their cash flows suffer from the additional cost of fuel. But if the price of jet fuel goes down, the airline that hedged will wish it had not, though its earnings do not suffer. It will regret having hedged, but its cash flow is not affected. It is likely to meet its budget targets and earnings expectations, assuming no other adverse events occur. So, from an accounting perspective, hedging can look like a very good strategy. From an economic perspective, however, the lost opportunity to increase the company's cash flow by not hedging when the price of jet fuel decreases is just as significant of a loss as the realized loss that occurs by not hedging when jet fuel goes up. Of course, the airline does not know which way the price of jet fuel will go. Interestingly, most airlines do a certain amount of hedging, but they do not hedge all of their fuel needs.[1]

It is, therefore, important to keep in mind that hedging is a decision to take a risk — the risk that the adverse outcome will occur — so protection is needed. Much of the remainder of this chapter will look at the various reasons for why risk management and hedging are worthwhile endeavors. Or perhaps why they are not.

6.1 Risk Management and Hedging in the Modigliani-Miller Framework

In order to understand how risk management could help the shareholders, we must first take a look at what types of financial decisions help shareholders and which types have no effect. Let us start by considering how the use of debt affects a company. When a company borrows money, it engages in a loan on behalf of the shareholders. The obligation might be in the form of a long-, intermediate-, or short-term bond or loan. The company enters into a formal agreement in which the lender advances cash to the company, and the company in return promises to pay back the loan at a particular rate of interest. Later in this course we will spend a lot of time discussing loans in which the rate adjusts periodically, but for now, let us focus on fixed-rate loans. The loan agreement specifies a specific fixed interest rate. The repayment terms can vary widely. Some loans require only a single repayment of interest and principal at the maturity date. Other loans require only the periodic payment of interest with a lump sum principal paid when the loan matures. Still others require periodic payments of both principal and interest. When a company takes out a loan, the creditors stand first in line for their

---

[1] I suspect the reason they do not like to hedge everything or nothing is that they do not want to risk being completely wrong, even if sometimes they would be completely right. They probably feel better being partly wrong and partly right. As we will discuss later in this chapter, it makes more sense to hedge risks over which you have no competitive advantage and retain risks over which you do. Hence, airlines should hedge all of their fuel price risk.

share of the company's cash. In other words, the creditors get paid before the shareholders, and if there is not enough money to pay the creditors, the shareholders get nothing. As a result of the positioning of the creditors before the shareholders, the risk to the shareholders increases with the use of debt. This increased risk results in an increase in the volatility of the returns to the shareholders. This concept gives rise to the term *leverage* to describe how shareholder returns are amplified both upward and downward by the use of debt.

The increased risk to the shareholders is, of course, a benefit as well as a cost. We illustrate this point in Exhibit 6-1 with two companies that have identical assets that produce identical annual net operating income, assumed to be all cash, of either $2,500 in what we refer to as a "good" year or −$1,000 in what we refer to as a "bad" year. The companies have total assets of $10,000. Company LC, representing the levered case, is financed with $4,000 of debt at 4% interest and $6,000 of equity. Company UC, representing the unlevered company, is financed completely with $10,000 of equity.[2] We shall initially assume that there are no taxes and that all earnings to the shareholders are distributed as dividends.

	Good Year		Bad Year	
	Company LC	Company UC	Company LC	Company UC
Net Operating Income	$2,500	$2,500	−$1,000	−$1,000
Return on Assets	$2,500/$10,000 = 25%	$2,500/$10,000 = 25%	−$1,000/$10,000 = −10%	−$1,000/$10,000 = −10%
Less Interest	−$160	−$0	−$160	−$0
Net Income	$2,340	$2,500	−$1,160	−$1,000
Return on Equity	$2,340/$6,000 = 39%	$2,500/$10,000 = 25%	−$1,160/$6,000 = −19.33%	−$1,000/$10,000 = −10%

Note: Company L has $4,000 debt at 4% interest and $6,000 of equity; Company U has no debt and $10,000 of equity;
Expected returns based on equal likelihood: LC, 9.83%, UC, 7.5%

Exhibit 6-1. Comparison of Incomes of Levered and Unlevered Companies under No Taxes

---

[2]Instead of being two companies, they could be the same company under different financing assumptions.

Notice that in the good year the return on assets is 25% ($2,500/$10,000) for both companies, but the company with debt (LC) earns 39% for its shareholders, while the all-equity company (UC) earns only 25%, which is the same return on equity as the return on assets. Leverage causes the return on equity to be substantially more than double the return on assets. In a bad year, the company with debt has a return on equity of −19.33%, while the all-equity company has a return on equity of −10%, again the return on assets. If the two events are considered equally likely, the expected returns on equity would be 0.5(39%) + 0.5(−19.33%) = 9.83% for the leveraged company and 0.5(25%) + 0.5(−10%) = 7.5% for the unlevered company, the same as the expected return on assets.

Exhibit 6-2 illustrates the effect by which leverage transmits a return on assets (ROA) to a return on equity (ROE) over a range of ROA from −100% to 100%. Notice that the levered company earns a much higher rate of return than the ROA in years in which ROA is up and a much lower (more negative) return in years in which ROA is down.

Thus, leverage magnifies gains and losses and is clearly beneficial to companies that do an effective job of investing in high quality productive assets. Nonetheless, leverage is a double-edged sword in that it brings greater risk to the shareholders. In good years, they do better. In bad years, they do worse.

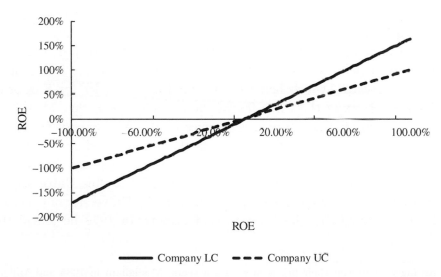

Exhibit 6-2. ROE of Levered and Unlevered Companies over a Wide Range of Net Operating Incomes

So the obvious question is how much debt a company should have. The financial economists Franco Modigliani and Merton Miller (M&M) won Nobel Prizes for their explanation of how companies decide how much debt to use in relation to equity.[3] This problem, which is called the *capital structure decision*, had always been considered to be a major question for companies. Perhaps surprisingly, their article (Modigliani-Miller, 1958) did not actually specify how much debt companies should use in relation to equity. In fact, they found that the amount of debt a company uses does not matter. A few years later, they published a second paper (Miller-Modigliani, 1961) that showed that dividend policy does not matter either. In other words, whether a company pays a dividend or retains and reinvests its earnings does not matter. In the sense of not mattering, they meant that shareholders were neither helped nor hurt. Thus, M&M argued that any amount of debt in relation to equity is as good as any other and that whether a company pays dividends, whether it pays high or low dividends, and whether it increases or decreases its dividends does not matter. In other words, shareholders cannot be helped or hurt by any particular capital structure or dividend policy.

Who Were Modigliani and Miller?

Franco Modigliani was born in Rome in 1918. He entered the University of Rome at the age of 17 with the intention of becoming a lawyer, but his interests quickly turned to economics. The Fascist movement in Italy at that time had a repressive effect on economics, however, and Modigliani moved to Paris in 1938, enrolled in school there, but eventually returned to Rome to complete his law degree. Fearing the onset of war, the now-married Modigliani moved to New York and enrolled in the New School of Social Research, which had been founded as an outlet for European economists escaping the three fascist dictatorships of Hitler, Mussolini, and Franco. Modigliani studied economics at the New School for Social Research, now known as the New School, and received his doctorate in 1944. He had begun teaching at the New Jersey College for Women in 1941 and moved to Bard College, a division of Columbia University, in 1942. He later received a fellowship to study at the University of Chicago, and he also taught at the University of Illinois. In 1952 he joined the

---

[3]Interestingly, they won their prizes in separate years, Modigliani in 1985 and Miller in 1990. The Nobel Prize primarily reflects a single accomplishment but does consider other achievements of the candidate.

faculty of the Carnegie Institute of Technology, now known as Carnegie-Mellon, where he co authored his famous papers on capital structure with Merton Miller. He moved to MIT in 1962 and remained there until his death in 2003 at the age of 85. Modigliani, who became a naturalized citizen of the United States in 1946, was also known for his studies on the life cycle of consumption and savings. In 1985 he received the Nobel Prize in Economics for "his pioneering analyses of saving and financial markets," which helped understand why people save at different rates at different points in their lives and why some countries have different saving rates than others. And as a rare accomplishment for a scholar, in 1997 he published an article on risk-adjusted performance measurement with his granddaughter, Leah, an investment strategist with Morgan Stanley Dean Witter.

Merton Miller was born in Boston in 1923 and received a bachelor's degree from Harvard in 1943. He initially worked for the U.S. Treasury Department and the Federal Reserve but returned to school and received a PhD in economics from Johns Hopkins University in 1952. He taught for one year at the London School of Economics and then joined the faculty of the business school at Carnegie Mellon where he connected with Franco Modigliani and wrote the two classic papers on capital structure. In 1961 Miller joined the business school of the University of Chicago, where he taught until officially retiring in 1993, though he continued to do some teaching for a few more years. In 1990 he shared the Nobel Prize with Harry Markowitz and William F. Sharpe, who were being recognized for their work in portfolio theory and the Capital Asset Pricing Model. The Nobel Committee noted that the award for all three was "for their pioneering work in the theory of financial economics." A long-time advocate of free markets, Miller was very active professionally until his death in 2000. He was also known as a tremendous fan of American football, as evidenced by his many years as a Chicago Bears season ticketholder.

At the time the M&M results were first published, they were considered shocking. Economists had observed that companies generally devote a great deal of time to capital structure and dividend decisions, and yet M&M were telling them that this time was wasted. There were, however, important assumptions that M&M made that played a role in their conclusions. Among others, they assumed perfect markets, which meant that there are no taxes or transaction costs and that every market participant had full access to all information. They also assumed that managers act in the best interests of shareholders. None of these assumptions is strictly true, and the impacts of these assumptions can range from immaterial to highly significant. Let us first take a look at the essence of the M&M argument in perfect markets. The implications are important for risk management. Then we will introduce market imperfections.

Modigliani and Miller viewed a company like a pie. Large companies are large pies and small companies are small pies. The shareholders and creditors supply capital to the company and have a claim on the assets. Of course, the creditors have the first claim; the shareholders get whatever is left after the creditors' claims are met. So the claims are like the slices of the pie, as illustrated in Exhibit 6-3. The creditors' slice is marked with a C, and the shareholders' slice is marked with an S.

We have drawn this pie so that the creditors' claim is about a fourth. In other words, this company finances its assets with about 75% equity and 25% debt.

The M&M argument is essentially the simple principle that how you slice the pie does not matter. It is the size of the pie that counts. If companies make good decisions on the asset side of the balance sheet, the pie will grow and, given the fixed nature of the creditors' claims, the shareholders will benefit, as shown in Exhibit 6-4. Here the drawing endeavors to show a larger pie but with the creditors' claims the same size as in Exhibit 6-3. The growth in the size of the pie comes from making good investments in assets. When companies do that, the creditors continue to get the same payments, so the benefits of successful investments go to the shareholders. Notice that because the size of the piece that goes to creditors is constant, the ratio of debt to equity decreases for successful companies. Naturally, the pie will

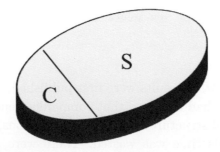

Exhibit 6-3. A Company as a Pie with Capital Supplied by Creditors and Shareholders

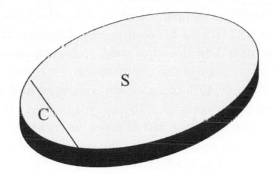

Exhibit 6-4. A Company that Grows the Pie

shrink for companies that are not successful, whereupon the ratio of debt to equity will increase.

Nonetheless, debt does have an advantage over equity. The creditors and shareholders of a company have required rates of return, which are the returns on their investments that they require to justify investing in the company. Required rates of return are determined by the risk. Because creditors have priority over shareholders, the risk is lower. Thus, creditors require a lower rate of return than do shareholders. When companies make investments in products and services, they must generate a sufficient return to pay their suppliers of capital. This return is known as the *cost of capital*. The required return to creditors is the *cost of debt*, and the required return to shareholders is the *cost of equity*. Thus, debt is cheaper than equity. But if that point gets you to thinking that debt would be preferred over equity since it is cheaper, that is only half the picture. M&M show that the risk of the shareholders' return increases as more debt is added. They claim that the increased risk completely offsets the benefit of using a cheaper source of capital.

The foundation on which the M&M argument is based is the principle of arbitrage, which will also be the foundation of much of the material that composes the remainder of this book. M&M show that if there were an advantage to using debt, such as the beneficial effects of leverage, then shareholders of companies that had no debt, and hence were not taking advantage of the fact that debt is cheaper than equity, could issue personal debt and effectively achieve the same result.[4] In other words, a shareholder of a company that finances say 40% of its capital with debt is equivalent to a

---

[4]When investors issue debt and use it to buy shares of stock, it is called margin trading or trading on margin.

shareholder in an identical company with no debt who buys the shares using 40% personal debt and 60% of his own money. Likewise, if the shareholder of a company that uses debt does not want to be responsible for any debt, he can buy some of the debt of the company. So, for example, a shareholder of a company that funds 40% of its assets with debt and 60% with equity can effectively turn his investment into one with no debt by purchasing $40 of the company's debt for every $60 of stock he owns in the company. By being a shareholder he is responsible for the company's debt, but by owning the debt, that responsibility is effectively offset.

The overall result is that M&M make a reasonable case that companies cannot do anything for their shareholders that the shareholders cannot do for themselves. With respect to financing, the ability of individuals to buy and sell securities means that individuals can engage in financing transactions as easily as companies. Individuals cannot, however, buy assets and make them productive the way companies can. Thus, on the left-hand side of the balance sheet, companies can engage in productive activities and create value for shareholders. On the right-hand side of the balance sheet, they cannot — at least according to M&M.

We could continue to explore this issue, but we do not have the time and space and it goes beyond our needs for the subject of risk management. It is one of the most important concerns in corporate finance. What matters to us is if and how the irrelevance of capital structure applies in risk management. Can companies do something for shareholders that they cannot do for themselves? A literal interpretation of the M&M argument is that they cannot. For example, consider an airline that hedges its fuel costs. Does that benefit its shareholders? The M&M argument would say that it does not. Shareholders of an airline can hedge energy costs by engaging in derivative contracts based on the price of energy. Can shareholders of a corporation hedge interest rate and foreign exchange risks? Of course, they can.

So, yes, the shareholders can engage in similar transactions as companies, *but only to a limited degree*. Companies are generally in a better position to hedge. They usually have more resources and the economies of scale to set up the systems necessary to execute and monitor hedge transactions. Also, companies know how much hedging to do. Do airline shareholders know how much to hedge to replicate the hedging that the airlines they own would do? They would probably not. The same is true for corporations hedging interest rate and foreign exchange risks. Shareholders are not likely to be able to hedge as precisely and effectively as companies. Thus, while there is certainly some truth for the M&M position — shareholders can and do engage in their own risk management transactions — they are not likely to be able to do it as well and as precisely as the companies they invest in.

Just as a heads-up, we will return to the M&M argument a little later. Recall that M&M's position applies to the capital structure of the company. They would not deny that asset investments can create wealth for their shareholders. The very concept of net present value, where a company makes an investment in a product or service that produces cash that has a greater present value on a risk-adjusted basis than the present value of the cash paid out to make the investment, is an indication of how assets can create value.

6.2 Tax and Bankruptcy Justifications for Risk Management and Hedging

One of the key assumptions in M&M's argument is no taxes. When we introduce taxes, however, the game changes completely, because the interest on debt is traditionally deductible on federal income taxes. Thus, the cost of using debt is partially subsidized by the government, or more precisely, the taxpayers. M&M were criticized for ignoring this point, and in response, they then wrote another article (Modigliani-Miller, 1963) that incorporated taxes. Once you introduce taxes, the substitution of tax-deductible debt for equity creates a preference for debt over equity. Without any factor to offset this effect, the amount of debt a company should use would be 100% of its financing. Of course, a company cannot be owned entirely by its creditors, so we are left with the conclusion that the company would have almost all of its financing supplied by creditors but would retain a small amount of equity. Some limiting factors have been introduced, but first let us take a look at the implications of taxes for the question of whether risk management is valuable for shareholders. Let us first see how taxes create a preference for debt over equity and how risk management can exploit that preference.

6.2.1 *Interest Tax Shield*

Let us look again at Companies LC and UC. Recall that in a good year, each company earns net operating income of $2,500. Let us now assume a tax rate of 30%. Exhibit 6-5 shows the income statements for both companies now that we impose taxes.

Note that while the levered company has lower net income, it also has lower taxes. Specifically, its tax bill is $48 lower, which is precisely equal to the amount of debt times the interest rate times the tax rate: $4,000(0.04)(0.30) = $48.

	Company LC	Company UC
Net Operating Income	$2,500	$2,500
ROA	$2,500/$10,000 = 25%	$2,500/$10,000 = 25%
Less Interest	−$160	−$0
Taxable Income	$2,340	$2,500
Tax (30% of taxable income)	$702	$750
Net Income	$1,638	$1,750

Exhibit 6-5. Income for Levered and Unlevered Companies with Net Operating Income of $2,500 and a 30% Tax Rate

In a world with taxes, all companies are clearly worth less because they have less money to pay to their creditors and shareholders. In the no-tax world, both companies had $2,500 to distribute to their suppliers of capital. The creditors of the levered firm got $160 and the shareholders had a claim on the remainder. When we introduce taxes, the government takes out $702 form the levered firm's cash flow leaving $1,798 to be distributed to the creditors and shareholders. The government takes out $750 from the unlevered firm's cash flow, leaving $1,750 to be distributed to the creditors and shareholders. So both companies have less cash for their suppliers of capital, but the levered firm has more cash than the unlevered company. As noted the greater amount of cash is precisely equal to the amount of debt times the interest rate times the tax rate.

Let us see how this implication affects the value of the company. The expected operating income is $0.5(\$2,500) + 0.5(-\$1,000) = \$750$. Let us assume that this amount is a perpetuity, meaning that the same amount is expected to occur every year.[5] Let us first step back to the no-tax case. If the unlevered company is worth $10,000, its value is clearly $10,000 and the cost of capital, which equals the cost of equity, is $750/$10,000 = 0.075, or 7.5%. In equation form,

$$V_U = \frac{\$750}{0.075} = \$10,000 \text{ (no taxes)}$$

If we introduce taxes, we do not change the risk, but the expected amount of capital available for distribution is now only $525, based on the government

---

[5]This amount is an expected amount. Variation is certainly allowed, but what we need is the expected amount. We have introduced no growth to the company's cash flows. Doing so simplifies things, but the point is correct even if the company grows.

taking $225 in taxes (30% of $750 expected taxable income). Thus, the value of the unlevered company is

$$V_U = \frac{\$525}{0.075} = \$7,000 \text{ (with taxes)}.$$

For the levered firm, however, the taxable income is $750 - \$160 = \$590$, and the tax bill is $\$590 \times 0.30 = \$177$, which is $48 less. So the creditors get $160 in interest, the government gets $177, and the shareholders have a claim on the rest, $413. In total the firm gets to keep $160 + \$413 = \$573$ and pay its suppliers of capital. The value of the levered firm will be based on discounting $573, which is comprised of $525 of net operating income after taxes and $48 of reduced taxes due to interest. The appropriate discount rate for the latter is the interest rate on the debt of 4%. The former would continue to be discounted at 7.5%. Thus, the value of the levered company is

$$V_L = \frac{\$525}{0.075} + \frac{\$48}{\$0.04} = \$8,200 \text{ (with taxes)}.$$

Or in general,

$$V_L = V_U + \tau_c B \text{ (with taxes)},$$

where τ_c is the corporate tax rate and B is the amount of bonds, the company's debt.

Thus, the company is worth more with leverage than without. The increase in value over that of the unlevered company is τ_C and is called the *interest tax subsidy* and sometimes the *interest tax shield*. It is the value of issuing debt worth B, paying interest at the rate r, deducting that interest to reduce taxes by the amount $rB\tau_C$, repeating every year, and finding the present value of this annual reduction in taxes by discounting at the rate r, in other words, $rB\tau_C/r - B\tau_U$. Thus, without any limiting factors, which we will cover later, we see that debt has an advantage over equity. The interest tax subsidy makes debt essentially a cheaper form of financing than equity. In other words, $1 paid in interest to creditors costs less than a dollar due to the tax deductibility of interest, whereas $1 paid in dividends costs a full dollar.

What does this result mean for risk management? Well for one, it means that companies need to take advantage of the interest tax subsidy to at least a minimum extent. Even companies like Microsoft, Google, and Apple, all of which generate enormous amounts of cash from the sale of their products and services, should do so. They hardly need more cash, and yet they issue debt, because they know how attractive debt is. But what about other companies that are not quite as financially secure as these companies? When they issue debt, they increase the risk to the shareholders and to their existing creditors. If they do a good job of managing the risk, in particular, hedging high and unwanted risks, they are in a better position to issue debt and take advantage of the interest tax subsidy. If they do not control their risks, it will be difficult to issue debt or to add more debt to existing debt. The stockholders, as represented by management and the board of directors, may not want to issue more debt. Moreover, the creditors are more likely to place restrictions on the company's ability to pile on more debt, but they may be more willing to allow additional debt if the company does a good job of controlling its risks. We will return to this point later when we discuss debt capacity.

6.2.2 *Bankruptcy and Financial Distress*

We have mentioned that in the absence of factors that could limit the use of debt, companies might want to issue massive amounts of debt to take full advantage of the interest tax subsidy and have its valuable benefits accrue to the holders of the small shareholder investment that remains. If your intuition about the advisability of this strategy bothers you, you are not alone. Normally when companies have extremely large amounts of debt, it is not because debt has been issued and used to repurchase equity but rather because poor performance has eroded the equity to the point that very little remains of the owners' investment. If your gut feeling tells you that a lot of debt and very little equity is a bad thing, you are correct. But you may not be correct for the right reason.

When a company declares bankruptcy, it has not necessarily irrevocably failed. Bankruptcy is a formal legal process in which a company places the government between itself and its creditors. It is a type of time-out in which the company uses the government to force the creditors to hold their claims in abeyance. During that time, the company attempts to repair whatever problems it has and develop a plan to pay its creditors over an extended period of time.

Bankruptcy is quite a profitable activity for certain entities, such as bankruptcy lawyers and consultants. In September 2008, the 158-year old investment banking firm Lehman Brothers filed for bankruptcy, listing assets of $691 billion and liabilities of $613 billion. Although not technically bankrupt since its book assets exceeded its book liabilities, Lehman was nonetheless unable to generate the cash to cover its obligations. The company emerged from bankruptcy in 2012, but by 2013, legal costs had run up to more than $2 billion, and they continue to grow as Lehman exists today as a liquidating trust operating with the objective of eventually terminating the company.

These legal fees, along with court costs, constitute a concept called bankruptcy costs. In effect, the external parties that are paid as a result of a bankruptcy have an implicit investment in a company. They have no explicit capital invested, but they benefit enormously from bankruptcy. In effect, they have a claim on the pie represented by the company's assets, but they have no capital at risk. Moreover, their claims are superior to those of the creditors.

Paying out a portion of a company's assets to parties that have no capital at risk is a heavy cost, and it is reasonable to assume that such a cost should be avoided. Hence, it is in the shareholders' interests to avoid bankruptcy. The bankruptcy costs should be compared to the interest tax subsidy. Companies should use as much debt as possible to take advantage of the interest tax subsidy, but the more debt a company uses, the more likely bankruptcy becomes. A company must decide on the amount of debt it should use that balances the benefits of the interest tax subsidy against the expected bankruptcy costs.

A concept similar to the notion of bankruptcy costs is the cost of financial distress. When companies become financially strained, they lose suppliers, creditors, customers, and employees. Even if they do not ultimately file for bankruptcy, the loss of these entities on which a company depends can be very costly. Hence, companies should not only attempt to avoid bankruptcy, they should also try to avoid the period of financial distress that often precedes bankruptcy.

The costs of bankruptcy and financial distress are both based on expectations of the direct costs conditional on bankruptcy or financial distress and the probability of either bankruptcy or financial distress. By stabilizing a company's cash flows, risk management can lower the probability of bankruptcy and financial distress, thus lowering the expected costs of bankruptcy and financial distress. In so doing, a company can use more debt and take greater advantage of the interest tax subsidy, and thereby increase the value of the company.

Exhibit 6-6 illustrates the capital structure tradeoff in the absence of risk management. We illustrate a hypothetical company worth $10,000 unlevered with taxes. As the company adds debt, replacing equity with debt, the value of the company increases due to the interest tax subsidy but so do the bankruptcy and financial distress costs. The vertical axis is the value of

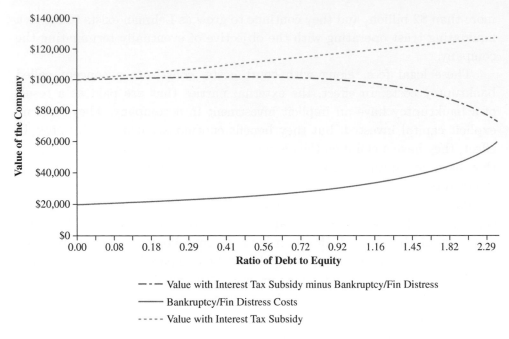

Exhibit 6-6. Tradeoff of Interest Tax Subsidy with Bankruptcy and Financial Distress Costs

the company, while the horizontal axis is the ratio of debt to equity.[6] The upward sloping line at the bottom is the expected bankruptcy costs, which obviously rise with higher debt in relation to equity. The top line, which is monotonically increasing, is the value of the company taking into account only the interest tax subsidy. The middle line reflects both the interest tax subsidy and the expected costs of bankruptcy and financial distress. Although it is not easy to pinpoint the exact optimum, this line reaches its peak at a ratio of debt to equity of about 0.33. In other words, in this example when there is $1 of debt to $3 of equity, the value of the company is maximized at a little under $102,000, as the marginal gain from the interest tax subsidy equals the marginal cost of bankruptcy and financial distress at that point.

---

[6]The ratio of debt to equity is based on the market value of the debt divided by the market value of the equity after accounting for the interest tax subsidy but not accounting for bankruptcy/financial distress costs. It is circular to account for the bankruptcy/financial distress costs in determining the debt/equity ratio because the debt/equity ratio is a determinant of the bankruptcy and financial distress costs.

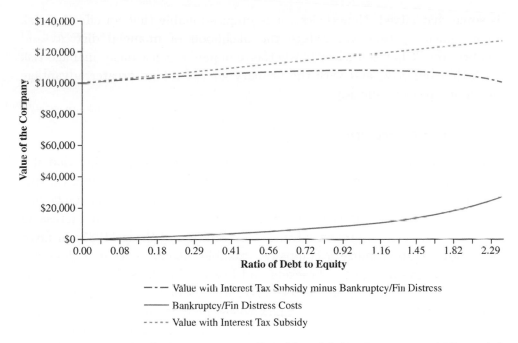

Exhibit 6-7. Tradeoff of Interest Tax Subsidy with Bankruptcy and Financial Distress Costs when Practicing Risk Management

Now look at Exhibit 6-7. Here we incorporate risk management by assuming that the probability of bankruptcy and financial distress is reduced by half.

Here the expected bankruptcy costs are considerably lower. As such, the value of the company is maximized at a much higher level of debt, a debt-to-equity ratio of about 0.62, thereby increasing the captured value of the interest tax subsidy. Here the maximum value of the company is about $108,000. This gain is close to 6% of the value of the company. Of course, practicing risk management does entail a cost, which would need to be compared to the gain in the value of the company.

Do not obsess with the exact numbers in these two figures. They are merely presented for illustrative purposes and to assist you in grasping the concept. The actual determination of these numbers for a real company would certainly be very challenging. But then, companies face similar challenges all of the time. Companies make many decisions under risk that are based solely on estimates, some of which may be merely educated guesses.

There have been some empirical studies on whether companies manage risk with the objective of lowering the costs of financial distress. The evidence is somewhat mixed. Nonetheless, it is unquestionable that an effective risk management system will reduce the likelihood of financial distress and bankruptcy. What is unclear is whether companies consciously manage risk with that objective and with the primary goal of taking greater advantage of the interest tax subsidy.

6.2.3 *Tax Convexity*

The tax systems used in many countries are progressive, meaning that if a taxpaying entity is more successful and therefore moves into a higher taxable income category, it pays taxes at a higher rate. This type of tax rate schedule has the characteristic of convexity, meaning that it increases at an increasing rate. As such, one argument advanced by Smith and Stulz (1985) in favor of hedging is to stabilize a company's taxable income so that it does not fluctuate between high tax brackets and low tax brackets. In a good year, a company jumps into a higher tax bracket. In a bad year, it jumps into a lower bracket. The reduction in taxes when the company falls into a lower tax bracket is more than offset by the increase in taxes when it jumps into a higher tax bracket. Moreover, if the company has really bad years in which it loses money, it does not have negative taxes. A loss simply eliminates the tax but does not result in the government paying the company. There are some provisions that permit carrying losses forward and offsetting future gains, but there are limitations and a company that loses money for a number of years, which is not uncommon, will effectively be unable to use its losses to offset gains in other years. By stabilizing income, a hedge can eliminate these fluctuations into high and low tax brackets and reduced overall taxes.

Exhibit 6-8 illustrates a hypothetical case based on a tax rate schedule in which a company pays tax at a 25% rate for all income up to and including $400. All income above $400 is taxed at a rate of 30%. Make sure you understand that if the company earns income above $400, the entire income is not taxed at 30%. Rather the first $400 is taxed at 25% and the excess is taxed at 30%. The exhibit shows a company with two possible levels of taxable income, $100 and $500.

Let us leave debt out of the picture, so this is an all-equity company. Let us assume the risk-free rate is 3%, that investors require an after-tax return of 8%, and that all income is cash. Assuming a perpetuity, the value of the company is

$$\frac{0.5(\$75) + 0.5(\$370)}{0.08} = \$2,781.25.$$

Taxable Income	Probability	Marginal Tax Rate	After-tax Income
$100	0.5	0.25	$100 − $100(0.25) = $75
$500	0.5	0.30	$500 − $400(0.25) − $100(0.30) = $370

Exhibit 6-8. Illustration of Tax Convexity

Suppose the company can hedge the pre-tax value of its income and lock in a taxable income that keeps the company in the 25% bracket. So, let us assume the company hedges the pre-tax income to $200. Its after-tax income would be $200 − $200(0.25) = $125.00. Since the company is hedged, this value can be discounted at the risk-free rate to obtain:

$$\frac{\$125}{0.03} = \$5,000.$$

This value is considerably higher. Though the example is quite simple and no firm would truly remain risk free or even want to, hedging keeps the company from leaping into higher tax bracket in which the additional taxes are far more than the lower taxes it pays when it bounces into a lower bracket. This result is strictly driven by the progressive tax structure.

The argument makes sense on the surface. The numbers certainly check out. But when considering the current tax structure, the argument is not quite so strong. For one, corporate tax rates are not particularly progressive. Currently in the U.S., there are levels of income at which hedging moves a company into a lower bracket, as in this example, but it is also possible that hedging does not change the bracket. Moreover, there are typically not many different corporate tax brackets. As of 2018, in the U.S., all corporate taxable income is taxed at a 21% rate, so there is only one bracket and clearly no tax convexity under current laws, although there was a progressive convex corporate tax schedule in the past. Empirical studies have also shown little support for the possibility that tax convexity motivates hedging. Of course, small companies that are taxed as proprietorships would be subject to multiple brackets.

6.3 Risk Management and Corporate Investment and Financing Decisions

In this section, we take a look at some factors that can motivate a company to engage in risk management to support its investment and financing decisions.

Recall that the M&M argument acknowledges that investment decisions can create value for shareholders, but that financial decisions may not.

6.3.1 *The Underinvestment Problem*

We ordinarily think that when companies have opportunities to invest in assets that create wealth, they would do so, but in practice, they might not. Failing to do so is called underinvestment, and it would tend to occur when companies are in dire financial straits with a high possibility of bankruptcy. In such situations, the benefits of successful investment accrue largely to the creditors. The shareholders are so far behind the creditors that they have little chance of receiving any benefit from investing in the project, and yet they would risk most if not all of the capital required for the investment.

In corporate finance courses, we refer to attractive investment opportunities as *positive net present value* or *positive-NPV projects*. Positive-*NPV* projects are those in which the risk-adjusted present value of expected future cash flows exceeds any and all cash outflows made to initiate the project and cash outflows to be made at any later date. When companies are nearly bankrupt, they know that the benefits of positive-*NPV* projects will typically go the creditors, with little if any left over for the shareholders. This expectation can destroy the incentive for the company to take on these projects. Yet, from a societal standpoint, companies should take on such projects. Bessembinder (1991) has advanced the idea that risk management can help companies avoid getting into situations in which the company is in such dire financial straits that it has lost the incentive to take on attractive projects.

The empirical evidence on this motivation is somewhat mixed, but there is little doubt that companies prefer not to get into deep financial difficulties, and it is likely that avoiding financial problems is a primary motivator for risk management. Reducing underinvestment may not be a specific objective of risk management, but it likely to be a benefit.

6.3.2 *Turning a Bad Investment into a Good One*

When a company analyzes an investment project, it presumably calculates the *NPV*. This calculation is an estimate of expected cash inflows and outflows. If the risk-adjusted expected inflows exceed the risk-adjusted expected outflows, the *NPV* is positive and the project is favorable. Most companies know, however, that these estimates incorporate risk only to a modest degree. The discount rate used to bring future cash inflows and outflows to their current values is set at a rate appropriate for the risk. The higher the risk, the higher the discount rate. A project with high uncertainty of cash inflows and low uncertainty of cash outflows or high uncertainty of cash outflows and low uncertainty of cash inflows can have a positive *NPV* and yet present considerable risk that the project will turn out to be adverse. Herein lies a major reason why risk management can be valuable.

Consider the following example. Suppose an airline is entertaining a proposal to provide transportation services for a sports team for the following year. The team has proposed that to pay the airline a flat rate of $10 million, an amount that can be treated as certain. The airline estimates that it will have non-fuel costs of $1 million for certain. The fuel cost estimate, however, is highly uncertain. Current estimates are $8 million but the airline expects that fuel costs will either remain at $8 million or increase to $12 million with equal probability. Fuel costs will be discounted at a rate of 10%. To simplify things, all cash flows are assumed to occur in one year.

Exhibit 6-9 illustrates the *NPV* possibilities. We see that the *NPV* will be about $1.381 million if fuel costs stay at $8 million, but *NPV* will be −$2.2 million if fuel costs go up to $12 million. The *NPV* is the probability weighted average, $0.5(\$1,381,019) + 0.5(-\$2,225,545) = -\$437,063$. Thus, it would appear that the airline will have to decline to do the project.

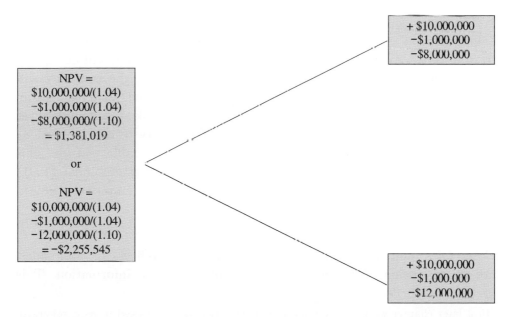

Exhibit 6-9. Estimation of Airline NPV from Team Transportation Project Proposal

The airline knows that the revenue offered by the team is non-negotiable. As an alternative, the airline takes into account its ability to hedge its fuel costs. Let us say a hedge will lock in the fuel costs at $8.5 million.[7] Now, all cash flows will be certain and can be discounted at the risk-free rate. The *NPV* is

$$NPV = \frac{\$10,000,000}{1.04} - \frac{\$1,000,000}{1.04} - \frac{\$8,500,000}{1.04} = \$480,769.$$

Now the project is attractive. Here is a good example of why the M&M argument does not contradict our conclusion that risk management is a good practice. M&M agree that value is created by making good asset investments, meaning those in which the risk-adjusted present value of the cash inflows exceeds the risk-adjusted present value of the cash outflows. If those investments can be improved by controlling certain risks, then M&M would argue that risk management is valuable. The M&M position relates only to financing, not to the investment in assets, and it requires that the company be able to engage in these risk management activities more effectively than the shareholders.

6.3.3 *Improving Credit Quality and Increasing Debt Capacity*

We have previously alluded to the fact that risk management can help a company avoid getting into financial difficulty. One benefit to the company from having a solid financial position is that its credit rating will be higher, so lenders will be more willing to extend credit. Thus, the company will have the ability to raise additional debt if and when it needs to. This feature, called debt capacity, is generally considered quite valuable. Companies never know when additional funds will be needed. The ability to raise capital by borrowing quickly and at low cost is considered a valuable feature. This attraction of risk management has been advanced by Bessembinder (1991) and Leland (1998), and has been generally supported by empirical studies.

6.3.4 *Information Asymmetry and Signaling*

Companies, and more specifically the high-ranking officers of companies, are in possession of a considerable amount of private information. This

---

[7]In a later chapter we will determine the amount that can be locked in as it relates to the current amount, $8 million in this problem. We have conservatively assumed that the locked-in amount is higher than the current amount, but that is not always the case.

information reflects what the company knows or expects will happen over the near future. Shareholders, creditors, and investment professionals do not have access to this information. This information asymmetry can create problems. While companies want to keep some information private, they want other information to be public because that information should improve investors' opinions of the company and raise the stock price. Yet, companies are not always believable. They constantly issue positive statements, even when times are difficult. And even when acknowledging underperformance and financial difficulties, they tend to convey optimism for the future. It is difficult for the shareholders, creditors, and investment professionals to know what to believe.

DeMarzo and Duffie (1995) have proposed the idea that companies that practice risk management send more believable signals to the public. It is easier to have confidence in companies that practice risk management, because investors and creditors know that the company is doing its best to maintain a strong financial position. Accordingly, companies may even be able to issue new debt or equity on more favorable terms. There is some empirical support for this argument.

6.3.5 *Risk Management to Support Internal Financing*

When companies need cash, they consider four sources of financing: selling an asset, issuing new debt, issuing new equity, and using internal financing. There are often limits to the ability to sell an asset, as most assets are needed and those that are not have probably already been disposed of. Of the three remaining sources, internal financing is usually preferred. In the accounting vernacular, internal financing is referred to as retained earnings. A better way to describe it is to refer to it as corporate savings. Just as an individual saves money, perhaps investing in a bank CD or short-term investments, a company can also save money, usually by holding cash and marketable securities. Those savings need not even have arisen from earnings not distributed. They may have come from asset sales made or equity or debt issued in the past. In short, companies typically look to their savings first before raising new capital in the debt and equity markets, as it is considered less costly and less cumbersome.

For reasons that are probably idiosyncratic, many companies use their internal financing to finance new asset acquisitions. Some companies have been known to finance their research and development (R&D) budgets strictly with internal financing. Thus, to provide a sustained level of growth, companies must generate sufficient cash from their sales. Froot, Scharfstein, and Stein (1993) propose that risk management can help stabilize the cash flow that is used to support internal financing. The empirical evidence seems to support this notion. In fact, the idea is quite intuitive. Companies that practice risk management would almost surely have more stable cash flows. It is common that companies draw most of their financing internally. Companies with stable cash flows can engage in long-term plans for sustained growth. Risk management supports the financing that leads to reinvestment and growth.

6.4   Risk Management and Competitive Advantage

It is relatively intuitive to believe that companies should take risks in which they have a competitive advantage and avoid risks in which they do not. Competitive advantage refers to the ability of a company to provide high quality products and services that are in strong demand by customers and clients and are preferred over those of the company's competitors. In other words, given that a company specializes in a particular line of business, it should have expertise in that line of business and should be capable of accepting and managing risks in its core business. In all likelihood, however, it does not have expertise in other areas that affect its business.

For example, airlines should be capable of transporting people, their luggage, and cargo from one place to another in a safe and timely manner. They should not be able to forecast fuel prices, exchange rates, and interest rates, all of which affect their business. Hence, airlines should hedge these risks, as they are not competitive risks. Airlines should be capable of taking the competitive risks that are involved in running their flights on schedule, dealing with weather, mechanical issues, and competitors.[8]

Tech companies such as Microsoft, Apple, and Google do not have much exposure to energy prices, nor commodities at all, but they have large global operations and receive cash flows in foreign currencies, and they have some interest rate exposure. These companies should have a competitive advantage in providing their specialized software and hardware but not in forecasting exchange rates and interest rates. Hence, they should hedge their exchange rate risk and also their interest rate risk.

---

[8]Of course, one can argue that airlines cannot predict the weather, but they have access to as much if not more weather information as anyone else and more importantly, they have the strategies for responding to weather-driven problems.

6.5   Managerial Motivations

For all of the solid business reasons for managing risk, there is yet another class of reasons that motivates risk management that may not be quite as justifiable but are perhaps even more likely to be true. We know that corporate management does not always act in the best interest of shareholders. The loss in value that shareholders incur from managerial self-motivation is called agency costs. Executives, more generically referred to as managers, act as agents for shareholders. They are compensated in a variety of ways, some of which are specifically designed to motivate managers to put the shareholders' interests in front of theirs. Nonetheless, often managers still put their own interests first.

The Poster Child for Agency Costs

Tyco International Ltd. is an Irish based company with a large U.S. operation headquartered in Princeton, New Jersey. It was founded in 1960, is the owner of the ADT line of security products and services, and it also makes hundreds of other products for a variety of uses related to safety and security. As of 2016, Tyco is part of a single company called Johnson Controls.

In 1976 a 30-year old auditor named Dennis Kozlowski, who had been raised in a tough Polish-Italian neighborhood in Newark, New Jersey, began working at Tyco. Just 14 years later, he was named President and CEO and by 1992, he had the added title of Chairman of the Board. During the 1990s, Tyco experienced tremendous growth but near the end of that decade, problems started to emerge. As his own wealth grew, Kozlowski acquired an affinity for art. He purchased $13 million of paintings, including some by Renoir and Monet, and had them shipped to a Tyco office in New Hampshire instead of his New York apartment. The significance of a seemingly minor shipping diversion is that New Hampshire has no sales tax, while New York does. In 2002 the New York district attorney was investigating high end art purchases and discovered the sale. Kozlowski was then indicted for avoiding more than $1 million in sales tax. In June he resigned from Tyco. But his problems were just starting.

In September 2002 a New York Grand Jury returned a 39-count indictment against Kozlowski and CFO Mark Swartz, alleging that they had engaged in fraud. Among other charges, Kozlowski and Swartz were believed to have paid themselves with Tyco money without authorization, engaged in securities fraud, and falsified records.

In a trial that lasted six months, it was revealed that Kozlowski had an extremely lavish lifestyle that while not strictly illegal, may have been supported with Tyco funds. It was alleged that Kozlowski had used Tyco money in furnishing his New York apartment and a home in Nantucket. Among other luxuries, Kozlowski had a $6,000 shower curtain, a $15,000 umbrella stand, a $2,000 wastebasket, and almost $3,000 in coat hangers. But what topped all of this is that he had gotten Tyco to pay half of the cost of a $2 million Roman-themed party on his wife's 40th birthday on the island of Sardinia. The entertainment included a $250,000 fee to pop star Jimmy Buffett for a one-hour performance. Videotapes and photos suggested that the affair was a Roman orgy party, but that was a bit of an overstatement. Nonetheless, the jurors did see a portion of the tape. In the end, however, the case was declared a mistrial due to a juror receiving threats.

Kozlowski's second trial resulted in convictions on 22 counts in June of 2005. He was sentenced to 8 1/3 to 25 years. He served a portion of his sentence in a minimum security prison in New York and was conditionally released in January 2014.

Well, there are agency costs, and then there is theft. Executives are always well-paid and their free tickets to the Super Bowl, access to celebrities, and travel on private jets are standard practices for wealthy and successful people. Some of these costs are the responsibility of the company. Business executives are essentially on call 24/7, and they are constantly selling the company. There is clearly a line between payments that are established by policy and approved by the board and those that board members know nothing of. But for sure, videos of toga parties do not make shareholders happy.

One way in which managers put their own interests first is by causing the company to take less risk than it should. While that may sound strange, it is actually consistent with the idea of managers acting in their own best interests and not those of their shareholders. Managers have a very high percentage of their personal wealth tied up in the company. Moreover, they are usually highly compensated with shares and options, thereby tying their wealth even more to the company. Thus, managers, unlike shareholders, tend to be poorly diversified, and unlike shareholders, there is little they can do about it. To offset this concentration of risk, managers often cause the company to take lower risks, which can be done in two primary ways. One is to cause the company to diversify. As noted by Smith and Stulz (1985), another way is to reduce the risk by hedging.

Diversification at the level of the company does very little if anything for shareholders, because the shareholders could achieve the same risk reduction by merely diversifying their portfolios. If companies diversify, they provide no real gains to shareholders and to the detriment of shareholders, they fail to concentrate on what they do well. Thus, diversification can be very costly to shareholders. There is empirical evidence that diversified companies sell at a lower price, which is called the diversification discount.

Engaging in risk management and hedging activities can be beneficial to shareholders for a variety of reasons discussed as in this chapter, but the primary reason why companies manage risk may well be due to executives attempting to reduce their own personal risk. Thus, when companies hedge because of managerial motivations, they clearly are not putting their shareholders first. Granting options to managers can alleviate this risk somewhat. Options are more beneficial the more volatile the underlying. Hence, if managers own options they will be less inclined to lower the risk of the company.

The empirical evidence generally supports the notion that managers do often hedge for personal reasons rather than because it is in the best interests of the shareholders.

6.6 Practical Reasons for Risk Management and Hedging

Economists have devoted a great deal of energy to studying the reasons for why an organization should practice risk management and hedging. As documented in the preceding sections, the empirical evidence is somewhat mixed. There are many good conceptual reasons for practicing risk management and indeed managers may have personal reasons, but ultimately most companies probably do so for very practical reasons.

As you probably know, most companies spend a great deal of time planning. They prepare budgets and make preparations for actions they will take in the future. These plans and budgets are quite specific, but realistically, everyone knows that there is enough uncertainty in the future to derail a company's expectations, perhaps quite significantly. Risk management can facilitate the planning and budgeting process. When companies can lock in prices and rates, it is much easier to prepare budgets and make plans for the future. Having a degree of certainty or at least a sense that the risk is under control can also take some of the pressure off management and employees and remove the fear of wage freezes and layoffs.

Most reasonably large companies are also organized into semi-autonomous entities that are sometimes called divisions, departments, subsidiaries, or groups. Let us just refer to all of these entities as divisions. As these divisions can engage in quite different activities, they take different degrees of risk. As such, a company will oftentimes allocate capital to its divisions according to the risks that the divisions are taking. Those that take more risk will require more capital. Risk management also helps companies allocate capital within the divisions of a company by forcing the company to identify, measure, and manage the respective risks of the divisions. In a similar vein, performance evaluation of each division is facilitated by risk management. Performance evaluation should be based on the risk taken and capital allocated.

Companies also can justify the practice of risk management to preserve their image and reputation. When companies sustain significant losses due to poor risk management or no risk management, they may incur costs that go far beyond the direct financial costs. Shareholders, creditors, financial analysts, customers, suppliers, employees, and regulators can lose faith in the company's ability to operate successfully in the long run. The support of these stakeholders is important, and a reputation lost is difficult to get back. Risk management can certainly make it easier to avoid losing reputation and the confidence of stakeholders.

Finally, we should add that risk management can facilitate a corporate culture in which all employees from top to bottom are cognizant of the risks around them and what they can do to control those risks. An emphasis on risk management at the top of the company can inculcate all employees to be aware of and manage the risks around them that are not worth taking.

6.7 On the Whole, Does Risk Management Add Value to a Company?

There have been about 10 major studies that look at whether the practice of risk management benefits shareholders. The overwhelming majority, but not all, shows that risk management is beneficial to shareholders in that it increases the value of the company. Yet, the question is a very difficult one and not easy to empirically test. Companies engage in many activities that are related to risk but do not necessarily involve consciously managing risk. For example, if a company decides to exit a market in which the risk has increased, it may be consciously making nothing more than a product decision, even though it is reducing the overall risk of the company. It is extremely difficult to categorize the decisions companies make into those that directly involve the practice of risk management and those that have other motivations.

Most of the studies have attempted to determine if the use of derivatives adds value to the shareholders.[9] Yet, the use of derivatives does not automatically imply a conscious decision to manage risk. Remember that risk management means to identify the risk tolerance, measure the risk, and align the desired risk with the risk taken. Companies that use derivatives could be using them for nothing but speculation. Moreover, there are so many differences between companies that it is difficult to accurately control for these differences. In addition, risk management is not a binary variable. We cannot divide the universe of companies into those that manage risk and those that do not. Many companies manage risk to a degree but stop short of having a fully coordinated effort to align the risk taken with the risk desired.

Thus, it is not likely that one can really identify for sure if companies that manage risk have higher values. It is also not likely that the empirical findings mentioned in this section can be relied upon. At this point, we must use more intuition than to lean on scientific evidence. And the intuition almost surely points in a positive direction. It is difficult to conceive of an argument against the desirability of identifying risk tolerance, deciding on the risk being taken, and aligning the risk being taken with the desired risk. Risk management is a disciplined practice that attempts to keep the company on the right track as it pursues its objectives.

We have cited plenty of good reasons to manage risk and a few that are not so good. Most companies could surely justify managing risk for at least some of the good reasons given here. Of course, many do so for some of the bad reasons, but that is not a justification to reject risk management.

6.8 The Value of Risk Management to Society

In this chapter, we have been discussing the value of risk management to a company, but what about the value to society? As citizens of a country, should we want a company to practice risk management? The answer sounds like "yes", but not so fast. From a societal point of view, it seems that we

---

[9] A good survey article is Aretz and Bartram (2010).

should be concerned with systemic risk, the potential failure of a large set of interconnected companies that threatens the health of an entire economy. It is tempting to think that if each company practices risk management, the systemic risk of an economy is lower, but that might not be true.

Systemic risk is a function of the risk taken by the various economic units and their interconnectivity. The interconnectivity derives from the extent to which they engage in relationships with each other. Obviously there is a great deal of interconnectivity. Company A borrows money from Bank B, which engages in a derivative transaction with hedge fund C, which has a large investment in Company A and Bank B. If one party fails, the other party can be heavily dependent on money owed to it by another company. This type of scenario can cause a string of failures.

A company can indeed be practicing risk management and can still take very high risks, either consciously or subconsciously. A company can believe that it has its risk under control and yet it does not. It seems intuitive that if companies devote some time and effort to measuring and managing their risks, they are less likely to get into the kinds of financial straits that end up leading to systemic problems.

6.9   Chapter Summary

In this chapter, we essentially asked the question, "Does risk management matter?" In other words, does risk management do anything for shareholders that they cannot do themselves? There are plenty of actions shareholders can take through diversifying their portfolios, engaging in derivatives transactions, and using borrowed funds to buy stock that affect the risks of their investments. But we argued that companies can generally do many of these things better than their shareholders can. Companies are in a better position to know the risks to which they are exposed that affect the shareholders and how much exposure the shareholders have.

We discussed the fact that it appears that risk management can benefit the shareholders by providing better control of credit risk, which lowers the probability of bankruptcy and financial distress and leads to the ability to borrow more and take advantage of the interest tax subsidy. We also saw that risk management can turn a bad investment into a good one by stabilizing cash flows at a level that leads to positive value for an investment, rather than taking too much risk that can make the investment unfavorable. We argued that risk management can stabilize the flow of internally generated cash, which can be beneficial to support growth. We also saw that risk management can better enable companies to selectively choose the risks they are best suited to take, which are the risks in which they have a competitive advantage. Those risks for which they do not have a competitive advantage can then be eliminated or at least reduced. We also mentioned that risk management can reduce taxes if the company's tax rate schedule is sufficiently convex and if its income is quite volatile. We also stated that risk management can reduce the underinvestment problem in which a financially struggling company may choose not to engage in attractive investment opportunities because they primarily benefit the creditors. Risk management can also reduce information asymmetry and improve the quality of the signals that companies send to stakeholders.

We found that many companies engage in risk management primarily through managers' self-motivation. Given the high concentrated risk that managers have in their personal wealth, they may choose to do an excessive amount of hedging, which would be bad for shareholders. Managers may hedge risks that shareholders would prefer they take. We also noted that there are many practical reasons for managing risk. Risk management facilitates planning, capital allocation, performance evaluation, the protection of reputation, and the inculcation of a risk culture that permeates the company and makes all employees aware of risks that the company is exposed to but should not take.

Finally, we noted that it is difficult to prove that risk management benefits companies and society as a whole. We tend to believe that it does, but proving it beyond a reasonable doubt is very hard to do. Therefore, we are at least somewhat required to take it on faith that risk management is worth doing. But our intuition is a strong supporter of the value of risk management.

6.10 Questions and Problems

1. Identify the advantage and disadvantage of financial leverage. Illustrate this point in the context of a levered company with $100,000 of assets financed by $45,000 of debt at 5% interest and $55,000 of equity in comparison to an unlevered company under the assumption that the assets generate a return of (a) 10% in a good year and (b) −10% in a bad year.
2. Briefly explain what the Modigliani-Miller (M&M) theory implies about the value of risk management.
3. Explain why the tax deductibility of interest is an advantage in financing a company. Then illustrate the effect with a company worth $600,000, divided into $250,000 of equity and $350,000 of debt at 4.2% interest.

Compare the value of the firm to the alternative of having zero debt under an expected net operating income of $75,000, a risk-free rate of 4%, and a tax rate of 34%.

4. What is meant by the costs of bankruptcy and financial distress?

5. How do the costs of bankruptcy and financial distress relate to the determination of an optimal capital structure, and where does risk management fit into this explanation?

6. Explain how tax convexity can justify hedging. Illustrate the point with a firm with equally likely taxable incomes of $1,500 and $6,000, in perpetuity. The tax rate is 25% on the first $4,000 of taxable income and 35% on all income above $4,000. Assume that hedging will stabilize taxable income at $2,000. Assume an all-equity firm with a discount rate of 7% and a risk-free rate of 4%. Explain why the tax convexity argument may not hold in practice.

7. What is the underinvestment problem and how does risk management reduce the magnitude of this problem?

8. How can risk management convert an unattractive investment in assets into an attractive one? Illustrate the point with the following example. A company is considering investing $100,000 into a one-year project that is expected to generate $9,000,000 of cash revenues every year for certain. Cash costs, however, can vary between $7,000,000 and $12,500,000 with equal probability. The discount rate is 10%, and the risk-free rate is 4%. Costs can be hedged to a value of $8,500,000. Show how the *NPV* is improved by hedging the costs.

9. How can risk management create value by increasing debt capacity?

10. What is information asymmetry and how can risk management reduce the problem it causes?

11. How does risk management support internal financing?

12. How can risk management give a company a competitive advantage?

13. What factor might motivate managers to hedge, even if not in the best interests of their shareholders?

14. What practical reasons are there for engaging in risk management?

15. Why is it difficult to determine if risk management adds value for a company?

16. Is risk management beneficial to society as a whole?

Part III

Managing Market Risk

Chapter 7

Measuring Financial Market Risk

Only those who risk going too far can possibly find out how far one can go.

T. S. Eliot
1888–1965

We now start Part III, which deals with managing market risk. The unit consists of four chapters. This chapter is the first, of course and it provides an introduction to the tools used in measuring market risk. Recall that market risk is the risk arising from movements in interest rates, exchange rates, commodity prices, and stock prices. These types of risks are those that arise from the volatility of prices and rates in their respective markets. In measuring these risks, we will use a number of risk management models. Risk management models have much in common with many financial models, but they do have some important differences. Most financial models are designed to capture the relationship between expected return and risk and, in so doing, they help us determine a fair price for an asset. For that reason, they are often called pricing models. The primary objective of risk management models is not the pricing of assets, but the measurement and control of the risks arising from those assets. Also, pricing models typically assume that market participants act rationally and align their desired risks with their risk tolerances. Risk management models make no such assumptions. The desired risks and risk tolerances are exogenous factors determined by risk managers, CEOs, or whoever is responsible for determining the amount of risk taken by the entity. Risk management models provide guidance on how to measure and control risk, so that the risk taken can be aligned with the desired risk for a given market participant.

Anyone who has studied finance will obtain some exposure to certain basic tools of risk measurement. In all likelihood, the first notion that a finance student gets of risk is the idea that the returns on assets are derived from an underlying probability distribution. Thus, the concept of probability is likely to be one's first formal educational exposure to the notion of risk.[1] A probability distribution is a mathematical function that describes the likely outcomes of a random variable. But let us first make sure we know what a random variable is.

A random variable is a measure that can take on multiple values and is at least partially if not completely unpredictable. There are many examples of random variables in life, and as mentioned, some are almost completely random, some are partially random and partially predictable due to the ability to observe their properties, and some are partially random and partially predictable due to the ability to influence their outcomes. As an example of a completely random variable, suppose you go to a popular restaurant and do not have a reservation. From your perspective, the amount of time you have to wait for a table is a completely random variable. It is a function of how many people want to eat at that restaurant at around the same time and also the quality of the service provided by the restaurant. Note that the variable — your waiting time — is random *from your perspective*. It can be influenced by the restaurant, but to you, it is random. The second type of random variable has a modest degree of predictability due to your ability to collect information on it. The weather is an example of such a random variable. Very near-term weather is relatively predictable, since one can usually observe weather patterns in nearby areas that experience the weather before your area does. Finally, we mentioned the possibility of a random variable over which you have some control. A good example is your health. It is not completely possible to take actions that guarantee a healthy life, but such actions do alter the probability in your favor. Risk management is an attempt to alter the probability distribution of outcomes in such a way that the outcomes are characterized by the degree of risk that the risk taker wishes to take. Oftentimes market risk management deals with the first situation, the completely unpredictable random variable. As we saw in

---

[1] As we saw in Chapter 2, we are constantly exposed to risk in life. We employ concepts of probability at an early age, such as when a perfectly calm baby cries when handed from its mother to a total stranger. The baby's innate risk monitoring system says that there is uncertainty over what will ensue and there is a distinct possibility of something bad, or at least, uncomfortable, happening.

Chapter 4, interest rates, exchange rates, commodity prices, and stock prices are largely random.

As noted above, random variables are characterized by probability distributions. A probability distribution is a mathematical specification of the statistical properties of a random variable. A probability distribution gives us information on the average value of the random variable, its volatility, its higher order parameters such as skewness or kurtosis, and it also enables us to make statements about the likelihood that a value of the random variable will be above a given value, below a given value, or between two given values.

There is just one fairly major problem with probability distributions in practice: almost always we do not know the true probability distribution for the random variable of interest. Those few occasions where we do know the probability distribution often involve experiments we construct and therefore control, such as card games and rolls of a die. When operating in business and especially in the financial market environment, we almost never know the true probability distribution that we face moving ahead. Certainly we can collect data and observe the historical statistical properties, and from there we can make statements with a measurable degree of confidence about what the probability distribution *was*. But we can rarely, if ever, say with confidence that the historical probability distribution is the same as the one looking ahead. Thus, we can seldom be sure that we know what the true probability distribution is.

Moreover, to know the true probability distribution, two pieces of information are required: we must know the type of distribution and, conditional on that information, we must know the parameters of the distribution. There are many types of distributions. We have already mentioned the normal, but you have probably heard of the *t-distribution*, the *chi-square distribution*, and the *F-distribution*. You may have heard of the *Weibull distribution*, the *beta distribution*, the *Poisson distribution*, the *binomial distribution*, the *hypergeometric distribution*, the *gamma distribution*, and many more. Each distribution has certain parameters that characterize it. For example, for a normal distribution, we need to know the expected return and variance, and for the Weibull distribution, we need to know some parameters called shape scale.

If the risk is reflected in a series of repeated exposures, we need to know if the risk is independent. We often use the expression *independent identically distributed*, sometimes referred to as *iid*, to describe repeated exposures to the same probability distribution with the same parameters. In real markets, the distributions and their parameters do often change. These concerns are the simple realities of risk management. We will address some of these issues in this chapter. Others belong in advanced courses and books.

As mentioned, we often describe random variables by various statistical measures. We have previously talked about average returns and standard deviations. We have also related the statistical properties of one random variable to those of another through a linear measure called correlation. These concepts are reasonable measures of association for many continuous random variables, such as prices and interest rates. Equipped with the foundations of these measures, we have been able to understand the concept of beta, the sensitivity of an asset's return to a market factor. These measures are useful tools, but they are not sufficient to successfully practice risk management. We will enhance these statistical measures with the material in this chapter.

As noted, this chapter deals only with market risk. Chapters 8, 9, and 10 cover the instruments called forwards and futures, swaps, and options, that are used to manage market risk. We shall cover credit risk in Chapter 11. It presents an entirely different set of measurement problems, and that can wait.

7.1 Value-at-Risk

In recent years, one statistical measure has gained widespread usage, albeit not without considerable controversy. That measure is called *Value-at-Risk*, sometimes referred to as *VaR* and occasionally *VAR*. As a very loose definition, *VaR* is a measure of the risk that exists in the negative tail of the distribution of gains and losses. Of course, this definition is pretty vague, and we will need to be far more precise. For now, however, let us provide a little perspective on how this measure came about.

Sir Dennis Weatherstone was formerly the Chairman of the Board and CEO of JP Morgan & Co., now J.P. Morgan Chase. In the early 1990s, Weatherstone sensed that the company was engaged in a great deal of derivatives trading that, through the high degree of leverage and potential inattentiveness of some individuals, could endanger the organization. He asked for a report at 4:15 p.m. each day indicating the company's exposure and potential for loss over the next day. He did not say how to measure this risk, leaving that up to his subordinates, who then came up with the concept of *VaR*.

As a formal definition, J.P. Morgan Chase defines *VaR* in its annual report (FY 2017 Annual Report, p. 289) as

> *the dollar amount of potential loss from adverse market moves in an ordinary market environment*

The company goes on to describe it in more detail. Let us see here, however, if we can consolidate the concept into a concise but reasonably comprehensive definition.

> *Value-at-risk is the minimum loss that would be incurred over a specified time horizon with a fixed probability in a normal market environment.*

Now, let us work through that definition carefully. First, we note that *VaR* is a *minimum loss*. This notion means that it is the smallest amount that can be lost under the conditions specified. Second, *VaR* is associated with a *specified time horizon*. What we mean by this concept is a certain future time period such as one day, one week, two weeks, one month, one quarter, or one year. Third, the definition refers to a *fixed probability*, which means that this probability reflects the likelihood that the stated *VaR* is the minimum loss over the given time period. The complement is considered to be the confidence level. Thus, a fixed probability of 5% means that there is a 5% chance that losses in excess of the stated *VaR* will occur, and the complement, 95%, is the confidence level. Finally, the definition refers to a normal market environment. While *VaR* is designed to reflect the potential for large losses, that potential is constrained to normal markets. What we mean by "normal markets" in a bit vague. We do not necessarily mean a market in which returns are normally distributed. We mean basically that our expectations of the distribution and its characteristics are realized. But we do not mean that large losses cannot occur. They certainly can occur, even in normal markets.

J.P. Morgan Chase measures its *VaR* daily with a confidence level of 95%. As of December 31, 2017, J.P. Morgan Chase reported that its *VaR* was $29 million. This number means that the company believes that there is a 5% chance that it would experience a one-day loss in excess of $29 million. While *VaR* is normally expressed in currency units, it is important to put the number in perspective. On that date, J.P. Morgan Chase reported total assets of $2.5 trillion, equity of $229 billion, and total revenue for the year of almost \$100 billion. Hence, \$29 million does not on the surface seem large, though obviously the potential loss is more than \$29 million.

The probability level and its complement, the degree of confidence, is a decision that must be made by the user. The most common levels are 5% probability (95% confidence) and 1% probability (99% confidence). Some investment management firms use one standard deviation, which is about 16% (84% confidence). Let us make sure we understand what information is being communicated by the probability and confidence levels. Using the J.P. Morgan Chase *VaR* of \$29 million for one day at a 5% probability, we are saying, as stated above, that on about 5% of all days, the bank would be expected to lose more than \$29 million. In a complementary sense, the confidence level of 95% means that 95% of the time, the bank's daily trading profits and losses would be better than a loss of \$29 million. It is important to be careful with the language. If we say something like "95% of the time, the bank will lose no more than \$29 million," the statement can be interpreted as meaning that on all days in which the bank loses money, the losses are less than \$29 million on 95% of them. This interpretation is incorrect, as it incorporates only the days in which the bank incurs losses. In fact, the 95% confidence level reflects also the days on which the bank makes money. Given a positive expected return, on far more than 50% of the days, the bank does not lose money.

Exhibit 7-1 visualizes the basic concept of *VaR*. This graph is a normal distribution, though we will talk about whether the distribution has to be

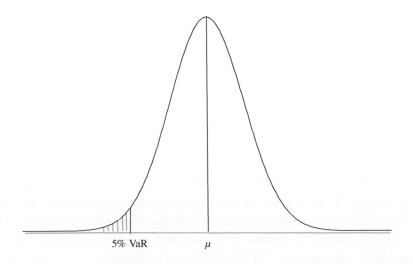

Exhibit 7-1. 5% Value-at-Risk (VaR) Given a Probability Distribution

normal later in this chapter. The distribution is centered on its expected value, denoted as μ. As you know from studying statistics, the variation around the expected value is determined by the volatility or standard deviation. The small lined area is the location in which 5% of the outcomes would fall. Thus, the *VaR* is the point at which 5% of the outcomes would be lower.

Talking about *VaR* is one thing: estimating *VaR* is another. Indeed, coming up with the *VaR* number is quite challenging, as we shall see in the next section.

7.1.1 *Estimating VaR*

VaR numbers, just like expected returns, volatilities, and correlations, do not reveal themselves to us. We have to estimate them. Estimation almost invariably starts with past data but typically requires intuition, a modest element of forecasting, and a great deal of educated guesswork. Those who do the best job of these activities will likely do the best job of managing risk.

One of the first steps in the process is to identify risk factors, which are the underlying sources of risk. Some risk factors are fairly obvious. A domestic stock held in a portfolio is its own risk factor, because the stock return is the source of risk. A foreign stock, however, has two risk factors: its return in the foreign currency and also the exchange rate. A bond can have multiple sources of risk. It will be affected by interest rates as well as credit risk. We will cover credit risk later, so let us leave that risk out of the picture. Nonetheless, the term "interest rates" encompasses a tremendous number of types of rates. There are short-, intermediate-, and long-term interest rates, but even these terms are quite vague, since there is no clear dividing line between short- and intermediate-term, and between intermediate- and long-term. There are also domestic interest rates and foreign interest rates. There are interest rates on government debt, interest rates on foreign debt, interest rates on corporate debt, interest rates on mortgages, and interest rate on other personal debt.

A second step in the process is typically to obtain a recent history of data of the risk factors. This recent period is called the *historical period* or *lookback period*. We will discuss this notion in more detail in the next sections.

There are three general methods of estimating *VaR*: the *analytical method*, the *historical simulation method*, and the *Monte Carlo simulation method*. We shall now take each in turn.

7.1.1.1 *Analytical Method*

The analytical method, also known as the *parametric method* and the *variance-covariance method*, is based on the assumption of a normal distribution. It essentially involves finding the critical point in Exhibit 7-1. This procedure is done "analytically," mean that it is done via a formula that incorporates the characteristics of the distribution.

Let us start by assuming that we either know or have estimates of the expected value, $E(R_p)$, and volatility, σ_p of the portfolio of assets. These values are based on a specific time horizon, as noted in the definition. Of course, how we get that knowledge or those estimates is a question we shall return to momentarily. First, let us assume that $E(R_p)$ and σ_p are based on rates of return. In other words, they are not the expected value and volatility of profits. Then we must decide on what probability level we wish.

For a normal distribution and a 5% probability/95% confidence level, the difference between the expected value and the *VaR* is 1.65 standard deviations. In other words, if you move leftward from the expected value, a shift of 1.65 standard deviations will take you to the point at which 5% of the distribution is left of that point. For a 1% probability/99% confidence level, the difference is 2.33 standard deviations. We shall identify this adjustment value (1.65 or 2.33) with the Greek symbol chi, χ. Our estimate of the *VaR* in terms of rate of return, VaR_r, is:

$$VaR_r = E(R_p) - \chi\sigma_p. \tag{7.1}$$

This value will generally be negative. Because *VaR* is always understood to reflect a loss, however, we automatically change the sign. One simple way to take care of this problem is to restate the above equation as

$$VaR_r = \chi\sigma_p - E(R_p). \tag{7.2}$$

We then multiply this amount by the size of the assets subject to this risk. So, for a portfolio valued at V_p, *VaR* is found as

$$VaR_P = VaR_r V_p.$$

So this process is what we mean by estimating *VaR* analytically. Recall that we also said that this estimation method is called the parametric method. The word "parametric" relates to the word "parameter." The parameters of the distribution are the expected value and volatility. Thus, this method directly uses the parameters of the distribution. We also referred to the estimation method as the variance-covariance method. The standard deviation is the square root of the variance, and it will incorporate the covariances among the component assets. We will explain this point with the example that follows.

While most portfolios are broadly diversified as a result of holding a large number of securities, we will need to look closely at the components in order to fully illustrate how *VaR* works. Therefore, we will illustrate *VaR* with a portfolio of only two assets, specifically a $300 million portfolio that is 75% invested in the exchange traded fund called the Vanguard Total Stock Market Index and 25% invested in the exchanged traded fund called the Vanguard Total Bond Market Index. These two ETFs are themselves broadly diversified, so this combination should be a well-diversified portfolio of stocks and bonds. We shall refer to the stock ETF by its ticker symbol, *VTI*, and the bond ETF by its ticker symbol, *BND*. We shall now need estimates of the expected returns and volatilities of *VTI* and *BND* and incorporate these estimates appropriately weighted in the 75%–25% proportions to obtain the expected return and volatility of the portfolio.

The analytical method tells us nothing about how to obtain the expected values and volatilities. Almost always we start with a series of historical returns. We shall collect the daily prices and dividends of the two ETFs over a two-year period. We chose to start with January 2, 2016, and end on January 2, 2018. There are 504 daily prices. To save space, in Exhibit 7-2 we present data for the first and last few observations and for a few observations in which dividends were paid. The columns also include our return calculations. Full information details are provided in the accompanying spreadsheet,

	VTI			BND		
Date	Closing Price	Dividend	Return	Closing Price	Dividend	Return
1/4/16	102.74	0.000	NA	80.72	0.000	NA
1/5/16	102.97	0.000	−0.0012	80.82	0.000	0.0012
1/6/16	100.95	0.000	−0.0134	81.18	0.000	0.0045
...	...	...	...	...	...	...
3/14/16	103.07	0.000	−0.0012	81.90	0.000	0.0022
3/15/16	102.24	0.480	−0.0034	81.82	0.000	−0.0010
...	...	...	...	...	...	...
3/31/16	104.82	0.000	−0.0011	82.81	0.000	0.0019
4/1/16	105.48	0.000	0.0063	82.73	0.173	0.0011
...	...	...	...	...	...	...
12/28/17	137.76	0.000	0.0022	81.44	0.000	−0.0006
12/29/18	137.25	0.000	−0.0037	81.57	0.000	0.0016
1/2/18	138.22	0.000	0.0071	81.34	0.000	−0.0028

Exhibit 7-2. Daily Price and Return Data on VTI and BND

"Chapter 7 VaR Calculation Support.xlsx", available at the web site for this book (https://www.worldscientific.com/worldscibooks/10.1142/11321).

The *VTI* ETF consists of almost 4,000 individual stocks. When these stocks pay dividends, typically on a quarterly basis but in different months, Vanguard accumulates the dividends and pays them out quarterly, near the end of each quarter.[2] As you can see, it paid a dividend of $0.48 on March 15. Other dividend payments are incorporated as well but not shown in the snapshot above. The *BND* ETF contains almost 7,000 different bonds, which make their interest payments at various times. Vanguard accumulates these dividends and pays them monthly. We see above the dividends of $0.163 on April 1, 2016. Other dividend payments are incorporated into the data but on dates not shown.

To illustrate a calculation, the VTI return on March 15, 2016 is found as

$$\frac{102.24 + 0.48}{103.07} - 1 = -0.0034,$$

Note the inclusion of the dividend in the numerator. Likewise, the *BND* return on April 1, 2016 is

$$\frac{82.73 + 0.173}{82.81} - 1 = 0.0011.$$

If a dividend is not paid on a given day, we simply divide that day's price by the previous day's price, or in other words, we essentially insert a dividend of zero.

Let us start by computing some descriptive statistics. We have covered these points in Chapter 3, so we shall just show the results below with some basic indications of how these estimates are calculated. The subscripts "V" and "B" are used for the *VTI* and *BND* ETFs.[3]

Average Return:

$$\bar{R}_V : \frac{-0.0012 + \cdots + 0.0071}{503} = 0.0007$$

$$\bar{R}_B : \frac{0.0012 + \cdots - 0.0028}{503} = 0.0001$$

---

[2]In other words, some stocks pay dividends in March, June, September, and December. Others pay them in January, April, July, and October, and others in February, May, August, and November. Thus, it is a virtual certainty that in every single month there will be at least one stock paying dividends.

[3]These results are calculated on a spreadsheet, so they may not be precisely equal to the same results calculated manually.

$$Volatility:$$

$$\sigma_V : \sqrt{\frac{(0.0022 - 0.0006)^2 + \cdots + (0.0071 - 0.0006)^2}{502}} = 0.0067$$

$$\sigma_B : \sqrt{\frac{(0.0012 - 0.0000)^2 + \cdots + (-0.0028 - 0.0000)^2}{502}} = 0.0019$$

$$Correlation:$$

$$\rho_{VB} = \frac{\{(0.0022 - 0.0006)(0.0012 - 0.0000) + \cdots (0.0071 - 0.0006)(-0.0028 - 0.0000)\}/502}{(0.0068)(0.0020)} = -0.2141$$

We typically express return statistics on an annual basis. We annualize the average returns by multiplying by the approximate number of trading days in a year, 250. We annualize the volatility by multiplying by the square root of 250. The correlation does not need to be annualized, as it is the same regardless of whether the data are daily or annualized. Exhibit 7-3 presents these statistics that we will be using.[4]

Now that we have these estimates we can presumably proceed — but wait. We have to ask ourselves if these estimates are realistic. In fact, they really are not. The previous two years were somewhat abnormal, particularly in that the stock market performed exceptionally well with relatively low volatility. Based on historical performance over a long period of time, we should probably use an average return of about 10% for stocks and a volatility of about 20%. For bonds we should use about 5% with a volatility of about 8%. Of course, these are subjective values, but the point is an

Statistic	Annualized Value
Average returns	$\bar{R}_V = 0.1723$ $\bar{R}_B = 0.0302$
Volatility	$\sigma_V = 0.1065$ $\sigma_B = 0.0305$
Correlation	$\rho_{V,B} = -0.2141$

Exhibit 7-3. Annualized Statistical Estimates for VTI and BND

---

[4]Again, due to spreadsheet precision, annualization may not lead to precisely the same figures if done manually.

Statistic	Annualized Value
Expected returns	$E(R_V) = 0.10$ $E(R_B) = 0.05$
Volatility	$\sigma_V = 0.20$ $\sigma_B = 0.08$
Correlation	$\rho_{V,B} = -0.18$

Exhibit 7-4. Statistical Inputs for VTI and BND

important one. We cannot simply use recent history. We can start with recent history, but we have to ask ourselves whether the recent history is realistic. Also, assume we think the correlation estimate is a little too high, so we change it to -0.18. Exhibit 7-4 summarizes these estimates of the statistical inputs we shall use. The average returns are now denoted as expected returns.

Practitioners will have good estimates from data available to them and can incorporate judgement about whether they anticipate stronger or weaker markets and more volatile and less volatile markets. Our objective is to illustrate the procedure, so any reasonable estimates will suffice.

Now we need to know what these estimates imply about the expected return and volatility of our $300 million portfolio that consists of 75% VTI and 25% BND. The calculations are below:

$$E(R_p) = w_V E(R_V) + w_B E(R_B)$$
$$= 0.75(0.10) + 0.25(0.05) = 0.0875$$

$$\sigma_p = \sqrt{w_V^2 \sigma_V^2 + w_B^2 \sigma_B^2 + 2 w_V w_B cov_{V,B}}$$
$$= \sqrt{(0.75)^2(0.20)^2 + (0.25)^2(0.08)^2 + 2(0.75)(0.25)(-0.18)(0.20)(0.08)}$$
$$= 0.1477$$

Now we must take into account that we need a daily *VaR*. Thus, we divide the annual expected return by 250 and the annual volatility by the square root of 250 to obtain

$$E(R_p) \,|\, \text{daily} = \frac{0.0875}{250} = 0.00035$$

$$\sigma_p \,|\, \text{daily} = \frac{0.1477}{\sqrt{250}} = 0.009342.$$

So, our portfolio is assumed to have an expected return of 0.035% and a volatility of 0.9342% on a daily basis. Now, it is simple to calculate a 5%

VaR. First, we find the *VaR* expressed as a return:

$$1.65\sigma_p - E(R_p) = 1.65(0.009342) - 0.00035 = 0.010564921.$$

We then multiply this amount by the size of the portfolio, $300 million, to obtain the estimate of our 5% daily *VaR*:

$$\$300,000,000(0.010564921) = \$4,519,476.$$

Thus, we would report that our daily analytical *VaR* at 5% is $4,519,476. Let us just round off to $4.5 million. We interpret this number to mean that we would expect to lose at least $4.5 million on 5% of all trading days, which is roughly once a month.

There are some slight variations of this procedure, which lie mainly in the interpretation of *VaR* in a statistical sense. The first variation, called the *mean-adjusted VaR* and sometimes *relative VaR*, interprets the *VaR* as the minimum amount relative to the expected future value of the portfolio rather than relative to the current value. In the previous few paragraphs we estimated *VaR* relative to the current value. So, when we said the VaR is $4.5 million, that value is a loss of $4.5 million from the current value of $300 million. The mean-adjusted *VaR* expresses the *VaR* relative to the expected value of the portfolio. For a portfolio value of V_P with an expected return of $E(R_p)$, the expected future value is $V_P(1 + E(R_p))$. The level of the portfolio that defines the mean-adjusted *VaR* is expressed as $V_P^* = V_P(1 + R^*)$ where R^* is the return that would take the current level of the portfolio, V_P, down to the VaR_p. Then $VaR_p = E(V_P) - V_P^*$. By definition, $R^* = E(R_p) - \chi\sigma_p$. Substituting we obtain, $VaR_p = V_P\chi\sigma_p$. Thus, in this example, the mean-adjusted VaR_p would be $300,000,000(1.65)(0.009342) - \$4,624,209$. So, is the *VaR* $4.6 million, or what we previously estimated, $4.5 million?[5] The answer is fairly simple. Our standard *VaR* estimate, rounded to $4.5 million, means that there is a 5% chance that the portfolio value will fall below the original value, $300 million, by more than $4.5 million. For the mean-adjusted *VaR*, note that the expected value of the portfolio is $300,000,000(1.00035) = $300,105,000. Under this specification, the interpretation is that there is a 5% chance that the portfolio value will fall below the expected portfolio value of $300,105,000

---

[5] Perhaps not surprisingly the difference in the two *VaR* numbers is precisely the expected return times the size of the portfolio, which sounds exactly like what it means when we say "mean-adjusted."

by more than \$4.6 million (rounded). The mean-adjusted VaR is the same concept as the *VaR*, but it expresses the deviation from the expected value.

Yet, another approach is to assume a zero expected return. Note that we had obtained an expected return of 0.035%. Some risk managers assume that this number is so close to zero that it can be safely assumed to be zero. In that case, both of the interpretations explained above lead to the same *VaR*, \$4.6 million. Thus, the zero-mean *VaR* is the standard *VaR* under the assumption of a zero expected return, and therefore, equals the mean-adjusted *VaR*.[6] There are significant conveniences of the assumption of zero expected return, but the zero-mean *VaR* has the deficiency that it implies that the annual expected return is 0.00%. Even a small daily return of 0.035% implies a reasonable annual expected return of 8.75%. Our overall preference is to use the first method we presented with a non-zero expected return.

The analytical method is straightforward and simple, which is due to its assumption of a normal distribution. That assumption will also come in handy later when we illustrate how *VaR* can be broken down into its components. But this advantage is also its disadvantage: the assumption of normality. In the next section we will look at a *VaR* estimation method that makes no assumption about the distribution. And while the analytical method can be characterized as simple, it does require the determination of portfolio variance for what might be thousands of components in real portfolios. Fortunately, computers are good at doing these kinds of computations.

A weakness of the analytical method is that the normal distribution assumes a linear and symmetric relationship between a change in the risk factor and the price of the security. Linearity and symmetry mean that the expected return and volatility are reasonably sufficient characterizations of how the price will change. For a stock, that assumption is not necessarily a major problem, but for bonds and options the relationship is definitely not linear.[7] Option returns are highly skewed, because an option has a

---

[6]There is one major convenience of the zero expected return assumption: you can convert a daily *VaR* to an annual *VaR* by multiplying it by the square root of the number of trading days in a year. This simple operation is not possible when the expected return is not zero, because the formula for *VaR* contains both the expected return and volatility, and the annual expected return is adjusted to the daily expected return by dividing by the number of trading days. The annual volatility is adjusted to the daily volatility, however, by dividing by the square root of the number of trading days.

[7]We are not dismissing the potential for stock returns to be skewed or to have a surprisingly large number of negative tail outcomes. We will discuss this point later.

limited loss of the premium. Bond returns are also somewhat skewed, because bond prices pull toward their par value. When skewness is a factor in describing returns, the expected return and volatility will not be sufficient to capture movements in returns. In addition, and perhaps most importantly, the normal distribution does not characterize most financial market returns. In particular, there are usually far more tail events than would be predicted by the normal distribution.

7.1.1.2 *Historical Simulation Method*

The historical simulation method positions the current portfolio at the beginning of a chosen historical period. It then determines the *VaR* based on the performance that the portfolio would have had during that period. This *VaR* estimate then becomes the *VaR* moving forward from the current point in time.

Clearly the historical simulation method does not rely on the assumption of a normal distribution. It simply takes whatever distribution of returns that occurred in the chosen historical period and inserts the current portfolio into that distribution to determine how it would have performed. Exhibit 7-5 shows a portion of the 503 portfolio returns on the *VTI* and *BND* ETFs that we drew from for the previous two years and the portfolio return based on a weighting of 75% *VTI* and 25% *BND*. The dates we show are the dates of the three largest and three smallest portfolio returns.

Since there are 503 returns, the cutoff for the lowest 5% would be at $503(0.05) = 25.15$. Thus, we want a value between the 25th and 26th lowest returns. The 25th lowest return is -0.0080 and the 26th lowest is -0.0075,

Date	VTI Return	BND Return	Portfolio Return $(0.75 \times$ VTI Return $+ 0.25 \times$ BND Return)
6/24/16	−0.0364	0.0056	−0.0259
9/9/16	−0.0249	−0.0044	−0.0198
1/13/16	−0.0258	0.0025	−0.0187
...	...	...	...
11/7/16	0.0221	−0.0013	0.0162
3/1/16	0.0238	−0.0033	0.0170
1/29/16	0.0248	0.0029	0.0193

Exhibit 7-5. Returns on Portfolio for Three Lowest and Three Highest Return Days

both rounded numbers. The Excel function = Percentile.EXC(data,cutoff) interpolates and generates the value -0.007873871. Changing the sign and multiplying by the $300 million value of the portfolio gives us the *VaR* estimate of

$$0.007873871(\$300,000,000) = \$2,362,161.$$

Let us round that number off to $2.4 million.

The first thing we should notice is that this number is considerably lower than the *VaR* estimated using the analytical method ($4.5 million). The reason should be obvious. The historical simulation method takes the actual recent history. Recall that in the recent historical period, we obtained a higher expected return and lower volatility of the stock ETF and a lower expected return and lower volatility of the bond ETF than we believed to be true looking ahead. Thus, for the analytical method we adjusted the expected returns and volatilities of the two ETFs.

Exhibit 7-6 shows the distribution of returns overlaid with a normal distribution. While it is apparent that the distribution is not perfectly normal, it is not far removed from normal. It should be remembered that each historical simulation period is unique, so the differences between the sample distribution and a normal distribution can vary widely.

Recall that earlier in this chapter we mentioned the *VaR* of J.P. Morgan Chase. The company stated in its 2017 annual report that it uses the

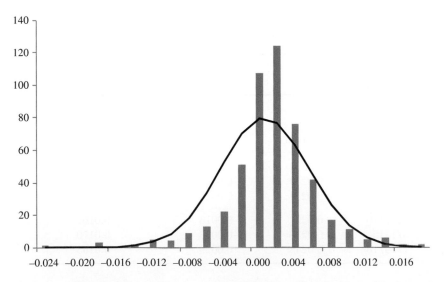

Exhibit 7-6. Distribution of Returns from Historical Simulation Overlaid with Normal Distribution

historical simulation method with 12 months of data. One advantage of using the historical simulation method is that no one can criticize you for being unrealistic. The method obviously incorporates events that actually happened. Yet, the trade-off is that you can be criticized for assuming that history repeats itself. Consider for example, the nearly 25% drop in the Dow Jones Industrial Average on October 19, 1987. A 25% decrease in one day is so far into the tails of the distribution that it defies any reasonable assumption of normality. If a day like that were included in a historical simulation, it would likely bias the results. Of course, one could discard such an extreme day, but there are other large movements of which it would be difficult to decide whether to discard. For example, there have been 19 days in history in which the S&P 500 has fallen in the range of −7% to −21%. Should these be discarded? They are certainly quite extreme. There is no clear answer. In addition, we should keep in mind that *VaR* is designed to help us manage tail risk. The problem is that it does this well only under normal market conditions, and sometimes we do not know if a market is normal but simply falling steeply or whether it is abnormal.

Next, let us take a look at a method that blends both the analytical and the historical simulation methods.

7.1.1.3 *Monte Carlo Simulation Method*

Monte Carlo simulation has been used for many years in scientific research. Originally referred to simply as simulation and also as statistical sampling, the technique got its geographical name from the casinos in Monte Carlo, Monaco. Monte Carlo simulation involves the generation of random outcomes according to a pre-specified probability distribution. These outcomes are then sorted and the *VaR* is obtained from the left tail of the sample of outcomes.

The Origins of Monte Carlo Simulation

Monte Carlo simulation originated in the physical and mathematical sciences. Suspend your common sense for a moment and assume that you have no idea what fraction of the time a coin toss will land on heads. To resolve this mystery, you propose to toss the coin many times and count the number of heads. You really do not know how many times it will take to answer the question, but you sense that when the fraction of tosses that land on heads starts to stabilize, you will probably have the answer. Now you have some sense of what Monte Carlo simulation does.

In the 18th century, the French scientist George Louis LeClerc, Comte du Buffon, proposed a problem to which the answer was not at all obvious. Take a needle, measure the length, and position two identical parallel lines a distance apart equal to the length of the needle. Randomly but blindly toss the needle in the general direction of the lines. Now, we want to know what fraction of the time the needle will intersect either line. It can be proven mathematically that the answer is $2/\pi$. To prove this result, LeClerc tossed baguettes, which seems a like a terrible waste of excellent French bread, but discovered that the fraction of times the needle intersected a line was approximately 0.63662, which is $2/\pi$. This type of experiment was perhaps one of the first examples of simulation.

In the early 1930s the Italian physicist Enrico Fermi used a random procedure to study the subject of neutron diffusion, which is the science of how neutrons react when they come into contact with various objects. Fermi generated numerous random outcomes according to a statistical distribution and tabulated them with an adding machine. At the time, this procedure was known as statistical sampling, meaning that it generated samples from a statistical distribution. About 10 years later Fermi became involved in the Los Alamos project that led to the first atomic bomb. The team of rock-star scientists included such notable geniuses as John Von Neumann, Stanley Frankel, Edward Teller, Stanislaw Ulam, and Nicholas Metropolis. Following the war, there was substantial interest in the kinds of complex computational problems that arose in nuclear physics. In addition, it had become apparent that new machines were being developed that would have the ability to do the massive numbers of computations required for these kinds of problem. Of course, these machines were the forerunners of today's computers.

According to Metropolis himself, he suggested that the procedure be called Monte Carlo simulation. As he tells it, Ulam had an uncle who was always borrowing money to go to Monte Carlo and gamble. It apparently reminded Metropolis that the random outcomes of this statistical sampling process were not unlike the random outcomes at Monte Carlo. This process, which has since come to be known as Monte Carlo simulation, has gone on to be widely used in the sciences as well as in finance, where the random outcomes of prices and rates can be difficult to analyze.

Reference: N. Metropolis, "The Beginning of the Monte Carlo Method," *Los Alamos Science*, Special Issue (1987), pp. 125–130 and R. L. Harrison, "Introduction to Monte Carlo Simulation." *AIP Conference Proceedings* (January 5, 2010, pp. 17–21 (available at National Institute of Health Public Access site)

Any type of probability distribution can be used, but since this is a basic introduction, we will use the simplest method, the normal distribution. We will also use the same parameters we used for the analytical method. There are two ways to approach a portfolio simulation problem. One way is to simulate from the portfolio distribution. The other is to simulate the individual securities and combine the results into portfolios. It is much easier and faster to simulate the portfolio than to simulate the individual securities, but it is important to know how to do both approaches. Each simulation is a random return from a distribution that has an expected value of the expected return and a standard deviation of the volatility. For the portfolio simulation, the portfolio expected return would be set at 8.75% and the volatility at 14.77%. These values would be converted to their daily values of 0.035% and 0.9342% respectively. Random values can then be simulated from the normal distribution with inputs of an expected value of 0.035% and a volatility of 0.9342%. Of course, these values are based on the adjusted expected values and volatilities, not the historical ones.

Alternatively, we could simulate the distribution of each component security. This method has considerably more flexibility but is more complex and time-consuming. Recall in using the analytical method that we assumed that the *VTI* distribution has an expected return of 0.10 and a volatility of 0.20. These values are equivalent to daily expected return and volatility of about 0.0004 and 0.0126, respectively. We assumed that the *BND* distribution has an expected return of 0.05 and a volatility of 0.08. These values are equivalent to daily expected return and volatility of 0.0002 and 0.0051, respectively. We also assumed that the correlation between the *VTI* and *BND* returns is −0.18. This correlation will have to be taken into account. We cannot simply generate independent returns.

For a given simulation, let us assume that the variable we wish to simulate is simply referred to as x. We assume that x follows a normal distribution with expected value $E(x)$ and volatility of σ_x. If we are simulating daily returns, we will assume that $E(x)$ and σ_x are already stated as daily values. To simulate a set of random returns with this property, let us start with the concept of a standard normal value, commonly referred to as a z-variable. This variable has an expected value of 0 and a standard deviation of 1. For the first simulation, we draw a random value from this distribution and call it z_1. To convert z_1 to our first simulated value x_1, we multiply z_1 by σ_x.[8] At this point, we have forced the simulated value to have the desired volatility σ_x, but the expected value is still zero. To force the expected value to equal the desired expected value, we simply add $E(x)$. Thus, for the kth simulated value z_k, we obtain x_k as follows:

$$x_k = z_k \sigma_x + E(x).$$

We can verify that the simulated value x_k has the desired return and volatility as follows.[9]

$$
\begin{aligned}
E(x_k) &= E(z_k \sigma_x + E(x)) \\
&= E(z_k \sigma_x) + E(x) \\
&= \sigma_x E(z_k) + E(x) \\
&= 0 + E(x) = 0 \\
\sigma^2(x_k) &= \sigma^2(z_k \sigma_x + E(x)) \\
&= \sigma_x^2 \sigma_{z_k}^2 + 0 \\
&= \sigma_x^2.
\end{aligned}
$$

Thus, it would appear that we can simulate the returns on *VTI* and *BND* in that manner by changing x to the return on *VTI* and creating another variable to represent the return on *BND*. But, we have not yet incorporated the correlation between *VTI* and *BND*. Let us assume that we generate a standard normal value z_V that will be used to produce the return on *VTI* and another standard normal z_B that will be used to produce the return on

---

[8]The volatility of $z_1 \sigma_x$ is found as follows. First, find the variance of $z_1 \sigma_x$, which is Variance$(z_1 \sigma_x) = \sigma_x^2$Variance$(z_1) = \sigma_x^2$. The volatility is, thus, σ_x.

[9]These results make use of several key statistical rules: (1) the expected value of a constant times a random variable is the constant times the expected value of the random variable, (2) the expected value of a constant is the constant, (3) the variance of the sum of two random variables is the sum of the variance of the two random variables plus twice the covariance, (4) the variance of constant times a random variable is the constant squared times the variance of the random variable, and (5) the variance of a constant is zero and the covariance of a constant with anything else is zero.

BND. Let us now specify a slightly modified value of z_B, called z_B^*, which is determined as follows:

$$z_B^* = \rho_{VB} z_V + z_B \sqrt{1 - \rho_{VB}^2}.$$

Here we have ρ_{VB} as the correlation. The expected value and variance are[10]

$$E(z_B^*) = E\left(\rho_{VB} z_V + z_B \sqrt{1 - \rho_{VB}^2}\right)$$

$$= \rho_{VB} E(z_V) + \sqrt{1 - \rho_{VB}^2} E(z_B)$$

$$= 0 + 0 = 0$$

$$\sigma_{z_{B^*}}^2 = Var\left(\rho_{VB} z_V + z_B \sqrt{1 - \rho_{VB}^2}\right)$$

$$- \rho_{VB}^2 \sigma_{z_V}^2 + \left(1 - \rho_{VB}^2\right) \sigma_{z_B}^2 + 2cov\left(\rho_{VB} z_V, z_B \sqrt{1 - \rho_{VB}^2}\right)$$

$$= \rho_{VB}^2 + 1 - \rho_{VB}^2 + 2\rho_{VB} \sqrt{1 - \rho_{VB}^2} cov(z_V, z_B)$$

$$= 1 + 2\rho_{VB} \sqrt{1 - \rho_{VB}^2} cov(z_V, z_B)$$

$$= 1.$$

Now let us find the correlation between z_V and z_B^*:

$$\rho_{z_V z_{B^*}} = \frac{cov(z_V, z_B^*)}{\sigma_{z_V} \sigma_{z_{B^*}}}$$

$$= \frac{cov(z_V, \rho_{VB} z_V + z_B \sqrt{1 - \rho_{VB}^2})}{1}$$

$$= \rho_{VB} cov(z_V, z_V) + \sqrt{1 - \rho_{V,B}^2} cov(z_V, z_B)$$

$$= \rho_{VB} \sigma_{z_V}^2 + 0$$

$$= \rho_{VB}.$$

This result means that the two simulated standard normal variables will have the desired correlation. When we transform these variables into the returns on *VTI* and *BND*, the values will retain this desired correlation.

---

[10]For the results below, keep in mind that z_V and z_B have zero covariance.

We have left out just one formal step, which is how we generated the standard normal values, z_V and z_B. Most companies will use specialized risk management software, but there are two methods that can be used in Microsoft Excel. Excel contains a function that generates a uniformly distributed random variable between 0 and 1 called RAND(). A uniform random variable is one in which all values are equally likely. If you generate 12 independent uniformly distributed values, sum them up and subtract 6.0, you obtain a random variable that has an expected value of 0, a variance of 1, and is symmetric.[11] While these properties are not absolutely sufficient to establish that the distribution is normal, they are reasonably sufficient. A second method in Excel is the function NORMSINV(RAND()), which produces a z-value for a given uniformly distributed random variable obtained from the RAND() function.

So, now we know how to simulate two correlated random variables. As noted above, we could simply simulate the portfolio return, but maximum flexibility is achieved by simulating individual components of the portfolio. That is because one can assume different types of distributions. We will not do that here, but we do need to know that this can be done.

One final decision that has to be made when doing Monte Carlo simulation is how many returns to generate. There is no definitive rule. The only satisfactory guideline would be to keep generating returns until the results stabilize. Here we will generate 10,000 returns.

So, we start with the first simulation. We generate the first return on *VTI* and the first on *BND*, using the inputs noted above and making the adjustment that forces the returns to have the desired correlation. We then combine the returns into the portfolio by weighting the *VTI* return by 0.75 and the *BND* return by 0.25. We do this procedure 10,000 times and now have a series of 10,000 returns. We then sort the 10,000 returns from lowest to highest. A portion of these sorted simulated returns is shown in Exhibit 7-7. Notice that there is no "Date" column, as in the historical simulation. In Monte Carlo simulation we are just generating values without regard to specific dates. Also, the portfolio return is sorted, so we see the bottom three

---

[11]With U_H and U_L the upper and lower limits of the uniform distribution, from statistical theory, the expected value is $(1/2)(U_H + U_L)$, and the variance is $(1/12)(U_H - U_L)^2$. Thus, the expected value of the sum of the 12 values is $12(1/2)(1 - 0) = 6.0$. Subtracting 6.0 gives an expected value of 0.0. The variance is $12(1/12)(1 - 0)^2 = 1.0$.

VTI Return	BND Return	Portfolio Return
−0.0448	0.0041	−0.0355
−0.0444	−0.0037	−0.0341
−0.0429	−0.0006	−0.0313
. . .	. . .	. . .
0.0467	−0.0066	0.0356
0.0426	0.0089	0.0371
0.0476	−0.0021	0.0372

Exhibit 7-7. Simulated Returns on Portfolio for Three Lowest and Three Highest Return Days

and top three portfolio returns. The bottom three and top three returns on the component securities may not necessarily be the three lowest and three highest portfolio returns.

With 10,000 returns, the 5th percentile would be at the $10,000(0.05) = 500^{\text{th}}$ portfolio return. In this case, the value is −0.0149252. Multiplying by the \$300,000,000 portfolio size gives a *VaR* estimate of

$$0.0149252(\$300,000,000) = \$4,478,016.$$

Rounding off, we get our 5% *VaR* estimate of \$4.5 million. Perhaps not surprising, this value is very close to the value we obtained using the analytical method (\$4,519,476). Indeed, that method assumed a normal distribution with the same parameters used here.

Exhibit 7-8 shows the histogram of our 10,000 simulations overlaid with a normal distribution. We used a normal distribution simulator, but the sample is not perfectly normal though it is reasonably close. A simulation is just a sample, and some variation is expected from sample to sample.

The advantage of the Monte Carlo simulation method is its tremendous flexibility. You can assume any type of distribution, as long as you can estimate its parameters and simulate its outcomes. In addition, it is quite adept at accommodating a multitude of positions and complex portfolios, such as would be the case with a mixture of securities and derivatives. Its primary disadvantage is that it requires that the user pre-specify the parameters of the distribution. Thus, these parameters have to be estimated. At one time, Monte Carlo simulation was considerably an extremely slow method, but that was in the days in which computers were much slower than they are today.

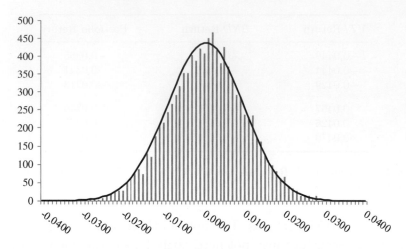

Exhibit 7-8. Histogram with Simulated Returns

7.1.2 *Strengths and Limitations of VaR*

VaR has many attractive features but also many weaknesses. Its widespread use suggests that its attractive features have overcome the limitations. Nonetheless, there are many staunch critics of *VaR*, and as such, it remains quite controversial. This controversy is a bit puzzling, however, because the use of *VaR* as a risk measurement tool should be no more controversial than using such simple statistics as expected returns, volatilities, betas, and probabilities of default, which are all widely and routinely used and seldom associated with controversy. The assumptions necessary to use these risk measures are no less onerous than those required to use *VaR*. The criticisms of *VaR* appear to have arisen because *VaR* purports to measure risk in the tails but does so only when the number and magnitude of tail events is not abnormal relative to the historical past or a pre-specified probability distribution. Because *VaR* is not structured to help manage the risk of cataclysmic events, its use in that manner has been problematic. Let us take a more formal look at its strong and weak points with a goal toward using it properly and recognizing when it is not enough.

7.1.2.1 *The Strong Points of VaR*

So, let us first look at the positives. *VaR* is relatively easy to understand. Although it relies on statistical theory, the interpretation is relatively simple. For our analytic *VaR* of \$4.5 million, one need simply understand that it means that there is a 5% chance that on a given day, we will lose more than

$4.5 million. And because *VaR* is so easy to understand, it is also easy to communicate. Conveying information is very important in an organization with substantial resources exposed to risk. Oftentimes the top-level decision makers and the governing board are not technically oriented. Yet, almost any reasonably educated person can interpret what it means to say that there is a 5% chance of losing at least $4.5 million on a given day.

VaR also provides the ability to separate risks, which we will discuss in more detail later. This feature leads to two more attractions. For one, it can be used in capital allocation, which is the process in which units within an organization are allotted a certain amount of capital to support them for the risk they take. Riskier units would be allotted relatively more capital than less risky units. Following on that theme, riskier units would also be expected to outperform less risky units over the long run. Thus, performance can be evaluated by adjusting for the *VaR* or capital allocated based on *VaR*. Hence, *VaR* can be used in performance measure.

It is also relatively easy to evaluate whether the *VaR* measure is accurate, a process called *backtesting*. For example, we found an analytical *VaR* of about $4.5 million. Thus, we would expect that 5% of the time, we would experience daily trading losses of at least $4.5 million. So, for example, moving forward on that basis, we would determine if the number of days of trading losses in excess of $4.5 million is statistically close to 5% of the total number of trading days. For example, suppose we move forward through the next 250 trading days. If $4.5 million is the *VaR*, we would expect to have losses of at least that amount on $250(0.05) = 12.5$ trading days. So, on roughly 12 to 13 trading days we would expect losses of at least $4.5 million. Of course, if the actual number of such days were 10 or 14, we might not reject the model. In fact, we can use statistical analysis to determine whether a slight deviation is reason to reject the model. We will not cover the specifics of this type of test here.

Orange County California and Value-at-Risk

The Orange County Investment Portfolio (OCIP) is a pool of funds invested on behalf of various units of the Orange County government. Because of its massive size and economies of scale, OCIP also accepts funds from other government units in California. In 1995 Orange County, California filed for bankruptcy as a result of an approximately $1.6 billion loss in its highly leveraged $7.5 billion portfolio. Orange County's elected treasurer, Robert Citron, had engaged in a series of layered reverse repurchase agreements. A reverse repurchase agreement, referred to as a reverse repo, is a financial transaction in which the holder of a security sells the security to a financial institution and agrees to buy it back at a specified later date. In essence, it is a loan with the security pledged as collateral. Mr. Citron took a large number of U.S. treasury notes from the OCIP assets and used them to borrow additional funds, which were invested in more treasury notes, which were then used to borrow more funds that were invested in additional treasury notes. The strategy was, thus, a layered series of investments that ultimately turned the $7.5 billion of assets into a $22 billion portfolio, funded by the original $7.5 billion in equity and the remainder in debt created through the reverse repos.

The strategy worked well for a few years. The portfolio generated a substantially greater return than other funds that used short- and intermediate-term instruments. Of course, this result was achieved because the portfolio was so highly leveraged and interest rates went down. As a result of the declining interest rates, the securities rose in value and with the substantial leverage, the rates of return were amplified.

Eventually, however, interest rates began to increase and the fund started to incur substantial losses that eventually ran up to about $1.6 billion. In spite of still having about $5 billion in equity in the fund, the county filed for bankruptcy. In response it made numerous budget cuts, won some lawsuits, and emerged from bankruptcy just six months later.

Professor Philippe Jorion, a resident of Orange County, a finance professor at the University of California at Irvine, and an expert on risk management and in particular Value-at-Risk, undertook an investigation of the fiasco. He determined that the annual *VaR* at 5% for Orange County at the time of the event was approximately $1.6 billion, which was roughly the same as the loss incurred. There is no particular connection between the fact that the *VaR* and the loss were about the same. *VaR* is, after all, the minimum loss that would be sustained. But the significance of the *VaR* number is that 5% of time, about once every 20 years, *the fund would be expected to incur a loss of at least $1.6 billion.* Such a number is staggering. A low-risk money market fund operated by a local government simply would not be expected to lose $1.6 billion, what more a larger amount. In fact, what is essentially a money market fund and more or less risk-free should never lose any money. When a government entity, entrusted as stewards of the public's money, loses that much money, there is a tremendous betrayal of trust. As Jorion explains, however, a simple calculation of the *VaR* would have at least run up a red flag.

Source: Philippe Jorion. *Big Bets Gone Bad: Derivatives and Bankruptcy in Orange County. The Largest Municipal Failure in U.S. History* (1995) San Diego: Academic Press.

Finally, for better or for worse, *VaR* is widely accepted by regulators. Banking and securities regulators generally approve, if not require, that banks report their *VaRs*. In the U.S., SEC disclosure rules that require the reporting of derivatives exposure permit the use of *VaR* as one of several acceptable risk measures. We will cover this topic in Chapter 13.

7.1.2.2 *The Weak Points of VaR*

In the unlikely event that you have not already noticed, *VaR* is quite subjective in that the user must make many choices. Recall that the user determines the horizon, the confidence level, and the method by which *VaR* will be calculated. If the analytical method is used, the user must come up with estimates of the average return and volatility. If historical data are used as the basis for these estimates, how far back would one go to collect the data? In addition, historical data can be collected daily, weekly, monthly, quarterly, or yearly. Although daily is probably the most popular, there are some circumstances in which daily data would not be available. How much judgement should be used in overriding historical estimates that may seem anomalous? If the historical simulation method is used, the risk manager must decide on the lookback period and whether any abnormal events should be discarded or underweighted. If the Monte Carlo simulation method is used, one must decide on the distribution, the input parameters, and the number of simulation runs.

VaR: An Opposing View

The trader, quantitative analyst, professor, and philosopher Nassim Nicholas Taleb has become famous among other things for his sharp criticisms of the use of *VaR*. While Taleb has no general problem with quantitative analysis, he has strong reservations about how *VaR* is sometimes used.

Taleb argues that there is substantial risk in using *VaR*, risk that he believes is even greater than the risk that *VaR* is designed to measure. He goes so far as to assert that risk managers who use *VaR* are guilty of malpractice.

His primary concern is a very important point: *VaR* is used to measure tail risk, but it is not well-designed to measure tail risk. As we noted in the definition, *VaR* is a measure that specifies the risk under *normal conditions*. "Normal conditions" does not necessarily mean that returns are distributed normally, but it means that the markets are functioning as they should, there is reasonable liquidity, investors are not panicking, and most importantly, there are no abnormal events occurring in the markets, the economy, and the world itself. The existence of any of these conditions defines abnormal markets and leads to returns that often occur in the left tail of the distribution. Yet, the left tail of the distribution is precisely the place where *VaR* is used.

Taleb notes that critics often say that VaR "works reasonably well" or "works on average," but these terms characterize an aggregation of conditions and say very little about the extreme events that often cause problems. As they say about averages:

> *A person two meters tall should be able to safely cross a stream that has an average depth of 1.5 meters.*

> *If you have one hand in the freezer and the other in the oven, on average you are comfortable.*

And in finance, if a trader earned a return of 25% a year for nine years but then on the 10th year loses all of his money, his average annual return would be a respectable 12.5%. Yet he would be bankrupt!

Taleb has used the allusion to the concept of a black swan as illustrative of this kind of risk. Before Europeans came to Australia, no one had seen a black swan. All swans in Europe were white. The term "black swan" was used to represent an event that no one had ever experienced and as such was, seeing a black swan considered to be impossible. But when the first Europeans arrived in Australia, they found black swans. The term then came to represent an event considered impossible but which did eventually occur. As Taleb points out, just because you are not dead does not mean you are immortal. Market crashes and crises are the black swans that are not accommodated in standard statistical models.

Taleb has made a career of betting on black swans and it has been alleged that he has made much money from these bets. No one knows for sure. But for certain, Taleb has brought an awareness of the dangers of putting too much faith in quantitative models, and in particular, *VaR*.

Do Taleb's arguments mean that we reject *VaR*, or as the saying goes, throw the baby out with the bathwater? Most experts would not agree with that statement. Most would agree that to go through life trying to anticipate black swans will result in a lot of lost bets and wasted precautions. Knowing you are not immortal just because you have not died yet does not mean that you should spend your life preparing to die the next day. Clearly we have to use *VaR* with considerable caution, supplementing it with other methods. And even then, we cannot assure ourselves that unanticipated tail events will not destroy the entity, any more than we can be sure that leading a healthy lifestyle will give us a long happy life.

Sources: Taleb, Nassim Nicholas. *The Black Swan: The Impact of the Highly Improbable*. New York: Random House (2007).

Taleb, Nassim Nicholas. *Fooled by Randomness: The Hidden Role of Chance in the Markets and in Life*. New York: Texere (2001).

A major criticism of *VaR* is that it underestimates tail events. This problem primarily occurs because of the use of the normal distribution, which implies only a very low likelihood of extreme losses. Moreover, the normal distribution is symmetric, when in fact, there are often far more losses than gains in most financial markets. Therein lies another criticism of *VaR*: it is exclusively focused on left tail events and gives no weights to large right tail events, meaning gains

VaR also generally fails to account for the liquidity of assets. We will cover liquidity risk in Chapter 12, but you should be aware that some assets have low liquidity. As such, the quoted prices for the assets can be misleading in that they may not indicate the possibility that the price would have to be lowered further in order to sell out of a position. Although it is technically feasible to incorporate this factor into a *VaR* analysis, it can be difficult in that some portfolios have thousands of positions and the liquidity effect cannot always be observed unless the asset is offered for sale.

VaR also fails to take into account *correlation risk*. Correlation risk is the risk that arises from the instability of correlations among assets, which have a tendency to rise during times of volatile markets. In other words, during market crises, correlations tend to rise toward 1.0, meaning that almost all assets fall in sync.[12] It is possible to account for this risk in a *VaR* analysis, but it is challenging to do so.

Another problem with *VaR* is the perhaps simply misunderstood belief of what it stands for. Without naming names, a Wall Street Journal reporter, commenting on the *VaR* reported by Goldman Sachs, stated that *VaR* is "the average sum it could lose on any given day." In Section 7.3.2, we will cover the notion of the average sum a company could lose, but that measure is *not VaR*. There is also a tendency on the part of non-experts to think of *VaR* as the maximum amount that could be lost. The maximum amount that could be lost is the entire capital of the organization.

Another major problem with *VaR* is the potential for overreliance on it. If a risk manager believes that the company's *VaR* is acceptable, she might proceed with an unjustified degree of confidence. Perhaps this criticism arises because *VaR* attempts to encapsulate a tremendous amount of information within a single number. Naturally a good risk manager will not make this mistake. She will rely on a lot of information that goes beyond *VaR*, some of which we cover in later sections. But for some reason, *VaR* has taken considerable criticism for being a one-dimensional measure that is used to the exclusivity of alternative risk measures, intuition, experience, and just plain good judgment.

7.1.2.3   *The Verdict: Is VaR Worth Using or Not?*

As noted at the beginning of Section 7.1.2, *VaR* has taken a tremendous amount of criticism. Some of it is justified. Users of any model need to know the model's weaknesses. Yet, its weaknesses are not unique to *VaR*. Virtually any financial model will exhibit these same weaknesses. Take, for example,

---

[12]Technically a group of assets that have less than perfect correlations among themselves but which almost all fall during a crisis does not mean that the correlations all become a perfect 1.0. Less than perfect correlation does not mean that two assets cannot move together. Indeed, they will move together part of the time. But when all assets move together at the same time, the situation is described as the correlations moving to 1.0. This characterization is not precisely what is happening, but the terminology is used nonetheless and widely understood.

the multistage dividend discount model. This model uses the widely accepted assumption that a stock price is the present value of all future dividends. Nonetheless, the model user has to divide the future up into different stages of growth. Within each stage, it assumes the same growth rate. It also has to assume a terminal stock price or a constant rate of stable growth at the end of the final stage on to infinity. Finally, it requires a discount rate that reflects the time value of money and the risk.

Whew! Those are a lot of assumptions. And yet this model has not even come close to taking the heat that *VaR* takes, in spite of undoubtedly being used much more.[13] Perhaps the reason *VaR* is so highly criticized is that it is believed to be widely used as a one-size fits all risk measure. It is indeed widely used, but virtually no one uses it to the exclusion of other information, not to mention experience, intuition, and judgment. Moreover, anyone who criticizes *VaR* should themselves never use estimates of volatility because these estimates require the same assumptions. It is virtually impossible to find an expert on risk management or even financial markets in general who does not use volatility. In short, the old expression *people who live in glass houses shouldn't throw stones* is very applicable to the risk management debate. If *VaR* is not appropriate, then let someone come up with a better measure.

VaR is clearly an important measure to learn and use. But it does not tell us everything we need to know. There are a number of variations and extensions of *VaR* with which we should become familiar.

7.1.3 *Variations and Extensions of VaR*

VaR is just a single statistic taken from information about a probability distribution. If we have the necessary information, there is more that we can do with it.

7.1.3.1 *Standalone VaR*

Recall in our example that the portfolio consists of 75% of our money in the *VTI* ETF and 25% in the *BND* ETF. We can dig a little deeper and take a look at the components of *VaR*. As an example, in its 2017 annual report,

---

[13]There are far more securities analysts than risk managers. Even the securities analysts that do not use the model have to use some kind of model that also requires extremely tenuous assumptions.

mentioned earlier, J.P. Morgan Chase states that its *VaR* breaks down as follows:

Fixed income	$28 million
Foreign exchange	$10 million
Equities	$12 million
Commodities & other	$7 million
Credit portfolio	$7 million
Consumer & community banking	$2 million
Corporate	$4 million

Of course, these numbers add up to $70 million. We mention that the company reported that its *VaR* was $29 million. So what is the difference? It is the diversification effect. The company reported that diversification across these units lowered the overall *VaR* by $41 million to $29 million. Thus, there was a substantial million diversification benefit. An individual *VaR* is referred to as a *Standalone VaR*. *VaR* is said to have the mathematical property of subadditivity, a concept that means that a function has a smaller value than the sum of its components.

Let us take a look at the analytical *VaR* for our example of the *VTI* and *BND* portfolio. Recall that with the 75-25 allocation, we have $225 million in the *VTI* ETF and $75 million in the *BND* ETF. The expected returns and volatility we use were shown in Exhibit 7-4. We combined those parameters to obtain the portfolio expected return and volatility and then converted these numbers to daily estimates. Now we need to convert the individual ETF annual parameters to daily parameters.

$$VTI: \bar{R}_V = \frac{0.10}{250} = 0.0004, \quad \sigma_V = \frac{0.20}{\sqrt{250}} = 0.0126$$

$$BND: \bar{R}_B = \frac{0.05}{250} = 0.0002, \quad \sigma_B = \frac{0.08}{\sqrt{250}} = 0.0051$$

Using the daily expected return and volatility as specified earlier we have the 5% *VaR* for each as:

$$VTI \ VaR = \$225{,}000{,}000(1.65(0.0126) - 0.0004) = \$4{,}605{,}982$$

$$BND \ VaR = \$75{,}000{,}000(1.65(0.0051) - 0.0002) = \$611{,}131.$$

Notice how if we add the numbers up we get $5,217,113, which is significantly higher than the analytical *VaR* found at the portfolio level, $4,519,476. The difference, $697,637, is the diversification benefit. Naturally, it arises because of the less-than-perfect correlation of the two assets.

We could also obtain the standalone *VaR*s using the historical simulation or Monte Carlo simulation methods. In the former case, we would assume a $225 million investment in the *VTI* ETF and a $75 million investment in the *BND* ETF at the beginning of the lookback period. Then we would roll through the historical period for each security separately and estimate the *VaR* in the manner described previously. The standalone *VaR*s for *VTI* and *BND* are found by extracting the 5th percentile of each of their respective historical samples of returns and multiplying by $225 million and $75 million, respectively. We obtain

$$VTI: \$2{,}254{,}926$$

$$BND: \$232{,}722.$$

The total of the standalone *VaR*s is $2,487,698. Thus, the diversification benefit is $125,537 and is obtained by subtracting the historical simulation *VaR*, $2,362,161 from the sum of the *VaR*s of the two assets.

Likewise, for the Monte Carlo simulation method, we can determine the *VaR* for the components separately. The answers are:

$$VTI: \$4{,}629{,}889$$

$$BND: \$622{,}686.$$

Again, these numbers are very close to the analytical *VaR*, because they were generated from a normal distribution with the same parameters. The total of these numbers is $5,252,575. Since the analytical *VaR* for the portfolio was $4,519,476, the diversification benefit is $774,559.

The standalone *VaR* can be useful in examining the risk of certain divisions of an organization, but it does not give the full picture of the entity's risk any more than an individual stock gives the full picture of a portfolio. Thus, the full *VaR* must be monitored. Fortunately, this feature is a characteristic of *VaR*, or more accurately, a characteristic of having diversified assets.

7.1.3.2 *Average Loss, Given Loss*

The information required to estimate *VaR* also permits the estimation of the notion of the average loss. This number answers the question, "If we lose money, how much do we lose on average?" This figure is an interesting and useful one, because it conditions the risk manager to know what loss is likely to occur on average, that is, when a loss is incurred.

The analytical method does not lend itself easily to this type of calculation. It requires either a fairly complex integration procedure or the use of a distribution called the half-normal distribution, which is a distribution of one-half of the normal and is commonly used for evaluating random variables that are absolute values. These methods are beyond the scope of this book.

The historical method can, however, be easily adapted to give the average loss. We simply add the returns for all of the days in which the returns are negative and divide by the number of days in which the returns are negative. We then multiply by the portfolio size of $300 million. The answer is $993,912. A similar method is used to get the average loss for the Monte Carlo simulation. The simulated returns are evaluated to determine the average of all returns that are negative. The average is then multiplied by $300 million. The answer is $2,194,762.[14] Of course, we would expect the result using Monte Carlo simulation to be greater, because we used greater volatility than occurred in the historical lookback period.

7.1.3.3 *Conditional VaR*

Sometimes we may wish to know the average loss when the *VaR* is exceeded. This concept is referred to as the *Conditional VaR*, the *Expected Shortfall*, the *Tail Loss*, and the *Average Tail Loss*.

Again, with the analytical method it is somewhat complex, as it requires evaluation of a complex integral. There are some approximating shortcuts, but we will not cover them here. Let us simply take a look at how this value is obtained using the historical simulation method. Here we simply take the average return of all the returns that are lower than the critical return that determines the *VaR*. We then multiply that average return by the portfolio size. In our example, the answer is $3,686,962. Using Monte Carlo simulation, we once again average the simulated returns that are lower than the *VaR*. The answer is $5,696,735. Again, we should not be surprised that this number is larger, because the Monte Carlo method uses greater volatility than occurred in the historical lookback period.

We emphasize that it is not possible to identify the largest possible loss other than to say that it is the entire equity of the organization. Conditional *VaR* does provide an estimate of the average loss when *VaR* is exceeded and

---

[14]Incidentally, this answer would be a good estimate of the value that would be obtained with the more complex analytical method.

therefore can be a useful number in giving a perspective on the expected loss for those occasions when the loss exceeds the *VaR*.

7.1.3.4 *Incremental or Delta VaR*

Sometimes a risk manager may want to know how the *VaR* would change if the portfolio allocation changed. For example, our portfolio consists of 75% *VTI* and 25% *BND*. Suppose the portfolio manager is considering increasing the allocation to 80% *VTI* and 20% *BND*. Such a possibility gives rise to the obvious question of how much the *VaR* would change. Clearly it would increase, because funds are being allocated from the lower risk investment to the higher risk investment. This question is important because many companies have *VaR* limits and could be near those limits.

The concept of incremental or delta *VaR* gives us this answer. The incremental *VaR* is calculated by estimating the *VaR* of the existing portfolio and then re-estimating under the assumption that the change has been implemented. We will omit the details, as they simply involve re-doing what we have previously done with an 80% allocation to *VTI* and 20% to *BND*. Exhibit 7-9 summarizes the results.

Again, not surprisingly, the Analytical and Monte Carlo methods gave reasonably close values. Also, notice that the incremental *VaR* is negative across all three methods. This makes sense. The portfolio is re-allocated form a lower risk ETF to a higher risk ETF.

7.1.3.5 *Marginal or Component VaR*

Marginal or component *VaR* is a very similar concept to incremental *VaR* but makes use of calculus to reflect the impact of small changes in a position. Using our two security case as an example and using the analytical method approach, let us write out the formula for the *VaR* in terms of the

	Existing *VaR*	*VaR* under New Allocation	Incremental *VaR*
Analytical Method	$4,519,476	$4,835,501	−$316,025
Historical Simulation Method	$2,362,161	$2,459,233	−97,072
Monte Carlo Simulation Method	$4,478,016	$4,810,740	−$332,724

Exhibit 7-9. Incremental VaR for Increase to 80% Allocation in VTI

components, identified as $MVaR_p$:

$$VaR_p = -V_p(E(R_p) - \chi\sigma_p)$$

$$= -V_p\left(w_V E(R_V) + w_B E(R_B) - \chi\sqrt{w_V^2\sigma_V^2 + w_B^2\sigma_B^2 + 2w_V w_B cov_{VB}}\right).$$

Let us take the first derivatives with respect to the allocations, w_V and w_B and denote these terms as the marginal *VaRs* with respect to V and B, $MVaR_v$ and $MVaR_B$:

$$MVar_V = \frac{\partial VaR_p}{\partial w_V}$$

$$= -V_p\frac{\partial\left(w_V E(R_V) + w_B E(R_B) - \chi\sqrt{w_V^2\sigma_V^2 + w_B^2\sigma_B^2 + 2w_V w_B cov_{VB}}\right)}{\partial w_V}$$

$$= -V_p\left(E(R_V) - \frac{\chi}{\sigma_p}[w_V\sigma_V^2 + w_B cov_{VB}]\right)$$

$$MVar_B = \frac{\partial VaR_p}{\partial w_B}$$

$$= -V_p\frac{\partial\left(w_V E(R_V) + w_B E(R_B) - \chi\sqrt{w_V^2\sigma_V^2 + w_B^2\sigma_B^2 + 2w_V w_B cov_{VB}}\right)}{\partial w_B}$$

$$= -V_p\left(E(R_B) - \frac{\chi}{\sigma_p}[w_B\sigma_B^2 + w_V cov_{VB}]\right).$$

In spite of appearances, these values are relatively easy to calculate. Doing so, we obtain \$6,085,530 for *VTI* and −\$178,685 for *BND*. It may seem confusing that one number is positive and one negative and that the two numbers are so far apart. The fact that the *VTI* marginal *VaR* is positive indicates that if the weight assigned to *VTI* increases, then the overall *VaR* will increase. The negative marginal *VaR* for *BND* means that if the weight assigned to *BND* is increased, then the overall *VaR* will decrease. These results should make sense. The *VaR* will be a reflection of the risks of the two ETFs and their correlation. *VTI* is clearly a riskier ETF, so if we increase our allocation to *VTI*, the overall *VaR* will increase. If we increase our allocation to *BND*, the less risky ETF, the overall *VaR* will decrease. There is one small technicality, however, in that a partial derivative is based on changing one thing and holding everything else constant. So, for example, we could not change the weight in *VTI* from 0.75 to say, 0.76, without changing the weight of *BND* from 0.25 to 0.24.

When there are J assets, the formula for marginal VaR of asset j, denoted here as $MVaR_j$ is

$$MVaR_j = V_p \left(\left(\frac{\chi}{\sigma_p} \right) \left(w_j \sigma_j^2 + \sum_{\substack{i=1 \\ i \neq j}}^{J} w_i cov_{ji} \right) - E(R_j) \right)$$

where $i = j$. In our example, this formula was applied with two assets so $J = 2$, and doing so leads to the formulas above.

It turns out that marginal VaR has an extremely convenient characteristic. The weighted sum of the marginal $VaRs$ equals the total VaR where the weights are the portfolio allocations. We will skip the mathematical proof of this result, but for a portfolio of J assets, here is the formula

$$VaR_p = \sum_{j=1}^{J} (MVaR_j) w_j,$$

where $MVaR_i$ is the marginal VaR for asset j and w_j is the percentage allocation to asset j.

In our example, we calculated the two marginal $VaRs$ above. Multiplying by the respective weights of the assets gives,

$$\$6{,}085{,}530(0.75) - \$178{,}685(0.25) = \$4{,}519{,}467,$$

which is the total analytical VaR as derived earlier.

The magnitudes of the marginal $VaRs$ can be somewhat difficult to interpret. Being derived from a calculus derivative, they reflect only an infinitesimal change to the differentiating variable, the weight. Nonetheless, they can be used to approximate the change in VaR from a change in the weight. Let us change the allocation to VTI by $+0.05$, which requires that we reduce the allocation to BND by 0.05. We will skip the calculations, but if you go back through the analytical method, you will see that the daily expected return will change to 0.00036 and the daily volatility will change to 0.0099869.[15] Recalculating the VaR using these parameters gives.

$$\$300{,}000{,}000(1.65(0.0099869 - 0.00036)) = \$4{,}835{,}501,$$

---

[15]This example is a good reminder that the marginal VaR for any one asset cannot truly be considered on an isolated basis, that is, without taking into account the fact that the allocation to the other asset must change. Thus, we have to incorporate both marginal $VaRs$.

subject to round-off error. The increase in *VaR* is \$316,025, which is the incremental *VaR*. Now let us estimate the new *VaR* using the marginal *VaRs*. We use the following formula,

$$\Delta VaR_p = MVar_1(\Delta w_1) + MVaR_2(\Delta w_2).$$

Plugging in our values,

$$\Delta VaR_p = \$6,085,530_1(+0.05) - \$178,685)(-0.05) = \$313,211.$$

This estimate is off by \$2,814, which is about 0.01% of the true *VaR*.

Marginal *VaRs* are not necessarily good approximations of the change in *VaR* if a weight were changed by a large amount, but the marginal *VaRs* are reasonably good and simple measures of which asset has the greater impact on *VaR*, here clearly the *VTI* ETF.

7.1.3.6 *Relative VaR*

It is also possible to adapt *VaR* to a benchmark. For example, consider the portfolio we have been working with in which 75% of the funds are invested in the *VTI* ETF and 25% are in the *BND* ETF. Suppose this allocation represents the current allocation of a portfolio that has as a benchmark an allocation of 50% *VTI* and 50% *BND*. In other words, the portfolio manager's performance will be compared to the benchmark.

Now let us create a benchmarked portfolio consisting of long our 75-25 portfolio and short the 50-50 portfolio. For example, suppose the *VTI* went up 1% and the *BND* went down 0.2%. Then the long position would have a return of $0.75(0.01) + 0.25(-0.002) = 0.007$. The benchmark would have a return of $0.50(0.01) + 0.50(-0.002) = 0.004$. Thus, our benchmarked portfolio would have a return of $0.007 - 0.004 = 0.003$. We can then proceed to conduct VaR analysis using any of the three methods on this benchmarked portfolio, though the historical simulation method is the best candidate method. This *VaR* concept is known as *relative VaR*.

This benchmarked portfolio captures a notion called *ex ante tracking error*. Tracking error is the difference between a portfolio and its benchmark. *VaR* analysis provides a means of analyzing and controlling ex ante tracking error.[16]

---

[16]In case you are wondering whether there is an ex post tracking error, there is indeed. It is performance analysis, the process in which ex post performance is compared to a benchmark portfolio.

7.1.3.7 *Delta-Normal VaR*

We have previously mentioned that options are non-linear instruments that are not well-adapted to the analytical method of *VaR*. The analytical method relies on the assumption of normality and the fact that the characteristics of the normal distribution can be completely described by the expected value and volatility. The non-linearity of an option's price and the consequential skewness of option returns can impart a substantial bias when applying changes in the underlying.

Recall that a call option pays off the greater of the underlying price minus the exercise price or zero. We illustrated this point in Chapter 4 with the hockey stick graphs. These figures depict the payoffs of an option at expiration. For option positions not held to expiration, the prices do not conform to the hockey stick graphs but the graphs are somewhat similar, though they are curved lines instead of the straight lines in the hockey stick graphs. We will take up this point in Chapter 10 when we study options. For now, however, you need to simply understand that option returns on a day-to-day basis are quite skewed and clearly not normally distributed. Thus, the analytical method of VaR is somewhat problematic when applied to options.

Nonetheless, there is an approximation method that is based on reasonable theoretical arguments. For small changes in the value of the underlying, the option price will behave in an approximately linear fashion with the underlying according to a concept known as the option delta, which ranges between 0 and 1. We will study option deltas extensively in Chapter 10. For now, just be aware that the change in the option price will be approximately the delta times the change in the underlying price. Letting c_t and c_{t+1} be the option prices at time t and $t+1$, S_t and S_{t+1} be the underlying price at times t and $t+1$, and Δ_c be the delta of the call, we have the approximation

$$c_{t+1} - c_t \approx (S_{t+1} - S_t)\Delta_c.$$

The left-hand side is the change in the option price from t to $t+1$. The right hand side indicates that the change in the option price is approximately the change in the underlying price times the option delta. Therefore, the return on the option can be expressed as

$$R_c = \frac{c_{t+1} - c_t}{c} \approx \frac{(S_{t+1} - S_t)\Delta_c}{c_t} = R_s \left(\frac{S_t \Delta_c}{c_t} \right).$$

If we need the volatility, we can express it as follows. First, take the variance:

$$\sigma_c^2 = Variance\left(R_s\left(\frac{S_t\Delta_c}{c_t}\right)\right)$$

$$= \left(\frac{S_t\Delta_c}{c_t}\right)^2\sigma_S^2.$$

In other words, the variance of the return on the call is the expression in parentheses squared times the variance of the stock. The volatility is then the square root of this expression. We will also need the expected return, and it is found as

$$E(R_c) = Expected\ Value\ of\left(R_s\left(\frac{S_t\Delta_c}{c_t}\right)\right)$$

$$= \left(\frac{S_t\Delta_c}{c_t}\right)E(R_s).$$

We would then proceed to use the analytical method with the option treated as any other security whose payoffs are linear. Because the delta is derived from calculus and is therefore based on the change in the option price for a very small change in the underlying price, the assumption is appropriate if the underlying changes by only a very small amount.

As we will cover in more detail in Chapter 10, for large changes in the underlying the delta will not be a very good approximation of the change in the option price. It can be improved by adding a second-order term called gamma. This approach leads to the use of delta and gamma to approximate a linear relationship between the option price and the underlying price. When applied to *VaR*, this approach is known as the delta-gamma-normal approach.

The historical method simply draws the returns from the actual distribution of historical returns. Hence, there is no distributional assumption and, therefore, no reason to worry about whether option returns are normally distributed. The Monte Carlo method requires only a distributional assumption about the underlying. Once we obtain a simulated value of the underlying price, we can obtain the corresponding option price from an option pricing model, which we cover in Chapter 10.

7.1.3.8 *Cash Flow at Risk (CFaR)*

In implementing *VaR*, it is necessary that the user be able to determine the values of the assets fairly easily. What may seem obvious is really not so.

Securities that trade in active markets, such as stocks, many bonds, and all exchange-traded derivatives are fairly easy to value. Many other financial assets have known cash flows and determining a value is mainly an exercise in applying a discount rate. Loans, real estate, and virtually all physical assets do not trade in active, liquid markets, so it is difficult to apply *VaR* to them. As a result, *VaR* is used almost exclusively by financial companies and almost always applied only to their portfolios of traded, liquid securities.

For non-financial corporations, Cash-Flow-at-Risk, or *CFaR* is a useful variation of *VaR* that accounts for the risk associated with cash flows. Inadequate cash flow can cause a liquidity crisis that can endanger the solvency of a company. *CFaR* can be used to characterize the risk that cash flow will be insufficient to avert a crisis.

Let us define H as the company's cash flow. Suppose the company feels that if its cash flow is below H_L, it will be in a financial crunch, meaning that it will have to make significant adjustments to be able to survive. It will not be insolvent at that point, but insolvency will certainly be a near-term possibility. Thus, H_L is a critical level of cash flow that the company wants to be comfortably above. Let $E(H)$ and σ_H be the expected value and volatility of its cash flow. *CFaR* allows a company to make a statement about the risk of the difference between its actual cash flow and the critical cash flow, H_L. Applying the same calculation that we did in *VaR*, we obtain a level of cash flow for a 5% tolerance of $1.65\sigma_H - E(H)$. This value would be the point at which the probability is 5% that the cash flow will be less than this value. From here we subtract the critical cash flow to obtain the *CFaR*. Thus,

$$CFaR = E(H) - 1.65\sigma_H - H_L.$$

Consider a company in which the expected cash flow ($E(H)$) is $50 million, the volatility of cash flow (σ_H) is $15 million, and the critical level is $5 million. Then *CFaR* is

$$CFaR = \$50 - 1.65(\$15) - \$5 = \$20.25.$$

Adding the distress level, we see that at cash flow of $25.25 million, the distress level will be exceeded by $20.25. Thus, there is a 5% chance that the cash flow will exceed the distress level by less than $20.25 million. Exhibit 7-10 illustrates the process. The distribution is centered at the expected value of $50 million. Moving over 1.65 standard deviations, we reach a level of $25.25 million. At that point, we have a cushion over the distress level of only $20.25 million. The interpretation is that there is a 5%

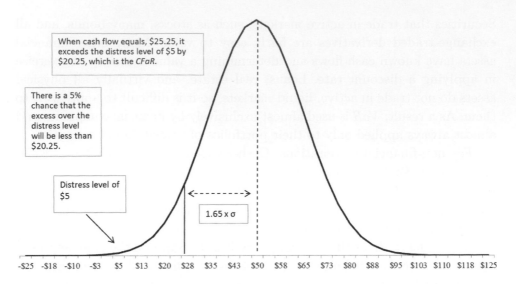

Exhibit 7-10.   Cash-Flow-at-Risk

chance that the cushion will be less than $20.25 million, which includes those outcomes in which the cash flow is below the critical level.

Thus, there are two distinctions between *VaR* and *CFaR*. *VaR* deals with the risk of changes in the values of the company's assets, while *CFaR* deals with the risk of cash flows generated by the company's assets. Another distinction is that *VaR* reflects an absolute level of value, while *CFaR* reflects a margin over a critical level.[17]

7.1.4   *Scenario Analysis and Stress Testing*

Many risk managers engage in an exercise called *scenario analysis*, which proposes that certain economic scenarios might occur and then attempts to determine how the portfolio would perform under these proposed scenarios. In effect, the risk manager identifies certain situations that could plausibly happen in the market and determines how the portfolio would have performed. For example, a manager might propose that an increase in the Fed Funds rate might occur simultaneously with an announcement of a change in the leadership of China. Neither event is likely to be catastrophic for

---

[17]Cash-flow-at-risk does not necessarily have to reflect a margin. In this example, we could have not subtracted the critical level of $5, and we would obtain $25.25. Then we would say that there is a 5% chance that cash flow would be less than $25.25. *VaR* could also be expressed relative to a critical level, but it traditionally is not.

markets and not necessarily even stressful, but both have at least a modest long-ranging significance. The risk manager would think through the possible implications for the financial markets and the company's portfolio. In some cases, the risk manager will propose extreme scenarios that might impose enormous stress on all financial markets. The manager would then attempt to determine how the portfolio would perform. Banking regulators commonly use stress tests to identify if the banking system is capable of handling the kinds of extreme scenarios that occur in financial crises.

For example, suppose we take a look at the worst days in the historical lookback period of our *VTI* and *BND* ETF portfolio. The worst day for the *VTI* ETF was a decrease of 3.64%. On that day, however, the *BND* ETF increased by 0.56%, leading to an overall loss of 2.59% ($-0.0364 * 0.75 + 0.0056 * 0.25$) or \$7,765,497 based on the \$300 million portfolio size. The worst day for the *BND* ETF was a loss of 0.99%, but on that day the *VTI* went up by 1.24%, leading to a gain of 0.68% ($0.0124 * 0.75 - 0.0099 * 0.25$) or a gain of \$2,049,783. Notice the effects of diversification. The two ETFs have a low correlation and, thus, when one performs poorly there is a reasonable chance that the other will perform well. If, however, we assume that the two worst days occurred on the same day, we would have a portfolio return of $0.75(-0.0364) + 0.25(-0.0099) = -0.0298$, which is a loss \$8,930,695. Such scenarios are often constructed so that the diversifying effects do not occur and that both markets incur significant losses simultaneously.

A variation of scenario analysis is a procedure called *stress testing*. Stress testing involves proposing an extreme scenario in which there are substantial pressures across multiple markets. Suppose we double the worst *VTI* return from -2.35% to -4.70%, and we also double the worst *BND* return from -1.11% to -2.22%. The portfolio return would be $0.75(-0.0470) + 0.25(-0.0222) = -0.0408$, a loss of \$12,232,590.

In some cases, a risk manager might propose historical scenarios, meaning to position the current portfolio within a period of history. Of course, that is precisely what the historical simulation approach does but only over a limited recent period. Let us roll the clock back a little further to September 29, 2008, a day in which the S&P 500 fell 8.81%. The *VTI* ETF fell 6.58% and the *BND* ETF rose 0.49%. Thus, the portfolio return would have been $0.75(-0.0658) + 0.25(0.0049) = -0.0481$, a loss of \$13,335,000.

After conducting these analyses, the risk manager must decide if these losses could be tolerated, regardless of how unlikely some of the scenarios may be. This point leads us into our final sub-section in this material on *VaR*: what to do about it when it is too high.

7.1.5 *Responding to an Unacceptable an VaR*

If the risk manager finds that the *VaR* is unacceptably high, there are several actions that can be taken. Clearly the need to reduce the *VaR* suggests that the company should shift some its exposure to a lower risk level. Consider two assets, A and B, in which the risk of A is higher than the risk of B. It would seem that the company could reduce its overall risk by reducing its exposure to A and increasing its exposure to B, but it is not that simple. The company must take into account the correlation between the assets and the expected returns on the assets. The best way to achieve this risk reduction is to use the marginal *VaR*, as discussed in Section 7.1.3.5, which gives the risk manager an indication of which assets have the greatest impact on *VaR* and in what direction. Marginal *VaR* takes into account not only the volatility but also the correlation and the expected return.[18]

Another possibility is to put on a hedge. A hedge is simply a variation of a portfolio reallocation in the sense that it adds a position to the portfolio that when properly structured contributes negative *VaR* and thereby reduces the overall *VaR*.

Another approach to addressing an unacceptably high *VaR* is to add more equity capital. The additional equity is designed to provide a greater cushion to cover losses. In some cases, this action can also reduce the *VaR*. For example, the *VaR* is not always calculated based on all assets, in particular those that are fairly illiquid but which are not intended to be traded. A good example is real estate. A company could, however, with some delay convert that asset to cash. The *VaR* of its portfolio of tradeable assets would stay the same, but there would be more equity in the form of cash to cover losses. A company could also inject more equity and hold it in cash or short-term liquid assets. Again, if cash or these liquid assets are incorporated into the *VaR* calculation, the *VaR* would change.

This section completes our discussion of Value at Risk. We will move on by examining an issue that commonly arises in risk management but gets less attention than it should.

---

[18]Incremental *VaR* could also be used, but there are an infinite number of potential incremental *VaRs* for most portfolios that contain many assets. The marginal *VaR* is easily calculated for each asset and provides a quick snapshot of the relative contribution of each asset to *VaR*. Thus, marginal *VaR* makes it easy to rapidly determine which assets have the most impact on *VaR*. There are still an infinite number of possible changes that can be made, but marginal *VaR* points the risk manager in the correct direction whereas incremental *VaR* does not.

7.2 Quantity Risk

When a company knows that it has a certain exposure, it may not appreciate the fact that it has solved only half of the problem of managing the risk. For example, consider a company that currently has 80,000 troy ounces of silver in its inventory.[19] It plans to sell all 80,000 ounces at a later date. Fearing a decrease in the price of silver, it considers putting on a hedge. It would need to take on derivatives exposure that would be the right size to balance its 80,000-ounce exposure. Each silver futures contract at the Chicago Mercantile Exchange covers 1,000 troy ounces of silver, so it could sell 80 contracts and cover the exposure, provided the expiration date is the day on which the sale will be made. Let us assume it is.

In this problem there is no uncertainty about the size of the position. The company holds 80,000 ounces for certain. But many exposures involve uncertainty quantities. For example, when a farmer plants a crop, he does not know the amount of the crop that will ultimately be harvested, called the crop yield. Crop yields are affected primarily by weather and plant diseases. If a farmer wanted to put on a hedge before the crop is harvested, he has the problem of not knowing how much of the crop will be harvested, so he does not know how many futures contracts to sell. When a multinational corporation considers the exchange rate risk of cash flows that will arise from future foreign sales, it does not know how much cash it will generate. When a company knows that it will issue debt at a future date and is concerned about the possibility that interest rates will increase before it borrows the money, it may not know how much it will ultimately have to borrow.

In these situations, the entity faces an extra type of risk called *quantity risk*. It is challenging enough having to deal with the risk of price fluctuations, but on top of that, quantity risk means that you do not even know how much exposure you have. This problem arises because the exposure itself is an uncertainty that will be resolved at a future date. Moreover, quantity risk can interact with market risk, as we will see in the following example.

Consider a U.S. hotel company that has operations in Western Europe and generates cash flows in euros. We will simplify the problem by assuming that the company estimates that there is a 50% chance that its European cash flow will be €150 million and a 50% chance that it will be €50 million.

---

[19]A troy ounce is a little less than a standard ounce. 80,000 troy ounces weighs about 5,485 pounds or a little more than 12,000 kg.

The expected cash flow, $E(H)$, and volatility of cash flow, σ_H, will be

$$E(H) = €150(0.5) + €50(0.5) = €100$$

$$\sigma_H = \sqrt{(€150 - €100)^2(0.5) + (€50 - €100)^2(0.5)} = €50.$$

Suppose it wishes to hedge by going short forward contracts on the euro. In other words, by doing this, it will obligate itself to deliver a certain number of euros at a future date, for which it will receive an exchange rate agreed on in advance. Let us assume that rate is $1.30. Now the problem is, how many euros should it go short in a forward contract? It will receive either €150 or €50, and its expected number of euros is €100 million. The size of the hedge is unclear.

Now, let us add a further complication. It is reasonable to assume that when the euro is strong, fewer Americans will travel to Europe and stay in these hotels. Thus, euro revenue will be down. When the euro is weak, more Americans will travel to Europe and stay in these hotels. Thus, euro revenue will be up. Let us propose that exchange rates of $1.10 or $1.20 with equal probability will be associated with euro revenue of €150 million, while exchange rates of $1.40 or $1.50 with equal probability are associated with euro revenue of €50 million. Using S_T as the symbol for the spot exchange rate, the expected exchange rate and volatility are, thus,

$$E(S_T) = \$1.40(0.25) + \$1.50(0.25) + \$1.20(0.25) + \$1.10(0.25) = \$1.30$$

$$\sigma_{S_T} = \sqrt{\begin{array}{l} (\$1.40 - \$1.30)^2(0.25) + (\$1.50 - \$1.30)^2(0.25) \\ + (\$1.20 - \$1.30)^2(0.25) + (\$1.10 - \$1.30)^2(0.25) \end{array}} = \$0.1581.$$

Exhibit 7-11 summarizes the problem and provides further analysis. First, let us assume that the company enters into a short forward contract for the expected cash flow in euros of €100 at a forward price of $1.30 ($F = 1.30$). Let us assume the forward contract settles in cash. Ignoring any costs of delivery, we can treat physical delivery and cash settlement contracts as generating the same outcome.

Consider the first outcome, a cash flow in euros of €50 million and an exchange rate of $1.40. The cash flow converts to €50($1.40) = $70 million. With a forward rate of $1.30, the forward contract pays off €100($1.30 − $1.40) = −$10. Thus, the overall net cash flow is $70 − $10 = $60. If the contract calls for physical delivery, the company would need to deliver €100 million. Since it generated only €50 million, it would need to buy €50 million at the market price of $1.40. So, the €50 million it generated

Cash Flow in € (H)	Exchange Rate of € (S_T)	Dollar Value of Cash Flow (millions) (HS_T)	Payoff of Forward Contract (millions) ($-100(S_T - F)$)	Net Cash Flow after Hedge (millions) ($HS_T - 100(S_T - F)$)
€50	$1.40	$70	−$10	$60
€50	$1.50	$75	−$20	$55
€150	$1.10	$165	$20	$185
€150	$1.20	$180	$10	$190

Exhibit 7-11. Cash Flow from Hedge of €100 Million with Forward Contract at $1.30

would be delivered for $1.30, amounting to $65 million. Then it would have to buy €50 million at $1.40 and delivery them for $1.30, a loss of $0.10 per euro, for a total loss of $5 million. Thus, its total cash flow is $65 million − $5 million = $60 million.

Notice the third column, which is the unhedged position. Its expected value and volatility are

$$E(HS_T) = \$70(0.25) + \$75(0.25) + \$165(0.25) + \$180(0.25) = \$122.50$$

$$\sigma_{HS_T} = \sqrt{\begin{array}{l}(\$70 - \$122.50)^2(0.25) + (\$75 - \$122.50)^2(0.25) \\ + (\$165 - \$122.50)^2(0.25) + (\$180 - \$122.50)^2(0.25)\end{array}}$$

$$= \$50.31.$$

The hedge should improve those numbers, but it does not. The expected value and volatility of the fifth column, which reflect the overall position of spot and forward, are

$$E(HS_T - 100(S_T - F)) = \$60(0.25) + \$55(0.25) + \$185(0.25) + \$190(0.25)$$

$$= \$122.50$$

$$\sigma_{HS_T - 100(S_T - F)} = \sqrt{\begin{array}{l}(\$60 - \$122.50)^2(0.25) + (\$55 - \$122.50)^2(0.25) \\ + (\$185 - \$122.50)^2(0.25) + (\$190 - \$122.50)^2(0.25)\end{array}}$$

$$= \$65.05.$$

The expected value is the same but the volatility is greater. Not much of a hedge.

The actual cash flows are €150 million and €50 million. We will skip the calculations, but you might wish to verify that the expected cash flows are still $122.50, but the volatility with a hedge of €150 million is $72.59 and the volatility with a hedge of €50 million is $57.61, which are both higher than the volatility of the unhedged position. So, how do we get the volatility down, which is the objective of hedging, in light of quantity risk?

We have to incorporate the volatility of the quantity *and* price risk along with their covariance. Letting H be the cash flow in units of the foreign currency and S_T be the exchange rate, we will construct a model that will tell us the optimal size of the forward contract to use. Let this optimal size be denoted as Q. Denote the overall cash flow as $HS_T + Q(S_T - F)$ where F is the price of a forward contract starting at time 0 and expiring at time T. Let $\sigma^2_{HS_T + Q(S_T - F)}$ be the variance of the overall position. Since Q and F are constants, we can write the variance as $\sigma^2_{HS_T + QS_T}$.

Now we specify how the variance is made up of the component variances and covariances. Following the same procedure that we do for a two-asset portfolio, we have

$$\sigma^2_{HS_T + QS_T} = \sigma^2_{HS_T} + Q^2 \sigma^2_{S_T} + 2cov_{HS_T, QS_T}$$

$$= \sigma^2_{HS_T} + Q^2 \sigma^2_{S_T} + 2Q cov_{HS_T, S_T}.$$

We wish to minimize this variance by choosing the optimal level of Q. Thus, we differentiate $\sigma^2_{HS_T + QS_T}$ by Q, set the result to zero, and solve for Q:

$$\frac{\partial \sigma^2_{HS_T + QS_T}}{\partial Q} = 2Q \sigma^2_{S_T} + 2cov_{HS_T, S_T}$$

$$2Q \sigma^2_{S_T} + 2cov_{HS_T, S_T} = 0.$$

The solution is

$$Q = -\frac{cov_{HS_T, S_T}}{\sigma^2_{S_T}}. \tag{7.3}$$

The second derivative is

$$\frac{\partial^2 (2Q \sigma^2_{S_T} + 2cov_{HS_T, S_T})}{\partial Q^2} = 2\sigma^2_{S_T}.$$

Since variances are positive, the second derivative is positive, so the solution is a minimum. Our formula above for Q, thus, tells us the appropriate size of the forward contract to minimize the variance.

To use this formula in our problem, we will need $cov(CR,R)$, which is found as follows:

$$cov_{HS_T,S_T} = (\$70 - \$122.50)(\$1.40 - \$1.30)(0.25)$$
$$+ (\$75 - \$122.50)(\$1.50 - \$1.30)(0.25)$$
$$+ (\$165 - \$122.50)(\$1.10 - \$1.30)(0.25)$$
$$+ (\$180 - \$122.50)(\$1.20 - \$1.30)(0.25)$$
$$= -7.25.$$

Recalling that we previously found $\sigma^2_{S_T} = (0.1581)^2 = 0.025$. Now plugging into the formula for the optimal Q:

$$Q = -\frac{cov_{HS_T,S_T}}{\sigma^2_{S_T}}$$

$$= -\frac{-7.25}{0.025} = 290.$$

Thus, the hedge should be long 290 euros, a number that may seem strange. The company receives euros, but to hedge, it should be long euros. Moreover, it will receive no more than 150 million euros and yet the hedge should be for 290 million euros. If that is confusing, however, just look at Exhibit 7-12, which shows the standard deviation for various sizes of the forward contract. It bottoms out at 290, just as the formula said it would. The formula took into account the fact that there is a relationship between the exchange rate and the cash flows. Remember that when the exchange rate is high, the

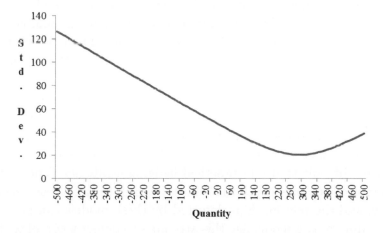

Exhibit 7-12. Optimal Size of Forward Contract for Quantity Risk Hedge

cash flow in euros is low and vice versa. Thus, there is a bit of a natural hedge. Revenue is partially stabilized by virtue of this inverse relationship. Nonetheless, the magnitudes of the revenues and exchange rates and their covariance must be taken into account, and the formula does just that. Of course, in practice, this relationship must be estimated from historical data, and the estimated relationship must be expected to hold in the future.

Minimizing risk is not necessarily the objective of all hedges, but it is a reasonable one in many cases. More formal hedging models would account for the decision maker's risk tolerance and any constraints. This is an advanced topic that we will not cover here.

7.3 Statistical Sensitivity

Some hedging strategies set as an objective the direct effect of a variable on the rate of return on the company's stock. For example, consider the following multiple regression:

$$R_t = b_0 + b_1 v_{1t} + b_2 v_{2t} + \cdots + b_M v_{Mt} + e_t.$$

Here the dependent variable is the return on the stock, which is measured at various time points denoted as time t. The return on most stocks have been shown to be affected by a number of well-known variables such as the return on the market, possibly a return on an industry index, a measure of the company's size, and factors that reflect premiums for value and growth stocks. These variables would be entered on the right-hand side. If a company were concerned about a particular source of risk, let us say the yen-euro exchange rate, it would enter the percentage change in that exchange rate on the right-hand side. Let us say that variable is v_j, where j is one of the independent variables from 1 to M. Then the coefficient b_j is commonly referred to as the firm's currency beta with respect to that particular currency.

Knowledge of a parameter such as the currency beta enables firms to determine the impact of the risk factor on their stock return. Such variables are commonly used in scholarly research and they can reveal a great deal about how exchange rates or other variables affect shareholder wealth, but they can be difficult to use in practical hedging strategies. There are many strict statistical requirements that must be met to use these results with reliability, and the relationships detected by these models can be extremely unstable. Moreover, a model like this attempts to detect a complex stream of relationships that can easily break down. For example, the effect of exchange rate changes manifests in changes in foreign cash flows and possibly even in domestic cash flows, as companies gain or lose domestic sales due to exchange rate changes. These cash flows can then convert into equity through the complex process in which investors predict future dividends, the growth rate of dividends, and discount by their required rates of return. Instead of trying to encapsulate the relationship between a variable and the equity return with a beta coefficient, most companies simply attempt to gauge the relationship between the variable and their cash flows, letting the rest of the valuation process play out on its own.

Some companies may use cash flow as the dependent variable, in which case the coefficients of the regression independent variables tell the sensitivity of cash flow to each respective source of risk. Knowing this sensitivity, the risk manager can get a better idea of how large of a hedge to put on.

7.4 Nonlinear Exposure

Most approaches to risk management assume that the relationship between the risk factor and the risk, as exemplified by a variable like the company's cash flow, is linear. Linear models have two primary implications. They mean that at a given condition, an upward move in the risk factor elicits a response to the risk that is equivalent in magnitude to an equivalent move in the opposite direction of the risk factor. In other words, the effect is the same whether the risk factor moves up or down. A second implication is that the response of the risk to a change in the risk factor is the same at any level of the risk factor. When either of these conditions is violated, the risk is said to be non-linear. These points may seem confusing, but they will be clarified with an example.

The panels of Exhibit 7-13 illustrate cases of linear and non-linear exposures. The risk factor is labeled the exchange rate and the risk is the cash flow. In Panel A, the change in the cash flow relative to the exchange rate is the same at all points along the line. In addition, at any given point, the change in cash flow from an increase in the exchange rate is of the same magnitude but opposite direction as the change in cash flow from a decrease in the exchange rate of the same amount. This statement is, of course, nothing more than a verbalization of what we mean by a linear relationship between two variables. In Panel B, however, the change in the cash flow relative to the change in risk is not the same at the two indicated points. Moreover, at any given point, the change in cash flow from an increase in the exchange rate is in the opposite direction but not of the same magnitude

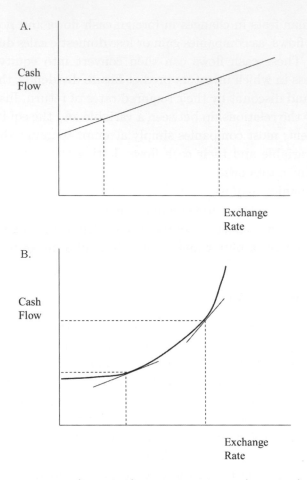

A.

Cash
Flow

Exchange
Rate

B.

Cash
Flow

Exchange
Rate

Exhibit 7-13. Linear (Panel A) and Non-Linear (Panel B) Exposures

as the change in cash flow from a decrease in the exchange rate. Note the
tangent lines, and as such, they indicate that linearity holds only for an
extremely small change in the exchange rate. Of course, this is the concept
of a calculus derivative. A linear relationship along a tangent line is relevant
if the independent variable changes only by an infinitesimal amount. But in
practice, infinitesimal changes are rare. Hence, for most reasonable changes,
non-linearity is often the case.

Now let us look at an example. Consider an American tour company
that advertises heavily in Europe for the purpose of providing customized
tours to European citizens visiting the U.S. When the euro is strong, more
Europeans come to the U.S. for vacations and when it is weak, Europeans
tend to stay in Europe. Therefore, the euro and the company's dollar cash

Exchange Rate	Cash Flow
$0.80	$7.50 million
$0.90	$9.00 million
$1.00	$10.00 million
$1.10	$10.50 million
$1.20	$10.75 million

Exhibit 7-14. Relationship between U.S. Tour Company's Cash Flow and the Euro

flow are directly related. But the relationship will weaken somewhat at higher rates. In other words, at very high rates, a stronger euro imparts a positive but weaker relationship between that currency and the company's cash flow. Exhibit 7-14 provides the basic data.

Let us say that currently the euro is at $1.00 and, therefore, the cash flow is $10 million. Suppose the euro goes up to $1.10, a change of $0.10. Then, we can measure the upside sensitivity as

$$\frac{\$10.5 - \$10.0}{\$1.10 - \$1.00} = 5.00.$$

The downside sensitivity for an equivalent move downward in the exchange rate is

$$\frac{\$9.0 - \$10.0}{\$0.90 - \$1.00} = 10.0.$$

In other words, for an exchange rate move of $0.10, which is 10%, in either direction, the response is much greater for a decrease in the exchange rate.

Now let us position ourselves at an exchange rate of $0.90 and calculate the upside and downside sensitivity,

$$\frac{\$10 - \$9}{\$1.00 - \$0.90} = 10.00 \text{ (upside)}$$

$$\frac{\$7.5 - \$9}{\$0.80 - \$0.90} = 15.00 \text{ (downside).}$$

Not only are the upside and downside sensitivities different at an exchange rate of $0.90, but the upside sensitivity at $0.90 is different from the upside sensitivity at $1.00 and the downside sensitivity at $0.90 is different from the downside sensitivity at $1.00.

So, now let us consider the implications for designing a risk management strategy. When the exposure is linear, the strategy is relatively simple.

The response coefficient, which is the change in the cash flow divided by the change in the risk factor, serves to indicate how much exposure to take in an offsetting derivatives transaction. The size of the necessary derivatives position would remain the same over all levels of the exchange rate. When the response is not the same in both directions, then the hedge will not be equally effective for exchange rate increases and decreases. In addition, when the response is not the same at all levels of exchange rates, the size of the derivatives position will need to be modified in accordance with the level of exchange rates. Hedges of non-linear exposures are less reliable and more difficult to manage. Doing so effectively is quite an advanced topic that we shall not take up at this introductory level.

7.5 Sensitivity Measures of Interest Rate and Equity Risk

In this section we examine how bonds and stocks respond to the factors that are the sources of their risk. For bonds, we will be examining how their prices change in response to changes in interest rates. For stocks, we will look at how their rates of return respond to changes in the market and potentially other factors that affect their returns. We first look at the effect of short-term interest rates.

7.5.1 *Short-Term Interest Rate Risk*

In this section, we will take a look at the two primary ways in which the prices of short-term fixed income instruments are related to short-term interest rates. There are two types of short-term instruments, one based on a discount of the interest off of the face value and the other based on an addition of the interest to the price. The first method, called *discount pricing*, is used in the U.S. Treasury bills market and a few other money markets. Letting B = the price of the instrument, r_D = the discount rate, h = the number of days in the life of the instrument, and assuming a par value of 1, we have the following formula for the price:

$$B = 1 - r_D \left(\frac{h}{360} \right).$$

As an example, consider a 90-day discount instrument with a discount rate of 2%. What is the price per par value of 1?

$$B = 1 - 0.02 \left(\frac{90}{360} \right) = 0.9950.$$

This result means that you would buy the instrument for \$0.995 per \$1 par. If you held it for 90 days, it would pay off the par value of \$1. So, how well did the investment do? To answer that question, we annualize the 90-day rate of return by multiplying by the number of 90-day periods in a year.[20]

$$\left(\frac{1}{0.9950} - 1\right)(365/90) - 1 = 0.0204.$$

Why Sometimes 360 and Sometimes 365?

One of the most confusing points that students of finance have to learn is how in some cases a year is considered to be 360 days and in some cases 365 days. In this vignette, we will try to gain some clarity.

Interest is the foundation of financial transactions. Determining the interest on a loan is a necessary computation, but one that can be difficult. For example, \$100 compounded annually at 4% for five years grows to a value of $\$100(1.04)^5 = \$121.67$. What seems like an easy computation to anyone with a calculator, a computer, or even just a mobile phone with a calculator app becomes quite difficult if you take these devices away. Back in the "olden" days, to facilitate interest calculations, banks tended to make short-term loans for periods such as 30, 60, 90, or 180 days, and they assumed there were 360 days in a year. They also tended to use interest rates like 4%, 6%, and 8%. Thus, a 90-day loan at 6% would require the repayment of interest at the rate of $6\% \times 90/360 = 1.5\%$. A bank could then simply apply the decimal 0.015 to the loan principal. For say a \$100 loan, the interest is \$1.50. In other words, by assuming 360 days and making loans be for a number of days that could be evenly divided into 360, interest can be more easily calculated. These practices began in short term money markets such as commercial paper, U.S. treasury bills, and Eurodollars, all of which were in existence well before electronic calculators. Not surprisingly, tradition dies a slow death. In this case, tradition never died. While today money market securities oftentimes have maturities that are not evenly easily divided into 360, the use of 360 days has persisted in the money markets.

There is, however, a subtle lesson in this antiquated method. Suppose a 180-day pure discount instrument is priced at a rate of 5%. For a \$1 face value, what would it cost? Using the formula as demonstrated in the text,

---

[20]Some people annualize returns by assuming that the return over 90 days is reinvested and compounds for 365 days. In that case, the return would be $(1/0.995)^{365/90} - 1 = 0.0205$.

you would pay $1 - 0.05(180/360) = 0.975$. This result means that you would invest $0.975 and receive back $1 at maturity. Recognizing that the 180-day assumption was a convenience that was useful in the days before electronic calculators, let us assume that the financial world decides to eliminate the use of 360 days in the computation and switch to 365. What would happen? Take a moment and think about this question. Your first response might be wrong.

Interestingly, most people think that the price would go to $1 - 0.05(180/365) = \$0.975342$. If that's what you thought, you are 100% wrong, and when you are 100% wrong in the financial world, someone who is 100% right will be eager to do a transaction with you, as it will be very profitable for that person and a big loss for you. We have just presented a good example of how too many finance students simply learn formulas and do not consider the intuition.

The price of anything — *absolutely anything* — is determined by supply and demand, that is, how much people are willing to pay to buy it and how much sellers demand to sell it. If buyers and sellers agreed on a price of $0.975 under a 360-day assumption, then that price would continue to hold under a 365-day assumption. After all, the underlying economics of the instrument have not changed. It is still a discount instrument that will pay $1 in 180 days. What would change is the discount rate, which would be $1 - r(180/365) = \$0.975$. Then r would be 0.050694. This discount formula is nothing but a quoting convention. Supply and demand for the instrument determine the price. Indeed, supply and demand determine the price of everything that trades in a competitive market.

Finally, let us note why we use 365 to determine the effective annual rate. We must account for the fact that there are 365 days in a (non-leap) year. To do otherwise would be to assume that there are five days in a year in which interest is omitted. No one gets free interest, so we must use 365 when we annualize a return over a shorter period.

Now let us look at the other type of short-term fixed-income security, the add-on instrument. A typical type of add-on instrument is a Eurodollar. Assuming $1 is invested at a rate of r_A for h days, the amount that will be paid at maturity is the future value, FV,

$$1\left(1 + r_A\left(\frac{h}{360}\right)\right) = FV,$$

So, if you invest \$1 for 90 days at 2%, the FV is

$$1 + 0.02 \left(\frac{90}{360} \right) = 1.005,$$

The annualized rate of return would be

$$\left(\frac{1.005 - 1}{1} \right)(365/90) = 0.0203,$$

Now let us look at the interest sensitivity of each type of security. First, let us simplify the formula a little by letting $h/360 = \tau$, the maturity. The pure discount bond price is

$$B = 1 - r_D \tau.$$

Let us take the derivative of the discount bond price with respect to a change in the rate, r_D, and then divide by the price, B:

$$\frac{dB}{dr_D} = -\tau$$

$$\frac{dB}{dr_D} \left(\frac{1}{B} \right) = - \left(\frac{1}{B} \right) \tau$$

$$\frac{dB}{B} = -\tau \left(\frac{1}{B} \right) dr_D.$$

The left-hand side represents the percentage change in B for an infinitesimally small change in r_D, as represented on the right hand side by dr_D. The right-hand side indicates that this value will be the negative of the maturity times one divided by the price times the infinitesimal interest rate change.

Now we do the same for the add-on instrument. First, we have to assume that the add-on instrument is contractually obligated to pay the amount $1 + r_A \tau$ at maturity, where τ is $h/360$. Of course, discounting that amount to the present naturally produces the current value of 1: $(1 + r_A \tau)/(1 + r_A \tau) = 1$. If the discount rate changes, however, the numerator remains constant and the denominator changes. So, let us designate the fixed numerator as r_A^*. So now we differentiate the price, B, with respect to r_A:

$$\frac{dB}{dr_A} = \frac{d}{dr_A} \left(\frac{1 + r_A^* \tau}{1 + r_A \tau} \right) = \frac{-(1 + r_A^* \tau)\tau}{(1 + r_A \tau)^2}$$

$$= -\frac{(1 + r_A^* \tau)\tau}{(1 + r_A \tau)^2} = \frac{-B\tau}{1 + r_A \tau}$$

$$\frac{dB}{B} = -\tau \left(\frac{1}{1 + r_A \tau} \right) dr_A,$$

The difference in the case of the discount instrument is that here the maturity τ is adjusted by the factor $1 + r_A \tau$ and in the former case, the maturity τ is adjusted by the original price, B. Since $1 + r_A \tau$ is more than 1 and B is less than one for a discount bond with face value of 1, the relative price change for an add-on instrument is less than for a discount instrument if the change in the rate is still the same.

Now let us examine the prices of these two instruments over a wide range of interest rate changes. Exhibit 7-15 shows the prices of these two short-term instruments with the rate ranging from 1% to 3%.

The add-on bond is higher priced only by construction. It is set at a price of $1 and pays off $1(1+0.02(90/360)) = $1.0050, whereas the discount bond pays $1 at maturity and sells for $0.995. From the lines above, we can see that the price sensitivity is virtually the same. More importantly, however, the price sensitivity is not particularly high. For example, if the discount rate goes from 2% to 3%, a tremendously large change, the prices go from $0.9950 to $0.9925 for the discount bond and from $1 to $0.9975, which are both very small changes, around a quarter of a percent. Of course, keep in mind that the yields on the two bonds might not necessarily be the same or change by the same amount, so comparisons of discount and add-on instruments are somewhat limited.

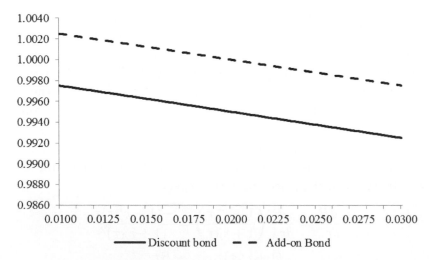

Exhibit 7-15. Prices of Short-Term Discount and Add-on Instruments for Range of Rates

The reason the prices of these instruments are not very sensitive to interest rate changes is that they are short-term instruments. Holding everything else constant, price sensitivity is lower the shorter the maturity. If these bonds had longer maturities, their price sensitivities would be much greater. Let us now look at the price sensitivities of intermediate- and long-term bonds.

7.5.2 *Intermediate- and Long-Term Interest Rate Risk*

As noted in the previous section, if these instruments had longer maturities, they would have greater price sensitivity. Suppose in the examples above, the bonds matured in 3,600 days or approximately 10 years. There is no reason to show the details, but you should go back and re-work the examples above. You would get a price of $0.8333 for the discount bond. The add-on bond is constructed with an initial value of $1. Recall that for 90-day maturities, the prices of both instruments changed by roughly 0.25% for an increase in the discount rate from 2% to 3%. For our 3,600-day bonds, the discount bond price would change by roughly 0.25% if the discount rate went from 2% to about 2.02%. The 3,600-day add-on bond would have its price fall about 0.25% if the discount rate went from 2% to about 2.03%. In other words, approximately the same relative price change that occurred with a move 2% to 3% on the discount rate on the 90-day securities would occur on the long-term securities with a move of just two to three basis points.[21]

Price sensitivity on long-term bonds is attenuated somewhat by the payment of periodic coupon interest. Holding everything else constant, a bond is less price sensitive the higher the coupon. Thus, both coupon and maturity have effects and those effects are opposite: low maturity and high coupon bonds have the least sensitivity and low coupon and long maturity bonds have the greatest sensitivity. The concept of duration captures both effects simultaneously.

7.5.2.1 *Duration*

Let us now consider a coupon bond that pays interest at the rare c_b at times $t = 1, 2, \ldots, T$, has a maturity of T, a discount rate of y, and a face value of 1. The counter t represents the time to each payment date in years. Thus, if $t = 1$, the payment occurs in one year. If $t = 2$, the payment occurs in two

---

[21]Recall from Chapter 4 that a basis point is 1/100 of a percent. So 1% is 100 basis points. If a rate of 1% goes up to 1.01%, it has increased by one basis point.

years, etc. Hence, T is the maturity of the bond in years.[22]

$$B = \sum_{t=1}^{T} c_b (1+y)^{-t} + 1(1+y)^{-T}.$$

The symbol "y" is used for the discount rate, because in practice this rate is commonly referred to as the *yield* or *yield to maturity*. Now, let us take the derivative with respect to the yield:

$$\frac{dB}{dy} = \frac{d\left(\sum_{t=1}^{T} c_b(1+y)^{-t} + 1(1+y)^{-T}\right)}{dy}$$

$$= -\left(\frac{t\sum_{t=1}^{T} c_b(1+y)^{-t} - T(1+y)^{-T}}{(1+y)}\right).$$

Now divide by the price B:

$$\frac{dB}{dy}\left(\frac{1}{B}\right) = -\left(\frac{1}{1+y}\right)\left(\frac{\sum_{t=1}^{T} tc_b(1+y)^{-t} - T(1+y)^{-T}}{B}\right).$$

It is traditional to define the term in large parentheses on the right-hand side as duration:

$$DUR = \frac{\sum_{t=1}^{T} tc_b(1+y)^{-t} - T(1+y)^{-T}}{B}.$$

With respect to its mathematical definition, duration is a weighted average of the times to each cash flow on a bond, as shown below:

$$DUR = \sum_{t=1}^{T} t\frac{c_b(1+y)^{-t}}{B} + (1)\frac{(1+y)^{-T}}{B}$$

$$= \sum_{t=1}^{T} tw_t \quad \text{where}$$

$$w_t = \begin{cases} \dfrac{c_b(1+y)^{-t}}{B} & \text{for } t < T \\[2mm] \dfrac{(1+c_b)(1+y)^{-t}}{B} & \text{for } t = T. \end{cases}$$

---

[22]If the payments occurred at six-month intervals, as they commonly do in the United States, then the formula would be adjusted so that the coupon rate and yield would be multiplied by 0.5.

In other words, duration is a weighted average of the times to maturity, as represented by the t's that run from $1, 2, \ldots$ to T. Each weight is the present value of the cash flow that occurs on that date divided by the overall price of the bond. Note that the cash flows are the coupons, c, plus the final cash flow at maturity representing the face value of 1. The duration is interpreted in years.

Now going back to the partial derivative formula above,

$$\frac{dB}{dy}\left(\frac{1}{B}\right) = -\left(\frac{1}{1+y}\right)DUR.$$

In some cases, the formula is simplified by defining a concept called modified duration as

$$DUR_m = \frac{DUR}{1+y},$$

such that

$$\frac{dB}{dy}\left(\frac{1}{B}\right) = -DUR_m. \tag{7.4}$$

This expression will come in very handy in a moment. First, however, let us illustrate how to calculate duration in Exhibit 7-16. Here we have a 10-year bond with coupon of 5% and yield of 5.25%.[23]

In the present value column, we calculate the present value of each cash flow that is shown in the column directly to the left. The sum is the price of 0.9809. In the last column on the right, we multiply each value t by the appropriate weight. Taking the fifth year payment for example, we have $5(0.0387 = 0.1936$, subject to rounding. The sum of the weighted values of t is 7.9325. Dividing this sum by the price gives the duration of 8.0867. Dividing the duration by 1 plus the yield of 0.0525 gives the modified duration (Mod Dur in the table) of 7.6833.[24]

Duration is widely used as a measure of the sensitivity of the price of the bond to a change in the yield. Manipulating Equation (7.4) for the partial

---

[23]The table has rows that accommodate up to 15 payments, but there are none beyond the 10th.

[24]Incidentally, the duration of a zero-coupon bond is its maturity. This statement is, more or less, true by definition. It makes only one payment, so a weighted average of that one payment date gives the payment date or maturity. The formula for the duration of a coupon-bond will also produce the maturity as the duration.

Maturity	10		
Coupon	0.05		
Yield	0.0525		

t	Cash Flow	Present Value	t * PV
1	0.05	0.0475	0.0475
2	0.05	0.0451	0.0903
3	0.05	0.0429	0.1287
4	0.05	0.0407	0.1630
5	0.05	0.0387	0.1936
6	0.05	0.0368	0.2207
7	0.05	0.0349	0.2446
8	0.05	0.0332	0.2656
9	0.05	0.0315	0.2839
10	1.05	0.6295	6.2946
	Sum	0.9809	7.9325
	Duration		8.0867
	Mod Dur		7.6833

Exhibit 7-16.   Calculation of Duration

derivative with respect to the yield, we have

$$\frac{dB}{dy} = -DUR_m B$$

$$\frac{dB}{B} = -DUR_m dy$$

$$dB = -DUR_m dy B.$$

The second equation is an approximation of the percentage change in the price of the bond, and the third is an approximation of the change in price. Of course, the use of calculus implies that the change in the yield is infinitesimally small. As such, for finite changes in the yield, we usually write the above expressions as

$$\frac{\Delta B}{B} \approx -DUR_m \Delta y$$

$$\Delta B \approx -DUR_m \Delta y B,$$

where the differentials are replaced by deltas so as to recognize that the change in yield might not be infinitesimal, and the equals sign is replaced by an approximately equals sign.

Let us now apply these equations. For the example bond, let us presume that the yield instantaneously changes by 0.005, which is 50 basis points, or

$1/2\%$. The duration formula estimates the change in price to be

$$\Delta B \approx -DUR_m B \Delta y$$
$$= -(7.6833)(0.9809)(0.005)$$
$$= -0.3768.$$

Since the original price is 0.9809, the new price should be

$$B + \Delta B - 0.9809 - 0.03768 = 0.9425.$$

The actual new price can be found be recalculating it, as in Exhibit 7-15, with a yield of $0.0525 + 0.005 = 0.0575$. The result is 0.9441. There is, thus, a small difference of 0.0016.

Exhibit 7-17 illustrates the relationship between the bond price and its yield over a wide range of yields. As you can see, the relationship is not linear. The use of calculus approximates a linear relationship by assuming a very small (infinitesimal) change in the independent variable, in this case the yield. Since duration is based on calculus, the duration approximation will be less accurate when the yield change in greater. In that case, it may be necessary to use a second-order adjustment called convexity. In most practical situations, however, convexity adds very little to the improvement in the approximation, because the yield changes that could reasonably occur over only an instant in time are too small to require the use of convexity.

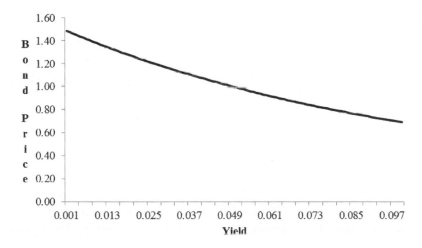

Exhibit 7-17. Bond Price vs. Yield
Maturity of 10 years, coupon of 5%, yield of 5.25%, annual payments

Thus, duration will suffice as a measure of the price sensitivity of a bond in most cases.[25]

At this point you may be wondering why we require an approximation to the new bond price when we know the precise formula. The benefit of the duration approximation is that it is a linear measure of price sensitivity and facilitates the use of derivatives. For example, suppose you hold a bond and wish to hedge it with a bond futures contract. The duration of a futures will be related to the change in the yield in the same manner as the duration of the bond. Thus, using $f_0(T)$ to represent the futures price at time 0 of a contract expiring at time T,

$$\Delta f_0(T) \approx -f_0(T) DUR_{mf} \Delta y.$$

A reasonable hedging strategy would be to use N_f futures to bring the overall duration to zero. We add the durations of the two positions weighted by the prices to get $DUR_m B + N_f f_0(T) DUR_{mf}$. We could then set this value to zero and solve for N_f. We will get into this approach more formally in the next chapter when we cover forward and futures hedging.

7.5.2.2   *Limitations of Duration*

Duration is widely used in the world of bond portfolio management. Nonetheless, it has many restrictions. Since duration is a function of time itself, the duration of a bond is only its duration for that instant in time. As it moves forward in time, all of the time-based calculations are no longer valid. That means if a hedge is put in place based on duration, that hedge would need to be re-evaluated more or less continuously to determine if the new duration requires an adjustment to the derivatives position in order to keep the risk of the bond and futures positions balanced. Of course, continuous rebalancing is not possible, so some loss of accuracy has to be tolerated.

In addition, duration is based on the assumption that one can capture the complexity of interest rate changes by a simple measure, the change in the yield. Although use of a single measure, the yield, to price bonds is a common simplification, the price of a bond is really a function of many interest rates. For example, a five-year bond with coupons in one, two, three, four, and five years will have its price determined by discounting the respective coupons at the respective one-, two-, three-, four-, and five-year rates. That price then

---

[25]When we get to options, we will require a second-order adjustment to the price sensitivity measure.

determines the yield, which is a single discount rate that when applied to all coupons and the par value forces the present value of the coupons and face value to equal the price. Duration is based on a yield change, when in fact what is really changing is the entire array of interest rates.

This "array of interest rates" is referred to as the term structure of interest rates. It is a graph of the relationship between rates on bonds by their maturities over a range of maturities and is usually constructed using government bonds so as to virtually eliminate the effect of any threat of default on the rates and to focus only on interest rate changes in the absence of credit risk changes.

The duration concept assumes that all rates change by the same amount. Such a case is depicted in Exhibit 7-18. The rate is on the vertical axes, and the maturity of the bond is on the horizontal axis. The lower curve is the current curve. Notice that the curve is upward sloping, indicating that longer-term bonds require a higher rate, which is often but not always the case. The arrows indicate a parallel shift to a higher curve. In other words, every rate on the lower curve changes by the same amount and produces the higher curve. This type of shift could also be downward. In either case, duration assumes a parallel shift.

Other types of shifts, however, are quite possible. Exhibit 7-19 shows a shift in the curvature of the term structure. The initial condition is the lower curve, which is steadily downward sloping. Notice the shift to the higher curve, which not only is upward sloping but also is quite steep at the low end.

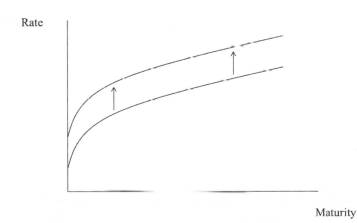

Exhibit 7-18. Parallel Shift in the Term Structure

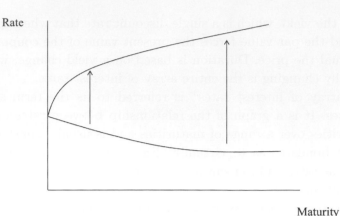

Rate

Maturity

Exhibit 7-19. One Type of Non-Parallel Shift in the Term Structure

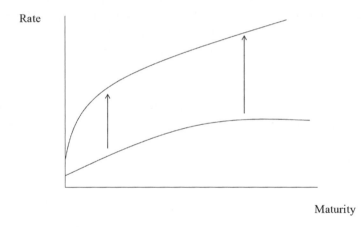

Rate

Maturity

Exhibit 7-20. Another Type of Non-Parallel Shift in the Term Structure

Exhibit 7-20 shows another type of non-parallel shift. Note that here the term structure remains upward sloping but becomes much steeper.

These types of term structure shifts are common, but they are essentially precluded by the concept of duration. The implications for risk management are that duration-based hedges will be less effective in the presence of these non-parallel shifts.[26]

---

[26]To get an idea of the kinds of shifts that have occurred historically in the term structure, see the web site http://stockcharts.com/freecharts/yieldcurve.php. It has an applet called the Living Yield Curve, which illustrates how the yield curve has changed starting from 1999.

7.5.3 *Equity Risk*

It turns out that we have already covered this topic in a different context in Chapter 3. In Section 8 of that chapter, we discussed the relationship between risk and return. We illustrated how that relationship manifests in the capital asset pricing model that relates the expected return to the systematic risk, which is known as the beta. The beta is a sensitivity measure in that it shows how the expected return on a stock responds to changes in the market risk premium as indicated by the difference between the expected return on the market and the risk-free rate. And as we mentioned in that section, multifactor models that reflect additional effects that can also drive returns are also widely used. The relationship of the return to each factor is a sensitivity measure. Thus, there are market betas, industry betas, growth betas, size betas, and factor betas that reflect the sensitivity of return to the market, industry, growth, size, and various other factors.

7.5.4 *A Note on Derivatives Risk*

Options, futures, forwards, and swaps also have sensitivity measures. Futures, forwards, and swaps have a linear relationship to the values of their underlyings, but options have non-linear relationships. These measures are referred to as deltas, gammas, and vegas. These concepts will be covered in detail in Chapter 10.

7.6 Chapter Summary

This chapter deals with the process of measuring financial risk, which is a critical first stage in managing it. We devoted a great deal of this chapter to understanding the concept of Value-at-Risk or *VaR*. As we saw, *VaR* is a measure of the likelihood of extreme losses. More precisely, *VaR* measures the minimum loss that will be incurred over a particular time horizon a specified percentage of the time. It reflects a point in the tail of the distribution. We saw how *VaR* is estimated, how it is used, and what are its strengths and limitations. We also examined related techniques such as standalone *VaR*, average loss given loss, conditional *VaR*, incremental or delta *VaR*, marginal and component *VaR*, relative *VaR*, delta-normal *VaR*, and cash-flow-at-risk or *CFaR*. We also looked at how *VaR* is often supplemented with scenario analysis and stress testing. We then examined the topics of quantity risk, statistical sensitivity, and nonlinear exposures. Then we looked at risk measures for interest rate risk, equity risk, and (briefly) derivatives risk.

7.7 Questions and Problems

1. Define the concept of Value-at-Risk. Then, (a) break down the elements of the definition and explain each of them carefully, (b) identify what *VaR* is and what it is not, and (c), make up an example and explain what it means.

2. What do we mean by a risk factor with regard to *VaR*?

3. Explain how the analytical method is used to estimate *VaR*, and in particular, explain how to estimate the volatility when there are multiple assets.

4. Consider a portfolio with expected annual return of 10.5% and volatility of 32.75%. Determine an analytical VaR for one month at 5% for a portfolio worth $125 million.

5. What is the primary advantage and disadvantage of the analytical method?

6. Explain how the historical simulation method is used to estimate *VaR*. Construct an expository example, but it is not necessary to show the details of the historical sample.

7. What is the primary advantage and disadvantage of the historical simulation method?

8. Explain how the Monte Carlo simulation method is used to estimate *VaR*. Construct an expository example, but it is not necessary to actual show the details of the simulation. Be sure that you explain how to handle the correlations between assets.

9. What is the primary advantage and disadvantage of the Monte Carlo simulation method?

10. What are the overall strengths and weakness of *VaR*? With respect to the weaknesses, how does *VaR* compare with other financial models?

11. Interpret the following information. A portfolio is comprised of five asset classes. The *VaR*s of the asset classes are $1.2 million, $1.8 million, $3.5 million, $2.9 million, and $1.4 million. The *VaR* of the entire position is $9.1 million.

12. Explain the concept of average loss, given loss and how it is computed.

13. Explain the concept of conditional *VaR*, also known as expected shortfall, tail loss, and average tail loss.

14. What does the measure called incremental or delta *VaR* tell us?

15. Explain the concepts of marginal *VaR*, also known as component *VaR*. Explain why marginal *VaR* may misstate the change in the *VaR* for a change in the weights of the asset classes.

16. How can the concept of relative *VaR* assist in understanding how a portfolio can deviate from its target benchmark?

17. How does a risk manager adapt the analytical method for use when the portfolio contains options?

18. Explain how Cash-Flow-at-Risk works as the primary alternative to *VaR* for non-financial companies.

19. Determine the quarterly *CFaR* for a company with an expected cash flow per quarter of €22 million, a volatility of €3 million, and a critical level of €12.5 million. Provide a verbal interpretation of the *CFaR* number such that senior management could understand.

20. How are scenario analysis and stress tests used to supplement *VaR*?

21. Suppose a risk manager finds that the VaR is uncomfortably high. What are the alternative methods for responding in an appropriate manner to control the risk?

22. What is quantity risk and why is it such a challenging problem for risk managers?

23. Consider a U.S. company that generates cash flows in British pounds. There are three possible outcomes as identified below.

Outcome	Probability	Pound	Cash Flow
1	0.40	$1.40	100
2	0.35	$1.35	110
3	0.25	$1.30	120

Assume a forward contract can be created at a price of $1.35. Determine the optimal foreign currency hedge. Find the volatility of the overall position and compare it to the volatility of the unhedged position. Also, construct a hedge based on the expected cash flow and compare its volatility to that of the optimal hedge. Round all hedge quantities to the nearest integer.

24. How can statistical regression models be used in managing risk?
25. What are the two characteristics of nonlinear exposure?
26. Suppose a company expects the following cash flows based on an underlying interest rate

Interest Rate	Cash Flow
0.04	94.0
0.05	98.0
0.06	100.0
0.07	101.5
0.08	102.0

   Show the two properties of non-linearity, using the 6% rate as the starting point and also examining from rates of 5% and 7%.
27. Find the price and non-compounded rate of return for a discount zero coupon bond of 180 days maturity with a 4% discount rate and also the payoff value and non-compounded rate of return for an add-on zero coupon bond with a rate of 5%. Assume a face value of 1 for both bonds.
28. Find the price and modified duration of a five-year bond with annual coupons of 4.2%, a face value of 1, and a yield of 4.6%.
29. Consider a five-year bond with an annual coupon of 3%, a face value of 1, and a yield of 4%. The price and modified duration of this bond are 0.9555 and 4.5284, respectively. Now, suppose the yield increases by 50 basis points. Find the duration estimate of the new price and compare it to the actual new price. Explain why there is a difference and what could make the difference be larger or smaller.
30. Why do the different possible types of term structure shifts make duration hedging more difficult?

Chapter 8

Managing Market Risk with Forward and Futures Contracts

It is often said in the derivatives business that you cannot hedge history.

Dan Goldman
Risk Management for the
Investment Community
(Risk Products Financial
Products Guide)
1999, p. 16

Chapter 8 is the first of three chapters that get into the meat and bones of risk management. Specifically, we will take a careful look at the types of derivative contracts that are used to manage financial risk. This chapter deals with forwards and futures, while the next, Chapter 9, deals with swaps, and after that we have Chapter 10, which covers options. We have already introduced these instruments in Chapter 4, though we did not get too far into them. After a brief review of the definition and characteristics of forward and futures contract, we will dive into the process of determining the price and value of a contract. Then we will look at applications in risk management. We will follow these steps first for forwards and then for futures.

Before we get started, however, it will be beneficial to review the definition of a derivative. In Section 4.4 of Chapter 4, we defined a derivative as

> ... a contract between two parties that provides for a payoff at a future date that will be determined by the value of an underlying asset, rate, other derivative, or risk factor.

If you do not remember what all of these terms refer to, it would be very important to go back to Chapter 4 before you go one step further.

8.1 Forward Contracts

We initially identified forward contracts as one of three types of forward commitments, the other two being futures contracts and swaps. As indicated, we will cover forwards and futures in this chapter and swaps in the next. In many ways, forward contracts are the foundations of all derivatives, and they are certainly the simplest.

8.1.1 *Formal Definition of a Forward Contract*

As a formal definition of a forward contract, we present the following:

> *A forward contract is a derivative in which one party, the buyer or long, agrees to purchase an underlying asset from or make a fixed payment to a counterparty, the seller or short, at a future date, and that seller agrees to sell the underlying asset or make a variable payment to the buyer or long at the specified future date.*

A forward contract is, thus, a commitment on the part of two parties, one party to buy the underlying and the other to sell it, or as a slight variation, for one party to make a fixed payment and the other to make a variable payment. The latter alternative is the cash-settled version of the former.[1] In the former case, there is a specific underlying asset, such as a stock, bond, currency, or commodity that will be delivered from the short to the long. In the latter, there is just an exchange of cash payments in which at least one payment is fixed and the other is determined by an underlying factor. If these points seem confusing, they will be clearer when we get more specific in the next section.

8.1.2 *Basic Structure and Characteristics of Forward Contracts and Markets*

When the two parties agree to engage in a forward contract, one party takes the position of the buyer or long and the other assumes the role of the seller or short. In a physical delivery contract, the long agrees that at expiration, it will accept delivery of the underlying asset from the short and pay the short a fixed price established when the contract is written. In a cash settlement contract, the long agrees that at expiration it will pay the short a fixed price and accept a cash payment of the spot price of the underlying from the short.

---

[1]Cash-settled forwards are sometimes called *contracts for differences* and *non-deliverable forwards*.

Forward contracts are customized agreements created in the over-the-counter market between dealers and end users. At this time, they are not generally subject to clearing and settlement in the way that swaps have become under recent new regulations, though eventually clearing and settlement are likely to become a routine part of the forward market.

In Chapter 4 we described the basic structure of a forward contract. We specified that the contract is initiated on day 0 and expires at a future time T, which is the number of years from day 0. The price the two parties agree on at the start of the contract is called the *forward price*, and we denoted it as $F(0, T)$. We specified that the spot price when the contract is initiated is S_0, and when the contract expires, the spot price is S_T. We explained that at expiration, the buyer receives a payoff equivalent to $S_T - F(0, T)$. With a delivery contract, this payoff arises from the fact that at expiration, the long pays the short $F(0, T)$ and receives from the short the underlying asset, which is worth S_T. With a cash settled contract, the short simply pays the long the cash amount of $S_T - F(0, T)$. Thus, the payoff to the long is $S_T - F(0, T)$, and the payoff to the short is $-(S_T - F(0, T))$, regardless of whether it is a delivery or cash settlement contract. Note that this payoff can be positive or negative. Also, note that the payoff to the long is the mirror image of the payoff to the long. From this point forward, we will treat forward contracts as physical delivery contracts unless otherwise specified. As can be seen in Chapter 4, the payoffs are linear. You may wish to re-examine the graphics of those payoffs, Exhibits 4-17 and 4-18.

Recall that in Chapter 5, we discussed the size of the OTC derivatives market as represented by the data collected by the Bank for International Settlements (BIS). We noted that at the end of 2017, the total notional was about \$531 trillion, and the total market value was \$11 trillion. At that time, interest rate forwards had notional of about \$68 trillion and a market value of about \$112 billion. Currency forwards had notional of about \$51 trillion and about \$1.1 trillion of market value.[2] In addition, there are equity and commodity forwards, but the BIS reports the sum total of both equity forwards and swaps, \$3.2 trillion notional and \$197 billion market value, and

---

[2]The currency figures are slightly distorted by the inclusion of a special type of trade called a forex swap. We will cover currency swaps in the next chapter, but they are not the same as a forex swap, which is a transaction to go long a currency forward with one expiration and short an otherwise identical currency forward with another expiration. In the futures markets, these types of analogous types of transactions are called spreads. Whenever the BIS began collecting this type of data, it chose to include forex swaps with forwards. Hence, for consistency it continues to do so.

both commodity forwards and swaps, \$1.3 trillion notional with market value not reported. Based on notional, interest rate forwards make up about 16% of the OTC interest rate derivatives market, with the lion's share being interest rate swaps, about 75%, and the rest being options. Currency forwards (and forex swaps) make up about 58% of the OTC currency derivatives market, with the rest split between swaps and options.

We now move into the valuation and pricing of forward contracts.

8.1.3 *A General Framework for Valuation and Pricing*

Forward contracts are simply agreements between two parties to do a transaction at a future date. They require no upfront payment from one party to the other. Thus, a forward contract is not a security. In fact, it is not even an asset. If you buy an asset from someone, you pay them money and you acquire something of value. In accounting terms, it goes on your balance sheet holdings as an asset. You own it in the same way that you own a car, a book, a watch, or a share of stock. In contrast, when a forward contract is created, you do not pay anything for it: you simply agree to buy the underlying later at the price you agree on, $F(0, T)$. This point establishes the first principle of forward contract valuation:

The value of a forward contract at the time it is created is zero.

We denote this statement in the following manner:

$$V_0(F(0, T)) = 0. \tag{8.1}$$

This statement specifies that the value of a forward contract at time 0 (the 0 subscript) when the forward price is $F(0, T)$ is zero.

We previously stated that at expiration the forward contract pays off the spot price minus the forward price. Thus, we say that the contract value at expiration is

$$V_T(F(0, T)) = S_T - F(0, T). \tag{8.2}$$

Later we will learn how to determine the value of a forward contract during its life.

Now what we need to do is to *price* the forward contract, meaning to determine the price $F(0, T)$ to which the two parties agree. The underlying foundation of forward pricing, indeed all derivative pricing, is the principle of *arbitrage*. Recall that this principle means that two identical assets must have the same price, a point called, rather obviously, the law of one price.

To apply that principle here, we will replicate a forward contract using other assets. This type of transaction is called a *replicating strategy*. We will then ensure that the replicating strategy also has zero value at the start. From there we shall be able to derive the forward price.

If you have studied finance in any previous course, you may have virtually equated the concept of *price* with that of *value*. The distinction typically arises in security analysis, where an analyst may conclude that based on expectations of future cash flows, growth rates, a price-earnings ratio, and a risk-adjusted discount rate, a stock has a value of say, $40. The price at which the stock trades, however, could differ from its value. If the stock is selling at more than $40, an analyst would recommend selling the stock. If it is selling for less than $40, an analyst would recommend buying the stock. So, there is a differential between price and value when a security is deemed to be mispriced. Nonetheless, price and value are on the same order of magnitude in that the price will not likely stray too far from its value. With forward contracts, however, price and value are two concepts that are on entirely different orders of magnitude, as we will see in the next section.

8.1.3.1 *Pricing a Forward Contract*

Let us start with an example of an asset worth S_0 that makes a cash payment to its holder of cf_t at a point in time t years from now. This asset could be a bond that makes an interest payment or a stock that makes a dividend payment of cf_t. For any asset that does not make any such payment, we can still use the concept of cf_t, but we just assume its value is zero. Let there be a forward contract on this asset with a price of $F(0, T)$. Recall that we know that the forward contract will pay the long $S_T - F(0, T)$ at time T. Now let us see how we could replicate the payoff of the forward contract by using the asset.

To create the replicating strategy, we need only introduce one more asset, a risk-free bond that pays interest at the rate r. Consider the following strategy:

Buy the asset, paying the spot price of S_0.

Borrow the present value of $F(0, T)$, which is $F(0, T)/(1 + r)^T$. This loan will require that you repay $F(0, T)$ in T years. Refer to this as your first loan.

Borrow the present value of cf_t, which is $cf_t/(1 + r)^t$. This loan is set up for you to pay it back in t years. Refer to this as your second loan.

Now, recall that the asset makes a payment, like a dividend, cf_t to its owner in t years. When you receive this amount, remember that your loan is due and requires a payment of cf_t. So, use this money to pay off your loan. Now look at what happens T years later.

You own the asset worth S_T
You pay back the first loan, thereby having a cash flow $-F(0, T)$

Thus, at time T, you have an asset worth S_T and pay out cash worth $F(0, T)$. The total value of your position is, thus, $S_T - F(0, T)$, which is precisely the payoff of the forward contract. Thus, this strategy replicates the forward contract. Therefore, the value of the replicating strategy at time 0 must equal the value of the forward contract at time 0. The value of the replicating strategy at time 0 is

S_0, representing the asset you have purchased
$-F(0, T)/(1 + r)^T$, representing the first loan you took, the minus sign indicating a liability
$-cf_t/(1 + r)^t$, representing the second loan you took out, the minus sign indicating a liability.

Thus, the overall value of your position at time 0 is

$$S_0 - F(0, T)/(1 + r)^T - cf_t/(1 + r)^t.$$

As noted, this value must be zero, because this strategy replicates the payoff of the forward contract, which has a value of zero at time 0, and there is no cash taken in or paid out at time 0. So, we set this equation to zero and solve for $F(0, T)$.

$$F(0, T) = \left(S_0 - cf_t/(1 + r)^t\right)(1 + r)^T. \tag{8.3}$$

And we see that the forward price is the value compounded to expiration of the difference between the spot price and the present value of the cash payment. This formula gives the price on which the two parties would agree. It can be referred to as the equilibrium price or the fair price. Most importantly, it is the arbitrage-free price, a point that we need to make perfectly clear.

We will show why there is no other admissible price, but first let us take apart the formula and consider the intuition. Again, looking at Equation (8.3), let us take the case in which there is no interim cash flow.

Thus, let $cf_t = 0$. Then the formula obviously reduces to

$$F(0,T) = S_0(1+r)^T. \tag{8.4}$$

Here we see that the forward price is the spot price compounded to expiration at the risk-free rate. There is a simple intuitive explanation of this equation. If you go long a forward contract, at time T you will end up paying $F(0,T)$ and receiving the asset, which will be worth S_T. If instead, at time 0 you buy the asset, you will pay S_0 at the start and end up owning the asset worth S_T. In both cases, you end up owning the asset. In the former case, you expended no money at time 0 but you paid $F(0,T)$ at time T. In the latter case, you expended S_0 at time 0 and no money later. Since you end up in the same position with either strategy, what you pay to get there needs to be equal. Hence, S_0 must equal the present value of $F(0,T)$, or alternatively, $F(0,T)$ must be the compound future value of S_0.

Another interpretation of this equation is that when going long the forward contract, you avoid the opportunity cost of having the spot price, S_0, tied up for the period to time T. Hence, the forward price must reflect that benefit and it does this by equaling the spot price compounded at the risk-free rate. In essence, to go long in the forward market you have to agree to pay a little more for the right to keep your money longer.

Of course, these examples were explained for the case of $cf_t = 0$. What about when that is not true? Now, the strategies of going long the forward contract or long the asset are not the same. When you go long the asset, you receive any cash payments it makes, and you get a chance to reinvest that cash. As such, the effective price paid at expiration using the forward contract, $F(0,T)$ must be reduced by the compound value of the cash payment. In essence, by going long the forward contract you do not receive any of the cash payments the asset would make. Thus, the price you agree to pay at expiration is discounted to reflect that fact. So, you will really pay $F(0,T) - cf_t(1+r)^{T-t}$. When discounted back to the present, this amount must equal S_0. Setting these values equal and solving for $F(0,T)$ gives the full formula, including the effect of cf_t, as shown above in Equation (8.3).

8.1.3.2 *Numerical Example of Pricing a Forward Contract*

Now, let us look at a simple example. Consider a stock priced at $100 that pays a dividend of $2 in nine months. The risk-free rate is 5%. We wish to price a one-year forward contract. This scenario is shown in Exhibit 8-1.

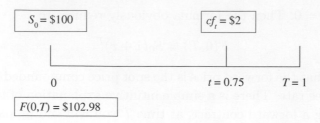

Exhibit 8-1. One-Year Forward Contract with Asset at 100 and Cash Payment of 2 in 0.75 Years

The forward price of the contract is

$$F(0, 1) = (\$100 - \$2/(1.05)^{0.75})(1.05)^1 = \$102.98.$$

Observe that we discount the spot price by the present value of the cash payment and then compound this result to expiration for one year at (the risk-free rate. Alternatively, we could have compounded the cash payment to expiration for three months and subtracted from the compounded value of the spot price, that is,

$$F(0, 1) = \$100(1.05)^1 - \$2(1.05)^{0.25} = \$102.98.$$

Clearly these types of calculation are easy, indeed some of the easiest of all financial calculations.

8.1.3.3 *Why the Formula Price Must be the Only Fair Price*

Now let us think about why any other price that the two parties would agree on could not be correct. We have just established that the buyer agrees at the start of the contract to pay $102.98 at the expiration, and the seller should agree to accept that amount. What if they agree on a different price, say $104? This price is obviously too high. Intuition should tell you that the buyer has agreed to pay too much, and the seller has been fortunate enough to commit to delivering the underlying and receiving more than the fair price. Since we said that the formula price, here $102.98, is the arbitrage-free price, a price of $104 must admit an arbitrage opportunity. And since the buyer agreed to pay too much, the seller should be able to take advantage of the buyer. Indeed he can, so let us see how that happens.

First, we need to think about what the seller should do. If a price is too high, one should sell it. If it is too low, one should buy it. Here the price is too high, so the seller — or any other person willing to do the arbitrage — will sell it. Of course, selling this forward contract by itself will not be an arbitrage transaction. Arbitrage transactions are supposed to have no risk.

Selling a forward contract by itself is not at all risk-free. In fact, it has quite a bit of risk. An arbitrageur will eliminate this risk, however, by buying the underlying asset. Moreover, he will use borrowed funds to do so, and thereby avoid having to put up any capital of his own.

So in this case, let the arbitrageur sell the forward contract at $104 and borrow $100 at the risk-free rate of 5%. He will use the funds to buy the asset. The loan will obligate him to pay back $105 in one year. In nine months, he will collect the cash payment of $2 and will reinvest it at 5% for three months, which means it will grow to a value of $2.02 ($2(1.05)^{0.25}$). Now look at what the arbitrageur does at expiration:

Deliver the asset in fulfillment of the forward contract and receive $104
Withdraw the reinvested value of the cash payment of $2.02
Pay off the loan value of $105

The net of these cash flows is $104 + $2.02 − $105 = $1.02. Notice that $1.02 happens to be the difference between the fair forward price ($102.98) and the actual forward price of this contract ($104). So the arbitrageur collects a profit of $1.02, without putting up any of his own money and without assuming any risk. Notice that we never had to determine the spot price at expiration, which is the source of risk. It did not matter to the arbitrageur. He owns the asset and is obligated to deliver it and accept $104 regardless of where the spot price is. The combined actions of arbitrageurs doing this transaction will push the forward price down from $104 until it hits the equilibrium price of $102.98, at which no further arbitrage is profitable.

Now consider what happens if the forward price is too low, say $102. Intuition suggests that if something is priced too low, it should be bought. So an arbitrageur would go long the forward contract, but of course, that would entail risk. So, the arbitrageur hedges it by going short the underlying asset.

Let us talk a bit about short selling. Securities can be borrowed and sold, with an obligation to buy the security back at a later date. Generally short selling is done in anticipation of buying the security back at a lower price. While a party is holding a short position in a security, that party must pay to the lender of the security any dividends if the security is a stock or any interest payments if the security is a bond. Paying these dividends is called *making restitution*.[3] Some assets, however, cannot be sold short or at least cannot be done so in a cost-effective manner. Borrowing commodities,

---

[3]The short seller must make restitution because the lender of the securities expects to receive any dividends or interest, but the security has been borrowed and sold to someone else, who also expects to receive any dividends or interest.

for example, can be very difficult, mainly because most commodities are very expensive to move around. If there is insufficient short-selling ability, the arbitrage process can be hampered, leading to the potential for forward prices to fall below their fair levels as given by the formula. In the absence of market participants who can sell short, however, there is another means of accomplishing the arbitrage. Parties who own the asset can simply sell it from their respective portfolios. Let us make the assumption that these parties step in the market and execute the arbitrage.

So, if the forward price is at $102, which is below the fair value of $102.98, an arbitrageur who owns the asset proceeds to sell it at the spot price of $100, and goes long the forward contract at $102. He then invests the $100 at the risk-free rate of 5% for one year. During the one-year life of this forward contract, the arbitrageur will forgo the cash payment of $2 in nine months. Adding three months' interest to that, the amount foregone as of the contract expiration is $2.02 $(=\$2(1.05)^{0.25})$. At expiration, the arbitrageur will be required to buy the asset at a price of $102. Thus, the asset will return to the arbitrageur's portfolio, where it would have been had he not done the arbitrage. But, had the arbitrageur kept the asset in his portfolio instead of selling it and getting it back through the forward contract, he would have $2.02 from collecting the cash payment and reinvesting it to pick up a little interest. But in addition, the arbitrageur will have $105 from having invested the spot price received from the sale of the asset at 5% for one year. Thus, he will have $105 and will have paid out $102, for a net of $3. Given that he gave up $2.02 in reinvested cash payments, he nets a risk-free gain of $0.98, which is precisely the amount by which the contract price was below the fair price. The combined actions of all arbitrageurs executing this strategy will push the forward price up from $102 to $102.98, at which point no further arbitrage profit is possible.

8.1.3.4 *Forward Contract Pricing with other Cash Flows and Costs*

In the development of the forward pricing model, we assumed that the underlying would make only one payment during the life of the forward contract. This assumption may not be true, particular if the contract is not very short term. Indeed, in the example we used, if the asset were a stock in U.S. markets, it would almost always make four dividend payments, not one, in a year. But no problem. The adjustment is easily accommodated. In the formula as derived above, we subtracted the present value of the cash payments from the spot price. Suppose there are n cash payments,

$cf_1, cf_2, \ldots, cf_T$ that occur at times $t = 1, 2, \ldots, T$, respectively. Let us denote their collective present value as simply

$$PVCF(0,T) = \sum_{t=1}^{T} cf_t/(1+r)^t. \tag{8.5}$$

Our forward price formula is now,[4]

$$F(0,T) = (S_0 - PVCF(0,T))(1+r)^T. \tag{8.6}$$

This formula reduces to the previous case when there is but one cash flow.

There is yet another type of cash flow that could occur on an asset. Securities like stocks and bonds make payments like dividends and interest. Some assets, however, are expensive to hold and incur costs while you own these. These costs are often called *storage costs*. Physical commodities have these storage costs. Let us denote the present value of the storage costs as $PVSC(0,T)$. The exact value of $PVSC(0,T)$ would be found by taking each cost, positioning it as it occurs over the period from time 0 to time T, and discounting each cost to time 0 at the risk-free rate. Note that the cash payments as described above that have present value of $PVCF(0,T)$ are the benefits of holding the asset, and they enter the pricing formula with a minus sign. The rationale for a minus sign was explained in Section 8.1.3.1, so you may wish to review it. Storage costs are the opposite of benefits: they are the costs of holding the asset. Thus, they will enter the formula with a positive sign. While we can express the cash flows on a present value basis, it is traditional to express the storage costs on a future value basis. Thus, we have $FVSC(0,T)$, which equals $PVSC(0,T)(1+r)^T$. Then the forward pricing formula is

$$F(0,T) = (S_0 - PVCF(0,T))(1+r)^T + FVSC(0,T). \tag{8.7}$$

And a well-known alternative and equivalent formula is

$$F(0,T) = S_0(1+r)^T + (FVSC(0,T) - FVCF(0,T)), \tag{8.8}$$

where we see that the present value of the cash flows inside the large parentheses in Equation (8.7) have been pulled out and compounded to their future value by the interest factor.

---

[4] We did not specifically prove this formula the way we did when we had one cash payment, but if you repeat that strategy with the only difference being to take out loans that correspond to the other cash payments in the way the first one did, you will get this result.

The combined effect of cash flows, storage costs, and the interest rate applied to the spot price encapsulates a concept called the *carry* and sometimes *cost of carry*. As noted in the above paragraph, there are costs to storing an asset. In addition, there is an indirect cost amounting to the interest lost on the funds tied up in the purchase of the asset. This interest is reflected in the application of the interest factor, $(1+r)^T$, to the spot price. In contrast to these costs is the direct benefit of holding an asset, meaning any cash flows paid by the asset, which are reflected in the term $PVCF(0,T)$. Notice, then that the forward price reflects the spot price plus any costs of holding the asset minus any benefits. The net of these costs and benefits is sometimes referred to as the *carry*. If that net carry is negative, then it is commonly referred to as the cost of carry, as it is effectively a cost. We say that it costs money to carry the asset.

Working from Equation (8.8), the expression $S_0(1+r)^T$ can be written as $S_0 + S_0((1+r)^T - 1)$. While that looks like a strange, albeit accurate, transformation, let us use it to rewrite Equation (8.8) as

$$F(0,T) = S_0 + \big(S_0(1+r)^T - 1\big) + FVSC(0,T) - FVCF(0,T). \qquad (8.9)$$

Now our formula for the forward price is a simple expression: the spot price plus the term in large parentheses. That term is the cost of carry, which reflects three components: the accumulated interest lost on the money tied up in the spot price, the accumulated storage costs, and the negative of the accumulated cash flows generated by the asset. Thus, in simple verbal terms: the forward price is the spot price plus the cost of carry. Looking at it that way, let us rewrite the pricing equation as

$$F(0,T) = S_0 + FVCC(0,T), \qquad (8.10)$$

where $FVCC(0,T)$ stands for the accumulated cost of carry from time 0 to time T and equals $(S_0(1+r)^T - 1) + FVSC(0,T) - FVCF(0,T)$. Again, it is the future value of the interest foregone, the cost of storage, subtracting out the cash flows.

8.1.3.5 *A Note on Backwardation and Contango*

At this point, we need to take a brief timeout and discuss some common terminology used in pricing forwards and futures. When the forward (or futures) price exceeds the spot price, the market is said to be in *contango*.

When the forward price is less than the spot price, the market is said to be in *backwardation*, and occasionally the word *inverted* is used to describe such a market. A contango market will arise when the costs of holding the asset exceed the benefits, and a backwardation or inverted market occurs when the benefits exceed the costs. Notice that in Equation (8.10), the forward price will exceed the spot price if $FVCC(0, T)$ is positive, in which case we call this a contango market. If $FVCC(0, T)$ is negative, we call it a backwardation market. Recalling that $FVCC(0, T)$ is the interest lost on the money tied up in the spot price plus the storage costs net of cash flows, $FVCC(0, T)$ can be negative if the cash flows exceed the interest and storage costs. While the terms backwardation and contango are not particularly important in understanding these markets, they are so widely used that so you should become familiar with them.

In addition, the terms *normal contango* and *normal backwardation* are also commonly used to describe certain market conditions. A *normal contango* market is one in which the forward or futures price exceeds the expected spot price, while a *normal backwardation* market is one in which the forward or futures price is less than the expected spot price. To examine which situation arises under what condition, let us recall that by definition the spot price of an asset is found by taking the expected future spot price and discounting it by a rate that is the sum of the risk premium and the risk-free rate. It must also be the case that the spot price will reflect storage costs and cash flows received, because owning an asset can incur costs and can realize cash benefits, such as dividends. Letting $FVRP(0, T)$ be the future value of the risk premium, we can see that

$$S_0 = \frac{E_0(S_T) - FVRP(0, T)}{(1 + r)^T} + PVCF(0, T) - PVSC(0, T),$$

which can be rewritten as

$$S_0(1 + r)^T = E_0(S_T) - FVRP(0, T) + (1 + r)^T \left(PVCF(0, T) - PVSC(0, T)\right)$$
$$= E_0(S_T) - FVRP(0, T) + FVCF(0, T) - FVSC(0, T).$$

Here the spot price is expressed completely in terms of future values of the terms on the right-hand side. Now let us re-state Equation (8.8) as

$$S_0(1 + r)^T = F(0, T) + FVCF(0, T) - FVSC(0, T).$$

Comparing this equation and the one above it, we see that they both have the same term on the left-hand side, so the right-hand sides must be equal. Thus,

$$F(0,T) = E_0(S_T) - FVRP(0,T). \qquad (8.11)$$

Thus, the forward price is not, in and of itself, an estimate of the expected future spot price. It is certainly influenced by the expected future spot price, but it does not equal the expected future spot price. If you used the forward price as an estimate of the expected future spot price, you would be biased on the low side by the amount of the risk premium. Thus, the forward price would seem to imply the condition of normal backwardation. This conclusion begs the obvious question of how normal contango could occur.

A market in which holders of the asset demand a risk premium is typically considered to be a market of normal backwardation. Holders of assets expect to earn a risk premium. That point certainly makes sense. When they hedge, however, they go short the forward contract and thereby transfer the risk to holders of long positions in the forward contracts. To get derivative market investors to be willing to go long forward contracts, the forward price must be discounted. In effect, the forward price is lower by the risk premium. The risk premium is, thus, transferred from the spot market to the derivatives market.

Normal contango would be one in which the risk premium is reversed. Such a conclusion seems to make no sense. After all, Equation (8.11) seems correct. Risk premiums are positive so how could the forward price exceed the expected future spot price? But there is yet one additional benefit of holding the asset, a concept called the *convenience yield*. It is a somewhat difficult and murky notion. It will play a role in forward market pricing, but it is more commonly discussed in the context of futures markets. We will take up this concept in Section 8.2.2.5. It will explain how normal contango can occur. You probably cannot wait, but you really need to.

8.1.3.6 *Valuation of Forward Contracts*

In the previous section we showed how to price a forward contract, which means how to determine the fixed price to which the two parties would agree on at the start of the contract. As demonstrated, this price would eliminate any possibility of one party engaging in an arbitrage against the other. We previously stated that the value of a forward contract at the start is zero, Equation (8.1), and that the value of the forward contract at expiration is the difference in the spot price at expiration and the forward price, Equation (8.2). Now we will determine the value of the contract during its life, that is, between 0 and T.

Determining the value of a forward contract during its life is important for three reasons. First, it is simply important that a party that holds a long or short position in the forward contract knows whether the contract is making money or losing money. The contract started with a value of zero. You can think of this condition as like being at the water's level. Now, later during the life of the contract, you want to know whether you are above water or below water. The only way to know if you are above water or below water is to determine the value of the forward contract. A second reason is that accounting rules require that the forward contract be assigned a value and placed on the balance sheet. When the contract is initiated, it has no value; thus, it is not an asset or a liability. But when its value becomes something other than zero it becomes an asset if its value is positive or a liability if its value is negative. We will take up derivatives accounting in Chapter 15 and see this point in more detail. A third reason is that one of the parties may wish to terminate the contract early. We will discuss this point in Section 8.1.6.

The value of anything is what it is worth to the owner. That is, it represents the cash that could be recovered if this "thing" is sold. Consider a forward contract as in the example above that enables you to buy an asset for $102.98 in one year when the current value of the asset is $100. We showed that a forward price of $102.98 is an arbitrage-free price under the current conditions. What if immediately after entering into the contract, the spot price rose sharply, say to $104? It should be apparent that a contract to buy the asset at $102.98 with the asset currently at $104 is worth more than its starting value of zero. While the asset may fall in value before expiration, there is a simple method by which the holder of the forward contract can lock in the value. He can sell a new forward contract to deliver the asset at the same date as on the original contract. Let us see how this process works.

The original forward contract has a price of $F(0, T)$, which was agreed upon at time 0. Let us remind ourselves of the formula for the forward price. As we showed in Section 8.1.3.5, the formula that accounts for cash flows and storage costs is Equation (8.7), repeated here:

$$F(0, T) = (S_0 - PVCF(0, T))(1 + r)^T + FVSC(0, T).$$

Now let us position ourselves at an arbitrary time t^*, which is between 0 and T. Since T is the number of years of the contract's life, t^* can also be thought of as the number of years that has elapsed since the contract was initiated. Thus, $T - t^*$ is the number of years of life remaining.[5] A new forward contract for delivery of the asset at time T would have the price $F(t^*, T)$ as shown below:

$$F(t^*, T) = (S_{t^*} - PVCF(t^*, T))(1 + r)^{T - t^*} + FVSC(t^*, T). \qquad (8.12)$$

This is just the same formula we previously developed for pricing a forward contract, Equation (8.7), but now positioned at time t^*. In other words, the zero has been replaced by t^*.[6] If the holder of the original long forward contract enters into a new forward contract to deliver the asset at T, he will lock in the difference in the two forward prices, $F(t^*, T) - F(0, T)$. That is, after entering into the second contract, he is contractually obligated to buy the asset at T at the price $F(0, T)$ from the first contract and contractually obligated to sell the asset at T at the price $F(t^*, T)$ from the second contract. Thus, he will net the amount $F(t^*, T) - F(0, T)$ at T. When he adds the new forward contract to his holdings, the overall value of his position is the sum of the value of his long position (the first forward contract) minus the value of the short position (the second forward contract). But the value of the newly initiated second forward contract is zero. (Remember that the value of any forward contract when initiated is zero.) Therefore, the value of the original forward contract at this interim time t^* is the present value of $F(t^*, T) - F(0, T)$:

$$V_{t^*}(F(0, T)) = (F(t^*, T) - F(0, T))/(1 + r)^{T - t^*}. \qquad (8.13)$$

The above statement is read as "The value at time t^* of a forward contract initiated at time 0 and expiring at time T is the present value from the expiration time T to the current time t^* of the difference in the price of a newly initiated forward contract and the price of the original forward contract."

8.1.3.7 *Forward Contract Valuation Example*

Now let us take the example we previously used and determine the value of the contract at a point during its life. Recall that this contract was initiated at time 0 when the asset was at \$100. The contract would expire in one

---

[5] Just a reminder, when we say "years" we can mean a fraction of a year. Something that happens in six months is 0.5 years from now.

[6] You might notice that the exponent on the $(1 + r)$ term is $T - t^*$ whereas previously it was T. Technically, it was previously $T - t^*$ and t^* was simply zero.

year. The risk-free rate was 5%. The asset would make a cash payment to its owner of $2 in nine months. The present value of this cash flow is

$$PVCF(0,1) = \$2/(1.05)^{0.75} = \$1.93.$$

The original forward price is, therefore,

$$F(0,1) = (\$100 - \$1.93)(1.05)^1 = \$102.98.$$

Of course, this is the result we previously obtained. Now let us move forward three months and assume that the asset is selling for $98. What is the value of the original forward contract, $V_{0.25}(0,1)$? So, now we have $S_{t^*} = \$98$ and $t^* = 0.25$. We need to price a brand new forward contract that has the same delivery date as the original contract. This contract would, therefore, expire in nine months, and the $2 cash payment would occur in six months. Thus, $T - t^* = 1 - 0.25 = 0.75$ and $t - t^* = 0.75 - 0.25 = 0.5$. The present value of the cash flow is

$$PVCF(0.25,1) = \$2/(1.05)^{0.5} = \$1.95.$$

The price of a new forward contract would, therefore, be

$$F(0.25,1) = (\$98 - \$1.95)(1.05)^{0.75} = \$99.63.$$

Exhibit 8-2 shows the setting. We wish to value the original forward contract at time $t^* = 0.25$.

And the value of the original forward contract would be

$$V_{0.25}(0,1) = (\$99.63 - \$102.98)/(1.05)^{0.75} = -\$3.23.$$

So this contract has gone from an initial value of zero to a negative value of $3.23. In essence, it has gone underwater. These computations are done, as they traditionally are, from the perspective of the long, but they could be

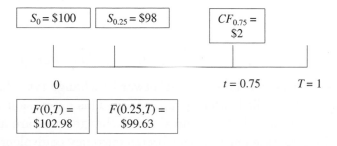

Exhibit 8-2. Valuation of a Forward Contract during its Life

done from the perspective of the short. It should be apparent to the short that the contract value has gone from $0 to a positive $3.23.

The framework used here is relatively general. In the next two major sections, we will apply this framework to the pricing and valuation of currency and interest rate forwards.

8.1.4   *Valuation and Pricing of Currency Forwards*

In July of 1944, representatives of 44 allied nations held a three-week meeting at a hotel in Bretton Woods, New Hampshire and decided how the international monetary system would be reconstructed in light of the impeding defeat of the Axis powers. Guided to a great degree by the celebrated British economist John Maynard Keynes, the countries decided to fix their exchange rates in relation to each other and in relation to the price of gold. Gold was, thus, viewed as the single unifying currency. The dollar was pegged at 35 to an ounce of gold. Ultimately the Bretton Woods system failed, as does virtually any system that attempts to control prices in capitalistic and free market economies. In 1971 U.S. President Richard Nixon suspended the convertibility of dollars to gold. The major currencies began to trade freely against each other and by 1973, the Bretton Woods system was more or less an historical artifact.

With fluctuating exchange rates now the norm, forward and futures contracts on currencies began trading. As mentioned in Section 8.1.2, forward contracts are the most common form of OTC currency derivative, accounting for about half of OTC currency derivatives.

As we saw in Section 8.1.3, a forward price is determined by taking the spot price, subtracting the present value of all future cash payments the asset will make during the life of the contract, compounding that difference at the risk-free rate for the life of the contract, and subtracting the future value of any storage costs that would be incurred in holding the asset over the life of the contract. Currency forwards are priced in the same manner, but the formula looks deceptively different.

8.1.4.1   *Pricing Currency Forwards with Interest Rate Parity*

The relationship between the spot and forward exchange rates has acquired a specific name. It is called *interest-rate parity*. This expression means that after taking into account interest rates, the exchange rates are at parity, or equivalence. Interest rate parity is the foreign currency equivalent of the cost of carry model. Let us see how interest rate parity is obtained.

A currency forward contract calls for the delivery of a foreign currency at the expiration date. A currency can be held just like any other asset, but you should not think of holding a currency as though you might obtain some foreign currency cash for a trip. In the world of international finance, foreign currency is held in the form of bank deposits that pay interest in the foreign currency at whatever risk-free rate prevails in that country. We have been using r as a symbol for the risk-free rate. Now we need to make a distinction between the domestic and foreign risk-free rates. Let r_d be the domestic rate and r_f be the foreign rate.

Now let us consider the following transactions:

(1) Borrow S_0 units of your domestic currency at the rate r_d.
(2) Purchase one unit of the foreign currency.
(3) Sell a forward contract to deliver $1(1+r_f)^T$ units of the foreign currency at time T at the rate $F(0, T)$.
(4) Hold the currency for the period from 0 to T, accruing interest at the rate r_f.
(5) At time T, you will have $1(1+r_f)^T$ units of the foreign currency.
(6) Deliver the $1(1+r_f)^T$ units of currency in fulfillment of your obligation on your short forward contract and receive $(1+r_f)^T F(0, T)$.
(7) Pay back the amount due on your loan of $S_0(1+r_d)^T$.

You invested no funds, incurred no risk, and ended up with a cash flow of $(1+r_f)^T F(0, T) - S_0(1+r_d)^T$. The first expression, $(1+r_f)^T F(0, T)$, is the funds received from delivering $(1+r_f)^T$ units of the asset and receiving the forward price of $F(0, T)$. The second expression, $-S_0(1+r_d)^T$, is the interest and principal payback from borrowing S_0. Since you invested no money and took no risk, you must ultimately receive no money. Thus, this cash flow at T must equal zero. Under these conditions, the payoff has to be zero. Setting it to zero and solving for the forward rate gives[7]

$$F(0, T) = S_0 \left(\frac{(1+r_d)^T}{(1+r_f)^T} \right). \tag{8.14}$$

In words, the forward rate is the spot rate compounded to expiration by the domestic risk-free rate and discounted to expiration by the foreign risk-free rate. This formula is called *interest rate parity*. It essentially says that after

---

[7]In the world of foreign currency, the price of a currency is called its exchange rate. Hence, we more commonly use the terms spot rate and forward rate over spot price and forward price.

adjusting for the interest rates in the two countries, the forward and spot rates are equal.

If the actual forward rate were higher than the rate in Equation (8.14), there would be an opportunity to make an arbitrage profit. A rate too high would suggest that the arbitrageur would sell the forward contract and buy the currency, while a rate too low would mean that the arbitrageur would buy the forward contract and sell the currency. The relative amounts bought and sold would have to be consistent with the risk-free rates and reflect the accumulation of interest at the domestic or foreign rate.[8] Transactions to capture arbitrage profits in currencies are called *interest arbitrage* and sometimes *covered interest arbitrage*.

Taking Your Money Elsewhere for a Better Rate

Interest rates in various countries are never equivalent, and in some cases the differences can be quite large. As I write this book, U.S. short-term interest rates are around 2%. Let us assume 2.5% on a bank CD. In Argentina, the rate is about 23%. U.S. investors might be tempted to put their money into Argentine savings accounts. Let us see what could happen.

At this time, the exchange rate is about 28 Argentine pesos per U.S. dollar. Let us say you have a $10,000 deposit in a U.S. bank. Dissatisfied with the 2.5% rate you are getting, you convert it to ARS280,000 (280,000 Argentine pesos) and are happy with the promised rate of 23% on a CD at a leading Argentine bank. Argentina is a country with great wine, incredible beef, fabulous scenery in Patagonia and elsewhere, a rich and colorful history of rancheros and gauchos, you loved *Evita*, and the tango is your favorite dance. An occasional trip to Buenos Aires to check on your money would be well worth it. What could possibly go wrong?

Well, Argentina has about a 26% inflation rate and considerable economic instability. When you take your money out, the exchange rate could fall quite a bit lower, meaning that while you held Argentine pesos, their value could be dropping, and you would then get fewer dollars. Had you left your $10,000 in your U.S. bank, it would be worth $10,000(1.025) = $10,250 in one year. Your Argentine peso CD of

---

[8]In other words, if you buy or sell one unit of the currency, the accrual of interest will make that unit grow to $(1 + r_f)^T$ so this amount would be set as the notional of the forward contract. If you arrange the forward contract to have a notional of 1, then you would need to start by buying $1/(1 + r_f)^T$ units of the currency so it would grow to one unit.

ARP280,000 would grow to a value of 280,000(1.23) = ARP344,400. But if the exchange rate is above 344,400/10,250 = 33.60, meaning that you now have to tender more than 33.60 pesos to get a dollar, your money will be worth less than $10,250 when converted back to the dollar. In short, there is considerable risk. You are long that currency in the hope that the exchange rate does not damage your position too much, while you collect that 23% interest.

Of course, you could hedge the conversion of the peso to U.S. dollars by selling a forward contract. Using the formula in the book, the forward rate would be 28(1.23)/(1.0250) = 33.60. In other words, you could lock in the conversion back to the dollar at 33.60 pesos per dollar. And when you do, your 344,400 pesos will be worth 344,400/33.60 = 10,250 (subject to some rounding). In other words, you get only a 2.5% return on your money.

So if you eliminate the currency risk, you net only your local risk-free rate. If you bear the currency risk, anything is possible, including large gains but also including large losses.

So, don't try this. I do not want you to have to say, "Don't cry for me, Argentina."

Alternatively, we can look at the formula in the following manner:

$$F(0,T) = \left(S_0(1 + r_f)^{-T}\right)(1 + r_d)^T. \tag{8.15}$$

Here we see that the spot rate is discounted by the foreign risk-free rate, and then this adjusted spot rate is compounded at the domestic risk-free rate. This construction is consistent with what we have previously shown for the more general case: the spot price is reduced by the present value of any cash benefits paid and the difference is compounded at the risk-free rate.

If you work in the world of foreign currency markets, you may see further variations of this formula. Sometimes the formula is approximated as follows:

$$F(0,T) \approx S_0(1 + r_d - r_f)^T. \tag{8.16}$$

And when interest is paid using the add-on method as in the LIBOR markets, the formula becomes

$$F(0,T) = S_0\left(\frac{1 + r_d(h/360)}{1 + r_f(h/360)}\right), \tag{8.17}$$

where h is the number of days to expiration.

An important characteristic of foreign currency is that it is as easy to quote the first currency in terms of the second as it is to quote the second in terms of the first. For example, if the euro is trading at $1.10, one could also say that the dollar is trading at $1/\$1.10 = €0.909$. If the rate is expressed that way, the formula would be inverted. To now, we have assumed that the quote S_0 is the price in domestic currency of a unit of foreign currency. If we invert S_0, we obtain the quote in terms of the price of a unit of domestic currency in units of foreign currency. In that case, we invert the two interest rate factors and the resulting forward rate is in units of foreign currency per unit of domestic currency. Thus, re-writing our original formula with the exchange rate inverted, we obtain

$$\frac{1}{F(0,T)} = \left(\frac{1}{S_0}\right)\left(\frac{(1+r_f)^T}{(1+r_d)^T}\right). \tag{8.18}$$

Thus, the resulting forward rate is also expressed as units of foreign currency per unit of domestic currency.[9]

In all cases, we see that if the exchange rates are adjusted by the interest rates in the two countries, the forward and spot rates are the same, hence, the use of the word "parity." This point is best illustrated by writing the pricing equation in the following manner:

$$F(0,T)(1+r_f)^T = S_0(1+r_d)^T. \tag{8.19}$$

As we mentioned in Section 8.1.3.1, the difference between the forward price and the spot price has traditionally given rise to some confusion and outright mistakes regarding whether forward rates are equal to expected future spot rates. For currencies, an implication of this mistaken view is that if the forward rate exceeds the spot rate, the expected future spot rate is higher than the current spot rate. This statement is simply not true. Let us write the interest rate parity equation as follows:

$$\frac{F(0,T)}{S_0} = \left(\frac{1+r_d}{1+r_f}\right)^T. \tag{8.20}$$

It should be obvious that if the forward rate exceeds the spot rate, then the numerator of the right-hand side must exceed the denominator. There is

---

[9]It has become customary in the foreign currency markets to quote five currencies in terms of the dollar per unit of that currency: the euro, Canadian dollar, Australia dollar, New Zealand dollar, and British pound. All other currencies are traditionally quoted as units of the foreign currency per dollar. Nonetheless, any quote can be inverted.

only way in which the numerator on the right-hand side can exceed the denominator and that is if $r_d > r_f$. For all positive values of T, any other explanation is a mathematical impossibility.

When the forward rate exceeds the spot rate, it does give rise to the expression that the currency is selling at a forward premium, meaning that it is more expensive to lock in a future purchase of the currency than it is to buy the currency now. Likewise, when the forward rate is less than the spot rate, the currency is said to be selling at a forward discount, meaning that it is cheaper to lock in the future purchase of the currency than to buy it today.

8.1.4.2 *A Currency Forward Pricing Example*

Suppose the spot rate for British pounds is $1.52. Let us assume the U.K. risk-free interest rate is 3.5% and the U.S. interest rate is 2.75%. We will assume these rates are in compound interest form and not add-on (LIBOR) interest. Thus, we should use Equation (8.14). The forward rate for a six-month contract will be

$$F(0, 0.5) = \$1.52 \frac{(1.0275)^{0.5}}{(1.035)^{0.5}} = \$1.51.$$

Note that if we quoted the spot rate in terms of pounds per dollars, we would have $1/\$1.52 = £0.6579$. Then the forward rate would be

$$F(0, 0.5) = £0.6579 \frac{(1.035)^{0.5}}{(1.0275)^{0.5}} = £0.6603.$$

And finally, note that $1/£0.6603 - \$1.51$, the forward rate obtained using the indirect approach.

8.1.4.3 *Valuing Currency Forwards*

Using the same approach taken in the general case, we can value a currency forward during its life by determining the rate on a new contract that will call for delivery of the currency at the same time as the old contract and then finding the present value of the difference. Thus, positioning ourselves at time t^* where t is between 0 and T, we find the rate on a new forward contract.

$$F(t^*, T) = S_{t^*} \left(\frac{(1 + r_d)^{T - t^*}}{(1 + r_f)^{T - t^*}} \right). \tag{8.21}$$

And the discounted difference between this forward rate and the original forward rate provides the value of the original forward contract.

$$V_{t^*}(F(0,T)) = (F(t^*,T) - F(0,T))/(1 + r_d)^{T-t^*}. \qquad (8.22)$$

8.1.4.4 *Currency Forward Valuation Example*

Now let us place a value on our original forward contract presented in Section 8.1.4.2. Recall that in that example, we created a six-month forward contract on the British pound denominated in U.S. dollars. The spot rate was $1.50, the British interest rate was 3.5%, and the U.S. interest rate was 2.75%. We found that the forward rate was $1.51. Now let us move one month ahead and assume that the spot rate is $1.55. So, now $t^* = 1/12 = 0.083$ and $S_{t^*} = \$1.55$. The new forward rate on a contract that expires in five months is

$$F(0.083, 0.5) = \$1.55 \left(\frac{(1.0275)^{5/12}}{(1.035)^{5/12}} \right) = \$1.55.$$

And the value of the original forward contract is

$$V_{0.083}(0, 0.5) = (\$1.55 - \$1.51)/(1.0275)^{5/12} = \$0.0305.$$

In other words, the party that went long the original forward contract is obligated to accept delivery of the British pound in six months for which he will pay $1.51. Now one month later, the pound is at $1.55. The party can then sell a new forward contract obligating him to deliver the British pound in five months for which he will be paid $1.55. Thus, he has locked in a gain that discounted back to the presented is $0.0305. If the notional were £10 million, the total value of the contract would be £10,000,000($0.0305) = $304,809.[10]

8.1.5 *Valuation and Pricing and Pricing of Interest Rate Forwards*

Forward contracts in which the payoff is determined either directly or indirectly by interest rates can be designed in one of two ways. One is that the underlying can be a bond. In that case, the forward contract pays off based on the price of the bond, and pricing and valuation of the contract would be

---

[10]Again, we are rounding off these values, so they may not appear to be completely precise, but they are far more accurate than values calculated manually.

done as described above. The bond would make interest payments and would have no other cash flows or carrying costs. To find the forward price, the bond price would be reduced by the present value of the interest payments on the bond during the life of the forward contract and the remaining value would be compounded by the risk-free rate over the life of the contract. Since interest rates determine bond prices, this type of forward would be indirectly driven by interest rates. In practice, however, the forward market for bonds is not very large. There is a very active futures market for bonds, however, and we cover that topic in Section 8.2.

The other type of structure for a forward contract based on an interest rate is a cash-settled contract in which the payoff is based directly on the interest rate.[11] This type of contract is called a *forward rate agreement* or *FRA*. This contract is a good example of why we have to admit that not all derivatives are based on an underlying asset, with emphasis on the word "asset." An interest rate is not an asset, yet it is the underlying for an FRA, and as we will see in the next two chapters, it is the underlying for commonly used swaps and options. Thus, we have to refer to interest rate derivatives as being based on an underlying, not an underlying asset.

An FRA is quite simply just a cash-settled forward contract in which the underlying is an interest rate. The interest rate in an FRA can be any one of the thousands of interest rates, but typically it is LIBOR. As described in Chapter 4, LIBOR, which stands for London Interbank Offer Rate, is the rate on a dollar borrowed by one London Bank from another. LIBOR loans are available in all major currencies, but typically when you say "LIBOR," you mean "dollar LIBOR." A dollar LIBOR loan was originally, and still is, known as a Eurodollar. The Chicago Mercantile Exchange's futures contract on this rate is called the Eurodollar futures. There are, however, also euro LIBOR, yen LIBOR, sterling LIBOR, etc. that represent loans in other currencies. LIBOR is, however, unique to London (the "L" stands for "London," after all), which is the primary financial center of the world.

The interest in Eurodollar loans is based on the add-on method. Thus, for a \$1 loan, the interest will be $\$1L(h/360)$ where L is the rate and h is the number of days of the loan. So for a \$1 loan, the payoff h-days later is $\$1(1 + L(h/360))$.

---

[11]There are also futures contracts in which the payoff is based on an interest rate. We will cover these instruments in Section 8.2.

When an FRA is constructed, the two parties agree on the underlying rate and the expiration. For the underlying rate, there is multitude of LIBORs that could be used, each one differing by maturity of the underlying rate. For example, there are Eurodollar loans with maturities of one, two, three, four, and six months, etc. The rates that banks are offering to pay are widely disseminated on financial news and quote services and web sites.[12] Rates for other maturities can be obtained by inquiring directly with the banks.

So, let us use the letter "h" to represent the number of days in the Eurodollar loan for which the rate is the underlying in the FRA, and "T_m" to equal the number of days until the FRA expires. Thus, for example, if a party wanted an FRA expiring in 42 days on 90-day LIBOR, then $T_m = 42$ and $h = 90$. It will be extremely important to keep these numbers straight. Once the FRA is set up, h will not change. Until it expires, the FRA will always be on h-day LIBOR, but the expiration of the FRA will start off as T_m days. A day later the FRA will expire in $T_m - 1$ days, a day after that $T_m - 2$, etc. Exhibit 8-3 illustrates the basic time layout of an FRA.

Here we observe that the FRA expires in T_m days and the underlying Eurodollar matures h days later, which is $T_m + h$ days after time 0. We will need to keep the point $T_m + h$ in mind as it will play an important role in pricing the FRA. The reason is that an FRA is technically based on a forward rate. If you make a Eurodollar loan, as a lender, initiated at time 0 with a maturity of $T_m + h$, then T_m days later, your loan would have a maturity of h days. If you attempted to sell that loan to someone else, the rate you would get would be the rate on a new h-day loan on day T_m and that rate determines the payoff of the expiring FRA. In the example of the

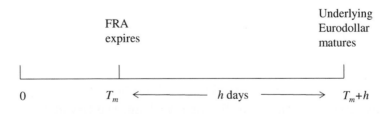

Exhibit 8-3. Time Layout of an FRA

[12]For example, the *Wall Street Journal* provides quotes on dollar, euro, pound, and yen LIBOR for various maturities up to one year at http://online.wsj.com/mdc/public/page/2_3020-libor.html.

42-day FRA that is based on 90-day LIBOR, $T_m + h$ is $42 + 90 = 132$. Thus, when the FRA expires in 42 days, the rate on a new 90-day LIBOR loan is the underlying rate that determines the payoff of the FRA.

FRA Terminology

The discussion of the terms of FRAs can get complicated. For example, a 42-day FRA in which the underlying is 90-day LIBOR effectively has an underlying of 132-day LIBOR. That is a lot of days and dates to keep track of. To keep this information clear, the FRA market has developed some simple terminology and notation.

Most FRAs are set up to expire in a certain number of months, and the underlying rate is identified by the number of months. So, for example, FRAs usually have maturities of Y months where $Y = 1, 2, 3, \ldots, 12$ months and the underlying rate is Z-month LIBOR where Z is $1, 2, 3, \ldots, 12$ months. The FRA is identified as a $Y \times (Y + Z)$ LIBOR. The "$\times$" is pronounced as "by." Here are some examples:

An FRA expiring in 1 month where the underlying is 3-month LIBOR is called a 1×4 FRA ("1 by 4")
An FRA expiring in 4 months where the underlying is 2-month LIBOR is a 4×6 FRA ("4 by 6")
An FRA expiring in 7 months where the underlying is 3-month LIBOR is a 7×10 FRA ("7 by 10")

8.1.5.1 *The Payoff of an FRA*

Now let us set up some notation for the relevant rates. The FRA is arranged at time 0. Let the rate agreed on at time 0 be denoted as $R(T_m, h)$. This rate is the fixed rate on the FRA, and it is interpreted as the rate on an FRA initiated on day 0 that expires in T_m days in which the underlying is h-day LIBOR. It is the unknown for which we will solve. At time 0, we can look in the market and observe the rate on T_m-day LIBOR loans, denoted as $L_0(T_m)$, and the rate on $T_m + h$-day LIBOR loans, denoted as $L_0(T_m + h)$. These two rates compose a small portion of the LIBOR term structure. When the FRA expires at time T_m, the rate on h-days loans can be observed and it is denoted as $L_{T_m}(h)$. Notice the notational pattern. The subscript denotes the point in time at which the rate is observed and the symbol in parentheses is the number of days of the loan. We do not subscript $R(T_m, h)$, because it does not change.

As with any forward contract, an FRA requires no up-front payment. Thus, its initial value is zero, which we state formally as

$$V_0(T_m, h) = 0.$$

Now let us specify the payoff of the FRA as the value on day T_m of the FRA established on day 0 and expiring on day T_m as $V_{T_m}(T_m, h)$. Thus, at time T_m, the FRA expires and the short pays the long the following amount per notional of one unit[13]:

$$V_{T_m}(T_m, h) = \frac{\left(L_{T_m}(h) - R(T_m, h)\right)\left(\frac{h}{360}\right)}{1 + L_{T_m}(h)\left(\frac{h}{360}\right)}. \qquad (8.23)$$

In the numerator, the first term, $L_{T_m}(h)$, is the underlying LIBOR at the FRA maturity. That number is the uncertainty in the FRA, and its value is revealed at day T_m. The second term, $R(T_m, h)$, is the fixed rate agreed on when the contract was initiated on day 0. It is the rate for which we are going to solve. The term $h/360$ is an adjustment factor reflecting the custom that the quotes are annual rates, so these annual rates must be adjusted for the relevant fraction of the year, $h/360$, of course using the customary 360-day year assumption. The denominator $1 + L_{T_m}(h)(h/360)$ is a discount factor. Dividing by this term converts the numerator to a present value. But why this discount factor is applied is not obvious. Let us explain.

The rate, $L_{T_m}(h)$, that determines the value of the FRA at expiration is a rate that is established between borrowing and lending banks in London on day T_m. These parties are not involved in the FRA in the same way in which an option on Apple Computer's common stock involves two parties neither of whom is Apple Computer Company. As explained earlier in this book, derivatives are created in markets external to the underlying market. The parties to the derivative simply observe the underlying market and extract the necessary prices and rates for use in their contracts. The parties to the LIBOR loan — the loan, not the FRA — created that rate on day T_m in London, and their agreement was that the rate would determine the interest due on the loan on day $T_m + h$. The parties to the FRA, however, use that rate

---

[13]In other words, the actual payoff would be this formula times the notional. The notional represents a specified number of units in the designated currency. An FRA pays off based on the difference between interest rates, with this difference applied to a notional in much the same way that a bond or loan makes interest payments based on the face value or loan amount.

on day T_m to determine the payoff on day T_m, not day $T_m + h$. Thus, in the case of the loan, the rate is applied and the interest at that rate is paid on day $T_m + h$. In the case of the FRA, the rate is applied and the payment based on that rate is made on day T_m. As such, it is entirely appropriate on the FRA to discount the payoff from day $T_m + h$ back to day T_m. The appropriate rate to use in discounting the payoff is h-day LIBOR on day T_m, $L_{T_m}(h)$. The process in which the rate is determined at the beginning of the settlement periods and the payment is made at the beginning of the settlement period is called *advance set, advance settle*. Shortly we will contrast this method with *advance set, settlement in arrears*, which is used for interest rate swaps and options.[14]

Consider the following example. Let us assume that an FRA is created with a maturity of six weeks. Six weeks is 42 days, so $T_m = 42$. The underlying is 90-day LIBOR, so $h = 90$. Thus, the payoff formula will be

$$V_{42}(42,90) = \frac{(L_{42}(90) - R(42,90))\left(\frac{90}{360}\right)}{1 + L_{42}(90)\left(\frac{90}{360}\right)}.$$

Let us assume that the notional is $50 million and that the rate the two parties agree on is 3.25%. We are working toward determining this rate given the information available in the market at the time the contract is created, but this will come in the next section. Now let us roll forward to day 42, at which time the FRA is expiring. We look into the LIBOR market and observe that 90-day LIBOR is at 3.5%. The payoff from the short to the long will be

$$V_{42}(42, 90) = \left(\frac{(0.035 - 0.0325)\left(\frac{90}{360}\right)}{1 + 0.035\left(\frac{90}{360}\right)}\right) \$50,000,000 = \$30,979.$$

It should be apparent that anyone taking a long position in an FRA is doing so because it wants to receive a positive payoff arising from an increase in interest rates increase such that the rate is above the contractual rate. Anyone taking a short position will receive a positive payoff if interest rates fall below the contractual rate.

---

[14]There is no clear reason why advance set, advance settle is used in the FRA market and advance set, settle in arrears is used in the interest rate swaps and options market. Your author has a hypothesis that the FRA market evolved out of the currency forward market, where settlement is done on the expiration day (advance set, advance settle), whereas the interest rate swaps and options market evolved somewhat separately and settled the same way in which the underlying LIBOR loans settle: advance set, settle in arrears.

8.1.5.2 *Pricing an FRA*

Now let us identify how the fixed rate is determined. It is entirely possible to value an FRA by engaging in a replicating portfolio of Eurodollar transactions, one with a maturity of m days and one with a maturity of T_{m+h} days. There is, however, a simpler way to do it. Note in Exhibit 8-4, we have the layout of the payoffs of an FRA to pay fixed and receive floating.

Breaking down the floating and fixed components, we have

$$\frac{L_{T_m}(h)\left(\frac{h}{360}\right)}{1 + L_{T_m}(h)\left(\frac{h}{360}\right)} \text{ (floating)}$$

$$-\left(\frac{R(T_m, h)\left(\frac{h}{360}\right)}{1 + L_{T_m}(h)\left(\frac{h}{360}\right)}\right) \text{ (fixed)}$$

If we wanted to know what these amounts were worth at time $T_m + h$, we would compound them from T_m to $T_m + h$ at the rate $L_{T_m}(h)$. So let us do that and then observe Exhibit 8-5, which illustrates the equivalent value payoffs moved forward to time $T_m + h$. Note, however, that we added a 1 and subtracted a 1. Thus, we have not changed the net payment, but we will help ourselves with this little trick.

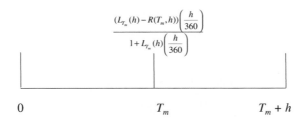

Exhibit 8-4. Payoffs of FRA to Pay Fixed and Receive Floating

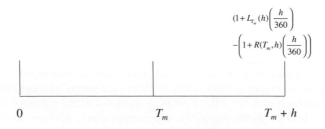

Exhibit 8-5. Payoffs of FRA to Pay Fixed and Receive Floating with Payment Compounded to Time $m + h$ with Added Notional

In other words, Exhibit 8-4 illustrates the determination and payment of the rate at the beginning of the settlement period, a process we referred to as advance set, advance settle. In Exhibit 8-5, we took the payment at time T_m and rolled it forward to time $T_m + h$, compounding by the appropriate interest factor. From the perspective of someone at time 0, both amounts are equivalent in value. For example, there is no difference in €100 one year from now and €102 two years from now if the interest rate is 2%.

Now, notice that the floating and fixed payoffs, expressed at time $T_m + h$, are

$$1 + L_{T_m}(h) \left(\frac{h}{360} \right) \quad \text{(floating)}$$

$$- \left(1 + R(T_m, h) \left(\frac{h}{360} \right) \right) \quad \text{(fixed)}.$$

Now, let us discount the floating payment value at $T_m + h$ back to time T_m. The appropriate rate for discounting over that period is $L_{T_m}(h)$. When we do the discounting, notice what we obtain:

$$\frac{1 + L_{T_m}(h) \left(\frac{h}{360} \right)}{1 + L_{T_m}(h) \left(\frac{h}{360} \right)} = 1.$$

So we know that the value at time T_m of the floating payment is 1. Then we simply discount the value 1 back from time T_m to time 0,

$$\frac{1}{1 + L_0(T_m) \left(\frac{T_m}{360} \right)} \tag{8.24}$$

The above equation is the value of the floating payment at time 0, with the addition of a hypothetical notional of 1 added at time $T_m + h$.

As we said above, the value of the fixed payment at time $T_m + h$ with hypothetical notional of 1 is $1 + R(T_m, h)(h/360)$. We then simply discount this value all the way back to time 0,

$$\frac{1 + R(T_m, h) \left(\frac{h}{360} \right)}{1 + L_0(T_m + h) \left(\frac{T_m + h}{360} \right)} \tag{8.25}$$

Because the FRA involves no net outlay or inflow of cash at time 0, the present value of the fixed payments, plus hypothetical notional of

1 at time $T_m + h$, must equal the present value of the floating payments, plus hypothetical notional of 1 at time $T_m + h$. Setting Equation (8.24) equal to Equation (8.25), we have

$$\frac{1 + R(T_m, h)\left(\frac{h}{360}\right)}{1 + L_0(T_m + h)\left(\frac{T_m + h}{360}\right)} = \frac{1}{1 + L_0(T_m)\left(\frac{T_m}{360}\right)}.$$

And solving the above for the fixed rate on the FRA gives

$$R(T_m, h) = \left(\frac{1 + L_0(T_m + h)\left(\frac{T_m + h}{360}\right)}{1 + L_0(T_m)\left(\frac{T_m}{360}\right)} - 1\right)\left(\frac{360}{h}\right) \qquad (8.26)$$

Equation (8.26) is, thus, the equation that determines the appropriate fixed rate on an FRA. Interestingly, it is a very simple equation and analogous to one commonly used in the bond market. The above equation produces what is commonly referred to as the *forward rate*.

The calculation of this rate is quite easy, as Exhibit 8-6 illustrates.

Thus, the two parties would agree on a fixed rate on the FRA of 3.25%. This rate is the only one that would eliminate any possibility of arbitrage.

Objective: Find the fixed rate on an FRA expire in 42 days in which the underlying is 90-day LIBOR and the term structure of LIBOR is as follows:

        42-day rate: 2.79%
        132-day rate: 3.11%

Inputs:

        $T_m = 42$
        $h = 90$
        $T_m + h = 42 + 90 = 132$
        $L_0(T_m) = 0.0279$
        $L_0(T_m + h) = 0.0311$

Results:

$$R(42, 90) = \left(\frac{1 + 0.0311\left(\frac{132}{360}\right)}{1 + 0.0279\left(\frac{42}{360}\right)} - 1\right)\left(\frac{360}{90}\right) = 0.0325.$$

Exhibit 8-6. FRA Pricing Example

Forward Rates in the Bond Market

In studying bond markets, it is customary to learn the concept of a forward rate. Suppose rates were quoted on a compounded basis. Thus, a rate such as 3% compounded annually on $1 invested for two years would produce a value of $1(1.03)^2 = 1.0609$.

If the term structure of zero coupon rates is 3% for two-year investments, and 3.5% for five-year investments, we might wish to determine the three-year forward rate two years hence. What we mean here is that if we entered into a forward transaction on a zero coupon bond that committed us to buying a three-year bond in two years at a rate locked in today, what is the rate we would lock in? It is widely taught in investment classes that the rate is found as

$$\sqrt[3]{\frac{(1.035)^5}{(1.03)^2}} - 1 = 0.0383.$$

This result arises from the fact that if we bought a two-year bond at the rate of 3% and entered into a forward contract that committed us to buying a three-year bond in two years, that bond would have a rate of 3.83%. After five years, an initial investment of $1 would grow to $1(1.03)^2(1.0383)^3 = \$1.1875$. Alternatively, if we bought a five-year bond at 3.5%, $1 would grow to 1.1875, subject to rounding. These strategies are equivalent, so 3.83% is the appropriate forward rate.

The only difference between this type of problem, which is commonly encountered in courses on investments or fixed income markets, and the FRA problem, is that the interest is computed on a compounding basis in the former and on an add-on basis in the latter.

8.1.5.3 *Valuation of an FRA*

Now we need to examine how to value the FRA at a point during its life. We wish to value the FRA at time t^*, which is after the initiation date, time 0, but before the expiration date, time T_m. On that day, the observable LIBORs are $L_{t^*}(T_m - t^*)$ and $L_{t^*}(T_m + h - t^*)$. Notice what this information represents. The rate $L_{t^*}(T_m - t^*)$ is LIBOR on day t^* for a loan of $T_m - t^*$ days, and the rate $L_{t^*}(T_m + h - t^*)$ is the rate observed on day t^* for a loan of $T_m + h - t^*$ days. The first referenced loan starts at the valuation date, t^*, and matures at the maturity of the FRA, T_m. The second referenced loan starts at the valuation date, t^*, and matures at the maturity date of the FRA underlying, $T_m + h - t^*$.

First we find the value on day t^* of the floating payment plus the hypothetical notional, which is just a slight variation of Equation (8.24),

$$\frac{1}{1 + L_{t^*}(T_m - t^*)\left(\frac{T_m - t^*}{360}\right)}. \tag{8.27}$$

Recall that the value at day T_m of the floating payment plus hypothetical notional is 1. The above equation simply discounts that value back to day t^*.

The value of the fixed payment is just a slight variation of Equation (8.25),

$$\frac{1 + R(T_m, h)\left(\frac{h}{360}\right)}{1 + L_{t^*}(T_m + h - t^*)\left(\frac{T_m + h - t^*}{360}\right)} \tag{8.28}$$

Here we are just discounting the day T_m value of the fixed payment plus hypothetical notional back to day t^*.

Now we can determine the value of a pay-fixed, receive-floating FRA on day t^* as Equation (8.27) minus Equation (8.28),

$$V_{t^*}(T_m, h) = \left(\frac{1}{1 + L_{t^*}(T_m - t^*)\left(\frac{T_m - t^*}{360}\right)}\right)$$
$$-\left(\frac{1 + R(T_m, h)\left(\frac{h}{360}\right)}{1 + L_{t^*}(T_m + h - t^*)\left(\frac{T_m + h - t^*}{360}\right)}\right) \tag{8.29}$$

Note that if we were at expiration, t^* would equal T_m and Equation (8.29) would be equivalent to the payoff value, Equation (8.23). In addition, if we were at time 0, just set t^* to 0, substitute Equation (8.26) for $R(T_m, h)$ and you would obtain a value of zero, just as you should.

Now let us continue the problem we worked in Exhibit 8-6 and find its value 18 days later. The result is in Exhibit 8-7.

8.1.6 *Terminating Forward Contracts*

In Sections 8.1.3.5, 8.1.4.3, and 8.1.5.3, we discussed how to value a forward contract. Recall that the value at initiation is zero, and the value at expiration is the payoff, based on the relationship of the original price or rate in relation to the price or rate at expiration. We worked three examples of

Objective: An FRA on 90-day LIBOR was created 18 days earlier at a fixed rate of 3.25%. The FRA expires in 24 days. The notional is $30 million. The current term structure is as given below. Find the value of the FRA to the holder of the long position.

24-day rate: 2.85%
114-day rate: 3.19%

Inputs:

$T_m = 42$
$h - 90$
$t = 18$
$T_m - t = 42 - 18 = 24$
$T_m + h - t = 42 + 90 - 18 = 114$
$L_{t^*}(m - t^*) = 0.0285$
$L_{t^*}(m + h - t^*) = 0.0319$

Results:

Applying Equation (8.29) to the notional of $30 million:

$$V_{t^*}(T_m, h) = \left(\left(\frac{1}{1 + 0.0285 \left(\frac{24}{360}\right)} \right) - \left(\frac{1 + 0.0325 \left(\frac{90}{360}\right)}{1 + 0.0319 \left(\frac{114}{360}\right)} \right) \right) \$30{,}000{,}000$$

$$= \$1{,}907$$

So the value of the FRA at time t^*, 18 days into its life with 24 days remaining, is $1,907.

Exhibit 8-7. FRA Valuation Example

forward contracts valued during their lives, the first being a generic forward contract, the second a currency forward contract, and the third being an interest rate forward contract or FRA. In Section 1.3.5 we mentioned that one reason why a party needs to value a forward contract is to terminate it early.

Forward contracts are generally undertaken with the objective of both parties holding the position to expiration. But in some cases, one party, usually the end user, decides that it no longer needs the forward contract. Such a decision is not unlike the holder of a stock deciding that she wants to sell it. The sale at this time might not have been planned when she bought the stock, but circumstances change. Stock markets are generally quite liquid, so selling most stocks is not difficult. The forward market, however, is not the same type of market as the stock market. Remember that forward contracts are OTC contracts. Nonetheless, there is no reason why a party to a forward contract cannot go back to the original counterparty and arrange an offset, which has the same effect as selling it.[15]

To offset with the original counterparty, the two parties simply need to agree on the value of the forward contract. Using the FRA valuation problem in Exhibit 8-7, we found that the FRA is worth \$1,907 to the holder of the long position. Thus, the FRA is worth −\$1,907 to the holder of the short position. The two parties can do an offset by having the holder of the short position pay the holder of the long position \$1,907. This arrangement cancels the contract.

We should also note that any forward contracts that are cleared through a clearinghouse would have their values computed on a day-to-day basis and their positions marked to market. Thus, a party holding a forward contract with a value of \$100 one day and \$101 the next would receive a payment of \$1 from the short. The contract would then be re-written at the new forward rate. This process would continue every day until expiration. Daily settlements of forward contracts are not widely done, but they are likely to increase in the future due to increasingly strong regulations being applied.

8.1.7 *Off-Market Forward Contracts*

We have noted that forward contracts have an initial value of zero. That characteristic is by custom, but it is not mandatory. A contract can be structured so that it has a non-zero value at the start. Such a transaction is called an off-market FRA. In the FRA example worked above, the rate for a zero-value FRA was 3.25%. This result means that if the two parties agree that the short will pay the long a payment of 3.25% and the long will accept a payment of the 90-day LIBOR at expiration of the FRA, the exchange is fair. Neither side can earn an arbitrage profit off of the other. The value of each side of the transaction is the same, so no exchange of money is necessary at the start. Suppose, however, that the two parties agreed on a rate of 3.15%. Your intuition should tell you that the long now has an advantage over the short. The long agrees to pay a fixed rate of 3.15% and accept LIBOR when the appropriate fixed rate is 3.25%. To offset this positive value at the start to the long, the long has to pay the equivalent amount of money to

---

[15]We have also previously mentioned that the party wanting to get out of the forward contract can enter into a new offsetting forward contract with a different counterparty. The market risk offsets, but there is still credit risk in that one counterparty might not pay its obligated amount. Offsetting with the same original counterparty is preferred.

the short. Likewise, a rate in excess of 3.25% would make the value of the contract positive to the short and negative to the long, in which case the short would have to pay the equivalent amount of money to the long at the start.

To see this effect, recall that in determining the initial rate on the FRA we specified the value of the overall replicating position that we set to zero. Looking at the problem from the perspective of the long, we take the value of the floating payment and subtract the value of the fixed payment:

$$\frac{1}{1 + L_0(T_m)\left(\frac{T_m}{360}\right)} - \frac{1 + R(T_m, h)\left(\frac{h}{360}\right)}{1 + L_0(T_m + h)\left(\frac{T_m + h}{360}\right)} = 0.$$

We then solved for $R(T_m, h)$. If the two parties agree on a different rate, however, then we insert the rate they agree on for $R(T_m, h)$ and solve for the right-hand side, which will not be zero unless the parties agree on the fair market rate, 3.25% in our example. In Exhibit 8-8, we examine the FRA we have worked on assuming an off-market rate.

Objective: Find the amount by which one party would pay the other for an off-market FRA in which the fixed rate is set at 3.30%. The notional is $30 million, the FRA expires in 42 days, the underlying is 90-day LIBOR, and the term structure of LIBOR is as follows:

> 42-day rate: 2.79%
> 132-day rate: 3.11%

Also determine which party pays the other.

Inputs:

> $T_m = 42$
> $h = 90$
> $T_m + h = 42 + 90 = 132$
> $L_0(T_m) = 0.0279$
> $L_0(T_m + h) = 0.0311$

Results:

$$\$30,000,000 \left(\frac{1}{1 + 00279\left(\frac{42}{360}\right)} - \frac{1 + 0.0330\left(\frac{90}{360}\right)}{1 + 0.0311\left(\frac{132}{360}\right)} \right) = -\$3,800$$

Because this number is negative, the value is positive to the short and negative to the long. Therefore, the short pays the long $3,800 at the start.

Exhibit 8-8. Off-Market FRA Valuation Example

8.1.8 *Applications of Forward Contracts in Risk Management*

Forward contracts are extremely useful in risk management, inasmuch as they lock in a future rate or price. While we cannot say for sure whether a decision maker would want to lock in a future rate or price and if so, how much of the exposure he would want to hedge, we can certainly show how to do so if he wants to.

8.1.8.1 *Locking in the Conversion Rate on Foreign Cash Flows*

Exhibit 8-9 illustrates a hedge of foreign currency cash flows by a multinational company.

The type of hedge described here for XYZ is a common one used in the pharmaceutical industry. Merck in fact pioneered this type of hedge in the

---

Scenario: XYZ Pharmaceuticals Corporation is a fictional U.S. company with a subsidiary in the U.K. that generates cash flows in British pounds. At the end of each calendar year, XYZ converts all excess cash back into U.S. dollars to fund its U.S. dollar-based research for the following year. As part of its planning process, XYZ believes that it will generate about £60 million the next year, which it will repatriate into U.S. dollars at the end of the year. The current spot rate for the pound is $1.50 and the forward rate is $1.55. XYZ is concerned that if the pound decreases in value relative to the dollar, the company will generate an insufficient amount of cash to fund its research and will have to raise funds elsewhere or delay some of its research. How can it manage this risk?

Solution: XYZ is effectively long £60 million. That is, it owns or is quite certain it will have a position of £60 million by year-end. As noted, a weakening of the pound relative to the dollar will result in a loss that can affect the cash flow it converts back to dollars to use to support its research. Therefore, selling £60 million in the forward market at the rate of $1.55 will guarantee that it will convert the pounds at a rate of $1.55. Thus, it enters into a one-year forward contract at a rate of $1.55 with a counterparty currency derivatives dealer. This contract obligates XYZ to deliver £60 million in one year and requires the dealer to pay XYZ $1.55 per pound. XYZ, therefore, knows that it will receive £60,000,000($1.55) = $93,000,000. Note that XYZ does not benefit if the pound increases and assumes some credit risk. These points are not addressed here, but they will become relevant when we discuss options in Chapter 10 and credit risk in Chapter 11.

Exhibit 8-9. Hedging Future Foreign Currency Cash Flows

1980s. Its foreign cash flows support its U.S.-based dollar research. If Merck does not sustain these foreign cash flows, it will have to cut its research.[16]

8.1.8.2 *Locking in the Purchase Price of Foreign Products*

In Exhibit 8-10, we examine a hedge of a company that purchases materials from a company in another country and must pay in the seller's currency.

As previously mentioned, forward contracts are the most widely used currency derivative. They have considerable flexibility, and the market has functioned extremely well. There are many dealers competing with one another. It is a popular and effective means of locking in the future sales or purchase price of a foreign currency.

8.1.8.3 *Locking in the Fixed Rate on a Loan*

Now let us now look at an example of the use of an FRA in Exhibit 8-11.

Scenario: Lucerne Technologies (LuTek) is a fictional Swiss high-tech company that quite naturally has its finances denominated in Swiss francs. It routinely purchases raw materials from a German firm and pays in that firm's currency, the euro. In the course of planning for the next year, LuTek anticipates purchasing materials currently costing €10 million. The current exchange rate is SF0.7/€. Thus, LuTek is currently looking at a cost of €10,000,000(0.7) = SF7 million. LuTek would like to eliminate the risk that the euro will increase relative to the Swiss franc, causing the materials to end up costing more. The rate on a one-year forward on the euro is SF0.72. What is LuTek's exposure and how does it eliminate the risk?

Solution: LuTek pays in euros. Thus, you should think of it as short euros. So if the euro goes up, the purchases will cost more in its home currency, the Swiss franc. Because LuTek is short euros, it needs to go long a forward contract on the euro. If the euro increases, LuTek would benefit from the long forward position. It finds a dealer and enters into a long forward contract to purchase €10 million in one year at the forward rate of SF0.72. Thus, when the contract expires, it purchases the €10 million, paying SF0.72 for an effective cost of €10,000,000(SF0.72) − SF7,200,000. It then has the euros it needs to pay the German firm. Again, note that there is credit risk, and there is also an opportunity cost if the euro decreases.

Exhibit 8-10. Hedging Future Purchases in a Foreign Currency

---

[16]See Lewent and Kearney (1990).

Scenario: U.S. Toys (USTOY) is a fictional U.S. toy manufacturer that routinely borrows money on a short-term basis at a fixed rate by issuing single-payment promissory notes. This type of loan is one in which the bank advances the money to the borrower, and the borrower pays back the loan plus interest with one payment at the loan maturity date. In planning for the next year, USTOY anticipates borrowing $30 million in July to be paid back 180 days later. The loan will be made at 180-day LIBOR plus 200 basis points at the time it is taken out. With planning for the next year being done in October, the company knows that this loan will occur about nine months later, at which time it will borrow $30 million and pay back the $30 million plus interest at LIBOR plus 200 basis points 180 days after the loan begins. USTOY is concerned about the interest rate on such loans increasing over the next nine months, and it would like to eliminate this risk. It knows that a long position in FRAs would enable it to benefit from an increase in interest rates, and this benefit can offset the increased rate on the loan. The current FRA rate is 4.5%. Thus, USTOY goes long a $30 million FRA at this rate. Determine the payoff of the FRA and the effective loan rate at expiration regardless of the value of LIBOR.

Solution: Now assume it is nine months later and the FRA is expiring. Let LIBOR be represented by the unspecified rate L. The loan rate will, therefore, be $L + 0.02$. The FRA payoff will be

$$\$30,000,000 \left(\frac{(L - 0.045)\left(\frac{180}{360}\right)}{1 + L\left(\frac{180}{360}\right)} \right).$$

It will receive this money when the FRA expires. If $L > 0.045$, let us assume it can invest this money at LIBOR (in reality it might have to earn a little less than LIBOR). If it is negative, assume it can borrow this at LIBOR (in reality it would borrow at more than LIBOR). One-hundred eighty days later, the payoff would grow to

$$\left(\$30,000,000 \left(\frac{L - 0.045}{1 + L(180/360)} \right) \left(\frac{180}{360} \right) \right) \left(1 + L\left(\frac{180}{360} \right) \right)$$

$$= \$30,000,000 \, (L - 0.045) \left(\frac{180}{360} \right).$$

With respect to the loan, USTOY borrows $30 million and pays back $30,000,000(1 + (L + 0.02)(180/360))$. Adding the FRA payoff, the net amount it will pay out is

$$\$30,000,000(1 + (L + 0.02)(180/360)) - \$30,000,000(L - 0.045(180/360))$$

$$= \$30,000,000(1 + 0.065(180/360))$$

Thus, it locks in 6.5%. Any additional rate it might have to pay to borrow and cover a negative payoff on its FRA or any reduction in the rate at which it could lend a positive payoff would be reflected in an adjustment upward from 6.5%, but if the difference were known, the uncertainty would still be eliminated.

Exhibit 8-11. Using an FRA to Lock in a Future Borrowing Rate

This completes our material on forward contracts. We now move on to their first cousins, futures contracts.

8.2 Futures Contracts

In Chapter 4 we introduced futures contracts, and in Chapter 5 we covered the unique characteristics of futures markets. Here we will take a brief review of the salient points from those sections.

8.2.1 *Formal Definition of a Futures Contract*

As a formal definition of a futures contract, we present the following:

> *A futures contract is a standardized derivative created on an organized exchange in which one party, the buyer or long, agrees to purchase an underlying asset or make a fixed payment at a future date with a counterparty, the seller or short, who agrees to sell the underlying asset or make a variable payment at that future date, and in which the parties are subject to a daily settlement procedure in which gains and losses are allocated from one party to the other.*

This definition is remarkably similar to that of a forward contract. Indeed, futures contracts are really just forward contracts that have been standardized, are created on an organized exchange, and are subject to the daily settlement procedure that we illustrated in Chapter 5. In contrast, forward contracts are customized between the parties, do not trade on an exchange, and are not generally subject to a daily settlement procedure.

Some of these clauses must be qualified, however, because recently regulatory and likely upcoming changes may ultimately bring forward market trading to mandatory clearing and settlement through clearinghouses. Forward contracts may also someday be largely traded on electronic exchanges. But forward contracts are still distinct from futures contracts in that forwards are customized. That is, with forwards, the two parties negotiate and agree on all of the terms of the contract. Futures contracts are authorized by futures exchanges that specify that futures contracts are available on only certain underlyings and have only certain expirations. In addition, futures exchanges are heavily regulated and generally most new contracts have to be approved by regulators. Forward contracts are far less restricted. Also, futures contracts tend to have smaller notionals than forward contracts.

The size of the exchange-traded derivatives market is reported in volume. In Chapter 5 we presented this data. As a reminder, in 2017, futures accounted for about 14.8 billion contracts out of the total exchange-listed derivatives volume of about 25.2 billion contracts, the remainder of course coming from options.

8.2.2   *Pricing a Futures Contract*

A straightforward comparison of forward contracts with futures contracts in which the only difference between contracts is the daily settlement on the futures would reveal that differences could exist between futures prices and forward prices. We will not illustrate a formal proof of this fact, but we will walk through a heuristic explanation.

Let us say that a forward contract and a futures contract are created at the same time with the same expiration on the same underlying. The forward will be settled at expiration, and the futures will be subject to a daily settlement. Let us assume the initial forward and futures price is the same, say $100. At expiration, suppose the spot price is $105. Then, the forward contract will settle at expiration for a profit of $5. The futures contract will generate a profit of $5, but this amount will be realized over the life of the contract in positive and negative increments that add up to $5. Positive cash flows that arise from the daily settlement and accrue to the holder of the long position from increases in the futures price can be reinvested to earn interest. Negative cash flows that accrue to the holder of the short position from increases in the futures price will result in the loss of interest. As a result, when futures prices and interest rates are positively correlated, it will be beneficial to be the holder of a long position. As such, futures have a benefit over forwards from the daily settlement, and futures prices will be higher than forward prices. When futures prices and interest rates are negatively correlated, it will be beneficial to be the holder of a short position. Losses to the short occur when interest rates are falling, and gains occur when rates are rising. As such, futures are disadvantaged over forwards from the daily settlement, and futures prices will be lower than forward prices. If there is no correlation between futures prices and interest rates, neither type of contract has a benefit over the other and their prices will be the same. A further condition that makes their prices equivalent is the extremely low interest rates that have existed since around 2009. Zero correlation between futures contracts and interest rates can also arise from virtually zero volatility of interest rates during this period as well. Of course, it should be obvious that if forward contracts are settled on a daily basis, forward prices will also equal futures prices.

The effect of daily settlement is complex and not incorporated into the standard cost of carry models that we have presented. A far more complex model is required, and we will not cover this topic in this book. The differences in prices between daily-settled futures and settled-at-expiration forwards would not likely be material anyway. Thus, we will proceed under the assumption that futures are priced by the cost of carry, which indeed is the model most widely used in the futures industry. As a result of this convenience, we will not need to cover futures pricing in much depth, as it is already well-covered in Section 1 in the context of forwards.

In addition, we should keep in mind that the daily settlement of futures markets is a significant benefit in mitigating credit risk. Futures prices, thus, can deviate from forward prices due to credit risk, though it is impossible to say in which direction, as this depends on the relative credit risks of each party. We will ignore credit risk until Chapter 11.

There are, however, some unique features of futures contracts that do need to be discussed. For some types of underlyings, notably bonds and stock indexes, futures contracts are more widely used than forward contracts.

8.2.2.1 *Pricing Short-Term Interest Rate Futures*

Futures on short-term interest rates began with the initiation of the U.S. Treasury bill futures contract of the Chicago Mercantile Exchange in 1976, a contract calling for physical delivery of 13-week treasury bills, which are pure discount securities issued by the U.S. government in original maturities of 13, 26, and 52 weeks. As described in Chapter 7, they use the discount method of interest computation, whereby a rate times the maturity in days divided by 360 is subtracted from the face value. When the bill matures, it pays its face value. Thus, the interest is deducted from the face value, and the instrument matures to its face value, thereby earning its interest through price appreciation. When the futures contract was launched in 1976, there were \$161 billion of Treasury bills outstanding and the U.S. national debt was about \$620 billion. As of June, 2018, there is \$2.2 trillion of Treasury bills outstanding and the U.S. national debt is about \$21.2 trillion, but there is no longer a Treasury bill futures contract? That seems strange.

Well, in 1982, the CME introduced a cash-settled Eurodollar futures contract that has been tremendously successful. In 2015, it traded almost 587 million contracts. Its success has relegated the Treasury bill contract to nothing but a historical footnote. When it was designed, the Eurodollar contract was modeled after the T-bill contract, and oddly enough, this design gave it an interesting quirk. Recall from Chapter 7 that we talked about discount and add-on interest. As described in the previous paragraph, T-bills use the discount interest method. When the CME designed the T-bill futures, it specified that the discount method would be used. As illustrated in Chapter 7, Eurodollars use the add-on interest method, whereby the interest is based on the rate times the number of days to maturity divided by 360 and is added to the price to equal the face value that is paid at maturity. The CME, however, designed the Eurodollar futures to pay off based on the *discount* method. In other words, the futures contract does not pay off the same way as the spot. Why the CME did this is unclear, but in all likelihood, the CME felt that users of CME contracts were familiar with the T-bill discount method and less familiar with the Eurodollar add-on method.

As a result of this disparity between the futures and spot pricing structures, there is a bit of a disconnection between Eurodollar spot and Eurodollar futures markets. The exact details can be quite complex and can lead to the requirement that an adjustment term be incorporated. We will not get into those details here, as the issue is beyond the scope of this book, and the adjustment is relatively small. Suffice it to say that the Eurodollar futures cannot be technically priced by the cost of carry model. Most market participants simply determine the forward rate in the LIBOR market, which is the same as Equation (8.26) used in FRA pricing, and then find the Eurodollar futures price using the discount method. The quoted price is 100 minus the discount rate, but the actual contract price is found applying the discount rate to the face value in the discount manner, not the add-on manner as is done in the Eurodollar spot market.

Now let us look at Exhibit 8-12, which is just a variation of Exhibit 8-4, where we priced an FRA.

Why the confusion? Which is the real price? It turns out that the characteristics of the contract as chosen by the CME make it easy for a trader to think quickly in a fast-moving market. Each contract covers $1,000,000 of Eurodollars. Thus, as shown above, a quoted rate of 3.25 implies a trade price of $991,875, based on applying the price computed above of 99.1875 per 100 to a face value of $1,000,000. Suppose the rate goes up to 3.26. Re-computing the price gives,

$$100 - 3.26 \left(\frac{90}{360} \right) = 99.1850.$$

Objective: Find the quoted and actual prices on a Eurodollar futures contract that expires in 42 days in which the underlying is 90-day LIBOR and the term structure of LIBOR is as follows:

> 42-day rate: 2.79%
> 132-day rate: 3.11%

Inputs: (Referring back to the FRA pricing material)

> $T_m - 42$
> $h = 90$
> $T_m + h = 42 + 90 = 132$
> $L_0(T_m) = 0.0279$
> $L_0(T_m + h) = 0.0311$

Results:

$$R(T_m, h) = \left(\frac{1 + 0.0311(132/360)}{1 + 0.0279(42/360)} - 1 \right) (360/90) = 0.0325$$

The quoted price based on par value of $100 will be

$$100 - 3.25 = 96.75.$$

The trade price per 100 par will be

$$100 - 3.25 \left(\frac{90}{360} \right) = 99.1875.$$

The standard contract size for the Eurodollar futures is $1,000,000, so the actual trade at which the contract is recorded is, 99.1875% of $1,000,000 or $991,875.

Exhibit 8-12. Eurodollar Futures Pricing Example

So, the trade price is $991,850, which is $25 lower. The CME designed the contract in this way so that each basis point move amounts to $25 of price change. So, if the rate goes up one basis point, the price goes down $25. This result is simply a mathematical result from designing the contract such that it covers $1,000,000 of Eurodollars and each basis point, which is 1/10,000 of $1, is multiplied by the factor 90/360. In effect, $(1/10,000)(90/360)(\$1,000,000) = \$25$.

In the global futures markets, there are a variety of short-term interest rate futures contracts. We cannot cover them all here. As noted, the Eurodollar contract of the CME is the most widely traded short-term interest-rate futures contract, the reason of which is that it is easily used by OTC dealers to hedge their interest rate forwards, swaps, and options. Now let us turn to futures contracts on bonds.

8.2.2.2 *Pricing Bond Futures*

The first futures contract on a bond was the Chicago Board of Trade's Treasury bond futures created in 1977.[17] The contract, based on a hypothetical Treasury bond with minimum maturity of 15 years, has been one of the most successful of all futures contracts in terms of trading volume. Its status as the most active bond futures contract has, however, been supplanted by its first cousin, futures on U.S. Treasury notes, which have maturities of from two to 10 years. Both T-note and T-bond contracts share some important characteristics that can be quite confusing.

Let us start by examining how these instruments are quoted. In pre-calculator days, Treasury notes and bonds were designed to be quoted in units of $100 par and fractions of 32^{nds}. Thus, you might see a price of 104-29, which means 104 plus 29/32 of par.[18] The fraction 29/32 is 0.90625, so the price is 104.90625. Based on $100 par, the price is $104.90625. So, if an investor held $10,000 par of these notes, the value would be $10,490.625. Because of calculators, the system of pricing in 32^{nds} has outlived its usefulness, but not surprisingly, it continues to be used. Thus, T-bonds and T-notes are still quoted in 32^{nds}. Likewise, futures on T-bonds and T-notes are also quoted in 32^{nds}.

Another complicating factor in the bond market is that the price is often quoted without the effect of any interest that has accumulated since the last interest payment. T-notes and T-bonds pay interest semiannually. In the world before calculators, it was more difficult to determine bond prices when the bond was not trading on a coupon payment date, which is nearly always the case. Back in the olden days, this problem was solved by quoting the bond price without the interest that had accrued since the last coupon payment date. Thus, a quote like 104-29, as mentioned above, would almost surely not be the full price you would pay. The interest accrued since the last coupon date would be added. This characteristic, like the use of 32^{nds}, is also an anachronism that probably should be terminated. But of course, it is still used. And the fact that the quoted price does not include the

---

[17]By the way, the terms *interest rate futures* and *bond futures* are often used interchangeably. In this book, we shall tend to use the former to refer to short-term futures and the latter to refer to intermediate- and long-term futures. Strictly speaking, both terms are appropriate in both situations.

[18]So 104-29 is not the arithmetic problem of 104 minus 29, which equals 75, but rather 104 plus 29/32. Also, be prepared for the fact that in the bond market, you will sometimes see the quote as 104.29, which is not 104 and 29/100. It is 104 and 29/32.

accrued interest makes futures price calculations a little more complex. We will bypass that problem by assuming that we know the full price of a bond and do not have to add on accrued interest because it is already in the price.

Exploiting Options Embedded in Futures Contracts

As described in the text, bond futures contracts commonly contain certain flexible conditions that can be exploited by the holder of the short position. These conditions are referred to as *options*. They are not strictly options in the manner in which a call or a put might be created between a buyer and a seller, but they do have much in common with traditional options. They give the holder certain flexibility, and the holder must pay for them. The options are commonly referred to as *delivery options*.

There are three primary classes of delivery options: the quality option, the location option, and the timing option. Timing options can be further divided into the accrued interest option, the wild card option, and the end-of-the-month option.

Quality options are represented by the right of the short to deliver any one of several varieties of the underlying. For example, settlement of a treasury note contract with a $6^1/2$ to 10-year maturity requirement can be met by delivering any treasury note with maturity in that range. Obviously a $6^1/2$-year bond is not the same bond as a 10-year bond. Also, many commodities have multiple grades. For example, settlement of a Soft Red Winter wheat futures contract on the Chicago Mercantile Exchange can be done by delivering a variety of wheat called #2 soft red winter wheat, with the alternative of #1 soft red winter wheat, and also #1 and #2 hard red winter wheat, #1 and #2 northern spring wheat, and #1 and #2 dark northern spring wheat can be delivered. In some cases, there are price adjustments if the quality difference is large.

Contracts also often have a location option, which permits delivery in multiple locations. The CME wheat contract mentioned above can be settled by delivery of the wheat at specific locations in Chicago, as well as locations in Indiana and Ohio. Financial instruments are delivered through an accounting entry, so there is no location issue.

As noted there are three types of timing options. The accrued interest option arises, because in many contracts, the short has the right to deliver on any day in the expiration month. A treasury bond could have an attractive coupon rate in relation to the cost of financing the bond that could make it worth holding on to for as long as possible, thereby delivering near the end of the month. The wild card option exists in U.S. treasury futures markets due to the fact that the futures markets close in the afternoon thereby locking in the delivery price, but the short can make a delivery decision until well into the evening. If the bond price falls sharply after the futures market closes, the short can benefit by buying the bond and delivering it at the locked-in price. The end of the month option exists because many contracts trade up through about three weeks of the expiration month but permit delivery any day of the expiration month. The day for any deliveries made in the last week is set on the last trading day. Thus, the delivery price is frozen. The short can then observe bond prices during the last week and buy a bond and deliver it for an extra profit if the price falls sufficiently.

These options offer attractive investment opportunities to holders of short positions. Holder of long positions are not, however, naïve. They know that these options are attractive to the shorts, so the futures price will be lower to the long. Thus, the short pays for these options by receiving a lower price when he opens a short position.

Source: Chance and Hemler (1993)

Finally, let us note that there are a variety of T-bonds and T-notes with different maturities. Suppose the contract specifies that the short will deliver a 7-year T-note. Stop. We immediately have a problem. T-notes are issued with original maturities of 2, 3, 5, 7, and 10 years. Unless a 7-year note is being issued on the expiration day or unless a 10-year note will have a maturity of precisely 7 years on the futures expiration day, there is no underlying. To accommodate this restriction, the contract allows a maturity with a range, say 7–10 years, technically $6\frac{1}{2}$ to 10. Now, clearly a bond with a maturity of 7-years is quite different from a bond with a maturity of 10-years. In addition, the eligible deliverable bonds have different coupons. Hence, the set of eligible deliverable bonds can be quite diverse.

When it created the contract, the Chicago Board of Trade recognized this problem and created a linear adjustment factor that would purport to make all deliverable bonds roughly equivalent. The contract specifies a standard coupon rate. Let us use 6%, which is the current rate used. The conversion factor is associated with a particular deliverable bond. If the deliverable bond has a coupon of 6%, the conversion factor is 1.0. If the deliverable bond has a coupon rate more (less) than 6%, the conversion factor is greater (less) than

1.0. Thus, delivering a bond with a coupon greater (less) than the standard coupon rate results in getting paid more (less) money than you would if you delivered a bond with the standard coupon. The conversion factors also take into account maturity. For a coupon greater (less) than 6%, delivery of a longer-term bond results in a greater (lower) conversion factor and, thus, a higher payment from the long to the short. The conversion factor system is an attempt to make all deliverable bonds equivalent. It is a relatively crude method, as it does not make all bonds completely equivalent. Nonetheless, it is pretty much the best method available.

Further complicating the matter is the fact that the short has the choice of which bond to deliver, and he does not have to tell the long which bond he intends to deliver until a few days before the expiration. Thus, anyone attempting to price the futures could have some difficulty identifying the underlying. Yet another complication is that there is a period of time, roughly one week, during which the short can make delivery. Thus, not even the expiration day is clear.

You would think that with all of these complications, Treasury bond and note futures would not be widely used. On the contrary, these contracts are very widely traded. These complicating features actually attract traders who are eager to profit off of their ability to analyze these complex characteristics and take advantage of those who either ignore these features or fail to take their significance seriously.

As we noted above, the conversion factor system does not make all bonds equivalent. Some are cheaper to deliver than others. The holder of the short position will deliver the bond that is the cheapest. At any given time, there is a fairly straightforward calculation to identify the cheapest to deliver. Whatever bond is the cheapest to deliver plays the role of the underlying. Then, the futures price is found simply as the spot price plus the cost of carry. The cost of carry reflects the risk-free rate of interest, net of the value of any coupons paid on the bond during the life of the futures. Thus, the futures contract is priced the same way in which we described the pricing of a forward contract. We will not get into the details of calculating accrued interest or the conversion factor. Exhibit 8-13 illustrates the process heuristically, letting *CF* represent the conversion factor.

From the above, one can solve for the futures price. While this procedure is the standard methodology used in practice, there are some issues being overlooked in this standard model. For example, there is the likelihood of another bond becoming the cheapest to deliver, and a trader would need to consider the various delivery options.

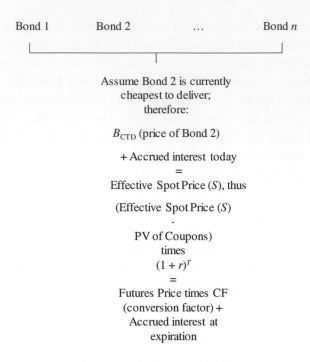

Bond 1   Bond 2   ...   Bond *n*

Assume Bond 2 is currently
cheapest to deliver;
therefore:

B_{CTD} (price of Bond 2)

+ Accrued interest today

=

Effective Spot Price (S), thus

(Effective Spot Price (S)

-

PV of Coupons)
times
$(1 + r)^T$

=

Futures Price times CF
(conversion factor) +
Accrued interest at
expiration

Exhibit 8-13. Pricing Bond Futures

Futures contracts on government bonds have been the most actively traded. In contrast, futures contracts on corporate and municipal bonds have not been particularly successful. Government bonds have a much more liquid market, and there are just enough but not too many bonds to support a futures contract. There are an extremely large number of highly diverse corporate and municipal bonds, and most are not highly liquid. There have been some attempts to create futures on bond indexes, but these efforts have not been very successful.

8.2.2.3 *Pricing Currency Futures*

Currency futures contracts were actually the first financial futures contracts. Launched in 1972, they brought futures trading out of its formerly isolated world of commodities to what was then referred to as the ultimate commodity — *money*. Prior to that time, the center of the financial markets was the New York Stock Exchange. Chicago was known for its commodity markets. Commodity trading and financial trading were entirely separate industries. With the creation of currency futures at the Chicago Mercantile Exchange, a marriage of financial and commodity markets began to take place.[19] Since that time, these markets have become increasingly integrated.[20]

Pricing currency futures is done the same way as pricing currency forwards, using Equation (8.14) and its variants that follow. The currency futures markets are not as large as the currency forward markets, but they are, nonetheless, widely used by hedgers, speculators, and OTC dealers. You may wish to review Section 8.1.4.2 on currency forward pricing.

8.2.2.4 *Pricing Equity Futures*

The class of instruments known as equity futures comprises futures on stock indexes and on individual stocks. Futures on individual stock, however, have never gained much traction, but stock index futures have been extremely successful since they were launched in 1982. The most popular indexes for futures trading are the S&P 500, the Nasdaq 100, and such foreign stock indexes as the Kospi 200 in South Korea and the Euro STOXX 50 in Europe.

As we described in Section 8.1.3.1, a futures contract is priced by taking the spot price, reducing it by the present value of the cash payments it makes over the life of the contract, and compounding that value forward to the expiration at the risk-free rate. We repeat here the pricing Equation (8.3),

$$F(0,T) = \left(S_0 - cf_t/(1+r)^t\right)(1+r)^T.$$

For equity futures, the cash flows are the dividends on the underlying stocks that compose the index. The index can be constructed and held in the form of a portfolio, typically called a basket, or a mutual fund, or an exchange-traded fund (ETF). Any time any stock in the index pays a dividend, the index itself effectively pays a dividend through the basket, the mutual fund, or the ETF.[21]

Suppose there are N dividends of $D_1, D_2, \ldots, D_N$ to be paid over the life of the derivative and times $1, 2, \ldots, N$, respectively. We assume these

---

[19]The Chicago Board Options Exchange was also created in 1972 by the Chicago Board of Trade, and it too helped bring commodity and financial markets together.

[20]In recent years, the term *financialization* has come to be used in a pejorative manner to describe the process by which financial institutions increasingly dominate the commodity markets, and in particular, the energy markets.

[21]Mutual funds typically accumulate the dividends and either declare a fund-level dividend that is distributed to the fund's shareholders or reinvested in additional shares on a monthly basis. ETFs typically accumulate dividends and distribute them to their holders on a quarterly basis.

dividends are known in advance.[22] The present value of the dividends is

$$\sum_{n=1}^{N} \frac{D_n}{(1+r)^n}.$$

Thus, the pricing equation for stock index futures is

$$f_0(T) = \left(S_0 - \sum_{n=1}^{N} \frac{D_n}{(1+r)^n} \right) (1+r)^T. \tag{8.30}$$

We use a lower case f to denote the futures price, in contrast to the upper-case F to denote the forward price. Because futures prices change during the life of the contract, a result of the daily settlement, we subscript the futures price. We did not do that for forward prices, as they remain fixed.

Sometimes a slightly simplifying assumption is used. The dividends on stocks and stock indexes are often subsumed within a single ratio called the *dividend yield*. Let us use δ as the dividend yield. In that case, we can write the pricing formula as follows:

$$f_0(T) = \left(\frac{S_0}{(1+\delta)^T} \right) (1+r)^T. \tag{8.31}$$

Yet another alternative is that the dividends are treated as occurring more or less continuously. Such an assumption is not completely realistic, but most broadly diversified indexes have at least one stock paying a dividend on any given day. Thus, there is a fairly steady stream of dividends. By incorporating a continuous dividend yield, the dividends are treated as a constant continuous percentage of the stock price. Under this assumption, one would typically let the risk-free be expressed in continuous form, $r_c = \ln(1+r)$. Letting, δ_c be the continuous yield, the formula then becomes

$$f_0(T) = S_0 e^{-(\delta_c - r_c)T}. \tag{8.32}$$

Now take a look at the example in Exhibit 8-14.

The differences in these prices can be a source of confusion. After all, by the law of one price, there can be only a single price for the futures. The example is not calibrated, however, to precision. The present value of the dividends is a rough estimate that is not set such that its effect is the same as using the dividend yield. Dividend yields are estimates and not precise

---

[22]There are some modest complicating factors when the dividends are unknown, but they can be accommodated. The effect of dividend uncertainty is a more advanced topic than can be covered here in this book.

Objective: Price a futures contract that expires in 60 days in which the underlying is a stock index ETF priced at 125.38. There are three different dividend assumptions:

(1) The ETF pays a single dividend in 45 days of 0.95.
(2) The ETF has an annual dividend yield of 1%.
(3) The ETF has a continuously compounded dividend yield of 0.99%

The discrete risk-free rate is 2.5% and the continuous rate is $\ln(1.025) = 2.47\%$.

Inputs:

$$S_0 = 125.38$$
$$T = 60/365 = 0.1644$$
$$D_1 = 0.95$$
$$t_1 = 45/365 = 0.1233$$
$$\delta = 0.01$$
$$\delta_c = 0.0099$$
$$r = 0.025$$
$$r_c = 0.0247$$

Results:

$$F(0, 0.1644) = \left(125.38 - \frac{0.95}{(1.025)^{0.1233}} \right) (1.025)^{0.1644} = 124.94$$

$$F(0, 0.1644) = \left(\frac{125.38}{(1.01)^{0.1644}} \right) (1.025)^{0.1644} = 125.68$$

$$F(0, 0.1644) = 125.38 e^{-(0.0099 - 0.0247)(0.1644)} = 125.69$$

Exhibit 8-14. Stock Index Futures Pricing Example

dividends, so it is the latter two answers that are likely to be slightly off from an estimate based on discounting the specific dividends. Note that the second case, the discrete yield, and the third case, the continuous yield are extremely close, which occurs because the risk-free rate and dividend yield in the discrete case are calibrated to their continuous equivalents, and the difference that remains is a round-off error.

8.2.2.5 *Pricing Commodity Futures*

For the most part commodity futures are storable assets, meaning that they can be bought and held in the same way that a stock, bond, or currency can be bought and held. Thus, we can price a commodity futures contract with the cost of carry model. Most commodities, however, incur significant storage costs that must be factored into the pricing model. For example, one cannot simply buy and store gold, oil, silver, wheat and most other commodities without incurring costs.

In Section 8.1.3.4, we derived the forward price with carrying costs as Equation (8.7), repeated here

$$F(0,T) = (S_0 - PVCF(0,T))(1+r)^T + FVSC(0,T).$$

Commodities do not make interest or dividend payments, so it would appear that we could drop the expression, $PVCF(0,T)$, leaving

$$F(0,T) = S_0(1+r)^T + FVSC(0,T).$$

But there is one complication. Notice in the equation directly above that $F(0,T)$ *has* to be more than S_0. We factor up S_0 by the interest rate and add the future value of storage costs. So, indeed $F(0,T)$ must be more than S_0. Right? Well, guess what? In practice, it is not always the case, at least not always for some commodities. In other words, futures prices behave as though there are some cash payments made by the underlying. Yet, there are not. What possible explanation can there be?

The explanation lies in the existence of a somewhat abstract concept: a non-monetary benefit to holding the underlying that is known as the *convenience yield*. The notion of a convenience yield is a hypothesis that certain assets provide a benefit to their owners that cannot be measured in monetary terms. Convenience yields most often arise when an asset is in short supply. When this situation occurs, the parties astute enough (or lucky enough) to own it have a valuable asset. They have something others want and cannot easily obtain without paying an unusually high price. We know the spot price would be high in such a situation, and indeed it could exceed the futures price. How can this be? The above equation ought to accommodate any situation and yet, the spot price cannot exceed the futures price in this equation.

While the explanation described here is a common one, it can be shown to be illogical. A current shortage is nothing more than a market condition in which the price is abnormally high due to low supply relative to demand. If the cost of carry model holds and someone buys this expensive asset, sells a futures and stores it, he will earn a negative return. Thus, when an asset is in short supply, there is a strong disincentive to store it. By storing it, you take it off the market with the expectation of making it available to sell in the future. Unless the shortage is expected to continue, there is no incentive to store the asset. With the unusually high spot price, it is better to sell it. Thus, the futures price will be said to have a convenience yield embedded within it. A convenience yield is a non-monetary benefit from owning the asset during times of low supplies.

Another possible explanation for a convenience yield is the inability to borrow the asset and sell it short. Short selling is associated primarily with financial assets but not commodities. The cost of carry model requires the ability to sell short essentially without restrictions. If the futures price is too low relative to the model price, an arbitrageur borrows the asset, sells it short, and buys the futures. But if the asset cannot be sold short, the arbitrageur cannot borrow the asset. When that happens the futures price remains low, as there is no arbitrage force to bring it back in line. With an abnormally low futures price, the spot price can easily be above it. Arbitrageurs who own the asset, however, have the opportunity to sell it, buy the futures, and capture the arbitrage profit. When the futures expires or the arbitrage position is terminated, the arbitrageur will end up capturing the arbitrage profit and getting the asset back in his portfolio, leaving him exactly where he was before the arbitrage but with the arbitrage profit in his pocket.

Thus, there can be a substantial advantage to owning assets whose supplies can be curtailed by a variety of market forces and which are not easily sold short. Agricultural commodities can have poor growing seasons, and energy supplies can be disrupted by geopolitical events. Hence, the convenience yield is primarily associated with these types of instruments. Financial assets do not have this problem.

Thus, the cost of carry model for such assets will look like the following:

$$F(0,T) = S_0(1+r)^T - FVCY(0,T) + FVSC(0,T). \qquad (8.33)$$

where $FVCY(0,T)$ is the convenience yield valued at expiration. An example is provided in Exhibit 8-15.

8.2.3 *Using Futures Contracts*

As you know by now, this is a book for end users, primarily graduate business students. Such students will typically assume the roles of buyers of derivatives from dealers. The majority of end users work for corporations, but some work in the investment management industry or for corporate pension funds. Most corporate end users do not use futures. Instead they prefer forwards, swaps, and OTC options. The investment management industry does, however, use futures. In addition, the broker-dealer firms in the financial industry are major users of futures. In this section, we will

Objective: Price a futures contract on a commodity currently selling for €75 in which the risk-free interest rate is 3% and the contract expires in 60 days. Every 25 days, the commodity holder will have to pay a fee of €1.05 in storage costs for each unit of the commodity. Any storage costs accumulated but not yet paid are found by prorating. In addition, there is an estimated convenience yield of €0.25 in present value terms.

Inputs: There is a slight twist to this problem. The formula in (8.33) specifies the storage costs as a future value. Thus, we have to convert the information about the costs into a future value. A cost of €1.05 every 25 days would mean a cost on the 25th and 50th days and on day 60, there would be an accumulated cost of $(10/25)$ €1.05 = €0.42. So, the future value of the storage costs would be based on €1.05 compounded for 35 days, €1.05 compounded for 10 days and €0.42.

$$1.05(1.03)^{35/365} + 1.05(1.03)^{10/365} + 0.42 = 2.53$$

To explain, we incurred an outright cash cost of €1.05 on day 25, the amount of which we must compound to day 60 to reflect the loss of interest on this money. We also incurred a cost of €1.05 on day 50, the amount of which we must compound to day 60 to reflect the loss of interest on this money. Finally, as of day 60 we would owe €0.42 for the final 10 days of storage. In addition, to use Equation (8.33), we need the convenience yield in future value terms. Thus, we compound €0.25 for 60 days:

$$0.25(1.03)^{60/365} = 0.25.$$

Thus,

$S_0 = €75$
$r = 0.03$
$T = 60/365 = 0.1634$
$FVCY(0,T) = €0.25$
$FVSC(0,T) = €2.53$

Results:

$$F(0,T) = 75(1.03)^{60/365} - 0.25 + 2.53 = 77.64.$$

Exhibit 8-15. Pricing a Commodity Futures Contract

examine three uses of futures contracts that are mostly applicable to the investment management industry. We noted earlier that Eurodollar futures are widely used, but much of this use is by OTC dealers who hedge their positions. We have already talked a little about dealer hedging, and we will return to the topic in the options chapter.

Before we get into examples, it is important to understand some concepts that arise in the use of futures in hedging. The first concept is the difference between the spot and futures price, which is referred to as the *basis*. In fact, in the practice of hedging we often say that the hedger is *speculating on the basis*. Let us see what this expression means.

Define the basis at any time t as the spot price minus the futures price,

$$BASIS_t = S_t - f_t(T). \tag{8.34}$$

So let us say that a hedge is put in place at time t and taken off at a later time, t^*. The basis at time t^* is

$$BASIS_{t^*} = S_{t^*} - f_{t^*}(T).$$

The net profit from a short hedge, which is a strategy in which you own the asset and sell a futures, is by definition

$$\prod_{t,t^*} = (S_{t^*} - S_t) - (f_{t^*} - f_t).$$

The first term in parentheses is the profit from buying the spot at time t and selling it at t^*. The second term arises from selling the futures at time t and buying it back at time t^*. Rewriting this expression, we have

$$\prod_{t,t^*} = (S_{t^*} - f_{t^*}) - (S_t - f_t)$$

$$= BASIS_{t^*} - BASIS_t. \tag{8.35}$$

So we can see that the overall gain or loss from a hedge is the change in the basis. If we were short the asset and hedged by going long the futures, a strategy called a long hedge, Equation (8.35) would have signs changed but the concept would be the same: the profit would be the change in the basis.

If the hedge is held to expiration, $t^* = T$, the spot and futures prices converge. Thus,

$$BASIS_T = S_T - f_T(T)$$

$$= S_T - S_T = 0.$$

In that case, the profit is

$$\prod_{t,T} = BASIS_T - BASIS_t$$

$$= 0 - BASIS_t$$

$$= -BASIS_t.$$

So the profit is the negative of the original basis. Most futures hedges do not result in holding the position to expiration. Rather, the futures position is closed out prior to expiration. Thus, there is some risk in that the basis could widen or shrink based on investors' perceptions of carrying costs and convenience yields.

As a result of the likelihood that a hedge is not held to expiration and the potential for unpredictable changes in the basis, a futures hedge is often described as *speculating on the basis*. And although speculating on the basis still sounds like speculation, the risk of the basis is far less than the risk of the spot price, as can be seen here. Let σ_S^2 be the variance of the spot price, σ_f^2 be the risk of the futures price, σ_b^2 be the variance of the basis, and $\text{cov}_{S,f}$ be the covariance of the spot and futures prices.[23] Then,

$$\sigma_b^2 = \sigma_S^2 + \sigma_f^2 - 2\text{cov}_{S,f}.$$

This expression will not universally lead to a lower variance of the basis than the variance of the spot. But if the correlation is quite high and the futures variance is fairly close to the spot variance, the basis variance will tend to be lower than the spot variance. In other words, the covariance term will more than dominate the futures variance, bringing the basis variance down to a level below the spot variance. These conditions are nothing more than the logical statement that if there is not a futures contract available on the underlying being hedged, a substitute futures contract could be used but should have a variance close to that of the spot and a very high correlation with the spot. Such a hedge is called a *cross-hedge*.

In the forward market, these issues do not tend to arise, inasmuch as a forward contract tends to be customized to the needs of the end user. Thus, the forward contract would likely expire exactly when the user wants to take off the hedge and the underlying will be precisely the asset being hedged. Nonetheless, futures hedges have other advantages. They are typically available in smaller unit sizes, and they are marked to market daily, thereby reducing any potential for the counterparty defaulting. In short, the distinctions between forward and futures contracts that we outlined in Chapter 5 can make one type of contract preferable over another, but the circumstances in which one is preferred over the other do vary. Let us now look at some examples using futures.

---

[23]This expression arises from the fact that the variance of the basis is the variance of the expression $S - f$. The variance of $S - f$ is the variance of S plus the variance of f minus (because of the minus sign in front of f) twice the covariance between S and f.

8.2.3.1 *Adjusting the Duration of a Bond Portfolio*

Consider a bond portfolio manager who has J bonds in a portfolio. The price of each bond is denoted as B_j, where $j = 1, 2, \ldots, J$. The value of the portfolio is, therefore,

$$V_p = \sum_{j=1}^{J} B_j.$$

The modified duration of each bond is denoted as DUR_{mj}. It represents the weighted average of the durations of the component bonds, with the weights being the relative market values of the respective bonds. In other words, if the market value of one bond is 2% of the total market value of the portfolio, the bond is said to have a weight of 0.02, which is represented symbolically as B_j/V_p. The overall modified duration of the portfolio is a weighted average of the modified durations of the component bonds in the following specification:

$$DUR_{mp} = \sum_{j=1}^{J} DUR_{mj} \left(\frac{B_j}{V_p} \right).$$

Now suppose we have a portfolio with modified duration of DUR_{mp}. Suppose that we have a forecast of the bond market that suggests that we should change our duration to DUR_{mp}^T. Here the T denotes the target duration. Obviously we could sell some bonds and replace them with other bonds such that the overall duration is changed to the target duration. But another method is to overlay the portfolio with a futures contract. Since we add futures positions without paying cash, we can effectively add or subtract risk as reflected in duration without having to disrupt the bond portfolio or come up with additional funds. The securities can remain in place and the futures contract will change the overall duration to the desired level.

Because the price of a bond futures contract will respond to changes in interest rates, it has, in essence, a duration that is conceptually the same measure as the duration of a portfolio of bonds. Given an interest rate change, the duration of a futures is the duration of the bond underlying the futures as though the bond were positioned at the futures expiration. So, for example, a futures contract expiring in 75 days in which the underlying is a 10-year note will have a duration that reflects the price sensitivity of that 10-year note in 75 days. Thus, the duration is a type of forward duration. We will denote the duration of the futures as DUR_m^f. We will not cover the computation of this duration, as it is slightly more complex than for an ordinary bond and is a topic for a fixed-income course. The value of the portfolio is the sum of the value of the bonds and the value of the futures. Of course, the value of the futures is zero when marked to market, but we will need to incorporate the change in value when the interest rate changes. We write the value of the portfolio consisting of bond and futures as

$$V_{pf} = V_p + v_f N_f.$$

This statement says that the value of the portfolio is the sum of the values of the bonds in the portfolio plus the value of the futures, v_f, times the number of futures contract, N_f. If we differentiate this equation with respect to the yield y, we obtain

$$\frac{\partial V_{pf}}{\partial y} = \frac{\partial V_p}{\partial y} + N_f \frac{\partial v_f}{\partial y}.$$

In Chapter 7, we presented the following equation that relates the duration of a financial instrument to the price of the financial instrument and the yield change:

$$\frac{\partial B}{\partial y}\left(\frac{1}{B}\right) = -DUR_m.$$

This equation will hold as well for the overall value of the portfolio and for the futures price as follows:

$$\frac{\partial V_{pf}}{\partial y}\left(\frac{1}{V^{pf}}\right) = -DUR_{mp}$$

$$\frac{\partial f}{\partial y}\left(\frac{1}{f}\right) = -DUR_{mf}.$$

We want to set the overall portfolio duration to a target duration, so let us specify that $DUR_{mp} = DUR_{mp}^T$. Substituting these equations into the equation for $\partial V_{pf}/\partial y$, recognizing that $B = V_{pf}$, and solving for N_f, we obtain

$$\frac{\partial V_{pf}}{\partial y} = \frac{\partial V_p}{\partial y} + N_f \frac{\partial v_f}{\partial y}$$

$$-DUR_{mp}V_{pf} = -DUR_m V_p + N_f(-DUR_{mf})f$$

$$-DUR_{mp}^T V_{pf} = -DUR_m V_p - N_f DUR_{mf} f.$$

The solution is

$$N_f = \left(\frac{DUR_{mp}^T - DUR_{mp}}{DUR_{mf}}\right) \frac{V_{pf}}{f}. \qquad (8.36)$$

This formula tells us how many futures contracts we need to trade to adjust the portfolio duration from DUR_{mp} to DUR_{mp}^T. The intuition is fairly simple. If we want to increase the risk of the portfolio, then D_{mp}^T is greater than DUR_{mp}. In that case, the numerator in parentheses is positive. All other terms are positive so N_f will be positive. That means we go long futures. Adding a long futures position to an existing long position adds duration and, therefore, adds risk. Obviously, if we want to reduce risk we need to lower the duration, so the target duration would be lower than the current duration. Then, we should short the futures. The sign of N_f will then be negative, telling us that we are shorting futures. If we wish to completely eliminate the risk, the target duration is zero, and the formula becomes

$$N_f = -\left(\frac{DUR_{mp}}{DUR_{mf}}\right) \left(\frac{V}{f}\right). \qquad (8.37)$$

An example is provided in Exhibit 8-16.

8.2.3.2 *Minimum Variance Hedging*

In some cases, the objective of hedging is to minimize the risk of the portfolio. In Chapter 7 we discussed this approach when covering quantity risk. At this point, we will not assume any quantity risk, but we will address how portfolio risk can be minimized. We will also connect this approach with the strategies in the previous section on using duration.

Objective: A bond portfolio worth $100 million has a modified duration of 8.5 years. The manager wants to use futures contracts to change the duration. Each futures contract has a price of $1 million and a modified duration of 3.5. How many futures would be needed to change the portfolio duration to (a) 10 and (b) zero? Round your answer to the nearest integer numbers of contracts.

Inputs:

$$V_p = \$100{,}000{,}000$$
$$f = \$1{,}000{,}000$$
$$D_{mp} = 8.5$$
$$D_{mf} = 3.5$$
$$\text{(a) } D_{mp}^T = 10$$
$$\text{(b) } D_{mp}^T = 0$$

Results:

$$\text{(a) } N_f = \left(\frac{10 - 8.5}{3.5}\right)\frac{\$100{,}000{,}000}{\$1{,}000{,}000} = 43$$

The manager would buy 43 contracts.

$$\text{(b) } N_f = -\left(\frac{8.5}{3.5}\right)\frac{\$100{,}000{,}000}{\$1{,}000{,}000} = -243$$

The manager would sell 243 contracts.

Exhibit 8-16. Adjusting the Risk of a Bond Portfolio

Let S_0 be the spot price and f_0 be the futures price. Let V be a portfolio consisting of one unit of the asset and N_f futures:

$$V = S_0 + N_f f_0.$$

The variance of this portfolio will be

$$\sigma_{S,f}^2 = \sigma_S^2 + N_f^2 \sigma_f^2 + 2N_f \, \text{cov}_{Sf}.$$

If we want to have the lowest possible variance, we try to minimize this equation. To do that, we differentiate the equation with respect to N and set the derivative to zero,

$$\frac{\partial \sigma_{S,f}^2}{\partial N_f} = 2N_f \sigma_f^2 + 2\text{cov}_{Sf} = 0.$$

The solution is

$$N_f = -\frac{\text{cov}_{Sf}}{\sigma_f^2}. \tag{8.38}$$

This equation may seem familiar from statistics classes. The value of N_f is equivalent to the slope of a regression of the spot price on the futures price. In other words, the beta or slope coefficient of a regression is the covariance between the dependent variable and the independent variable divided by the variance of the independent variable.[24] For this solution to be a minimum rather than a maximum, the second derivative must be positive. Differentiating the first derivative with respect to N,

$$\frac{\partial^2 \sigma_{S,f}^2}{\partial N_f^2} = 2\sigma_f^2.$$

Since variance is always positive, this expression is positive, and it is confirmed that the solution is a minimum.[25] Of course, recall that the covariance is the correlation times the product of the two standard deviations. An example is provided in Exhibit 8-17.

8.2.3.3 *Adjusting Stock Portfolio Risk with Stock Index Futures*

Suppose a portfolio manager owns a stock portfolio worth S_0, which has a beta of β_s. The manager wishes to adjust the beta to a target beta of β_p^T. A futures contract exists and has a price of f_0 and a beta of β_f. How can the manager use futures to change the beta from where it is to the target beta?

First, let us write down the relationship between the portfolio beta in dollars and the components of the portfolio under the assumption that the portfolio contains one asset, the stock, and N_f futures:

$$\beta_p V_p = \beta_s S_0 + N_f \beta_f f_0.$$

The left-hand side is the dollar portfolio beta and the value of the portfolio, which is V_p, but $S_0 = V_p$, because the value of the futures is zero. Now, consider that we want the portfolio beta, β_p, to equal the target beta, β_p^T.

---

[24]This equation can also be shown to equal the equation for converting a bond portfolio from its current duration to a duration of zero. This makes sense. Zero duration would minimize the variance for sure.

[25]Be aware that sometimes the regression is specified in terms of price changes or rates of return, instead of the level of the price.

Objective: A U.S. grain dealer currently holds an inventory of sorghum, a grain used in the production of ethanol and as livestock feed. The current price of sorghum is $225 per metric ton, and the standard deviation is $25. Operational necessities force the dealer to hold various amounts of sorghum for periods of time, thereby leaving itself exposed to decreases in the price of sorghum. There is no sorghum futures contract, but corn is widely used as a substitute in cross hedging. The current price of corn futures is about $393 per 5,000 bushels, which is about 127 metric tons. The standard deviation of the price is estimated at $15. The dealer currently has an inventory of 15,000 metric tons. The correlation between sorghum and corn futures is estimated at 0.48. (a) How many futures contracts of corn would minimize the overall risk? Round the answer to the nearest integer contract. (b) What is the overall standard deviation of the value of its position after the hedge is put into place?

Inputs:

$S_0 = \$225 \times 15{,}000 = \$3{,}375{,}000$ (price per metric ton times # of metric tons)

$f_0 = \$393 \times 127 = \$49{,}911$ (price per contract times # of metric tons per contract)

$\sigma_S^2 = (\$25)^2(15{,}000)^2 = 140{,}625{,}000{,}000$ (variance of price times # of metric tons held)

$\sigma_f^2 = (\$15)^2(127)^2 = 3{,}629{,}025$ (variance of contract price # of metric tons per contract)

$\rho = 0.48$

Results:

(a) Let us first convert the variances to standard deviations:

$$\sigma_S = \sqrt{140{,}625{,}000{,}000} = 375{,}000$$

$$\sigma_f = \sqrt{3{,}629{,}025} = 1{,}905$$

Then the solution is

$$N = -\frac{\text{cov}_{S,f}}{\sigma_f^2}$$

$$= -\frac{0.48(375{,}000)(1{,}905)}{3{,}629{,}025} = -94$$

So the dealer would sell 94 contracts.

(b) $\sigma_{S,f}^2 = \sqrt{140{,}625{,}000{,}000 + (-94)^2(3{,}629{,}025) + 2(-94)(0.48)(375{,}000)(1{,}905)}$

$= 328{,}976$

Note that this volatility is lower than the original volatility, which is the volatility of the spot, 375,000.

Exhibit 8-17. Minimum Variance Hedging

So we set $\beta_p = \beta_p^T$ in the above equation and solve for N_f.

$$N_f = \left(\frac{\beta_p^T - \beta_s}{\beta_f} \right) \frac{S_0}{f_0}. \tag{8.39}$$

In many cases, the futures contract will be based on a market index, so it would reasonable to assume that $\beta_f = 1$. Notice that if we wish to increase the target beta, then $\beta_p^T > \beta_f$ and the sign of N_f will be positive. This makes sense. We want to increase the risk. We are long the asset, so to increase the risk we should add long exposure through a long futures position. Similarly, if we wish to decrease the risk, the target beta will be lower than the current beta, so N_f will be negative. If we want to completely eliminate the risk, we set the target beta to zero and obtain

$$N_f = -\frac{\beta_s}{\beta_f} \frac{S_0}{f_0}. \tag{8.40}$$

An example is provided in Exhibit 8-18.

Objective: The manager of a €475 million stock portfolio with a beta of 0.9 wishes to temporarily change the beta. A stock index futures contact, $\beta_f = 1$, traded with a price of €355,000. (a) How many contracts should he buy or sell to change the beta to 1.1? (b) How many contracts should he buy or sell to lower the beta to 0.0? Round both answers to the nearest integer.

Inputs:

$$S_0 = €475,000,000$$
$$f_0 = €355,000$$
$$\beta_s = 0.9$$
$$\beta_T = \text{(a) 1.1, (b) 0.0}$$
$$\beta_f = 1.0$$

Results:

(a) $N_f = \left(\dfrac{1.1 - 0.9}{1.0} \right) \left(\dfrac{€475,000,000}{€355,000} \right) = 268.$

Given the desire to increase the risk, the number of contracts is positive, meaning to buy futures.

(b) $N_f = \left(\dfrac{0.0 - 0.9}{1.0} \right) \left(\dfrac{€475,000,000}{€355,000} \right) = -1,204.$

Given the desire to reduce the beta risk, the number of contracts is negative, meaning to sell futures.

Exhibit 8-18. Changing the Beta of a Stock Portfolio

8.3 Chapter Summary

In this chapter, we examined the pricing, valuation, and use of forward and futures contracts. Recall that these contracts require no up-front investment, and they commit one party to buying and the other to selling the underlying at a fixed price at the expiration of the contract. Forward contracts are customized, while futures contracts are standardized, traded on a futures exchange, and subject to a daily settlement. We saw that both contracts are priced by an arbitrage strategy that results in the price equaling the spot price minus the present value of any benefits offered by the asset compounded at the risk-free rate minus the compound value of any costs of holding the asset. In addition, with some futures contracts, there is the possibility of a convenience yield, a non-monetary return that arises from holding an asset that is in short supply and/or cannot be sold short. We closely examined forward and futures contracts on currencies, bonds, interest rates, stock indexes, and commodities. Forward contracts are widely used in the corporate world, while futures are more commonly used in the asset management industry to either eliminate or modify the risk.

8.4 Questions and Problems

1. In what way is a forward or futures contract a firm commitment? How can this commitment be avoided?
2. How does a cash settlement at expiration of a forward contract result in economic equivalence to physical delivery, ignoring transaction costs?
3. Provide a conceptual explanation of the value of a forward contract under the following circumstances: (a) at initiation, and (b) at expiration. Justify why the value is as you say it is.
4. Explain in words the formula for the value of a forward contract under the assumption that the underlying makes cash payments but has no storage costs. Explain why the cash payments are handled in the formula the way in which they are.
5. Reconsider your answer in Question 4 to account for storage costs and also identify what we mean by the cost of carry.
6. Explain the concept of convenience yield and modify your answer in Question 5 to account for the effect of a convenience yield.
7. Consider a 160-day forward contract on an asset priced at $135. The asset generates cash flows of $1.50 in 40 days and $1.75 in 120 days. It incurs storage costs of $1.25 in 60 and 120 days, that is, every 60

days. The future value of the convenience yield is found to be $2.87. The risk-free rate is 3.55%. Find the forward price.

8. If the forward price in the market is different from the model forward price, explain how an arbitrageur will take action. Cover the two cases of an overpriced forward and an underpriced forward. Identify what happens to bring the market price to the model price.

9. Explain the concepts of (a) backwardation vs. contango and (b) normal backwardation vs. normal contango.

10. Provide a conceptual explanation of how to determine the value of a forward contract during its life.

11. Consider a $20 million notional forward contract established today at a price of $452.50. The contract expires in 250 days. Now we move forward 100 days. The price of a new forward contract is $452.19. The risk-free rate is 1.75%. Find the value of the contract to the long.

12. Explain how the interest rate parity formula is derived.

13. Suppose you are a currency trader in South Korea. The exchange rate for the Korean won relative to the U.S. dollar is 1,114.95. This figure is Korean won (KRW) per U.S. dollar (USD). Assume the Korean annually compounded risk-free rate is 1.5%, while the U. S. rate is 0.5%. Find the forward rate in KRW for a six-month contract.

14. A U.S. trader enters into a long one-year forward contract on the Russian ruble at a rate of $0.0161. Now, three months later, the forward price of a ruble expiring at the same time is $0.0166. The U.S. interest rate is 0.65%, and the contract notional is $30 million. Find the value of the contract.

15. Why does the payoff formula for an FRA reflect a discount factor?

16. Provide a conceptual explanation of how the price of an FRA is determined.

17. Find the fixed rate on a 120-day FRA on 90-day LIBOR given the following information: 120-day LIBOR is 4.26% and 210-day LIBOR is 4.74%.

18. Provide a conceptual explanation of how the value of an FRA is determined.

19. Suppose a corporation enters into an FRA that expires in 180 days and the underlying is 30-day LIBOR. The fixed rate is found to be 3.22%. Now roll ahead 72 days, and determine the value of the FRA if the rate for 108 days is 3.15% and the rate for 138 days is 3.08%. The notional is $28 million.

20. Explain the role of the value of a forward in terminating a position early.

21. What is an off-market FRA?

22. Consider an FRA expiring in 90 days based on 180-day LIBOR that is constructed based on the following term structure: 180-day LIBOR = 2.77%, 270-day LIBOR = 2.85%. The notional is $17.5 million. The formula fixed rate is 2.97%, but the parties set the fixed rate at 3.25%. With this being an off-market forward, determine how much money one party owes the other and identify which party pays.

23. Consider a Danish company that has a substantial operation in the U.S. and receives cash flows in U.S. dollars. It anticipates the receipt of $100 million in one year. The current forward rate for its current, the Danish krone (DKK), is 6.6814 per USD. Explain how it would use a forward foreign currency hedge to eliminate the exchange rate risk.

24. A Peruvian company buys raw materials from a European company and pays in euros. It anticipates that in six months it will buy 20 million units of the material and will pay a price of €2.55 per unit. The current six-month forward exchange rate is that one Peruvian sol = 0.2621 euros. Explain the risk faced by the Peruvian company and how it can hedge that risk.

25. A U.S. company plans to borrow $15 million in 180 days at 90-day LIBOR plus 2.5%. Identify the risk and explain how it could use a 180-day FRA on 90-day LIBOR at the rate of 4.72% to eliminate the risk.

26. Identify the primary differences in futures and forwards.

27. Explain how the daily settlement on futures can make futures prices be higher or lower than forward prices.

28. The term structure of LIBOR is 2.29% for 60 days and 2.72% for 150 days. Find the quote price of a Eurodollar futures and convert to the trade price. Then let the rate decrease by five basis points and show that the change in the trade price is $-5(\$25) = -\$125$.

29. Explain how bond futures contracts with multiple deliverable bonds are priced.

30. Consider a stock index at 1,422.15 that is expected to pay a dividend of $3.40 in 10 days and in 100 days. (a) Find the price of a futures contract on the index that expires in 120 days. The risk-free rate is 2.88%. (b) Find the price if instead the dividend is quoted as a continuously compounded yield of 1%.

31. Why is a futures hedge concerned essentially a speculative position in the basis?

32. Suppose you hold a bond portfolio worth $75 million, with a modified duration of 5.87 years. You are concerned about the outlook for an

interest rate increase and would like to lower the duration. A futures contract priced at \$125,500 with a modified duration of 6.44 is available. (a) How many futures contracts would you need to trade and would you be long or short if you want to lower the duration to 3.25? (b) How many futures contracts would you need to trade and would you be long or short if you want to completely eliminate the risk?

33. An investor holds an asset worth \$850,000 and wishes to hedge it so as to minimize the risk. The asset has a correlation with a futures contract of 0.63 and a volatility of \$25,000. The futures contract has a volatility of \$4,500. How many futures contracts should the investor sell to minimize the risk? Determine the volatility of the hedged position and compare it to the volatility of the unhedged position.

34. Consider a stock portfolio worth \$350 million with a beta of 1.15. A futures contract that will hedge the portfolio has a beta of 1.0 and a price of \$155,000. (a) How many contracts should be used and should they be bought or sold to increase the beta to 1.35? (b) How many contracts should be used and should they be bought or sold to reduce the beta to zero? In both cases, round to the nearest integer number of contracts.

Chapter 9

Managing Market Risk with Swaps

You can think of a derivative as a mixture of its constituent underliers much as a cake is a mixture of eggs, flour, and milk in carefully specified proportions. The derivative's model provides a recipe for the mixture, one whose ingredients' quantities vary with time.

Emanuel Derman
Risk magazine
July, 2001, p. 48

In Chapter 8 we examined forward and futures contracts. Recall that these derivatives are contracts in which two **parties** agree that one party will buy an asset from another at a future date at a price they agree on at the start. Forward and futures contracts are sometimes called forward commitments, because they are agreements that commit each party to a transaction in the future at a price they agree on when the transaction is initiated. Swaps extend the idea of a commitment made in advance for a single transaction to a commitment made in advance for a *series of transactions* at different dates. Thus, in some sense a swap can be viewed as a portfolio of forward or futures contracts, though we will illustrate this point in more detail later and show that there are some technical differences.

9.1 Formal Definition of a Swap

As a formal definition of a swap, we present the following:

> *A swap is a derivative contract in which two parties, the buyer and the seller, agree to exchange a series of cash flows at specified future dates with at least one cash flow series being variable and determined by the future course of an uncertain price or rate and the other cash flow series being either fixed or variable and based on the future course of a different price or rate.*

Now let us carefully work through that definition. As with all derivative contracts, there are two parties, one party typically referred to as the buyer and the other, the seller. The two parties agree to exchange a series of future cash flows at specified dates. At least one cash flow is variable and determined by a price or rate. This cash flow series will typically be based on the price of an asset or on an interest rate or on an exchange rate. We note that the other cash flow can also be variable and if so, it would be determined by a different price or rate. Oftentimes, however, the other series is fixed, meaning that the two parties agree to a fixed rate in advance. Thus, in most swaps one party is said to pay a floating or variable rate and the other pays a fixed rate, though in some swaps, both pay floating rates.[1] A party, such as an end user, can be on either side of the transaction. Thus, one party can pay floating while the other pays fixed, or one party can pay fixed while the other pays floating. Or one party can pay a particular floating rate while the other pays a different floating rate. Although we will illustrate the purpose of swaps in more detail later, it is useful to see here that swaps can be used to shift the risk away from exposure to a particular price or rate. If a party is exposed to a specific price or rate, it could enter into a swap to receive or pay that price or rate and pay or receive a fixed rate or pay or receive a different price or rate.

The terminology of a party being *long* or *short* can get a bit confusing in swaps. The party referred to as long is usually the one paying a fixed price or rate, while the short pays a floating or variable price or rate. But if both rates are variable, neither can truly be referred to as long or short. In that case, we usually identify the parties in some other way, such as by name or generically as, say, party A and party B. When referring to the two parties or sets of payments, we often use the terms *sides* or *legs*. There is a fixed side or leg and a floating side or leg.

Swaps can be set up to settle completely in cash. Indeed, most swaps are settled in cash. It is much easier to make a payment based on the

---

[1]It may seem to be an omission that we have not mentioned the possibility that both sides pay the same or different fixed rates. Consider a case where the two parties each agree to make payments to each other at a rate of 3%. An arrangement of this sort would accomplish nothing, as both parties would pay each other the same amount on all of the payment dates. Suppose, however, that party A agrees to pay party B a series of 3% payments and party B agrees to pay party A a series of 4% payments. Clearly party A is getting the better end of the deal. It has effectively created a 1% annuity. There would be no reason for party B to do this transaction unless party A paid party B the present value of a series of 1% payments. Thus, such swaps have no purpose and are not done. At least one party always pays a variable or floating rate.

price of an asset or rate than to deliver the underlying asset or whatever asset determines the underlying rate. Cash settlement fulfills the financial objective of a swap without incurring the costs of delivering assets.

9.2 Basic Structure and Characteristics of Swap Contracts and Markets

Swaps are strictly over-the-counter contracts. They involve two parties, one typically an end user and the other a dealer. Normally the end user approaches the dealer with a particular risk it needs to reduce or eliminate. Swap dealers make markets in swaps by quoting prices or rates for either side of the transaction.[2] Being OTC instruments, swaps are extremely flexible and can be tailored precisely to an end user's needs. The payment dates and final maturity can be set at whatever dates the end user desires.

The most common underlyings of swaps are interest rates, exchange rates, stock prices or stock indexes, and commodity prices.[3] There are rather significant differences in the types of swaps as categorized by the underlying price or rate, and as such, we cannot give a good general characterization of all swaps. We will cover details of these four types of swaps based on their underlyings in this chapter.

In Chapter 5 we discussed the size of the OTC derivatives market based on the Bank for International Settlements (BIS) survey data. We reported that in December 2017, the total notional of OTC derivatives was about $531 trillion, while the total market value was $11 trillion. Interest rate swaps compose about $319 trillion notional and about $6.7 trillion of market value. Currency swaps are about $25.5 trillion notional with about $989 billion market value. The BIS continues to group equity swaps and forwards together, and this total is about $3.2 trillion notional and $197 billion market value. Commodity forwards and swaps are also grouped together and make up $1.4 trillion notional with market value not reported. Clearly interest rate swaps are the largest component of the general category of swaps.

---

[2]We would be remiss, however, if we failed to acknowledge the enormous selling effort that dealers make in attempting to convince end users to engage in swaps. Recall the example at the beginning of this book in which the newly appointed corporate CEO is courted by a dealer bank selling swaps. High pressure can be placed on end users, but of course, no one can force an end user to sign a derivative contract.

[3]Credit is also an underlying in swaps, and indeed credit default swaps are an important instrument in financial markets. We will cover credit default swaps in Chapter 11 where we will see that they are somewhat misnamed and are not really much like swaps.

The Big Bang of Swaps

It is rare in the financial world that we can trace a privately constructed financial instrument to its origin, meaning to identify the first parties who did a particular type of transaction. But for swaps, there is widespread agreement that the origins trace back to a transaction conducted in 1981 between IBM, the World Bank, and the no-longer-existent investment bank of Salomon Brothers.

The World Bank is a bank that extends credit to countries that have difficulty borrowing in traditional financial markets. These countries are often developing and economically weak countries that use the funds to invest in projects that will hopefully improve their economies. The World Bank is owned by the governments of 188 countries.

There are widely divergent versions of why in 1981 the World Bank needed to borrow German marks and Swiss francs but could not do so attractively, and why IBM needed U.S. dollars but could not borrow attractively. Regardless of the reason, Salomon Brothers came up with the solution. Since the World Bank could borrow attractively in the U.S. and IBM could borrow attractively in Germany and Switzerland, it occurred to someone that the two countries could take out loans in their preferred markets and swap the currencies obtained from their up-front payments. Thus, IBM borrowed in Germany and Switzerland and through a swap, it paid the proceeds of those loans to the World Bank up front. The World Bank in turn borrowed in U.S. dollars and paid the proceeds of that loan to IBM. Each entity effectively took out a loan in one currency and using a swap, converted it to a loan in another currency. Hence, the first currency swap came in with a (big) bang.

There is no documented history on when someone got the idea of making both currencies be the same and having one set of payments be at a fixed rate and one at a floating rate. But whenever someone did, the first interest rate swap was born.

Let us now take a look at the special characteristics of the four primary types of swaps.

9.2.1 *Interest Rate Swaps*

As demonstrated above, interest rate swaps are the largest component of the swaps market. They are widely used by corporations to modify the payment patterns of their loans, as for example converting a floating-rate loan to a fixed-rate loan. We will see an example of how this objective is achieved later.

In order to understand how interest rate swaps fit into the general concept of a swap, it will be beneficial to go back a couple of pages and re-read the definition of a swap. We need to modify that definition so that it characterizes an interest rate swap. Unfortunately, there are many varieties of interest rate swaps, so it will be difficult to create an all-encompassing definition. It will be far better to lay a foundation by identifying the definition and characteristics of the most common type of swap, which is called a *plain vanilla swap* and sometimes just a *vanilla* swap. That definition is as follows:

> *A (plain) vanilla interest rate swap is a swap in which the buyer or long agrees to make a series of fixed interest payments based on an agreed-upon notional to the seller or short at specified future dates, with the seller or short agreeing to make a series of floating interest payments on that same notional with the payments determined by the course of a specified underlying rate.*

In other words, a vanilla interest rate swap is a fixed-for-floating swap. One party pays a fixed rate, and the other pays a floating rate. The terms *long* and *short* work perfectly well for vanilla swaps. The buyer is long the floating rate, and thereby benefits from an increase in the floating rate, while the seller is short the floating rate and benefits from a decrease in the floating rate.

The underlying rate in most plain vanilla swaps is LIBOR. As explained in previous chapters, LIBOR, the London Interbank Offer Rate, is the rate at which a London bank borrows from another London bank. The primary currency in which these transactions are conducted is U.S. dollars. Thus, there is dollar LIBOR, but in addition, there are also euro LIBOR, yen LIBOR, and sterling LIBOR, as well as LIBOR for other currencies. Dollar LIBOR is sometimes referred to as the Eurodollar rate. Swap dealers, in fact, often use Eurodollar futures to hedge their swaps.

Recall in Chapter 8 that we discussed the FRA market, which is more or less just the market for swaps with one payment. We designated the symbol $L_0(T_m)$ as the rate on day T_m of T_m-day LIBOR. Thus, today we might look up the rate on 90-day LIBOR and denote it as $L_0(90)$. In addition, we could look up the rates on 30- and 60-day LIBOR as well as other rates with maturities 30 days apart up to 360 days. Interest on a loan based on LIBOR would be determined based on the number of days divided by 360.

In the case of FRAs, the date T_m is the maturity and payment date of the FRA. As noted, all swaps make payments on a series of specified dates. These dates are commonly separated by one month, three months, or six months, though any set of dates can be specified. The end user typically specifies the dates, because it is usually employing the swap to hedge a risk that involves rates that are set on certain dates. When engaging in a vanilla swap, the dealer quotes the fixed rate that one party will pay with an understanding that the other party will pay the floating rate. Thus, it is not necessary to quote the floating rate. In Section 9.3, we will cover how the dealer determines the fixed rate.

The dates on which the payments are made are called the *settlement dates*, and the periods between these settlement dates are called the *settlement periods*. The floating rate is set at the beginning of the settlement period and the payment is made at the end of the period, the method of which we referred to in Chapter 8 as advance set, settlement in arrears. Let us assume that the swap is set up at time 0 with settlement dates denoted as $T_1, T_2, \ldots, T_m$. We can treat these dates as days from day 0, and they are h days apart. Thus, T_1 might be 180, T_2 might be 360, etc. On day 0, the first floating rate is set at $L_0(T_1)$, the current T_1-day rate that is set in London by banks borrowing from each other. The fixed rate on the swap, as quoted by the dealer, is $FS(0, T_m)$. Exhibit 9-1 illustrates the sequence of payments from the point of view of the long and is based on a notional of \$1.

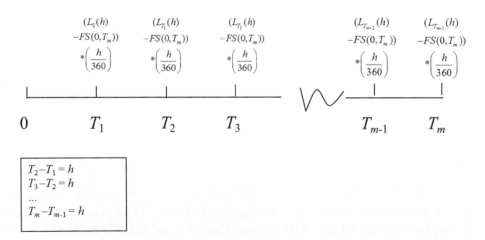

Exhibit 9-1. Structure and Cash Flows of a Plain Vanilla Swap from the Perspective of the Buyer

Any other notional can be accommodated by multiplying the payments by the notional.[4]

Note first that the cash flows, which are written above the time line, occur at the series of points, $T_1, T_2, \ldots, T_m$. The box in the lower left corner indicates that these points are equally spaced with the interval of h days. Now observe the first payment, which is denoted as $(L_0(h) - FS(0, T_m)) * (h/360)$. Remember that this exhibit is shown from the point of the view of the buyer, who pays a fixed rate. Thus, the buyer pays $FS(0, T_m)$ to the seller, which explains the minus sign in front of $FS(0, T_m)$. The seller pays floating to the buyer. The floating rate paid at time T_1 is the rate that was set at time 0, which is $L_0(h)$. After adjusting by the $h/360$ factor, the cash flow from the perspective of the buyer is $(L_0(h) - FS(0, T_m)) * (h/360)$. This equation specifies not only the amount of the cash flow to the buyer, but it even suggests the manner in which the payment is made. The buyer does not independently pay $FS(0, T_m)$ times $h/360$ to the seller, and the seller does not independently pay $L_0(h)$ times $h/360$. The two parties simply determine the net amount, and a single payment is made from one party to the other.[5] Thus, if $(L_0(h) - FS(0, T_m)) * (h/360)$ is positive, meaning that $L_0(h)$ exceeds $FS(0, T_m)$, the net is positive and the seller pays the buyer the net amount. Otherwise, the net is negative, and the buyer pays the seller.

Note that the initial floating rate, $L_0(h)$, is set at time 0, the day the swap starts.[6] Thus, the first payment is not subject to any uncertainty. But on day T_1, the two parties observe in the market that the h-day LIBOR is now $L_{T_1}(h)$. This new value of h-day LIBOR sets the rate for the next payment. Notice in Exhibit 9-1 that the next payment, made at T_2, is $(L_{T_1}(h) - FS(0, T_m)) * (h/360)$. Then on that date, we observe a new value

---

[4]Here we have assumed that both the fixed and floating payments are done by applying the days/360 adjustment. It is quite common that the fixed rate is adjusted using 365 days. In addition, some swaps involve the floating payments being done on one day and the fixed on another. Also, in some swaps the day counts are based on the assumption of 30 days in a month. Thus, payments done on the 15th of each quarter would be adjusted by 90/360, not the actual number of days divided by 360. These factors would require some additional notation in the figures and adjustments to the pricing and valuation formulas that we will present later, but they would not complicate the calculations. We will leave off these adjustments in order to make the basic ideas much clearer.

[5]As mentioned, some swaps do not have to have the fixed and floating payments on the same day. One might be quarterly and one semiannually. Thus, the parties cannot always net the payments.

[6]Technically there is a two-business-day period between the rate set day and the initiation day. Also, all rate resets occur two business days before the respective settlement day.

of h-day LIBOR, which determines the payment at T_3. This process continues until the last payment, $(L_{T_{m-1}}(h) - FS(0, T_m)) * (h/360)$, which is made on the termination date of T_m.

As noted, the process in which a rate is determined at the beginning of the settlement period and payment is made at the end of the settlement period is called *advance set, settle in arrears*. This arrangement is the most common in swaps, and the reason is quite simple: advance set, settle in arrears is the most common method used in floating-rate loans. Typically a rate is observed in the LIBOR market and used to set the rate on a loan. Interest then accrues at that rate, and the interest is paid at the end of the period. You may remember from Chapter 8, however, that with FRAs the rate is determined and set on the same day, a process referred to as *advance set, settle in advance* or *advance settle*.[7] As a result, FRA payments based on h-day LIBOR are discounted for h days. So FRAs and swaps on LIBOR are not structured quite the same way. When we cover interest rate options, we will see that they are structured like swaps, that is, advance set, settled in arrears.

Let us take a look at how swap payoffs are determined in Exhibit 9-2.

It is extremely important to note that interest rate swaps do not involve any payment of notional. For example, an interest rate swap with notional of

---

Objective: Consider a vanilla interest rate swap based on 90-day LIBOR with notional of $25 million and fixed payments of 3.5%. The 90-day floating rate at the last settlement date is 2.92%. Determine the current payment for the party paying fixed and receiving floating.

Inputs:

Notional:	$25 million
Fixed rate:	3.5%
Floating rate for current payment:	2.92%

Results:

$$\$25,000,000(0.0292 - 0.035)\left(\frac{90}{360}\right) = -\$36,250$$

Thus, party paying fixed and receiving floating has to pay the counterparty $36,250.

Exhibit 9-2. Vanilla Interest Rate Swap Payoffs

---

[7]Depending on the perspective, one could call it *set in arrears, settled in arrears*.

$50 million merely involves a series of net interest payments (floating minus fixed) applied to the $50 million notional. Indeed, it would be absurd to have an exchange of notionals. At the end of the life of the swap, why would one party pay $50 million to the other party, who would immediately pay $50 million to the first party? Such an exchange would serve no purpose. Nonetheless, the implicit element of the notional plays an important part in swap pricing. We defer a full discussion of this point until the pricing material in Section 9.3, but let us see now what happens if we insert a notional into the problem.

Suppose the end user, the party who is long the swap in Exhibit 9-1, considers an alternative way of structuring the transaction. Let us say the end user takes out a $1 loan at a rate of $FS(0, T_m)$ with payments made on the dates indicated in Exhibit 9-1. The end user will receive $1 at time 0 and pay back $1 at time T_m. Assume that the lender is the dealer. Assume also that at time 0 the end user takes the $1 proceeds from the loan and makes a floating-rate loan to the dealer that pays interest at h-day LIBOR and matures at time T_m. Thus, the end user pays and receives $1 at times 0 and T_m. If the opposite party in these two loans is the same party, these transactions are called parallel loans, and they are often believed to be the progenitors of swaps. Exhibit 9-3 illustrates how parallel loans are effectively equivalent to vanilla swaps.

Observe that at time 0, there is a cash inflow of 1, arising from the issuance of the fixed-rate loan of principal 1, and a cash outflow of 1, arising from the creation of the floating-rate loan of principal 1. Thus, the net cash flow at time 0 is zero. At the maturity of the two loans, time T_m, there is a cash inflow of 1, arising from the payoff of on the floating-rate loan the party holds, and a cash outflow of 1, arising from the repayment of the fixed-rate loan. Thus, there is zero net cash flow at maturity from the principal payments. On the settlement dates there are cash flows arising from the payment of fixed interest on the fixed-rate loan and the receipt of floating

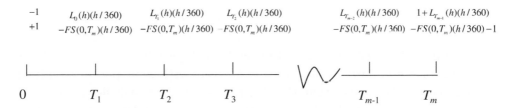

Exhibit 9-3. Fixed- and Floating-Rate Parallel Loans

interest on the floating-rate loan. The net of all of these cash flows is the same as the payments on a vanilla swap.

Nonetheless, there is an important distinction between parallel loans and vanilla swaps. Borrowers can default on principal payments on loans. Thus, the party above who is expecting to receive a principal payment of 1 at T_m will not be paid if the issuer defaults. In contrast, a swap specifies no principal payments at all. Thus, there is no concern over the credit risk of the principal in a vanilla swap. Now we are not saying that there cannot be defaults on the net swap payments, and we will discuss this matter in Section 9.6 and in more detail in Chapter 11 when we discuss credit risk. But in an actual interest rate swap, there cannot be default on the principal, because there is no principal payment.

Although we will cover how swaps are used in a Section 9.7, it is worthwhile here to consider the purpose of swaps. Let us go back to Exhibit 9-1 and imagine that the end user has a floating-rate loan in which it pays h-day LIBOR with payments on days $T_1, T_2, \ldots, T_m$. Fearing an increase in interest rates, the end user would prefer a fixed-rate loan. By engaging in the swap in Exhibit 9-1, the end user can effectively convert the floating-rate loan into a fixed-rate loan. The end user pays the appropriate floating LIBOR rate to its creditor on each payment date, the loan rate is reset, and a new rate goes into effect, thereby setting the rate for the next loan interest payment. Simultaneously, the end user receives the same floating LIBOR payment on the swap, the swap rate is reset to the same rate on the loan that will determine the next swap payment, while simultaneously making payments to the swap dealer at the fixed rate. Thus, the floating payments cancel, and the end user synthetically converts the floating rate loan into a fixed rate loan at the swap fixed rate, $FS(0, T_m)$. An actual loan would probably involve the party paying a spread over LIBOR but that spread would be fixed and would net out that the borrower would effectively pay the swap fixed rate plus a constant spread.

Before we leave this introductory section on interest rate swaps, look again at Exhibit 9-1. There are some exceptions to the general layout as we have shown here. For one, the settlement periods might not always be h days apart, as specified here. Doing so enables us to consistently use $h/360$ as the adjustment. For whatever the settlement periods are, we would use the appropriate number of days during a given settlement period to adjust the payments. Also, note that the diagram shows the cash flows from the perspective of the long, that is, the party paying fixed and receiving floating. If we were interested in viewing the swap from the other party's perspective, we would simply put a negative sign in front of each cash flow, which would correctly adjust for the fact that the other party receives the fixed rate and pays the floating rate. In addition, for a notional of more than \$1, we would simply multiply the cash flow in the figure by the notional. And finally, let us note that the fixed rate on the swap, $FS(0, T_m)$, is determined by pricing the swap, a process we will study in Section 9.3.1.

9.2.2 *Currency Swaps*

While we started Section 9.2 with interest rate swaps, we could just as easily have started with currency swaps. By the time we get to the end of this section you will see why, but in short, an interest rate swap is just a special case of a currency swap in which both currencies are the same.

Let us start with a definition of a currency swap:

A currency swap is a special form of an interest rate swap in which one party agrees to make a series of interest payment to the other at specified future dates in one currency, with the other party agreeing to make a series of interest payments to the first party in a different currency.

The key characteristic is that one party makes interest payments in one currency and one makes interest payments in another currency. Recall that with vanilla interest rate swaps, one payment is fixed and one is floating. With currency swaps, the interest payments are based on interest rates in the different countries. Thus, both payments can be floating or both could be fixed or you could have one floating and one fixed. You might also note that we do not refer to a given party as the buyer or long and the other as the seller or short. One party is long one currency and the other party is long the other currency. In turn, each is short the opposite currency. So, the two parties are each both a buyer and a seller.[8] By the way, currency swaps are occasionally called *cross-currency* swaps.

Another seemingly unusual characteristic of currency swaps is that they *can* be set up to involve the exchange of notionals. Recall that in vanilla interest rate swaps, an exchange of notionals would merely involve each party giving the other the same amount of money at the same time. As you will see, that arrangement is not what happens in currency swaps. We will focus

---

[8]Such is the perhaps somewhat confusing nature of currency transactions. When we get to currency options, we will see that the holder of a call on one currency can also be viewed as the holder of a put on the other currency.

almost exclusively on currency swaps that involve an exchange of notionals, as this type of currency swap is more common.

So, let us identify four types of currency swaps: (1) pay domestic currency floating, receive foreign currency floating, (2) pay domestic currency floating, receive foreign currency fixed, (3) pay domestic currency fixed, receive foreign currency floating, and (4) pay domestic currency fixed, receive foreign currency fixed. For clarity, let us add a subscript d for domestic and f for foreign. We will assume that the LIBORs in the two currencies are the relevant floating rates. Thus, we will denote the floating rates at time 0 as $L_{0,d}(h)$ and $L_{0,f}(h)$ and the fixed rates as $FS_d(0, T_m)$ and $FS_f(0, T_m)$. Again, we will cover how these fixed rates are determined in the pricing section. You will note that, ignoring the d and f subscripts, we are using the same symbols that we used for the fixed rates on interest rate swaps. As we will see later in this chapter, the fixed rates on currency swaps are indeed the same as the fixed rates on interest rate swaps.

Currency swaps have two notionals, one in each currency. We will set the domestic notional to 1. Let us assume the spot rate for the two currencies is S_0. Thus, the foreign notional is $1/S_0$. Let us think about that point for a moment.

Suppose the domestic currency is the U.S. dollar and the foreign currency is the British pound. Let the exchange rate be \$1.60, meaning that 1 British pound costs \$1.60. The inverse of \$1.60 is 1/\$1.60 = £0.625. Thus, \$1 notional on the domestic side of the transaction implies that the foreign notional is £0.625. At the start of the swap, there is an initial exchange of currencies, but the value of the swap is zero, because the two currencies are made equivalent in value by setting the notionals in this manner.

Exhibit 9-4 illustrates the payments on a currency swap in which one party pays floating in its domestic currency on notional of 1 and receives floating in the foreign currency on notional of $1/S_0$.

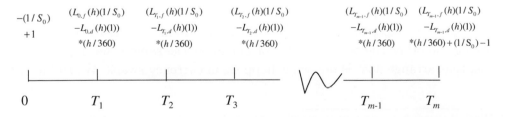

Exhibit 9-4. Structure and Cash Flows of a Currency Swap Paying Domestic Floating and Receiving Foreign Floating

Notice as with interest rate swaps that the floating rates are set in advance and settled in arrears and that the respective notional payments are made at the beginning and at the end of the swap. At the beginning, the two amounts, -1 and $1/S_0$, are equivalent, but they are not likely to be at the end, because the exchange rate will surely have changed over the life of the swap.

Note also that the party receiving foreign floating must pay the foreign notional at the start and receives the foreign notional at the end. This party also receives the domestic notional at the start and pays the domestic notional at the end. Looking at it this way, we see that this party has executed the equivalent of two transactions. One is to issue a bond in domestic currency and use the proceeds to buy a foreign bond. These points will apply equally to the remaining currency swaps that we cover in the next three exhibits.

Exhibit 9-5 illustrates a currency swap paying domestic floating and receiving foreign fixed.

The only difference with Exhibit 9-4 is that the payment received is at the foreign fixed rate rather than at the foreign floating rate.

Exhibit 9-6 illustrates a currency swap in which the party pays domestic fixed and receives foreign floating. Note that the party pays the same rate,

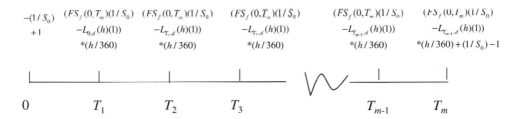

Exhibit 9-5. Structure and Cash Flows of a Currency Swap Paying Domestic Floating and Receiving Foreign Fixed

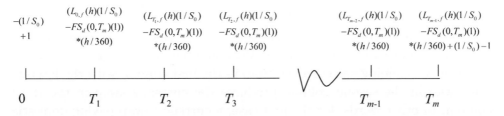

Exhibit 9-6. Structure and Cash Flows of a Currency Swap Paying Domestic Fixed and Receiving Foreign Floating

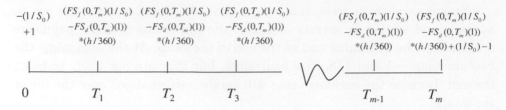

Exhibit 9-7. Structure and Cash Flows of a Currency Swap Paying Domestic Fixed and Receiving Foreign Fixed

$FS_d(0, T_m)$, the domestic fixed rate, on all payments and receives the foreign floating rate in arrears.

Finally, Exhibit 9-7 illustrates a currency swap in which the party pays domestic fixed and receives foreign fixed. Notice here that it appears as if the same payments are being made, but keep in mind that the foreign payments are in the foreign currency and the domestic payments are in the domestic currency, and also that the domestic and foreign fixed rates are not likely to be the same. Moreover, when the foreign payments are translated into the domestic currency, the changing nature of the exchange rate will make the value of the foreign payments fluctuate. In addition, the values of all payments in each of the above illustrated swaps vary with changes in interest rates. Thus, we can see that all currency swaps have two sources of uncertainty: interest rates and exchange rates.

Let us now take a look at any actual calculation of a currency swap payment. Exhibit 9-8 illustrates the calculation of payments for the four types of currency swaps.

It should be noted that currency swaps are not typically netted. Each party pays in the respective currencies. The calculations above do net the amounts, so as to arrive at the overall value of the payment.

Now take a look Exhibit 9-9, which illustrates a very important point: how currency and interest rate swaps are related to each other. In the first column we list the four types of currency swaps, as identified a few pages back. In the second column we list various ways to structure an interest rate swap. We refer to the swap as "domestic" in that it is executed within the party's domestic market and is denominated in the party's domestic currency. Combining the currency swap in the first column with the interest rate swap in the second column produces the currency swap in the third column. In other words, for the first case, a currency swap paying domestic floating and receiving foreign floating is combined with a domestic interest rate swap to pay domestic fixed and receive domestic floating. Therefore,

Objective: Consider currency swaps based on 90-day LIBOR with notionals of $25 million and £20 million. The U.S. and U.K. swap fixed rates are 3.22% and 3.85%, respectively. The U.S. and U.K. floating rates, which were set at the last settlement date, are 3.95% and 4.15%, respectively. The current exchange rate for the pound is $1.28. Determine the current net payments in dollars for the party paying in dollars and receiving in pounds for the four kinds of swaps:

> Swap 1: Pay dollars fixed, receive pounds fixed
> Swap 2: Pay dollars fixed, receive pounds floating
> Swap 3: Pay dollars floating, receive pounds floating
> Swap 4: Pay dollars floating, receive pounds fixed

Inputs:

	U.S.	U.K.
Notional:	$25 million	£20 million
Fixed rate:	3.22%	3.85%
Floating rate for current payment:	3.95%	4.15%

Results:

Swap 1

$$£20,000,000(0.0385)\left(\frac{90}{360}\right)(\$1.28) - \$25,000,000(0.0322)\left(\frac{90}{360}\right) = \$45,150$$

Swap 2

$$£20,000,000(0.0415)\left(\frac{90}{360}\right)(\$1.28) - \$25,000,000(0.0322)\left(\frac{90}{360}\right) = \$64,350$$

Swap 3

$$£20,000,000(0.0415)\left(\frac{90}{360}\right)(\$1.28) - \$25,000,000(0.0395)\left(\frac{90}{360}\right) = \$18,725$$

Swap 4

$$£20,000,000(0.0385)\left(\frac{90}{360}\right)(\$1.28) - \$25,000,000(0.0395)\left(\frac{90}{360}\right) = -\$475$$

Exhibit 9-8. Currency Swap Payoffs

Currency Swap	Plus Domestic Interest Rate Swap	Equals Currency Swap
(1) Pay domestic floating, receive foreign floating	Pay domestic fixed, receive domestic floating	(3) Pay domestic fixed, receive foreign floating
(2) Pay domestic floating, receive foreign fixed	Pay domestic fixed, receive domestic floating	(4) Pay domestic fixed, receive foreign fixed
(3) Pay domestic fixed, receive foreign floating	Pay domestic floating, receive domestic fixed	(1) Pay domestic floating, receive foreign floating
(4) Pay domestic fixed, receive foreign fixed	Pay domestic floating, receive domestic fixed	(2) Pay domestic floating, receive foreign fixed

Exhibit 9-9. The Relationship of Currency Swaps to Interest Rate Swaps

the pay domestic floating leg on the currency swap and the receive domestic floating leg on the interest rate swap offset, leaving a position of paying domestic fixed and receiving foreign floating. Note that currency swap (1) is thereby converted to currency swap (3), and currency swap (2) can be converted into currency swap (4). Likewise, we could reverse the direction. Currency swap (3) could be converted into currency swap (1), and currency swap (4) could be converted into currency swap (2).

If you are wondering whether currency swap (1) can be converted into currency swap (2) and currency swap (3) can be converted into currency swap (4), indeed they can. An end-of-chapter problem asks you to do this, so be thinking. And if you are wondering if (1) can be converted into (3) and (2) into (4), you will get that question too, and it requires an extra step.

Finally, let us note that, as we said earlier, interest rate swaps are just special cases of currency swaps in which both currencies are the same. In that case, the exchange rate is implicitly 1 and the foreign notional is 1 with domestic notional of 1. So a floating-for-fixed currency swap would simply become a floating-for-fixed interest rate swap.

As you can imagine, the direct relationship between currency swaps and interest rate swaps means that we will have to take into account the pricing of interest rate swaps when we price currency swaps. This topic is covered in detail in Section 9.3.2.

9.2.3 *Equity Swaps*

Equity swaps, which are often referred to as **total return swaps** and sometimes **asset swaps**, are swaps in which the underlying is a stock or stock index.[9] Let us define an equity swap in the following manner.

> *An equity swap is a swap in which one party agrees to make a series of payments to another party based on the performance of a stock or stock index at a series of specified future dates with the latter party agreeing to make a series of payments to the former party that are based on another stock or index or a floating interest rate or a fixed interest rate.*

---

[9]Interest rate swaps are not asset swaps, because the underlying is an interest rate and not an asset. Currency swaps can be viewed as asset swaps, in the sense that the underlying currency is an asset, but they are never referred to as asset swaps. Asset swaps are almost always equity swaps, though it is possible for bonds to be used in asset swaps. Sometimes a fixed- or floating-rate bond is purchased and a swap is used to convert it into a floating- or fixed-rate bond. Later when we study credit risk, we will learn that total return swaps involving bonds are one form of credit derivative. And in Section 9.2.4, we will cover commodity swaps, which are also asset swaps.

An important characteristic of equity swaps that distinguishes them from interest rate or currency swaps is that they pay *a rate of return* based on a stock or stock index. They do not pay the *value* of the stock or stock index. For ease of exposition, let us simply refer to the underlying as a stock, though it could be a stock index, which is just a portfolio of stocks. The sequence of values of the stock is $S_0, S_{T_1}, S_{T_2}, \ldots, S_{T_m}$. Thus, over the course of the swap, the receiver of the equity side of the swap will receive payments of $(S_{T_1}/S_0) - 1, (S_{T_2}/S_{T_1}) - 1, \ldots, (S_{T_m}/S_{T_{m-1}}) - 1$. These amounts are the rates of return on the stock from period to period. These returns will be multiplied by the notional, which we assume is \$1 or one unit of a different currency.

As mentioned in the definition, an equity swap can involve two different equities. That is, both sides could pay the return on an equity. In that case, we will differentiate the two equities by referring to the prices as $S1$ and $S2$. Thus, the rates of return over the swap life would, therefore, be expressed as

$$(S1_{T_1}/S1_0) - 1, (S1_{T_2}/S1_{T_1}) - 1, \ldots, (S1_{T_m}/S1_{T_{m-1}}) - 1 \quad \text{and}$$
$$(S2_{T_1}/S2_0) - 1, (S2_{T_2}/S2_{T_1}) - 1, \ldots, (S2_{T_m}/S2_{T_{m-1}}) - 1.$$

Exhibit 9-10 illustrates an equity swap from the perspective of the party paying the return on stock 2 and receiving the return on stock 1. The notional is \$1 on both sides. Note that there is no day count adjustment as in interest payments. Stock returns are simply whatever they are whereas interest rates are stated as annual rates and must be adjusted by the length of the period.

As we briefly mentioned, the return on a stock can be swapped for either a floating or fixed return. Exhibit 9-11 shows the structure of an equity swap to receive the return on a stock and pay the floating rate. Notice that the floating interest rate is precisely the same as in the interest rate swap and that it must be adjusted by the factor $h/360$. Because there is only one equity, we need not make the $S1$, $S2$ distinction.

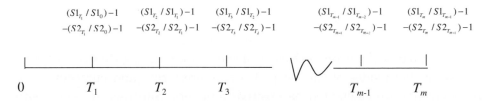

Exhibit 9-10. Structure and Cash Flows of an Equity Swap to Pay the Return on Stock 2 and Receive the Return on Stock 1

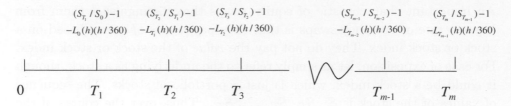

Exhibit 9-11. Structure and Cash Flows of an Equity Swap to Pay a Floating Rate and Receive the Return on a Stock

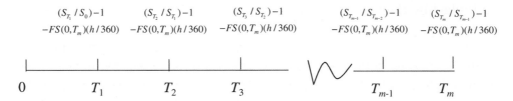

Exhibit 9-12. Structure and Cash Flows of an Equity Swap to Pay a Fixed Rate and Receive the Return on a Stock

A swap to pay fixed and receive the equity return is depicted in Exhibit 9-12. We use the same symbol for the fixed rate as we used in interest rate and currency swaps. As we shall see later, indeed this rate is the same rate in those swaps.

As with currency swaps, it should be apparent that equity swaps can be related to interest rate swaps. An equity swap to pay fixed and receive the equity return can be constructed by combining the equity swap to pay floating and receive the equity return with an interest rate swap to pay fixed and receive floating. The pay floating and receive floating legs cancel, leaving the entity paying fixed and receiving the equity return. While this swap would not ordinarily be constructed by combining the other two swaps, it is useful to see that how one type of swap can be created from another.

Exhibit 9-13 illustrates the computation of an equity swap payoff on a settlement date.

Equity swaps have an unusual feature not seen in interest rate, currency, or commodity swaps. Because an equity return can be negative, it is possible that one party will pay on both sides of the swap, meaning that the other will receive on both sides of the swap. With interest rate and currency swaps, all payments are calculated as positive numbers. Subtracting one positive number from another can produce a positive or a negative net payment. As we shall see later, commodity swaps will also always have one payment

Objective: Consider a group of equity swaps in which the fixed rate is 2.77%, and the floating rate is 2.95%. The notional is $50 million. There are two equity indexes. Index1 was at 455.87 at the beginning of the period and is now at 459.33 at the end of the period. Index2 was at 1,766.81 at the beginning of the period and is now at 1,779.99 at the end of the period. The interest rate is 90-day LIBOR. Find the current payments for the following three equity swaps:

> Swap 1: Pay fixed, receive return on Index1
> Swap 2: Pay floating, receive return on Index1
> Swap 3: Pay return on Index2, receive return on Index1

Payments are made at quarterly intervals.

Inputs:

Notional:	$50 million
Fixed rate:	2.77%
Floating rate for current payment:	2.95%
Values of Equity Index1:	from 455.87 to 459.33
Values of Equity Index2:	from 1,766.81 to 1,779.99

Results:

Swap 1
$$\$50,000,000\left(\left(\frac{459.33}{455.87}-1\right)-0.0277\left(\frac{90}{360}\right)\right)=\$33,244$$

Swap 2
$$\$50,000,000\left(\left(\frac{459.33}{455.87}-1\right)-0.0295\left(\frac{90}{360}\right)-1\right)=\$10,744$$

Swap 3
$$\$50,000,000\left(\left(\frac{459.33}{455.87}-1\right)-\left(\frac{1,779.99}{1,766.81}\right)-1\right)=\$6,506$$

In all three swaps, the party receives a net payment. Of course, the counterparty would make these payments.

Exhibit 9-13.   Equity Swap Payoffs

positive and one negative, netting out to either a positive or a negative net payment. But with an equity swap, a negative equity return means that a negative number is subtracted from a negative number, producing an even greater negative number. In effect, one party makes both payments, so there is no netting.

For example, in Exhibit 9-13 above, suppose Index1 went down instead of up. Instead of going from 455.87 to 459.33, let us assume it went to 452.75.

The calculations would now be

Swap 1

$$\$50,000,000 \left(\left(\frac{452.75}{455.87} - 1 \right) - 0.0277 \left(\frac{90}{360} \right) \right) = -\$688,453$$

Swap 2

$$\$50,000,000 \left(\left(\frac{452.75}{455.87} - 1 \right) - 0.0295 \left(\frac{90}{360} \right) \right) = -\$710,953$$

Swap 3

$$\$50,000,000 \left(\left(\frac{452.75}{455.87} - 1 \right) - \left(\frac{1,779.99}{1,766.81} - 1 \right) \right) = -\$715,191$$

Notice how large and negative the payments are. In Swaps 1 and 2, this party has to make the fixed payment but *receives a negative equity payment*. Therefore, it effectively *makes*, not receives, the equity payment. In Swap 3, this party makes a payment on Index B, which went up, and receives the payment on Index1, which went down. Therefore, the party makes a payment on Index1 as well as on Index2.

You may have noticed that we have omitted the incorporation of dividends into swap payments. We discussed this point when covering forwards and futures. Equity swaps may or may not include dividends in their specified payments. When they do, the swaps are often referred to as total return swaps. The assumptions about how dividends are paid that we made when discussing forwards can be applied to equity swaps, though there are some complications that we will not take up here.

Equity swaps are valuable tools for an equity portfolio manager. They allow very easy transfer of risk. We will get into the pricing and use of equity swaps in later sections.

9.2.4   *Commodity Swaps*

Commodity swaps are swaps that involve payments tied to commodities such as oil and gold. Probably not surprisingly, oil is the most important and widely used commodity and oil swaps are fairly commonly used. As with currencies and equities, commodities are assets, but commodity swaps are structured somewhat differently from currency and equity swaps. With currency swaps the payment is an interest rate in the foreign currency. With equity swaps, the payment is an equity return. With commodity swaps, the payment is the actual commodity itself or an equivalent value in cash, in other words, the price of the commodity.

We define a commodity swap as follows:

> *A commodity swap is a swap in which one party, the buyer or long, agrees to make a series of fixed payments to the seller or short at specified future dates, with the seller or short agreeing to make a series of payments equal to the price of an underlying commodity.*

Let us identify the sequence of prices of the commodity as S_0, S_{T_1}, $S_{T_2}, \ldots, S_{T_m}$. Commodity swaps are almost always structured so that one party pays a fixed price and the other pays the price of the commodity, or equivalently, delivers the commodity. We will designate the fixed price on the commodity swap as $FS_c(0, T_m)$. This payment is not an interest rate, so it does not have to be adjusted by the factor $h/360$. This fixed price is on the order of magnitude of the price of the commodity. Exhibit 9-14 shows the structure of a commodity swap to pay fixed and receive the commodity, or a cash equivalent.

In the illustration above, the sequence of commodity prices can represent either a cash payment made by the short to the long or it can represent the actual delivery of the commodity. In a commodity swap, the notional is expressed in units of the commodity. In the example above, we use a notional of 1, as in, say, one barrel of oil. Thus, at each settlement date, the long receives one barrel of oil worth the price indicated. Alternatively, the long could simply receive the price of one barrel of oil in cash.

Exhibit 9-15 illustrates a payment at a settlement date of a commodity swap.

In these subsections, we have laid out the structure of each of the four types of swaps. We shall now learn how the swap fixed prices and rates are determined. Then we shall cover how swap values are determined during the life of the swap.

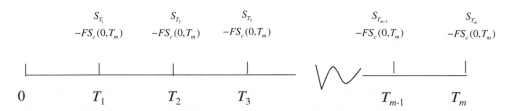

Exhibit 9-14. Commodity Swap to Pay a Fixed Rate and Receive the Price of the Commodity

Objective: Consider a commodity swap on 14,500,000 units of the commodity. An end user pays a fixed rate of $71.15 per unit. On the settlement date, the price of the commodity is $72.50. Determine the payment from the perspective of the end user.

Inputs:

Notional:	14,500,000 units
Fixed price:	$71.15
Floating price for current payment:	$72.50

Results:

$$14{,}500{,}000(\$72.50 - \$71.15) = \$19{,}575{,}000$$

Thus, the party receives a payment of $19,575,000, which occurs as a result of the commodity price exceeding the fixed price and the difference applied to the notional of 14.5 million units of the commodity.

Exhibit 9-15. Commodity Swap Payoffs

9.3 Swap Pricing and Valuation

In Chapter 8, we examined the pricing of forward contracts. We noted that in forward contracts, neither party pays any money to the other at the start. As such, the contract initiates with a value of zero. The correct forward price is the price that forces the value of the contract to be zero at the start. As time elapses and the underlying rate or price changes, we saw that the values of forward contracts move either up (above zero) or down (below zero). These characteristics apply equally to swaps, though the process is slightly more complex. Nonetheless, swap pricing and valuation are still fairly simple, requiring only some time value of money calculations.

As you should recall, derivative pricing is based on the principle of arbitrage, or as some say, no arbitrage. In pricing the swap, we will find the fixed rate that prevents either party from earning an arbitrage profit off of the other.

9.3.1 *Pricing and Valuation of Interest Rate Swaps*

The fixed rate on a vanilla interest rate swap is the rate that makes the present value of the fixed payments equal the present value of the floating payments. Given a particular fixed rate, it is easy to find the present value of the fixed payments. The process is precisely the same as finding the price of a bond, given a known coupon and maturity. The fixed rate is analogous to the coupon rate. But finding the present value of the floating payments is not so straightforward. Other than the first floating payment, all of the subsequent floating payments are unknown. They will not be determined until the swap progresses through its life. Thus, pricing a vanilla swap would seem to be difficult.

But wait a minute and think.

Why would valuing a vanilla swap be any more difficult to price than a stock? Financial analysts and investors value stocks all of the time. Expected future dividends and capital gains are no more certain than are the floating payments on a vanilla swap. In fact, dividends and capital gains are a lot less certain, because equity returns are riskier than interest rates. So the problem of pricing a swap cannot be any more difficult than valuing stocks. In fact, as we will see, it is much easier.

Let us start with a small diversion that will be immensely helpful. Consider a floating rate security in which the coupon rate is set at LIBOR.[10] A floating rate security is a bond or note in which the issuer borrows a principal amount, makes periodic interest payments at the floating rate, and then pays back the principal. The periodic payments follow the advance set, settlement in arrears structure in which the rate is set at the beginning of the interest payment period, interest accrues through the period, and the rate is paid at the end of the period.

To keep things simple let us assume a three-year floating rate note that pays interest at annual LIBOR. Let L_0 be the one-year LIBOR in effect at time 0. At the end of the first year, a new LIBOR of L_1 will go into effect, and at the end of the second year, a new LIBOR of L_2, will go into effect. These rates are annual rates, so we do not need to adjust them by the day-count factor since that factor would simply be 360/360. By making these rates annual, we can leave off this factor and have one less term to distract us. There is an important point to make here, day-count factors are not critical to understanding the issue, and by now you should remember to include them where appropriate.

This floating-rate note has a principal of 1 and will be paid off at the end of the third year. Exhibit 9-16 shows the stream of payments and the market value to the holder of this note.

---

[10]Coupon rates are often tied to LIBOR but usually in the form of LIBOR plus a fixed spread. We could incorporate that spread here, but because it is constant, it would add nothing to the analysis and clutter things up with an additional and unnecessary symbol.

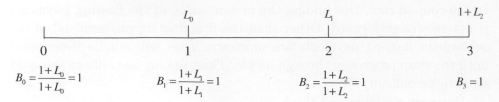

Exhibit 9-16. Cash Flows on and Value of a Three-Year Floating Rate Note Paying LIBOR

The numbers above the time line represent the stream of payments. So at time 1, the holder receives L_0, which was established at time 0. The rate is then reset at time 1 to L_1. At time 2, the holder receives L_1, which was established at time 1, and then the rate is reset to L_2. At time 3, the holder receives L_3, which was established at time 2, plus the repayment of the principal of 1. The numbers below the time line represent the market values of the floating rate note at times 0, 1, 2, and 3. Let us start at time 3 and work backwards.

When the note matures at time 3, it is worth its face value of 1, as indicated by the notation $B_3 = 1$. Stepping back to time 2, the note is worth the discounted value of the remaining cash flows, which are the terms in the numerator, $1 + L_2$. The appropriate discount rate is the current one-period rate, L_2.[11] Thus, the time 2 value is $B_2 = (1 + L_2)/(1 + L_2) = 1$. Now, do not forget what we have just determined: *the note is worth its face value of 1 at time 2.* Stepping back to time 1, the value of the note is, again, the discounted value of the remaining payments. The upcoming payment at time 2 is L_1, but we do not know the payment at time 3. Fortunately, it does not matter, because we already determined that the value of the note at time 2, which is 1, equals the value of the remaining payment and the final principal repaid at time 3. So we can discount $1 + L_1$ at the rate L_1 for one period giving a value of 1: $B_1 = (1 + L_1)/(1 + L_1)$. Stepping back to time 0 and applying the same point, we find that the value of the note at time 0 is 1, its face value. That is, $B_0 = (1 + L_0)/(1 + L_0) = 1$.

---

[11]We are making the convenient assumption that LIBOR is the appropriate discount rate to use in discounting LIBOR-based cash flows. On the surface, this point seems correct. But if the note is issued by company that does not have the same credit quality as the banks borrowing at LIBOR, then the cash flows would have to be discounted at a higher rate to reflect credit risk. Moreover, that rate might change as the company's credit risk changes. We avert this problem by assuming that the floating-rate security is issued by a bank that can borrow at LIBOR. Alternatively, we could add a spread to the specified coupon and make that spread be constant.

Now, let us pause and make sure you understand what we just showed. At time points 0, 1, and 2, we found the value of the floating-rate note by discounting the sum of the next coupon payment and the market value. You may ask, "Why the market value?" There are several ways to help you see the answer to that question. If this asset were a stock, we would naturally discount the market value.[12] So, why not with a floating-rate note? Another way of looking at this point is that the market value of 1 at time 2 reflects the repayment of principal at time 3, the market value of 1 at time 1 reflects the value at time 1 of all of the remaining payments, and the market value at time 0 reflects the market value of all of the remaining payments. We have just seen that the value of a floating-rate note on any rate reset date is its principal value. This point is consistent with the primary objective of a floating-rate note, which is to have a coupon that adjusts to market conditions so as to keep the value of the security from wandering too much from par. Will the value stray from par? Yes, it will, and we will incorporate that point a little later when we look at valuing the swap between payment dates. For now, just look back at Exhibit 9-16 and imagine that you are at a point between payment dates, and you want to value the floating rate security. You do that by discounting the upcoming payment plus the market value of 1 at the next payment date. The discounting equation will have a numerator equal to 1 plus the upcoming coupon and the denominator will be the 1 plus appropriate discount rate for the remaining time to the next payment. We will return to this point later.

So what is the purpose of this diversion into floating rate securities? Well, we are going to be able to treat a swap like a floating-rate security offset by a fixed-rate security. Of course, you may notice an immediate problem in that the floating-rate security has principal paid at maturity while a swap does not have a principal payment at maturity. But likewise, a fixed-rate security has a principal paid at maturity and a swap does not. Recall that we explained in Section 9.2.1 how an interest rate swap can be viewed like issuing one security and using the proceeds to buy another. So, if we issue a fixed-rate note of maturity T_m, with payments to be made at $T_1, T_2, \ldots, T_m$,

---

[12]For example, if today you owned a non-dividend paying stock that was expected to be worth $50 one year from now and the discount rate is 14%, its value today would be $50/1.14 = $43.86. If the stock were expected to pay a $2 dividend in one year, its value today would be ($50 + $2)/(1.14) = $45.61. Notice how the dividend is analogous to the upcoming floating coupon and the stock price is analogous to the value of the floating rate security. The stock value is always the discounted value of the expected future price of the stock and the upcoming dividend.

with a rate equal to the fixed rate on the swap, $FS(0, T_m)$, and we use the proceeds to buy a floating-rate note with the same maturity, same payment dates, and payments made at LIBOR, we shall replicate a swap to pay fixed and receive floating.

The Financial Crisis that began in 2008 raised some new issues about what LIBOR really means when used as a proxy for the nearly risk-free rate. As a result, some changes in the way in which swaps are priced have begun to emerge. We will take up these issues later in this chapter. For now, our objective is to understand the mechanics of swap pricing.

9.3.1.1 *Interest Rate Swap Pricing*

To price a swap, we need to find the fixed rate such that the present value of the fixed payments equals the present value of the floating payments. To start, let us consider what information we have. We will know the term structure of interest rates for LIBOR of various maturities corresponding to the swap payment dates. For example, we would know $L_0(T_1), L_0(T_2), \ldots, L_0(T_m)$. That is, we would know the rate at time 0 for LIBOR loans of maturities $T_1, T_2, \ldots, T_m$. To simplify the notation a bit, let us define the present value factors associated with these rates and dates as follows in Exhibit 9-17. We will then use the present factor notation in the fourth column instead of the present value formula in the third column.

Now, let us designate the symbol, $Bfix_0$, as the value of a fixed rate note with the same terms as the fixed side of the swap with the notional added:

$$Bfix_0 = FS(0, T_m) \left(\frac{h}{360} \right) \sum_{t=1}^{m} PVF(0, T_t) + (1)PVF(0, T_m).$$

Period	Rate	Present Value Factors	Notation
T_1	$L_0(T_1)$	$\dfrac{1}{1 + L_0(T_1)\left(\frac{T_1}{360}\right)}$	$PVF(0, T_1)$
T_2	$L_0(T_2)$	$\dfrac{1}{1 + L_0(T_2)\left(\frac{T_2}{360}\right)}$	$PVF(0, T_2)$
$\ldots$	$\ldots$	$\ldots$	$\ldots$
T_m	$L_0(T_m)$	$\dfrac{1}{1 + L_0(T_m)\left(\frac{T_m}{360}\right)}$	$PVF(0, T_m)$

Exhibit 9-17. Present Value Factors for Time 0 LIBOR with Various Maturities

Note that each payment is $FS(0, T_m)$ multiplied by $h/360$ and then multiplied by the present value discount factor for the date on which the payment occurs. The term $FS(0, T_m)(h/360)$ has been pulled out to the left of the summation sign because it is a constant. The final principal payment, the "1" in parentheses, is multiplied by the discount factor for the maturity T_m. Somewhere in finance courses, you have likely encountered roughly this same concept: it is nothing more than the price of a fixed-rate bond, here with the coupon rate set at $FS(0, T_m)$.

We already learned that at the start of a swap the present value of the floating-rate payments, assuming a final notional payment of 1 at maturity, is 1. Therefore, we do not need to employ a formula at all for its value. Using $Bflt_0$ as that price, we write that result as

$$Bflt_0 = 1.$$

The value of the swap to receive floating and pay fixed is, therefore,

$$VS_0(T_m, h) = Bflt_0 - Bfix_0.$$

Because neither party pays the other anything at the start, this value has to be zero. We, therefore, set this amount to zero:

$$VS_0(T_m, h) = Bflt_0 - Bfix_0 = 0$$

$$0 = 1 - \left(FS(0, T_m) \left(\frac{h}{360} \right) \sum_{t=1}^{m} PVF(0, T_t) + (1)PVF(0, T_m) \right)$$

We then solve for the fixed rate:

$$FS(0, T_m) = \left(\frac{1 - PVF(0, T_m)}{\sum_{t=1}^{m} PVF(0, T_t)} \right) \left(\frac{360}{h} \right) \tag{9.1}$$

Here we see that the fixed rate on the swap is just a simple present value calculation. The numerator is 1 minus the present value factor for the last payment, and the denominator is the sum of all of the present value factors. The result is then annualized using the factor $360/h$. This calculation could hardly be any easier.

So now let us put our formula to work. Exhibit 9-18 presents a swap with four payments, starting in 180 days and spaced 180 days apart.

Objective: Consider a swap with four payments occurring in 180, 360, 540, and 720 days. The term structure of LIBOR is provided below. Find the fixed rate on the swap.

Term	Rate
180	3.00%
360	3.35%
540	3.40%
720	3.45%

Inputs:

First find the present value factors:

$$PVF_0(0,180) = \frac{1}{1 + 0.0300\left(\frac{180}{360}\right)} = 0.9852$$

$$PVF_0(0,360) = \frac{1}{1 + 0.0335\left(\frac{360}{360}\right)} = 0.9676$$

$$PVF_0(0,540) = \frac{1}{1 + 0.0340\left(\frac{540}{360}\right)} = 0.9515$$

$$PVF_0(0,720) = \frac{1}{1 + 0.0345\left(\frac{720}{360}\right)} = 0.9355$$

Results:

$$FS(0,T_m) = \left(\frac{1 - 0.9355}{0.9852 + 0.9676 + 0.9515 + 0.9355}\right)\left(\frac{360}{180}\right) = 0.0336$$

Exhibit 9-18. Vanilla Interest Rate Swap Pricing Example

Thus, the annually quoted rate would be 3.36%.

How Swap Rates are Quoted

In the example above, the swap rate is determined to be 3.36%. So, let us say an end user contacts a dealer and asks for a quote on the swap in question. You might think the dealer would respond, "three point thirty-six percent." No, it is not that simple. First of all, let us remember that the dealer is indeed, well, a dealer. A dealer stands ready to take either side of the transaction. When trading securities or derivatives, a dealer quotes a bid and an ask price, the former being the price at which it is willing to buy and the latter being the price at which it is offering to sell. For a swap, the dealer quotes the fixed rate he will pay when the end user wants to pay floating and the fixed rate he is willing to accept if the end user wants to pay fixed. The magnitude of the spread between the fixed rate the dealer is willing to pay and the fixed rate it is asking to receive is the spread. The spread is determined by a number of factors, but for vanilla swaps, the spread is extremely small, owing to very heavy competition. Let us assume the spread is two basis points that, is 0.02% or 0.0002. Thus, when the dealer determines that 3.36% is the appropriate fixed rate, he would quote 3.35% and 3.37%, meaning that if the dealer pays fixed, it would pay 3.35%, and if the dealer receives fixed, it would accept 3.37%.

But wait. He does not actually quote the rates that way.

When a dealer quotes a rate, there is always some confusion about the length of time the quote is good. While a car dealer might quote you a price that is good for a week or so, a dealer in financial instruments cannot afford to fix a price for *any* period of time. Prices and rates in the market can move very quickly, literally in fractions of a second. To protect itself and give its quote a sense of permanence, the dealer quotes the swap bid and ask in basis points over the rate on a Treasury security of equivalent maturity. Thus, the rate on a one-year swap would be quoted as spread over the rate on one-year treasury securities. So for example, if the rate on one-year treasury notes were 3%, the swap would be quoted as 0.35% and 0.37%. And in fact, the percentage sign would not be mentioned. Thus, the quote would be 0.35 and 0.37, and further simplified to 35 and 37. Written out, it would commonly be stated as $TSY_1 + 35$ and $TSY_1 + 37$.

9.3.1.2 *Interest Rate Swap Valuation*

Of course, as we have emphasized, the value of the swap when it is initiated is zero, because neither party pays anything to the other at the start. As soon as anything changes, either an interest rate or the passage of time, the value of the swap will no longer be zero. The swap value, often called the *mark-to-market value*, will either become positive to the buyer and negative to the seller, or negative to the buyer and positive to the seller.

We need to be able to determine the value of a swap for several reasons. In Chapter 13, we cover derivatives accounting and learn that swaps have to be reported as assets or liabilities on balance sheets and the changes in their values must be reflected in income statements. When the swap value is zero at the start, it is neither an asset nor a liability, so it does not go on the balance sheet. When that value becomes positive, the swap is now an asset and there has been a gain. When the swap value becomes negative, the swap is now a liability and there has been a loss. A second reason why we need to know the value of the swap is that we simply need to know how our position is changing. Anyone who takes a position in a financial instrument should know if the investment is increasing in value or decreasing in value. A portfolio manager frequently checks the values of her portfolio. In most cases, checking the values of securities is relatively easy, but because swaps are customized and do not trade in the market the way a share of Google trades with a virtually continuous series of values, determining swap values requires a little more effort. But again, it is not particularly difficult and considerably more reliable than the estimates of the value of Google stock that are made by financial analyst.

While end users can obtain a swap quote from a dealer or a pricing service, it would behoove the end user to know how swap values are computed. If a quote provided by a dealer seems out of line, an end user should be able to do his own calculations and challenge the dealer. Fortunately, as with pricing a swap, valuing a swap entails nothing more than a time value of money calculation.

Recall that in the pricing illustration we structured the swap to have a series of payments at times $T_1, T_2, \ldots, T_m$. Let us assume that we are at an arbitrary point in time t^*, which is part of the way between the last payment date, T_{u-1}, and the upcoming payment at T_u. For example, if the last payment was the third payment, it was made at T_3, so $u - 1 = 3$. The upcoming payment is the fourth and will be made at T_4 with $u = 4$.

We now have a new term structure of interest rates, $L_{t^*}(T_u), L_{t^*}(T_{u+1})$, $\ldots, L_{t^*}(T_m)$. The upcoming payment will be at the rate $L_{T_{u-1}}(h)$. This rate is the h-period rate that was set at time T_{u-1}, the time of the last payment, and will be paid at time T_u.

Now let us think about how we could determine the value of this swap that we set in place at time 0 when we are now at time t^*, which is between payments $u - 1$ and u. For notational purposes, let us denote this value as $VS_{t^*}(T_m, h)$. The scenario we face is illustrated in Exhibit 9-19. To simplify

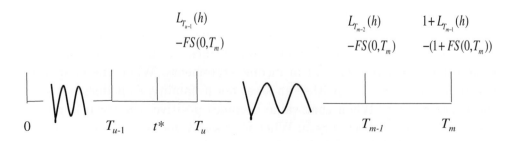

Exhibit 9-19. Vanilla Interest Rate Swap Valuation Setting

the notation a bit and avoid crowding, we have omitted the day count adjustment, but we will incorporate it into the formulas.

Now recall that we determined that the value of the floating payments plus the hypothetical notional equals 1 at any payment date. At time t^*, we know what the next floating payment will be, because that rate was set at the last payment date. Therefore, we can simply discount 1 plus the next floating payment back to t^*:

$$Bflt_{t^*} = \frac{1 + L_{T_{u-1}}(h)\left(\frac{h}{360}\right)}{1 + L_{t^*}(T_u - t^*)\left(\frac{T_u - t^*}{360}\right)} \tag{9.2}$$

The value at t^* of the fixed payments plus hypothetical notional is easy to determine and equal to

$$Bfix_{t^*} = FS(0, T_m)\left(\frac{h}{360}\right)\sum_{t=u}^{m}\frac{1}{1 + L_{t^*}(T_u - t^*)\left(\frac{T_t - t^*}{360}\right)}$$

$$+ \frac{1}{1 + L_{t^*}(T_m - t^*)\left(\frac{T_m - t^*}{360}\right)} \tag{9.3}$$

Thus, the value of the swap to pay fixed and receive floating is, therefore, Equation (9.2) minus Equation (9.3),

$$VS_{t^*}(T_m, h) = \left(\frac{1 + L_{u-1}(h)\left(\frac{h}{360}\right)}{1 + L_{t^*}(T_u - t^*)\left(\frac{T_u - t^*}{360}\right)}\right) - FS(0, T_m)\left(\frac{h}{360}\right)$$

$$\times \left(\sum_{t=u}^{m}\frac{1}{1 + L_{t^*}(T_u - t^*)\left(\frac{T_i - t^*}{360}\right)} + \frac{1}{1 + L_{t^*}(T_m - t^*)\left(\frac{T_m - t^*}{360}\right)}\right) \tag{9.4}$$

An example applying this formula is provided in Exhibit 9-20.

Before we leave the subject of interest rate swap valuation, it is important to understand the source of value for interest rate swaps. As we know, a swap has zero value at the start. Value then arises through the life of the swap as a result of changes in interest rates and the passage of time. Since we decomposed a swap into a floating-rate bond and an opposite position in a fixed-rate bond, the value of a swap arises from relative differences in the value of these floating- and fixed-rate bonds.

It is tempting to think that a pay-fixed, receive-floating interest rate swap becomes valuable when interest rates increase. An increase in interest rates would appear to benefit floating-rate bonds. The rate adjusts upward, so that would appear to benefit the party receiving a floating rate on the swap. An increase in interest rates also benefits the payer of the fixed rate.

Objective: Consider the swap we priced in the previous example. Let us now position ourselves 400 days into the life of the swap. The second payment was made 40 days earlier and there are 140 days until the next payment. Let us assume that the rate on the upcoming payment, established 40 days ago, is 2.80%. This payment will be made in 140 days. The term structure is

Term	Rate
140	2.96%
320	2.88%

Let the notional be $20 million. The fixed rate was established at 3.36%. Find the value of the swap.

Inputs:

$$L_{t^*}(140) = 2.96\%$$
$$L_{t^*}(320) = 2.88\%$$

Now find the present value factors:

$$PVF_{t^*}(0, 140) = \frac{1}{1 + 0.0296\left(\frac{140}{360}\right)} = 0.9886$$

$$PVF_{t^*}(0, 320) = \frac{1}{1 + 0.0288\left(\frac{320}{360}\right)} = 0.9750$$

Note that from a notational perspective, time 0 is time t^*. Time t^* reflects the time since we originated the swap. Discounting will come from a point after t^* back to t^*.

Results:

Thus, the value of the swap to receive floating and pay fixed with a $20 million notional is

$$VS_{t^*}(T_m, h) = \$20,000,000 \left(\frac{1 + 0.0280\left(\frac{180}{360}\right)}{1 + 0.0296\left(\frac{140}{360}\right)} \right.$$

$$\left. - \left(0.0336\left(\frac{180}{360}\right)(0.9886 + 0.9750) + (1)0.9750 \right) \right)$$

$$= -\$111,754$$

Exhibit 9-20. Vanilla Interest Rate Swap Valuation Example

Fixed-rate bonds fall in value when interest rates increase. So, indeed an increase in interest rates increases the value of the floating side and decreases the value of the fixed side, both of which are beneficial to the fixed-payer, floating-receiver. When we discuss the use of swaps to adjust duration, we will get a better picture of how this value arises. We will see that gains and losses in swap value arise far more from the fixed than from the floating side, a fact that could surprise you.

9.3.1.3 *How Interest Rate Swaps are Related to FRAs*

In Chapter 8 we discussed FRAs, which are forward contracts on interest rates. Now in Chapter 9, we are discussing interest rate swaps. An interest rate swap is like a combination of FRAs. So there should be a connection between FRAs and swaps.

First, however, let us note an important difference. Recall that FRAs are based on the principle of advance set, advance settle. Thus, if an FRA on 90-day LIBOR were expiring today and using L to represent today's 90-day LIBOR, the short would owe the long $L(90/360)/(1 + L(90/360))$. Remember that we discounted the payoff over the upcoming period, in this case a 90-day period, to reflect the fact that the London Eurodollar market generates the rate L today in anticipation that the interest will be paid in 90 days. It should be easy to see, however, that if FRAs were structured to pay L in 90 days, the method known as advance set, settlement in arrears, the value of the payment would not be discounted and would equal $L(90/360)$. So, whether a party receives $L(90/360)/(1 + L(90/360))$ today or $L(90/360)$ in 90 days is immaterial. The present value of $L(90/360)$ to be received in 90 days is $(L(90/360))/(1 + L(90/360))$. Swaps are based on advance set, settlement in arrears, so this apparent difference in swaps and FRAs is really not a difference in terms of pricing and valuation.

If we construct a series of FRAs with different expiration dates that corresponded to the swap payment dates, it might appear that we have replicated a swap with an FRA, but we have not. At least not precisely. Each FRA would have a different fixed rate, while the fixed rate would be the same for all payments in the swap. For example, go back to Exhibit 9-18, wherein we constructed a two-year swap with payments spaced 180 days apart with the underlying being 180-day LIBOR. We found the fixed rate to be 3.36%. The fixed rate on FRAs of 180, 360, and 540 days would be as follows[13]:

$$\left(\frac{1 + 0.0335(360/360)}{1 + 0.03(180/360)} - 1 \right) \left(\frac{360}{180} \right) = 0.0365$$

$$\left(\frac{1 + 0.0340(540/360)}{1 + 0.0335(360/360)} - 1 \right) \left(\frac{360}{180} \right) = 0.0339$$

$$\left(\frac{1 + 0.0345(720/360)}{1 + 0.0340(540/360)} - 1 \right) \left(\frac{360}{180} \right) = 0.0343$$

---

[13]Note that there are only three FRAs, while there are four payments in a swap. The first payment in a swap involves no uncertainty. The floating rate is already known, because it is set at the initiation date of the swap. We will address this point momentarily.

So, in this swap one party agrees to pay 3.36% and receive LIBOR on each of the various settlement dates, while in the analogous series of FRAs, the party would be paying 3.65%, 3.39%, and 3.43% and receiving LIBOR on the various expiration dates.[14]

But suppose we constructed each FRA at the rate of 3.36%. For example, if the first FRA rate should be 3.65% and the long pays only 3.36%, clearly that FRA does not have zero value at the start. It is what we called an off-market FRA. Intuitively, we would think its value is positive to the long. It should pay 3.65% but pays only 3.35%. To determine the value of the FRA we apply Equation (8.27) of Chapter 8,

$$V_{t^*}(T_m, h) = \left(\frac{1}{1 + L_{t^*}(m - t^*)((m - t^*)/360)} \right)$$
$$- \left(\frac{1 + R(T_m, h)(m + h)/360}{1 + L_t(m + h - t^*)(m + h - t^*)/360} \right)$$

Here $m = 180$, $t^* = 0$, $R(T_m, h) = 3.36\%$, and $L_0(m) = 0.03$. Valuing these three FRAs, we obtain

$$V_0(180, 180) = \left(\frac{1}{1 + 0.0300(180/360)} \right) - \left(\frac{1 + 0.0336(180/360)}{1 + .0335(360/360)} \right) = 0.0014$$

$$V_0(360, 180) = \left(\frac{1}{1 + 0.0335(360/360)} \right) - \left(\frac{1 + 0.0336(180/360)}{1 + 0.0340(540/360)} \right) = 0.0001$$

$$V_0(540, 180) = \left(\frac{1}{1 + 0.0340(540/360)} \right) - \left(\frac{1 + 0.0336(180/360)}{1 + 0.0345(720/360)} \right) = 0.0003.$$

Now recall that the swap also contains a payment in 180 days that is known for certain. The party that pays fixed and receives floating pays 3.36% and receives the initial 180-day rate of 3%. This combination of payments has a current value of

$$\frac{(0.03 - 0.0336)(180/360)}{1 + 0.03(180/360)} = -0.0018$$

Adding up these four values, we obtain $0.0014 + 0.0001 + 0.0003 - 0.0018 = 0.0000$. So indeed the combination of the three FRAs at the rate of 3.36% and the initial payment are equivalent to a swap. They have zero value at the start.

---

[14]And do not think that the swap rate of 3.36% is an average of these three rates. That average of these FRA rates is 3.49%.

We mentioned that if the three FRAs were constructed separately and priced at zero value at the start, they would have rates of 3.65% for the 180-day maturity, 3.39% for the 360-day maturity, and 3.43% for the 540-day maturity. By pricing these FRAs at a rate of 3.36%, which is lower than all of these FRA rates, we see that they all have positive values. There is no requirement that an FRA has to be priced at zero initial value. It is simply customary to do so. Remember that when an FRA is priced at a rate that implies a non-zero value at the start, it is referred to as an *off-market FRA*. Thus, a swap is a combination of off-market FRAs plus the net of an initial pair of known payments that correspond to the first payments of the swap, which themselves are known.

9.3.1.4 *Using Forward Rates to Price Interest Rate Swaps as Expectations*

Some people prefer to price interest rate swaps as expectations of future spot rates. For example, consider the interest rate swap we have been illustrating. One party pays 3.36% and receives a series of floating payments. The first floating payment in 180 days is known, because it is set by observing the current 180-day rate. The remaining payments will be determined later. Some people consider pricing a swap to be a process of simply discounting the expected future payment. Well, that would be a problem here, because we do not know the expected future floating rates. Forward rates, however, are commonly used as though they were expected future spot rates. In fact, in Chapter 8 we discussed how forward currency rates are often treated as expected future spot currency rates. We explained that forward rates are not really expected future spot rates, in spite of considerable belief among professionals and academics. Nonetheless, you can value a swap as the discounted expected future payoffs where the forward rates are treated as expected spot rates and the current spot rates for the various maturities are used to discount these expected future payments.[15]

First, we recognize that the value of the first payment of 3.36% fixed for 3% floating, as calculated in Section 9.3.1, is −0.0018. These payments are known as they have already been set. For the second payment on the swap, the rate is determined in 180 days and occurs in 360 days. As an estimate of that expected spot rate, we can use the forward rate for transactions to

---

[15]When forward rates are used as expected future spot rates, we are employing a method of pricing known as *risk neutral pricing*. This concept is widely used in pricing options, and we will discuss it when we cover options.

start in 180 days at 180-day LIBOR, which is 3.65%. For the expected spot rate in 360 days, we use the forward rate for transactions to start in 360 days at 180-day LIBOR, which is 3.39%. For the final payment, set in 540 days and occurring in 720 days, we use the forward rate for transactions to start in 540 days at 180-day LIBOR, which is 3.43%. Of course, these rates are the rates on FRAs as explained in the last section. Thus, the discounted expected value of these three payments is

$$\frac{0.0365 - 0.0336}{1 + 0.0300(180/360)} = 0.0014$$

$$\frac{0.0339 - 0.0336}{1 + 0.0335(360/360)} = 0.0001$$

$$\frac{0.0343 - 0.0336}{1 + 0.0340(540/360)} = 0.0003$$

These results are the same amounts we obtained in the previous section. They add up to 0.0018. Combined with the initial payment of 3.36% fixed for 3% floating, which has a value of -0.0018, the overall total value is 0.0000, which is indeed the value of the swap.

To recap, what we have done in Section 9.3.1 is the pricing and valuation of vanilla interest rate swaps. Pricing a vanilla swap means to determine its fixed rate. We do that by determining the fixed rate that sets the value of the swap to zero at the start. As soon as interest rates change and/or time elapses, the value of the swap moves to a positive value for one party and corresponding negative value to the counterparty. Thus, we need to know how to value a swap at any point in its life, and we did that with Equation (9.4). If that equation is applied at time 0, it will equal zero. An end-of-chapter problem asks you to show this point.

This relationship between interest rate forwards and interest rate swaps also suggests that futures and swaps should be related. Indeed, they are. As we have previously noted, many dealers use interest rate futures to hedge interest rate swaps. Moreover, interest rate swap pricing is often done using the rates implied by interest rate futures. While there is a slight bias when futures rates are used for forward rates, the bias can be corrected.

9.3.2 *Pricing and Valuation of Currency Swaps*

As described earlier in this chapter, currency swaps are really just interest rate swaps in which the two parties make payments in different currencies. It follows that interest rate swaps are just currency swaps in which both sides make payments in the same currency. Pricing and valuation of currency swaps is relatively simple and essentially follows the same formulas used to price interest rate swaps, with one additional step of converting the payments to a common currency.

As we have previously mentioned, currency swaps can involve the payment of notional on both legs. Alternatively, currency swaps can be constructed to not involve the payment of notional. We shall assume that the notional is paid. We will discuss the case of no notional later in this section.

Recall from Section 9.2.2 that one can design a currency swap four different ways. First, let us assume that the party in question will pay in the domestic currency and receive payments in the foreign currency. Therefore, it can

> Receive foreign floating, pay domestic floating
> Receive foreign floating, pay domestic fixed
> Receive foreign fixed, pay domestic floating
> Receive foreign fixed, pay domestic fixed

And if we reversed things, the party could pay in the foreign currency and receive in the domestic currency. Let us hold that combination to the side, however, and focus on paying domestic currency and receiving foreign currency using the four structures shown above.

Now, given what we know about interest rate swaps, we can apply those formulas to value the domestic payments of the currency swap. In the interest rate swap formulas, we added hypothetical notionals of 1 to both the fixed and floating side. When we do that with currency swaps, these notionals are not hypothetical and they are not offsetting. For example, a notional of $1 does not offset a notional of €1, except in the unlikely case that the pound sells for $1. Hence, the addition of notionals to the problem of pricing currency swaps means that the notionals are actually paid.

9.3.2.1 *Currency Swap Pricing*

We will use the subscript d to indicate the domestic side of the transaction and f to indicate the foreign side of the transaction. Let us first look at the pricing of the domestic leg of the swap. The fixed rate on the domestic side of a currency swap is simply an adaptation of Equation (9.1), adding the subscript d to distinguish this, the domestic side, from the foreign side, which we will cover next:

$$FS_d(0, T_m) = \left(\frac{1 - PVF_d(0, T_m)}{\sum_{t=1}^{m} PVF_d(0, T_t)} \right) \left(\frac{360}{h} \right) \qquad (9.5)$$

Thus, if a currency swap has a fixed domestic payment, it will be at the rate given in Equation (9.5). If the currency swap has a floating domestic payment, there is no pricing required. The payments will simply be made at the appropriate floating rate. In the example, we have been working with here in the exhibits, the 180-day spot rate is 3% and that rate will be the first floating payment. Of course, the remaining domestic floating payments will be determined as time evolves. The present value of the floating payments plus the notional of 1 is 1 unit of the domestic currency at time 0 and at all payment dates.

In working with the foreign side of a currency swap, we facilitate the process by positioning ourselves as though we are in the foreign country and are pricing an interest rate swap in that country. In that case, the fixed rate on the foreign side of a currency swap is likewise an adaption of Equation (9.1), using the subscript f:

$$FS_f(0, T_m) = \left(\frac{1 - PVF_f(0, T_m)}{\sum_{t=1}^{m} PVF_f(0, T_t)} \right) \left(\frac{360}{h} \right) \tag{9.6}$$

Of course, if the foreign payments are floating, we do not do any specific pricing. The floating payments start off at the current spot rate for the upcoming period, and the remaining floating payments are determined as time evolves. The present value of the floating payments plus the notional of 1 unit of the foreign currency is 1 unit of the foreign currency at time 0 and at all payment dates.

Keep in mind, however, that when working with the foreign side of the currency swap, we are assuming a notional of 1 unit of foreign currency. The actual foreign notional will be determined by the exchange rate when the swap is initiated. Nonetheless, the fixed rate, Equation (9.6), is still valid, as the size of the notional does not affect the fixed rate on a swap.

As explained in Section 9.2.2, the notionals on a currency swap are determined by applying the current spot exchange rate. Normally the end user approaches the dealer and requests a currency swap with a particular notional in one currency. The corresponding notional in the other currency is determined by simply applying the exchange rate. Thus, if the British pound is selling for $1.55, and the end user wanted a notional of £10,00,000, the equivalent dollar notional would be £10,00,000($1.55) = $15,500,000. So pricing a currency swap includes determining the notional in one currency, given the notional in another. Exhibit 9-21 illustrates a currency swap pricing example.

Objective: This example extends the interest rate swap example in Exhibit 9-18. Consider a swap with four payments occurring in 180, 360, 540, and 720 days. The term structure of LIBOR is re-stated below. The domestic rates are the same as in Exhibit 9-18, and the foreign rates are shown below. The exchange rate is 1.45 domestic per foreign. Find the fixed rate and the domestic notional if the end user wants 10,000,000 units of foreign notional.

Term	Domestic Rate	Foreign Rate
180	3%	4.40%
360	3.35%	4.70%
540	3.40%	4.90%
720	3.45%	5%

Inputs: The domestic present value factors were found in Exhibit 9-18. They are

$$PVF_{d,0}(0, 180) = 0.9852$$

$$PVF_{d,0}(0, 360) = 0.9676$$

$$PVF_{d,0}(0, 540) = 0.9515$$

$$PVF_{d,0}(0, 720) = 0.9355$$

The foreign present value factors are

$$PVF_f(0, 180) = \frac{1}{1 + 0.0440(180/360)} = 0.9785$$

$$PVF_f(0, 360) = \frac{1}{1 + 0.0470(360/360)} = 0.9551$$

$$PVF_f(0, 540) = \frac{1}{1 + 0.0490(540/360)} = 0.9315$$

$$PVF_f(0, 720) = \frac{1}{1 + 0.0500(720/360)} = 0.9091$$

Results: We found the domestic fixed rate in Exhibit 9-18 as 3.36%. Thus, $FS_d(0, T_m) = 0.0336$. The foreign fixed rate is, therefore,

$$FS_f(0, T_m) = \left(\frac{1 - 0.9091}{0.9785 + 0.9551 + 0.9315 + 0.9091} \right) \left(\frac{360}{180} \right) = 0.0482$$

As noted, the foreign notional is 10,000,000 units of the foreign currency. Therefore, the domestic notional will be the domestic equivalent, which is

$$10,000,000(1.45) = 14,500,000$$

Thus, the swap will involve making payments on 14,500,000 units of domestic currency and receiving payments on 10,000,000 units of foreign currency. If the domestic payments are fixed, the rate will be 3.36%. If the foreign payments are fixed, the rate will be 4.82%. If the payments are floating, no rate is specified, but the first floating payment will be at the 180-day domestic floating rate of 3% and the 180-day foreign rate of 4.40%. The remaining floating payments will be determined as time elapses.

Exhibit 9-21. Currency Swap Pricing Example

9.3.2.2 *Currency Swap Valuation*

As with interest rate swaps, we need to know how to value currency swaps. The basic procedure is the same as in valuing interest rate swaps. For the domestic payments, we position ourselves in the domestic country and find the present value of the payments. For the foreign payments, we position ourselves in the foreign country and find the present value of the payments. Of course, these payments can be fixed or floating. A given swap to pay domestic and receive foreign will involve only two sets of payments, domestic floating or fixed and foreign floating or fixed. We determine the appropriate values, convert the foreign payments to domestic, and then net them out.

So, let us recall Equations (9.2) and (9.3), which give the value of the floating and fixed payments on an interest rate swap, assuming notionals of 1 are added to both sides. We adapt those equations with the d and f subscripts to value a swap at time t^* with the upcoming payment being payment u and the previous payment being payment $u - 1$:

$$Bflt_{d,t^*} = \frac{1 + L_{d,u-1}(h)\left(\frac{h}{360}\right)}{1 + L_{d,t^*}(T_{u-t^*})\left(\frac{T_u-t^*}{360}\right)}$$

$$Bfix_{d,t^*} = \sum_{t=u}^{m} \frac{FS_d(0,T_m)\left(\frac{h}{360}\right)}{1 + L_{d,t^*}(T_t - t^*)\left(\frac{T_t-t^*}{360}\right)} + \frac{1}{1 + L_{d,t^*}(T_m - t^*)\left(\frac{T_m-t^*}{360}\right)}$$

$$Bflt_{f,t^*} = \frac{1 + L_{f,u-1}(h)\left(\frac{h}{360}\right)}{1 + L_{f,t^*}(T_{u-t^*})\left(\frac{T_u-t^*}{360}\right)}$$

$$Bfix_{f,t^*} = \sum_{t=u}^{m} \frac{FS_f(0,T_m)\left(\frac{h}{360}\right)}{1 + L_{f,t^*}(T_t - t^*)\left(\frac{T_t-t^*}{360}\right)} + \frac{1}{1 + L_{f,t^*}(T_m - t^*)\left(\frac{T_m-t^*}{360}\right)}$$

$$(9.7)$$

These equations may look like a lot of math, but the third equation is the same as the first, just replacing the domestic inputs by the foreign inputs. Likewise, the fourth is the same as the second, replacing the domestic inputs by the foreign inputs. In short, we more or less just work two interest rate swap examples, one as though we are within the domestic country and one as though we are within the foreign country. These values are based on notionals of 1, so we then convert them to their actual notionals. We then convert the foreign value to its domestic equivalent and net the difference. These steps are likely to sound more complex than they are. We illustrate with Exhibit 9-22.

Objective: Consider the currency swap we priced in the previous example. As with the interest rate swap valuation example, let us now position ourselves 400 days into the swap. The second payment was made 40 days earlier and there are 140 days until the next payment. Let us assume that the upcoming floating domestic payment, established 40 days ago, is 2.80%, while the upcoming floating foreign payment is 4.2%. These upcoming payments will be made in 140 days. The domestic notional is 14,500,000, and the foreign notional is 10,000,000. The exchange rate is 1.42 domestic per unit foreign.

The term structures are

Term	Domestic Rate	Foreign Rate
140	2.96%	4.45%
320	2.88%	4.89%

As with the interest rate swap, notice why we need the 140- and 320-day rates. There are 140 days until the upcoming payment and 320 days to the last payment. If there were more than two payments remaining, we would need the rates for days to each of those payment dates. The domestic fixed rate was established at 3.36% and the foreign fixed rate was 4.82%. Find the value of the four possible currency swaps, paying domestic and receiving foreign, and then find the values if we were paying foreign and receiving domestic.

Inputs:

We previously found the domestic present value factors:

$$PVF_d(0, 140) = 0.9886$$

$$PVF_d(0, 320) = 0.9750$$

The foreign present value factors are

$$PVF_f(0, 140) = \frac{1}{1 + 0.0445(140/360)} = 0.9830$$

$$PVF_f(0, 320) = \frac{1}{1 + 0.0489(320/360)} = 0.9583$$

Results: Now let us apply the floating and fixed formulas to find the present value of the domestic and foreign payments for all possible swaps.

$$Bflt_{d,t^*} = \frac{1 + 0.0280 \left(\frac{180}{360}\right)}{1 + 0.0296 \left(\frac{140}{360}\right)} = 1.0025$$

$$Bfix_{d,t^*} = \frac{0.0336 \left(\frac{180}{360}\right)}{1 + 0.0296 \left(\frac{140}{360}\right)} + \frac{0.0336 \left(\frac{180}{360}\right)}{1 + 0.0288 \left(\frac{320}{360}\right)} + \frac{1}{1 + 0.0288 \left(\frac{320}{360}\right)} = 1.0080$$

$$Bflt_{f,t^*} = \frac{1 + 0.042 \left(\frac{180}{360}\right)}{1 + 0.0445 \left(\frac{140}{360}\right)} = 1.0036$$

$$Bfix_{f,t^*} = \frac{0.0482 \left(\frac{180}{360}\right)}{1 + 0.0445 \left(\frac{140}{360}\right)} + \frac{0.0482 \left(\frac{180}{360}\right)}{1 + 0.0489 \left(\frac{320}{360}\right)} + \frac{1}{1 + 0.0489 \left(\frac{320}{360}\right)} = 1.0051.$$

Exhibit 9-22. Currency Swap Valuation Example

These are the values of the payments per notional of 1. We now convert them to their values given the actual notionals:

Domestic floating:	1.0025(14,500,000) = 14,535,678
Domestic fixed:	1.0080(14,500,000) = 14,616,700
Foreign floating:	1.0036(10,000,000) = 10,036,316
Foreign fixed:	1.0051(10,000,000) = 10,051,047

The two foreign values are in the foreign currency, so let us convert them to domestic currency so that we can net them with the domestic payments.

Foreign floating in domestic currency:	10,036,316(1.42) = 14,251,569
Foreign fixed in domestic currency:	10,051,046(1.42) = 14,272,487

Now we can net the domestic and foreign legs and derive the value in the domestic currency. For swaps to pay domestic and receive foreign:

Receive domestic floating, pay foreign fixed:	14,535,678 − 14,272,487 = 263,191
Receive domestic floating, pay foreign floating:	14,535,678 − 14,251,569 = 284,110
Receive domestic fixed, pay foreign fixed:	14,616,700 − 14,272,487 = 344,213
Receive domestic fixed, pay foreign floating:	14,616,700 − 14,251,569 = 365,131

If we were paying domestic and receiving foreign, the values would be the negatives of the values above:

Pay domestic floating, receive foreign fixed:	−263,191
Pay domestic floating, receive foreign floating:	−284,110
Pay domestic fixed, receive foreign fixed:	−344,213
Pay domestic fixed, receive foreign floating:	−365,131

Exhibit 9-22. (*Continued*)

Currency swaps such as these that include the payment of notionals at the expiration are used primarily to hedge a bond issue or a loan with a fixed principal payment at the end. We will illustrate this type of application later in this chapter. There are also currency swaps that do not specify payment of the notionals at the end, but these swaps are not widely used. They are best suited for hedging a sequence of cash flows, but this type of swap is not common in this situation as most companies tend to prefer forward contracts.

9.3.3 *Pricing and Valuation of Equity Swaps*

As described in Section 9.2.3, equity swaps involve one party paying the return on a stock or stock index and the other paying either a fixed rate, a floating rate, or the return on a different equity index. To put equity swaps in perspective, let us think about them in comparison to interest rate and currency swaps. An interest rate swap can be replicated by issuing a fixed-rate bond and using the proceeds to buy a floating-rate bond, or vice versa. A currency swap can be replicated by issuing a fixed- or floating-rate bond in one currency and using the proceeds to buy a fixed- or floating-rate bond in another currency. As we will show, an equity swap can likewise be replicated, but the replication process is a little more complex and requires some adjustments as we move through time.

An equity swap is not a swap to pay the *value* of a stock or stock index. An equity swap is a swap that pays the *return* on a stock or stock index. Let us now determine how to replicate an equity swap. First, we will work with equity swaps that involve receipt of the equity return and payment of a fixed rate. Recall that we denoted the settlement dates on a swap as $T_1, T_2, \ldots, T_m$. At time 1, the party will receive a payment of $S_{T_1}/S_0 - 1$. This expression is the rate of return on the stock or index over the period from T_0 to T_1. Notice that no day count adjustment is required. If a stock goes from 100 to 101 over this period, the return is 1%. There is no reason to multiply by the number of days divided by 360.[16] If this party pays a fixed rate, it will pay $FS(0, T_m)h/360$. We used the designation $FS(0, T_m)$ as the symbol for the fixed rate on interest rate and currency swaps. It might occur that perhaps we should use a slightly different symbol for equity swaps. As a sneak preview, we will go ahead and inform you that the same fixed rate for interest rate and currency swaps applies to equity swaps. You will see that point for sure momentarily. So, there is no need to create a new symbol for something that is precisely the same as something we have already used.

9.3.3.1 *Equity Swap Pricing*

Now let us see how to replicate an equity swap with a notional of $1. Let us refer to the stock as an index. Investment in such an index could be done with an ETF on the index, an index mutual fund, or by holding a portfolio that is identical to the index. Now we do the following transactions.

- Issue a loan of $1 paying interest at the rate $FS(0, T_m)$ with payments on the swap settlement dates and principal to be repaid at the maturity of the swap. Use the proceeds of $1 to invest in the index.
- At time T_1, we will have stock worth S_{T_1}/S_0 and will pay the interest on the loan, $FS(0, T_m)h/360$. We sell the stock and withdraw the return,

---

[16]In simple terms, when pricing stocks, investors already take into account the period of time. Interest rates, however, are always stated on an annual basis. Therefore, it is necessary to account for fractions of a year when computing interest.

$S_{T_1}/S_0 - 1$, leaving \$1 (that is, $(S_{T_1}/S_0) - (S_{T_1}/S_0 - 1) = 1$), which is invested back into the stock.

- At time T_2, do precisely the same thing we did at time 1 and continue to do the same thing at each settlement date up to T_m, whereupon we use the final \$1 to pay off the loan.

It should be apparent that the cash flows at the settlement dates are precisely the cash flows from an equity swap. The party receives the return on the stock and pays the fixed rate on the loan. The overall investment required to initiate this strategy at time 0 is

$$1 - \left(FS(0, T_m) \left(\frac{h}{360} \right) \sum_{t=1}^{m} PVF(0, T_t) - (1) PVF(0, T_m) \right).$$

The "1" is the investment of our capital. The expression in large parentheses is the value of the loan that we issue.[17] Because an equity swap involves no investment of capital, this expression must equal zero. Setting the expression to zero and solving it for $FS(0, T_m)$ give us

$$FS(0, T_m) = \left(\frac{1 - PVF(0, T_m)}{\sum_{t=1}^{m} PVF(0, T_t)} \right) \left(\frac{360}{h} \right) \tag{9.8}$$

Do not be surprised if this equation looks familiar. It is Equation (9.1), the equation for the fixed rate on interest rate swaps, which is also the same fixed rate for currency swaps. As we said earlier, we do not need a new symbol for the fixed rate on an equity swap.

If an equity swap is structured to involve receipt of the equity payment and payment of a floating rate, no pricing is required. The floating payment will simply be based on LIBOR. One obvious way to see this result is to see how an equity swap to pay fixed and receive equity can be converted into an equity swap to pay floating and receive equity.

Swap 1: Swap to pay fixed and receive equity plus
Swap 2: Swap to pay floating and receive fixed equals
Swap 3: Swap to pay floating and receive equity

---

[17]Notice that we have factored out the coupon rate and the time adjustment, $h/360$ from the right of the summation sign, because these terms are constant through the entire summation. Therefore, we can bring them to the left of the summation and multiply them by the sum of the present value factors.

Swap 1 is the equity swap we have been working with. Swap 2 is a vanilla interest rate swap. Swap 3 is the equity swap we desire. Thus, equity and interest rate swaps are naturally connected.

Now consider a swap to pay the return on one equity index and receive the return from a different index. Let us call the first index Index1 and the second Index2. Look back at Equation (9.8), which gives the fixed rate for an equity swap. That equation incorporates no characteristics of either Index1 or Index2. Therefore, the characteristics of the stock have no bearing on the terms of a swap involving the stock.

Let us construct the following transactions:

Swap 1: Swap to pay fixed and receive the return on Index1 plus
Swap 2: Swap to pay the return on Index2 and receive fixed equals
Swap 3: Swap to pay the return on Index2 and receive the return on Index1

In short, there is no pricing requiring. A swap to pay the return on one stock and receive the return on another is an even exchange. The parties simply agree to make the future payments to each other.

9.3.3.2 *Equity Swap Valuation*

As with interest rate and currency swaps, we will need to know how to value equity swaps. Again, let us position ourselves at time t^*, with the last payment being at T_{u-1} and the next payment at T_u. First, let us work with the swap to pay fixed and receive the equity return. The equity portion of this return is equivalent to investing $S_{l^*}/S_{T_{u-1}}$ in the index. If we made that investment at time T_{u-1} we would have shares worth $(S_{t^*}/S_{T_{u-1}})S_{T_u}/S_{l^*} = S_{T_u}/S_{T_{u-1}}$ at time T_u. Then if we liquidate the stock and withdraw $S_{T_u}/S_{T_{u-1}} - 1$, we would have \$1.

Let us then reinvest the \$1 in the index, just as we described when illustrating the pricing of equity swaps. The fixed portion of the equity swap is equivalent to having a loan with interest payments of $FS(0, T_m)h/360$ and principal of \$1 due at T_m. Thus, the value of this swap is

$$VS_0(T_m, h) = \frac{S_{l^*}}{S_{T_{u-1}}} - \left(FS(0, T_m) \left(\frac{h}{360} \right) \sum_{t=u}^{m} \frac{1}{1 + L_{t^*}(T_t - t^*) \left(\frac{T_t - t^*}{360} \right)} \right.$$

$$\left. + \frac{1}{1 + L_{t^*}(T_m - t^*) \left(\frac{T_m - t^*}{360} \right)} \right) \tag{9.9}$$

All we did was borrow the present value of the fixed payments that appear in Equation (9.4). If the payment side involves floating payments instead of fixed, we can borrow the present value of the floating payments that appear in Equation (9.4) and obtain

$$VS_0(T_m, h) = \frac{S_{t^*}}{S_{T_{u-1}}} - \left(\frac{1 + L_{u-1}(h)\left(\frac{h}{360}\right)}{1 + L_{t^*}(T_{u-t^*})\left(\frac{T_u - t^*}{360}\right)} \right) \qquad (9.10)$$

We have one more swap to value, the swap to pay one equity and receive another. We know that the expression $S_{t^*}/S_{T_{u-1}}$ represents the investment required to replicate the equity return. We call one equity Index1 and another Index2 and designate their values as $S1$ and $S2$ with appropriate time subscript. So the value of this swap to pay the return on Index2 and receive the return on Index1 would be

$$VS_0(T_m, h) = \left(\frac{S1_{t^*}}{S1_{T_{u-1}}} \right) - \left(\frac{S2_{t^*}}{S2_{T_{u-1}}} \right). \qquad (9.11)$$

Now we turn to an equity swap valuation example in Exhibit 9-23.

There are some variations of equity swaps. One in particular is quite interesting and practical. Suppose we were using an equity swap to replicate the performance of an investment in an index. The results produced by an equity swap as shown here will not exactly achieve this result. An equity swap structured in this manner will produce the results from a constant investment of $1 (or other currency unit) in the index. This point should be obvious. At each settlement date, the party receiving the equity returns gets the one-period rate of return based on an investment of 1 unit of currency. But if you actually invested say $1 in an index and it earned 2% one period and 3% the next, you would have $1(1.02)(1.03) = 1.0506 after two periods, because after the first period you have $1.02 invested. This point is commonly described as *the power of compounding*. The equity swap described here is based on withdrawal of the periodic rate of return. We will not get into this advanced topic, but be aware that it is possible to design the equity swap to accommodate this factor.

Another point of concern in an equity swap is dividends paid on the index. Dividends provide an element of complexity that we shall not address here, but they can be accommodated under most reasonable assumptions about how dividends are paid.

9.3.4 *Pricing and Valuation of Commodity Swaps*

In an interest rate swap, the underlying is an interest rate. In a currency swap, the underlyings are interest rates in two countries as well as the

Objective: Consider the vanilla interest rate the swap we priced earlier in this chapter, which had settlements in 180, 360, 540, and 720 days. The fixed rate was 3.36%. Then, 400 days into the swap, we determined its value. The second payment was made 40 days earlier and there are 140 days until the next payment. As before, we assume that the upcoming payment, established 40 days ago, is 2.80%. This payment will be made in 140 days. The final payment will occur in 320 days. The term structure and the present value factors previously found were

Term	Rate	Present Value Factor
140	2.96%	0.9886
320	2.88%	0.9750

Let the notional be $20 million. Now let us value the three types of equity swaps. First consider Index1 that was at 1,542.55 on the last payment date and today is at 1,551.19. Now consider Index2 that was at 12,447.16 on the last payment date and today is at 12,568.93.

Swap 1: Pay fixed, receive return on Index1
Swap 2: Pay floating, receive return on Index2
Swap 3: Pay return on Index2, receive return on Index1.

Inputs:

The index values are

$$Index1: \quad S1_{T_{u-1}} - 1,542.55; \ S1_{t^*} = 1,551.19$$
$$Index2: \quad S1_{T_{u-1}} = 12,447.16; \ S1_{t^*} - 12,568.93$$

The other values are the same as in the earlier example.

Results:

The value of the equity swap to pay fixed and receive the equity return (Index1) is

$$VS_{t^*}(T_m, h) = \$20,000,000 \left(\frac{1,551.19}{1,542.55} - (0.0336) \left(\frac{180}{360} \right) (0.9886 + 0.9750) + (1)0.9750 \right)$$
$$- \ \$48,943$$

The value of the equity swap to pay floating and receive the equity (Index1) return is

$$VS_{t^*}(T_m, h) = \$20,000,000 \left(\left(\frac{1,551.19}{1,542.55} \right) - \left(\frac{1 + 0.0280 \left(\frac{180}{360} \right)}{1 + 0.0296 \left(\frac{140}{360} \right)} \right) \right)$$
$$= \$62,811$$

The value of the swap to pay the return on Index2 and receive the return on Index1 is

$$VS_{t^*}(T_m, h) = \$20,000,000 \left(\left(\frac{1,551.19}{1,542.55} \right) - \left(\frac{12,568.93}{12,447.16} \right) \right)$$
$$= -\$83,637$$

Exhibit 9-23. Equity Swap Valuation Examples

exchange rate. In an equity swap, the underlying is the return on a stock or stock index. Commodity swaps are perhaps most closely related to equity swaps, but they do not pay off a rate of return. Instead they pay off the price of the underlying commodity.

Let us continue with the assumption that the swap has settlement dates of $T_1, T_2, \ldots, T_m$. At each date, one party pays the other the price of the commodity. So on these respective dates, the prices are denoted as $S_{T_1}, S_{T_2}, \ldots, S_{T_m}$. Of course, these prices are unknown when the swap is initiated. The other party pays a fixed price, which will designated as $FS_c(0, T_m)$.[18] In short, one party is buying a unit of the commodity from the other at each of the settlement dates at a price agreed on when the swap is negotiated.

Recall from Chapter 8 that most commodities incur storage costs, which we encapsulated into a concept known as the cost of carry reflecting the net overall costs of holding the asset. The symbol $FVSC(0, T)$ was used to represent the future value of the storage cost over the period of 0 to T. With a commodity swap, there will be multiple periods over which storage costs are accumulated and paid. Thus, we should consolidate the storage costs into a single future value, obtained by compounding them until the expiration. We shall, however, have to incorporate a means of replicating them over each of the time periods. Let us let SC_t be the storage cost paid at time t, which reflects the storage of the commodity from period $t-1$ to t. So we have storage costs of $SC_1, SC_2, \ldots, SC_m$ at times $T_1, T_2, \ldots, T_m$, respectively. We can find their future value at time T_m by compounding their values to time T_m at the risk-free rate. Their value at time T_m is

$$FVSC(0, T_m) = \sum_{t=1}^{m} SC_t(1 + r)^{(T_m - T_t)/360}$$

If the storage cost is the same every period, then SC_t is simply SC for all t. In that case, we can pull out the SC term from the right side of the summation sign. Then we are simply finding the future value of an annuity of SC.

9.3.4.1   *Commodity Swap Pricing*

Let us proceed to create a strategy that replicates the payoffs of a commodity swap. We then set the value of that strategy to zero, and solve for the fixed

---

[18]Up until now, this symbol has always stood for a rate, but in commodity swaps, the symbol is a price.

rate. First, we buy m units of the commodity, that is, one unit for each of the m settlements. At each settlement date, we will sell one unit, thereby collecting the spot price at the respective date, and this procedure replicates the cash flow from the commodity. At time 0 we shall also construct a series of loans. In one set of loans, we are the borrower and in another we are the lender. These loans replicate the fixed payments and the storage costs. Let us see how that replication is done.

First, we shall use LIBOR-style interest rates. In a commodity swap, we will have to pay a fixed rate of $FS_c(0, T_m)$ at each of the times $T_1, T_2, \ldots, T_m$. To replicate these swap payments, we take out individual loans maturing at these dates where each loan has a face value of $FS_c(0, T_m)$. The total value of these loans at time 0 is

$$FS_c(0, T_m) \left(\sum_{t=1}^{m} \frac{1}{1 + L(0, T_t)(T_t/360)} \right).$$

As each loan matures, we pay it off, thereby paying out $FS_c(0, T_m)$ at each of the dates $T_1, T_2, \ldots, T_m$. This sequence of payments replicates the fixed payments of the commodity swap. We can think of the above equation as the debt taken out that is equivalent to the fixed payments on the commodity swap. Paying back that series of loans replicates the fixed payments on the commodity swap.

By owning various units of the commodity, however, we will incur storage costs. These costs are not paid by either party to a swap, so to replicate the swap we have to remove the effect of these costs. We do so by making a series of loans, that is, as the lender. We want each loan to mature on one of the dates $T_1, T_2, \ldots, T_m$ and pay off an amount equivalent to the storage costs. Thus, we make a series of loans as a lender that have a present value of

$$PVSC(0, T_m) = \sum_{t=1}^{m} \frac{SC_t}{1 + L(0, T_t)(T_t/360)}.$$

Thus, as each of these loans matures, the payoff will give us the money to pay the storage costs. We shall need to know the future value of these storage costs, and this is easily found as

$$FVSC(0, T_m) = PVSC(0, T_m)\left(1 + L(0, T_m)\right) T_m/360$$

So, now let us recap the strategy we have constructed to replicate the commodity swap. We buy m units of the asset, borrow an amount equivalent to the fixed payments on the swap, and lend an amount equal to the storage costs. Thus, the total value of our position at time 0 is

$$mS_0 - FS_c(0, T_m) \left(\sum_{t=1}^{m} \frac{1}{1 + L(0, T_t)(T_t/360)} \right) + FVSC(0, T_m) \qquad (9.12)$$

Since a commodity swap does not require any initial outlay or generate an inflow, its initial value is zero. Thus, we set this amount to zero and solve for $FS(0, T_m)$ to obtain:

$$FS_c(0, T_m) = \frac{mS_0 + FVSC(0, T_m)}{\left(\sum_{t=1}^{m} \frac{1}{1 + L(0, T_t)(T_t/360)} \right)} \qquad (9.13)$$

This equation has a fairly simple interpretation. Starting with the numerator on the right-hand side, we take the value of the assets, add the storage costs, and then through the denominator, we gross this value up to the maturity date by dividing by present value factor for the respective settlement dates.[19] Recall that this general procedure is how we price forwards and futures. Exhibit 9-24 presents a commodity swap pricing example.

9.3.4.2 *Commodity Swap Valuation*

Now let us take a look at how a commodity swap would be valued. Again, we position ourselves at time t^*. The last payment was at time T_{u-1} and the next is at time T_u. The current spot price is S_{t^*}. At this point we have already sold off $u - 1$ units of the commodity, so the commodity swap is equivalent to holding $m - (u - 1)$ units of the commodity, borrowing the remaining fixed payments, and lending the remaining storage costs. Recall Equation (9.12) that gives the value of the replicating portfolio at time 0. Let us adapt this value to position the swap at time t^*:

$$VS_{t^*}(T_m, h) = (m - (u - 1))S_{t^*} - FS_c(0, T_m)$$

$$\times \left(\sum_{t=u}^{m} \frac{1}{1 + L(t^*, T_t)((T_t - t^*)/360)} \right) + FVSC(t^*, T_m)$$

$$(9.14)$$

And of course, we would multiply by the notional as expressed by number of units of the commodity. Now let us look at a valuation example in Exhibit 9-25.

---

[19]Multiplying by present value factors discounts a value. Dividing by present value factors compounds the value.

Objective: Consider a commodity swap with four payments occurring in 180, 360, 540, and 720 days. The term structure of LIBOR and present value factors are provided below, and they are the same ones we have previously been using. The future value of the carrying costs is in the last column. We will assume the carrying costs are fixed at $1.00 for each 180 days. We incur the cost every 180 days. Thus,

Term	Rate	PVF
180	3.00%	0.9852
360	3.35%	0.9676
540	3.40%	0.9515
720	3.45%	0.9355

The commodity sells for $125 today. Find the fixed rate on the swap.

Inputs:

First we need to find the future value of the storage costs. We must take into account the fact that we start by purchasing four units of the commodity and then we sell one unit at each of the next three settlement dates. Thus, on day zero we own four units, on day 180, we sell one unit and then own three. On day 360 we sell one unit and then own two. On day 540, we sell one unit and then own one. So we carry four units for the first 180 days, three units from day 180 to day 360, two units from day 360 to day 540, and one unit from day 540 to day 720. At a cost of $1 per unit per 180 days, our costs are $4 on day 180, $3 on day 360, $2 on day 540, and $1 on day 720.

We simply find the present value of the storage costs and then compound that value to the end of the life of the contract. The present value is

$$\$4(0.9852) + \$3(0.9676) + \$2(0.9515) + \$1(0.9355) = \$9.68$$

The future value at 720 days is easily found. We divide this amount by the present value factor for 720 days (or multiply by $1 + 0.0345(720/360)$):

$$\frac{\$9.68}{0.9355} = \$10.35$$

All input values are given above

Results:

$$FS_c(0, T_m) = \frac{4(\$125) + \$10.35}{0.9852 + 0.9676 + 0.9515 + 0.9355}$$

$$= \$132.91$$

Thus, with this commodity selling at $125, a swap with fixed payments in 180, 360, 540, and 720 days would be engaged at a fixed price of $132.91. The party that goes long the swap would agree to pay $132.91 a unit for the commodity at each of the four settlement dates.

Exhibit 9-24. Commodity Swap Pricing Example

Objective: Consider the same commodity swap previously priced at $132.91. Now we move 400 days into the life of the swap. The second payment was the previous payment and the third payment is the upcoming payment. Thus, $m - (u - 1) = 4 - (3 - 1) = 2$. Now let the new spot price be $130 and assume the notional is 100,000 units of the commodity. Recall that we previously had the new set of interest rates, which were as follows.

Term	Rate	Present Value Factor
140	2.96%	0.9886
320	2.88%	0.9750

Assume that storage costs for units held for a fraction of a period are charged on a prorated basis.

Inputs:

Now we shall need to compute the future value of the remaining storage costs. To replicate the swap on day 400, we shall need two units of the commodity. We will sell one of them on day 540 and the other on day 720. So there will be a storage cost incurred on day 540 for two units held for 140 of 180 days. So that cost will be $2(140/180)\$1.00 = \$1.56$ on the next settlement date, which is in 140 days. On day 720, we shall have a cost of $1, covering one unit held from day 540 through day 720. We first find the present value of the storage costs to day t^*, which is day 400:

$$\$1.56(0.9886) + \$1(0.9750) = \$2.51$$

We then compound to the expiration:

$$\frac{\$2.51}{0.9750} = \$2.58$$

Results:

We need the value of two units of the commodity, minus the value of a loan to pay $132.91 at each of the remaining two settlement dates, plus the future value of the storage costs.

$$VS_{t^*}(T_m, h) = 100{,}000(2 * 130 - \$132.91(0.9886 + 0.9750) + \$2.58)$$

$$= \$158{,}180$$

Thus, with this commodity selling at $125, a swap with fixed payments in 180, 360, 540, and 720 days would be engaged at $132.91. The party long the swap would agree to pay $132.91 a unit for the commodity at each of the four settlement dates. At this point, 400 days into the life of the swap with the commodity price at $130 and two settlement dates remaining, the value of the swap would be $158,180, based on 100,000 units of the commodity.

Exhibit 9-25. Commodity Swap Valuation Example

9.4 Terminating Swaps

We have spent a great deal of time discussing the valuation of a swap during the life of the swap. We mentioned that swaps have to be accounted for in financial statements, and we also noted that anyone taking a position in a swap should want to know what the swap is worth at any time during its life. One cannot simply look at a swap the way one looks up the price of a stock. The swap must be valued by determining the present value of the remaining net payments, and we covered how to do that for interest rate, currency, equity, and commodity swaps. But there is yet another reason, and a very important one, for wanting to know the value of a swap, and that is for termination purposes.

You might recall that in Chapter 8 we discussed the termination of FRAs. When a party to an FRA wants to terminate it before expiration, that party can go back to the dealer and ask for a buyout. Alternatively, the party can do an offsetting transaction with another party, which as we noted would negate the risk but would leave the potential for default. You may wish to review the FRA material on terminating a position in Section 8.1.6.

The same considerations hold for swaps. As we have described much earlier in this book, swaps are usually initiated by end users who engage the services of a swap dealer. Dealers do not typically ask end users for offsets. The end user wants the swap, so the dealer would not be servicing its customer very well if it wanted to back out of the swap before the swap matures. Almost always, a termination occurs because the needs of the end user have changed. For whatever reason that the end user put the swap in place, that reason no longer holds. As an example, an end user with a floating rate loan that engages a vanilla swap to effectively pay fixed and receive floating thereby converting the floating-rate loan to a fixed-rate loan might need to terminate the swap early. For example, suppose the end user decides to pay the loan off before maturity? Or what if the end user decides it wants to convert the loan back to floating? Suppose an investment manager engages in a swap to pay a floating rate and receive an equity return, thereby implicitly converting a portion of his floating rate bond portfolio into equity. Now at a later point, the manager might prefer to have the floating rate exposure back with a reduction in the equity exposure. In both cases, the end user could terminate the original swap.

Recall that in Exhibit 9-20, we estimated the value of a plain vanilla swap to pay fixed and receive floating as −$111,754. If the party wanted to terminate that position, it would go back to the dealer and ask for an offset.

The dealer would quote a value of $-\$111,754$. The negative sign means that the position is in the red to the end user and in the black to the dealer. Therefore, the end user could terminate the position by paying the dealer $111,754.

In Exhibit 9-23, we examined the valuation of equity swaps. Consider the swap to pay floating and receive the return on Index1. We estimated its value at $62,811. If the end user wanted to terminate that swap, the dealer would pay the end user $62,811.

Recall that we mentioned that a party could offset the swap with a different party. In the vanilla swap in Exhibit 9-20, the end user is paying fixed and receiving floating with a particular dealer. Let us refer to that dealer as dealer A. If the end user wanted to offset with a different party, it would find another dealer, which we shall call dealer B, and engage in an offset. The swap with dealer B involves the end user paying floating and receiving fixed on the same settlement dates as in the original swap. The floating rates offset, leaving the dealer with paying a fixed rate that will be higher than the original fixed rate. You should not be surprised to know that the annuitized value of the difference in the fixed payments is the value of the swap, here $-\$111,754$. Nonetheless, both swaps remain in place. The net amount of the fixed and floating payments must be made on both swaps. Therefore, the end user faces some credit exposure. If one counterparty fails to pay, the end user cannot use that as an excuse to default to the other counterparty. A similar point would apply to the equity swap or any other swap that is offset in this manner.

Most swaps are terminated with the original dealer rather than offset with a third party. The main reason for going to a third party is for competitive purposes. If the end user goes back to the dealer for a termination, the dealer knows that it is important to the end user to terminate. Thus, the dealer might try to gouge the end user by quoting a biased termination value. This is why it is important to the end user to know how to calculate the value of a swap. A third party could potentially give it a better quote. But in spite of this point, most swaps are offset with the original dealer, partly out of convenience and partly to remove the credit risk.

9.5   Extensions and Variations of Swaps

The swaps previously covered are certainly the most common. There are, however, a number of extensions and variations of these standard swaps. In the following subsections, we will lightly discuss them. At this level of the subject of financial risk management, we will not provide complete coverage and examples of their use. So, in other words, we do not cover pricing and valuation in any detail, though we will verbally describe the basic ideas. Our objective here is to obtain awareness of the features that distinguish these types of swaps from standard swaps.

9.5.1 *Basis Swaps*

In Chapter 8, we talked about the basis, which is the difference between the spot price and the futures price. We noted that a hedge is sometimes referred to as speculating on the basis. We also noted how in some cases, there is no futures contract that exactly matches the spot price. An alternative futures contract that is highly correlated can sometimes be used with success. This type of transaction was referred to as a cross hedge. The basis is the relationship between two prices. For a cross hedge, the basis is the relationship between the futures price of the contract you are using and the spot price that determines the original exposure.

A similar notion applies in the swaps market but in slightly different way. Recall that we spent a good bit of time on vanilla swaps, which are swaps of a fixed rate for a floating rate or vice versa. The fixed rate was usually LIBOR for whatever currency that applies given the country the party is in. A basis swap is a swap of one floating rate for another in the same currency. A common type of basis swap is dollar LIBOR swapped against the U.S. Treasury bill rate. Recall that dollar LIBOR is sometimes referred to as the Eurodollar rate. The spread between the Eurodollar rate and the Treasury bill rate is called the TED spread, where TED stands for T-bills over Eurodollars. Because the T-bill rate, the rate at which the U.S. government borrows for less than a year, is virtually the lowest rate in the financial world, the Eurodollar rate, which is the rate at which London banks borrow, is typically higher. As this spread widens, it normally reflects a growing concern about the stability of the financial system.[20]

A basis swap on the TED spread would involve paying LIBOR and receiving the T-bill rate or vice versa. Because of the way in which the TED spread reflects credit risk in the economy, basis swaps are primarily speculative instruments. Pricing and valuation of such a swap would be easy. A basis swap to pay LIBOR and receive the T-bill rate is equivalent to a

---

[20]Check the following link for a current graph of the TED spread: http://www.macrotrends.net/1447/ted-spread-historical-chart. Note how sharply it rose in 2008.

vanilla swap to pay LIBOR and receive a fixed rate and a vanilla swap to receive the T-bill rate and a fixed rate. The fixed rates do not offset, however. The fixed rate paid against LIBOR would have to exceed the fixed rate paid against T-bill because the party receiving LIBOR would get a larger floating payment than the party receiving T-bill. The fixed rate paid against LIBOR is found in the same way we presented in Section 9.3.1. The fixed rate paid against T-bill would be found the same way we found it for LIBOR, except that we would use the T-bill term structure. The spread between the fixed rates will be added to the T-bill floating payment or deducted from the LIBOR floating payment. In other words, one party pays T-bill plus a spread and the other party pays LIBOR, which should make sense because the T-bill rate is below LIBOR. Or one party could pay LIBOR minus a spread and the other pay T-bill. Valuation of the swap would be done by finding the value of a LIBOR-based swap, as shown in Section 9.3.1, and comparing it to the value of a T-bill based swap, found the same way as that of LIBOR-based swap but using the T-bill term structure. The difference would be the value of the basis swap.

Basis swaps can also be structured to involve a given floating interest rate for one maturity swapped against the same interest rate but a different maturity. For example, one rate might be 30-day LIBOR and the other 90-day LIBOR. The settlement period might be 30 or 90 days.

9.5.2 *Forward Swaps*

As noted, the most common use of a vanilla swap is to convert a floating-rate loan to a fixed-rate loan. Rarely are loans ever taken out on the spot. They usually require some advance planning as well as paperwork. When a company knows in advance that it will take out a floating-rate loan, it may begin thinking about whether it will use a swap to convert it to a fixed rate loan. The company may wish to lock in the fixed rate on the swap in advance of when it takes out the loan. It can do this by engaging in a forward swap. A forward swap is, thus, simply a forward contract to enter into a swap.

A forward swap is easily priced using the standard approach explained in Section 9.3.1 but with one twist. Instead of using spot rates, we use forward rates. For example, if we wanted to enter into a swap to start in one year, with payments six and twelve months after the swap starts, we would need the forward rates for transactions starting in one year and ending in 18 months and the forward rates for transactions starting in one year and ending in 24 months. Valuation before the swap is initiated is slightly more complex but not difficult.

Misusing Forward Swaps

(This story is a true one involving litigation in which the author served as an expert witness for the bank).

A small business arranged a floating rate loan to finance an expansion project. The loan was to start about six months later. Wanting to convert the loan to a fixed rate loan, the company entertained the possibility of engaging in a forward swap with a major U.S. dealer bank. By doing a forward swap for the approximately six-month period, the effective fixed rate on the swap would be locked in from the start. The alternative of waiting six months and starting the swap when the loan started would have exposed the company to the risk of rising interest rates during the six-month period.

The forward swap committed the company to engage in a pay-fixed, receive-floating swap at a locked-in rate about six months later. Soon after the forward swap was engaged, interest rates began to rise. Several months into the forward swap with a few more months to go before the loan started and the forward swap expired, the forward swap had risen substantially in value. But a rare and an unforeseen circumstance then occurred.

The purpose of the loan was to finance a real estate purchase. Before all real estate transactions occurred, a title search is required. A specialized title attorney examines historical records to make sure that all of the previous transactions for that property are legal and that no third party should be able to step in and claim that the property is his and therefore being sold improperly. Most title searches turn up nothing. On a rare occasion, something happens. This case was one of those times.

As a result of the title issue, the sale of the real estate was canceled. As such, the bank would not be able to make the loan, since there was no property that would stand as collateral. Further complicating matters was the fact that the forward swap, which had been positive in value to the borrower, then turned negative, a result of rapidly falling interest rates.

Thus, the loan that the swap was supposed to hedge did not occur, but the company was engaged in a forward swap committing it to initiating the swap at the date it would have otherwise. This commitment was deeply in the red for this small company, to the tune of almost $2 million.

The company refused to pay to get out of the forward swap and sued the bank, claiming that the company did not know what it was doing when it engaged in the forward swap and that the bank took advantage of it. It also claimed that the bank profited excessively from the transaction.

In fact, the bank did not profit at all, as it had hedged its exposure. Its gain on the forward swap was matched by hedging transactions. Also, it was noted that the bank had made presentations to the company on the risk of the transaction. Moreover, when the first indications occurred that the loan and real estate transaction would not happen, the bank encouraged the company to close the swap. The company chose not to do so, hoping the market would turn around. But perhaps the most significant piece of evidence was an email from the company to the bank indicating that the company had done transactions like this before and knew exactly what it was doing.

A local judge ruled in favor of the bank without even going to trial.

Before leaving this section on forward swaps, we need to alert you to the fact that in Chapter 10 we will encounter options on swaps, which are called swaptions. Because we have not covered options yet, we cannot say anything substantive about swaptions. But keep in mind that forward swaps commit you to enter into a swap. As we will see in Chapter 10, swaptions give you the right but not the obligation to enter into a swap.

9.5.3 *Amortizing Swaps*

In all of the interest rate swap examples we have done, each of the loans is what is called a bullet loan. This characterization means that the loan is paid off entirely at its maturity. That is, no portion of the loan principal is paid before maturity. Thus, during the life of the loan, interest payments are made, but the principal does not go down. The vanilla swaps done here are designed to convert a floating-rate bullet loan to a fixed-rate bullet loan or vice versa. In the financial world, however, many loans are amortizing loans. For example, the periodic payments in mortgages include a contribution to paying down the principal balance. Many other loans amortize according to a schedule. The standard vanilla swap is not appropriate for such a loan. Fortunately, swaps for amortizing loans, which are called amortizing swaps, can be constructed, provided the amortization schedule is known. The formulas are a bit more complicated, but for the most part, they involve simply weighting the present value factors by the loan balance.

9.5.4 *Adjustable Interest Rate Swaps*

Some floating-rate loans do not simply involve setting the rate at the beginning of the period and paying the interest at the end of the period.

They specify that the rate is set only for a period and then it is reset, possibly several times, before the interest is paid. For example, consider a loan with quarterly payments made on the 15th of January, April, July, and October. Let the rate be set on the 15th of January, from which point interest begins to accrue. On the 15th of February, the rate is reset and interest continues to accrue. On the 15th of March, the rate is reset again, and interest continues to accrue. On the 15th of April, the accrued interest is paid. So on April 15, the interest paid reflects compounding interest at three different rates during the quarter. If a loan is structured in this manner, it would be important that a swap designed to convert it to a fixed rate loan be structured in that same manner.

The fixed rate on such a swap is the same as that of a standard swap. The reason is that to price the swap we equated the present value of the fixed payments plus notional to the present value of the floating payments plus notional, which equals the notional regardless of whether the swap is standard or adjustable. Valuation of such a swap is somewhat more complex, but it relies on the principal that the floating side plus notional is worth its notional value on a payment date. At any time prior to the payment date, the floating side plus notional is worth the notional plus whatever interest has accumulated since the last payment date. With these points in mind, it is simple to discount the values back to the point of valuation.

There is an important version of an adjustable rate swap that is called an *overnight index swap* or OIS swap. Here the underlying is typically the overnight rate at which banks borrow money from each other. In the U.S., this rate is called the Federal funds, or Fed funds, rate. An OIS swap changes the rate daily, accumulating interest until the scheduled payment date. We will return to the notion of an OIS rate when we discuss the credit risk of swaps in Section 9.6.

9.5.5 *Diff Swaps*

Diff swaps, sometimes called *rate diff swaps*, are variations of currency swaps in which the payments are made in the same currency. While this structure would sound like an interest rate swap, diff swaps still involve interest rates in different countries. Thus, for example, a party might enter into a swap to pay a floating rate in dollars with payments made in dollars and receive a floating rate in euros but with payments made in dollars.

Recall that there are basically three underlyings in currency swaps: the domestic interest rate, the foreign interest rate, and the exchange rate. Rate diff swaps have an implicit fixed rate of currency conversion and, thus, eliminate the third source of uncertainty. Their primary use is to speculate on movements of interest rates in two countries without speculating on the currency risk.

9.5.6   *Constant Maturity Swaps*

Constant maturity swaps, sometimes called *CMS*, are swaps in which the underlying is the rate on an instrument of a constant maturity that is usually longer than the settlement period. Oftentimes, the rate underlying a CMS is referred to as the *CMT rate* where "CMT" refers to Constant Maturity Treasury. The notion of a constant maturity treasury is that of a U.S. Treasury security with constant maturity. Of course, no security has constant maturity, as time increments continuously, but the U.S. Treasury publishes an estimate of the rate on such a security if it existed. Such a rate is obtained by interpolation of the rates with surrounding maturities.

A constant maturity swap enables the receiver or payer of the floating rate to set the maturity or duration at a constant value that would usually be more than the length of the settlement period. Thus, it can be used to change the duration of a bond portfolio to a constant level. A CMS swap also has the unusual feature that the maturity of the underlying, the so-called constant maturity, is typically longer than the settlement period. Thus, for example, a swap might settle every 180 days with the underlying being the five-year CMT rate.

There are many other varieties of swaps that we will not cover here. This is an introductory book and is designed for end users. The material in Section 9.5 is aimed at giving you some exposure to a few of the more popular varieties of swaps. If you encounter other varieties, you will need to spend some time on your own learning about them, but this book will give you the foundational knowledge to do so.

9.6   Swap Credit Risk and Mark-to-Market

Swaps are characterized by bilateral credit risk, which means that each party assumes some risk from the other. As a result, these risks are partially offsetting. For example, recall that when we calculated the value of the vanilla swap in Exhibit 9-20, we found a value of −$111,754 from the perspective of the party paying fixed and receiving floating. The point in time in which this value was calculated was 400 days into the life of the swap. The last payment was 40 days ago, day 360, the upcoming payment occurs in 140 days, day 540, and there is a final payment 180 days after the next one, or 320 days from today and 720 days after the swap was created. At this point, the party paying fixed owes $111,754 more than the party paying floating, but no payment is due at the current time. Nonetheless, the party paying fixed could declare bankruptcy due to this debt and others it may have. If the party owing more on the swap does not declare bankruptcy, there is no current formal obligation, but there is the risk that future obligations might not be met.

On a payment date, whichever party owes more on the current payment could default to the other. Only the net amount owed is subject to default. The remaining payments enter into the picture only if a party declares bankruptcy or announces its inability or renounces its commitment to make one or more remaining payments.

It is important to see the bilateral nature of the credit risk. Recall that from the perspective of a given party, let us say it is you, the swap could have positive or negative value. If it has positive value, the counterparty owes you more than you owe it. If it has negative value, you owe more than the counterparty owes you. If market conditions change, however, a positive value swap can become a negative value swap and vice versa, in which case the party facing the credit risk changes.

You should also be able to see that there is current credit risk and potential credit risk. Current credit risk applies only at the time a payment is due. Potential credit risk applies to payments that are to come later.

Typically a swap has the greatest exposure to credit risk in the middle of its life. In the latter part of its life, the remaining payments are small. Of course, a swap could have high exposure early in its life, but it is generally assumed that no one would enter into a swap if the risk of default early in its life were high.

How does one go about managing swap credit risk? We have an entire chapter (Chapter 11) devoted to credit risk, so we are not going far into the subject here. At a first level of protection, most parties try to engage in swaps only with the most creditworthy counterparties. Other require that collateral be posted with a third party. In other words, the counterparty to whom the value is negative would typically post some money up to the full negative value with a third party. Another method of managing the credit risk is to mark a swap to market. As an example of how marking to market is done with swaps, consider a two-year swap with semiannual payments and a requirement that the parties mark-to-market each month. Once a month, the parties will determine the value of the swap, and the party owing the greater amount will pay it to the counterparty. The two parties will then reprice the swap to the new market rate. They will then repeat that procedure every month. In other words, the parties will settle up every month and basically re-write the swap as a new swap.

In the U.S., the Dodd-Frank Act went into effect in 2010. Part of its objective was to provide more oversight of the swaps market and to reduce systemic risk. As a result, the new law essentially requires that most swaps be executed on organized facilities, which are called *swap execution facilities* (SEFs) and *designated contract markets* (DCMs). These facilities provide quotation systems in which parties can shop for the best quotes. These transactions that run through SEFs and DCMs will be cleared by one of several clearing entities and will require margins and daily mark-to-market. These swaps are then essentially regarded as default-free, at least based on the experience of nearly 100 years of clearinghouses.

LIBOR Swaps and OIS Discounting

We illustrated in this chapter how the LIBOR-based cash flows in a swap are discounted at LIBOR. This procedure is particularly convenient for the floating payments, because it means that the floating payments plus notional have a value of the notional on any reset date. The assumption underlying the discounting of any series of cash flows is that the discount rate should reflect the risk of the cash flows. On the surface, it seems that LIBOR should reflect the risk of floating payments based on LIBOR. Hence, LIBOR would seem an appropriate rate at which to discount the payments on a swap. LIBOR is viewed as a reflection of a AA-rated (pronounced "double-A rate") London bank. Such banks would seem to be safe, right?

Well, the Financial Crisis of 2008 changed the way of thinking about this issue. The banks that borrowed at LIBOR were not nearly as low risk it had been thought. Discounting by LIBOR, therefore, implicitly imposes a risk premium, reflecting a possibility that the payments will not be made. In other words, LIBOR could no longer be viewed as a risk-free rate. Prior to the enactment of the Dodd-Frank Act, many swaps were collateralized and were virtually risk-free, but discounting at LIBOR penalized them. After Dodd-Frank, most swaps have become collateralized, and therefore LIBOR is no longer viewed as the appropriate rate at which to discount cash flows.

The rate generally used by the market for discounting is called the Overnight Indexed Swap rate, or OIS rate. It is essentially the rate on risk-free money loaned overnight from bank to bank. In the U.S., that rate is essentially the federal funds rate, which is the rate at which high quality banks lend overnight. Of course, these banks are subject to default but the extremely short-term nature of this type of lending virtually removes that risk. During the Financial Crisis, the LIBOR-OIS spread was between 300 and 400 basis points, implying a 3–4% premium for the bearing of credit risk. Discounting LIBOR cash flows by OIS rates raises the value of the fixed and floating payments on risk-free swaps because a lower discount rate is used, but it causes some complexity in that the value of the floating payments plus notional no longer equals the notional. In that case, the floating side of a swap is usually valued by using the forward rates as projected floating rates.

Notwithstanding the discounting of essentially risk-free swap cash flows at the OIS rate, there are swaps themselves in which the floating cash flows are based on the OIS rate. Such cash flows accumulate interest at daily floating rates. We discussed this type of floating structure when we covered adjustable interest rate swaps. They are not particularly difficult to value and have the convenience that the cash flows and the discount rate are the same.

We should note that non-collateralized swaps and those not secured through clearinghouses are still appropriately discounted at LIBOR.

But for whatever it is worth, the spread between LIBOR and OIS rates, which widened so much during the crisis, has gone back to nearly zero, meaning that there is virtually no difference between the results using LIBOR or OIS discounting.

Source: Smith (2011, 2013).

While almost all swaps are required to be cleared, some exceptions exist. End users employing swaps for hedging purposes can be exempted, but these exceptions can be nullified if the swap dealer as counterparty is required to clear swaps. Small financial institutions, meaning those with less than $10 billion of assets, can also get exceptions. In addition, swaps involving foreign counterparties may be permitted exceptions depending on the constraints imposed by the counterparty's regulatory requirements.

Swaps, and indeed all derivatives, that are not executed through clearinghouses would entail some credit risk. As such, accounting rules now require adjustments to the values of swaps that are called *credit value adjustments* (CVA) and *debit value adjustments* (DVA), two concepts that are the mirror image of each other. One party makes a CVA and the other would make a DVA.

9.7 Applications of Swaps in Risk Management

In this final section of the chapter, we will take a look at specific examples of the use of swaps. We will cover at least one use of each of the four types of swaps.

9.7.1 *Converting a Floating-Rate Loan into a Fixed-Rate Loan*

Most corporate loans are made at floating rates. The reason is that banks prefer to make floating-rate loans, because their funding is at floating rates. By making floating-rate loans, banks pass on their interest rate risk to companies.

A good argument can be made that banks are uniquely qualified to manage interest rate risk and should, therefore, manage that risk and offer fixed-rate loans. Banks do indeed offer some fixed-rate loans, but most corporate loans of reasonable size are at floating rates. As an alternative, banks typically offer floating-rate loans through their lending divisions and then offer interest-rate swaps separately through their derivatives divisions. In effect, a borrower would take out a floating-rate loan with one part of the bank, a lending group, while engaging in a swap to pay fixed and receive floating with another part of the bank, a derivatives group. One might logically ask why there appears to be more people involved in such a transaction than are necessary. If the bank did its own interest-rate hedging, it could offer fixed-rate corporate loans. The answer most likely lies in the fact that the bank can earn a profit off of *both* transactions that is more than it could earn if it offered the two transactions as a simple fixed-rate loan. Of course, the end user is free to shop around, but in most cases, the swap is done with the lending bank.[21]

Exhibit 9-26 illustrates such a transaction. The end user, which is likely to be a corporation, takes out a floating-rate loan at LIBOR plus a spread

---

[21]Think of buying a large appliance such as a refrigerator from an appliance store. The store offers delivery and installation, the latter of which is not much more than plugging the new refrigerator in. The dealer does charge a fee for this service. You could do the delivery yourself or you could hire a company to do it and possibly get a better deal. But in all likelihood, you will have the dealer do it.

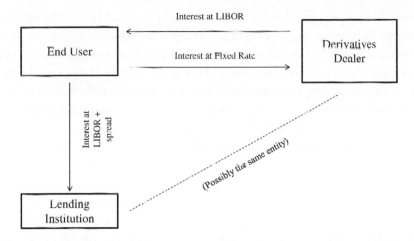

Exhibit 9-26. Converting a Floating-Rate Loan to a Fixed-Rate Loan

from the lending institution.[22] It simultaneously engages in an interest rate swap with a derivatives dealer. The swap results in the end user paying a fixed rate and receiving a floating rate. The interest the end user receives from the dealer offsets the interest paid to the lending institution. The end user is protected against increases in LIBOR, because any higher rate paid on the loan will be offset by a higher floating payment from the swap dealer. Netting it all out, the end user pays the swap fixed rate plus the spread.

The above transaction is one of the most common in the entire financial markets. Indeed, its simplicity is undoubtedly one of the reasons why swaps have been so widely embraced by corporate end users since swaps premiered in the early 1980s. There are some arguments in favor of this pair of transactions over a direct fixed-rate loan on the basis of the fact that the end user faces some credit risk and can earn a return to compensate it. In other words, a fixed rate loan plus the credit spread is believed to be at a lower rate than it would be if the bank simply offered a fixed rate loan in the first place. This argument might well be true, but corporate end users are typically not in the best position to evaluate whether the credit risk is worth it. Hence, corporate end users should have other reasons for engaging in swaps.

---

[22]The end user pays a spread, because it does not have the high credit quality of a London bank, which is what LIBOR is based on. Most end users have to pay a spread over LIBOR to reflect the credit risk they impose on the lender.

One justification for this transaction might be that the corporation fears an increase in interest rates. This reason might be a good one for the strategic use of swaps, meaning that the end user routinely engages in swaps to convert floating-rate loans to fixed-rate loans. But if the end user engages in tactical swap trading, meaning that sometimes it does swaps and sometimes it keeps the loan rates fixed, it is engaged in a form of interest-rate market timing. Such a strategy is unlikely to be very effective, as corporate end users are probably not able to time interest rate markets. Even banks and professional traders are not able to do so very effectively.

Again, the best justification for end users engaging in swaps is likely to be that end users want to remove the risk over which they have no control in order to focus on the risks on which they have competitive expertise. Thus, a large global company such as Toyota might wish to consistently rid itself of the interest rate risk of its floating-rate loans doing the kinds of swaps shown in Exhibit 9-26.

9.7.2   *Adjusting Bond Portfolio Duration*

Bond portfolio managers can use swaps to adjust the duration of a bond portfolio. Examining how this is a done is a very useful exercise in understanding the interest rate risk in swaps. Let us first consider a pay-fixed, receive-floating interest rate swap. Earlier in this chapter, we illustrated how this instrument is like issuing a fixed-rate bond and using the proceeds to buy a floating-rate bond. We know how to measure the duration of a fixed rate bond, as this concept was covered in Chapter 7. Recall that duration is a type of present value-weighted time to maturity. So now let us think about the duration of a floating rate bond.

First, let us assume there is virtually no possibility of default, so this is essentially a AAA-rated bond. The basic idea behind a floating rate bond is that the coupon adjusts to the current rate in the market on every coupon payment date, forcing the bond price to go back to its par value. Floating rate bonds are, thus, designed to provide some stability to the price. If the coupon were paid continuously, the coupon rate would adjust continuously and the bond price would always be at its par value, but of course, that is not possible.

Consider a floating rate bond that pays a coupon of c_b and matures in T years, the next coupon payment date. T could be less than a year. On that date, the price will go back to par. Thus, in T years the holder will have a claim of c_b plus 1. Assume that the bond yield is y. Thus, the bond price is

$B = (1 + c)/(1 + y)^T$. Let us find the duration by differentiating the bond price with respect to the yield,

$$\frac{dB}{dy} = \frac{-(1 + c)T(1 + y)^{T-1}}{(1 + y)^{2T}}$$

$$= -B\left(\frac{T}{1 + y}\right).$$

A floating rate bond is basically a zero coupon bond with face value $1 + c$ that is renewed period after period. The duration of a zero coupon bond is the maturity, T. Modified duration is defined as $DUR_m = -(dB/dy)/B$. Doing the math, we obtain

$$DUR_m = -\frac{dB}{dy}\Big/B$$

$$= -B\left(\frac{-T}{1 + y}\right)\Big/B. \qquad (9.15)$$

Thus, the modified duration is

$$DUR_m = \frac{T}{1 + y}. \qquad (9.16)$$

So the modified duration of a floating rate bond is its duration, which is the maturity, divided by one plus the yield.

Since a vanilla swap is equivalent to issuing a floating-rate bond and using the proceeds to buy a fixed-rate bond, we can say that the duration of a floating-for-fixed swap is the duration of a floating-rate bond minus the duration of a fixed rate bond. So now let us look at how to adjust the duration of a portfolio of bonds using swaps.

Let B be the portfolio value, DUR_B be the portfolio duration, DUR_T be the target duration, P be the notional of the swap and DUR_s be the duration of the swap. The target duration times the portfolio value will be made up of the duration of the bond portfolio times its value plus the duration of the swap times its notional,

$$B * DUR_T = B * DUR_B + P * DUR_S.$$

Solving for P, we obtain

$$P = B\left(\frac{DUR_T - DUR_B}{DUR_S}\right). \qquad (9.17)$$

Objective: A portfolio manager holds a $30 million bond portfolio with a modified duration of 7.5. He wants to reduce the duration to 6.5 by using swaps. The duration of the fixed-rate bond implicit in the swap is 1.25. The floating-rate bond implicit in the swap has a yield of 6% and makes its first payment in six months. Assume a pay-fixed, receive-floating swap. How would the manager use swaps to change the duration of the portfolio? Explain your answer.

Inputs:

B:	$30 million
DUR_B:	7.5
DUR_T:	6.5

In addition, the floating rate bond pays interest every six months and has a yield of 6%. We need to first find the duration of the floating rate component of the swap, which is the reset period of one-half year divided by one plus the yield. It will be

$$\frac{0.5}{1.06} = 0.4717$$

Given that the fixed side of the swap has a duration of 1.25, the overall duration of the pay-fixed, receive-floating swap is

$$0.4717 - 1.25 = -0.7783.$$

Results:

The notional required to change the portfolio duration from 7.5 to 6.5 is

$$P = \$30,000,000 \left(\frac{6.5 - 7.5}{-0.7783} \right) = \$38,545,455.$$

The duration of the swap is negative, which means that instead of moving inversely with interest rates, the swap moves directly with interest rates. This result is logical, because it is a pay-fixed, receive-floating swap. As rates go up, the higher rates benefit the floating side and reduce the value of the fixed side. A bond portfolio with positive duration is inversely related to interest rates. A swap with negative duration will reduce that sensitivity. Hence, the notional is positive. Interestingly, if we had specified a pay-floating, receive-fixed swap, the swap duration would have been positive and the formula would have given a negative notional, which would be a signal to do the opposite. Thus, the formula will always tell you whether to pay fixed, receive floating or do the opposite.

Exhibit 9-27. Using Vanilla Swaps to Adjust Portfolio Duration

This formula applies regardless of whether it is the duration or the modified duration. It gives us the notional of a swap with a duration of DUR_s that would change the portfolio duration to the target duration. Exhibit 9-27 illustrates the use of this formula.

This example provides a good opportunity to see the source of value in an interest rate swap, a topic we covered in Section 9.3.1.2. As we saw in this section, the duration of a floating rate security is a little less than the length of the reset period. Thus, a swap with payments every six months would have a duration of less than six months for its floating payments. The duration of the fixed side of the swap would correspond to the duration of the implicit fixed-rate bond that replicates the fixed payments. Thus, the fixed duration will almost always be considerably more than the floating duration. We know that interest rate sensitivity is directly related to duration. Hence, the fixed side of the swap is far more sensitive than the floating side. As a result, changes in interest rates will impart more value to the fixed side than to the floating side. So, as interest rates increase, the value of a pay-fixed, receive-floating swap will increase, but will do so more as a result of the decreased value of the fixed payments than the increased value of the floating payments.

9.7.3 Converting a Domestic Bond Issue into a Foreign Bond Issue

Currency swaps are most often used in conjunction with issuing a bond in one currency and using the swap to effectively convert it to a bond in another currency. A common situation of this sort is when a company needs funding in a foreign currency. For example, a company may be planning an expansion into a foreign market. It will incur significant cash outlays in the foreign currency and, thus, needs a supply of foreign cash. It could issue a bond in the foreign country denominated in the foreign currency, but it is less known in that country than in its own domestic market. Thus, it will often find that it is more efficient and less costly to issue the bond in its own market in its own currency and use a currency swap to convert the bond to the foreign currency it needs. Exhibit 9-28 illustrates how this is done.

One other consideration is that the company has assumed some credit risk from the swap. The dealer could default to it. As such, the company should get a better rate than it would if it issued the bond in euros.

9.7.4 Asset Allocation of an Equity Portfolio using Swaps

Asset allocation is an investment strategy in which portfolio managers decide on how their portfolios will be allocated among broad classes of investments.

Objective: A U.S. corporation needs €150 million to finance expansion into European markets. It has decided to issue a bond in the U.S. and use a currency swap to convert the bond to euros. We want to create three diagrams illustrating the flow of cash, one at the issue date, one representing each interest payment date, and one at the maturity date. Let us assume that the bond will pay interest at a fixed rate. We also need to find the domestic notional. In addition, let us consider how the answer would differ if the bond were designed to pay floating interest. The exchange rate is $1.067.

Inputs:

Foreign notional:	€150,000,000
S_0 (spot exchange rate):	$1.067

Results:

We need to find the domestic notional. It would be

$$(€150,000,000)\$1.067 = \$160,000,000$$

(with some rounding off). At the issue date, the company issues the bond in U.S. dollars for $160,000,000. It then engages in a currency swap and pays the dealer the notional of $160,000,000. In turn, the dealer pays the company the euro notional of €150,000,000. The company now has the euros it needs to finance its expansion.

(a) At Issue Date

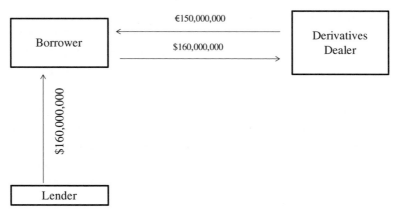

At the interest payment dates, the company will pay the interest on its bond to its U.S. investors. It will receive U.S. dollar interest from the swap dealer and pay interest in euros to the swap dealer. The problem stated that the interest would be fixed on the loan, so the swap would be a fixed-pay swap. The fixed rate on the loan and the fixed rate on the swap are not likely to be the same, but the difference is a constant spread. Alternatively, the loan could have floating interest in which case the swap would be structured to have floating interest. Again, there would probably be a spread on the loan.

Exhibit 9-28. Converting a Domestic Bond Issue to a Foreign Bond Issue

(b) Interest Payment Dates

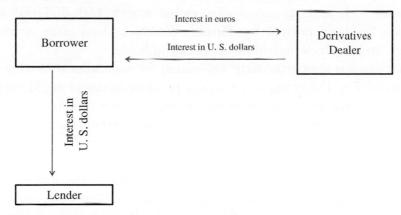

At maturity of the bond and expiration of the swap, the parties do the opposite of what they did at the issue date. The company pays back the dollar principal of the bond. It receives the same dollar principal from the swap dealer and pays the swap dealer the euro principal.

(c) Bond maturity and swap expiration

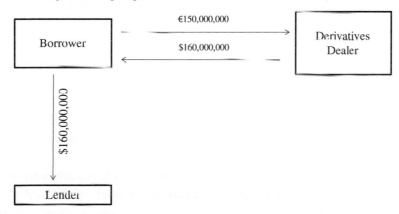

The net effect of the bond and swap is that the company receives the euros it needs at the start and can carry on with its expansion. It effectively pays interest in euros, though it may have an additional premium of the fixed rate on its loan versus the fixed rate on the swap but this premium is in dollars, so it faces no additional currency risk. At maturity of the bond, it receives the dollar notional from the derivatives dealer and uses this amount to pay off its bond. It also pays the derivatives dealer the euro notional. The company has effectively issued a bond in euros.

Exhibit 9-28. *(Continued)*

Stocks and bonds are the broadest classes, but within those classes are other sub-classes such as large-cap stocks, global stocks, high-dividend stocks, corporate bonds, municipal bonds, etc. Within a given class, a manager will then decide which individual securities to hold.

Equity swaps are particularly well-suited for asset allocation changes in equity portfolios. For example, an equity portfolio manager could engage in a swap to pay the return on an equity index and receive a fixed or floating rate. This strategy would result in a shift of the portfolio away from equity in the direction of bonds. An equity portfolio manager with funds invested in one particular equity asset class could engage in an equity swap to pay the return on an equity index representing that equity asset class and receive the return on an equity index representing a different equity asset class. These transactions can be very attractive in lieu of selling off some of the equity and investing in a fixed income security, a floating rate security, or another equity index. A swap would have lower transactions costs and could probably be arranged much faster than the time it would take to do the transactions in the spot market. Also, many portfolios are managed by different managers. For example, a pension fund might have an equity manager and a fixed income manager. If it wanted to change the asset allocation the traditional way of buying and selling securities, it would force the two managers to do their respective trades. There would likely be some advantage to having each manager focus on security selection and not have to worry that the allocation to his asset class will be increased or decreased, which would require him to execute some additional trades. An equity swap would allow an overall portfolio manager to reallocate the portfolio without disturbing the asset class managers.

There is little need to illustrate this procedure, as it is fairly simple. There are, however, some special considerations associated with equity swaps. Recall that we previously mentioned that in equity swaps that pay the rate of return on a constant notional, the settlement cash flows would not exist if the transactions were done in the securities. Thus, if a manager reduces its equity exposure using a swap, it will have to make cash payments of the return on the stock, which it would not be making if it sold the stock. In addition, an equity swap involves the rate of return on a constant investment one unit, whereas an equity portfolio return is based on its own accumulated value. Thus, there are some cash-flow factors and modest differences that a portfolio manager would need to consider, but these can be handled.

9.7.5 *Hedging the Future Purchase of a Commodity*

Commodity swaps are excellent tools for locking in the future price of a commodity. If a company knows that it will be buying a certain number of units of the commodity on a periodic schedule, a commodity swap can be easily structured to hedge against increases in the price of the commodity. A classic example is the purchase of jet fuel by airlines. All an airline would need to do is get a swap created that calls for the purchase of a certain number of gallons of jet fuel at specific dates for however long the company wants to put the hedge in place.

Constructing a commodity swap to perfectly hedge, however, is virtually impossible. Let us take a look at an example. The U.S. government web site (http://www.transtats.bts.gov/fuel.asp) provides data on U.S. airline purchases and use of fuel. In 2015, Delta Airlines purchased approximately 3.37 billion gallons at an average cost per gallon of $2.31. Thus, its total expenditure on jet fuel was about $7.79 billion. Delta purchases fuel each month. In 2015, it averaged around 280 million gallons a month ranging from a high of almost 329 million gallons in August, 2015 to a low of around 230 million gallons in February, 2015. These numbers are, however, not necessarily consistent from year to year. They depend on the economy and in particular on the amount of summer vacation travel people do.

Airlines can hardly hope to match their purchases with swaps that cover the precise number of gallons they will need. In particular, for a hedge to be very effective, they cannot just hedge a month in the future. Thus, airlines would tend to make reasonable estimates of their monthly or quarterly consumption and have swap dealers design swaps that provide the best terms possible. Still, their forecasts are not perfect, so an airline might sometimes over-hedge and sometimes under-hedge. If it under-hedges, it has some unhedged purchases to make in the spot market, and these purchases will be made at the spot price at the time of the purchase. If it over-hedges, it will have speculated with a portion of the swap. Of course, if prices rise, that speculation will be profitable, but if they fall, the airline will take a loss on the over-hedged portion of the notional. What we have just described is the concept of quantity risk, which we covered in Chapter 7.

In practice, most airlines do not hedge anywhere near all of their consumption. Perhaps the reason is that they do not want to lose money on these derivatives or be accused of speculating. And yet, they are speculating by leaving most of their positions unhedged.

Commodity swaps have an interesting variation that helps hedgers achieve an imperfect albeit reasonably satisfactory result. Many commodity swaps are based on the average price of the asset during the settlement period. Thus, at the settlement the hedger buys the commodity at the average price. The pricing and valuation of these swaps is more complex but can be done.[23]

We should also note that commodity swaps can be structured for actual delivery of the commodity or for cash settlement. Cash settlement is typically more attractive. For example, a global energy user will likely have a need for the oil in many different locations. As such, a swap to settle in cash would work best. The swap holder would receive the commodity price less the fixed price it agreed to pay. Any profit or loss would arise from increases or decreases in the price of oil. The swap buyer would then buy the oil on the spot market. Profits from the hedge would effectively adjust the price paid for the oil. If oil prices rise, the higher price paid in the spot market would be partially offset by the profits from the swap. If oil prices decrease, the losses on the swap would effectively raise the lower price paid on the spot market. In both cases, the hedger would end up paying roughly where it expected to pay, the fixed price of the swap.

9.8   Chapter Summary

This chapter has been a long one, one of the longest in the book. There is a reason for that. Swaps are the most widely used derivative instrument. It is extremely important for end users to have a good understanding of how swaps are priced, valued, and used. Therefore, there is much to be learned.

We saw that because swaps involve no initial exchange of money, they have zero value. As such, the fixed price or rate for a swap is identified as the price or rate that leads to zero value at the start. With the value of the swap at zero, changes in the underlying and the passage of time lead to changes in the swap value. We learned how to determine the fixed price or rate for the swap and how to identify the value of the swap during its life. We examined interest rate, currency, equity, and commodity swaps.

In addition, we look at several applications of swaps. In all cases, we saw that swaps are used to alter the risk of a position. Interest rate swaps can be used to change a floating-rate loan to a fixed-rate loan or to alter the duration of a bond portfolio. Currency swaps can be used to change the

---

[23]Your author covers this topic in Chance (1996).

issue of a bond in one currency to a bond in another currency. Equity swaps can be used to alter the asset allocation of a portfolio involving equities. Commodity swaps can be used to lock in the price for future purchase of a commodity. These uses are common ones but certainly not the only ones.

9.9 Questions and Problems

1. How does a swap differ from a forward contract?
2. What are the four categories of underliers of swaps?
3. What is a vanilla interest rate swap?
4. How is the floating interest rate determined and how is the interest paid on a vanilla interest rate swap? This question is in regard to the beginning or end of the settlement period. How does this method differ from the method used in FRAs?
5. Determine the net payment due at this time on an interest rate swap in which the fixed rate is 3.77%, the floating rate is 3.13%, the underlying rate is 180-day LIBOR, and the notional is $32 million. Identify which party makes the net payment and which receives it.
6. Explain how interest rate swaps are like two loans.
7. Explain how currency swaps are related to interest rate swaps.
8. Why do currency swaps typically involve the payment of the notionals while interest rate swaps do not.
9. You are given the following information. The rates are based on 90-day LIBOR and Euro LIBOR.

USD notional:	$25,000,000
EUR notional:	€22,100,000
Exchange rate:	$1.08
EUR fixed rate:	2.25%
EUR floating rate:	2.14%
USD fixed rate:	1.97%
USD floating rate:	1.88%

Calculate the net values of the payments in dollars on the following swaps:

(a) pay dollars fixed, receive euros fixed
(b) pay dollars fixed, receive euros floating
(c) pay dollars floating, receive euros floating
(d) pay dollars floating, receive euros fixed.

Round to the nearest dollar or euro.

10. Explain how the following currency swaps can be converted into other currency swaps.

    (a) A currency swap to pay domestic floating and receive foreign floating to a currency swap to pay domestic floating and receive foreign fixed

    (b) A currency swap to pay domestic fixed and receive foreign floating to a currency swap to pay domestic fixed and receive foreign fixed

11. Explain how an equity swap is similar to but different from an interest rate swap.

12. Name at least three types of series of cash flows that can be paid or received when the other leg is an equity return.

13. Calculate the payoff of the following equity swaps if the equity leg is a stock index that went from 752.14 at the beginning of the settlement period to 744.87 at the end, and the notional is $15 million. Explain why the payments are the signs they are.

    (a) Receive equity, pay a fixed rate of 2.37% based on 90-day LIBOR

    (b) Receive equity, pay a floating rate, currently 1.98%, based on 90-day LIBOR

    (c) Receive equity as described above and pay the return on a different equity index that went from 1,222.90 at the beginning of the period to 1,187.52 at the end.

14. Of the three swaps, interest rate, currency, and equity, which is most like commodity swaps?

15. Find the payoff of a commodity swap on 10,000 units of a commodity priced at $4.55, with the fixed rate at $4.17. The party pays the fixed rate and receives the commodity price.

16. Explain in words how a vanilla interest rate swap is priced.

17. Find the fixed rate on a vanilla interest rate swap based on the following term structure where the underlying is 60-day LIBOR:

Days	Rate
60	0.0422
120	0.0426
180	0.0435
240	0.0447

18. Suppose you have engaged in a £18 million notional pay-fixed, receive-floating vanilla swap. The fixed rate is 2.76%. You have three payments remaining, one in 35 days, one in 125 days, and one in 215 days. The underlying is 90-day LIBOR. The upcoming floating payment is 2.27%. The term structure is as follows:

Days	Rate
35	0.0299
125	0.0315
215	0.0331

Find the value of the swap.

19. Use the term structure in Problem 17 and show how that swap is priced as a combination of off-market FRAs.

20. Using the term structure in Problem 17, demonstrate that the expected value of the payments in the swap is zero, using the forward rates as expected spot rates.

21. Find the fixed rates on currency swaps involving notional of USD35 million swapped against Swiss francs (CHF). Determine the CHF notional if the exchange rate is CHF1.1300 per USD. The term structures for USD and CHF are given below:

Days	USD	CHF
180	0.027	0.011
360	0.029	0.016

22. Using the swap in Problem 21, now assume you are 35 days into the swap and the term structure is given below. The new exchange rate is 1.1392.

Days	USD	CHF
145	0.0295	0.0119
325	0.0318	0.0201

Find the values in USD of the following four swaps:

(a) Pay USD floating, receive CHF floating
(b) Pay USD floating, receive CHF fixed
(c) Pay USD fixed, receive CHF floating
(d) Pay USD fixed, receive CHF fixed

23. Use the term structure information in Problem 17 and work the following pricing problems on equity swaps.

    (a) Price an equity swap to pay fixed and receive the equity return, where the equity is at 984.49.
    (b) Price an equity swap to pay fixed and receive floating.
    (c) Price an equity swap to pay the return on an equity index that is at 2247.81 and receive the return on the equity index that is at 984.49.

24. Using the term structure in Problem 17, roll forward 40 days and use the following term structure to value the three equity swaps indicated. The notional is $10 million.

Days	Rate
20	0.0429
80	0.0433
140	0.0439
200	0.0451

    (a) An equity swap to pay fixed and receive the equity return. The index started at 984.49, as indicated in the previous problem, and is now at 998.15.
    (b) An equity swap to pay floating and receive the equity return. Use the levels in part (a).
    (c) An equity swap to pay the return on an index that started at 2,247.81 and is now at 2,291.66 and receive the return on the index with levels indicated in part (a).

25. Use the term structure in Problem 17 and find the fixed rate on a commodity swap that involves paying a fixed price with payments on the four dates indicated in that term structure where the commodity is currently priced at $32.57 and the storage cost is $0.25 every 60 days.

26. Use the information in the previous problem and find the value of the swap after the first two payments have been made and there are 25 days until the next. The spot price is now $34.01 and the swap covers 150,000 units of the commodity. The term structure is as follows:

Days	Rate
25	0.0449
85	0.0458

Storage costs for part of a period are paid on a prorated basis.

27. Describe the two ways of terminating swaps and discuss the pros and cons of each

28. What is a basis swap? What type of basis swap would enable one to speculate on the creditworthiness of London banks?

29. Explain how a party can pre-establish a fixed rate for a swap to be engaged in the future.

30. Explain how swaps can be structured to accommodate amortizing fixed income securities, such as mortgages.

31. What adjustments are required for interest rate swaps in which the underlying rate on a loan being hedged by the swap compounds through the interest accrual period?

32. Explain how interest rate swaps can be arranged to speculate or hedge on differences in interest rates across countries with no currency risk.

33. What is a CMT rate and how is it used in CMS swaps?

34. What type of credit risk is assumed in interest rate swaps and when is this risk typically the greatest?

35. Explain how a vanilla swap can be used to convert a fixed-rate loan into a floating-rate loan?

36. The manager of a bond portfolio worth $125 million wants to use swaps to change its modified duration of 8.55. The floating side of the swap has a yield of 2.75% and a reset period of three months. The fixed side of the swap has a modified duration of 3.35. Find the size of the notional on the swap to (a) change the modified duration to 5, and (b) change the modified duration to zero.

37. Explain how a currency swap can be used to effectively convert a bond issued in one currency into a bond issued in another currency.

38. Explain how an equity portfolio manager can use equity swaps on indexes to change the asset allocation from 60% large-cap, 40% small-cap to 55% large-cap, 45% small-cap.

39. Explain how a commodity swap can be used by a jewelry manufacturer to lock in the purchase price of a series of future purchases of diamonds.

Chapter 10

Managing Market Risk with Options

Wall Street firms do not guess when they calculate the values of bonds and options, even though many corporate treasurers still do. Guessing went out of fashion about ten years ago — ever since the derivative products markets began to flourish.

> Andrew J. Kalotay
> and George O. Williams
> "How to Succeed in Derivatives
> without Really Buying"
> *The Journal of Applied
> Corporate Finance*
> Fall, 1993.

Chapter 10 is the final chapter of a pedagogical trilogy on the three principal types of instruments used in market risk management. Chapter 8 was on forwards and futures, and Chapter 9 was on swaps. Because they are slightly more complex than forwards, futures, and swaps, we have saved options for last, though the wait should be worth it. What makes options more complex is that they have non-linear payoffs, meaning that their payoffs are not related to the underlying in the same way over the full range of possible underlying values at the expiration or settlement dates. In contrast, forwards, futures, and swaps have linear payoffs, meaning that the payoffs are the same function of the underlying regardless of the level of the underlying. If this point is not clear, do not worry. We will cover it in detail, and it will become clear. So, let us get started with understanding just what an option is.

10.1   Formal Definition of an Option

As with forwards, futures, and swaps, we need a good, clear formal definition of an option. So let us use this one:

> *An option is a derivative contract involving two parties, the buyer and the seller, in which the buyer pays a fixed sum of money to the seller and receives the right to buy or sell an underlying at a fixed price or rate or make an equivalent cash settlement either at or before a specific date.*

Now let us work through that definition.

First of all, quite naturally, an option is indeed a derivative contract, and it involves two parties that are referred to as the buyer and seller. The buyer is said to be the option holder and has a long position in the option. The seller is sometimes called the writer and is said to have a short position in the option. Notice that we stated that the buyer pays a sum of money to the seller. Unlike forwards, futures, and swaps, there is an exchange of cash at the start of the life of the option. The money paid from buyer to seller is referred to as the option premium but can also be simply called the option price. On some occasions, it might be referred to as the option value. Recall that in the study of forwards, futures, and swaps, what we call the price of the forward, futures, or swap is the fixed price or rate to which the two parties agree will be paid at expiration or settlement date. The value of a forward, futures, or swap is zero at the start and then rises above or falls below zero during the life of the contract. For options, the concept of value takes on a different meaning and one more like the meaning for securities. Just as a financial analyst might assess that the value of a stock is $25 but the stock is selling for $30, so might an options expert assess that the value of an option is $6 though it is selling for $5. Of course, prices are supposed to converge to values, but value is subjective. Nonetheless, the point is that the price and value are similar concepts and on the same order of magnitude for options and securities, but not for forwards, futures, and swaps.

The definition also states that in return for paying this sum of money, the buyer receives the right to buy or sell something. The word *right* is analogous to the word *option*. The buyer has a choice of whether to use the option. An option that conveys the right to buy something is referred to as a call, while an option that conveys the right to sell something is referred to as a put. If a call holder uses the option to buy the underlying, he is said to be exercising the option. If a put holder uses the option to sell the underlying, he is also said to be exercising the option.

In the definition we also mentioned buying the underlying, which is the case of a call, and selling the underlying, which is the case of a put. We also referred to the concept of an equivalent cash settlement. We have already discussed how forwards, futures, and swaps can settle in cash instead of delivery of the underlying. So too can options.

An option grants the right to buy or sell at a fixed price. That fixed price is called the *exercise price*, the *strike price*, the *strike*, and (somewhat rarely) the *striking price*. When the underlying is referred to as a rate such as an interest rate or a foreign exchange rate, we usually use the term *exercise rate* or *strike rate*.

Finally, we noted that the exercise of the option can be made either before or at a specific date. The option contract itself specifies which exercise style is applicable. Options that can be exercised at any time before they expire are referred to as *American options* and sometimes *American-style options*. Options that can be exercised only at the point of expiration are referred to as *European options* or *European-style options*. The point of expiration is a particular day that is referred to as the expiration, expiration day, expiry, and less often, the maturity or maturity date. The time period to the expiration is called the *time to expiration* or occasionally, the *expiration*.

10.2 Basic Structure and Characteristics of Option Contracts and Markets

Options are traded in both exchange-listed and over-the-counter markets. Exchange-listed options are standardized and trade on the major derivatives exchanges around the world. OTC options are customized and trade on a direct basis between counterparties, which are typically end users and dealers. The most common underlyings are individual common stocks, stock indexes, currencies, bonds, interest rates, and commodities. As we will see later in this chapter, there are also options on futures, forwards, and swaps.

In Chapter 5, we looked at the size of the derivatives markets. As of December, 2017, the global OTC derivatives market as reported by the Bank for International Settlements was about $531 trillion notional with market value of $11 trillion. Interest rate options account for about $39 trillion notional and about $719 billion market value. Currency options compose $10.7 trillion notional and $192 billion market value. Stock and stock index options make up $3.4 trillion notional and $378 billion market value. Commodity options make up $447 billion, but their market value is not collected by the BIS.

These numbers for OTC equity options, however, are relatively small, but that is because equity options are widely traded on derivatives exchanges. In Chapter 5, we reported global volume as provided by *Futures Industry* magazine. In 2017, options accounted for about 10.4 billion contracts of the 25.2 billion of exchange-listed derivatives volume.

10.3   Option Payoffs and Characteristics of Option Prices

In Chapter 4, Section 4.4.4, we introduced some basic concepts of options. In this section, we will review that material. We let T be the time to expiration of the option in years. Thus, an option expiring in 60 days will have $T = 60/365 = 0.1644$. We let X be the exercise price. We will start off with a generic underlying priced at S_0 when the option is initiated and at S_T at expiration. It is probably easiest to think of this underlying as a stock or stock index, though it could be an exchange rate or commodity price. When we discuss interest rate options, we will utilize the notation we used for FRAs and interest rate swaps. The prices of European calls and puts at time 0 are denoted $c_0(X, T)$ and $p_0(X, T)$. If these options are American-style, we use $C_0(X, T)$ and $P_0(X, T)$.

In Exhibit 4-19, we presented a graph of the profit from the purchase of a call option. We repeat that graph here as Exhibit 10-1. This example assumes a European call, and we shall discuss any difference that might arise for American calls. The graph shows the profit from the strategy on

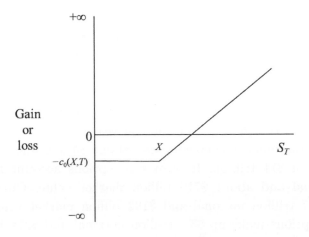

Exhibit 10-1. Profit Diagram for Buyer of a Call Option

the vertical axis, given the price of the underlying at expiration, S_T, on the horizontal axis.

This graph is one of several option graphs that are commonly referred to as a hockey stick graph, and it shows that if $S_T \leq X$, the profit is the loss of the premium, $-c_0(X, T)$. This result arises because in this circumstance, referred to as expiring out-of-the-money, the holder of the option will not exercise it. The option allows the holder to purchase the asset at X, but if $S_T \leq X$, the asset can be purchased at a lower or equal price in the market. Thus, the option holder would let the option expire unexercised. For the case in which the $S_T > X$, which we refer to as expiring in-the-money, the call holder will exercise the option, thereby purchasing the underlying for X. The holder will then be in possession of an asset worth S_T, having paid X for it. Thus, by virtue of having the option, the option holder possesses something of value of $S_T - X$. In the graph above, the profit for the in-the-money case, is $S_T - X - c_0(X, T)$. As you see, there is a range over which this profit is negative, which is where the underlying price does not exceed the exercise price by the amount of the premium.

We are interested in writing a statement that specifies the value of the option at expiration, which we specify as $c_T(X, T)$, given the value of the underlying, S_T. We can, therefore, write this value as

$$c_T(S_T, X) = Max(0, S_T - X) \tag{10.1}$$

This expression is read in the following manner: *the value of a European call option at expiration is the maximum of either $S_T - X$ or zero.* In other words, if $S_T > X$, then $S_T - X$ is positive. A positive number is greater than zero, so $S_T - X$ is the value of the call option. If $S_T \leq X$ then $S_T - X$ is either zero or negative. In that case, the value of the call option is zero.

Now, let us take a look at puts Exhibit 4-21 showed the profit for a put buyer. We repeat it here as Exhibit 10-2.

If $S_T \geq X$, the out-of-the-money outcome, the put option value is zero, and the profit is $-p_0(X, T)$, representing the loss of the premium on the put. If $S_T < X$, the in-the-money outcome, the put permits the holder to sell the asset for X when it is selling for less than X. By exercising the option, the holder nets a gain of $X - S_T$, representing the opportunity to sell an asset worth S_T for X. The profit is $X - S_T - p_0(X, T)$. Thus, the value of the put at expiration is $X - S_T$. Thus, we can write the value of the put at expiration as

$$p_T(X, T) = Max(0, X - S_T) \tag{10.2}$$

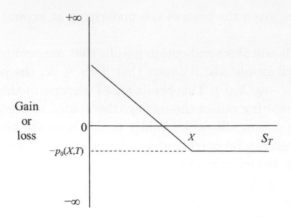

Exhibit 10-2. Profit Diagram for Buyer of a Put Option

This expression is read as follows: *the value of the European put at expiration is the greater of either zero or the exercise price minus the price of the underlying.*

The results presented above for both calls and puts were specified in terms of European calls and puts. If the options were American-style, the results would be the same. Though American options allow exercise before expiration, here we are looking at the value of the option only at expiration. Thus, there is no concept of early exercise once we are at the expiration. For American options, the prices of which are denoted in upper case letters, we can obviously make similar statements.

$$C_T(X, T) = Max(0, S_T - X) \tag{10.3}$$

and

$$P_T(X, T) = Max(0, X - S_T) \tag{10.4}$$

10.3.1 *Characteristics of Option Prices*

Let us now delve a little further into the characteristics of option prices. Our objective is to figure out what an option is worth prior to expiration. We position ourselves at time 0 with the underlying at S_0.

10.3.1.1 *Non-negativity*

The holder of an option is not required to ever exercise it. If the underlying is less expensive to buy at the market price than by exercising, the call holder would not exercise the option. Thus, the option will never be exercised when it would cost the holder more than the value of what he obtains. Therefore, the option can never have negative value. This statement is true for both American and European calls.

$$c_0(X, T) \geq 0$$
$$C_0(X, T) \geq 0$$

$$(10.5)$$

And likewise for puts, the holder cannot be forced to exercise it when the underlying can be sold for more in the market. Thus, the statement is also true for both European and American puts.

$$p_0(X, T) \geq 0$$
$$P_0(X, T) \geq 0$$

$$(10.6)$$

The fact that we are at time 0 is irrelevant. We could be at any time during the life of the option, and these statements would hold.

10.3.1.2 *American Options and European Options*

As you have heard, American options can be exercised at any time prior to expiration, whereas European options can be exercised only at expiration. You should think of an American option as a European option that has an additional feature — the right to exercise early — attached to it. Since no one can be forced to exercise an option, the early exercise feature cannot have negative value. As such, the value of an American option must be at least as much as the value of a European option. This statement is true for calls and puts. Therefore,

$$C_0(X, T) \geq c_0(X, T) \tag{10.7}$$

$$P_0(X, T) \geq p_0(X, T) \tag{10.8}$$

These statements do not mean that the right to exercise early has any value. Later we will see circumstances in which the right to exercise early has no value. As such, an American option will be worth the same as a European option. These statements simply mean that the right to exercise early cannot have negative value.

10.3.1.3 *Maximum Value*

A call option is a means of obtaining the underlying. Therefore, the value of the underlying establishes a maximum value for a call. Thus,

$$c_0(X, T) \leq S_0$$
$$C_0(X, T) \leq S_0$$

(10.9)

In other words, you would not pay more for the right to buy the underlying than you would for the underlying. For a European put option, the maximum value is the present value of the exercise price. This fact is true, because the underlying cannot go below zero, at which point the put is worth the exercise price. But the European put cannot be exercised early, so you have to discount the present value. For American puts, however, early exercise is possible, so the maximum value is the exercise price. Therefore,

$$p_0(X, T) \leq X/(1 + r)^T$$
$$P_0(X, T) \leq X$$

(10.10)

And the fact that we attach these statements to time 0 is irrelevant. They are true at any time in the life of the option.

10.3.1.4 *Relationship to Exercise Price*

For a call option, the exercise price is the hurdle over which the underlying must get in order for a call option to be exercised. It should be intuitive that the lower the hurdle, the easier it is for the underlying to get over it. Moreover, if the underlying is over the exercise price, the lower the exercise price the more in-the-money the option is and the less likely the option will fall out-of-the-money. While we generally say that a call option is worth more the lower the exercise price, it is possible that two options with the same exercise price could both be essentially worthless if the call is deeply out-of-the-money. Therefore, we have to admit this possibility. Thus, for two options with exercise prices X_L and X_H where X_L is the lower exercise price and X_H is the higher exercise price, we have the following principles for both European and American calls:

$$c_0(X_L, T) \geq c_0(X_H, T)$$
$$C_0(X_L, T) \geq C_0(X_H, T)$$

(10.11)

As noted, while the "greater than" sign (">") is usually applicable, deep out-of-the-money calls can have virtually equal value regardless of the exercise price, so we use the greater-than-or-equal sign, $\geq$.

For puts, the exercise price is the barrier below which the underlying must go for the put to be exercised. The higher the exercise price, the easier it is for the underlying to get under the hurdle and stay under the hurdle. When the underlying is below the hurdle, the higher the hurdle, the deeper in-the-money and the more valuable is the option. We would tend to say that the higher the exercise price, the more valuable is the option, but two very deep out-of-the-money puts with different exercise prices will both be worth essentially nothing. Therefore, we have to admit this possibility. Thus, we can say that for both European and American puts,

$$p_0(X_H, T) \geq p_0(X_L, T)$$
$$P_0(X_H, T) \geq P_0(X_L, T)$$

(10.12)

While there are more formal ways to prove these points, your intuition should be sufficient. Calls are generally more valuable with a lower exercise price meaning the right to buy at a lower price. Puts are generally more valuable with a higher exercise price, meaning the right to sell at a higher price.

Perhaps not surprisingly, all of the statements in this section apply at any time during the life of the option, not just at time zero.

10.3.1.5 *Effect of Time to Expiration*

Options are generally worth more the longer the time to expiration. Since the holder of an option is never forced to exercise it, additional time is usually worth more. This statement is definitively true for both American and European call options. Therefore, for two call options, one expiring at T_S and one expiring later at T_L, with $T_S < T_L$, we say

$$c_0(X, T_L) \geq c_0(X, T_S)$$
$$C_0(X, T_L) \geq C_0(X, T_S)$$

(10.13)

Put options are a different story, well, slightly different. For reasons that are beyond the scope of this material, a European put with a longer time to expiration can be worth less than one with a shorter time to expiration. This phenomenon occurs with certain deep in-the-money puts and somewhat results from the fact that a put option has a limit to its maximum value: it can never be worth more than its exercise price. Consequently, there is a limit to the gain from holding on to a put. If the put is American, however, it can always be terminated right away by exercising it. Thus, we can make the following statements:

$$p_0(X, T_L) \Leftrightarrow p_0(X, T_S)$$
$$P_0(X, T_L) \geq P_0(X, T_S)$$

(10.14)

And of course, these statements apply at any time in the life of an option.

10.3.1.6 *Put-Call Parity*

Put-call parity is an extremely important relationship between the price of a call and the price of a put. Suppose your friend constructs a portfolio that consists of one unit of the underlying that is priced at S_0, and one European put option with an exercise price of X that is priced at $p_0(X, T)$. Your friend will invest the cost of the underlying and the cost of the put, $S_0 + p_0(X, T)$. Think of this as the amount of money your friend puts up. Now suppose you buy a European call option on that underlying, which will cost you $c_0(X, T)$, and also buy a zero coupon bond that pays off the exercise price, X. This bond will cost you the present value of X, which is $X/(1 + r)^T$ where r is the risk-free rate, which is the yield or discount rate on the bond. If you find the notion of this bond confusing, just consider a simple example. Suppose the exercise price is £40 and the present value is £38. You simply buy a zero-coupon bond for £38 that will mature to a value of £40. The amount of money you put up is $c_0(X, T) + X/(1 + r)^T$.

Let us take a look at how these two portfolios perform, which is shown in Exhibit 10-3.

Notice that the two portfolios perform identically. When $S_T < X$, your friend will exercise the put, thereby selling the underlying for X, and your call will expire out-of-the-money but your zero-coupon bond will mature for a value of X. When $S_T \geq X$, your friend's put will expire out-of-the-money but his underlying will be worth S_T, while your bond will mature for a value of X, which you will use to pay the exercise price in order to exercise your call, thereby purchasing the underlying valued at S_T. In both outcomes, you and your friend end up in the same position.

Given that your friend's portfolio pays the same amount in all outcomes as yours, the initial values of these two portfolios must be the same. Hence,

$$S_0 + p_0(X, T) = c_0(X, T) + X/(1 + r)^T$$

(10.15)

	Initial Value	Value of Underlying at Option Expiration	
		$S_T < X$	$S_T \geq X$
Your friend's strategy (buy underlying and put)			
Underlying	S_0	S_T	S_T
Put	$p_0(X,T)$	$X - S_T$	0
Total	$S_0 + p_0(X,T)$	X	S_T
Your strategy (buy European call option)			
Call option	$c_0(X,T)$	0	$S_T - X$
Zero-Coupon Bond	$X/(1+r)^T$	X	X
Total	$c_0(X,T) + X/(1+r)^T$	X	S_T

Exhibit 10-3. Underlying plus European Put compared to European Call plus Zero-Coupon Bond

This relationship is known as *put-call parity*. It is one of the most enlightening relationships in the entire world of derivatives, as we will see here.

Now suppose there were a discrepancy between the cost of your friend's portfolio and the cost of your portfolio. Let us say that your friend's portfolio costs less to purchase than yours, meaning that the left-hand side of Equation (10.15) is less than the right-hand side. In the financial world, when something is too low, you buy it. When it is too high, you sell it. We cannot say exactly which of the four instruments is priced too high and which is priced too low, but it does not matter. What we know is that the underlying and put are priced too low and the call and bond are priced too high. So, we buy the underlying and put and sell the call and bond. Selling the bond means borrowing the present value of X and promising to pay back X. With the underlying and the put priced at less than the call and bond, buying the underlying and put and selling the call and bond will generate a net positive sum of money at the start. Now, let us look at what happens at expiration.

If $S_T < X$,

        Exercise your put, selling the underlying for X
        Use the amount X to pay off your bond
        Your call expires out-of-the-money
        Net payoff: 0

If $S_T \geq X$

> Your put expires out-of-the-money
> The call expires in-the-money, resulting in delivery of the underlying for which you receive X
> Use the X received from delivering the underlying to pay off the bond
> Net payoff: 0

Thus, the positions offset. You should have realized they would. If the portfolios as shown in the exhibit are equivalent, then going long one of them and short the other would result in an offset at expiration. But remember that you paid less for the underlying and put than you received for the call and bond. Thus, this difference between what you paid and what you received is yours to keep. Indeed, it is an arbitrage profit. You earned it without taking any risk or committing any funds of your own.

Given that investors throughout the market will recognize this opportunity, there will be an increased demand to purchase the underlying and put and an increased supply to sell the call and bond. This additional demand and supply will push up the cost of the underlying and put and push down the cost of the call and the bond. When the cost of the underlying and put equals the cost of the call and bond, the arbitrage opportunity is gone and put-call parity, Equation (10.15), is upheld. And naturally if the call and bond are worth less than the underlying and put, the call and bond will be purchased and the underlying and put will be sold to create the opposite arbitrage transaction that will still produce a positive cash flow up front and offsetting payoffs at expiration.

Observe in Equation (10.15) that the signs on each terms are positive. Positive signs mean long positions, that is, buying the instrument. Reading Equation (10.15), we say that a long position in the underlying and a long position in the put is equivalent to a long position in the call plus a long position in the zero-coupon bond. That should not be surprising, because we said that your friend's portfolio, long the underlying and long a put, is equivalent to your portfolio, long the call and long a zero-coupon bond. Using that knowledge, we can construct other equivalent combinations by simply doing some algebraic rearrangements. Let us isolate each of the four terms on the left-hand side:

$$S_0 = c_0(X, T) + X/(1 + r)^T - p_0(X, T)$$
$$c_0(X, T) = p_0(X, T) + S_0 - X/(1 + r)^T$$

$$p_0(X, T) = c_0(X, T) - S_0 + X/(1 + r)^T$$
$$X/(1 + r)^T = p_0(X, T) + S_0 - c_0(X, T)$$

The first equation above can be interpreted as follows: *a long position in the underlying is equivalent to a long position in the call, a long position in the bond, and a short position in the put.* The second equation is interpreted as follows: *a long position in the call is equivalent to a long position in the put, a long position in the underlying, and a short position in the bond.* The third equation is read as follows: *a long position in the put is equivalent to a long position in the call, a short position in the underlying and a long position in the bond.* The fourth equation is read as follows: *a long position in the bond is equivalent to a long position in the put, a long position in the underlying, and a short position in the call.* This fourth equation is particularly interesting in that the left-hand side, the bond, is risk-free. Therefore, the right-hand side must also be risk-free. It might not appear that a long put, long underlying, and short call are risk-free, but they are. They are not individually risk-free, but collectively they are. In fact, to adequately study this material, you should verify the above results for each of the four statements above. You should construct a table like Exhibit 10-3 in which your friend's portfolio is the left-hand side and your portfolio is the right-hand side. Do this for each of the four equations, and you should see the equivalence.

The right-hand side combinations are also known as *synthetics*. From the first equation above, we can see that a synthetic position in the underlying can be constructed by buying the call and bond and selling the put. A synthetic call can be constructed by buying the put and the underlying and selling the bond. A synthetic put can be constructed by buying the call and bond and selling the underlying. Finally, a synthetic risk-free bond can be constructed by buying the put and the underlying and selling the call.

It is also worthwhile to note that the four equations above can be multiplied by -1 to obtain the opposite results that are still as valid and easily interpretable.

$$-S_0 = -c_0(X, T) - X/(1 + r)^T + p_0(X, T)$$
$$-c_0(X, T) = -p_0(X, T) - S_0 + X/(1 + r)^T$$
$$-p_0(X, T) = -c_0(X, T) + S_0 - X/(1 + r)^T$$
$$-X/(1 + r)^T = -p_0(X, T) - S_0 + c_0(X, T)$$

Once again, we simply read minus signs as short positions and plus signs as long positions.

10.3.1.7 *Minimum Value*

In Section 10.3.1, we established that all options must have non-negative values. As a boundary on option prices, this statement does not help us much. It simply says that an option is worth at least zero. Fortunately, it is possible to establish a lower boundary that is higher than zero. In doing so, we narrow the range of possible prices. Consider a European call with exercise price X and expiration T. Suppose you and your friend are comparing investment strategies for speculating on a stock. You like call options, but your friend is convinced that buying the stock on margin, meaning to borrow money and buy the stock, is preferable. Specifically your friend borrows $X/(1+r)^T$ and uses the funds to buy the stock, which costs S_0. You, however, buy a European call option with an exercise price of X expiring at T and costing c_0. Exhibit 10-4 illustrates how each investment performs given the outcome that the stock price at expiration is less than X and the outcome that the stock price at expiration is greater than or equal to X.

Your friend invests a total of $S_0 - X/(1+r)^T$, while you invest c_0. We do not know the value of $c_0(X, T)$, but we can tell one thing for sure. Notice that if the "good" outcome occurs, meaning the stock ends up at or above X, your payoff is the same as the total value of your friend's strategy. If the bad outcome occurs, meaning that the stock price ends up below X, you end up with zero value, which sounds bad except that the value of your friend's strategy is $S_T - X$, and since this outcome is the one with S_T less than X, your outcome is better. Thus, your friend's strategy will never beat yours. It can match it, but it cannot beat it.

You must be feeling pretty smart, having outfoxed your friend, except that we did not address which strategy costs more. In fact, your strategy will

	Initial Value	Value of Stock at Option Expiration	
		$S_T < X$	$S_T \geq X$
Your friend's margin strategy (borrow cash and buy the stock)			
Stock	S_0	S_T	S_T
Loan	$-X/(1+r)^T$	$-X$	$-X$
Total	$S_0 - X/(1+r)^T$	$S_T - X$	$S_T - X$
Your strategy (buy a European call option)			
Call option	$c_0(X, T)$	0	$S_T - X$

Exhibit 10-4. Buying Stock on Margin Compared to Buying a Call

always cost the same or more. If you could ever implement your strategy for less than the cost of your friend's strategy, you could do your strategy and do the opposite of your friend's strategy. In that case, we just change the signs of your friend's strategy, so that when $S_T < X$, your combined positions are worth $0 - (S_T - X)$, which is positive, and when $S_T \geq X$ your combined positions are worth $S_T - X - (S_T - X) = 0$. Thus, at worst you end up with is nothing, but you sold your friend's strategy for more than you paid for yours. Arbitrageurs would take advantage of this opportunity unless your strategy costs more. Thus, we have to have $c_0(X, T) \geq S_0 - X/(1 + r)^T$.

The statement that $c_0(X, T) \geq S_0 - X/(1+r)^T$ looks like a nice minimum price for a call, but we can improve it a little. If $S_0 - X/(1+r)^T$ is negative, which is easily possible if X is high enough, then the statement becomes simply that the call price is more than a negative number. We already know that the call price cannot be negative. Thus, we can combine these points and obtain the minimum price of a European call:

$$c_0(X, T) \geq Max(0, S_0 - X/(1 + r)^T) \qquad (10.16)$$

The expression $Max(0, S_0 - X/(1 + r)^T)$ enables us to substitute zero for the lowest price if $S_0 - X/(1 + r)^T$ is negative. And as far as outsmarting your friend, your strategy is always at least as good as that of your friend's, but you will never be able to do it for less than what your friend pays.

This result holds for European calls. What about American calls? Well, they can be exercised at any time, so their lowest possible value is $S_0 - X$ if this value is positive and zero otherwise. So, let us make that statement in a formal manner:

$$C_0(X, T) \geq Max(0, S_0 - X) \qquad (10.17)$$

This expression is referred to as the *exercise value* and sometimes *intrinsic value* or *parity value* of a call option. Compare it to Equation (10.3), which is the value of the option at expiration. These statements look very much alike. In fact, they are the same except that Equation (10.3) refers to the exercise value at expiration, and Equation (10.17) refers to the exercise value prior to expiration.

Notice, however, that $S_0 - X$ is less than $S_0 - X/(1+r)^T$, so this lowest price for a European call is applicable to an American call.[1] After all, an

---

[1]In other words, since X is more than its present value, $X(1 + r)^T$, subtracting X means ending up with a smaller number.

American call could not worth less than a European call, a point we showed in Section 10.3.1.2. Thus, for American calls, we have the same statement:

$$C_0(X, T) \geq Max(0, S_0 - X/(1 + r)^T) \tag{10.18}$$

Now let us look at the corresponding principles for puts where we shall see something similar but with one difference. Let us say that your friend thinks that buying a put is the best way to take advantage of a decline in the price of a stock. You think selling short the stock is better. Selling short, however, involves considerable risk and your broker will require a cash deposit to cover potential losses. Let us say you deposit $X/(1 + r)^T$ into an account that will accrue interest at the rate r until time T. Exhibit 10-5 compares your position at time T with your friend's.

Notice in a down market $(S_T \leq X)$, your strategy and your friend's strategy produce the same result. In an up market $(S_T > X)$, however, your friend's strategy is better. It produces zero value, but your strategy produces a value of $X - S_T$, which is negative. So your friend's strategy always does at least as well as yours. Therefore, the initial value has to be at least as high:

$$p_0(X, T) \geq Max(0, X/(1 + r)^T - S_0) \tag{10.19}$$

For American puts, the story is a bit more complicated. First, let us establish that the lowest price for an American put is its exercise value,

$$P_0(X, T) \geq Max(0, X - S_0) \tag{10.20}$$

In other words, an American put would always have to sell for at least the amount for which it could be exercised. The value of exercising is based

	Initial Value	Value of Stock at Option Expiration	
		$S_T \leq X$	$S_T > X$
Your strategy (Invest cash and sell short the stock)			
Cash	$X/(1 + r)^T$	X	X
Short Stock	$-S_0$	$-S_T$	$-S_T$
Total	$X/(1 + r)^T - S_0$	$X - S_T$	$X - S_T$
Your friend's strategy (buy a European put option)			
Put option	$p_0(X, T)$	$X - S_T$	0

Exhibit 10-5. Investing Cash and Selling Short compared to Buying a Put

on the purchase of the stock for S_0 and sale of it for X. This formula gives us the *exercise value* of the put. And note that the exercise value at expiration, Equation (10.4), is the same as Equation (10.20), simply positioned at expiration.

The minimum value of the European put was shown to be $X/(1+r)^T - S_0$ or zero if this expression is negative. Now compare $X/(1+r)^T - S_0$ with $X - S_0$. Which is greater? It should be obvious that $X - S_0$ is greater than $X/(1+r)^T - S_0$. Remember that with calls, the minimum value of a European call was more than the exercise value of an American call. Since an American call cannot be worth less than a European call, the minimum value of an American call is the minimum value of the corresponding European call. That results was Equation (10.18). But with puts, the effect is opposite. The minimum value of a European put is less than the minimum value of an American put. Thus, the minimum value of a European put is Equation (10.19), and the minimum value of an American put is Equation (10.20).

10.3.1.8 *Effect of Early Exercise*

We have mentioned that American options can be worth more than European options, but in this section we will learn that this statement is somewhat restrictive. For options in which the underlying makes no payments, such as dividends or interest, nor does it have a convenience yield, there is no reason to exercise early. If it will never be exercised early, an American call would be worth no more than a European call. Now, in all likelihood you may believe these statements, but you probably took them at face value. Let us see why they are true.

Suppose you had a call on a non-dividend paying stock. If you are considering exercising it early, it must be in-the-money. And it is probably deep in-the-money. If you exercise it, you obtain $S_0 - X$. Yet, we just showed in the previous section that its minimum value is $S_0 - X/(1 + r)^T$, which is more than its exercise value. Thus, the call is worth more by selling it to someone else. If your intuition still tells you that the call should be exercised, then consider this fact: if you exercise the call, you must believe the stock is not going any higher. If you thought it was, the call would be better than the stock, as it offers a higher rate of return with less capital committed. But if you think the stock is going no higher, then why would you prefer the stock over the call? To acquire the stock by exercising the call, you will have to pay the exercise price. Thus, you would commit capital in the amount of X.

You would be no better off than holding on to the call or selling it than you would to commit capital to exercise it. So why give up your money early?

As a result of these points, *for an underlying asset that makes no cash payments or offers no convenience yield during the life of the option,*

$$C_0(X,T) = c_0(X,T)$$

(no cash payments or convenience yield on underlying)

(10.21)

In other words, American calls and European calls are worth the same value under these conditions. If the underlying is a dividend paying stock or any other asset that makes a cash payment, however, the decline in the price of the stock as the cash is paid will drive down the price of the call and can make early exercise justified. Hence, *for an underlying asset that makes cash payments or offers a convenience yield during the life of the option, early exercise can be justified, and hence,*

$$C_0(X,T) \geq c_0(X,T)$$

(cash payments or convenience yield on underlying)

(10.22)

The above statement is technically only true under certain circumstances. For example, it is possible that the dividends are not large enough to justify early exercise. Exactly when and whether to exercise early is an advanced subject that we cannot take up here, and it is not of much use to end users.

For puts, cash payments on the underlying make early exercise *more likely*. Cash payments such as dividends push down the price. If there is a dividend, for example, early exercise is more likely and if it occurs, it would most likely occur right after the stock pays the dividend. Thus, there is generally a premium for exercising early. But there is yet another reason why a put might be exercised early, even if there are no dividends.

If you own an American put on a stock, what is the best outcome, meaning the situation that produces the highest value of your put? Well, that would be bankruptcy. If the stock goes to zero, the put would be worth the exercise price, inasmuch as the put would allow you to sell a worthless share of stock at the exercise price X. If you hold a European put and the company goes bankrupt, your put would be worth its maximum value only by holding it to expiration. Right now, it would be worth only the present value of the exercise price. If the put is American, however, you can always exercise it and capture the full value X right now. So it would certainly be worth exercising early.

Without getting into details beyond where we are right now, we cannot prove that you might exercise a put early even if the company is not bankrupt, but that fact is the truth. Certain deep in-the-money puts are worth exercising early. The basic intuition is simply that the maximum value is fixed at X. Holding on to the put gives it no chance to get deeper in-the-money. Thus, we say that

$$P_0(X, T) \geq p_0(X, T) \tag{10.23}$$

In other words, American puts usually command a premium over European puts. While in this introductory book, we cannot demonstrate exactly when early exercise of puts would occur, that information is not all that important to end users.

10.3.1.9 *The Effect of Volatility*

One of the most important factors that drives the value of an option is the volatility of the underlying. Option values are directly related to the value of the underlying. This point is quite easy to see. Suppose at expiration the underlying can be either a value of 100 or a value of 50. A call option with an exercise price of 75 will, therefore, be worth either 25 or zero at expiration. Now let us impose a greater volatility of the underlying. Let us assume that it can be worth either 125 or 25. In that case, the call will be worth either 50 or zero at expiration. The in-the-money payoff is greater, but the out-of-the-money payoff is the same. So, the call option must be worth more if the volatility is greater. The argument holds equally well for puts. With an exercise price of 75, the put will be worth either zero or 25 with the lower volatility. With the higher volatility, the put will be worth either zero or 50. Clearly, higher volatility is beneficial for both calls and puts, and as such, one must pay a higher price for a call or a put on a more volatile asset, ignoring all other factors.

10.3.1.10 *The Effect of the Risk-Free Rate*

The effect of the risk-free rate of interest on option values is one of the more enigmatic but less important factors. Yes, we did say "less important." The simple facts are that call option values are directly related to the risk-free rate, while put option values are inversely related to interest rates. Understanding the reasons, however, is a bit challenging.

The principal reason that call options are directly related to the value of the underlying is that a higher risk-free rate saves money for holders of call options. They hold an economic interest in the value of the underlying but do so at lower cost. The money they save by holding the option rather than holding the underlying is worth more the higher the rate of interest. Holders of puts are hurt by a higher risk-free rate. While holding a put, the investor is losing interest he could be getting by exercising the put to sell the stock and capture the exercise price.

These explanations are, however, only part of the picture. There are several effects of interest rates on option prices that are relatively complex. Fortunately, the net overall effects are straightforward — call options are worth more with higher interest rates and put options are worth less.

But there is a key piece of knowledge out of all of this that is even more important. The effect of interest rates on calls and puts is relatively minor. It takes a fairly large change in interest rates to impart much of a change in the value of an option. And with that point, we move right into the subject of option valuation.

10.4   Option Valuation

In the previous two chapters of this book, we have covered how forwards, futures, and swaps are priced and valued. In the previous sections we examined some characteristics of the prices of options. In this section we will learn how option prices are determined. Understanding option pricing is important for end users for the same reasons that it is important to understand the pricing of forwards, futures, and swaps. End users need to know if they are paying good prices, and they need to know how to assign values to their options. In this section we will cover two main models for pricing options: the *binomial model* and the *Black-Scholes-Merton model*. We will also cover a variation of the Black-Scholes-Merton model, called the Black model.

First, however, let us make a note of an important point that distinguishes the pricing and valuation of options from pricing and valuation of forwards, futures, and swaps. Recall that forwards, futures, and swaps are instruments that have zero value at the start. They are simply agreements to do transactions at later dates at prices agreed to in advance. As such, their values started off at zero, and the price of a forward, futures, or swap was the fixed price or rate agreed on that would be paid at a later date for this future transaction or transactions. Options are not zero-value transactions at the start. The buyer of an option pays the price or premium to the seller of the option at the start, for which the option buyer gets to choose whether or not to exercise the option later. Hence, pricing and valuing an option means to determine the appropriate amount for the buyer to pay the seller at the start and at any time during the life of the option.

Of course, we must never forget that options pay off their exercise values at expiration, and that prior to expiration, their prices have the characteristics covered in the previous section.

10.4.1 *Binomial Option Valuation*

The binomial option valuation model is undoubtedly the simplest approach to valuing options. In fact, it is so simple that you might believe it has no practical use, but in fact, it is extremely practical, thanks to the speed of today's computers. The binomial model, sometimes known as the Cox-Ross-Rubinstein model for its discoverers, is based on the assumption that the stock can move one period later to only two prices, one higher than the current price and one lower.

So let us say the current stock price is S and it can go up by the factor u or down by the factor d to Su or Sd. These factors imply that the two possible rates of return, or percentage changes in the price, are $u - 1$ or $d - 1$. At the current time, there is a call option priced at c. If the underlying goes up to Su, the call will be worth c_u. If the underlying goes to Sd, the call will be worth c_d. Be careful and note that Su means S times u and Sd means S times d. But c_u does not mean c times u and c_d does not mean c times d. The u and d factors are one plus the return on the underlying if the underlying goes up and one plus the return on the underlying if the underlying goes down. In the example we will be doing, the underlying is at 50 and can go up by 20% to 60. Thus, $S = 50$, $u = 1.20$ and $Su = 60$. The underlying can go down to 40, so $d = 0.80$ and $Sd = 40$. But the call value does not go up and down by the same proportions as the underlying. Hence, we use the u and d as subscripts on the call to identify the outcome to which we are referring. When we assume that the option expires in one period later, we are working with the one-period version of the model.

Finally let us assume that the risk-free rate is 3%.

10.4.1.1 *One-Period Binomial Model*

Exhibit 10-6 illustrates this setting for a one-period model, meaning that we consider only the next movement of the underlying. We place the symbols for the call values in parentheses.

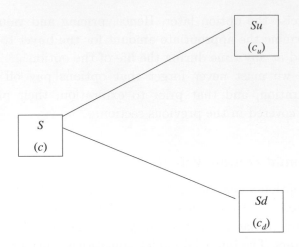

Exhibit 10-6. One-Period Binomial Option Pricing Setting

So at time 0, the asset and option are priced at S and c respectively. At time 1, the asset and option are priced at Su and c_u if the asset goes up and S_d and c_d if the asset goes down. These two outcomes at time 1 are often called *states*. The top state is often called the up-state with the bottom state called the down-state.

Now suppose we form a portfolio consisting of η (eta) units of the asset and one short call option with exercise price X. Shortly we will determine the value of η but for now just think of it as a certain number of units of the underlying that we would hold for each call option sold. The value of our position at the start is

$$V = \eta S - c. \tag{10.24}$$

The values of our position at time 1 for both states are

$$V_u = \eta Su - c_u$$
$$V_d = \eta Su - c_d.$$

Suppose we set these two equations equal to each other and solve for η:

$$\eta = \frac{c_u - c_d}{Su - Sd} \tag{10.25}$$

Even though we do not know which outcome will occur, setting the value of η to the right-hand side of this equation will hedge our overall position. That is, the value of our position in the up-state, V_u, will be the same as the value of our position in the down-state, V_d. If this strategy results in a perfect hedge, the value at time 1, either V_u or V_d since they are equal, should equal the starting value, V, compounded by the risk-free rate, r, for one period. So let us compound the current value to V_u by the interest factor:

$$V(1 + r) = V_u, \text{ thus}$$

$$(\eta S - c)(1 + r) = \eta Su - c_u.$$

The next step is to solve for c. While this step looks simple, we want to express our formula for c in the simplest and most intuitive way possible. The result is

$$c = \frac{\pi c_u + (1 - \pi)c_d}{1 + r}, \tag{10.26}$$

where

$$\pi = \frac{1 + r - d}{u - d}. \tag{10.27}$$

Now, if you try to solve for c, you might not obtain the form in (10.26), but do not fear. It is just a matter of algebra, but it is a little tricky. Do not worry about it.

Equation (10.26) is a very simple formula for the value of the call option at time 0. It takes the next two values and weights them by π and $1-\pi$ where π is given by (10.27). It turns out that π has the convenient characteristics of a probability. In fact, in Chapter 3, we already identified it as a risk-neutral probability. Like a probability, the value of π is between 0 and 1. Therefore, multiplying c_u and c_d by π and $1 - \pi$, respectively, is like taking a weighted average of the next two outcomes. In essence we are roughly taking a weighted expected call price one period later. Dividing by $1 + r$ discounts that expectation to the present. If this book were for an advanced course in option pricing, we would provide a more precise treatment of what π really is. We do not have to do that here. Nonetheless, you should know that the π is referred to as a *risk-neutral probability* and also occasionally as a *martingale probability*.

We now work a problem that illustrates the application of this formula in Exhibit 10-7.

As we see in Example 10-7, the option price at time 0 is a weighted average of the two possible option prices at time 1, which are €10 and €0.0. The weights are π and $1 - \pi$, which are 0.575 and 0.425, respectfully. This weighted-average time 1 price is then discounted at the risk-free rate to time 0 to obtain an option value of 5.58.

We have said that the price of the option should be the price given by the formula. If the option is trading for any other price in the market, then an

Objective: Find the price a one-period European call that has an exercise price of €50 in which the underlying is at €50 and can go up 20% or down 20% in one period. The risk-free rate is 3%.

Inputs:

$$S = €50$$
$$u = 1.20$$
$$d = (1 - 0.20) = 0.80$$
$$X = €50$$
$$r = 0.03$$
$$Su = €50(1.20) = €60$$
$$Sd = €50(0.80) = €40$$
$$c_u = \text{Max}(0, Su - X) = \text{Max}(0, €60 - €50) = €10$$
$$c_d = \text{Max}(0, Sd - X) = \text{Max}(0, €40 - €50) = €0$$

Results:

$$\pi = \frac{1 + r - d}{u - d} = \frac{1.03 - 0.80}{1.20 - 0.80} = 0.575$$

$$c = \frac{\pi c_u + (1 - \pi)c_d}{1 + r} = \frac{0.575(€10) + (1 - 0.575)€0.0}{1.03} = €5.58$$

Exhibit 10-7. One-Period Binomial Option Pricing Example

arbitrage possibility exists. Exhibit 10-8 illustrates the exploitation of such a situation.

Risk Neutral and Martingale Probabilities

The probability denoted by π and given as $(1 + r - d)/(u - d)$ is referred to as a risk neutral probability. Let us see why. Using the numbers in the example used here, an asset worth 50 can go up to 60 or down to 40, given the u and d factors of 1.20 and 0.8, respectively. Recall that the risk-free rate is 3%. Thus, $\pi = (1 + 0.03 - 0.80)/(1.20 - 0.80) = 0.575$.

Now, it is true by definition that the price of an asset is the expected future price discounted at the required rate of return. Suppose we treat the probability π as the probability of the up move. The expected price is, therefore, $(60(0.575) + 40(1 - 0.575)) = 51.50$. Then if we discount 51.50 at 3% for one period, we obtain $51.50/1.03 = 50$, which is the current price. This formulation of the current price is said to be the price as obtained by risk neutral investors. Risk neutral investors do not require a risk premium and, thus, they discount expected future prices at the risk-free rate. These probabilities are the ones that lead to the actual current price for risk neutral investors. Hence, they are called risk neutral probabilities.

Now, we know that investors are not risk neutral, so the idea presented here is a theoretical concept but it is in fact an extremely useful concept. We saw that it plays a key role in finding the option value that prohibits arbitrage. For investors who are not risk averse, suppose the required rate of return on the asset is 10%. Then the expected price at time 1 should be 50(1.10) = 55. We can then infer that the true probability of an up move would have to be 0.75: 0.75(60) + 0.25(40) = 55.

Risk neutral probabilities are also sometimes called martingale probabilities. A martingale is a random statistical process in which the expected return is the current price. While that point is not technically true here, the expected value of the future price is the current price, after adjusting for the time value of money. So, experts just call this process a martingale.

Objective: Continue with the problem in Exhibit 10-7 in which the option should be priced at €5.58. Suppose the call is selling for €6. Illustrate how an arbitrage profit can be earned.

Inputs: The actual price of the call is €6.

Results: The call is overpriced so sell it and buy η units of the asset

$$\eta = \frac{c_u - c_d}{Su - Sd} = \frac{10 - 0.0}{60 - 40} = 0.5$$

This result means that for every call sold, the arbitrageur should own 0.5 units of the asset. So, let us say the arbitrageur sells 1,000 calls. Then he should buy 500 units of the assets. The value of this position is

$$V = \eta S - c = 500(€50) - 1,000(€6) = €19,000.$$

So the arbitrageur will invest €19,000 of his capital in the trade. The arbitrageur will have a payoff of

$$V_u = \eta Su - c_u = 500(€60) - 1,000(€10) = €20,000 \text{ (if the asset goes to 60)}$$

$$V_d = \eta Sd - c_d = 500(€40) - 1,000(€0) = €20,000 \text{ (if the asset goes to 40)}$$

So regardless of the outcome, the arbitrage will get a payoff of €20,000, which is a return of

$$\frac{€20,000}{€19,000} - 1 = 0.053,$$

or 5.3%, which greatly exceeds the risk-free rate of 3%. In fact, the arbitrageur could borrow the €19,000 at the risk-free rate and not commit any of his funds.

Exhibit 10-8. One-Period Binomial Option Pricing Arbitrage Example

And not surprisingly, as long as the price is above 5.58, this type of trade would continue to be executed, placing downward pressure on the option price until it falls to the model price, at which point there is no further gain from arbitrage.

But what happens if the option were underpriced? In that case, we would need to buy the option and sell short the asset. In Chapter 8 we discussed the situation in which it might not be possible to borrow the asset and sell short. We mentioned that another alternative is for someone holding the asset to sell it and buy the option. When the option expires, the arbitrageur will have earned a profit and will have the asset back in his possession. An end-of-chapter problem covers this case.

The one-period model is extremely useful in enabling us to see how arbitrage forces the option price to converge to its model price, but it is an extremely simplified version of the real world. There is no way that the asset can move to only one of two prices. So now let us look at the two-period version of the model that we will use to value a two-period option, and which we will eventually use to divide a real option's life into a very large number of small sub-periods.

10.4.1.2 *Two-Period Model*

In the one-period example in the previous section, we had the option expire one period later. As such, the formulas for the options values in the time 1 up- and down-states are easy to determine. They are simply the exercise values. We then showed how an arbitrage-free portfolio can be developed with the result that the option price at the start has to equal the formula in Equation (10.26). Note that in that equation, there is nothing that requires that the option has to expire one period later. The formula requires the values of the call in the next period, c_u and c_d, but those values are not required to be the values at expiration. They are simply required to be known values. By the word *known*, we do not mean that we know which value will occur. We simply mean that we have to know the values of c_u and c_d, given the two states. Because of this fact, the model is extremely flexible and can be adapted to multiple periods.

There are two ways in which the one-period binomial model can be made into a two-period model. The first is to model an option that expires in two periods. The second is to divide the life of an option into two periods instead of one.

Let us take a look at the first approach. The second will be covered in Section 10.4.1.5. Recall that in the previous section, we developed a binomial model for valuing an option on an underlying priced at S that could go up to Su or down to Sd the next period, at which time the option would expire. We could think of that option as a one-period option. Now let us consider a two-period option, one that expires later than the option we valued in the previous section. Obviously this new option is a longer term option, and as we previously discussed, it would almost always be worth more.

Now we have to extend the binomial model one period. Consider the point at the end of the first period when the underlying went up to Su. Suppose from that point, the underlying can go up again or it can go down. The underlying would then be at Suu or Sud. Now consider the point at the end of the first period when the underlying went down to S_d. Suppose from that point, the underlying can go up again or it can go down. Then the underlying would be at Sdu or Sdd. It should be apparent that Sud is the same as Sdu.[2] Thus, two periods from the start, the underlying can be at Suu, Sud ($= Sdu$), and Sdd, so there are three unique outcomes. Associated with each outcome is a value for the call option: c_{uu}, c_{ud} ($= c_{du}$), and c_{dd} at the second period, c_u and c_d at the first period, and c at the start. In addition, at each time point, the hedge ratio is calculated as the difference in the next two option values divided by the difference in the next two underlying values, as shown originally in Equation (10.25). Adapted to the two-period model, we have

$$\eta_u = \frac{c_{uu} - c_{ud}}{Suu - Sdd} \tag{10.28}$$

$$\eta_d = \frac{c_{ud} - c_{dd}}{Sud - Sdd} \tag{10.29}$$

Exhibit 10-9 illustrates the process for the asset price and option value.

With this diagram, you should be able to see how the middle point at time 2, representing the underlying at Sud, is the same as the underlying at Sdu. The underlying can reach that point by going up by a factor of u and then down by a factor of d or by going down by a factor of d and up by a factor of u. This property is referred to as *recombination* in the sense

---

[2]This result is an example of the associative law of mathematics. S times u times d is the same as S times d times u.

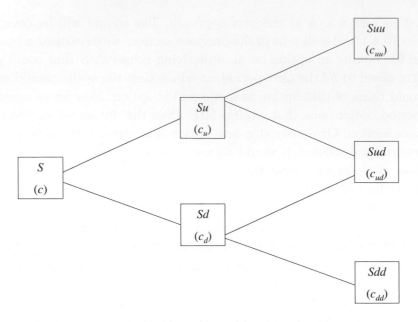

Exhibit 10-9. Two-Period Binomial Option Pricing Setting

that the tree *recombines*, meaning that it merges. Henceforth, and strictly for convenience, we will always use Sud and c_{ud} over Sdu and c_{du}.[3]

Now, it should be apparent that we can use Equation (10.26) at the time 1 up-state as well as the time 1 down-state to value the option as c_u and c_d, respectively, as follows:

$$c_u = \frac{\pi c_{uu} + (1 - \pi)c_{ud}}{1 + r} \tag{10.30}$$

$$c_d = \frac{\pi c_{ud} + (1 - \pi)c_{dd}}{1 + r} \tag{10.31}$$

Given the ability to calculate these two values, we can then apply Equation (10.26) in the normal manner. Given that u, d, and r are the

---

[3]There are some advanced option pricing models that do not possess the property of recombination. One obvious case is where the u and the d in the first period are not the same as the respective u and d in the second period. When a tree recombines there will be $n+1$ final outcomes for every n time steps. Here $n = 2$ and there are $2+1 = 3$ time steps. If a tree does not recombine, there are will be 2^n outcomes for n time steps. Thus, for $n = 2$ there would be $2^2 = 4$ outcomes. Consider a model with 10 time steps. There would be only 11 outcomes for a recombining tree, but $2^{10} = 1,024$ outcomes for a non-recombining tree. Obviously we prefer recombining trees.

Objective: Continue with the problem in Exhibit 10-7 in which the option expires in two periods. Find the value of the option and the number of units of the asset to hedge.

Inputs: Same as in Exhibit 10-7. In addition, the asset moves up or down in the second period by the same factors $u = 1.2$ and $d = 0.8$ as in the first period.

Results: We first need to find the values for Suu, Sud, and Sdd:

$$Suu = 60(1.2) = 72$$
$$Sud = 60(0.8) = 48$$
$$Sdd = 40(0.8) = 32$$

These are the values of the asset at time two. Then we need to find the corresponding option values at time two. Given that the option is expiring, its values are

$$c_{uu} = Max(0, 72 - 50) = 22$$
$$c_{ud} = Max(0, 48 - 50) = 0$$
$$c_{dd} = Max(0, 32 - 50) = 0$$

Then we back up to time one and find the two possible option values:

$$c_u = \frac{0.575(22.00) + (1 - 0.575)(0.00)}{1.03} = 12.28$$

$$c_d = \frac{0.575(0.00) + (1 - 0.575)(0.00)}{1.03} = 0.00$$

We then back up and find the time one option value

$$c = \frac{0.575(12.28) + (1 - 0.575)(0.00)}{1.03} = 6.86$$

The number of units of the asset to hedge at times 0 and time 1 is

$$\eta_u = \frac{22 - 0}{72 - 48} = 0.9167$$

$$\eta_d = \frac{0 - 0}{48 - 32} = 0.0000$$

$$\eta = \frac{12.28 - 0}{60 - 40} = 0.6141$$

Exhibit 10-10. Two-Period Binomial Option Pricing Example

same, the value of π will still be found with Equation (10.27). An example is given in Exhibit 10-10.

You should be able to see that by adding periods, we can value options with longer lives. We will, however, identify another benefit of adding periods. This feature will come in Section 10.4.1.5.

10.4.1.3 *Valuing Puts with the Binomial Model*

Valuing put options with the binomial model is extremely easy and requires only simple modifications. We will skip the details and provide a heuristic explanation.

When we valued calls, we constructed an arbitrage portfolio consisting of η units of the asset and one short call (-1 calls). When the option is a put, we also construct an offsetting position in the derivative. But since a put increases in value when the underlying goes down, a long position in the asset would be offset by a long position in the put. With a call, the option would be hedged by going long the underlying. As such, working through the arbitrage portfolio, we would find that if we are long one put, we should be long η units of the asset where η is given by

$$\eta = \frac{p_d - p_u}{Su - Sd} \tag{10.32}$$

Note that because a put attains a greater value when the underlying goes down than when it goes up, the numerator of (10.32) will be positive[4]:

$$p = \frac{\pi p_u + (1 - \pi)p_d}{1 + r} \tag{10.33}$$

Since u, d, and r are the same, the value of π will be the same as it was for a call, Equation (10.27). For the two-period model, the equations are easily extended to

$$\eta_u = \frac{p_{du} - p_{uu}}{Suu - Sdd} \tag{10.34}$$

$$\eta_d = \frac{p_{dd} - p_{du}}{Sud - Sdd}. \tag{10.35}$$

And the value of η at time 0 is given above as Equation (10.32). The values of the put at the various time points in the binomial tree are

$$p_u = \frac{\pi p_{uu} + (1 - \pi)p_{ud}}{1 + r} \tag{10.36}$$

---

[4]The equation for η for a put and η for a call would appear to be conflicting. The left-hand sides (η) are the same, but the right-hand sides are different. We could use a distinguishing p or c on the left-hand side, but to reduce the clutter, we will simply assume you can tell from the numerator of the right-hand side whether we are talking about puts or calls. And, be aware that the value of η for a put is not the same as the value of η for call. Nonetheless, the difference is only that the put hedge ratio is the factor -1 multiplied by the hedge ratio for the call.

$$p_d = \frac{\pi p_{ud} + (1 - \pi)p_{dd}}{1 + r}. \qquad (10.37)$$

In the next section, we will look at the early exercise of American puts and will need to apply these equations.

10.4.1.4 *Valuing American Options with the Binomial Model*

In Section 10.3.1.7 we discussed the potential for early exercise of calls and puts. We noted that in the absence of a cash payment such as a dividend on the underlying, a call will not be exercised early. It is possible to adjust the binomial model to account for dividends and, thereby, to observe how early exercise occurs. There are several potential adjustments, and they are somewhat complex. The material in this book is introductory and designed for end users, so we will not look at the early exercise of calls in the binomial model. We will, however, examine the early exercise of puts, as this type of problem is very easy to illustrate.

Consider a two-period binomial model with an American put. There are three potential states in which the put might be exercised early: (1) when the asset is at Su, (2) when the asset is at Sd, and (3) when the asset is at S, time 0 or the initial state of the model. The three outcomes at time 2 are all at expiration so early exercise is not relevant at that point. Assume we are at the time 1 up-state, where the asset is at Su. The holder of an American put has a choice of either not exercising it or exercising it. We know that if the put is not exercised, its value is the value of a European put at that point in the binomial tree, which was given above in Equation (10.36). It is possible, however, that the put could be worth more exercised, in which case, its value, using capital P_u for American puts, would be $Max(0, X - Su)$. Likewise, in the time 1 downstate, the value of an American put, P_d, would be Equation (10.37) if unexercised or $Max(0, X - Sd)$ if exercised. Thus, at time 1, we can say that the value of an American put would be

$$P_u = Max\left(X - Su, \frac{\pi P_{uu} + (1 - \pi)P_{ud}}{1 + r}\right) \qquad (10.38)$$

or[5]

$$P_d = Max\left(X - Sd, \frac{\pi P_{ud} + (1 - \pi)P_{dd}}{1 + r}\right) \qquad (10.39)$$

---

[5] We have used the upper-case P for the value at expiration. At that point, it is immaterial whether one uses the symbol for a European or American put, even when valuing a European put.

At time 0, the value of the American put will be

$$P = Max\left(X - S, \frac{\pi P_u + (1 - \pi)P_d}{1 + r}\right) \qquad (10.40)$$

In other words, the value of the put at time 0 will either be its current exercise value or the formula value, which takes a weighted average of the next two values and discounts that average back one period to the present. The process is illustrated with a numerical example, as presented in Exhibit 10-11.

We will not address the hedge ratio computation, but it would be done the same as for European options. Indeed, the formulas are precisely as the same. The values, of course, would differ slightly.

Earlier we said that there are two ways to create a two-period binomial model. One is to simply add periods and assume that the u and d factors are the same. The other is to take an option's life and divide it into binomial periods, which requires that we adjust the u and d factors. We will take this approach in the next section.

10.4.1.5 *Dividing the Life of an Option into Binomial Periods*

In the examples in the previous section, the life of the option was simply given as one "period" or two "periods." These so-called maturities are a bit nebulous. How long is a period? Options in the real world have maturities like three weeks, six months, and two years. Let us take a one-month option and attempt to model it with the binomial model. Suppose one binomial time period is specified to represent one month. As a result, the model we would be using would permit the asset to take on only two possible values one month later when the option expired. This kind of restriction is incredibly unrealistic and quite limiting. Using the example above, do we really believe that a $50 asset can be worth only $60 or $40 in one month? And a two-month option modeled with a binomial tree would have just three outcomes, here $72, $48, and $32. Proceeding in this manner, the only way to get a large number of outcomes would be to model a very long-term option.

A better approach would be to divide an option's life into smaller and smaller intervals. For example, a 30-day option could be viewed as having 30 binomial periods, each period representing one day. But for that matter, we could even divide a 30-day option into 60 periods, each representing one half day. If we take this approach, however, we cannot continue to use the factors u, d, and r in the same manner. In our example, u was 1.2. If we divided the option's life into smaller and smaller periods, we have to adjust u to smaller and smaller values. Likewise, we would have to do the same for d.

Objective: Continue with the problem in Exhibits 10-7 and 10-10 but make the option an American put with an exercise price of 50. For comparison, also consider a European put with an exercise price of 50. Find the values of the two options at the start.

Inputs: Same as in Exhibits 10-7 and 10-10.

Results: Recall the values for *Suu*, *Sud*, and *Sdd*:

$$Suu = 60(1.2) = 72$$
$$Sud = 60(0.8) = 48$$
$$Sdd = 40(0.8) = 32$$

The corresponding put values at time two are

$$p_{uu} = Max(0, 50 - 72) = 0$$
$$p_{ud} = Max(0, 50 - 48) = 2$$
$$p_{dd} = Max(0, 50 - 32) = 18$$

Then we back up to time one and find the option values unexercised. We will denote these as the value of the European versions of these options:

$$p_u = \frac{0.575(0.00) + (1 - 0.575)(2.00)}{1.03} = 0.83$$

$$p_d = \frac{0.575(2.00) + (1 - 0.575)(18.00)}{1.03} = 8.54$$

The corresponding American option values are found by comparing the exercise values at those points to these European option values. Thus, the values of the American options are

$$P_u = Max(50 - 60, 0.83) = 0.83$$
$$P_d = Max(50 - 40, 8.54) = 10.00$$

Thus, in the down-state of time 1, the put would be exercised because its value if exercised is 10, which is more than its value if not exercised, 8.54. In the up-state of time 1, the put would not be exercised, as it is out of the-money, so its value at that point is 0.83. Stepping back to time 0, the value of the put if it is European is

$$p = \frac{0.575(0.83) + (1 - 0.575)(8.54)}{1.03} = 3.99$$

If the option is American, its value if unexercised at time zero is

$$P = \frac{0.575(0.83) + (1 - 0.575)(10)}{1.03} = 4.59$$

Exhibit 10-11. Binomial Valuation of an American Put Option

The option could be exercised at time 0, however, so we must check to determine if it is optimal to do so. Its value at time 0 is, therefore,

$$P = Max(50 - 50, 4.59) = 4.59$$

Clearly it would not be exercised, as it is not in-the-money. Nonetheless, it is always necessary to check for whether it is worth exercising at time 0.

We see that the American put is worth 4.59, while its European counterpart is worth only 3.99. The difference is due to the fact that there is at least one outcome in which the option would be worth exercising early.

Exhibit 10-11. *(Continued)*

And obviously if r is the risk-free for one period, we cannot arbitrarily use the same value of r if we cut and slice the option's life into smaller and smaller periods.

To use the binomial model in this manner, however, we need benchmarks to enable us to properly account for u, d, and r. In the binomial model, the parameters u and d clearly define the maximum and minimum returns. For most assets there is no maximum return, and the minimum is usually -1.00, or -100%, and which occurs when the asset goes to zero. The up and down factors, however, do attempt to capture a sense of the volatility of the asset. We have already discussed volatility quite a lot in this book, and we have typically used the standard deviation to measure volatility. It is customary to speak in terms of the annual volatility. So let us say that σ is the measure of the volatility of the annual return on the asset. To adapt the binomial model for an option of a given maturity to a large number of time periods, we need a way to express u and d in such a manner that they are consistent with an annual volatility of σ. We will also define r as the annual risk-free rate, just as it has been in previous chapters, and we need a way to specify the interest rate for each period that is consistent with an annual rate of r.

Let us now define the expiration of the option in years as T. For example, an option expiring in 60 days would have $T = 60/365 = 0.1644$. Assume that we will be using n binomial periods. Then the length of each period is T/n. There are many formulas that would give us values for u and d that are consistent with a given annual value of σ, but here is a set that is widely used.[6]

$$u = e^{\sigma\sqrt{T/n}}$$
$$d = e^{-\sigma\sqrt{T/n}}$$

---

[6]Note that $d = 1/u$. In the example we used where $u = 1.2$ and $d = 0.8$, d would not be $1/u$.

Adjusting the risk-free rate is simple. Define r_b as the binomial risk-free rate for an annual risk-free rate of r. We would then have

$$r_b = (1 + r)^{T/n} - 1$$

Consider a call option in which the underlying is at 100, the exercise price is 100, the risk-free rate is 3%, the option expires in one year, and the volatility is 0.40. If we used one binomial period, the parameters would be

$$u = e^{0.4\sqrt{1/1}} = 1.4918$$

$$d = e^{-0.4\sqrt{1/1}} = 0.6703$$

$$r_b = (1.03)^{1/1} - 1 = 0.03$$

If we use two binomial periods, the values will be

$$u = e^{0.4\sqrt{1/2}} = 1.3269$$

$$d = e^{-0.4\sqrt{1/2}} = 0.7536$$

$$r_b = (1.03)^{1/2} - 1 = 0.0149$$

For 10 binomial periods, the values will be

$$u = e^{0.4\sqrt{1/10}} = 1.1348$$

$$d = e^{-0.4\sqrt{1/10}} = 0.8812$$

$$r_b = (1.03)^{1/10} - 1 = 0.0030$$

Notice that the u and d parameters move closer to 1, reflecting the smaller movements permissible when we shrink the time period. In addition, the interest rate gets smaller. Exhibit 10-12 is a graph of the price of this option using an increasing number of binomial time steps from one to fifty. With just one time step, the option price is 20.91. At 50 time steps, the option price is 17.04.

Two interesting patterns appear. First we see a trend toward convergence to a single value. Although the graph is not sufficiently detailed to permit determination of that value, we will learn in the next section that the value is 17.12. The second pattern we see is a bit of a zig zag. First down, then up, then down, then up. Indeed, the mathematical structure of this problem leads to the result that if the number of time steps is odd, the binomial model will overestimate the true value. If the number of time steps is even, the binomial model will underestimate the true value. Nonetheless, the errors from estimating the true value do shrink as the number of time steps increase.

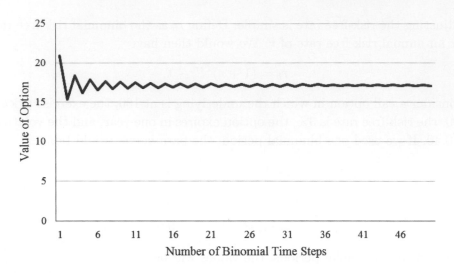

Exhibit 10-12. Binomial Value of European Call Option by Time Steps

As we said, the true value, which we will determine in the next section, is 17.12. So, how many time steps does it take for the binomial model to return a result of 17.12? Well, it takes between 800 and 900. That may seem like a lot, but it is not really a lot of work for a computer. In any case, we can bypass all of that calculating effort by using the Black-Scholes-Merton model.

10.4.2 *Black-Scholes-Merton Valuation*

The Black-Scholes-Merton model (BSM), also sometimes just called the Black-Scholes model, was developed in independent research conducted at the Sloan School of Management at MIT in the early 1970s. Fischer Black and Myron Scholes were working on a formula for the value of an option, while Robert Merton was working on the same problem in the same building but independently of Black and Scholes. The binomial model had not yet been discovered, and Black, Scholes, and Merton were working on the problem in a framework called *continuous time*. Continuous time essentially means that markets are open and trading at all times and that anyone can trade at any point in time with no costs and no taxes. In addition, borrowing and lending at the continuously compounded risk-free rate is available to all. Most importantly, they assumed that the volatility of underlying was known and constant.

How the Black-Scholes-Merton Model Was Discovered

The Black-Scholes-Merton model has been hailed as one of the greatest discoveries in the entire world of economics. Though not without its critics who believe that the model is based on flimsy assumptions and leads to dangerous actions that can destabilize the market, it has nonetheless been so widely used that it has become the go-to model for pricing options and managing risk. The origins of the model are told quite well in two books, *Capital Ideas: The Improbably Origins of Modern Wall Street* by Peter L. Bernstein (New York: The Free Press, 1992) and *Pricing the Future: Finance, Physics, and the 300-Year Journey to the Black-Scholes Equation. A Story of Genius and Discovery* by George G. Szpiro (New York: Basic Books, 2011). You might also find it interesting to read Fischer Black's own account in Black (1989).

We can hardly do justice to the story by trying to summarize it here, but let us try to get the basic idea of what happened. The seminal model was developed by a French doctoral student in mathematics, Louis Bachelier, who was studying at the University of Paris in 1900. Unfortunately, Bachelier's professors were not impressed with his work as it was largely considered applied rather than theoretical, and consequently, it essentially lay undiscovered for at least 60 years. Formal models were derived by the economists Case Sprenkle in 1961, James Boness in 1964, and Robert Merton working with Paul Samuelson in 1969. While each of these models made substantial progress toward solving the problem of pricing options, each model either had an unacceptable assumption or required information that was not readily available.

Fischer Black working with Myron Scholes at the Sloan School of Management at MIT began to explore the problem from a different perspective. Black and Scholes proposed that if the option could be combined with an offsetting position in the underlying, a balanced position could be obtained. This balance would eliminate the risk, thereby leaving a position that should earn the risk-free rate. Black and Scholes were then able to back into the value of a call that guarantees that this risk-free position earns the risk-free rate.

Working concurrently in the same building as Black and Scholes, Robert C. Merton tackled the same problem. Using a different approach but nonetheless relying on the notion that a risk-free portfolio of the underlying and the option would earn the risk-free rate, Merton derived the result using some fairly powerful mathematics. Although the model is more commonly known as the Black-Scholes model, it only seems fair to give Merton his due credit and call it the Black-Scholes-Merton model.

Interestingly, great discoveries are not always recognized as early as they should. Black and Scholes had considerable difficulty getting their article published in a scholarly journal, being rejected at least twice. Thanks to the intervention of a future Nobel Laureate, University of Chicago professor Merton Miller, the Black and Scholes article was eventually published in 1973 in the *Journal of Political Economy*, perhaps a somewhat odd home for an article on pricing financial instruments, but a home nonetheless. Interestingly, the delay in publication of the article resulted in the publication of an empirical study of the model by Black and Scholes in the *Journal of Finance* a year earlier. So, the model was essentially empirically tested before it was actually published. Merton's paper also appeared in 1973 in the *Bell Journal of Economics and Management Science*.

Unfortunately, Fischer Black died of cancer at the age of 57 in 1995. Two years later the Royal Swedish Academy awarded the Bank of Sweden Nobel Prize in Economics to Merton and Scholes. Nobel Prizes are not awarded posthumously, but special mention was noted of Black's contribution.

Of course, there is much more to this story. Just a few years later, Merton and Scholes were involved in a hedge fund that nearly brought down the financial system. You can read this story in Lowenstein (2000).

An important feature of the continuous time framework is that prices are smooth and while they are volatile, they cannot jump around abruptly. Just exactly how one defines the dividing line between a small but smooth move and an abrupt jump is an advanced mathematical concept that we need not address here. The mathematics required to have developed the BSM model is quite advanced, but the basic idea is simple and pretty much the same as the idea used in developing the binomial model, which is its discrete time analog. An investor holds a portfolio of assets and sells a European call option or buys a European put option. The investor then balances the number of units of the asset and the short call options in such a way that the risk is completely offset and eliminated. As such, the position is riskless and should earn the risk-free rate. From there, Black, Scholes, and Merton are able to solve for the value of the option that ensures that this riskless portfolio earns the risk-free rate. Of course, we will skip the math, but the formulas for calls (c) and puts (p) are

$$c_0(X, T) = S_0 N(d_1) - X e^{-r_c T} N(d_2)$$
$$p_0(X, T) = X e^{-r_c T} N(-d_2) - S_0 N(d_1)$$
$$d_1 = \frac{\ln(S_0/X) + (r_c + \sigma^2/2)T}{\sigma \sqrt{T}} \qquad (10.41)$$
$$d_2 = d_1 - \sigma \sqrt{T}$$

The expressions $N(d_1)$ and $N(d_2)$ are the values taken from the normal probability distribution. They represent the probability that a value of d_1 (or d_2, or their corresponding negatives for puts) would be observed at random. The variable r_c is the continuously compounded risk-free rate, found as $\ln(1 + r)$ where r is the discrete risk-free rate. The variable σ is the volatility of the underling, and of course, S_0, X, and T are symbols we have used already in this chapter.

Computation of BSM values is quite straightforward. We first simply compute d_1 and d_2 and then determine the probability that one would observe values less than these values in a normal distribution, the familiar bell curve. Exhibit 10-13 shows a normal probability table using two-digit inputs with four-digit output. It permits the input of a generic random variable, z, that is considered to have an expected value of zero and a volatility of 1. The table then produces the normal probability, $N(z)$, which is the probability that a value of z or less would be observed at random. Here z is either d_1, d_2, $-d_1$, or $-d_2$, which by their specifications in the BSM formula are of the standard normal variety. So let us say we calculated the value of $N(d_1)$ from Equation (10.41) and obtained 1.1874. To use the table, we would have to round it to 1.19. To look up $N(1.19)$, we first look in the left column for the row that covers 1.1. We then move over to the column that covers 0.09. We then find that $N(1.19)$ is 0.8830. This result means that in a normal distribution, a value of 1.19 or less would be expected to occur 88.3% of the time.

Simple enough? Well, not exactly. There is a lot of rounding off going on. We rounded off the inputs to two digits, and the outputs in the table are rounded off to four digits. Moreover, if the calculations of d_1 and d_2, as well as the rest of the BSM formula are done manually, there is considerable room for error in the final answer. As an alternative, we can use Excel to obtain a more accurate estimate. Specifically, Excel has a function called *Normsdist* that provides the normal probability. If we enter the function "=normsdist(1.1874)" into a cell, it would return 0.882465. We might then

z	0.00	0.01	0.02	0.03	0.04	0.05	0.06	0.07	0.08	0.09
0.0	0.5000	0.5040	0.5080	0.5120	0.5160	0.5199	0.5239	0.5279	0.5319	0.5359
0.1	0.5398	0.5438	0.5478	0.5517	0.5557	0.5596	0.5636	0.5675	0.5714	0.5753
0.2	0.5793	0.5832	0.5871	0.5910	0.5948	0.5987	0.6026	0.6064	0.6103	0.6141
0.3	0.6179	0.6217	0.6255	0.6293	0.6331	0.6368	0.6406	0.6443	0.6480	0.6517
0.4	0.6554	0.6591	0.6628	0.6664	0.6700	0.6736	0.6772	0.6808	0.6844	0.6879
0.5	0.6915	0.6950	0.6985	0.7019	0.7054	0.7088	0.7123	0.7157	0.7190	0.7224
0.6	0.7257	0.7291	0.7324	0.7357	0.7389	0.7422	0.7454	0.7486	0.7517	0.7549
0.7	0.7580	0.7611	0.7642	0.7673	0.7704	0.7734	0.7764	0.7794	0.7823	0.7852
0.8	0.7881	0.7910	0.7939	0.7967	0.7995	0.8023	0.8051	0.8078	0.8106	0.8133
0.9	0.8159	0.8186	0.8212	0.8238	0.8264	0.8289	0.8315	0.8340	0.8365	0.8389
1.0	0.8413	0.8438	0.8461	0.8485	0.8508	0.8531	0.8554	0.8577	0.8599	0.8621
1.1	0.8643	0.8665	0.8686	0.8708	0.8729	0.8749	0.8770	0.8790	0.8810	0.8830
1.2	0.8849	0.8869	0.8888	0.8907	0.8925	0.8944	0.8962	0.8980	0.8997	0.9015
1.3	0.9032	0.9049	0.9066	0.9082	0.9099	0.9115	0.9131	0.9147	0.9162	0.9177
1.4	0.9192	0.9207	0.9222	0.9236	0.9251	0.9265	0.9279	0.9292	0.9306	0.9319
1.5	0.9332	0.9345	0.9357	0.9370	0.9382	0.9394	0.9406	0.9418	0.9429	0.9441
1.6	0.9452	0.9463	0.9474	0.9484	0.9495	0.9505	0.9515	0.9525	0.9535	0.9545
1.7	0.9554	0.9564	0.9573	0.9582	0.9591	0.9599	0.9608	0.9616	0.9625	0.9633
1.8	0.9641	0.9649	0.9656	0.9664	0.9671	0.9678	0.9686	0.9693	0.9699	0.9706
1.9	0.9713	0.9719	0.9726	0.9732	0.9738	0.9744	0.9750	0.9756	0.9761	0.9767
2.0	0.9772	0.9778	0.9783	0.9788	0.9793	0.9798	0.9803	0.9808	0.9812	0.9817
2.1	0.9821	0.9826	0.9830	0.9834	0.9838	0.9842	0.9846	0.9850	0.9854	0.9857
2.2	0.9861	0.9864	0.9868	0.9871	0.9875	0.9878	0.9881	0.9884	0.9887	0.9890
2.3	0.9893	0.9896	0.9898	0.9901	0.9904	0.9906	0.9909	0.9911	0.9913	0.9916
2.4	0.9918	0.9920	0.9922	0.9925	0.9927	0.9929	0.9931	0.9932	0.9934	0.9936
2.5	0.9938	0.9940	0.9941	0.9943	0.9945	0.9946	0.9948	0.9949	0.9951	0.9952
2.6	0.9953	0.9955	0.9956	0.9957	0.9959	0.9960	0.9961	0.9962	0.9963	0.9964
2.7	0.9965	0.9966	0.9967	0.9968	0.9969	0.9970	0.9971	0.9972	0.9973	0.9974
2.8	0.9974	0.9975	0.9976	0.9977	0.9977	0.9978	0.9979	0.9979	0.9980	0.9981
2.9	0.9981	0.9982	0.9982	0.9983	0.9984	0.9984	0.9985	0.9985	0.9986	0.9986
3.0	0.9987	0.9987	0.9987	0.9988	0.9988	0.9989	0.9989	0.9989	0.9990	0.9990

Exhibit 10-13. Normal Probability Table

round that number off to 0.8825. A difference from the table value of 0.0005 might not seem like much, but it can affect the value of the option quite notably.[7]

---

[7]Other mathematical routines are available, but we can stick with Excel here.

Some Bell Curve Trivia

The bell curve, sometimes called the normal probability distribution, is a widely known statistical benchmark that is used to establish the probability of something occurring. While it is not completely clear who first discovered the so-called bell curve, most of the credit is given to the German mathematician Karl Friedrich Gauss, who first wrote about it in 1809. In fact, the curve is often called the Gaussian curve. Interestingly, Gauss was such an honored citizen in the history of Germany that his face appeared on the 10 Deutschemark note along with a graph of the normal curve and also its formula. For a look at that specimen of this old piece of paper money, which has been supplanted by the euro, see

http://www.history.didaktik.mathematik.uni-wuerzburg.de/ausstell/ gauss/geldschein.html

Let's suppose for a presentation you wanted to draw the bell curve. Well it is not easy. But if you have a spreadsheet, you can program it. The curve specifies the probabilities for a value of a variable commonly called a z-statistic, which can run from $-\infty$ to $+\infty$. For all practical purposes, a z-value from -5 to $+5$ should be adequate. So, construct a range of values of z from -5 to $+5$ in increments of say, 0.10. That is $-5.00, -4.90, -4.80, \dots, 4.80, 4.90, 5.00$. You will have 101 lines in the spreadsheet. You can space them closer if you would like, and the smaller the increment, the smoother the curve. Let us say that the first value of z is -5 and it is in cell C8. In the adjacent cell, type the formula $=(1/\text{SQRT}(2*\text{PI}()))*\text{EXP}(-(\text{C8}^2)/2)$. This will produce a value of $f(z)$ of 1.48672E-06, which might be written differently depending on how you have the cell formatted. Now, copy that formula down the column through the z-value of $+5$. Then create a graph of the formula values. There you have it: a reasonably nice drawing of the normal curve!

One other point we might add about the normal curve is that even if the distribution you are drawing from is not normally distributed, the sample mean and sum are normally distributed, regardless of the distribution. This statement means that the data might be drawn from a highly skewed distribution, but the sum and the average will be normally distributed. So we could draw a sample, calculate its average, and then draw other samples and calculate their respective averages.

If we draw enough samples, the averages we obtain will plot out as a normal distribution centered around the population average. This famous result is known as the *central limit theorem*. It was first attributed to French mathematician Abraham de Moivre around 1733 and made famous by another French mathematician, Simon Laplace, in 1812. De Moivre in fact may even have discovered the normal curve itself in 1738, though full attribution is generally deferred to Gauss.

One more consideration in using the table is that the value of the input z, representing d_1, d_2, $-d_1$, or $-d_2$, could be negative. In that case, we simply change the sign and subtract the table value from 1. Thus, if the value of z is say -0.58, we look up the positive value 0.58, and we get a probability of 0.7190. We then subtract this value from 1 to obtain $1 - 0.7190 = 0.2810.$[8] The ability to make this simple adjustment occurs because of the symmetry of the normal curve, and this feature permits us to get by with only a single table containing positive values of z. Thus, in order to condense the table to a manageable size, the negative values are omitted, and the inputs are rounded to two decimal places. The latter constraint imposes some inaccuracy, but we can live with it. In real-world applications in your career, you should probably not do the table calculation.

We will work an example, the same one described in Section 10.4.1.5 that we used to see how the binomial value converges to the Black-Scholes-Merton value when we divided the option's life into smaller and smaller time periods. This example is done in Exhibit 10-14.

10.4.2.1 *Pricing Options when there are Carrying Costs and a Convenience Yield*

In Chapter 8 we learned how storage costs and convenience yields affect the price of a forward contract. We learned that storage costs increase the forward price and the convenience yield decreases it. There is a similar effect in options. With forwards we learned that one can simply take the spot price, deduct the present value of the convenience yield and add the present value of the storage costs, and then incorporate that adjusted price into the standard model. Or we can compound the spot price, deduct the future value of the convenience yield, and add the future value of the storage costs. Indeed, this is the case with options. Let $PVD(0, T)$ be the present value of the dividends

---

[8]The value obtained using Excel is 0.280957.

Objective: Price a European call option in which the underlying is at 100, the exercise price is 100, the risk-free rate is 3%, the option expires in one year, and the volatility of the asset is 0.4.

Inputs: First we must note that the interest rate was stated as an annual rate. The BSM model needs the interest rate to be continuously compounded. The conversion is simple: $r_c = \ln(1.03) = 0.029559$. Let us round to 0.0296.

$$S = 100$$
$$X = 100$$
$$r_c = 0.0296$$
$$T = 1.0$$
$$\sigma = 0.4$$

Results: First plug in to their respective formulas to obtain the values of d_1 and d_2.

$$d_1 = \frac{\ln(100/100) + (0.0296 + (0.4)^2/2)(1)}{0.4\sqrt{1}} = 0.2739$$

$$d_2 = 0.2739 - 0.4\sqrt{1} = -0.1261$$

For illustrative purposes, these values are shown to four decimal places, but they are retained in the computer to more significant digits. Feeding these values into Excel, we obtain the values of the normal probabilities of

$$N(0.2739) = 0.6079$$

$$N(-0.1261) = 0.4498$$

Plugging in to the call option formula, Equation (10.41), we then obtain the option value as

$$c = 100(0.6079) - 100e^{-0.0296(1)}(0.4498) = 17.12$$

And 17.12 is the number we mentioned in the previous section as the value to which the binomial price converges. The calculations here were done on a spreadsheet and no values were rounded. If the values of d_1 and d_2 were rounded to two decimal places and fed into Excel, from which we rounded the Excel probabilities, we would still obtain 17.12, though such accuracy is not always the case. If the values of d_1 and d_2 were rounded to two decimal places and looked up in a table, we would obtain an option value of 17.13. Larger round-off errors do occur in other problems.

Exhibit 10-14.   Calculation of the Black-Scholes-Merton Option Value

---

from time 0 to time T, $PVCY(0, T)$ be the present value of any convenience yield from time 0 to time T, and $PVSC(0, T)$ be the present value of the carrying costs from time 0 to time T. Thus, one would adjust the spot price from S to $S - PVD(0, T) - PVCY(0, T) + PVSC(0, T)$ and insert that price into Black-Scholes-Merton formulas as given in the previous section.

10.4.2.2 *Pricing American Options*

The BSM formula applies only to European options. If the options are American, the formula does not give an accurate answer, except in the case of call options in which there are no cash flows on the underlying. For example, the call options on a stock that does not pay a dividend during the life of the option would not be exercised early, so those options could be priced by the BSM model. There are more sophisticated versions of the BSM model that can price other cases of American options, but these models are required to make some extreme assumptions. The best approach for pricing American options is a binomial model with a large number of time steps.

10.4.2.3 *Implied Volatility*

The inputs for the BSM model are the value of the underlying, the exercise price, the risk-free rate, the time to expiration, the volatility, and the future dividends or interest, convenience yield, and carrying costs. The value of the underlying, the exercise price, the risk-free rate, and the time to expiration are observable values. There would be little, if any, disagreement between two parties on these values. The volatility, dividends and interest, convenience yield, and carrying costs, however, are not directly observable. Because dividends tend to be fairly stable, they can probably be reasonably forecasted. If the asset is a bond, interest payments would be known, subject only to possible default. The convenience yield can be difficult to estimate, but it is applicable only to certain storable assets. Carrying costs represent the costs of storing an asset, and they would be reasonably known. That leaves us with volatility as the only really problematic input.

Volatility represents the standard deviation of the return on the underlying. This parameter is a statistical characteristic of the distribution of the return on the underlying over the life of the option. The volatility is one piece of information required to price options that is not required to price forwards, futures, or swaps.[9] As such, it is a fairly onerous requirement and makes option pricing far more subjective than objective. Market participants will have different opinions on the future volatility of the asset, and the variety of opinions will lead to different opinions on the prices of options, which tends to stimulate trading.

---

[9]The reason volatility does not appear in formulas for pricing forwards, futures, and swaps is that their payoffs are linear. Because option payoffs are non-linear, the volatility is required to provide a more precise modeling of the statistical characteristics of the underlying.

If an option price is observed from a trade in the market or observed as a quoted price offered for purchase or sale, it is possible to infer the volatility that determined the price, given an acceptance of the option pricing model being used. This volatility is called the *implied volatility*. For example, consider the BSM formula, Equation (10.41). If we assume that the option price, c_0 or p_0, on the left hand side is observable through quotes or trades, we can presumably determine the value of σ that produced that price. Unfortunately, there is no simple algebraic rearrangement of the formula that will isolate σ on the left-hand side, given the call and put prices and the other inputs on the right-hand side. There are, however, iterative techniques that solve for this implied volatility.

All options with the same expiration on the same underlying should have the same implied volatility, but unfortunately, they do not. A plot of volatility against exercise price of a given option often produces a pattern generally known as the *volatility smile* though it is sometimes more of a skew, or smirk. The differences in these implied volatilities are generally thought to reflect the fact that the model does not capture all of the characteristics of options, or that it requires critically inaccurate assumptions. For example, the ability to trade continuously with no transaction costs is assumed by the model, but that assumption is hardly realistic.

The implied volatilities of options on the well-known S&P 500 index are consolidated into a single measure produced by the Chicago Board Options Exchange. This measure is called the VIX, which stands for volatility index, and its history is illustrated in Exhibit 10-15.

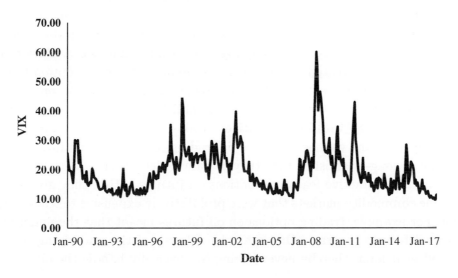

Exhibit 10-15. The CBOE Volatility Index (VIX)

You can think of the VIX as the expected volatility of the S&P 500 over the next month. As you can see the average level of the VIX has been about 20, suggesting that the average standard deviation of the S&P 500 has been about 0.20. It has reached a maximum of 59.89 in October 2008 and a minimum of 9.59 in October of 2017. The VIX is sometimes referred to as the *fear index*. A high level of the VIX relative to the average or recent past indicate that option traders feel that the market will become more volatile. Perhaps that is something to fear, though as we know, option prices are higher the more volatile is the underlying, and that is not necessarily something to be afraid of.

10.4.3 *Options on Forwards and Futures*

The BSM model in the form given in the previous sections is appropriate for pricing European options on assets. In addition to options on assets, there are options on futures and forwards. The exchange-listed options on futures markets was launched in 1982 in the U.S., and these instruments have been extremely successful in terms of usage. One probable reason is that the U.S. has traditionally had a separation of exchange-listed options and their underlyings. When floor trading was prevalent in the U.S., the ability to do arbitrage transactions between an option and its underlying required executing trades on different exchanges. Such transactions can be done rapidly but not as fast as they would if the options were traded on the same exchange as the underlying. For example, trading an option on the S&P 500 and trading the S&P 500 through either an index mutual fund or by building a mimicking portfolio would require transactions on the Chicago Board Options Exchange and exchanges that traded the stocks. Options on futures were then created by the futures exchanges. Thus, the option traded in the same physical area as the underlying futures. As such, options on futures began to trade very actively and established themselves as important instruments in the world of derivatives. Today, the volume of floor trading is swamped by the volume of electronic trading, but options on futures have become so long-established that they remain widely used.

Another attractive feature of options on futures is that they give access to some commodity markets that were prohibitively expensive to trade in the spot. For example, trading options on oil futures meant that the underlying is an oil futures contract. One can take delivery of the underlying futures and offset it later, thereby never having to physically handle the oil.

In addition, there are options on forwards that trade exclusively in the over-the-counter market. Options on futures and options on forwards would essentially be priced the same way and for the European versions of these options, they require only a modest adjustment to the BSM model. This adjusted model is often called the *Black model*, because Fischer Black developed it on his own. To understand the Black model, let us first assume that we have an asset that makes no cash flows nor does it have a convenience yield. We will also need to operate in a world with continuous compounding, so let the continuously compounded risk-free rate be r_c. Based on what we learned in Chapter 8, the futures or forward price would be the spot price compounded at the continuously compounded risk-free rate over the life of the option. Using the futures price, for example,

$$f_0(T) = Se^{r_c T}$$

If the futures contract and the option expire at the same time, an exercised call option would turn into a futures, which would immediately turn into the underlying asset. Thus, under these conditions, an option on the futures and an option on the asset would have the same price. We could, therefore, use the BSM model, but we might prefer to price the option off of the futures instead of the spot. In that case, the formula would be

$$c_0(X, T) = e^{-r_c T}\left(f_0(T)N(d_1) - XN(d_2)\right)$$
$$p_0(X, T) = e^{-r_c T}\left(XN(-d_2) - f_0(T)N(-d_1)\right)$$
$$d_1 = \frac{\ln(f_0(T)/X) - (\sigma^2/2)T}{\sigma\sqrt{T}} \tag{10.42}$$
$$d_2 = d_1 - \sigma\sqrt{T}$$

An illustration of the Black option value calculation is in Exhibit 10-16.

If the futures (or forward) and the option do not expire at the same time, the values of options on the futures (or forward) and options on the underlying asset will not be the same. Nonetheless, we would still use the Black model is illustrated here, with the time to expiration being that of the option and not the futures. Binomial models can also be adapted to options on futures, but that is an advanced topic that we do not cover here.

The Black model is frequently used to value another type of option that is widely traded and one of which we will cover in the next section: options on interest rates.

Objective: Continue with the problem in Exhibit 10-14. Price a European call option on a futures in which the underlying is at 100, the exercise price is 100, the risk-free rate is 3%, the option expires in one year, and the volatility of the asset is 0.4.

Inputs: From 10-14,

$$S = 100$$
$$X = 100$$
$$r_c = 0.0296$$
$$T = 1.0$$
$$\sigma = 0.4$$

First let us price the futures:

$$f_0(T) = 100e^{0.0296(1)} = 103.00$$

This result should not be surprising. We originally said that the annually compounded rate of interest was 3%, so 100 compounded for one year should be 103.

Results: First plug in to obtain the values of d_1 and d_2.

$$d_1 = \frac{\ln(103/100) + ((0.4)^2/2)(1)}{0.4\sqrt{1}} = 0.2739$$

$$d_2 = 0.2739 - 0.4\sqrt{1} = -0.1261$$

Feeding these values into Excel, we obtain the values of the normal probabilities of

$$N(0.2739) = 0.6079$$

$$N(-0.1261) = 0.4498$$

(If you were paying attention to Exhibit 10-14, you would see that these are the same values of d_1, d_2, $N(d_1)$, and $N(d_2)$). Plugging in to the formula, we then obtain the option value as

$$c = e^{-0.0296(1)} (103(0.6079) - 100(0.4498)) = 17.12$$

And this value, 17.12, is the same value we found in Exhibit 10-14.

Exhibit 10-16.   Calculation of the Black Option Value

10.5   Interest Rate Options

With the exception of options in which the underlying is a futures or a forward contract, all of the options we have covered have been options on assets. There are, however, options in which the underlying is an interest rate. The fact that these instruments exist should not be surprising to you. We have already covered futures, forwards, and swaps, which are derivatives in which the underlying is an interest rate, so naturally there is no reason why options on interest rates cannot exist.

Like its counterparts in the futures, forwards, and swaps markets, most interest rate options are based on LIBOR, either dollar LIBOR or LIBOR for another currency, for a given maturity.[10] Thus, an option might be on 30-day LIBOR. Let us take a look at how these options work.

10.5.1 *Payoffs of Interest Rate Options*

Consider an interest rate option on h-day LIBOR expiring in m days. Exhibit 10-15 shows the time line of this option. This graph is virtually the same as Exhibit 8-3, which pertained to FRAs. The underlying is a Eurodollar loan starting at day T_m and ending at day $T_m + h$. The option expires on day T_m, at which time the payoff is determined. The payoff is actually made, however, on day $T_m + h$. As such, interest rate options pay off like interest rate swaps: the rate is determined on one date, but the payment is made later, a process we referred to as advance set, settled in arrears. With FRAs, however, we found that the rate is determined on one day, and the payoff is made on that date, with the payoff discounted to reflect the time value of money, a process called advance set, advance settle. We saw that there is no economic difference in the two methods, as the discounting of the FRA payoff makes them equivalent. Exhibit 10-17 illustrates the time line.

To get started in understanding the payoffs, let us just use a generic symbol, L, to represent LIBOR at the expiration of the option. The exercise price of an interest rate option is not so much a price as it is a rate. We will use continue to use the symbol X but keep in mind that it is on the order

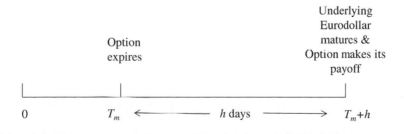

Exhibit 10-17. Time Layout of an Interest Rate Option

---

[10] Unless otherwise stated, here all references to LIBOR will be dollar LIBOR.

of magnitude of an interest rate. On the expiration day of an interest rate call option with an exercise rate of X, the value of the option, or its payoff, is determined by the formula

$$Max(0, L - X)\left(\frac{h}{360}\right)$$

This formula looks pretty much like the standard formula for a call, but there is one catch. You might notice that we did not write this as an equation with a left-hand side of "$c_T =$". The value of the option at the expiration T is not the above expression, *because interest rate options do not make their payoffs on the expiration day.* This amount will be paid h days later. Note also that this equation is the payoff for one unit of currency, so the total payoff would be found by multiplying this amount by the notional. Interest rate options are strictly cash-settled. They are, after all, simply payments of cash.

Exhibit 10-18 illustrates the calculation of the payoff for an interest rate call.

Objective: Consider an interest rate call that expires in 90 days in which the underlying is 180-day LIBOR. Let the exercise rate be 4.5% and the notional be $25 million. Calculate the payoffs for each of the following rates at expiration: (a) 4%, (b) 6%. Identify when the payoff occurs in relation to the day on which the option is initiated.

Inputs: Here $h = 180$. L will be represented by 4% and 6% in parts (a) and (b), respectively.

Results:

Part (a):

$$Max(0, L - X)\left(\frac{h}{360}\right)$$
$$= Max(0, 0.04 - 0.045)\left(\frac{180}{360}\right) \$25,000,000 = \$0$$

Part (b):

$$Max(0, L - X)\left(\frac{h}{360}\right)$$
$$= Max(0, 0.06 - 0.045)\left(\frac{180}{360}\right) \$25,000,000 = \$187,500$$

The payoff occurs 180 days after expiration. Since the option expires in 90 days, the payoff occurs 270 days after initiation.

Exhibit 10-18.   Calculation of the Payoffs for an Interest Rate Call

Objective: Consider an interest rate put that expires in 60 days in which the underlying is 90-day LIBOR. Let the exercise rate be 2% and the notional be $40 million. Calculate the payoffs for each of the following rates at expiration: (a) 1.5%, (b) 3.75%. Identify when the payoff occurs in relation to the day on which the option is initiated.

Inputs: Here $h = 90$. L will be represented by 0.015 and 0.0375 in parts (a) and (b), respectively.

Results:

Part (a):

$$Max(0, X - L)\left(\frac{h}{360}\right)$$

$$= Max(0, 0.02 - 0.015)\left(\frac{90}{360}\right)\$40,000,000 = \$50,000$$

Part (b):

$$Max(0, X - L)\left(\frac{h}{360}\right)$$

$$= Max(0, 0.02 - 0.0375)\left(\frac{90}{360}\right)\$40,000,000 = \$0$$

The payoff occurs 90 days after expiration. Since the option expires in 60 days, the payoff occurs 150 days after initiation.

Exhibit 10-19. Calculation of the Payoffs for an Interest Rate Put

The payoff expression above is for calls. Its counterpart for puts is

$$Max(0, X - L)\left(\frac{h}{360}\right),$$

and represent the amounts to be paid h days later. There is no physical delivery, as there is no underlying asset to deliver. It is simply a cash payment. Again, you would multiply this amount by the notional. Exhibit 10-19 illustrates the payoff of an interest rate put.

10.5.2 *Pricing Interest Rate Options*

Of course, the option buyer pays the option seller a premium at time zero. The determination of premiums on interest rate options is a fairly complex process, requiring the construction of an arbitrage-free model of the term structure of interest rates. What this statement typically means is that we construct a binomial tree model in which the prices of all assets and derivatives that are determined by interest rates are priced so as to preclude arbitrage. In addition, there are continuous time models for interest rate option pricing. One simplified procedure that is commonly used is to apply the Black model to price an interest rate option. The Black model is based on pricing a forward or futures rate. In an interest rate option, the underlying is a forward or futures price. Hence, many practitioners adapt the Black model to the case of pricing interest rate options. While the model is anecdotally believed to provide reasonable prices, there is no guarantee that the prices of interest rate options will be not arbitrageable against interest rate swaps and forwards. The only guarantee against that concern is to use a term structure model that is free of any opportunity for a market participant to earn an arbitrage profit. These topics are relatively advanced, however, and we shall not take them up here.

10.5.3 *Interest Rate Caps, Floors, and Collars*

Interest rate call options are often combined into portfolios of interest rate calls expiring at different times. Such a combination is called an *interest rate cap*. A combination of interest rate puts is called an *interest rate floor*. Although we will cover the application of interest rate caps and floors in detail in Section 10.8, we will provide a basic introduction here.

Interest rate calls are frequently used to protect floating-rate borrowers against rising interest rates. It should be apparent that if interest rates increase, borrowers with floating-rate loans have to pay more interest. But if those borrowers have interest rate calls, the calls can pay off and compensate them for the higher interest rate. In the opposite manner, lenders who extend credit at floating rates are hurt when interest rates fall. If they use interest rate puts, however, they can protect themselves against decreases in interest rates.

But most floating-rate loans have multiple payments. For example, suppose today that a company takes out a 90-day floating-rate loan with payments spaced 30 days apart. The rate is set today for the first 30 days. The interest then begins to accrue. After 30 days, the borrower pays the interest, and the rate is reset for the next 30 days. Then 30 days later, which is 60 days after the loan was taken out, the borrower pays the interest that accrues from day 31 through day 60. On day 60, the rate is reset, and interest begins to accrue. On day 90 the borrower pays the interest that has accrued from day 61 to day 90. The loan then matures and the borrower also pays back the principal. This description is for a fairly standard non-amortizing loan. Note that the rate is set today, so there is no risk of the interest owed in the first 30 days. But the rate will be re-set in 30 and 60 days, so there is risk of the rate increasing. Thus, there are two event dates.

A borrower might wish to hedge this risk by taking out an interest rate cap, which is a combination of interest rate calls with expirations timed to correspond to the rate reset days. Each component call in a cap is often referred to as a *caplet*. In this particular floating rate loan, an interest rate cap would contain two call options, one expiring in 30 days and one expiring in 60 days. Do not be confused by the fact that a loan with three payments would be hedged with a cap that contains just two call options. As noted, the initial rate is set today and poses no risk. The risk arises from the resetting of the rate in 30 and 60 days. Note too that the payoffs of the options, which are determined on days 30 and 60, actually occur on days 60 and 90. The options are, thus, structured like the loan. The rate is reset on days 30 and 60, and the interest is paid on days 60 and 90.

A lender is worried about a decrease in the floating rate. To hedge against a decrease, the lender might enter into an interest rate floor, which is a combination of interest rate put options that expire at the rate reset dates. The component put options in a floor are called *floorlets*.

Of course, as an alternative the two parties could simply agree on a fixed-rate loan, but many lenders simply through custom do not make many fixed rate loans. Banks in particular get so much of their funding at short-term variable rates that they prefer to pass on the interest rate risk to borrowers in the form of floating-rate loans. But as you know, banks offer interest rate swaps and FRAs, so it is not uncommon for a bank to arrange a floating-rate loan, while suggesting that the customer talk with the bank's derivatives group about a swap or FRA that would effectively convert the floating-rate loan to a fixed-rate loan.

A swap removes all of the risk of rising interest rates from a loan, effectively leaving a fixed-rate loan. Caps remove the upside risk but not the benefit of the downside. Caps, however, cost money in the form of a premium whereas swaps do not require an initial outlay. There is, however, another alternative that can remove some but not all of the upside risk and require a smaller premium if not zero initial outlay. This strategy is called an *interest rate collar* or just a *collar* and consists of financing the premium for buying a cap by selling a floor at a lower exercise rate. The cap costs money in the form of the cap premium, but the sale of the floor generates money. The premium from the sale of the floor can partially offset, exactly offset, or more than offset the premium from purchase of the cap. Most often, the premium on the floor is set to exactly offset the premium on the cap, which is done by choosing an appropriate floor strike.

When an end user wants to enter into an interest rate collar, it normally specifies the upper limit of the interest rate that it is willing to pay on its loan. That limit sets the strike on the cap. Let us say the current rate on a $20 million loan with payments in 180, 360, 540, and 720 days is 4%. The borrower is willing to bear the risk of paying up to 4.75%. The dealer would then calculate the premium on an interest rate cap with a strike of 4.75% and would run a computer program that plugs in various strike rates for the interest rate floor until it finds the one that generates the same premium as the cap. Let us say that the floor strike that generates a premium that exactly offsets that of the cap is 3.92%. Thus, the collar buyer has a combination of long calls struck at 4.75% and has sold a combination of puts struck at 3.92%.

Technically, the premium on the floor does not have to offset the premium on the cap. Assuming the cap buyer is satisfied with the call strike, he could want to earn more gains on the downside. In other words, his rate is capped at 4.75% but he cannot benefit from any rate decreases below 3.92%. Suppose he wants to lower the floor strike. As you know, a lower strike on a put lowers the premium, so the floor would not generate a premium high enough to offset that of the cap. The net result is that this collar, which is non-zero-cost, will require a net cash outlay. Of course, one other alternative that would permit a lower floor strike is to accept a higher cap strike. So if the cap buyer is willing to bear a little more risk of an interest rate increase, he can benefit from an interest rate decrease below 3.92%. Yet another possibility is that the cap buyer can set the floor strike higher than 3.92%, which combined with a cap strike of 4.75% will result in a net cash inflow at the start. This strategy, however, is not widely used. The most common strategy is when the floor and cap premiums offset, and this strategy is often called a *zero cost collar*. Let us now look at the payoffs of a collar.

With a cap strike of X_c and a floor strike of X_p, the payoffs of the collar for a notional of 1 are[11]

$$Max(0, L - X_c) - Max(0, X_p - L)$$
$$\text{(cap)} \qquad\qquad \text{(floor)}$$

---

[11]Of course, the actual payments would also have day count and notional adjustments.

This result applies to a single loan reset date, whereby the rate will be reset, and interest will accrue and be paid 30, 60, 90 days etc. later depending on whether the rate is a 30-, 60-, 90-day rate.

If $L > X_c$,

Caps pays $L - X_c$, floor pays zero

Net interest rate paid on loan plus collar: $L - (L - X_c) = X_c$

If $L < X_p$,

Cap pays off zero, floor pays $L - X_p$

Net interest rate paid on loan plus collar: $L - (L - X_p) = X_p$

If $X_p \leq L \leq X_p$

Cap pays zero, floor pays zero

Net interest rate paid on loan plus collar: L

The payoff is for a single given interest payment. The cap payoff is

$$\max(0, L_{T_m}(h) - X_c)\left(\frac{180}{360}\right).$$

The floor payoff is

$$\max(0, X_p - L_{T_m}(h))\left(\frac{180}{360}\right).$$

The loan interest is

$$L_{T_m}\left(\frac{180}{360}\right).$$

All of these payments occur at the same time, 180 days after the option expires and all would be multiplied by the face value of the loan, which is the notional of the collar. And recall that there are multiple options in the collar. Exhibit 10-20 shows the payoff of this strategy — loan plus collar — for a situation in which a company plans to borrow $20 million at a future date based on 180-day LIBOR. The strikes are 3.92% for the floor and 4.75% for the cap. The graph explores a range of rates from 2% to 7%, where the payoff is the total amount paid out.

Now we examine the special case of when the cap and floor strike are the same. So let us set a common strike on the cap and floor to simply X and for now, we use L as LIBOR at expiration. The cap payoff is $Max(0, L - X)$ and the floor payoff is $-Max(0, X - L)$. Thus, if $L \geq X$, the cap pays $L - X$

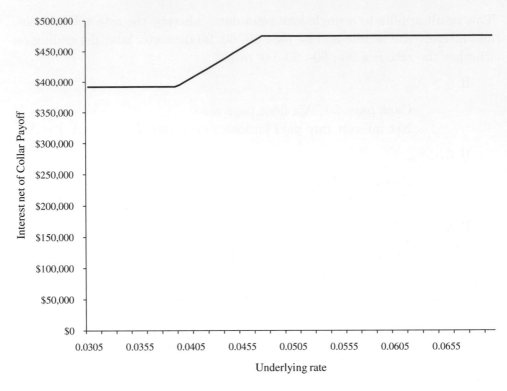

Exhibit 10-20. Payoff of Loan and Collar for a Given Payment Date

and the floor pays nothing for a total of $L - X$. If $L \leq X$, the cap pays nothing and the floor pays $-(L - X) = L - X$. So in all cases, the payoff is $L - X$. In some cases, this payoff is positive $(L > X)$ and in some, it is negative $(L < X)$. Combined with the payment of loan interest at L, the net interest paid is $L - (L - X) = X$. In other words, a same-strike collar results in the payment of interest at the rate X regardless of the actual rate in the market. Nonetheless, if the strike is the same on the cap and floor, the net premium is not zero. Depending on where the strike is set, the net premium will be positive or negative. This fact means that there must be a common strike that equates the floor and cap premium. That common strike is the swap rate. Recall that a swap results in the same payoff pattern, $L - X$ and requires no cash flow up front. Thus, this common strike must be the swap rate.

Finding that strike and verifying that it is the swap rate, however, is a bit problematic, because there is a subtle technical issue that we mentioned that arises in using the Black model to price interest rate caps. That problem manifests quite particularly in this situation. We noted earlier that the Black model is not specifically an arbitrage-free model. The Black model is designed to eliminate arbitrage between a forward contract on an asset, the asset itself, and an option on the asset. When using the Black model to price interest rate options, we insert a forward rate into the model in the place normally reserved for a forward price. This approach is a bit ad hoc, though widely used in the financial world, but it can get one into trouble if it is done indiscriminately. So, here we might find the rate that equates the premiums on the cap and floor but that rate is not the swap rate. This is a good example of how the Black model can fail and can result in the potential for an arbitrage profit for one party. Most firms handle this problem by finding the swap rate and then finding different implied volatilities that correctly price the cap and floor so that they produce the same premium. This procedure is called "calibrating the Black model." We will not cover it here, but do be aware that dealers are very careful to calibrate the Black model and you cannot expect an arbitrage opportunity.

It is important to note that while collars are most often used in interest rate risk management, they are also used in equity portfolio risk management. The investor in an equity portfolio will sometimes wish to protect a position against loss, which would ordinarily be done by purchasing a put. To offset the cost of the put, the investor might sell a call at a strike higher than the put strike. A computer can search for the strike in which the put premium offsets the call premium, resulting in a zero-cost equity collar. The investor then is protected against loss below the put strike but agrees to forego gains above the call strike. With interest rate collars, the party that initiates the transaction tends to set the cap strike at the desired level and then the dealer finds the appropriate floor strike. With equity collars, the party that initiates the transaction tends to set the floor strike at the desired level and then the dealer finds the appropriate cap strike.

10.6　Swaptions

To this point in the book, we have covered only one derivative at a time. In this section we merge some of the features of two different types of derivatives, swaps and options. But first let us recall that we described a derivative as having an underlying. We used that word *underlying* as a noun, because we did not want to have to say that a derivative is based on an underlying asset. The underlying need not be an asset. For a swaption, the underlying is another derivative.

10.6.1 *Basic Principles of Swaptions*

A *swaption* is simply an option on a swap. The word "swaption" certainly did not exist in the English language until this instrument was created. In fact, the word "swaption" is a merger of the words *swap* and *option*. The instrument was at one time referred to as a *swap option*, but that term was then shortened to just *swaption*.[12]

A swaption is an option to enter into a swap as either a fixed-rate payer or a fixed-rate receiver. A swaption to enter as a fixed-rate payer, and thereby a floating-rate receiver, is called a *payer swaption*. For reasons that will be demonstrated later, it is also referred to as a *put swaption*. An option to enter a swap as a fixed-rate receiver, and thereby a floating-rate payer, is called a *receiver swaption* and occasionally a *call swaption*. The underlying in a swaption is technically a swap, but more precisely, it is the fixed rate on a swap. Recall in Chapter 9 that we devoted a great deal of effort to learning how to determine the fixed rate on a swap. In actual markets, this rate might be observed on a terminal linked to the trading desks of various institutions, though that rate would still have to be found using the arbitrage-free methods we illustrated in Chapter 9. When a swaption expires, the holder observes this fixed rate on the underlying swap and decides whether to exercise the swaption.

Recall that in Chapter 9, the fixed rate on a swap of maturity T_m was denoted as $FS(0, T_m)$. As noted, this rate is determined by a formula that we covered in that chapter that takes into account the term structure. A payer swaption will be exercised when the swap rate in the market is above the strike rate. A receiver swaption will be exercised when the swap rate in the market is below the strike rate. Let us verify these two critical facts.

Suppose we enter into a European payer swaption with a strike rate of X. The swaption contract will specify the characteristics of the underlying swap, with all the necessary details such as the swap expiration, the underlying rate, and the settlement dates on which the swap payments will be made. At expiration, the swaption allows the holder to enter into the underlying swap as a fixed-rate payer at a rate of X. Note here that we will use day 0 as the expiration of the swaption and day T_m as the maturity date of the underlying swap. So let us assume that at expiration, the fixed rate on the underlying swap is $FS(0, T_m)$. For the case of $FS(0, T_m) > X$, consider the choice: we can enter into a swap to pay a fixed rate of X when the market fixed rate is

---

[12]Somewhat rarely there have been options on FRAs, which are known as fraptions.

$FS(0, T_m)$, or we can let the swaption expire. Using your intuition, it should sound like exercising the swaption is a good decision. If we can enter a swap to pay X when the market rate for that swap is higher, should we not prefer to enter into the swap by exercising the swaption than by engaging in the swap at the market rate? But what is the value of the swaption at the point of expiration? There is an easy way to obtain this answer.

Suppose we exercise the swaption, thereby entering into the swap to pay fixed and receive floating, and then we simultaneously enter into a swap at the market rate of $FS(0, T_m)$ to pay floating and receive fixed. Let us ignore the day count adjustment and the notional. Exhibit 10-21 illustrates the cash flows from combining a swap obtained from exercising a payer swaption with the same swap obtained at the market rate. The series of LIBORs on the various dates are denoted as $L_0, L_1, \ldots, L_{m-1}$.

Note that on each payment date the payments we receive will be

L_0, L_1, etc. $-X$, on the swap obtained by exercising the swaption

$FS(0, T_m) - L_0, L_1$, etc., on the swap created at the market rate

The net payment is $FS(0, T_m) - X$, which is a fixed amount. Thus, on each payment date, we will receive $FS(0, T_m) - X$ times the day count adjustment $(h/360)$ times the notional. In short, exercise of the swaption creates an annuity with payments on the swap payment dates.[13] Of course, if $FS(0, T_m) < X$, we would simply let the swaption expire. If we wanted to

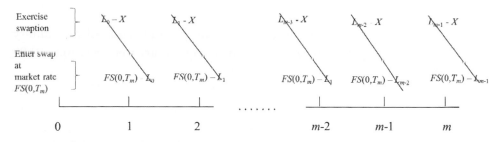

Exhibit 10-21. Cash Flows from Exercise of Payer Swaption plus Entering into a Swap at the Market Rate

---

[13]Recall that one of the most basic financial concepts is that of an annuity — a series of equal payments at specified times. Because X is stated in the swaption contract, and the market rate $FS(0, T_m)$ is determined on the swaption expiring date, exercise of the swaption and creation of the opposite creates a series of known payments.

enter into a swap to pay a fixed rate, it would be cheaper to enter into the swap at the market rate, which is lower than the swaption strike.

Let us denote $VPSW_{T_m}(T_m, h)$ as the value of the payer swaption at expiration when the day count between payment dates is h. We have

$$VPSW_{T_m}(T_m, h) = Max\left(0, (FS(0, T_m) - X)\right)\left(\frac{h}{360}\right)\sum_{t=1}^{m} PVF(0, T_t)$$

(10.43)

The expression $PVF(0, T_t)$ is simply the present value factor that discounts an amount at time T_t back to the present based on rates that comprise the term structure. The above expression is simply the present value of an annuity of either $FS(0, T_m) - X$ or 0, which is greater, based on notional of 1 and adjusted for the day count of h days. Exhibit 10-22 illustrates a payoff calculation for a swaption.

A receiver swaption would work just the opposite. It is an option to enter into a swap to receive fixed and pay floating. It would be exercised when the market swap rate, $FS(0, T_m)$, is below the swaption rate, X. If exercised, the holder would enter into a swap to receive X and pay L. The holder could then enter into the opposite swap in the market to pay $FS(0, T_m)$ and receive L. The floating payments would offset, leaving an annuity of $X - FS(0, T_m)$. Thus, the value of the receiver swaption at expiration would be

$$VRSW_{T_m}(T_m, h) = Max\left(0, (X - FS(0, T_m))\right)\left(\frac{h}{360}\right)\sum_{t=1}^{m} PVF(0, T_t)$$

(10.44)

And again, the above expression is simply the present value of an annuity of $(X - FS(0, T_m))(h/360)$ or zero, whichever is greater. Exhibit 10-23 illustrates the payoff of a receiver swaption.

For the payer swaption, the condition that $FS(0, T_m) > X$ is when the swaption is said to be in-the-money and, as with other options at expiration, it would be exercised. Otherwise, it is out-of-the-money and not exercised. Likewise, for a receiver options, the condition that $X > FS(0, T_m)$ is in-the-money, so the swaption would be exercised. Otherwise, the condition is out-of-the-money, and the swaption would not be exercised. Of course, these are the conditions at expiration. Some swaptions might even be American-style and would permit exercise prior to expiration.

In the development of the previous two equations for the values of payer and receiver swaptions at expiration, we stated that the holder of the

Objective: Find the payoff of an expiring payer swaption on $28 million notional with an exercise rate of 5.5% in which the underlying is a two-year swap with semiannual payments in 180, 360, 540, and 720 days. The term structure at expiration is the following:

180 days	5.6%
360 days	5.8%
540 days	5.9%
720 days	5.95%

Inputs: If the swaption is expiring and the term structure is given as above, we need to determine the fixed rate on the underlying swap. Let us first find the present value factors from the term structure:

$$PVF(0, 180) = \frac{1}{1 + 0.056\left(\frac{180}{360}\right)} = 0.9728$$

$$PVF(0, 360) = \frac{1}{1 + 0.058\left(\frac{360}{360}\right)} = 0.9452$$

$$PVF(0, 270) = \frac{1}{1 + 0.059\left(\frac{540}{360}\right)} = 0.9187$$

$$PVF(0, 360) = \frac{1}{1 + 0.0595\left(\frac{720}{360}\right)} = 0.8937$$

Results:

The swap rate is, thus,

$$FS(0, T_m) = \left(\frac{1 - PVF(0, T_m)}{\sum_{t=1}^{m} PVF(0, T_t)}\right)\left(\frac{360}{h}\right)$$

$$= \left(\frac{1 - 0.8937}{0.9728 + 0.9452 + 0.9187 + 0.8937}\right)\left(\frac{360}{180}\right) = 0.0570.$$

With an exercise rate of 5.5%, this swaption is obviously worth exercising. Its value is

$$VPSW_{T_m}(T_m, h) = Max\left(0, (0.0570 - 0.055)\right)\left(\frac{180}{360}\right)(0.9728 + 0.9452 + 0.9187 + 0.8937)$$

$$= 0.0037$$

In other words, exercising the swaption enables the holder to enter into a swap to pay a fixed rate of 5.5%. The market fixed rate is 5.7%. This difference, 0.2%, has the value of an annuity of four payments of half that amount (i.e., times $(180/360)$). The present value of these four payments is 0.0037 per $1 notional. For a notional of $28 million, the total value is $105,333.

Exhibit 10-22. Calculation of the Payoff of a Payer Swaption

Objective: Using the same data in Exhibit 10-22, find the payoff of an expiring receiver swaption with an exercise rate of 6% in which the underlying is a two-year swap with semiannual payments in 180, 360, 540, and 720 days. Again, the notional is $28 million.

Inputs: We know the present value factors from Exhibit 10-22, and we know that the fixed rate on a swap at this time with the above term structure is 5.7%.

Results:

With an exercise rate of 6%, this swaption is obviously worth exercising. Its value is

$$VRSW_{T_m}(T_m, h) = Max\left(0, (0.06 - 0.057)\right)\left(\frac{180}{360}\right)(0.9728 + 0.9452 + 0.9187 + 0.8937)$$

$$= 0.0056$$

In other words, exercising the swaption enables the holder to enter into a swap to receive a fixed rate of 6%. The market fixed rate is 5.7%. This difference, 0.3%, has the value of an annuity of four payments of half that amount (i.e., times (180/360)). The present value of these four payments is 0.0056 per $1 notional. For notional of $28 million, the payoff is $105,787.

Exhibit 10-23. Calculation of the Payoff of a Receiver Swaption

swaption would exercise if the swaption were in-the-money at expiration. We also said that the holder would enter into an offsetting swaption. Well, in fact, the holder does not have to enter into an offsetting swaption. We made that assumption here to facilitate valuation. If the swaption contract prescribes physical settlement, the holder would enter into the swaption upon exercise, but he does not have to offset the swaption. He can simply maintain the position in the swap obtained upon exercise. The assumption of entering into an offsetting swaption is not necessary but is a simple means of obtaining the value of the swaption at expiration.[14] The swaption contract can also specify cash settlement, meaning that upon exercise, the seller of the swaption simply pays the buyer the cash value as given by Equation (10.43) for payer swaptions or (10.44) for receiver swaptions.

---

[14]There is a very simple analogy using options on stocks. Say you own a call option with an exercise price of €60. At expiration the underlying stock is selling for €63. You can exercise and sell the stock, thereby capturing €3. Or, you can exercise and hold on to the stock, also realizing a gain of €3 but of course that gain is now at risk. Entering into an offsetting swap is like cashing out your gain in the same manner as exercising an option on a stock and selling the stock.

10.6.2 *Valuation of Swaptions*

Determining an appropriate price for a swaption is a somewhat advanced topic, and we will cover it only lightly here. Sometimes the Black model is used, whereupon the forward price that goes into the Black model is the fixed rate on the swap. The model provides a rough estimate, but the assumptions of the Black model deviate rather significantly from those that characterize the underlying swap.

An alternative approach is to view a swaption as an option on a bond. In fact, this approach will be quite useful in better understanding what a swaption is. Recall that Equation (10.43) gives the payoff of a payer swaption. Now, let us consider a bond that has coupon payment dates at the same time as the swaption and that the bond coupon rate is the exercise rate on the swaption. When interest is paid, the coupon rate is multiplied by the bond principal and also by the time adjustment factor, $h/360$. We will continue to assume $1 notional on the swap, and we will set the bond principal at $1. Now consider a put option on the bond with an exercise price of $1. The value of the bond at expiration of the swaption is

$$PVF(0, T_m) + X\left(\frac{h}{360}\right)\sum_{t=1}^{T_m} PVF(0, t))$$

Notice the components of this expression. $PVF(0, T_m)$ is the present value factor for the repayment of principal of $1 at time T_m. The remaining terms represent the present value of the coupons. The payoff at expiration of a put option on this bond is, therefore,

$$Max\left(0, \left(1 - \left(PVF(0, T_m) + X\left(\frac{h}{360}\right)\sum_{t=1}^{T_m} PVF(0, t)\right)\right)\right).$$

This expression follows the standard format for a put option that we covered early in the chapter: Max(0,exercise price − price of the underlying). Here the exercise price is 1, from which we subtract the price of the underlying. The resulting difference, if positive, gives the value of the swaption. Otherwise, the value is zero. Now remember that the formula for the fixed rate on the swap at expiration of the swaption is

$$FS(0, T_m) = \left(\frac{1 - PVF(0, T_m)}{\sum_{t=1}^{m} PVF(0, T_t)}\right)\left(\frac{360}{h}\right)$$

If we substitute this result into Equation (10.43), the formula for the value of a payer swaption at expiration, and do some algebraic rearrangements, we will get the formula above for the payoff of a put option on a bond. A similar procedure can be followed to demonstrate that a receiver swaption is equivalent to a call option on a bond.

Since payer swaptions are the same as put options on bonds and receiver swaptions are the same as call options on bonds, we could price them as though they were options on bonds. We would simply need to make the settlement dates on the underlying swaps line up with the coupon payment dates on the bonds, the coupon rate on the bond be the exercise rate on the swaption, the bond have a face value of $1, and the exercise price on the bond be $1. We did not spend much time talking about bond options in this chapter. They are a relatively advanced topic, owing as they do to some complexities caused by the fact that interest rates have certain characteristics that have to be modeled carefully and bond prices are required to converge to their par values at maturity. So we will not address those details at this introductory level.

10.6.3 *Use of Swaptions*

To understand how swaptions are used, it is first necessary to recall why swaps are used. We will focus on interest rate swaptions, as these are the most widely used of all swaptions, not surprisingly because interest rate swaps are the most widely used of all swaps. Recall that interest rate swaps are most often used to convert floating-rate loans to fixed-rate loans. When a borrower engages in a floating-rate loan, it often simultaneously enters into an interest rate swap to pay fixed and receive floating. The floating receipt on the swap balances the floating payment on the loan, leaving the borrower making a fixed payment on the swap.

As you have learned, a swaption is an option to enter into a swap. There are two common situations in which a party might wish to buy a swaption. One is in anticipation of taking out a floating-rate loan at a later date. The rate on the loan will be established at that later date, so the borrower assumes the risk of an increase in interest rates between now and when the loan is take out. By purchasing a payer swaption that expires on the day the loan begins, the borrower has the right to enter into a pay-fixed swap at that time. When that time arrives, the loan is started and the borrower exercises the swaption if the market fixed rate on that swap is above the swaption strike. Exercise of the swaption creates a pay-fixed swap that effectively converts the floating-rate loan into a fixed-rate loan. If the market fixed rate on the swaption expiration day is below the swaption strike, the borrower simply allows the swaption to expire unexercised, and he engages in a swap at the market fixed rate, which is more attractive. In order to create this possibility, the borrower has to pay cash up front to the seller of the swaption.

Another situation in which a borrower might wish to own a swaption is to have the right to convert the loan from floating to fixed at a favorable rate. For example, suppose at the time the loan is initiated, the borrower likes the current floating rate. Nonetheless, the borrower believes that at some later time, he may wish to convert the loan from floating to fixed. By purchasing a payer swaption that expires during the life of the loan, the borrower has the option to exercise the swaption and convert the floating-rate loan to a fixed-rate loan. This type of swaption would probably be American-style, as this type of swap would give the borrower the flexibility to exercise at a time it deems it most favorable. As long as interest rates remain low, the floating rate will remain low and the borrower will not likely want to exercise the swaption. If interest rates begin to rise, the borrower may decide he wishes to convert the loan to a fixed-rate loan. He can do so by taking the fixed rate on new swaps in the market. But if he owns a swaption, he can take a specified fixed rate. Thus, if the market fixed rate is higher than the swaption strike rate, he will exercise the swaption. He will then be paying a floating rate on the loan but receiving the same rate on the swap and paying the fixed rate established by the swap strike.

Suppose a borrower with a floating-rate loan has effectively converted the loan into a fixed-rate loan by engaging in a pay-fixed swap. Now, assume that at some point in the life of the loan, interest rates start to fall and the borrower believes that they will continue to fall. In that case, the borrower might wish to convert back to a floating-rate loan. If the borrower owns a receiver swaption, it can use it to convert the loan back to a floating rate at an established fixed rate. If the market fixed rate is lower than the swaption strike, the borrower would exercise the swaption, thereby establishing a new swap to receive fixed and pay floating. If the market fixed rate is higher than the swaption strike, the borrower would not exercise the swaption but would create a new swap at the more attractive market rate.

Thus, swaptions are useful to enter and exit swaps at attractive rates. Payer swaptions, like put option on bonds, pay off when interest rates increase, and thus, are useful in situations when interest rate increases will hurt a party. Receiver swaptions, like call options on bonds, pay off when interest rates decrease and, thus, are useful in situations when interest rate decreases will hurt a party.

10.7   Measuring and Controlling Option Risk

We have seen that options are valuable risk management tools for end users. They can be used to offset undesirable risks in hedging. But risk does not simply go away. Options transfer risks from one party to another. Thus, if hedgers use options to transfer risks, their counterparties must be taking on those risks. Those counterparties are usually the dealers, and they must find ways of transferring the risks to speculators.

Because options are clearly risky instruments, it is important to understand the nature of the risks they create, so that these risks can be used to set the overall risk of the entity to the proper level. In contrast to forwards, futures, and swaps that pay off linearly with respect to the underlying, options have non-linear payoffs that create risks that are a bit more complex to manage.

10.7.1   *The Greeks*

There are several key measures of option risk. These measures have been given Greek names, the primary ones of which are delta, gamma, and vega.[15]

10.7.1.1   *Delta*

Delta is the measure of an option's sensitivity to a change in the value of the underlying. Specifically,

$$\text{Delta} = \frac{\text{Change in value of option}}{\text{Change in value of underlying}}$$

But to quantify delta, we need to use an option pricing model. Given such a model, we obtain a formula for the value of the option in terms of the factors that affect the value of the option. We know that the value of the underlying is a critical factor. Delta quantifies how critical it is.

In Section 10.4, we covered valuation models that are typically used with options on assets. The first model we covered was the binomial model. Extracting the delta and other risk measures from a binomial tree is a somewhat more advanced topic that we will not cover in this book. The Black-Scholes-Merton (BSM) model is the other model we covered in Section 10.4. As explained in that section, the BSM model is used under the assumption of continuous time.

---

[15] As we shall see later, vega is not really a Greek name, but in the world of options, it has been unofficially inducted into the world of Greek names.

We gave the formula for the BSM model as Equation (10.41). It is repeated here with the notation slightly simplified in that we drop the time subscriptions and the X and T arguments in parentheses of c and p,

$$c = SN(d_1) - Xe^{-r_cT}N(d_2)$$

$$p = Xe^{-r_cT}N(-d_2) - SN(d_1)$$

$$d_1 = \frac{\ln(S/X) + (r_c + \sigma^2/2)T}{\sigma\sqrt{T}}$$

$$d_2 = d_1 - \sigma\sqrt{T}.$$

What we want to know is how a change in S affects the values of the call and put, c and p. We can use calculus to arrive at an approximation of that answer. We differentiate the BSM formulas for the call and put value with respect to S. The actual mathematical steps are somewhat complex, involving a lot of clever substitutions, but the end result is simple:

$$\text{Delta of call: } \Delta_c = \frac{\partial c}{\partial S} = N(d_1)$$

$$\text{Delta of put: } \Delta_p = \frac{\partial p}{\partial S} = N(d_1) - 1 = -N(-d_1)$$

$$(10.45)$$

So, perhaps interestingly, the normal probability measure, $N(d_1)$, is the measure of delta for a call and its counterpart, $1 - N(-d_1)$ or $-N(-d_1)$, is the delta measure for a put.

Exhibit 10-24 shows the relationship between delta and the value of the underlying. This example is an at-the-money call option in which the underlying is 50, the exercise price is 50, the risk-free rate is 2.5%, the time to expiration is 0.5, and the volatility is 0.45.

Note that because it is a probability number, delta is between 0 and 1. When the underlying is low relative to the exercise price, the delta is nearly zero. When the underlying is high relative to the exercise price, delta is close to 1. It has become a good general rule of thumb that an at-the-money option has a delta of 0.5.

Note that the delta of a put is expressed as $N(-d_1)$. Thinking about the normal curve, $N(d_1)$ is the area to the left of the point d_1. If we change the sign of d_1, we flip it to the opposite side of the origin, 0, and need the area to the left. Hence, $N(-d_1)$ is also $1 - N(d_1)$. Exhibit 10-25 shows the delta of a put plotted against the value of the underlying. The delta of a put is between 0 and -1. When the underlying is extremely high relative to the

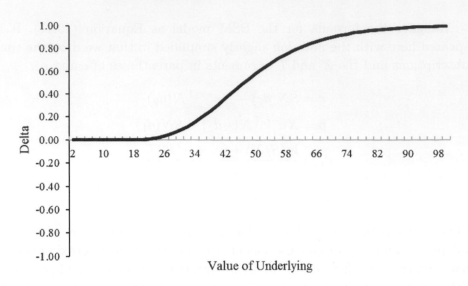

Exhibit 10-24.   Relationship between the Delta of a Call and the Value of the Underlying

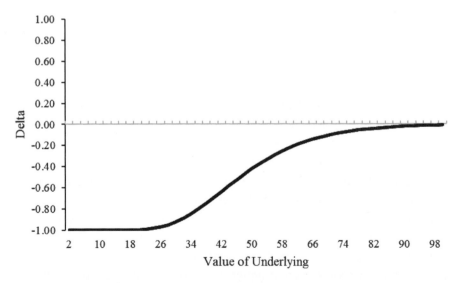

Exhibit 10-25.   Relationship between the Delta of a Put and the Value of the Underlying

exercise price, the put delta is close to 0. When the underlying is very low relative to the exercise price, the put delta is close to −1.

Deltas behave in a manner reflecting the likelihood of the option being exercised. For example, as shown above, a deep in-the-money call has a delta close to 1 while a deep in-the-money put has a delta close to −1. Deep in-the-money options generally have a high probability of being exercised. If a call is exercised, the holder will obtain the underlying, which has a delta of 1, meaning that it moves one-for-one with itself. If a put is exercised, the holder who does not own the underlying acquires a short position in it, which has a delta of −1, meaning that the position moves one-for-one opposite itself. Deep out-of-the-money options have a low likelihood of being exercised. Thus, if they expire unexercised they will have zero value and hence, a delta of zero, as shown in the above two graphs.

The above comments were made conditional only on the moneyness of the option. Time to expiration can also affect the likelihood of being exercised. Exhibit 10-26 shows the effect of time to expiration and moneyness on the delta of a call with an exercise price of 50 and an initial time to expiration of 0.5, or one-half year. The graph reads from left to right and shows three lines, one representing an option with the underlying at 60, one with the underlying at 50, and one with the underlying at 40. When the underlying is 40, the option is fairly deep out-of-the-money, and with a time to expiration of 0.5, the delta starts at 0.3075. By holding the underlying at 40 and with a shorter time to expiration, the delta progressively falls toward zero. When the underlying is at 60, the delta is 0.7798 when the time to expiration is at

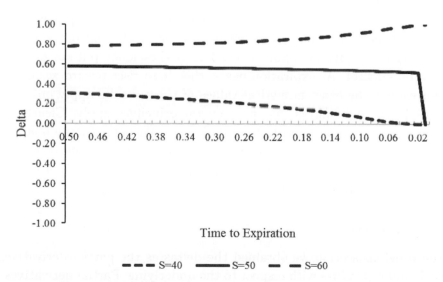

Exhibit 10-26. Relationship between the Delta of a Call, Value of the Underlying, and Time to Expiration

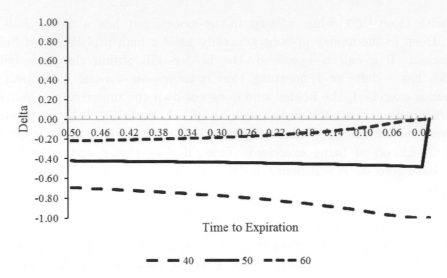

Exhibit 10-27. Relationship between the Delta of a Put, Value of the Underlying, and Time to Expiration

0.5. As time to expiration moves toward zero, the delta rises to 1.0. For the at-the-money call, in which the underlying is at 50, the delta starts off at 0.5786, but then falls toward zero. Indeed, an expiring at-the-money option has a delta of zero.

Exhibit 10-27 illustrates the same effect for a put. The in-the-money put starts off with a delta of −0.6925, which falls toward −1 as expiration nears. The out-of-the-money put starts off with a delta of −0.2202, which rises toward zero as expiration approaches. The at-the-money put starts off with a delta of −0.4214. As expiration nears, this delta rises toward zero.

Of course, the exact numerical values of these results apply only to the options in these examples, but the general principles apply. Clearly delta changes with moneyness and time to expiration. We cannot truly hold either constant, particularly time. In the next section, we look at a measure of how delta changes with the underlying. It turns out that there is more to what is going on than meets the eye.

10.7.1.2 *Gamma*

In the previous section we obtained the deltas as the partial derivatives of the call and put values with respect to the underlying. Partial derivatives, by definition, are based on the assumption that the underlying changes by a very small, i.e., infinitesimal, amount. But the price of the underlying may not change by such a small amount. Indeed, over a finite period of time, the price of the underlying will surely change by a finite amount. In mathematics, this concern arises when trying to estimate the value of a function when there is a finite change in the independent variable. The effect is estimated by using the second derivative. For options, the second derivative of the option value is a measure called the gamma.[16]

$$\text{Gamma of call: } \Gamma_c = \frac{\partial}{\partial S}\left(\frac{\partial c}{\partial S}\right) = \frac{\partial}{\partial S}\left(N(d_1)\right) = \frac{e^{-d_1^2/2}}{S\sigma\sqrt{2\pi T}}$$

$$\text{Gamma of put: } \Gamma_p = \frac{\partial}{\partial S}\left(\frac{\partial p}{\partial S}\right) = \frac{\partial}{\partial S}\left(N(-d_1)\right) = \frac{e^{-d_1^2/2}}{S\sigma\sqrt{2\pi T}}$$

$$(10.46)$$

Notice first that the call gamma and the put gamma are the same. Notice second that the denominator contains the expression, $\sqrt{2\pi T}$. Seeing the square root of T, the time to expiration, should not seem unusual, but it might strike you as a bit off that the square root of 2 times pi is in the formula. Well, without getting into the mathematical details, the formula that graphs the normal distribution for a variable d_1 incorporates the value of 2 times pi. In fact, the formula is almost exactly the one in Equation (10.46), as shown in Exhibit 10-28, which shows the relationship between the gamma of a call or put and the value of the underlying. Notice how the curve looks somewhat like the normal probability curve. In fact, the expression inside the formula, $\frac{e^{-d_1^2/2}}{\sqrt{2\pi}}$, *is* the normal curve. Thus, the graph for gamma is the normal curve times $\frac{1}{S\sigma\sqrt{T}}$. Clearly the gamma is largest when the underlying is in the middle range, and it is nearly zero for very large and very small values of the underlying. As a general rule, the gamma will be large when there is the greatest uncertainty about whether the option will expire in- or out-of-the-money.

Exhibit 10-29 shows the gamma for three options, one in-the-money, one at-the-money, and one out-of-the-money, as indicated by prices of the underlying of 60, 50, and 40, respectively. These gammas are illustrated as

---

[16]There is a great deal of math involved in taking that second derivative and simplifying it to the form above. Do not worry about these details.

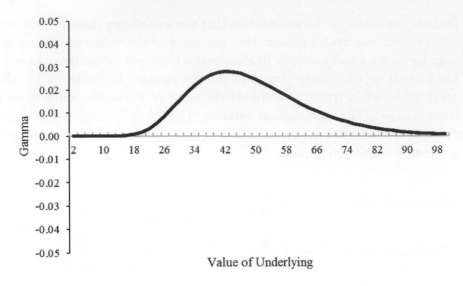

Exhibit 10-28. Gamma of a Call or a Put and the Value of the Underlying

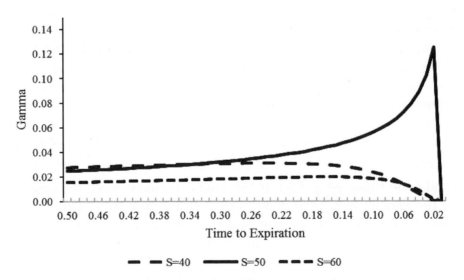

Exhibit 10-29. Gamma or a Call or Put by Moneyness and Time to Expiration

the option moves from a remaining life of 0.5 years to its expiration. Notice how at expiration, the far right point, the gammas all go to zero. Expiration represents the complete resolution of uncertainty. Note how the at-the-money option, the solid line representing an underlying price of 50, rises sharply as expiration approaches. For the at-the-money option, the uncertainty is greatest about whether it will expire in- or out-of-the-money. As expiration approaches, the uncertainty increases. Just before expiration, the gamma increases greatly. Then at expiration the gamma goes to zero. Remembering that gamma is the change in delta for a change in the underlying, we see that the delta becomes potentially quite unstable as expiration approaches for at-the-money options. As we shall see later, this instability causes problems when attempting to hedge positions in options. In short, gamma reflects the change in the value of the option that can arise from large changes in the value of the underlying.

10.7.1.3 *Vega*

We mentioned earlier that the value of an option is directly related to the volatility. The strength of this relationship is often measured by a concept known as vega. First, recall that the name of this section of the chapter is The Greeks. As it turns out, vega is not a Greek word. Vega is actually the name of one of the brightest stars in the sky.[17] Nonetheless, it has been adopted by the option community to represent the partial derivative of the option value with respect to the volatility and as such, it is commonly included as "one of the Greeks." The vegas of calls and puts are the same and are given as[18]

$$\text{Vega of call: } \frac{\partial c}{\partial \sigma} = \frac{S\sqrt{T}e^{-d_1^2/2}}{\sqrt{2\pi}}$$

$$\text{Vega of put: } \frac{\partial p}{\partial \sigma} = \frac{S\sqrt{T}e^{-d_1^2/2}}{\sqrt{2\pi}}$$

$$(10.47)$$

The relationship between vega and the value of the underlying is shown Exhibit 10-30. Note that as with gamma, the vega looks a bit like the normal curve, and indeed, examining Equation (10.47) shows that the formula is the same as that of the normal curve, simply multiplied by $S\sqrt{T}$. Note that vega is highest when the option is approximately at-the-money and nearly zero when deep in- or out-of-the-money.

---

[17]Vega is also a common Spanish surname, and it was also the name of a Chevrolet that was on the market from 1970–1977.

[18]There is no symbol for vega, since, as we noted, it is not a Greek letter. So we will just write out the word.

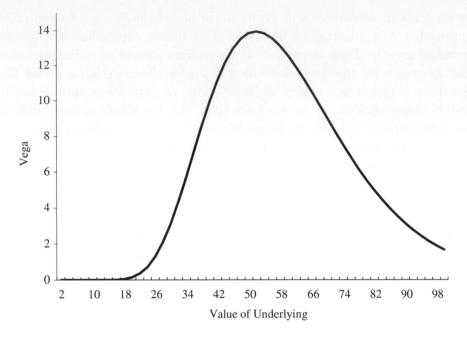

Exhibit 10-30. Vega and the Value of the Underlying

We will not show a graph of the relationship between vega and time to expiration, as it is easy to explain and is approximately the same regardless of moneyness. Vega declines toward zero as expiration approaches.

Vega and the Black-Scholes-Merton Model: Not Quite What it Seems

The value of an option as determined by the Black-Scholes-Merton model (BSM) clearly is a function of the volatility of the underlying. In fact, volatility is a major factor in determining option values, and it is the only value that goes into the model that is not clearly observable in the market. Different investors will have different opinions of its value, which makes for interesting trading possibilities.

Even though we calculate the vega and use it as a measure of how much the option value will change if volatility changes, technically the BSM model does not permit volatility to change. When using vega in this manner, we are violating an assumption of the model.

Here is an analogy. The famous Einstein equation $E = mc^2$ relates energy (E) as a product of the mass (m) and the square of the speed of light (c). We could differentiate this function with respect to c and obtain, $\partial E/\partial c = 2mc$, suggesting that an infinitesimally small change in the speed of light would produce a change in the energy of twice the product of the mass and the speed of light. But the speed of light is a universal constant of 299,792,458 meters per second. It does not vary, at least not in this universe. Thus, the partial derivative is meaningful only if we admit something that cannot happen.

When using the BSM we assume that the volatility cannot change, even though it really can. In a similar manner to the speed of light issue, we are corrupting the model. While the speed of light cannot change, we allow that possibility by taking the derivative with respect to c. While the volatility can change, the model assumes that it does not, and yet we allow that possibility by taking the derivative with respect to σ.

The problem is also analogous to assuming that one unit of currency invested at a rate r per year for T years will grow to $(1 + r)^T$ after T years. We would be assuming that r does not change.

And yet, this is what the options industry does. While there are models that incorporate changing volatility, they are so much more complex that we simply tend to use the vega from BSM. BSM is clearly not a perfect model, but it is a pretty widely used one, if not a pretty good one, provided its limitations are understood.

10.7.1.4 *Other Greeks*

Option prices are also related to the time to expiration. This effect is measured by the derivative of the option price with respect to the time to expiration, which is known by the Greek letter, *theta*. Option prices are characterized by the principle of time value decay, meaning that they lose value as they approach expiration. At expiration, the only remaining value is the exercise value. While an understanding of theta is important in trading options, we are studying these risk measures to understand how options react to factors that are uncertain, such as the price and volatility of the underlying. Time is not a factor of uncertainty. For example, an option that has 30 days until maturity as of today will become an option that has 29 days until maturity tomorrow. There is no doubt of this fact.

There is also another Greek measure known as *rho*, which reflects the sensitivity of an option price to the risk-free rate of interest. As noted earlier in this chapter, the effect of interest rates is quite small, so we will omit coverage here.

10.7.2 *Managing Option Risk*

Recall that derivatives dealers take positions in options to meet the needs of their clients. In doing so, they assume the risk transferred from their clients. These measures known as delta, gamma, and vega constitute the tools that they use in managing the risk that they assume. Let us take a look at how they do it. We will first look at the practice of delta hedging.

10.7.2.1 *Delta Hedging*

Suppose a dealer sells a call option to a client. The dealer now has an exposed position in the option. If the underlying goes up, the call value increases and the dealer incurs a loss. An unhedged position in a call exposes the dealer to unlimited loss, given that there is no upper limit on the value of the underlying. The dealer ordinarily protects itself by engaging in delta hedging.

Recall that the deltas of calls and puts were given in Equation (10.45). The call delta was denoted as Δ_c and it represents the change in the call value for a change in the value of the underlying. Let us assume the dealer sells one call option. Now let the underlying change by ΔS. Given the delta of the option, it would be expected to change by ΔS times Δ_c. Therefore, if we take a position in ω units of the underlying, with ω defined as the value of Δ_c, the effects will offset as shown below:

$$\omega(\Delta S) + (-1)(\Delta S)(\Delta_c) = 0$$

Thus, holding ω units of the asset where ω is the call delta will offset.[19]

Consider a call option in which the underlying is at 100, the exercise price is 100, the risk-free rate is 2%, the volatility is 0.35, and the option expires in 90 days. Thus, the time to expiration is $90/365 = 0.2466$. Plugging these values into the BSM model produces a call option value of 7.16 and a delta of 0.5459. To hedge a short position in one unit of the call, we would purchase $\omega = 0.5459$ units of the asset. The net value of this combination is

$$0.5459(100) - 7.16 = 47.43$$

Let us assume the underlying instantaneously increases from 100 to 101. Inserting the inputs into the BSM model with a new value of the underlying

---

[19]In other words, solving this equation for ω leads to $\omega = \Delta_c$.

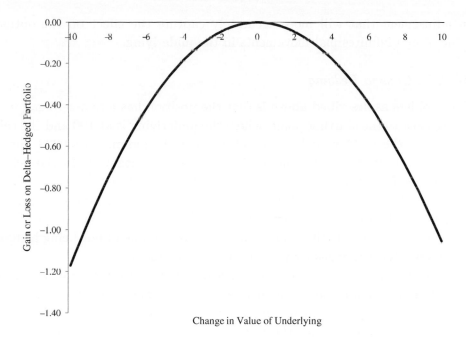

Exhibit 10-31. Changes in Value of Delta-Hedged Portfolio

of 101, we would obtain a new value of the call of 7.71. The new value of the delta hedged portfolio would now be

$$0.5459(101) - 7.71 = 47.42$$

The portfolio value is virtually unchanged. In Exhibit 10-31, we show the change in the value of this portfolio for a range of changes in the value of the underlying from -10 to $+10$.

For very small changes in the underlying the change in the value of the delta-hedged portfolio is nearly zero. But for larger changes, the delta-hedged portfolio is, well, not very hedged. For example, suppose we let the underlying go from 100 to 110. The option would change in value to 13.67, and the portfolio value would change to 46.38, a change of -1.05. The reason for this result is quite simple. Recall that the delta is the partial derivative of the value of the option with respect to the value of the underlying. A partial derivative is the slope of a tangent line, representing the change in the dependent variable for a very small — infinitesimal — change in the independent variable. Any change in the underlying that is more than infinitesimal will impart a change in the option that is not correct reflected in the delta. This problem leads us to the possibility of using gamma to make an adjustment that will more accurately capture the effect on the option value of non-infinitesimal movements in the underlying.

10.7.2.2 *Gamma Hedging*

The problem as described above is that the position has a non-zero gamma. Going back to the starting point, where the underlying is at 100 and the call is at 7.16, the BSM model would tell us that the gamma is 0.0228. Since we are short the call, the gamma of the position is negative. In the delta-hedged portfolio, we are long the underlying, but it has zero gamma. Thus, the call position and the underlying position combine to produce a negative net gamma. This negative gamma is what produces the concave shape of the curve in the above exhibit. And it exposes us to the risk of not being hedged if the underlying changes by more than a small amount.

In order to nudge this overall negative gamma to zero, we will have to add another instrument that has non-zero gamma. Thus, we shall need to add another option. To distinguish the original option from this newly added option, we shall call the original option "option 1" and this newly added option "option 2." We denote their values as c_1, c_2, their deltas as Δ_1, Δ_2, and their gammas as Γ_1, Γ_2. To distinguish the number of units of each, we will use ω_u for units of the underlying, and ω_1 and ω_2 for units of the original and the added option. But since we already said that we sold one unit of the original option, $\omega_1 = -1$, and we will actually not need the ω_1 symbol.

Now we need to know how many units of the second option to add. If we just set the overall gamma to zero, we may have a non-zero delta, so we need to jointly set the overall delta and gamma to zero. We do this by specifying the following equations:

$$\omega_u(1) - \Delta_1 + \omega_2\Delta_2 = 0 \text{ (set overall delta to zero)}$$

$$-\Gamma_1 + \omega_2\Gamma_2 = 0 \text{ (set overall gamma to zero)}$$

In the first equation the number of units of the underlying, ω_u, is multiplied by its delta of 1. The number of units of the first option is -1, which is multiplied by its delta, Δ_1. Then the number of units of the second option, ω_2, is multiplied by its delta Δ_2. The sum of these expressions is set to zero, thereby setting the portfolio delta to zero.

In the second equation, we have no terms for the underlying, as its gamma is zero. Then the number of units of the first option, -1, is multiplied by its gamma, Γ_1, and the number of units of the second option is multiplied by its gamma, Γ_2. The sum of these expressions is set to zero, thereby setting the portfolio gamma to zero. These two equations represent a system of two equations with two unknowns. Two equations and two unknowns means that they are solvable.[20] The simple approach is to noted that the second equation can be solved for ω_2:

$$\omega_2 = \frac{\Gamma_1}{\Gamma_2}.$$

This result can be substituted into the first equation to obtain its solution,

$$\omega_u = \Delta_1 - \left(\frac{\Gamma_1}{\Gamma_2}\right)\Delta_2$$

By holding these quantities of the underlying and the second option, we reduce some of the gamma risk.

So let us create another option on the same underlying, which would obviously have the same volatility. This option has to be different from the original option in some way. We shall make it have the same exercise price, 100, but an expiration of 30 days for a time to expiration of $30/365 = 0.0822$. Plugging the inputs into the BSM model gives a call price of 4.08, a delta of 0.5265, and a gamma of 0.0397. Recall that for the first option, the price is 7.16, the delta is 0.5459, and the gamma is 0.0228. Thus, the number of units of the second option and the underlying should be

$$\omega_2 = \frac{\Gamma_1}{\Gamma_2} = \frac{0.0228}{0.0397} = 0.5748$$

$$\omega_u = \Delta_1 - \left(\frac{\Gamma_1}{\Gamma_2}\right)\Delta_2 = 0.5459 - 0.5748(0.5265) = 0.2432$$

The value of the portfolio is, therefore,

$$0.2432(100) - 7.16 + 0.5748(4.08) = 19.5128$$

Now, as we did with the delta-hedged portfolio, let us assume a change in the underlying from 100 to 110. The original option, option 1, changed to a value of 7.71. We found that the delta-hedged portfolio dropped by 1.05.

---

[20] Do not go thinking that all systems of two equations and two unknowns have solutions. If the equations are linearly related to each other, there will be an infinite number of solutions. But for options, delta and gamma will not be linearly related to each other.

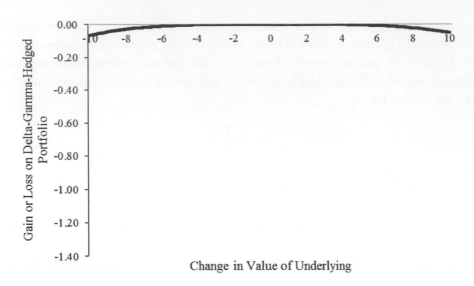

Exhibit 10-32. Changes in Value of Delta-Gamma-Hedged Portfolio

If we re-compute the value of option 2, we obtain 4.63. Thus, the value of the hedged portfolio is

$$0.2432(101) - 7.71 + 0.5748(4.63) = 19.5127$$

which is a change of -0.0001. Exhibit 10-32 is an extension of Exhibit 10-31. It shows the change in the value of the hedge portfolio for a range of prices changes of -10 to $+10$. The ranges of the vertical axes are the same.

Go back to Exhibit 10-31 and you will note that the changes in 10-32, the delta-gamma hedged portfolio, are much smaller. The accuracy of the hedge is much greater for a wider range of movements in the underlying.

To recap, delta hedging protects a position for very small changes in the value of the underlying. Large changes, which could occur over a short period of time but are also likely to occur over a longer period of time, will result in substantial deviations in the value of the portfolio when only delta is hedged. A gamma hedge, which requires the addition of another option, will protect against larger changes. Obviously, hedging the gamma is more involved than simply hedging the delta.

In addition, delta and delta-gamma hedges are correct only for an instant. The values of options, their deltas, and their gammas change with any change in the value of the underlying or simply the passage of time. Thus, in theory, the position must be revised instantaneously. Yet, such a strategy would require trading continuously. Clearly no one can trade continuously and the costs would be prohibitive. Thus, most option dealers monitor their deltas, put on gamma hedges when the gamma exposure is large, and revise the position when in their judgement the risks are too great.[21]

10.7.2.3 *Vega Hedging*

In addition to the potentially adverse effect of changes in the underlying, a change in the volatility can also result in losses to a dealer. The effect of volatility on the price of an option is captured by the vega, as illustrated above. As we noted, options are relatively sensitive to volatility and the effect is in a positive direction. Thus, if a dealer sells an option, it will be short vega and, therefore, exposed to increases in volatility, though it would benefit from a decrease in volatility. Hedging the vega of an option position requires the addition of another option so that the vega of the added option can be used to offset the vega of the position in place. Thus, if the dealer were delta-gamma hedging and wanted to vega hedge, it would require yet another option. There would now be three constraints, delta $= 0$, gamma $= 0$, and vega $= 0$, but there would be three unknowns: units of the underlying, units of the second option, and units of the third option. We will not go into the details of vega hedging, but the principle is pretty much the same as we have already explained with delta and gamma hedging.

10.8 Applications of Options in Risk Management

In this section we illustrate some examples of the use of options in risk management. Our discussion will cover interest rate options, currency options, commodity options, and swaptions.

10.8.1 *Interest Rate Options*

Consider a company that is developing its financial plans about a year ahead. It determines that it will need to borrow \$20 million in the form of a 180-day single payment note at LIBOR plus 300 basis points. This arrangement means that it will borrow \$20 million and 180 days later, it will pay back the \$20 million principal and interest at the rate of LIBOR $+$ 300 basis

---

[21]There is an old saying in the derivatives business: *the only perfect hedge is in a Japanese garden.* Though Brits are likely to argue that they have some perfect hedges too, the point is that rarely is a financial hedge absolutely perfect. Hence, there is a strong need for understanding what a perfect hedge is and how a hedge can deviate from perfection. Interpreting information of this sort is the job of a risk manager.

points. Let us say that the current 180-day LIBOR is 3.5%. The company is planning ahead and is concerned that in a year, interest rates will be much higher than they are. Fearing this possibility, it purchases an interest rate call option on LIBOR. Let us say it chooses an exercise price of slightly above the current LIBOR, say 3.6%. The dealer quotes it a price of 20 basis points, which is $20,000,000(0.0020)(180/360) = \$20,000$. Note that in quoting a rate as the cost of the option, the rate is quoted on an annual basis. Twenty basis points on $20 million is $20,000 when the rate is 180-day LIBOR. Now, let us consider a range of possible LIBORs at the expiration of the option, one year later.

Now we will examine some outcomes. The $20,000 premium paid for the option has to be accounted for in analyzing the overall cost of the loan. The option will be purchased now, but the loan will be initiated in one year. Thus, the $20,000 plus the interest thereon for one year effectively reduces the proceeds from the loan. Let us say that the company could earn 2% interest on $20,000 for one year, which amounts to $20,000(0.02) = \$400$. Thus, the effective cost of the option is $20,400, and the loan is effectively taken out for $20,000,000 - \$20,400 = \$19,979,600$.

Let us take one particular outcome, say that LIBOR is 3.9% at the option expiration. With the 300 basis points credit spread, the interest on the loan would be $20,000,000(0.039 + 0.03)(180/360) = \$690,000$. The option payoff would be

$$\$20,000,000 Max\,(0, 0.039 - 0.036) \left(\frac{180}{360} \right) = \$30,000.$$

So the net interest paid would be $690,000 - \$30,000 = \$660,000$. For any LIBOR above the strike of 3.6%, the net interest is capped at $660,000, making the effective loan rate be $(\$660,000/\$19,979,600)(360/180) = 0.0661$. Now, assume a LIBOR of 3.2%. The loan interest would be $20,000,000(0.032 + 0.03)(180/360) = \$620,000$. The option payoff would be

$$\$20,000,000 Max\,(0, 0.032 - 0.036) \left(\frac{180}{360} \right) = \$0.$$

So the net interest is $620,000 and the effective loan rate would be $(\$620,000/\$19,979,600)(365/180) = 0.0629$. Exhibit 10-33 illustrates the effective loan rate for a range of LIBORs.

The effective loan rate is capped at 6.67%. Now, flipping things around, lenders might use puts to protect against decreases in rates, but in practice

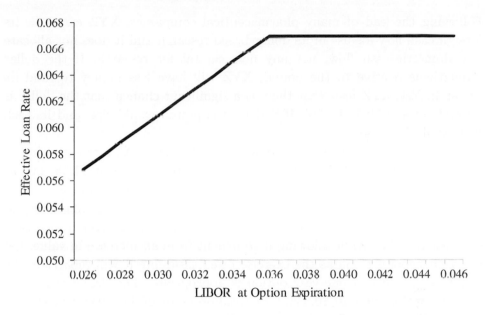

Exhibit 10-33. Effective Loan Rate Using Interest Rate Call

lenders simply make floating rate loans to reflect the fact that they borrow at floating rates.

As we described in Section 10.5.3, interest rate caps are applicable to hedging floating rate loans with multiple payments. On each reset date, a caplet pays off based on whether the rate in the market is above the strike rate. As such, a cap controls the interest cost on multiple reset dates in the same manner as the interest rate call in the example above controls the setting of the rate. And as we described in Section 10.5.3, collars are used to provide some of the benefits of caps without incurring the initial cash outlay. Recall that a collar is constructed by selling a floor at a lower strike than the cap strike, with the floor strike set at a level that generates the same premium as the cap. Thus, by buying a cap for a particular premium and selling a floor for the same premium, there is no initial cash cost. When LIBOR falls below the floor strike, however, the dealer exercises the floor and the borrower must make a payment that offsets the benefit of the lower interest rate on the loan.

10.8.2 *Currency Options*

Consider a fictional U.S. company called XYZ Pharmaceuticals that has a U.K. subsidiary that generates an estimated net cash flow of £60 million.

Following the lead of many pharmaceutical companies, XYZ earmarks its foreign cash flow for use in its dollar-based research and it does not allocate any domestic cash flow, nor any new capital for research. If the dollar strengthens relative to the pound, XYZ will have less money to fund its research. Yet, XYZ feels that there is a significant chance that the dollar is overvalued and likely to fall. If it does, the pound would rise, and its cash flow would increase.

The current spot rate is $1.50, so for £60 million, XYZ is expecting to receive $90 million. A forward contract could be created at $1.55, but as you recall, a forward contract would lock in the exchange rate. Given XYZ's feeling that the pound has a good chance of strengthening, it wants to benefit if that outcome occurs. Thus, a put on the pound will protect it against a decrease in value, while allowing it to benefit from an increase in value. Let us say it chooses $1.55 as the exercise rate. Assuming it will repatriate the funds in one year, a one-year option is appropriate. The dealer tells XYZ that the option will cost $0.045, for a total premium of $60,000,000 \times \$0.045 = \$2,700,000$. The payoff of the option will be

$$£60,000,000 Max(0, \$1.55 - S_T)$$

where S_T is the exchange rate of the pound in dollars at the option expiration.

It must also take into account the option premium of $2.7 million. Suppose the company could earn 2% on that money for one year. Then the premium effectively costs it $\$2,700,000(1 + 0.02) = \$2,754,000$. This amount will reduce the payoff of the option, as it was paid out to buy the option.

Now let us take a particular outcome, say an exchange rate of $1.52. The £60 million will convert to $£60,000,000(\$1.52) = \$91,200,000$. The payoff of the option will be

$$£60,000,000 Max(0, \$1.55 - \$1.52) = \$1,800,000.$$

So the total cash flow is $\$91,200,000 + \$1,800,000 - \$2,754,000 = \$90,246,000$. Now consider an outcome of $1.58. The £60 million will be worth $£60,000,000(\$1.58) = \$94,800,000$. The option payoff will be

$$£60,000,000 Max(0, \$1.55 - \$1.58) = \$0.$$

So the total cash flow will be $\$94,800,000 + \$0 - \$2,754,000 = \$92,046,000$. Exhibit 10-34 presents the results for a range of exchange rates between

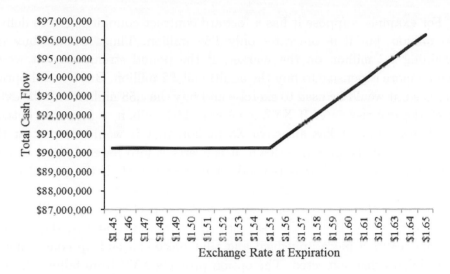

Exhibit 10-34. Effective Cash Flow Using Currency Put

$1.45 and $1.65. The put enables the firm to put a floor on the dollar value of its U.K. cash flow of $90,246,000.

This example applies to a one-time cash flow, such as XYZ repatriating its annual net cash flow all at once, say the end of the year. If conversion back to U.S. dollars were done say on a quarterly basis the company might consider a series of options expiring at various quarterly dates.

Call options on a currency would often be used when a foreign currency outflow is anticipated. An example there might be a company that needs to make some purchases of foreign materials that will be paid for in the foreign currency. A call option would enable the company to benefit if the currency strengthens, and this benefit would offset the higher cost of purchasing the materials.

There is one interesting characteristic of options that is particularly helpful when hedging. You may remember from Chapter 4 that we discussed quantity risk, which is the uncertainty of the amount of the exposure. In the example of XYZ Pharmaceuticals, we assumed that the £60 million figure was absolutely certain. It may have been obtained from historical experience combined with expectations of the future. Yet, in reality, there has to be some uncertainty in the amount of British pounds it expects to receive. With quantity uncertainty, options are far more beneficial than forwards. Let us assume that a put option on £60 million is compared with the alternative strategy of a short forward contract on £60 million at $1.55.

For example, suppose it has a forward contract committing it to deliver £60 million, but if it generates only £58 million. Thus, it must buy the remaining £2 million on the market. If the pound strengthens, it would become more expensive to buy the additional £2 million. But if a call option were used, it would be used to exercise and buy the £58 million and the extra £2 at the exercise rate. If XYZ generates £63 million, a forward contract would mean that it has an extra £3 million that it would convert at the market rate. If the pound is down, it converts it into fewer dollars, though that additional cash flow is beyond what it expected. If the pound is up, it converts it into more cash flow than expected. If its cash flow exceeds expectations, the forward contract is really no problem, as it will end up with more money. But if the cash flow is below expectations, the forward contract leaves a piece unhedged and that piece can end up converting to fewer dollars than expected. The option protects XYZ from falling short of its expected cash flow and does a better job than the forward, owing to its flexibility. In other words, if more cash flow is generated than required by the contract, that additional cash flow will be converted attractively at the exercise rate. Of course, that flexibility has a price, the premium paid for the option.

10.8.3 *Commodity Options*

A refiner buys oil and processes it into its principal components: heating oil, kerosene, and unleaded gasoline, which is primarily kerosene. A rising price of crude oil reduces the refiner's cash flow. Consequently, a call option on crude oil could be easily justified. Consider a refiner that anticipates purchasing 2 million barrels of crude in three months. The spot price is currently $42. The refiner decides to purchase a call on 2 million barrels that expires in three months and has an exercise price of $40. The dealer quotes it a price of $3.25, meaning that the total cost is $6,500,000. The option expires in three months. Assuming a 2% annual opportunity cost on the money, the effective premium is $6,500,000(1 + 0.02(3/12)) = $6,532,500$. The payoff of the option is

$$2,000,000 Max(0, S_T - \$40)$$

Let us now consider some outcomes. Suppose expiration arrives and the spot price of the oil is $52. The oil will cost the refiner 2,000,000($52) = $104,000,000. The option payoff is

$$2,000,000 Max(0, \$52 - \$40) = \$24,000,000$$

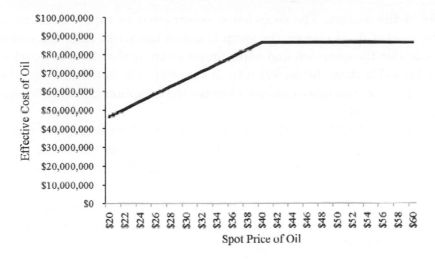

Exhibit 10-35. Effective Cost of Oil Using Call Option

Taking into account the premium, the total cost is $104,000,000 − $24,000,000 + $6,532,500 = $86,532,500. With a spot price of $35, the oil will cost 2,000,000($35) = $70,000,000. The option payoff is

$$2,000,000 Max(0, \$35 - \$40) = \$0$$

The total cost of the oil is $70,000,000 − $0 + $6,532,500 = $76,532,500. Exhibit 10-35 shows the net cost of the oil for a range of spot prices of $20 to $60. Notice how the total cost of the oil is maxed out at $86,532,500.

10.8.4 *Swaptions*

Because of the special characteristics of swaptions that we had to understand from the start, we have already covered some applications. Consider a company that uses floating-rate debt and always swaps it into fixed-rate debt. In planning for the next year, it anticipates that in six months it will issue a two-year semiannual coupon floating-rate note at LIBOR plus a credit spread and will use a swap to effectively convert it to a fixed-rate loan. So, over the next six months it faces the risk of increases in interest rates. If that happens, it will enter into a swap at a higher fixed rate than exists now. It learns that a swaption can be used to manage this risk. Specifically, a payer swaption would allow it to choose a strike rate that would enable it to enter into the swap at a fixed rate of the strike rate or a better rate if it exists in the market. The swaption is constructed to expire in six months. If the market fixed rate on the swap is above the strike rate, the company will exercise the swaption and enter into a swap at the strike rate, which is more favorable than the market rate. If the swap rate in the market is below the strike rate, the firm does not exercise the swaption and enters into the swap at the market rate.

In Exhibit 10-22 in Section 10.6.1, we presented an example of this sort. The payoff of a swaption depends on the entire term structure, so there are many possible outcomes and no single LIBOR rate. Nonetheless, the swaption will cap the fixed rate on a loan at the strike rate. If market rates on swaps are below the strike rate, the firm can obtain a lower effective fixed rate on the loan. Of course, the premium of the swaption will effectively raise the loan rate a bit.

10.9   Chapter Summary

You may have felt that this has been a long chapter. It certainly is, because there is a lot to cover with options. First you have to learn what they are. Then you learn some of the basic pricing rules, such as put-call parity, and then you identify the factors that affect the values of options. Then you study how options are priced by constructing an arbitrage portfolio. The binomial model is an excellent way to observe this principle. The Black-Scholes-Merton model extends the arbitrage pricing principle to continuous time. Then we presented interest rate options and their variants known as swaptions. Finally, we examined the key risk measures for options, known as delta, gamma, and vega, and illustrated how these concepts are used by dealers to hedge against changes in the value of the underlying and volatility. We concluded by looking at how options are used in solving common risk management problems.

This chapter concludes Part III of this book. Part III deals with managing market risk, wherein we examined some characteristics of market risk and then developed a foundational knowledge of the principal tools for managing market risk: forwards, futures, swaps, and options.

Part IV heads off in a different direction. Market risk is not the only risk we have to worry about. In particular, we will care greatly about whether a counterparty who owes us money will be able to pay us, which is what we call credit risk.

10.10 Questions and Problems

1. Explain how an option differs from a forward contract.
2. Suppose we are at the expiration of an option. Consider call and put options with exercise prices of $50. Determine the payoffs for the call and put given the following values of the underlying at expiration:

    (a) $45
    (b) $58

3. Consider the prices of options at time 0, which is prior to expiration. You are given the value of the underlying of S_0 and the exercise price of X, but we are not specifying if S_0 is above or below X. Identify the upper and lower limits of

    (a) European calls
    (b) American calls
    (c) European puts
    (d) American puts.

    Assume no cash flows, storage costs, or benefits on the underlying.
4. Explain in words how call and put options are related to their exercise prices.
5. Explain in words how call and put options are related to their times to expiration.
6. Consider an underlying priced at $42. The risk-free rate is 3.5%. European call and put options expiring in three months with exercise prices of $40 are priced at $4.12 and $3.50, respectively. Construct a risk-free strategy that will exploit mispricing. Determine the amount of the arbitrage profit and demonstrate that the strategy is risk-free. Assume that any asset can be bought or sold short.
7. Explain how to use put-call parity to create a synthetic short position in the underlying. Be sure to show that your synthetic short position precisely replicates the desired position.
8. Identify under what single condition an American call option will be exercised early and explain why this is true.
9. Explain why Americans put options might be exercised early. Contrast why early exercise is possible on put options but usually not on call options. Assume no dividends or cash flows on the underlying.

10. Explain why high volatility is a valuable feature of both a call and a put option.

11. Consider a stock priced at $125 that can go up by 15% or down by 10% in one period. At the end of that period, European call and put options struck at $120 expire. The risk-free rate is 3%.

    (a) Find the value of the call option today and the hedge ratio, which is the number of shares per short call.
    (b) Find the value of the put option today and the hedge ratio, which is the number of shares per long put.

12. Consider a stock priced at $75 that can go up by 25% or down by 15%. The risk-free rate is 2.5%. You are provided the value of the option, $7.203, and the hedge ratio 0.625. Construct an arbitrage portfolio that will earn better than the risk-free rate and demonstrate that indeed it will. Invest the proceeds from the arbitrage portfolio in risk-free bonds. Assume 1,000 options traded.

13. The diagram below shows a two-period binomial tree for a stock priced at $35. The risk-free rate is 2%. There are options with exercise prices of $112.

Time 0	Time 1	Time 2
		$125.44
	$112.00	
$100.00		$100.80
	$90.00	
		$81.00

    (a) Find the price of a two-period European call.
    (b) Find the price of a two-period European put.
    (c) Find the price of a two-period American put.

14. Consider a stock price at $85 with a volatility of 0.35. The risk-free rate is 3.25%. If you were going to do a five-period binomial model for a six-month option, what would be the u, d, and r parameters. Do not do the model. Just obtain the parameters to four decimal places.

15. Find the normal probability for the z values below using both manual calculations from the table provided in the text and using Excel.

    (a) $z = 1.2439$
    (b) $z = -0.8192$

16. Find the values of European put and call options if the underlying price is 38.5, the exercise price is 40, the continuously compounded risk-free rate is 2%, the volatility is 0.44, and the options expire in 71 days.

17. What effects do storage costs and a convenience yield have on Black-Scholes-Merton call option values?

18. What is the implied volatility of an option?

19. Consider an asset priced at $57.55 that has volatility of 0.3825, makes no cash payments, has no storage costs, and has no convenience yield. A futures contract expires in 44 days. A call option on the futures with exercise price of $55 expires 35 days. The continuously compounded risk-free rate is 1.95%. Determine the price of the option.

20. Consider interest rate calls and puts on notional of €25 million. The strikes are 4.5%. The underlying is 120-day euro LIBOR. Determine the payoffs if euro LIBOR on the expiration is the following in (a) and (b):

    (a) 4.65%
    (b) 3.99%
    (c) Identify when the payoffs are made.

21. Why are the Black-Scholes-Merton and Black not models not easily adaptable to pricing interest rate options?

22. Consider a borrower paying 180-day LIBOR plus 1.5% on $52.5 million. The borrower arranges a collar with the cap struck at 3.25% and the floor struck at 2.15%. Determine the total amount paid for each of the following values of LIBOR at the expiration of a caplet and floorlet, (a)–(e):

    (a) 4.00%
    (b) 3.51%
    (c) 2.75%
    (d) 1.95%
    (e) 1.75%
    (f) Comment on why some of these values are the same.

23. How is a zero cost interest rate collar constructed, in contrast to a collar with non-zero cost?

24. How are swaptions blend the features of both swaps and options? What are the two types of interest rate swaptions and under what conditions do they pay off?

25. Consider a swaption in which the underlying is a swap based on 90-day LIBOR with four payments. The notional is $15 million. Suppose we are at the swaption expiration and the term structure is as follows:

Days	Rate
90	.0322
180	.0328
270	.0334
360	.0337

Determine the payoffs for the following swaptions that differ by strike:

(a) Payer swaption with strike of 3.55%
(b) Payer swaption with strike of 3.21%
(c) Receiver swaption with strike of 3.44%
(d) Receiver swaption with strike of 3.15%

26. Explain in words how swaptions can be valued as options on bonds.

27. Explain how a corporate treasurer can use a swaption to hedge future floating-rate borrowings that it plans to convert to fixed-rate borrowings.

28. Explain what the delta of an option measures. Distinguish between the deltas of calls and the deltas of puts.

29. How do deltas of both call and put options change as (a) the underlying changes, (b) time elapses

30. Under what conditions can delta fail to reflect the change in an option price and how can a better estimate of the change be obtained using the gamma?

31. What does vega measure? How is the use of vega justified in a Black-Scholes-Merton world in which volatility is assumed to be constant?

32. Suppose you are a dealer and have sold 5,000 call options at an exercise price of $60 with an expiration of 65 days. The underlying price is $62.50 and has a volatility of 0.448. The continuously compounded risk-free rate is 3.2%. You wish to delta-hedge it by purchasing the underlying.

The price of the call is \$6.16 and its delta is 0.6333. These values were obtained using the Black-Scholes-Merton model. Answer the following questions:

(a) How many units of the underlying should you buy and what is the value of the delta-hedged portfolio at the start?

(b) Assume that the underlying increases by \$1. Using the Black-Scholes-Merton model, you would find that the option value would now be \$6.81. Determine the gain or loss on the delta-hedged portfolio.

33. Assume you are a dealer and have sold 10,000 call options at a price of \$5.24 with a delta of 0.5184 and a gamma of 0.0259. The underlying value is \$42.28 and has a volatility of 0.516. The options expire in 181 days. The continuously compounded risk-free rate is 2.65%.

(a) Suppose you construct a delta hedge using the underlying. Determine the change in the value of the hedge portfolio if the underling decreases by \$2, which will cause the option to fall to \$4.26.

(b) Instead of delta-hedging, suppose you had gamma-hedged, adding a call option with the same expiration but an exercise price of \$40. Its price is \$7.40, its delta is 0.6445, and its gamma is 0.0242. When the underlying decreases by \$2, the price of this option changes to \$6.16. Find the change in the delta-gamma hedged portfolio.

34. A corporation anticipates borrowing \$25 million at 180-day LIBOR plus 1.75% in 120 days. It is worried about an interest rate increase and buys a cap struck at 4.25% for \$55,000. The opportunity cost on its money is 2.5%. Use a spreadsheet to create a table and graph showing the effective annual loan rate. Use LIBORs of from 1% to 7% in 25-basis point increments.

35. Use the same information from Problem 34, but now have the firm sell a floor at the same premium with an exercise rate of 3.4%. Construct the same type of table but add a column for the floor payoff, and also generate a graph.

36. YYZZ is a U.S. manufacturer of electronic circuit boards. It has extensive global markets, including a strong reputation in Australia. It generates about \$A125 million (125 million Australian dollars) per year, which it

repatriates into U. S. dollars at the end of the year. It would like to hedge the value of the Australian dollar relative to the U.S. dollar.

(a) Explain how it could hedge its exposure to Australian dollars using puts.

(b) Assume that it buys a put on the Australian dollar denominated in U.S. dollars. The exercise price is $0.70. The current exchange rate is $0.75. Use a spreadsheet to construct a table showing the value of its cash for a range of values of the Australian dollar from $0.50 to $1.00 in increments of $0.025.

37. AuGold is an industrial manufacturer that uses a substantial amount of gold in its production process, but it knows that gold is a volatile commodity. It anticipates that in 180 days it will purchase 20,000 troy ounces of gold, and it is concerned that the price of gold might rise. The current spot price is $1,355.42. It would like to use options to protect it against increases in the cost of the gold it purchases.

(a) Explain how AuGold could use a call option on gold to provide the necessary protection.

(b) Assume a put option can be purchased for $1,250,000. It expires in 180 days and has an exercise price of $1,350. The opportunity cost on the money is 2% per 360 days. Construct a table showing the net overall cash flow for a range of prices of gold from $1,200 to $1,500 in increments of $25. Also, construct a graph of the results in your table.

Part IV

Managing Non-Market Risks

Chapter 11

Managing Credit Risk

Remember that credit is money.

Benjamin Franklin
Advice to a Young Tradesman (1748)

It is perhaps appropriate that the chapter on credit risk is Chapter 11 of this book. Normally in the financial world, when you say "Chapter 11," you are referring to the section of the U.S. bankruptcy code that specifies the legal statute under which a company can file for protection from its creditors. Owing money to other entities in excess of the equity of a company or individual is what results in bankruptcy. When one party owes money to another party, there is always the possibility of bankruptcy. Credit risk management is a critical process by which an organization manages the risk that the counterparty will not pay what it owes.

Chapter 11 begins a section called Managing Non-Market Risks. Recall that market risk is the risk that arises from movements in interest rates, exchange rates, commodity prices, and stock prices. Credit risk arises from the possibility that a party will be unable to pay an amount owed to another party. It is important to understand, however, that credit risk and market risk are not independent risks. In fact, they are often quite related. No one engages in a financial transaction with a near-immediate threat that one party will default. Credit risk tends to arise as market conditions change. Recall, for example, that a swap starts off with zero value. Neither party owes the other any money. As market conditions change, the swap value will move to the positive for one party and the negative for the other. The party owing the greater amount, to whom the swap value is negative, can become at risk of defaulting to the counterparty. But market conditions need not drive a party to default. A borrower can simply find that over time it becomes unable to generate the cash necessary to pay its obligations, regardless of what happens in the market.

Credit risk is also sometimes referred to as default risk and sometimes counterparty risk, though we will mostly call it credit risk. In all cases, we are talking about the possibility of one party defaulting to the other. So let us formally define credit risk:

> *Credit risk is the risk that a party that owes money to another party will be unable to pay.*

This sentence is an attempt at a concise definition, but be aware that credit risk is not just the failure to pay. It encompasses a set of conditions that characterize the likelihood that a party will pay. Hence, the word "risk" as used in the above definition. A party could weaken to the point where failure to pay an upcoming debt becomes increasingly likely. With further weakening of the party, the actual failure to pay may be a bit anticlimactic, as the parties might well have expected the default. The failure to pay might just confirm what everyone more or less knew was coming. But there can also be an additional uncertainty in that there can be recovery of a portion of the amount owed. How much is recovered is often unclear and unpredictable. Credit risk can also reflect a borrower's effort to restructure a debt, meaning that the borrower admits that he cannot pay what is owed when it is owed but does believe that he can pay the debt over a longer period of time. Let us now look a little further into what credit risk encompasses.

11.1   The Nature and Basic Characteristics of Credit Risk

Credit risk is probably one of the oldest risks known to human beings. It seems likely that prehistoric people lent assets to each other and learned pretty quickly that there was risk of non-repayment. Such a lesson will instill a sense that some protective measures should be used the next time. The Code of Hammurabi, written around 1780 B.C., specified conditions under which loans would be repaid:

> *88. A merchant may collect interest of thirty-three and one-third per cent on a loan of grain, and twenty per cent interest may be charged on a loan of silver.*

> *89. If a free person who has borrowed cannot repay the loan with silver but can repay it with grain, the merchant who made the loan is obligated to accept the grain at the rate of exchange set by the king; if the merchant*

tries to raise the interest-rate, that merchant shall forfeit both the capital and the interest.

92. If a merchant loans grain or silver at one rate but later tries to collect at a higher rate, that merchant shall forfeit both the capital and the interest.

Source: (Rummel at
http://history.hanover.edu/courses/excerpts/105hammurabi.html)

So, commerce in ancient Babylonia was clearly characterized by lending, albeit at extremely high rates of interest. Interestingly, these loans had the feature that one could repay a loan due in one commodity with a different commodity, which is a form of an option, and in particular, an option that is somewhat similar to the delivery options associated with some futures contracts.

11.1.1 *Expected Loss*

A good starting point in understanding credit risk is the notion of *expected loss*, a metric that describes the average amount an entity would expect to lose over a period of time. More formally,

> *Expected loss is the probability of default times the amount owed times the percentage of the amount owed that is not paid.*

The amount owed that is not paid reflects a concept called the *recovery rate*. Just because an entity defaults does not mean that the creditor receives nothing. The borrower will often have a modest amount of assets that can be used to at least generate a part of the amount owed.

The most important measure in understanding credit risk is the probability of default, which is sometimes referred to as the *hazard rate*. It is the probability that the event, in this case default, occurs given that it has not already occurred. As an example, let us assume that a creditor makes a $1,000 loan. It believes that there is a 90% chance that the borrower will pay back the loan in full and a 10% chance that the borrower will default. If default occurs, the credit believes that the borrower will pay back $200. Thus, $200 is the recovery and 20% is the recovery rate. The expected loss is, therefore,

$$\text{Expected loss} = 0.10 \times \$1,000 \times 0.80 = \$80$$

Alternatively, the expected payment is the complement, $920. The interpretation of these numbers is that if a large sample of loans with the same characteristics were made, the lender would on average lose $80 for every $1,000 owed.

11.1.2 *Accumulated Default Probability*

Most lenders attempt to make loans with a small probability of default. But a seemingly small probability of default can be a misleading measure. Over the life of a loan, a small probability of default can accumulate to a rather large probability of default. Consider a three-year loan with a 2% probability of default per year. Thus, in any given year, there is a 2% probability that the borrower will default. Exhibit 11-1 illustrates the possible combinations of default and no default over the three years. The term "Pr" means probability and refers to the probability of the path associated with it.

Each annual outcome involving no default has a 98% chance of occurring. Each annual outcome involving default has a 2% chance. If default occurs, the tree goes no further to the right. If default does not occur, the tree branches out to the right, reflecting the next period, up to the maturity of three years. The probability of three straight years of no default is the product of 0.98 three times, or 0.9412. Thus, the likelihood of default is the complement, 0.0588. The likelihood of not defaulting for two years and defaulting the third is $0.98 \times 0.98 \times 0.02 = 0.0192$. The likelihood of not

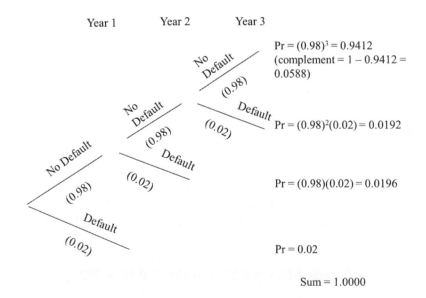

Exhibit 11-1. Combinations of Outcomes for Three-Year Loan with 2% Annual Probability of Default

defaulting the first year and defaulting in the second is $0.98 \times 0.02 = 0.0196$. And of course, the likelihood of defaulting in the first year is 0.02. The sum of 0.0192, 0.0196, and 0.02 is also 0.0588. Another way to obtain the answer is $1 - 0.98^3 = 0.0588$. With this simple formula in mind, note how a 2% annual probability of default translates into an 18% probability of default somewhere over 10 years:

$$1 - (0.98)^{10} = 0.1829.$$

Thus, what seems like a 98% nearly sure bet is actually much riskier than it seems.

11.2 Credit Risk as an Option

You will recall that Chapter 10 was devoted to options. As it turns out, there is also a great deal we can use from that chapter in understanding credit risk. You see, credit risk is itself an option. Recall that options are rights, representing the opportunities to make decisions that are in the best interest of the holder of the option. As we will see, the right to default is an option held by a party with limited liability. Using that theme, in this section, we will use the results of the Black-Scholes-Merton model to estimate the risk of default and what that risk costs in terms of money and yield.

11.2.1 *Stock as a Call Option*

Let us begin by assuming a corporation that has assets with a market value of A_0. The volatility of the return on these assets is σ_A. The company has one issue of zero-coupon debt of face value of Z that is due in T years. The continuously compounded risk-free rate is r_c. In other words, this company must repay Z in T years. In accordance with the rules of limited liability that apply to corporations, the company pays off its debt if its assets exceed the amount owed. If the assets are less than the amount owed, the company defaults and the assets are turned over to the creditors. The value of the assets at maturity of the debt is A_T. The value of the debt at time 0 is D_0, and the value of the stock at time 0 is S_0. Exhibit 11-2 illustrates this point.

In the rightmost column we specify the condition, $A_T > Z$, which means that the asset value is large enough to pay off the debt. In that case, the creditors receive the amount owed, Z, and the shareholders receive the remaining assets, $A_T - Z$. In the adjacent column, the condition $A_T \leq Z$ means that the asset value is not sufficient to pay off the debt. In that

	Value of Claim at time 0	Value of Assets at Maturity of Debt	
		$A_T \leq Z$	$A_T > Z$
Creditors' claim	D_0	A_T	Z
Shareholders' claim	S_0	0	$A_T - Z$
Total claims	$D_0 + S_0 = A_0$	A_T	A_T

Exhibit 11-2. Payoffs of Debt for a Corporation

Parameters	Standard Call Option	Stock as a Call Option on the Assets
Underlying	value of stock	value of assets
Exercise price	exercise price	face value of debt
Risk-free rate	risk-free rate	risk-free rate
Volatility	volatility of return on stock	volatility of return on assets
Time	expiration of option	maturity of debt

Exhibit 11-3. Standard Call Option on Stock vs. Stock as a Call Option on Assets

case, the creditors receive the assets and the shareholders receive nothing. Because of limited liability of the shareholders, however, the creditors accept the assets in full payment of the amount owed.

From Exhibit 11-2, we can see that the claims of the shareholders are isomorphic to those of the holder of a call option. Remember that a call option pays off $S_T - X$ if $S_T > X$ and zero otherwise. We see essentially that same result in Exhibit 11-2. The stock of the company pays off like a call option in which the underlying is the assets and the exercise price is the face value of the debt.

With this analogy in mind, we can map the basic elements of a standard call option to those of a share of stock viewed as a call option, as in Exhibit 11-3.

Each term in the standard model maps to a corresponding term in the model of stock as a call option on the assets. Because we know so much about options and in particular the Black-Scholes-Merton model, there are many interesting results we can derive that will give us a clearer understanding of what credit risk really is.

First, let us recall from Chapter 10 the principle of put-call parity:

$$p_0 + S_0 = c_0 + X/(1+r)^T.$$

We showed that a put and the underlying asset, as represented by the left-hand side, produce the same result as a call and a zero coupon bond with a face value equal to the exercise price of the option and maturing at the option expiration day, as represented by the right-hand side. This result was shown to hold because if $S_T > X$, the put expires worthless and the asset is worth S_T, for a total value of S_T, while the call expires in-the-money for a value of $S_T - X$ and the bond matures to a value of X, so the call and the bond likewise add up to S_T. If $S_T \leq X$, the put expires in-the-money for a value of $X - S_T$ and the underlying has a value of S_T, for a total value of X, while the call expires out-of-the-money for a value of zero and the bond matures to a value of X, for a total of X. Thus, under both outcomes, $S_T > X$ and $S_T \leq X$, each combination, put combined with underlying and call combined with bond, produces the same results at expiration. Since the two combinations produce the same results at expiration, they must have the same initial values, or otherwise the cheaper combination could be bought and the more expensive combination sold to generate an initial cash inflow but with offsetting results in expiration and, therefore, no further cash due in or paid out.

Using the mapping in Exhibit 11-3, we can rewrite put-call parity for the case of the stock viewed as a call option on the assets,

$$p_0 + A_0 = S_0 + Z/(1+r)^T \tag{11.1}$$

Note that we made no change of symbols for the put. We need to get an understanding of what this mysterious put option is. There are no put options in Exhibit 11-2, so where is this put option?

Remember that a put option is the right to sell an asset at a fixed price. Let us rearrange Equation (11.1) to isolate the stock price,

$$S_0 = A_0 + p_0 - Z/(1+r)^T$$

We now have the interpretation that the value of the stock consists of the value of the assets, this mysterious put option, and the value of a risk-free zero coupon bond. But by definition, we know that the stock value is equal to the value of the assets minus the value of the debt:

$$S_0 = A_0 - D_0.$$

Therefore, it must be true that

$$D_0 = Z/(1+r)^T - p_0. \tag{11.2}$$

That is, the value of the debt, which can potentially default, is the value of a default-free bond minus the value of a put option. This put option is the right held by the shareholders and granted by the creditors to turn over the assets of the company to the creditors in complete fulfillment of the shareholders' obligation to pay off the debt. This right is known in the legal world as limited liability, and it means that the personal assets of the shareholders cannot be taken by the creditors to fulfill the debt. The creditors agree to accept the value of the assets in full payment of the debt, even if the value of the assets is less than the amount owed. Thus, the creditors are essentially sellers of a put, which is held by the shareholders.

From Equation (11.2), we see that the value of a defaultable bond is less than that of a default-free bond maturing at the same time with the same face value. That result should make sense. A defaultable bond is logically worth less than a default-free bond, because there are some outcomes in which it will not pay off the full amount owed. The amount by which a defaultable bond is worth less than a default-free bond is the cost of credit risk. Now let us see how to use the Black-Scholes-Merton model to assign a price to the credit risk.

11.2.2   *Valuation of Stock as an Option*

Repeated below from Chapter 10 is the Black-Scholes-Merton (BSM) formula for the value of a call option:

$$c_0 = S_0 N(d_1) - X e^{-r_c T} N(d_2)$$

$$d_1 = \frac{\ln(S_0/X) + (r_c + \sigma^2/2)T}{\sigma\sqrt{T}}$$

$$d_2 = d_1 - \sigma\sqrt{T}.$$

Recall that S_0 is the value of the underlying asset at time 0, X is the exercise price, r_c is the continuously compounded risk-free rate, T is the time to expiration, and σ is the volatility of the return on the underlying. In treating stock as an option, we noted that the underlying is the value of the assets, A_0, the volatility is the volatility of the assets, σ_A, the exercise price is the face value of the debt, Z, which is the amount owed at maturity, T is the time to maturity of the debt, and the continuously compounded risk-free rate, r_c, is the same concept as in the standard model. Thus, we can write the formula for the value of stock when viewed as a call option on the assets, as

$$S_0 = A_0 N(x_1) - Z e^{-r_c T} N(x_2)$$

$$x_1 = \frac{\ln(A_0/Z) + (r_c + \sigma_A^2/2)T}{\sigma_A \sqrt{T}} \tag{11.3}$$

$$x_2 = d_1 - \sigma_A \sqrt{T}.$$

Using this result and the fact that $S_0 = A_0 - D_0$, we can derive a formula for the value of the bonds,

$$
\begin{aligned}
D_0 &= A_0 - S_0 \\
&= A_0 - \left(A_0 N(x_1) - Z e^{-r_c T} N(x_2) \right) \\
&= A_0 \left(1 - N(x_1) \right) + Z e^{-r_c T} N(x_2)
\end{aligned}
\tag{11.4}
$$

So, Equation (11.4) is kind of a Black-Scholes-Merton formula for the value of a bond that is subject to default.

11.2.3 The Price of Credit Risk in the Option Model

There are several ways in which we can measure the price of credit risk. By "price of credit risk" we mean what it costs in interest rate or in currency when there is credit risk as compared to a default-free bond. A widely used and traditional measure of credit risk is the *credit spread*. A second measure is the value of the put option held by the shareholders.

11.2.3.1 The Credit Spread

To measure the credit spread, first we must start with a benchmark, which will typically be the yield on a default-free security of a given maturity. This rate is the lowest rate in the market for a security of that maturity. It is also a rate that should reflect systematic changes in market conditions, and it should not be influenced by whatever is happening to the particular debtor in question. That is, if the debtor gets into financial trouble, it should have no effect on the benchmark. We then calculate the difference between rate on the debtor's security and the benchmark rate, for equivalent maturities.

The yield spreads on corporate and municipal bonds are widely followed in the U.S. and other countries. These bonds are often grouped into ratings classes. That is, the ratings assigned by such companies as Standard and Poor's and Moody's KMV represent collective groupings of bonds with similar likelihoods of default, at least in the assessment of the ratings companies. Yield spreads on a given rating class are indicative of the cost of credit risk. For example, suppose a 10-year U.S. Treasury bond is yielding 1.75% and a Baa-rated 10-year corporate bond is yielding 4.5%, the yield spread is 2.75%. We will have more to say about yield spreads and credit ratings in Section 11.4.1.1, but for now, just be aware that the spread is wider the greater the likelihood of default.

Now let us consider the bond we were examining that has a face value of Z, a price of D_0, and matures in T years. Let us calculate the yield spread as implied by the BSM model. Typical yield spreads in markets are done on a discrete compounding basis, but the BSM model uses continuous compounding, so we must do so as well. Let y_c be the continuously compounded yield. By definition, the yield is the discount rate that equates the price to its face value:

$$D_0 = Ze^{-y_c T}.$$

Solving for y_c gives

$$y_c = -\frac{\ln(D_0/Z)}{T} \tag{11.5}$$

And the yield spread is easily found as

$$y_s = y_c - r_c \tag{11.6}$$

Shortly, we shall illustrate this point with an example.

11.2.3.2 *The Value of the Implicit Put Held by the Shareholders*

Now, let us value the put option held by the shareholders that was granted by the creditors. Recall from put-call parity, $S_0 = A_0 + p_0 - Z/(1+r)^T$, so $p_0 = S_0 - A_0 + Z/(1+r)^T$. Note, however, that we used discrete discounting by applying the factor $1/(1+r)^T$. When working in the Black-Scholes-Merton world, we shall need to use continuous discounting. Therefore, the discount factor is e^{-r_cT}. Thus, $p_0 = S_0 - A_0 + Ze^{-r_cT}$.[1] Substituting from Equation (11.3), we have

$$p_0 = A_0 N(x_1) - Ze^{-r_cT} - A_0 + Ze^{-r_cT}$$
$$= Ze^{-r_cT}(1 - N(x_2)) - A_0(1 - N(x_1)) \tag{11.7}$$

Of course, as previously noted, a somewhat simpler way to value the put is through put-call parity. Here we express it using continuous discounting of the option exercise price, Z:

$$p_0 = S_0 - A_0 + Ze^{-r_cT}.$$

11.2.3.3 *The Probability of Default*

The probability of default is easily obtained from the BSM model. As it turns out, the value of $N(x_2)$ is the probability that stock will pay off and, thus, not default. So the probability of default is $1 - N(x_2)$ or $N(-x_2)$. There is, however, one catch. The term, x_2, calculated as

$$x_2 = x_1 - \sigma_A\sqrt{T}$$
$$\text{where } x_1 = \frac{\ln(A_0/Z) + (r_c + \sigma_A^2/2)T}{\sigma_A\sqrt{T}},$$

is based on the assumption that the expected return on the company's assets is the risk-free rate. This assumption is a convenient one that works correctly for valuing derivatives, but it does not accurately capture the likelihood of the option paying off, or conversely, expiring out-of-the-money. Thus, it will not accurately capture the likelihood of default.

Using the equations directly above, it can be shown that

$$x_2 = \frac{\ln(A_0/Z) + (r_c - \sigma_A^2/2)T}{\sigma_A\sqrt{T}}$$

The difference between x_2 and x_1 is the sign after the risk-free rate, which is positive for x_1 and negative for x_2. The risk-free rate, r_c, is the implied

---

[1] Because $r_c = \ln(1+r)$, the two present value factors, e^{-r_cT} and $1/(1+r)^T$ give equivalent values, so we have not changed the underlying economics.

expected return on the asset. Let us define the expected return on the assets as a new variable, μ_A.[2] Then we specify the probability of default as

$$\text{Probability of Default} = \Pr(A_T < Z) = 1 - N(x_{2A})$$

$$\text{where } x_{2A} = \frac{\ln(A_0/Z) + (\mu_A - \sigma_A^2/2)T}{\sigma_A \sqrt{T}}. \tag{11.8}$$

where $\Pr(A_T < Z)$ is formally stated as the probability that the asset value at the maturity of the debt is less than the amount owed.

11.2.3.4 *The Expected Loss, Given Default*

We will also be interested in quantifying the expected loss in terms of actual money. First, we shall take a look at the concept of *Expected Loss Given Default*. This measure is sometimes called *Loss Given Default* or LGD, but we should not forget that it is an expected loss, so we shall call it the former and use the symbol ELGD. It is based on the notion that if default occurs, we would like to know what loss to expect. It is defined as

$$\text{Expected Loss Given Default} = \text{ELGD}$$

$$= Z - E(A_T | A_T < Z).$$

In other words, ELGD is defined as the amount owed minus the expected value of the assets, given that the asset value is below the amount owed. To obtain the value $E(A_T | A_T < Z)$, we recognize the two collectively exhaustive conditions that make up the expected value of A_T:

$$E(A_T) = E(A_T | A_T \geq Z)\Pr(A_T \geq Z) + E(A_T | A_T < Z)\Pr(A_T < Z).$$

The first condition on the right-hand side is the expected value of the assets conditional that the value of the assets exceeds the amount owed, times the probability that the value of the assets exceeds the amount owed. The second condition is the one of interest, the expected value of the assets conditional that the value of the assets is less than the amount owed, times

---

[2]In corporate finance courses, this concept is known as the *cost of capital* and represents the rate of return a company must earn on its assets to pay the suppliers of capital, who are the creditors and shareholders, the return they expect given the risk they take.

the probability that the value of the assets is less than the amount owed. Rearranging the above equation, we have:

$$E(A_T|A_T < Z) = \frac{E(A_T) - E(A_T|A_T \geq Z)\Pr(A_T \geq Z)}{\Pr(A_T < Z)}$$

By definition, the expected value of the assets at T is

$$E(A_T) = A_0 e^{\mu_A T}$$

Thus,

$$E(A_T|A_T < Z) = \frac{A_0 e^{\mu_A T} - E(A_T|A_T \geq Z)\Pr(A_T \geq Z)}{\Pr(A_T < Z)}$$

Re-writing, we obtain

$$E(A_T|A_T \geq Z)\Pr(A_T \geq Z) = A_0 e^{\mu_A T} - E(A_T|A_T \geq Z)\Pr(A_T \geq Z).$$

Without getting into a formal proof, as it is beyond the scope of this course, we will state formally that the expression on the right-hand side after the minus sign, $E(A_T|A_T \geq Z)\Pr(A_T \geq Z)$, is equivalent to $A_0 e^{\mu_A T}N(x_{1A})$, where x_{1A} is the value of x_1 in Equation (11.3) with the cost of capital, μ_A, in place of r_c. Thus, the right hand side is equal to $A_0 e^{\mu_A T}(1 - N(x_{1A}))$. And we know that $\Pr(A_T < Z)$ is $1 - N(x_{2A})$. Thus, the Expected Loss Given Default is

$$ELGD = Z - E(A_T|A_T < Z) = Z - \frac{A_0 e^{\mu_A T}(1 - N(x_{1A}))}{1 - N(x_{2A})} \qquad (11.9)$$

Or alternatively, we can write it as

$$ELGD = \frac{Z(1 - N(x_{2A})) - A_0 e^{\mu_A T}(1 - N(x_{1A}))}{1 - N(x_{2A})}$$

11.2.3.5 *The Expected Loss*

We may also be interested in the Expected Loss (EL). It differs from the Expected Loss Given Default in that the Expected Loss takes into account all of the outcomes in which there is not a loss as well as the outcomes in which there is a default, while the Expected Loss Given Default considers only the outcomes in which there is a loss.

The Expected Loss is easily found as the ELGD times the probability of default:

$$EL = ELGD * \Pr(A_T < Z) = \left(Z - \frac{A_0 e^{\mu_A T}(1 - N(x_{1A}))}{N(x_{2A})} \right) N(x_{2A})$$

$$(11.10)$$

11.2.4 *A Comprehensive Credit Risk Pricing Example*

In Exhibit 11-4, we examine a credit risk problem and calculate the measures described above.

11.2.5 *The Effect of Changes in Inputs*

We have seen that the key outputs of this model are driven by the asset value, the amount of debt, the time to maturity of the debt, the risk-free rate, and the volatility of the assets. Changes in the values of these inputs can have a significant effect on the outputs.

We will focus on two key outputs, the yield spread and the probability of default, and we will examine three inputs, the ratio of debt to total assets, the volatility of the assets, and the maturity of the debt. The ratio of debt to total assets will be defined as the face value of the debt divided by the market value of the assets. Normally this measure, roughly called the debt ratio, is measured as either the book value of the debt divided by the book value of the assets or the market value of the debt divided by the market value of the assets. We do not have, nor do we need, the book value of the assets. Book value is a measure of the historical entries in the accounting statements. It is completely irrelevant in the assessment of credit risk. We could measure the market value of the debt divided by the market value of the assets, but there is a problem in that the market value of the debt is endogenous. It is one of the outputs of the model. Thus, we cannot exogenously specify it the way we can the face value of the debt. Thus, we will use the book value of the debt divided by the market value of the assets. This ratio will simultaneously capture the effects of two inputs, the market value of the assets and the face value of the debt. As noted, we will also look at the volatility of the assets and the maturity of the debt. We will not look at the effect of the risk-free rate, as it is well-known to have only a modest effect on Black-Scholes-Merton option values.

Objective: Determine the value of the stock, the value of the debt, the value of the implicit put option held by the stockholders, the yield spread, the probability of default, the expected loss given default, and the expected loss for a company with assets with a market value of $100,000, one issue of zero-coupon debt due in seven years with face value $45,000, volatility of assets of 0.35, and a continuously compounded risk-free rate of 3%. The expected return on the assets is 10%.

Inputs:

$$A_0 = 100,000$$
$$Z = 45,000$$
$$r_c = 0.03$$
$$T = 7$$
$$\sigma_A = 0.35$$

Results:

$$x_1 = \frac{\ln(100,000/45,000) + (0.03 + (0.35)^2/2)(7)}{0.35\sqrt{7}} = 1.5521$$

$$x_2 = 1.5521 - 0.35\sqrt{7} = 0.6261$$

$$N(1.5521) = 0.9397$$

$$N(0.6261) = 0.7344$$

$$S_0 = 100,000(0.9397) - 45,000e^{-0.03(7)}(0.7344) = 67,181$$

The value of the bonds is found as the difference in the market value of the assets and the market value of the stock.

$$D_0 = A_0 - S_0$$
$$= 100,000 - 67,181$$
$$= 32,819.$$

If the bonds were default-free, their value would simply be the face value discounted at the risk-free rate:

$$45,000e^{-0.03(7)} = 36,476.$$

The value of the implicit put is the difference in the value of the bonds if they were default-free and their value as defaultable bonds:

$$p_0 = 36,476 - 32,819$$
$$= 3,657.$$

The yield on the bonds is

$$y_c = -\frac{\ln(32,819/45,000)}{7} = 0.0451.$$

Exhibit 11-4. Comprehensive Credit Risk Pricing Problem

The yield spread is

$$y_s = 0.0451 - 0.03 = 0.0151.$$

Now we estimate the probability of default with the assumption that the expected return on the assets as 10%.

$$x_{1A} = \frac{\ln(100{,}000/45{,}000) + (0.10 + (0.35)^2/2)(7)}{0.35\sqrt{7}} = 2.0812$$

$$x_{2A} = 2.0812 - 0.35\sqrt{7} = 1.1552$$

$$N(2.0812) = 0.9813$$

$$N(1.1552) = 0.8760.$$

The probability of default is $1 - 0.8760 = 0.1240$. The Expected Loss Given Default is

$$ELGD = \frac{45{,}000(1 - 0.8760) - 100{,}000e^{0.10(7)}\,(1 - 0.9813)}{1 - 0.8760}$$

$$= 14{,}621.$$

The Expected Loss is

$$EL = 100{,}000e^{0.10(7)}(1 - 0.9813)$$

$$= 1{,}813.$$

Exhibit 11-4. (*Continued*)

Exhibit 11-5 shows the yield spread and probability of default plotted against the debt ratio, defined as face value of debt divided by market value of assets. First, notice a strong similarity between the two graphs. Indeed, the yield spread is driven heavily by the probability of default, though the recovery rate also plays a role. Both the yield spread and probability of default rise monotonically with the debt ratio. This result is what we should expect. Holding everything else constant, the more debt the company has, the riskier it is, and, thus, the higher is the yield spread and probability of default.

Exhibit 11-6 shows the yield spread and probability of default as they relate to the volatility of the return on the assets. You should think of the volatility of the return on the assets as a basic measure of the business risk of the company. It reflects the uncertainty of the products and services that the company provides. While these graphs are somewhat similar, but they are still a bit different. As we would expect, if the assets are riskier, the yield spread and the probability of default should be higher. The yield spread rises monotonically at an increasing rate, while the probability of default has an

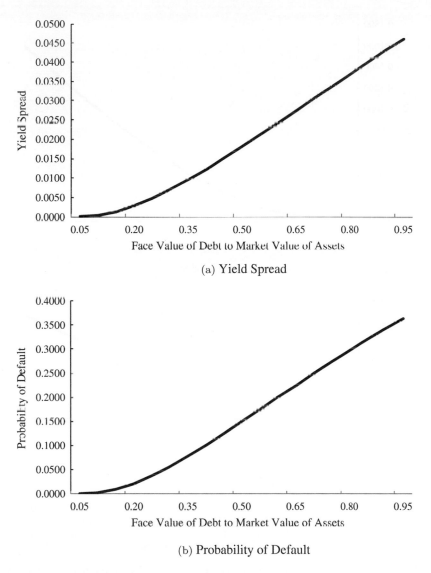

(a) Yield Spread

(b) Probability of Default

Exhibit 11-5. Yield Spread (a) and Probability of Default (b) by Debt Ratio

inflection point, a level at which it stops increasing at an increasing rate and begins to increase at a decreasing rate.

Exhibit 11-7 shows the yield spread and probability of default by the maturity of the debt. Here the yield spread rises sharply and then flattens out at around 10%, which occurs at a maturity of about 13 years. It then begins to fall with longer maturity. The probability of default rises monotonically but at a decreasing rate. The reason for this turnaround in the yield spread

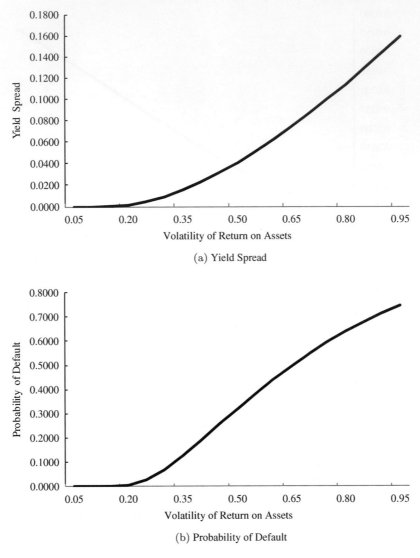

Exhibit 11-6. Yield Spread (a) and Probability of Default (b) by Volatility of Assets

is interesting. On the one hand, one tends to think that a longer maturity should result in an increased in the yield spread. After all, a longer maturity means more time to default. Such a result is clear in the range of zero to about 13 years. But beyond a point of maturity, the yield spread starts to decrease. This result is due to the fact that longer maturity can give a company more time to perform well. In other words, if a company begins to have trouble, the longer the maturity, the more likely it will have time to

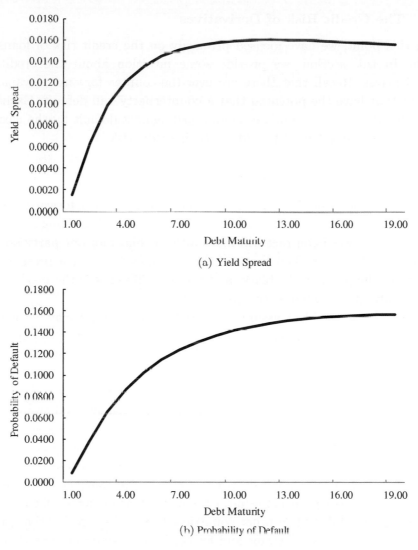

Exhibit 11-7. Yield Spread (a) and Probability of Default (b) by Debt Maturity

recover. This effect does not show up, however, in the probability of default. The probability of default does not incorporate the recovery rate. It is strictly a measure of the likelihood that the asset value will exceed the amount owed on the maturity date. The yield spread, however, does reflect the recovery rate. Thus, longer term debt can have a higher probability of default, but the amount recovered can be greater due to the longer time that the assets have to grow in value.

11.3 The Credit Risk of Derivatives

Until this point, we have focused primarily on the credit risk of loans and bonds. In this section, we provide some intuition about the credit risk of derivatives. Recall that there are over-the-counter forwards, swaps, and options that have the potential that a counterparty will default. Exchange-listed derivatives are essentially guaranteed against default by the clearing-houses, so we do not need to address their credit risk.

11.3.1 *Forward Contracts*

In Chapter 8 we studied forward contracts. Recall that a forward contract starts off with a zero value at the start. As the underlying changes and time elapses, the forward contract will move into the black for one party and into the red for the other. The party in the red owes more on a present value basis than the party in the black, and the net difference is the market value of the contract. So where is the credit risk?

The party in the black assumes the credit risk in that it may not get paid by the party in the red. Yet as long as the contract is prior to expiration, the amount owed is not currently due. Thus, there is no default. It is quite possible, however, that the party in the red will declare bankruptcy before the forward contract expires. In the U.S. the bankruptcy law was amended in 2005 to accelerate the termination of forward contracts and swaps. Thus, when a party files for Chapter 11, swaps and forward contracts are handled outside of the normal bankruptcy process. The market value is calculated and owed immediately by one party to another. This process prevents the defaulting party from sliding deeper in debt as the contract could become increasingly more negative in value as the underlying changes. Of course, this process can be different in other countries. But if this acceleration process is legal, the credit risk of swaps and forwards is considerably less than that of other general and secured creditors.

So at any given time, the current exposure in a forward contract is the market value, and that exposure is assumed by the party in the black. The exposure is not, however, a measure of the full credit risk. As we saw in previous sections, there are several ways to express that risk, such as the expected loss and the expected loss given default. Thus, just because one holds an outstanding forward contract with positive value does not mean that the likely loss is very great. The probability of default could be very low.

The credit risk in a forward contract is generally somewhat low, at least in relation to the notional principal. Parties typically do not enter into forward contracts unless the counterparty has low credit risk. Moreover, the market value of the contract is usually somewhat low relative to the notional. Remember that the market value is the present value of what one party owes minus the present value of what the other party owes. This net amount is almost always just a small fraction of the notional. There is an exception, however, because the notional is paid at the end of some currency swaps.

11.3.2 Swaps

The points regarding credit risk of forward contracts apply to the credit risk of swaps. Recall that forward contracts differ from swaps only on two dimensions. Swaps involve a series of payments, while forwards involve only one payment. Also, all swap payments are made at the same agreed-to-fixed rate, while the individual forward contracts that expire on the each of the swap payment dates would have different fixed rates. While these points are important in seeing the analogy, they do not materially change the credit risk characteristics of swaps and forwards. After the initiation date, a swap has a market value that is in the black to one party and in the red to the other. The party to which the value is in the black assumes the credit risk at that instant. The credit risk itself, however, is not just the exposure but reflects the likelihood of default. Moreover, the market value can flip over from red to black for one party and black to red to the other. And, the acceleration clause in the U.S. applies to swaps as well.

There is certainly more credit risk in swaps than in forwards, as swaps involve more payments and, therefore, will have more money to changing hands. But again, these payments are net payments. The credit risk of swaps is likely to be greatest during the middle of the life of the swap. Shorter-term swaps tend to have fairly low credit risk, because they are not generally engaged if the credit risk is high at the time the transactions are initiated. The credit risk is also somewhat lower during the latter part of the life of a swap, because there are fewer payments remaining.

The swaps industry has developed a measure called the credit value adjustment, or CVA, that is used in swap pricing and incorporates the value of default. The CVA is essentially the difference in the value of an instrument, such as a swap, based on the assumption that it is risk-free compared to its true value. Thus, CVA is the value, or conversely the cost, of the credit risk.

11.3.3 Options

While the credit risk of swaps and forwards is similar, the credit risk of options is structurally quite different. Recall that with an option, the buyer pays money at the start but has no further obligation. It has the right to exercise the option, but it has no obligation to do so, nor is there any additional money it has to pay. Therefore, the seller of the option assumes no credit risk. The buyer of the option holds an asset that has value during the life of the option and, therefore, the buyer assumes some credit exposure. Ultimately, however, the option might expire out-of-the-money and, therefore, have zero value. So the option holder assumes the credit risk that if he chooses to exercise the option, the option seller could default.

By way of comparison, the credit risk of forwards and futures is bilateral, meaning that each party assumes some credit risk from the other. Bilateral credit risk exists whenever each party owes money to the other. In forwards and swaps, each party agrees to make a payment to the other. Thus, there is a pair of bilateral payments and, thus, bilateral credit risk. With options, however, the credit risk is unilateral. In all cases, the credit risk is the market value multiplied by a factor to reflect the likelihood of default and the potential recovery.

It is also important to see that credit risk is related to market risk. As the market moves, the market value changes and creates the credit risk that one party assumes from the other.

11.4　Measuring and Managing Credit Risk

We have seen that with option models, credit risk can be quantified. We can talk about the expected loss, the expected loss given default, and the probability of default. These measures are useful, but they are only part of the toolkit used by credit analysts. Moreover, the inputs to the option model of credit risk can be difficult to obtain without applying further analysis.

One of the real challenges in measuring credit risk is the simple fact that credit losses are infrequent events. Consider a company that has never defaulted in its entire life. How does one go about estimating the likelihood of default in such a situation? Market risk, on the other hand, is assessed by analyzing the large quantities of data on the fluctuations in prices, interest rates, and exchange rates that are collected on a daily basis in the market. In other words, we have a great deal of information on the ups and downs of an interest rate, but we have little to no information on the frequency with which a party defaults.

Be that as it may, there is still a great deal of information on the frequency of defaults in general. Thus, it is possible to combine data for similar types of firms and firms with similar risk profiles. For example, one might ask the question: out of 1,000 industrial companies with solid financial characteristics, how many default in a given year? But how do we decide which companies should be grouped together? That task is typically done by rating agencies.

11.4.1 *Rating Agencies*

In the early 1900s, John Moody founded a company called Moody's Investor Services. Among the products he offered were ratings of the credit quality of U.S. corporate and municipal bonds. In the 1860s, Henry Varnum Poor began to publish a history of the U.S. railroad and canal industry and eventually began to collaborate with his son Henry W. Poor on manuals on railroads. In the early part of the 20th century, the Poors merged the company with a firm known as Standard Statistics Bureau, which had begun to publish ratings of bonds, and the company became known as Standard and Poor's, commonly referred to as S&P. In the 1960s, S&P was bought out by a major book publisher, McGraw-Hill. While there are several other companies that provide credit ratings, Moody's and S&P are the industry leaders. The rating companies have assumed such an important part in our markets that they are recognized by the federal government as Nationally Recognized Statistical Rating Organizations, or NRSROs. While the term "agencies" is widely used to characterize these companies, they are not agencies of any entity in any sense. They are private companies that provide opinions. Still, you will often hear of them referred to as ratings agencies.

11.4.1.1 *Credit Ratings*

Exhibit 11-8 gives Moody's and Standard and Poor's ratings categories. The name of the highest rating, Aaa for Moody's and AAA for S&P, is pronounced "Triple A." The second highest category, Aa2 for Moody's and AA+ for S&P, is pronounced "Double A2" and "Double A plus," respectively. Other categories have pronunciations such as "B double A2" (Baa2) for Moody's and "Double B plus," (BB+) for S&P. The industry has also adopted a subjective dichotomy in which all bonds rated Baa3 or BBB — or above are referred to as "investment grade," and the remaining lower-rated bonds are called "speculative," although there is some disagreement over exactly where the line is drawn. While the so-called investment grade bonds are considered relatively safe and speculative bonds are considered relatively risky, it is clear that one cannot easily split all bonds into two categories. The very notion that bonds are rated into these multiple categories belies any sense that there is an easy-to-discern dichotomy.

Moody's	Standard and Poor's
Aaa	AAA
Aa1	AA+
Aa2	AA
Aa3	AA−
A1	A+
A2	A
A3	A−
Baa1	BBB+
Baa2	BBB
Baa3	BBB−
Ba1	BB+
Ba2	BB
Ba3	BB−
B1	B+
B2	B
B3	B−
Caa1	CCC+
Caa2	CCC
Caa3	CCC−
Ca	CC
C	C
	D

Exhibit 11-8. Moody's and Standard and Poor's Ratings

Moody's and S&P do not reveal the methods they use to classify bonds, but researchers have been able to determine that bond ratings are fairly predictable based on standard financial ratios, which we will lightly discuss in a later section. Separate ratings are also given for short-term debt. The issuers of these securities pay Moody's and S&P to rate their debt, though in some cases, a company may choose not to pay to get rated in which case Moody's and S&P may decide to rate the company anyway.

Exhibit 11-9 shows the data reported by Standard and Poor's of average default rates by its rating categories from 1982 through 2010. A number of years ago, S&P did not use the plus and minus categories, so this data is based on ignoring the plusses and minuses. The column called "One Year" means that the percentage indicated is the percentage of bonds that defaulted with a year. The columns called "Five Years Later" and "Ten Years Later" indicate the percentage of bonds that defaulted five and ten years respectively after the bonds were rated in the category indicated in the left-most column. Notice that there are no defaults in the Aaa category in the

Rating Category	One Year	Five Years Later	Ten Years Later
AAA	0.00%	0.35%	0.72%
AA	0.02%	0.33%	0.77%
A	0.06%	0.53%	1.41%
BBB	0.18%	1.78%	3.76%
BB	0.72%	7.45%	13.33%
B	3.76%	18.32%	25.43%
CCC-C	26.78%	46.42%	51.03%
Investment Grade	0.10%	0.96%	2.11%
Speculative Grade	3.83%	15.29%	21.67%
All Bonds	1.52%	6.25%	9.18%

Global Corporate Average Cumulative Default Rates (1981–2016) as compiled by S&P. Data extracted from Table 24 in *2016 Annual Global Corporate Default Study and Rating Transitions*.

Exhibit 11-9. Default Rates by S&P Rating Category

year following the rating. Nonetheless, some of these bonds are downgraded and regardless of rating, 0.35% have defaulted within five years and 0.72% within 10 years. Notice also that in all cases, the percentage of defaults increases consistently by rating category.

When Moody's and S&P first began rating bonds about a hundred years ago, it was quite difficult to obtain information about the credit quality of a company. Moreover, there was very limited knowledge on what to do with this information. Credit analysis is an art as well as a science, and there was not much general knowledge of how to do it. Moody's and S&P not only had access to the financial information necessary to analyze the creditworthiness of a company, but they also employed personnel with the requisite expertise. Over the years, however, the knowledge of how to conduct credit analysis and even the knowledge necessary to unlock the mysteries behind Moody's and S&P's ratings has become more widespread. Credit analysis is widely taught in finance programs, and banks and other borrowers train their personnel how to do it. As such, the ratings provided by these companies do not really provide much additional information beyond what a good financial analyst could discern on her own. Nonetheless, the prestige and stature of these firms has increased over the years to the point that in the U.S. they are mentioned in many laws and are regulated by the SEC. Almost any lender or credit analyst would check the Moody's and S&P ratings before making a final recommendation.

Sub-Prime Mortgages and the Bankruptcy of Lehman Brothers

Lehman Brothers was founded in the middle of the 19th century by two German brothers who started a dry-goods store in Montgomery, Alabama. Since cotton is one of the most important raw materials in dry goods, the company participated in the strong growth of the cotton industry in the 19th century south. The firm also began speculating in the trading of cotton, and following the Civil War, it moved to New York where the financial markets were more active. The company became a financial institution, engaged primarily in trading and investment banking, eventually rising to become the fourth largest investment banking firm in the U.S. Its last highly successful year, 2007, saw Lehman earn revenues of $46 billion and profit of $4 billion.

But Lehman became heavily involved in the sub-prime mortgage market. Sub-prime mortgages were mortgages in which borrowers that had very low credit quality and a questionable likelihood of repayment were able to easily get mortgages to finance home purchases. Sub-prime mortgages were a response to the U.S. government's assertive stance that every American should own a home. Supported by the willingness of the two-government backed corporations, Fannie Mae and Freddie Mac, to buy the mortgages, Lehman and numerous other Wall Street firms willingly traded in sub-prime mortgages, knowing that they could easily sell the mortgages to Fannie Mae and Freddie Mac, if not other financial institutions.

But in 2007, the formerly booming U.S. house prices began to fall. Many sub-prime mortgages that were initially made at a low rate eventually required refinancing at a higher rate. With falling house prices, many homeowners went "underwater" meaning that they could not refinance since the values of the houses were less than the amount owed on the loans. It is believed that Lehman carried over $20 billion of these mortgages, which began to rapidly decline in value. And as with most financial institutions, much of Lehman's assets were financed by credit. Its creditors became very uncomfortable and exercised their rights to deny further credit and to reduce Lehman's credit balances. All of this was happening within six months of the bankruptcy of Bear Stearns, another major Wall Street investment banking firm which had been the fifth largest U.S. investment bank, and stresses and strains at many other major financial institutions.

Lehman looked hard for a company with which it could merge but was not successful. It also sought investors that would inject additional capital, but no one was willing to take the bet, given Lehman's precarious position. It asked that it be classified as a bank, whereupon it could borrow from the Federal Reserve, but the Fed would not agree. Lehman then attempt to sell itself to Barclays and Bank of America, but those banks wanted a government guarantee that they did not get. Other firms, such as Merrill Lynch, Washington Mutual, and AIG were also weakening and in danger of failing. The Fed and the U.S. Treasury had a lot to worry about. From January to July of 2008, Lehman's stock fell from just under $80 to about $20. And on September 15, 2008 Lehman filed for Chapter 11 protection listing assets of about $691 billion and liabilities of $619 billion. Though not technically bankrupt, Lehman was completely unable to meet its collateral requirements, as so many of its assets were insufficiently liquid. The Lehman bankruptcy sent shock waves into an already fragile financial system and accelerated what was then a financial weakening of the economy into a full-blown crisis. Further complicating matters was the fact that Lehman had over 900,000 derivative contracts in place.

As of this date, the Lehman bankruptcy is still the largest in history. Perhaps not surprisingly, the second largest was also a major player in the sub-prime mortgage crisis: Washington Mutual. Indeed, the Financial Crisis of 2008 and 2009 generated a large group of casualties of financial institutions that either died or were absorbed into stronger companies.

11.4.1.2 *Ratings Transitions*

Besides the ratings themselves and their corresponding probabilities of default, changes in ratings are useful information. They tell us the likelihood that a borrower will move from one rating category to another in a specified period of time. Because a change in rating is a significant piece of information, it is useful to know something about the likelihood that a borrower will undergo a change in its rating. This type of information is often shown in the form of a table called a *rating transition matrix*. Exhibit 11-10 shows a one-year rating transition matrix provided by S&P and published in its *2016 Annual Global Corporate Default Study and Rating Transitions*. The figures are based on data from 1981–2016.

The numbers in each cell represent the percentage of bonds rated according to the rating in the row that changed to the rating in the column

Rating	AAA	AA	A	BBB	BB	B	CCC/C	D	NR
AAA	87.05%	9.03%	0.53%	0.05%	0.08%	0.03%	0.05%	0.00%	3.17%
AA	0.52%	86.82%	8.00%	0.51%	0.05%	0.07%	0.02%	0.02%	3.99%
A	0.03%	1.77%	87.79%	5.33%	0.32%	0.13%	0.02%	0.06%	4.55%
BBB	0.01%	0.10%	3.51%	85.56%	3.79%	0.51%	0.12%	0.18%	6.23%
BB	0.01%	0.03%	0.12%	4.97%	76.98%	6.92%	0.61%	0.72%	9.63%
B	0.00%	0.03%	0.09%	0.19%	5.15%	74.26%	4.46%	3.76%	12.06%
CCC/C	0.00%	0.00%	0.13%	0.19%	0.63%	12.91%	43.97%	26.78%	15.39%

Average One-Year Corporate Transition Rates (1981–2016); Data extracted from Table 22 in *2016 Annual Global Corporate Default Study and Rating Transitions*.

Exhibit 11-10. Example of S&P Ratings Transition Matrix

within one year. The columns labeled "D" and "NR" mean that the bond defaulted or was not rated, respectively.[3]

We see that most bonds remain in the same rating class within a year. There is a slight tendency for higher rated bonds to move up and lower rated bonds to move down. S&P also publishes ratings transition matrices for three, five, and seven years. Over a longer period of time, ratings changes occur far more frequently.

11.4.2 *Quantifying Credit Risk*

The credit risk model that we discussed in Section 11.2.3 in which the Black-Scholes-Merton model is used to find the value of a bond subject to default and other useful information is one way to approach credit risk measurement on a case-by-case basis. It permits us to analyze one loan or derivative at a time. When there are multiple loans or derivatives, as there usually are, the situation gets a bit more complex. Moreover, there may be reason to believe that if one loan defaults, the condition that caused the default could affect other loans.

11.4.2.1 *The Single Loan Case*

Let us start with an example of a single loan, referred to as Loan A, in the amount of $20,000. We assess that the probability of default is 4.5%.

---

[3]Moody's withdraws a rating when it feels that it cannot obtain sufficiently accurate information, or the company is in bankruptcy, liquidation, restricting, or a write-down, though such an event would almost surely result in the company classified as having defaulted.

If default occurs, however, all is not lost. There is a 75% chance of recovering 10% of the amount owed, which is $2,000 implying a loss of $18,000, and a 25% chance of recovering 20% of the amount owed, which is $4,000 implying a loss of $16,000. Thus, with the probability of default at 4.5%, there is a 95.5% chance of losing nothing. The probability of recovering 10% of the amount owed and losing 90% is $0.045(0.75) = 0.03375$, which is based on a 4.5% chance of default and a 75% chance of recovering 10% of the amount owed. The probability of losing 80% of the amount owed is $0.045(0.25) = 0.01125$, based on a 4.5% chance of default and a 25% chance of recovering 20% of the amount owed. Thus, the distribution of possible credit losses is

Credit Loss	Probability
$0	0.95500
$16,000 (80% loss)	0.01125
$18,000 (90% loss)	0.03375

To verify that these numbers are correct, note that the probability of default is the sum of the probabilities of the two losses, 0.0125 and 0.03375, which add up to 0.045, as specified.

From here, we can calculate the expected credit loss, which is

$$\$0(0.95500) + \$16,000(0.011250) + \$18,000(0.03375) - \$788.$$

The loss given default is the expected value of the loss, given that default occurs. We find it by taking a weighted average of the two possible loss amounts. The weights are their probabilities of occurrence divided by the probability of default.

$$\$18,000 \left(\frac{0.03375}{0.01125 + 0.03375} \right) + \$16,000 \left(\frac{0.01125}{0.01125 + 0.03375} \right) = \$17,500.$$

In other words, the terms in parentheses, which calculate to 75% and 25%, respectively, indicate that if default occurs, there is a 75% chance of a loss of $18,000 and 25% chance of a loss of $16,000, which averages out to $17,500. So we might say that on average, we would expect to lose $788, and if a default occurs, we would expect to lose $17,500 on average.

11.4.2.2 *Two Independent Loans*

Now suppose we add a second loan, which we identify as Loan B. The face value is $12,000 and the probability of default is 6%. If default occurs, there is again a 75% chance of a 10% recovery, which is $1,200 implying a loss of $10,800, and a 25% chance of a 20% recovery, which is $2,400 implying a loss of $9,600. Thus, there is a 94% chance of no loss, a $0.06(0.25) = 0.015$ chance of a loss of 80%, and a $0.06(0.75) = 0.045$ chance of a loss of 90%. The distribution of possible credit losses is, therefore,

Credit Loss	Probability
$0	0.94000
$9,600 (80% loss)	0.01500
$10,800 (90% loss)	0.04500

And of course, 0.015 and 0.045 add up to 0.06, the probability of default. The expected credit loss is

$$\$0(0.94000) + \$9,600(0.015) + \$10,800(0.045) = \$630$$

The loss given default of the second loan is

$$\$9,600 \left(\frac{0.015}{0.015 + 0.045} \right) + \$10,800 \left(\frac{0.045}{0.015 + 0.045} \right) = \$10,500.$$

Adding up the expected losses, we obtain $788 + $630 = $1,418, but is this is the actual expected loss? It will be the expected loss only under one condition: that the default rates are independent. Let us first prove that indeed, $1,418 is the expected loss if the default rates are independent. Then, let us remove the assumption of independence.

Independence of default rates means that if one loan defaults, it has no effect on whether the other loan defaults. In short, we assume that the default probability of Loan B is the same regardless of whether Loan A defaults. Likewise, the default probability of Loan A is the same regardless of whether Loan B defaults. That is, if the probability of default of Loan B does not depend on whether Loan A defaults or vice versa, the loans are independent. If the probability of default of one loan is affected by whether the other loan defaults, the loans are not independent.

With two recovery rates possible, we will see that there are nine possible outcomes, as shown below[4]:

---

[4]The reason we know there are nine outcomes is that there are two loans, each with three outcomes (full recovery, 10% recovery, and 20% recovery). The nine outcomes derive from the expression $3^2 = 9$, where the exponent is the number of loans and the base is the number of possible outcomes.

Outcome	Result
1	Both loans pay off in full
2	Loan A pays off, Loan B defaults with 10% recovery
3	Loan A pays off, Loan B defaults with 20% recovery
4	Loan A defaults with 10% recovery, Loan B pays off in full
5	Loan A defaults with 10% recovery, Loan B defaults with 10% recovery
6	Loan A defaults with 10% recovery, Loan B defaults with 20% recovery
7	Loan A defaults with 20% recovery, Loan B pays off in full
8	Loan A defaults with 20% recovery, Loan B defaults with 10% recovery
9	Loan A defaults with 20% recovery, Loan B defaults with 20% recovery

Exhibit 11-11 shows the probability calculations and the losses under each of these conditions. For Loan A, the probability of default is 0.045, and the probability of a full payoff is $1 - 0.045 = 0.955$. For Loan B, the probability of default is 0.06, and the probability of a full payoff is $1 - 0.06 = 0.94$. If either loan defaults, the probability of a 10% payoff is 0.75, and the probability of a 20% payoff is 0.25. If A defaults with a 10% recovery, the loss is $18,000 (90% of $20,000), and with a 20% recovery, the loss is $16,000 (80% of $20,000). If B defaults with a 10% recovery, the loss is $10,800 (90% of $12,000), and with a 20% recovery the loss is $9,600 (80% of $12,000).

To verify this table, you should add up column 3 that shows the probabilities. The probabilities should and do indeed add up to 1. We can verify the expected loss by the product of the third and fourth columns:

$$0.8977(\$0) + 0.042975(\$10,800) + 0.014325(\$9,600)$$
$$+ 0.031725(\$18,000) + 0.001519(\$28,800) + 0.000506(\$27,600)$$
$$+ 0.010575(\$16,000) + 0.000506(\$26,800) + 0.000169(\$25,600)$$
$$= \$1,418$$

And this answer is the one we obtained earlier when simply adding the expected losses from each of the two loans, $788 + $630. The probability of default is $1 - 0.8977$, meaning 1 minus the probability of both paying off, which is 0.1023. This number is the probability of at least one default.

Outcome	Result	Probability	Loss
1	Both loans pay in full	$0.955 \times 0.94 = 0.8977$	$0
2	A pays off, B defaults with 10% recovery	$0.955 \times 0.06 \times 0.75 =$ 0.042975	$10,800
3	A pays off, B defaults with 20% recovery	$0.955 \times 0.06 \times 0.25 =$ 0.014325	$9,600
4	A defaults with 10% recovery, B pays in full	$0.045 \times 0.75 \times 0.94 =$ 0.031725	$18,000
5	A defaults with 10% recovery, B defaults with 10% recovery	$0.045 \times 0.75 \times 0.06 \times 0.75 = 0.001519$	$18,000 + $10,800 = $28,800
6	A defaults with 10% recovery, B defaults with 20% recovery	$0.045 \times 0.75 \times 0.06 \times 0.25 = 0.000506$	$18,000 + $9,600 = $27,600
7	A defaults with 20% recovery, B pays in full	$0.045 \times 0.25 \times 0.94 =$ 0.010575	$16,000
8	A defaults with 20% recovery, B defaults with 10% recovery	$0.045 \times 0.25 \times 0.06 \times 0.75 = 0.000506$	$16,000 + $10,800 = $26,800
9	A defaults with 20% recovery, B defaults with 20% recovery	$0.045 \times 0.25 \times 0.06 \times 0.25 = 0.000169$	$16,000 + $9,600 = $25,600

Exhibit 11-11. Probabilities of Default and Losses for Independent Loans A and B

The probability of two defaults is the sum of the probabilities of all of the outcomes in which there are two defaults (outcomes 5, 6, 8, and 9), which is $0.001519 + 0.000506 + 0.000506 + 0.000169 = 0.0027$, or 0.27%. The loss given default is

$$\frac{\begin{matrix} 0.042975(\$10,800) + 0.014325(\$9,600) + 0.031725(\$18,000) \\ + 0.001519(\$28,800) + 0.000506(\$27,600) + 0.010575(\$16,000) \\ + 0.000506(\$26,800) + 0.000169(\$25,600) \end{matrix}}{0.1023}$$

$$= \$13,856$$

Finally, we might wish to assemble the data into a Value-at-Risk table. To do so, we simply place the losses in order from largest to smallest and accumulate the probabilities, as shown in Exhibit 11-12.

The table cannot be arranged as neatly as does a VaR table based on market risk. With a market risk VaR, we have many more observations and can easily cut the line at the 5% or 1% point. Here the data are not

Loss	Probability	Cumulative Probability
$28,800	0.1519%	0.1519%
$27,600	0.0506%	0.2025%
$26,800	0.0506%	0.2531%
$25,600	0.0169%	0.2700%
$18,000	3.1725%	3.4425%
$16,000	1.0575%	4.5000%
$10,800	4.2975%	8.7975%
$9,600	1.4325%	10.2300%

Exhibit 11-12. Credit VaR for Independence of Default

sufficiently granular for a 1%, 5%, or even 10% cutoff. We can, however, make some useful statements such as "A 4.5% VaR is $16,000, which means that there is a 4.5% chance that we will lose at least $16,000. In real world situations, a creditor would use sophisticated software, there would be multiple loans, and there would be many recovery rates. Additional data points would provide further granularity, such that in all likelihood a 5% or 1% VaR could be obtained.

11.4.2.3 *Two Correlated Loans*

In the example we used above, the two loans were independent of each other. We know that is true, because the probability that B defaults was set at 6% without regard to whether A defaults. But loan defaults can be related to each other. Two companies might be in related industries, similar geographic areas, or they may simply have common exposure to a weakening economy or industry. Let us now incorporate this effect into our analysis. We will assume that if A defaults, the probability of B defaulting is 55%. If A does not default, we shall leave the probability of B defaulting at 6%. From this information, we can infer the overall probability of B defaulting:

Probability of B defaulting = Probability of B defaulting given that

A defaults

× Probability that A defaults

+ Probability of B defaulting given that
A does not default

× Probability that A does not default

$$= 0.55(0.045) + 0.06(0.955) = 0.08205$$

So the probability that B defaults is now 8.205%, but the usefulness of that number is a bit limited. Whether B defaults depends on whether A defaults. We incorporate this effect by repeating the previous analysis but using a probability of 0.55 for the likelihood of B defaulting if A defaults and 0.06 for the likelihood of B defaulting if A does not default.

When the probability of default of a given loan is not independent of whether another loan defaults, the loans are said to be correlated. We studied the concept of correlation earlier in this book. We learned that correlation is a measure of the linear association between two variables. The variables are correlated if it is possible to fit a straight line between them, even if the points do not all fall on the line, which is the largely hypothetical case of perfect correlation. The use of the term "correlation" in the context of loan defaults is not technically correct. There is no linear relationship in loan defaults. Yet, the term correlation has simply come to be used in this context, so right or wrong, we are compelled to use it. The most important point is that the probability of one party defaulting can be related to whether another defaults.

There are still nine outcomes as identified in the previous section, but the probabilities and losses are different as shown in Exhibit 11-13. The losses for each event are the same as in Exhibit 11-11, but many of the probabilities are quite different. For example, Outcomes 4 and 7, in which A defaults and B pays off, have considerably lower probabilities, and the probabilities of Outcomes 5, 6, 8, and 9 in which both default are considerably higher.

The probability of at least one default is still $1 - 0.8977 = 0.1023$. This figure is not different from the case of independence, simply because we specified that the probability of B defaulting if A does not default is 6%, the same as before. Nonetheless, the other events where there is at least one default clearly have different probabilities.

The expected loss is now:

$$0.8977(\$0) + 0.042975(\$10,800) + 0.014325(\$9,600)$$
$$+ 0.015188(\$18,000) + 0.01392188(\$28,800) + 0.00464063(\$27,600)$$
$$+ 0.005063(\$16,000) + 0.00464063(\$26,800) + 0.00154688(\$25,600)$$
$$= \$1,649$$

Recall that in the independence case, the expected loss is $1,418. So we see that indeed, correlation raises the risk. While the probability of at least one default is the same, the higher correlation increases the likely of more

Outcome	Result	Probability	Loss
1	Both loans pay in full	$0.955 \times 0.94 = 0.8977$	$0
2	A pays off, B defaults with 10% recovery	$0.955 \times 0.06 \times 0.75 = 0.042975$	$10,800
3	A pays off, B defaults with 20% recovery	$0.955 \times 0.06 \times 0.25 = 0.014325$	$9,600
4	A defaults with 10% recovery, B pays in full	$0.045 \times 0.75 \times 0.45 = 0.015188$	$18,000
5	A defaults with 10% recovery, B defaults with 10% recovery	$0.045 \times 0.75 \times 0.55 \times 0.75 = 0.0139222$	$18,000 + $10,800 = $28,800
6	A defaults with 10% recovery, B defaults with 20% recovery	$0.045 \times 0.75 \times 0.55 \times 0.25 = 0.004641$	$18,000 + $9,600 = $27,600
7	A defaults with 20% recovery, B pays in full	$0.045 \times 0.25 \times 0.45 = 0.005063$	$16,000
8	A defaults with 20% recovery, B defaults with 10% recovery	$0.045 \times 0.25 \times 0.55 \times 0.75 = 0.004641$	$16,000 + $10,800 = $26,800
9	A defaults with 20% recovery, B defaults with 20% recovery	$0.045 \times 0.25 \times 0.55 \times 0.25 = 0.001547$	$16,000 + $9,600 = $25,600

Exhibit 11-13. Probabilities of Default and Losses for Correlated Loans A and B

than one default. Recall that previously the probability of two defaults is 0.27%. Now it is the sum of outcomes 5, 6, 8, and 9, which is $0.0139222 + 0.004641 + 0.004641 + 0.001547 = 0.02475$, or 2.475%, almost ten times higher. The expected loss given default is found as

$$\frac{\begin{aligned} &0.042975(\$10,800) + 0.014325(\$9,600) + 0.015188(\$18,000) \\ &\quad + 0.01392188(\$28,800) + 0.00464063(\$27,600) + 0.005063(\$16,000) \\ &\quad + 0.00464063(\$26,800) + 0.154688(\$25,600) \end{aligned}}{0.1023}$$

$$= \$16,120$$

This number is considerably higher than in the independence case ($13,856), because the events in which both borrowers default now have a greater probability.

Loss	Probability	Cumulative Probability
$28,800	1.3922%	1.3922%
$27,600	0.4641%	1.8563%
$26,800	0.4641%	2.3203%
$25,600	0.1547%	2.4750%
$18,000	1.5188%	3.9938%
$16,000	0.5063%	4.5000%
$10,800	4.2975%	8.7975%
$9,600	1.4325%	10.2300%

Exhibit 11-14. Credit VaR with Correlated Default

Now we will construct a credit VaR. The losses associated with the nine outcomes are the same, but the probabilities of some are different. The credit VaR is shown in Exhibit 11-14.

Note here that a 4.5% VaR is the same as in the independence case, $16,000, but there are much higher probabilities of the largest losses. A 2.32% VaR is $26,800. In the independence case, the closest we could get to 2.32% is somewhere between a loss of $18,000 and one of $25,600. The highest loss, $28,800, now has a probability of 1.3922% versus 0.1519% when the loans are independent.

It is important to note that correlation is not the same as causality. Two random variables that are correlated simply have an association. There is no implication that one causes the other. For example, the U.S. economy performed exceptionally well in the eight-year period during which Michael Jordan led the NBA's Chicago Bulls to six championships. These events coincided, but one did not cause the other. In some cases, one event could cause another. Smoking causes lung cancer. Being overweight does cause high blood pressure. When causality exists, correlation will tend to be high, but high correlation does not mean causality.

Even with the concept of correlation used incorrectly with respect to the notion of a relationship between the likelihood of default for two borrowers, there need not be a cause and effect. There could be a common element driving the likelihood of default. It could be that two borrowers have a business relationship, such that if one defaults, it might cause the other to suffer and subsequently default. In that case, causality does exist. One default causes the other. Or, it might be that both companies are driven by similar economic factors, say retail sales or the price of energy. Or both companies might be located in the same geographic area, such that economic weakness in that area can spell trouble for both companies. Neither of those examples involve causality. In any case, it does not matter which causes which, and indeed it is possible to structure the problem so that we deal with the likelihood of A defaulting, given that B defaults. We can even find the probability that A defaults given that B defaults. It is the sum total of the probabilities of events 5, 6, 8 and 9: $0.01392188 + 0.00464063 + 0.00464063 + 0.00154688 = 0.02475$ divided by the probability that B defaults. So, we have $0.02475/0.08205 = 0.301645$. The probability that A defaults given that B does not default is the sum of the probabilities of events 4 and 7, $0.015188 + 0.005063 = 0.020251$, divided by the probability that B does not default. So, $0.020251/0.91795 = 0.022061$. We can verify that these numbers are correct by using them to obtain the probability of A defaulting, which we know is 0.045.

$$\text{Probability of A defaulting} = \text{Probability of A defaulting given that}$$
$$\text{B defaults}$$
$$\times \text{Probability that B defaults}$$
$$+ \text{Probability of A defaulting given that}$$
$$\text{B does not default}$$
$$\times \text{Probability that B does not default}$$
$$= 0.301645(0.082050)$$
$$+ 0.022061(0.91795) = 0.045$$

Clearly the correlation between two loans defaulting is an important concept to accurately measure. Moreover, it can be very difficult to measure. The Financial Crisis of 2008 is a good example of how experts underestimated the default correlation of loans

Credit Correlation and the AIG Bailout

In 2007 AIG was the largest insurance company in the world. It employed more than 100,000 people and generated revenue of over $100 billion and a profit of $6 billion. But in 1987, AIG made a strategic move that did not have to haunt it many years later. But it did. That year, the company created a financial products subsidiary called AIG Financial Products (AIGFP) and began selling credit default swaps. These instruments guarantee to a counterparty that any credit losses the counterparty incurred from a third party would be covered. Its AA rating helped it assure counterparties that it could pay in the event that these swaps were exercised due to default.

As an insurance company that began in Shanghai, China right after World War I, AIG was in the business of providing a broad range of insurance products and other financial services. Its decision to begin selling credit default swaps (CDS) in the late 1980s seemed like a natural extension of its business. The fundamental model on which insurance is sold is the principle of diversification: sell a lot of fire insurance policies but not to houses that are right next to each other. In other words, make sure your risks are spread out. Selling credit default swaps ought to work that way as well. Right? After all, whether one party defaults should not be influenced by whether another party defaults. If the risks are well diversified, the liability arising from the volume of claims should be a manageable and predictable number that can be factored into the premiums. Or so, the theory of insurance goes.

But AIG's credit default swaps were largely written on individuals and institutions that had a significant stake in the U.S. housing market. AIG's risk managers were surely aware of the concentrated nature of its risk, but they were confident that the U.S. housing market would remain strong. It always had been. And they felt that the risks were well diversified, as they always had been.

But that is not what happened. The bubble of house prices burst in 2007. House prices began to fall, and as a result, the large volume of high-risk, sub-prime mortgages that had been built up to finance housing growth began to backfire, resulting in increasing defaults and the threat of economic doom.

The pressure mounted on AIG, which had over $500 million of CDS on its books at the end of 2007. And in spite of its more than $6 billion profit in 2007, it posted a fourth-quarter loss of over $2 billion. Still, it had almost $1 trillion in assets, equity of about $100 billion, and a market cap of $188 billion. In the first quarter of 2008 it did not fare any better, with a loss of almost $8 billion, and its credit rating was lowered to A−. Then, its second-quarter loss came in at over $5 billion. Credit default swaps typically require the seller to post collateral, providing an assurance to the buyer that the payoffs could be made if the defaults occurred. Its counterparties began to demand that AIG post more collateral, but it simply did not have the cash. AIG desperately needed new capital, and no one was willing to provide it. The screws tightened, and in mid-September, its stock fell 88% in just six days.

In an attempt to raise capital, AIG was able to borrow a modest amount from its subsidiaries, albeit threatening their existence and the rest of its insurance business. Seeing the systemic threat to the American financial system, the U.S government lent AIG about $180 billion and became an owner of more than 80 percent of the company. AIG was effectively nationalized. Nonetheless, a few years later, AIG paid back the loan, and the government sold the shares for a profit of more than $20 billion.

So where did AIG go wrong? It believed that credit risk was diversifiable. It never imagined that defaults would grow to the wide scale that they did. Most of the time, that assumption is correct. Defaults tend to be localized or concentrated in industries. And although recessions do weaken many companies and individuals, rarely are defaults that wide scale. But in this case, they were. A failure to recognize credit correlation virtually destroyed this company and the global financial system.

11.4.3   *Internal Credit Risk Analysis*

In this day and age in which knowledge of financial analysis is widespread in the financial world, there are probably a few hundred thousand people who know how to do basically what Moody's and S&P do: assess the credit quality of a debtor. This type of analysis is done, among other ways, on an internal basis, meaning that the creditor analyzes the financial statements of the debtor. The principal financial statements are the income statement, the balance sheet, and the statement of cash flows. Entire books and courses are built on the subject of financial statement analysis, and we will not attempt to scale to that level of coverage here. We will just highlight some of the key ratios used in credit analysis.

Probably one of the most important is the debt ratio. Typically, the *debt ratio* is the ratio of total debt to total assets. Normally this measure is on a book value basis, but the market value of equity is often far in excess, though occasionally far below, book value. Market value is a more accurate measure as it provides a snapshot of what the equity is worth now, whereas book value is simply the accumulation of the effects of past events. Thus, the debt ratio is often estimated as

$$\text{Debt ratio} = \frac{\text{Book value of debt}}{\text{Book value of debt} + \text{market value of equity}}$$

Some calculations of the debt ratio use only long-term debt in the numerator, under the belief that short-term debt is typically not as critical a measure as long-term debt, as the latter represents a commitment over a long period of time.

Another key ratio used by credit analysts is *times interest earned*, computed as

$$\text{Times interest earned} = \frac{\text{Earnings before interest and taxes}}{\text{Total interest paid}}$$

Times interest earned is a measure of how many times a company's earnings before interest and taxes would cover its interest. It is also occasionally referred to as the *interest coverage ratio*. Also, sometimes the measure is adjusted to reflect cash flow, as earnings before interest and taxes (EBIT) is not cash flow. Adding back depreciation produces a slightly more accurate measure of cash flow. Thus, the numerator may reflect EBIT plus depreciation.

These two measures are the principal ones used in credit analysis, but analysts do look at more than just the amount of debt or interest. They will look at the company's profitability as indicated by such measures as its *return on assets*, *return on equity*, *gross profit margin*, and *net profit margin*.

When these ratios are computed, however, the major problem is having something to which one can compare them. Typically, one compares a company's ratio to that of the industry, but that approach can be problematic. Some industries are quite small. For example, Coca-Cola is in the beverage industry, but that industry consists largely of only three companies: Coca-Cola, Pepsi, and Dr. Pepper/Snapple. It is difficult to justify comparing Coca-Cola to such a small group, which is mostly driven by Coca-Cola itself. Even if the company itself were removed from the industry benchmark, the comparison is still not particularly appropriate, as there are only two competitors. In addition, just following an industry average may not be an adequate benchmark. An industry may be declining and while the company may be doing well against the industry, it may be doing poorly in general. The historical patterns in the ratio of a given company can provide useful information. For example, if times interest earned has been declining, there may be reason for concern. As it turns out, most analysts would simply state that they believe that they have a good feel for where these ratios should be.

11.4.4 *Commercial Credit Risk Models and Services*

Several major financial institutions provide quantitative credit risk models that generate statistical estimates of such factors as the probability of default, the expected loss, and credit VaR. Moody's KMV, CreditSuisse, and RiskMetrics, a spin-off of J. P. Morgan Chase, are among the better known providers. We will not cover these models here, but you need to be aware that it is possible to purchase estimates of these vital credit risk measures.

11.5 Basic Methods of Managing Credit Risk

There are a variety of fairly basic but well-accepted methods of managing credit risk. Many of these are extremely easy to administer. Some are more complex.

11.5.1 *Limiting Exposure*

One of the oldest and most fundamental techniques is to limit the amount of exposure to any one party. Clearly the credit risk of a single party is partly driven by how much exposure there is. Thus, a bank might not want to make another loan to a party to whom it is already highly exposed. This point does not mean that the loan should not be made but that the loan should perhaps be made by a different bank. This fundamental practice is nothing more than the principle of diversification. Parties exposed to credit should spread out the risk into a set of highly diverse obligors.

11.5.2 *Collateral and Marking-to-Market*

A second common practice in credit risk management is the use of collateral. Using collateral is the process by which certain assets of the obligor are pledged to cover potential credit losses. Assets that can serve as collateral range from cash to highly liquid short-term securities, to slightly less liquid intermediate- and long-term securities, to high illiquid securities such as a factory or real estate, which of course is the standard collateral for mortgages.

The quality of the collateral is a major factor that determines the amount of collateral required. Assets that are highly liquid and relatively low risk, such as U.S. treasury bills, provide the highest quality collateral. If the collateral is in the same amount as the credit exposure, one could argue whether the collateral should simply be liquidated and the credit not used.

In other words, if you need to borrow €20,000 and have to put up government securities worth €20,000, it would probably make more sense to liquidate the securities and not take out the loan. There are two responses to this concern. One is that seldom would a debtor have to deposit an equivalent amount of highly liquid low-risk collateral. In that case, the loan would essentially be risk-free and should cost the risk-free rate. Lenders are typically willing to absorb some credit risk in order to earn a return higher than the risk-free rate. When the collateral is not necessarily low risk or highly liquid, the creditor will require more of it, but in essence, the creditor is taking on the volatility and liquidity risks of the collateral. It is betting that if the debtor defaults, it can liquidate the collateral for an amount sufficient to cover the amount owed, but of course, this result is not guaranteed. The assets pledged as collateral can be simply recorded as such with documentation to support the creditor's claim, or they can be held with a third party.

Derivatives that have bilateral credit risk, which includes forwards, futures, and swaps, may require collateral by one or both parties. As described when covering the daily settlement process of futures markets in Chapter 5, futures contracts require that both parties post collateral in the form of margin deposits that must meet initial or maintenance margin requirements. Because the accounts are marked to market, neither party is ever in the black or red for more than the duration of a trading day. For OTC contracts that are not executed through a trading platform and cleared through a clearinghouse, however, one party is in the black with the other in the red. If the parties agree to require collateral, they may stipulate that both parties must set aside collateral or they may require simply that the party in the red must post collateral, while the party in the black does not have to. The amount posted can be the contract value or it can be less or more. For option contracts traded on exchanges, the clearinghouse requires that the seller post the premium received at the start and an additional amount to cover potential further losses. Likewise, for an OTC contract, the seller would have to post the premium and likely an additional amount.

As described earlier in the book, the Dodd-Frank Act of 2010 and similar regulations being enacted outside the U.S. encourage and ultimately require that a significant portion of all OTC derivatives be created on an exchange and cleared through a clearinghouse. Such a process would essentially result in the use of collateral for most OTC derivative transactions, with that collateral being maintained and managed by the clearinghouse.

Collateral is an extremely effective means of credit risk mitigation, but it can be extremely costly. It ties up funds that could potentially be used in more productive means. Although securities pledged as collateral may continue to earn interest, those securities are no longer available to provide a ready source of cash.

11.5.3 *Special Purpose Vehicles*

We might tend to believe that dealers worry about their end users defaulting, but end users may also worry about dealers defaulting. Most dealers are large banks and other investment-related firms. The end users that held derivatives with counterparties AIG, Lehman Brothers, Bear Sterns, and Merrill Lynch, all of which either failed, merged, or were bailed out, did not think they had anything to worry about as 2008 started. Little did they know: they had a lot to worry about. And those kinds of worries that banks can have are not limited to derivatives transactions. They can also be due to other transactions conducted across the many lines of business in these firms. To deal with that problem, dealers often created *special purpose vehicles* or *SPVs*. An SPV is a separate company, usually run as a subsidiary, that does nothing but engage in a particular type of transaction, such as derivatives. The parent company injects capital into this subsidiary, and the subsidiary is not responsible for the debt of the parent company. Thus, the subsidiary is considered a prime counterparty and typically receives a very high rating from the credit rating agencies. In this manner, a bank that finds itself crumbling under the weight of bad loans does not run the risk of taking down its derivatives operation. Moreover, the financial institutions not only inject capital, but they also stand behind the SPV with a willingness to provide additional capital. As such, counterparties to the derivatives transactions typically have no fear of entering into transactions with these SPVs. When used in creating these types of derivatives dealer subsidiaries, SPVs are sometimes called *Enhanced Derivatives Product Companies*, or EDPCs, although that term has been used a lot less in recent years.

Unfortunately, SPVs have been employed in an unscrupulous manner by some companies, such as Enron, which set them up largely to hide the massive amount of debt it carried so the parent company would look stronger. Accounting rules have improved since that time, however, and it has become more difficult to hide debt through off-balance sheet companies.

11.5.4 *Netting*

Most derivative contracts include a provision for *netting*. Netting is a process in which all of the obligations between two parties are offset against each other in the event of a declaration of bankruptcy. Many large end users will have multiple derivative contracts with a dealer. In addition, there may be loans and leases that create obligations from the end user to the dealer. If bankruptcy is declared by either party, the netting provision goes into effect. It specifies that the current market values of all transactions between the two parties is determined. The aggregate value of these transactions will lead to a single overall value owed by one party to the other. That amount will then become the claim in the bankruptcy process.

Netting is one of the simplest, least costly, and most effective means of mitigating credit risk. Let us see how it reduces the risk. Consider two companies, A and B, that are engaged in two transactions with each other. B holds an asset worth $10,000, which is a liability owed by A, and A holds an asset worth $15,000, which is a liability owed by B. Now consider these scenarios when one of the parties declares bankruptcy.

A declares bankruptcy: B is a creditor of A with a claim of $10,000. A, however, holds an asset worth $15,000 in the form of its claim on B. If these two claims are not linked to each other through a netting agreement, B might be obligated to pay A the $15,000 it owes, without regard to whether it gets paid the full $10,000.

B declares bankruptcy. Here, company A may be forced to pay the $10,000 it owes to B, while it holds a claim of $15,000 against B that is tied up in the bankruptcy process.

If the two parties had agreed to net, however, the resolution of their obligations would be much simpler.

A declares bankruptcy. B has no claim against A, and A simply holds an asset worth $5,000 representing its net claim against B.

B declares bankruptcy. A has a claim of $5,000 against B.

As you can see, in the absence of netting, the party owing the bankrupt party could be obligated to pay up the full amount without offsetting it against what the bankrupt party owes. A bankruptcy court can order liquidation of some or all assets, so the non-bankrupt party could have to pay up the full amount it owes and while waiting on its claim to be settled. In effect, what netting does is created collateral in the form of the counterparties' claims against each other. It links all derivative contracts between the two parties together. In some cases, the parties may agree to net *all* transactions, not just derivatives. In that case, loans and leases may be netted.

As previously noted, in the U.S., the Bankruptcy Prevention and Abuse Protection Act of 2005 specified that claims related to swaps and forwards in which the bankrupt party is in the red will accelerate, which means that these claims take priority over other claims. The justification for this change is that the market value of these claims fluctuates daily with the volatility of prices and rates. By accelerating these claims, they are settled faster and cannot get the bankrupt party further in debt as the bankruptcy process evolves.

11.5.5 *Capital and Liquidity*

Another method of credit risk management is the use of capital. Capital is the equity that backs up the debt. Capital does not reduce the credit risk. It provides only a buffer to absorb losses. But capital as a credit risk management tool is not widely understood. It is generally believed that if sufficient capital backs up the debt, credit losses are simply born by the shareholders and the company does not fall into bankruptcy.

But the process is a bit more complex than that. For one, capital is typically just an accounting number, usually reflecting the book value of the equity relative to the book value of the assets. Book value of equity does not pay off debt. Only cash can pay off debt. When a borrower is not technically bankrupt — assets exceed liabilities — it can still be unable to meet its obligations. For example, it might be unable to make a required interest or principal payment. In that case, it is illiquid. A company can have plenty of equity capital, but that capital can be tied up in extremely illiquid assets. Indeed, that is often the case with banks, as much of their capital is tied up in loans that cannot be called in for early repayment. Although capital receives a huge amount of emphasis in analyzing the credit risk of banks, liquidity is far more important, both for banks and non-banks.

Capital is highly regulated in the banking industry. Banks are required to maintain a certain amount of capital based on the riskiness of their assets. But again, an obligor's ability to generate cash from its assets is far more important than whether it has sufficient equity capital.

There is one final method of managing credit risk, but it has become so important in recent years that we devote a new section to it.

11.6 Credit Derivatives

The derivatives we have studied so far are all based on market risk, meaning the changes in interest rates, exchange rates, commodity prices, and stock prices. In this chapter we have identified credit risk as a distinct form of risk. Just as we have seen that there are derivatives based on market risk, it should not be surprising that it is possible to create derivatives on credit risk. These instruments, naturally called *credit derivatives*, enable the financial markets to separate market risk from credit risk. With credit derivatives, it is possible to trade credit risk separately from market risk, and thereby to hedge or speculate strictly on the credit risk of an entity.

The notion of a derivative product on credit is not a new one. We previously described how put options are like insurance, and we illustrated how the Black-Scholes-Merton model can be used to price the risk associated with the failure of an asset value to equal a desired minimum, such as the amount sufficient to pay off debt. Hence, virtually any form of an insurance policy is a form of a derivative. There have been some forms of credit insurance in the U.S. for many decades. For example, insurance has been available on municipal bonds since at least the early 1970s. Insurance on mortgages, referred to as private mortgage insurance, is widely used. The U.S. government agency known as Ginnie Mae, which stands for Government National Mortgage Association, guarantees the required payments on certain loans that are backed by the Federal Housing Authority and the Department of Veterans Affairs. So the notion of insuring against credit losses is not a new one.

In the U.S., insurance is a highly regulated business. Traditional insurance companies that provide life, auto, property, and health insurance are regulated by each of the 50 states. The reason for this regulatory structure is because insurance is heavily sold to the general public, and state governments have felt the need to protect consumers. Thus, to sell insurance in any of the 50 states, a company would have to obtain approval from that state's insurance regulatory board. When the derivatives industry began to grow, it started thinking about how it could insure against credit losses and avoid this heavy regulatory structure. It first realized that one instrument that already existed provided some protection against credit losses. It then created three more instruments. None of these were referred to as insurance. Even though they served a similar purpose, these instruments were not designed as consumer products. Hence, the avoidance of state regulation was not an attempt to sneakily escape regulation but rather an effort to stop the states from using their largely consumer regulatory powers to regulate a product not designed for consumers. We will now take a look at the four instruments that are classified as credit derivatives.

11.6.1 *Total Return Swaps*

In Chapter 9 we introduced equity swaps, which are swap contracts in which the payments made by one party are determined by the performance of a stock or stock index. An equity swap may or may not contain a provision to include dividends as part of the swap payment made by one party. When dividends are included, the swap is a total return swap. A total return swap pays the entire return, which consists of dividends and capital gains. Total return equity swaps are not credit derivatives, but when a total return swap is tied to a bond, a total return swap has an element of a credit derivative.

The total return on a bond is determined by three main factors: the present value of the interest, the present value of the principal repayment, and the credit risk. Interest and principal are promised payments, but credit risk can reduce the amount of interest and principal repaid. In addition, bonds have market values that are determined by discounting the remaining interest and principal payments at a rate appropriate to the risk. Thus, bond prices fluctuate when they trade in the market, and their values of course fluctuate whether they are traded or not. These fluctuations arise from changes in the appropriate discount rate, which reflects the opportunity cost of alternative and equivalent investments. In addition, changes in the perceived credit quality can affect the discount rate on a bond. For example, if S&P lowers the rating on a bond, the discount rate will increase and the bond price will decrease.

A total return swap in which one side pays the total return on a bond can be structured to pass on the credit risk from one party to another. Of course, a total return swap also passes on market risk, but that risk can be eliminated by using interest rate swaps. Exhibit 11-15 illustrates how a total return swap can function as a credit derivative. Credit derivatives are purchased by a protection buyer, the party exposed to the credit risk who is seeking protection. On the other side is a protection seller, the party willing to bear the credit risk. That party is likely to be a dealer, but it can also be any type of speculator, such as a hedge fund. The protection buyer holds a bond that is identified as the reference asset.

We see here that the protection buyer pays the total return to the protection seller. This total return is based on the market value of the bond. Thus, if the bond value changes due to the market's perception of a change in the credit quality, that change is effectively passed on to the protection seller.

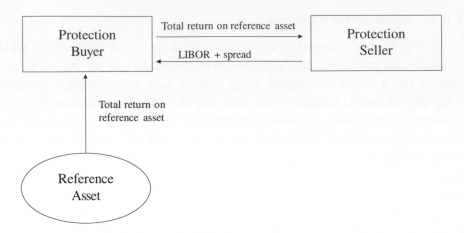

Exhibit 11-15. Total Return Swap on a Bond as a Credit Derivative

Note that the protection buyer receives LIBOR plus a spread. Thus, the protection buyer now holds the equivalent of a LIBOR-based floating-rate security. Of course, the protection buyer might not want a floating rate security, but if that is the case, it can engage in a vanilla interest rate swap to pay LIBOR and receive a fixed rate, thereby effectively turning it into a fixed-rate security.

Total return swaps can be used only for bonds that have a reasonable amount of liquidity. Clearly the bonds have to trade in a market that produces a price that can be considered an accurate gauge of its value. Highly illiquid bonds or non-tradeable fixed-income securities, which include standard loans, would not work for total return swaps. The total return must reflect the market's consensus of both the market risk and the credit risk.

11.6.2 *Credit-Linked Notes*

Credit-linked notes are a credit derivative that are based on the credit protection buyer issuing a fixed-rate security whose payoff is contingent on the payoff of the reference asset. They are best illustrated by referring to Exhibit 11-16.

The protection buyer holds the reference asset, a bond that makes interest and principal payments. For some bonds, principal payments are made only at expiration. For others, there could be a periodic principal payment or a deposit of money into a sinking fund that is used to pay off

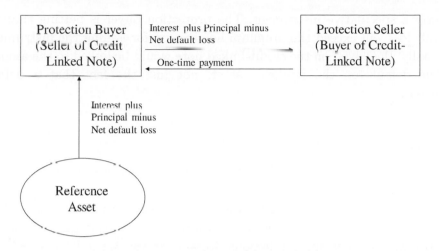

Exhibit 11-16. Credit-Linked Note

the principal at maturity.[5] Such payments are required by the terms of the indenture, so failure to do so means that the bond is in default. To purchase protection, the holder of the reference asset sells a credit-linked note to the protection seller. The credit-linked note specifies that the issuer will pass on the principal and interest less any credit loss to the protection seller, who is the buyer of the credit-linked note. Thus, if the reference asset fails to make a payment, the buyer of the credit-linked note assumes that loss. The holder of the reference asset has purchased the reference asset and sold a claim against it. If a credit loss occurs, it will stand to gain, because the difference in the amount it paid for the reference asset and the amount it received from the protection seller will be exceeded by the credit loss. In other words, let us say it pays $1,000 for the reference asset, he would likely sell it for less than $1,000, say $990, as the protection seller would have to charge a premium for assuming the risk. So, the protection buyer has paid $10 for the protection. If any credit loss occurs, it is likely to exceed $10. The market value of the bond he holds will fall, but the market value of the note he has issued will also fall. This type of instrument is

---

[5]Some bonds can be structured to amortize the principal over time, but this approach is not common. Some other bonds have sinking funds, which are accounts into which a portion of the principal is periodically deposited. By the time the bond matures, the sinking fund will have sufficient cash to pay it off.

strictly a speculative instrument. The protection buyer is betting that the default loss will exceed the premium he gives up for issuing the instrument. Normally, the payoff on the credit-linked note would be linked to the amount of the default on the reference asset, not just the fact that a default occurred.

Phileas Fogg Bonds

The origins of credit-linked notes may trace themselves back to bonds and notes structured so that the principal did not need to be repaid if something happened. The famous 19th century French science fiction writer Jules Verne must have been aware of these instruments, for he incorporated them into his famous literary classic *Around the World in 80 Days*. (Don't worry if you have not read or it seen the movie: no spoilers here.)

In this story set in 1872, wealthy Londoner Phileas Fogg makes a bet with his card-playing friends that he can circumnavigate the world in 80 days. The possibility of such a rapid passage had been suggested in a newspaper article about the opening of a new rail line in India. Of course, 80 days was the absolute minimum, but the cool and confident Fogg offered a wager of £20,000, about $1.6 million today, that he could do it. Fogg's trip would take him and his new assistant, a Frenchman named Jean Passepartout, (not coincidentally, Passepartout means to "travel all around"), on an exciting journey with many twists and turns. Although the original 1956 movie, starring David Niven as Fogg, took some Hollywood liberties and introduced a few variations into the story with Fogg traveling part of the way by hot air balloon, no such form of transport was mentioned by Verne.

When the challenge is announced, the story notes that England is a country full of people who love to bet. Not surprisingly, the public begins placing bets on whether Fogg will make it in 80 days. Some enterprising people issue "Phileas Fogg bonds" that would pay off based on whether Fogg makes it in 80 days. In effect, someone could borrow by issuing these bonds with repayment required only if Fogg makes it. Verne describes how the prices of these bonds rose and fell with expectations of Fogg's success. Interestingly, Fogg could have issued the bonds to hedge himself. If he made it, he would certainly become famous and probably greatly increase his earning power. If he failed to make it, he would have earned a windfall by borrowing money that he did not have to pay back.

We will not spoil the story by telling you whether Fogg made it. But we do know that this instrument is similar to credit-linked notes. If the underlying security fails by defaulting, the issuers of the notes do not have to pay off.

A credit-linked note can be created on virtually any instrument on which credit risk exists. Thus, the instrument can be instruments for which there are no active trading markets, such as loans.

11.6.3 *Credit Spread Options*

Earlier in this chapter, we mentioned the concept of a yield spread, which is the difference in the yield on a bond that can default and the yield on a bond that cannot default, such as a bond issued by the government. Yield spreads are sometimes referred to as credit spreads. Credit spreads fluctuate with investors' perceptions of the credit quality of the company. When the credit quality appears to deteriorate, the spread widens. A fluctuating credit spread presents the opportunity for speculative bets by those wishing to take a position on expected movements in credit spreads. Options are one way to make such a bet. In very simple terms, a credit spread option is an option that pays off based on the credit spread at a specific date. A credit spread option is illustrated in Exhibit 11-17.

For example, the spread on BBB-rated 10-year corporate bonds is typically around 1.5%. A party holding such a bond might buy a credit spread call option with an exercise rate of 1.5% expiring in two years. Two years later, if the spread on the bond is above 1.5%, the call pays off based on the difference between the spread and 1.5%. This difference would be multiplied by a notional amount and potentially another factor to reflect compensation for the higher discount rate on all future coupons and principal. If structured properly, the option payoff would compensate for any loss of value in the bond. Credit spread options will tend to be call options, paying off if the spread is above the exercise rate, rather than put options, because holders of bonds will tend to need protection against increases in the spread, which arise from increases in credit risk. The buyer of the credit spread option pays a premium at the start, and this premium may or may

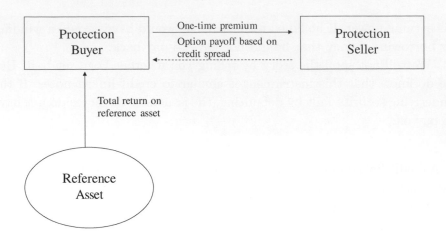

Exhibit 11-17. Credit Spread Option

not be exceeded by the payoff of the option. Of course, this option might also expire out-of-the-money in which case the buyer loses the premium.

Credit spread options can only exist on actively traded instruments, such as bonds of major corporations.

11.6.4 *Credit Default Swaps*

Total return swaps, credit-linked notes, and credit spread options have served a small number of participants as forms of credit derivatives. *Credit default swaps*, however, have become the most widely used credit derivative.

You may recall that we typically start our treatment of a derivative by defining what it is. In this case, however, we need to define what it is not. A credit default swap is really not a swap. As previously described, a swap is a series of payments from each of two parties to the other. Credit default swaps, also referred to as CDS, involve one series of payments made by the first party to the second and *could* lead to a series of payments by the second party to the first. As we previously mentioned, credit derivatives are variations of insurance, and the credit default swap is the best example. It mirrors very closely an insurance policy. Buyers of insurance policies pay periodic premiums and are compensated if a loss occurs. That is precisely what happens with a credit default swap. The primary difference between a CDS and an insurance policy is that the holder of a CDS does not need to have an insurable interest in the reference asset. For example, you can hold a life insurance policy on yourself and a person close to you or on whom you might be dependent. You cannot generally buy a life insurance policy on someone unrelated in any way to you. Thus, you cannot buy an insurance policy on the life of a decadent celebrity that you believe will not live long. You can, however, buy a CDS that pays off if a corporation defaults on a bond that you do not own. You do not have to be a shareholder or any other creditor of that corporation. You can be, in essence, a disinterested third party. There are some other minor technical differences in CDS and insurance policies, but the primary one is that in the U.S., CDS are not state-regulated whereas insurance is. So, let us try to construct a definition of a CDS:

> *A credit default swap is a derivative contract in which one party, the buyer, makes a series of payments to the other party, the seller, and receives a promise that the seller will compensate the buyer to a specified degree for a credit loss on a reference asset.*

Exhibit 11-18 illustrates a CDS. Notice that the protection buyer is receiving the total return on a reference asset, often called the *reference obligation*, which has been issued by a particular borrower referred to as the *reference entity*. This asset could be a bond or a loan, though it would tend to be a bond. The protection buyer pays a series of premiums amounting to a particular annual rate to the protection seller. The protection seller stands ready to compensate the protection buyer if a specified credit event occurs.

The payments made by the protection buyer are referred to as the *premium leg*, while the potential payment made by the protection seller is referred to as the *protection leg*. The payments made by the protection buyer

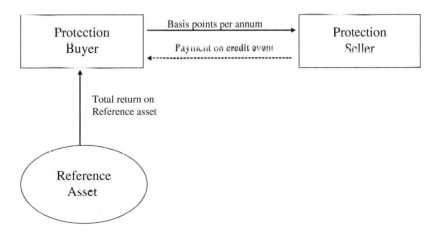

Exhibit 11-18. Credit Default Swap

are called the premiums. The reference asset is usually a senior unsecured bond, but the coverage provided by the CDS contract is not limited solely to this single instrument. Any instrument issued by the borrower that is equivalent or higher in priority is covered by the CDS. We will see shortly how the payoff is determined if there are multiple obligations.

There is a potentially confusing matter in the terminology of CDS. The credit protection buyer promises to make a series of payments, and as a result of engaging in a sequence of obligations, this party is referred to as short the CDS. The credit protection seller is said to be long the CDS. The credit protection seller can be thought of as long the company, because it benefits if the company does well. The credit protection buyer is short the company, because it benefits if the company does poorly.

The credit event can be a bankruptcy filing, a formal default, or a restructuring whereby the reference entity decides to repay in different terms than specified in the original credit agreement. A bankruptcy filing is a formal legal process in which a borrower invokes the bankruptcy laws to prevent creditors from temporarily enforcing their claims. During the bankruptcy period, the borrower attempts to work out a payment plan with the creditor and normally institutes changes in the company that are designed to enable it to operate profitably. A restructuring without a bankruptcy filing is an action taken by the borrower without the agreement of the creditors to extend the terms of the credit over a longer period or to modify the terms in some way such that the creditors are not paid back in the amounts and times they were promised. For some sovereign debt, a government might simply repudiate an obligation, such as when a rebellious group takes over control of the government and refuses to pay obligations of the previous government. Such an event would be a failure to pay even though the payment is not immediately due. Whether a credit event has occurred is not necessarily crystal clear. ISDA provides a group called the Determinations Committee that decides whether to declare that a credit event has occurred, thereby triggering the seller's obligation in a CDS.

There are two possible ways that payment from credit protection seller to credit protection buyers can be specified. One is in the form of a cash payment. In that case, there is a survey of financial institutions to determine an estimated market value of the reference instrument. In that case, the protection seller pays the protection buyer the amount the debtor owes minus the market value obtained from the survey. Another way to pay off is by physical settlement, in which case the protection buyer delivers the reference asset and is paid a pre-specified amount.

For most CDS, the payment from the buyer to the seller is made on the 20th of March, June, September, and December. In the early years of the market, the payments made by credit protection buyer were based on whatever rate was determined as appropriate given the risk. In recent years, the industry has settled on the use of just two payment rates, 1% and 5%. We will explain how these standardized coupons work in the next section where we cover pricing.

Of course, it should be apparent that the protection buyer's coverage is no better than the credit risk of the protection seller. As such, the protection seller needs a very strong credit rating. Moreover, it is not uncommon to require that the protection seller post collateral. This requirement makes a great deal of sense. Sellers of put options are required to post collateral, and CDS are very similar to put options. They allow their owners to be compensated when the value of an asset falls.

CDS that are on a particular borrower are referred to as *single-name CDS*. In addition, there are CDS on CDS Indexes, called *Index CDS*, which we will discuss later. There are also instruments called *tranche CDS*, which are on combinations of borrowers.

11.6.4.1 *Pricing CDS in the Black-Scholes-Merton Framework*

In Section 10.1, we covered how credit risk is an option held by the debtor and written by the creditor. We used an example in which a company had $100,000 market value of assets, and $45,000 face value of zero coupon debt due in seven years. The volatility of the assets was 0.35, and the risk-free rate was 3%. We found that the equity of that company is worth $67,181, and the market value of the debt is $100,000 - $67,181 = $32,819. The yield on the bond was 4.51% and the credit spread was 1.51%. With an expected return on the assets of 10%, the probability of default was 12.40%. All compounding is continuous.

So, now let us determine what a credit default swap would cost. Remember that a credit default swap would require a series of payments made by the creditor to the counterparty, a CDS dealer. The answer is really quite simple. If a risk-free borrower owed $45,000 in seven years, and the risk-free rate is 3%, the value of the bond would be

$$\$45,000e^{-0.03(7)} = \$36,476.$$

Because the value of the bond is $32,819, the difference, $36,476 - $32,819 = $3,657 is the credit premium. It is the amount that explains the difference in the value of a default-free bond and one that can default. Thus, it is equivalent to the present value of a series of payments made to insure against default risk. Hence, it is the CDS premium expressed on a present value basis. We will identify it as CDS_{PV}.

We then amortize this amount over the life of the CDS on a quarterly basis. For a seven-year CDS with quarterly payments, there will be 28 payments in all, and they will be spaced in annual increments of 0.25. We will denote the quarterly CDS payment as CDS_q. In other words, using simple formulas for the present value of an annuity of 28 payments with continuous compounding, we specify the following problem.

$$\$3{,}657 = CDS_q \left(\frac{1 - (1 + 0.03/4)^{-28}}{0.03/4} \right)$$

In other words, the CDS quarterly payment is CDS_q. The interest rate of 3% is specified as a quarterly rate, 0.03/4, and there are 28 quarters, so note that 28 is the exponent. The above formula says that the present value of the 28 payments of CDS_q must equal \$3,657. The bracketed term is the present value factor for an annuity. Solving for CDS_q, we have

$$CDS_q = \frac{\$3{,}657}{\left(\frac{1 - (1 + 0.03/4)^{-28}}{0.03/4} \right)}$$

$$= \$145.30.$$

In other words, if the interest rate is 3%, 28 quarterly payments of \$145.30 have a present value of \$3,657.

It is customary to express the CDS premium in basis points per annum, which we will denote as CDS_{bpa}. \$145.30 is expressed as \$581.20 per year, which is divided by the amount owed, \$45,000, to obtain \$581.20/\$45,000 = 0.012916, or 129.16 basis points per annum, or just 1.2916%.

Exhibit 11-19 shows the CDS rate in basis points per annum by the debt ratio as measured by face value of debt to market value of assets. We see that premium rises monotonically with the debt ratio. The example we use here is a debt ratio of 0.45 and the premium is about 129 basis points. At a debt ratio of 0.9, the premium is about 669 basis points. Naturally, the more debt the company has, the higher the rate, but the premium increases at an increasing rate.

Exhibit 11-20 shows the CDS premium by asset volatility. It increases with the volatility, but beyond a volatility of about 0.6, it increases at a

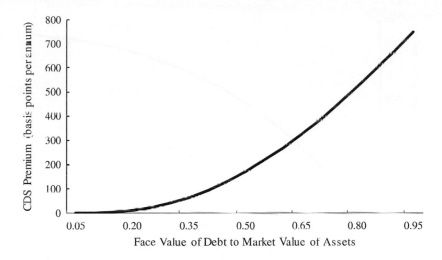

Exhibit 11-19. CDS Premium (Basis Points per Annum) by Debt Ratio

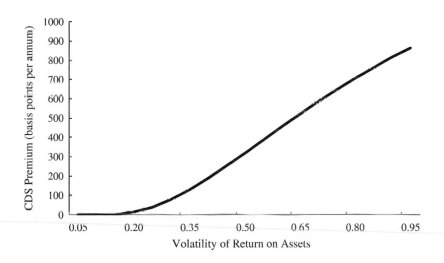

Exhibit 11-20. CDS Premium (Basis Points per Annum) by Volatility of Assets

decreasing rate. At our benchmark case with a volatility of 0.35, the premium is about 129 basis points. At a volatility of 0.7, the premium is about 586 basis points.

Exhibit 11-21 shows the CDS premium by maturity of the debt, which assumes that the CDS covers the entire term of the debt. Again, we see that

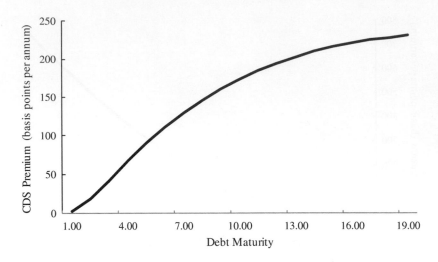

Exhibit 11-21. CDS Premium (Basis Points per Annum) by Debt Maturity

the premium monotonically increases, but after a point, around a maturity of about three years, it begins to increase at a decreasing rate.

We mentioned earlier that the CDS market has come to standardize the coupon rates on CDS to either 1% or 5%. Although most companies do not fall neatly into the two categories of low risk and high risk, it is customary to classify companies into the one or the other. Low risk companies will have CDS with coupons of 1%, while high risk companies will have CDS with coupons of 5%. In our example, the actual coupon required to insure against default was 1.29%. A CDS on this company would probably be priced with a 1% coupon. Thus, if a buyer purchased a CDS on this company with a 1% coupon, it would be paying less than it should be paying. To compensate for this discrepancy, the buyer would pay the seller a cash amount up front. A coupon of 1% on $45,000 would be $450 a year and $112.50 per quarter. The present value of 28 payments of $112.50 would be

$$\$112.50 \left(\frac{1 - (1 + 0.03/4)^{-28}}{0.03/4} \right) = \$2{,}832$$

Thus, the value of the buyer's payments is $2,832, when it should be $3,657. So the buyer would be underpaying and would need to make up the difference by paying the seller $826 up front. It should be apparent that if the true rate as determined by pricing the risk is more than 1%, the buyer will pay the seller a cash amount up front. If the true rate is less than 1%, the seller will pay the buyer a cash amount up front. If, for some reason, the bond in this example were priced at a 5% benchmark, the present value of the payments would be $14,159. At an equilibrium premium of only $3,657, the buyer would be greatly overpaying, so the seller would have to pay the buyer the difference.

The BSM model illustrated here is not typically used in pricing CDS, because most actual CDS are far more complex than what is assumed here. Here we allowed for a single issue of zero coupon debt. Most CDS provide coverage for multiple issues of a single entity. In that case, dealers price CDS by estimating the probabilities of default applied to the promised payments and discounting those values back to the present. This present value is the value of the expected payout of the CDS seller. From there it is easy to find the series of equivalent payments that the CDS buyer would make that has the same present value. The math is complex, but the dealers have the financial know-how and technology to do it.

11.6.4.2 *CDS Indexes*

A company called Markit has created a series of CDS indexes. Each index represents the credit risk of a particular group of entities. Markit has CDS indexes that cover obligors classified as North America Investment Grade, North America High Yield, Emerging Markets, Loan CDS, Municipal Bond CDS, and also CDS that cover Europe, Western Europe, Japan, Asia, and Australia. The North American and Emerging Markets group of indexes go by the name of *CDX*. For example, the North America Investment Grade index is identified as CDX.NA.IG. The North American High Yield Index is referred to as the CDX.NA.HY. The European, Australian, and Asian indexes are referred to as iTraxx indexes, such as iTraxx Europe and iTraxx Japan. Markit changes the composition of the indexes every six months and sometimes introduces new indexes within each category. The indexes contain anywhere from 14 to 125 entities. The maturities when launched are either three, five, seven, or ten years. Credit events include bankruptcy and failure to pay for all CDX indexes and bankruptcy, failure to pay, and restructuring for iTraxx indexes.

One slightly complicating factor with CDS indexes that one simply has to get used to is that some indexes are quoted on the basis of a spread and some on the basis of a price. When an index is quoted on the basis of a spread, the actual level of the index is the average spread of the entities in the index. All of the iTraxx indexes as well as the North American Investment Grade and North American Investment Grade High Volatility indexes are quoted on the basis of a spread. Thus, for example, the CDX.NA.IG might be quoted at 80.25, which means that the average spread on the entities in that index is 80.25 basis points.[6] A deterioration of the overall credit quality of the entities in the index will cause the index to increase. The North American High Yield, the Emerging Markets, and the CDX based on loans are quoted in terms of price with a starting price of 100. The price is 100 minus a present value adjustment that reflects how much the spread has increased. Thus, if the credit quality deteriorates, the spread goes up, causing the quoted price of the index to go down.[7]

Of course, an index by itself is just a measure of what is going on in the market. CDS indexes, however, have been assembled into units that trade, much like a stock mutual fund or ETF. There are dealers that make markets in these indexes. The prices of the indexes fluctuate as perceptions change regarding the credit risk of the components. When any entity defaults, the entity is removed from the index and settled as though it were a single-name CDS in proportion to its composition in the index.

11.6.4.3   *Who Trades CDS?*

Most non-financial corporate end users have little need for CDS. Indeed, most such firms are themselves the reference entities on which CDS are traded. They rarely if ever extend loans to the parties covered by CDS. They may extend trade credit, but it is unlikely that they would have enough exposure through trade credit to need the protection afforded by CDS. Thus, they would rarely if ever need to buy CDS. Selling CDS puts them in the position of assuming the credit risk of a third party. Such a strategy would be inconsistent with the objectives of most non-financial corporations. Financial end users, such as mutual funds, hedge funds, and banks and certain financial institutions might be easily exposed to the credit risk of the entities on which CDS exist or can be created. Hence, they may well be justified in purchasing credit default swaps.

But what kinds of parties would be on the other side? The sellers of credit protection. These parties assume the risk of default. In the early

---

[6]By the way, the industry uses the term "spread" to refer to the spread over the risk-free rate. In other words, the spread is the premium in basis points.

[7]If the inconsistency seems confusing, it is not the first time the financial world has done things this way. You may recall from previous coverage that U.S. Treasury bills, for example, are quoted on the basis of a discount rate, while U.S. Treasury notes and bonds are quoted on the basis of their prices.

days of credit default swaps, the risk was considered to be diversifiable. By assuming the credit risk of multiple relatively unrelated entities, a credit protection seller might believe it is well diversified. Credit losses would not likely be systemic. The Financial Crisis that broke in 2008 proved that point to be wrong. While some sellers are pure speculators, many others are dealers. Dealers that sell credit protection would typically not maintain that exposure. They would likely hedge it with CDS indexes that contain the reference entity. Yet, that still leaves the question of who ends up holding the credit risk. As with any risk, the ultimate holder of the risk is either a speculator, someone willing to take on the risk, or a party with the opposite risk. Many hedge funds and sophisticated investors are speculators, though they may hold broadly diversified exposures. A party with the opposite risk would have a position that would benefit if the reference entities gets into financial difficulty. Examples would be a short seller, the holder of a put, or the seller of a call, forward, futures, or swap on the reference entity. Any deterioration in credit risk that would increase the exposure of the seller of credit protection would also tend to damage the equity, so a party with any of those positions would have a partial hedge.

CDS also have an interesting, unusual, and to some, an unsettling feature. One could buy credit protection on an entity to which it is not otherwise exposed. For example, one might think that a credit protection buyer would be a party that has exposure to the risk of an entity, such as a party that owns the bonds of a reference entity or has made a loan to it. Buying a CDS would certainly make sense, as it would protect against credit losses. But one can also buy a CDS on an entity to which one has no exposure, thereby simply making a side bet that the reference entity will default. Although the CDS itself is no different from one in which the holder has exposure, in this case it is sometimes referred to as a *naked CDS*. Some have argued that no one should be allowed to take such a position, but that argument collapses on itself. Short sellers, holders of puts, and sellers of calls, forwards, futures, and swaps on the reference entity can take such positions. Such has been standard procedure in the financial markets for a very long time. The markets need these pure speculators, because they take on risk and provide liquidity to the market.

11.6.5 *Securitization and Collateralized Debt Obligations*

In the 1970s, the financial industry created a process called *securitization*, which involves the assembling of a portfolio of debt securities or receivables on which claims would be sold in the form of shares in the securitized instrument. These claims differ in the priority in which they received payments. The first type of securitized instrument was the mortgage-backed security. A financial institution would assemble a portfolio of mortgages and issue claims against these mortgages. The mortgages would typically be insured against credit losses, leaving only a risk known as prepayment risk. Prepayment risk is the risk that the mortgagor would pay off the mortgage early, which would occur if the mortgagor sold the house before the mortgage was paid off or refinanced the house at a lower interest rate than the one on the mortgage. The risk associated with mortgages due to selling a home before the loan is paid off is a fairly predictable and manageable risk. There is considerable demographic data on the rate at which homes are sold before mortgages mature. This risk is, thus, relatively predictable and diversifiable. But when a mortgage pays off before its maturity date due to the homeowner refinancing at a lower interest rate, the holder of the mortgage suffers a loss because it has to reinvest the funds in a lower interest rate environment. The claims issued against these mortgages in a mortgage-backed security have different priorities in terms of the absorption of losses due to prepayments. These claims are called tranches, tranche being a French word meaning a layer or a slice. These tranches are also sometimes referred to as *asset-backed securities.*

Mortgage-backed securities are widely seen in the financial markets, particularly in the U.S. Many of these securities are ultimately held by Fannie Mae and Freddie Mac, two publicly traded companies that receive an implicit guarantee by the U.S. government. Indeed, the U.S. government had to bail out these two companies during the financial crisis that began in 2008.

But mortgage-backed securities are not the only forms of securitization. Credit card receivables and other short-term receivables have been securitized. But by far the most widely known form of securitization is the collateralized debt obligation.

11.6.5.1 *Collateralized Debt Obligations (CDOs)*

The financial instrument known as a collateralized debt obligation or CDO has become widely used since the decade of the 1990s. It, too, is a form of a credit derivative. A CDO is fairly general name for a family of instruments that can include collateralized bond obligations, known as CBOs, and collateralized loan obligations, known as CLOs. A collateralized debt obligation is a type of investment fund that holds underlying securities that are subject to default and issues securities representing claims against the payoffs of the underlying securities but in which the securities it issues have different priorities of claims. If the underlying securities are bonds, the instrument is called a CBO. If the underlying securities are loans, it is called a CLO. Some CDOs, however, can hold both bonds and loans. Technically bonds and loans are the same concept, but they can have vastly different types of payments. Moreover, bonds are generally considered to be marketable instruments. They can be bought and sold, whereas loans are not usually marketable.

Although there can be more than three tranches, let us assume just three, and we will call them by their common names: the subordinated or equity tranche, the mezzanine tranche, and the senior tranche. For right now, these names will not mean much, but let us use them for identification purposes only. Examples that will show why these names are used will come. In addition, there can be more than three types of tranches, but we will stick with three for learning purposes.

Exhibit 11-22 illustrates how CDOs are generally organized. The CDO is created by a financial entity, such as when a bank purchases various assets that promise principal and interest payments but are subject to default. The CDO issues the three tranches called the senior, mezzanine, and equity tranches. Each tranche receives principal and interest but a portion of the defaults is deducted from the promised payments. The allocation of the

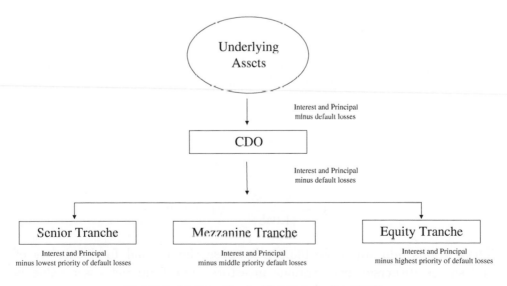

Exhibit 11-22. Basic Structure of a CDO

defaults is to the equity tranche first, the mezzanine tranche second, and the senior tranche last. We will illustrate this process with a detailed example later.

At first glance, a CDO bear some resemblance to a mutual fund. You probably know that most mutual funds hold stocks, bonds, or some combination thereof and sell shares on the fund, each share of which represents a claim on the underlying stocks and bonds. Owners of mutual funds effectively own fractional units of the stocks and bonds held by the funds. But that is where the analogy ends. Mutual funds pass their returns on to their shareholders directly and unaltered, except for the removal of a small fee. Many mutual funds also actively trade. CDOs also hold underlying securities and pass those returns on to their shareholders, but CDOs alter the returns. Let us explain how that is done.

Consider a very simple mutual fund that holds only three securities, each of which is a zero-coupon bond. One bond has a face value of $1,200 and matures in one year. The other has a face value of $2,400 and matures in two years. The third has a face value of $5,400 and matures in three years. Let us assume the first bond has a yield of 3.5%, the second a yield of 4.1%, and the third a yield of 4.5%, all of these rates based on discrete annual compounding. To keep things simple, we will organize the fund as a unit investment trust (UIT), which means that the trust will dissolve and return all remaining funds to its investors as of a certain date, here year three. If the fund were not organized as a unit investment trust, it would continue to operate ad infinitum and use the proceeds of repaid bonds to buy new bonds to keep the fund going. We need to avoid getting distracted with new bonds purchases, so a UIT is a structure that will achieve this objective. Think of it as just a mutual fund with a finite life. We will divide it into 100 shares.

Given their yields, the prices of the bonds at time zero are

$$B1_0 = \frac{\$1,200}{1.035} = \$1,159.42$$

$$B2_0 = \frac{\$2,400}{(1.041)^2} = \$2,214.67$$

$$B3_0 = \frac{\$5,400}{(1.045)^3} = \$4,732.00$$

These totals add up to $8,106.09. Suppose the mutual fund consists of 100 shares dispersed over various investors. The fund net asset value is obviously $8,106.09/100 = $81.0609.

Now, let us roll forward to time 1 when the first bond is due to be paid off. Let us assume that the bond defaults and pays only 60% of the face value. That means that the fund receives only $720 instead of $1,200 at time 1. Each of the 100 shares is paid $7.20 at time 1. At time 2, let us say that the second bond pays off fully. Each investor receives $2,400/$100 = $24 at time 2. At time 3, let us assume that the third bond defaults and pays only 40% of its face value. Thus, the bond loses $3,240, and each share receives $2,160/$100 = $21.60. Notice that each share was paid the same amount and, therefore, assumed an equal degree of credit risk.

Now assume that instead of a standard UIT, let us organize the fund as a CDO. We issue 100 shares divided into three tranches. As noted, the first tranche is called the equity tranche, and sometimes the *first-loss tranche*. We will set the terms such that the first tranche absorbs 60% of the default losses. The second tranche is called the *mezzanine tranche*. It will absorb 30% of the credit losses. The third tranche is called the senior tranche, and it assumes the remaining 10% of the credit losses.

When the first bond defaults, there is a total of $720 to disburse, and the loss is $480. Holders of the equity tranche bear 60% of the loss, so they forego $288($480 × 0.6). Holders of the mezzanine tranche bear 30% of the loss, so they forego $144($480 × 0.3). Holders of the senior tranche bear 10% of the loss, so they forego $48($480 × 0.10). The losses of the three tranches add up to $480. The gross ex ante payoff is split equally. Holders of each tranche would get $400 if paid in full, but the net payoff to the tranches is

$$\text{Equity tranche: } \$400 - \$288 = \$112$$

$$\text{Mezzanine tranche: } \$400 - \$144 = \$256$$

$$\text{Senior tranche: } \$400 - \$48 = \$352$$

The total disbursed is $112 + $256 + $352 = $720, the amount recovered after the default, but as you can see, the parties did not share equally in the credit losses. The equity tranche bore the brunt, and the senior tranche bore the lowest loss.

When the second bond pays off in full, the $2,400 is disbursed equally among the three tranches, so each gets $800. For the third bond, the gross payoff before default is $5,400/3 = $1,800, so each tranche is promised $1,800 if the bond pays in full. It does not, however, and the credit loss is $3,240. The equity tranche bears 60% of that total, which is 0.6 × $3,240 = $1,944. The size of that number should ring a bell. This amount is more than the equity tranche's share if the payoff were made in full. Indeed, some tranches can appear to be responsible for more than their share. Upon thinking about it, it is easy to see that this can be the case. If there is zero recovery, the equity tranche would technically have to absorb 60% of the full $5,400 loss, which is clearly more than its share of $1,800. CDO tranches, however, have limited liability, so clearly the structure of the contract has to limit the loss to the full amount owed, so that a tranche has a minimum final value of zero. In practice, there is typically a limit that prevents a tranche from absorbing all of the loss. Let us add that structure here. Let us say that the equity tranche can absorb all losses up to the amount it has been promised to receive. So, the equity tranche absorbs all of the amount it is promised of $1,800. With the total loss at $1,944, there is an additional $144 that spills over to the mezzanine tranche. The mezzanine tranche is required to absorb 30% of the loss, which is 0.30($3,240) = $972. Then, it must also absorb the $144 spillover, for a total loss of $972 + $144 = $1,116. The mezzanine tranche holder has been promised $1,800, and this amount is within its promised payment, so it absorbs this entire amount. But if the amount exceeded the promised amount $1,800, the remainder would spill over to the holder of the senior tranche. The senior tranche absorbs 10% of the loss, so it absorbs 0.1($3,240) = $324. So, for the third bond, the equity tranche receives nothing, the mezzanine tranche receives $1,800 − $1,116 = $684, and the senior tranche receives $1,800 − $324 = $1,476.

It is also possible that some of the tranches will have limits up to the full amount. In other words, the equity and mezzanine tranches could have limits that guarantee them at least a portion of the payoffs. In that case, the senior tranche bears a slightly higher risk, because the payments that go to the mezzanine and equity tranches will have to come from the senior tranche. Also, in practice, there often many more tranches than just these three. Moreover, each tranche may not share equally in gains, as here where we allotted an $1,800 payoff to each tranche for the third bond if paid in full. The structures can get quite complex. But the example here shows the basic idea, which is that the credit losses are not allotted equally or according to the amount invested. Instead, credit losses are allotted according to a formula that makes some tranches much riskier than others and some less risky. The total risk of the CDO is absolutely no different from that of the corresponding mutual fund, but every mutual fund share bears the same risk of credit losses. The exposure of any one investor varies only by the number of shares held, hence the amount of money invested. In CDOs, investors clearly do not bear equivalent credit risk.

If this arrangement makes it sound like a CDO is a complex structure, it usually is. But it is not illegal by any means. Investors who buy a given tranche know exactly how the credit losses will be allocated. The senior tranche is the safest, and it will have the highest price and lowest expected rate of return. The equity tranche is the riskiest, and it will have the lowest price and the highest expected rate of return. For the mezzanine tranche, the price and expected rate of return will fall somewhere in between those of the senior and equity tranches. In our example, the cost of the three bonds is about $8,100. Since the mezzanine tranche is in the middle in priority, its cost is likely to be about a third of $8,100, or $2,700. The senior tranche will cost more than $2,700, while the equity tranche will cost less. Actual pricing of CDOs is more involved than explained here. One would typically use Monte Carlo simulation or models that take into account the correlation among defaults. Analyzing the price of any tranche except the equity tranche also requires analyzing the other tranches, so that the potential for spillover is considered.

11.6.5.2 *Synthetic CDOs*

As you know, we have shown in this book that in the world of derivatives there are many ways to replicate a strategy. We can replicate a position in an asset by buying a forward or futures contract on the asset and investing the equivalent in the risk-free asset. We can also replicate a position in the asset by buying a call and a risk-free asset and selling a put, a result we obtained using put-call parity. These strategies are referred to as synthetic versions of the asset. There are synthetic calls, puts, futures, forwards, and swap. Therefore, it should not be surprising that a CDO can also be replicated by creating a synthetic CDO.

Exhibit 11-23 illustrates the structure of a synthetic CDO. There are two principal differences with a standard CDO. The CDO holds only default-free securities, such as U.S. treasury notes and bonds, but it sells credit default swaps. The combination of default-free bonds and CDS results in the equivalence of the underlying assets to a traditional CDO. Because the underlying assets are default-free, their interest payments would naturally be lower than if they carried the risk of default, but the periodic premiums received on the CDS increment the interest payments on the default-free assets, driving them up as though they were assets that could default, which would result in greater interest. And while the underlying assets do not

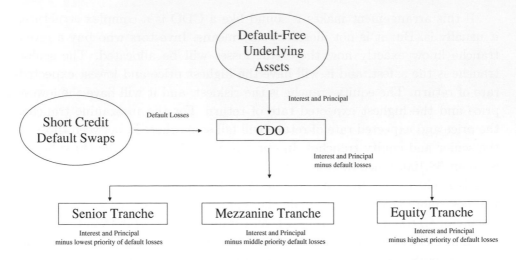

Exhibit 11-23. Basic Structure of a Synthetic CDO

default, the CDS will likely necessitate the assumption of some losses that have to be absorbed by the tranches of the synthetic CDO.

But why would someone create a synthetic CDO? The answer is the same as why any security or derivative would be created in a synthetic form: to exploit the perception of mispricing. For example, as we noted, one could buy a call and the risk-free asset and sell a put. If one could buy a put at a lower cost than the cost of buying the call and the risk-free asset and selling the risk-free bond, an arbitrage could be obtained by purchasing the cheaper asset and selling the more expensive asset. The payoffs offset to eliminate the risk, and the arbitrageur reaps a risk-free profit from the difference in the price paid and the price received for the offsetting positions.

So, likewise, an arbitrageur could buy the actual CDO and sell a synthetic CDO or do the opposite if mispricing warrants it and theoretically earn an arbitrage profit. Actually earning an arbitrage profit on a synthetic CDO is, however, more difficult to do than to explain. As an example, let us consider one bond, say a 10-year bond issued by Coca-Cola. Can this bond be perfectly replicated by purchasing a 10-year U.S. treasury bond and selling a credit default swap on Coca-Cola? Well, not exactly. Recall that a CDS pays off based on the default of multiple bonds of a given issuer. Coca-Cola could default on a different bond than the 10-year bond of interest here. Its default could occur on a bond that is due, while the 10-year bond is not due, and the CDS would pay off. Moreover, the different bonds issued by Coca-Cola could have different priorities and different recovery rates. Nonetheless, arbitrageurs do their best to take these differences into account, and as a result, there is a strong demand for synthetic CDOs.

Rating Agencies and CDOs

Moody's, Standard and Poor's, and the other ratings agencies make their money from providing credit ratings on fixed-income securities. The business is quite profitable. Issuers of these securities pay these agencies a considerable sum of money for each issue to be rated. As a result, there is the potential for a conflict of interest. Imagine a case in which restaurant inspectors were paid by restaurants. Nowhere has this problem been more evident than in the ratings assigned to CDOs by the agencies.

A CDO is divided into component tranches that vary in terms in how the credit risk is allocated. The senior tranches are safest, and the equity tranches are the riskiest. Each of these tranches is a fixed-income instrument, a type of bond that pays a return but is subject to losses due to defaults. The equity tranche absorbs credit losses first. When the limits are reached, the losses spill over into the mezzanine tranches. Where their loss limits are breached, the senior tranches start bearing losses. In the aggregate, the total credit risk of a CDO is the same as that of the underlying bonds, but the different tranches bear different degrees of credit risk.

The ratings agencies have been rating bonds for more than 100 years, so rating CDOs seems like a natural extension. But the Financial Crisis of 2008 revealed that the ratings agencies either were biased by their conflicts of interest with many of the CDO issuers, or they were sloppy in developing and testing their ratings, or they were simply ignorant, blindly applying old methods of analysis to what were new and considerably more complex instruments. There were more than 40,000 CDO tranches rated AAA/Aaa, a surprising number in light of the fact that fewer than 10 American companies were rated AAA. On the surface, a ratio of 40,000 to 10 might not be terribly askew in that a highly risky bond can be cut into tranches and the senior tranche would have considerably lower risk than the mezzanine tranche. But ultimately more than half the CDO tranches that were given the coveted AAA/Aaa rating became impaired in some way. So what went wrong?

First, it would appear that the agencies failed to appreciate the risk caused by high credit correlation. Their traditional approach to rating bonds was to rate a single bond in isolation. They did not traditionally rate portfolios of bonds, such as mutual funds. While analysis of a single bond would ordinarily take into account the potential for a weakening economy or industry, ultimately each rating stood on its own. But with CDOs, the ratings were of portfolios of bonds, so the correlation between their likelihoods of default became important, and the agencies had never truly mastered the art of predicting credit correlations. Further complicating things was the reallocation of risk created by the tranched structures. The potential for spillover effects was a new type of risk with which the agencies had little experience.

While regulators ultimately claimed that most of the blame was corruption caused by the conflict of interest, this is unlikely to be completely the case, if at all. CDOs were new instruments and although the agencies had more than 20 years of experience with mortgage-backed securities, the risk in those securities is prepayment risk, while the risk in collateralized debt obligations is credit risk. Moreover, the agencies were caught in a maelstrom, much like the rest of the world's investors and consumers. The Financial Crisis of 2008 was truly a unique event that had never been experienced before. But while the event was a painful one, it taught lessons to the agencies and the users of their ratings. For one, no rating system is perfect. Defaults will occur and will sometimes exceed the expected number of defaults. Moreover, they are not the fault of the ratings agencies or the issuers. Second, new and complex financial instruments cannot be subjected to traditional methods of rating. They must be scrutinized with the most powerful brainpower and technology and then questioned and re-questioned. If anything, the ratings of new instruments should be biased lower. Third, investors and regulators probably rely too much on ratings agencies. Relying on someone else to do what you should learn how to do yourself is a dangerous strategy.

It should be noted that it is possible to do the opposite type of structure with a synthetic CDO. One can hold a portfolio of bonds subject to default and buy CDS on those bonds. The CDS protect the bonds and make them essentially default free. The tranches of the CDO would then all virtually revert to equivalent and almost default-free status. Of course, you must be wondering why anyone would do such a transaction. Again, it is likely due to

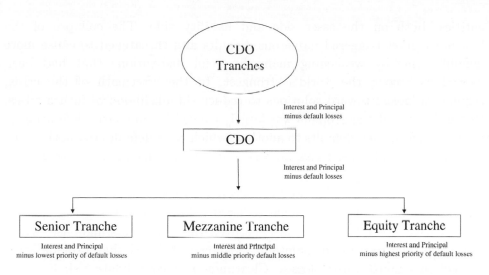

Exhibit 11-24. Basic Structure of a CDO^2 ("CDO-squared")

perceived mispricing that can lead to the creation of a default-free portfolio of bonds that earns a rate higher than the default-free rate.

11.6.5.3 CDO^2

In case you are looking for a footnote 2 in the title of this section, the "2" you see is not a footnote. It is the square. The instrument we are talking about is called a CDO-squared. CDO^{2}s ("CDO squareds") are CDOs of which the underlying assets are CDOs, as shown in Exhibit 11-24.

The underlying CDO tranches would not typically be structured to make up the entire CDO. For example, in the example we used earlier with a senior, mezzanine, and equity tranche, the CDO^2 would not generally buy up all of these tranches. If it did, it would absorb all of the credit risk and would just as well hold the underlying bonds. Instead a CDO^2 will tend to focus on one or more tranches of one or more CDOs but not all of the tranches.

It almost goes without saying that a CDO^2 is a complex security. The underlying securities are CDOs themselves, so they are complex and can be of fairly high or fairly low risk, with a likely preference for somewhat high risk. Then the tranches themselves further re-allocate the underlying risk.

11.7 Risk Management of Systemic Credit Risk

The financial crisis that began in the 2008 was largely a massive credit crunch. Many CDOs and CDS were found in the portfolios of bankrupt entities, both on the asset side and liability side. The collapse of the housing market triggered numerous defaults and threatened to cause more defaults, thereby weakening many financial institutions that had been viewed as among the world's strongest. In the aftermath of the crisis, regulators looked toward solutions to reduce the likelihood of future crises. Recognizing that the problem was largely caused by one party defaulting to another, which then defaults to another, which then defaults to another, the notion of systemic credit risk became a motivating factor in the search for solutions.

You will remember that we have already covered the concept of a clearinghouse, which is used for exchange-listed listed derivatives. All exchange-listed derivatives transactions are executed through a clearinghouse, which forces the two parties to maintain a balance of funds that provide some protection against future losses. Clearinghouses consolidate risk into one central entity. In doing so, they concentrate the risk, which adds some element of danger, but they also can be managed and closely monitored.

The Dodd-Frank Act of 2010 has essentially mandated that OTC derivatives be run through clearinghouses. The process of implementing that rule has been a slow one, but it is happening. Let us first look at how clearinghouses reduce systemic credit risk.

Let us start by considering a market consisting of three trading entities: ABC, XYZ, and JKL. Suppose that as a result of price movements, ABC owes XYZ $10,000, XYZ owes JKL $6,000 and JKL owes ABC $4,000. We will assume the parties have already engaged in bilateral netting, so that these amounts are the net amounts that each party owes the other after accounting for all of their mutual transactions. Bilateral netting is an important first line of defense against credit risk.

Exhibit 11-25 illustrates who owes what. The risks should be apparent. XYZ is counting on getting $10,000 from ABC. JKL is counting on getting $6,000 from XYZ. If XYZ is not paid by ABC, it might have to default to JKL. But JKL owes money to ABC, so there should be some way to offset, and indeed it is.

Exhibit 11-25. Bilateral Clearing Example

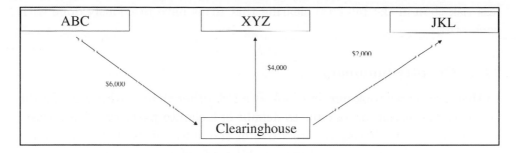

Exhibit 11-26. Multilateral Clearing Example

We now introduce the concept of *multilateral clearing*, sometimes called *multilateral netting*, which entails is the use of a clearinghouse. Exhibit 11-26 illustrates how the process works.

In Exhibit 11-25, we see that ABC owes \$10,000 and is owed \$4,000. With multilateral clearing, ABC owes the clearinghouse the net amount, \$6,000. XYZ is owed \$10,000 and owes \$6,000, so it has a claim of \$4,000 from the clearinghouse. JKL is owed \$6,000 and owes \$4,000 so it has a claim of \$2,000 from the clearinghouse. In effect, the clearinghouse collects \$6,000 from A and disburses \$4,000 to XYZ and \$2,000 to ABC. The amount of money that has to be collected is considerably less than in the bilateral clearing case. In effect, with bilateral clearing, the two parties simply clear with each other. With multilateral netting, all parties clear with the clearinghouse. As such, there is considerable potential for offsetting, given that these entities do multiple transactions with each other.

Multilateral clearing in today's market is primarily conducted at four dominant institutions: The LCH.Clearnet, also known as the London Clearinghouse, the Chicago Mercantile Exchange Clearinghouse, known as CME Clearing, the Intercontinental Exchange Clearinghouse, also known as ICEClear, and the Japan Securities Clearing Corporation. By far the largest of these is the LCH.Clearnet.

Multilateral clearing has been almost universally praised as reducing systemic credit risk, but it does concentrate the risk, thereby raising some concerns. In the example here, if ABC does not pay, then the clearinghouse has to make up the loss through reserve funds or insurance coverage. In the event of major defaults, the parties to whom the money is owed could end up absorbing losses, which would defeat the purpose of a clearinghouse. That has never happened, and in fact, has never come close to happening, but it does not mean that there is absolutely no risk. But there is unquestionably less risk than in the bilateral clearing that firms have previously done with each other.

11.8   Chapter Summary

In this chapter we took our first look at a risk other than market risk. Credit risk is the potential for loss due to default of a counterparty on a loan, lease, or derivative. Credit risk is surely one of the oldest risks that people have ever recognized. We saw how the probability of default is one measure of the credit risk, but that one should also take into account the amount of money at risk and the potential for recovering a portion of that money. Drawing on what we learned about options, we saw that equity in a company that has debt can be viewed as an option on the assets of the company written by the creditors. The possibility that the company would default and leave the creditors holding the assets, which are worth less than their claim, reflects the limited liability feature of corporate stock. The creditors must accept the assets in full payment. They cannot take other assets from the owners. We saw how we can apply the Black-Scholes-Merton model to price the credit risk.

We looked at how over-the-counter derivatives themselves have credit risk and how that risk is bilateral for forwards and swaps but unilateral for options. We then examined how the financial industry relies heavily on rating agencies, which analyze borrowers and classify them into certain categories that reflect relative credit risk. We also looked at how credit risk is managed, including limitations on exposure, collateral and marking-to-market, special purpose vehicles, netting, and using an adequate amount of capital. We examined how the concept of credit correlation refers to the potential for defaults on one claim can be associated with defaults on other claims. As such, if one loan defaults, it can increase the potential for another loan to default, owing to some common element of the two borrowers.

We then looked at several kinds of credit derivatives, with emphasis on credit default swaps. We saw how to price credit default swaps using the Black-Scholes-Merton model. We discussed how CDS trading is extremely popular, particularly in the form of indexes.

Finally, we examined how the use of clearinghouses can reduce systemic credit risk. We noted that clearinghouses do concentrate risk but that they have been completely successful in eliminating the risk that a party who makes money will not get paid.

11.9 Questions and Problems

1. How is credit risk different from but related to market risk?
2. Calculate the expected loss on a $15 million loan with a 2.5% probability of default and a recovery rate of 60%.
3. Consider a seven-year loan with a 1.25% probability of default per year. What is the probability that the loan will default over a seven-year period?
4. Explain why credit risk can be viewed as an option. How do the terms in the Black-Scholes-Merton option pricing model correspond to analogous terms when the stock of a company is viewed as a call option? What is the value of the analogous put option in this framework?
5. Consider a company with assets worth $12 million of market value and one issue of zero coupon debt with a face value of $5 million due in 10 years. The risk-free rate is 2.5% and the volatility of the assets is 0.32.

   (a) Find the value of the equity
   (b) Find the value of the debt and the portion of the value of the debt that is the risk premium.

6. Consider a company with assets worth $35.5 million market value with one zero-coupon debt issue with a face value of $24.5 million due in four years. The risk-free rate is 2%, and the asset volatility is 0.4. The following values are obtained in preliminary calculations:

$$x_1 = 0.9636, \quad x_2 = 0.1636$$
$$N(x_1) = 0.8324, \quad N(x_2) = 0.5650$$

   The value of the equity is $16,771,657. The expected return on the assets is 0.095. Find the following values:

   (a) The credit spread.
   (b) The probability of default
   (c) The expected loss given default
   (d) The expected loss

7. When credit risk is priced as an option in the Black-Scholes-Merton model, what factors result in an increase in the credit spread?
8. Explain why credit risk is greatest during middle of the life of a swap, in contrast to near the beginning or the end.

9. Why is credit risk unilateral in options in contrast to the bilateral nature of credit risk in forwards and futures?

10. Explain how S&P, Moody's, and the various credit rating companies provide information on the likelihood of default of a bond. How effective are these categories in assessing relative credit risk?

11. Consider a lender with two independent loans outstanding. The first loan, called loan F, is for $100,000 and has a 2.5% probability of default. The second, loan S, is for $150,000 and has a 4% probability of default. If default occurs, loan F has a 60% chance of a 25% recovery and a 40% chance of a 45% recovery. Loan S has a 60% chance of a 25% recovery and a 40% chance of a 45% recovery. Find the following:

    (a) Probability of at least one default
    (b) Probability of two defaults
    (c) Expected loss
    (d) Expected loss, given default
    (e) A cumulative distribution of losses such that a *VaR* could be determined

12. Following up on the loans in the previous problem, use the same two loans, but some different information. The probability of default for the second loan is 65% if the first loan defaults and 6.5% if the first loan does not default. Everything else is the same. Find the following:

    (a) Probability of default of the second loan
    (b) Probability of at least one default
    (c) Probability of two defaults
    (d) Expected loss
    (e) Expected loss, given default
    (f) A cumulative distribution of losses such that a *VaR* could be determined

13. What are the two key ratios that give an indication of the ability of a company to pay its debt? How does a credit analyst traditionally determine whether the values of financial ratios are strong enough?

14. Identify and briefly describe the five basic techniques for managing credit risk.

15. Suppose that bank A owes bank B £200,000 on one loan, bank B owes bank A £1.25 million on an option, and Bank A owes bank B £700,000 on another loan.

    (a) What is the net amount owed from one bank to another? Which bank owes the net to the other?
    (b) Assuming you got part (a) correct (check your answer if not), explain what would happen if A declares bankruptcy and, alternatively, if B declares bankruptcy.
    (c) How would an acceleration rule such as exists in the U.S. affect the payments in event of bankruptcy? Assume the acceleration rule applies to all derivatives.

16. How do total return swaps on bonds serve as a type of credit derivative?
17. Explain how a credit-linked note passes on credit risk from one party to another.
18. Describe how credit spread put and call options on a bond work? Give an example.
19. Explain how credit default swaps are similar to but different from insurance.
20. Consider a company with assets valued at $100 million and one issue of zero-coupon debt with face value of $65 million due in four years. The volatility of the assets is 0.45, and the risk-free rate is 2%. Answer the following questions.

    (a) Find the annual cost in basis points per annum to the nearest whole basis point of a credit default swap that makes quarterly payments.
    (b) Find the upfront payment and indicate who makes it if the CDS coupon is set at 5%.

21. What are the two methods of quoting CDS indexes and how does each method change if the credit quality of the underlying entities deteriorates?
22. Explain how collateralized debt obligations (CDOs) are able to take a portfolio of credit entities and divide the credit risk in such a manner that some of the CDO tranches are less risky and some are riskier than the entire portfolio.

23. Consider a CDO consisting of three bonds with information as given below:

Bond	Maturity	Face Value	Recovery Rate
1	2	$1,200	100%
2	4	$4,200	40%
3	7	$6,000	20%

The bonds are pooled into a CDO with three equal shares. The loss absorption is 70% on the equity tranche, 20% on the mezzanine tranche, and 10% on the senior tranche with all tranches limited to a maximum loss of the entire amount due. Determine how much each tranche receives for the following situations.

(a) The first bond pays off in full.
(b) The second bond defaults.
(c) The third bond defaults.

24. How do synthetic CDOs differ from standard CDOs?
25. How are CDO^2s different from CDOs?
26. What is systemic risk and why is it in the interest of society to reduce it?
27. Consider the following creditor-debtor relationships:

> B owes A €100
> A owes C €40
> D owes A €35
> C owes B €120
> C owes D €80
> D owes B €90

Create the amounts owed from whom to whom if these debts are processed through a multilateral clearinghouse. How is the risk reduced?

Chapter 12

Managing Operational and Other Risks

Risk can be managed with foresight. Damage can be controlled with hindsight. Your choice.

Coopers & Lybrand
Advertisement in *The Wall
Street Journal*,
December 7, 1995, p. A3

Chapter 12 is the second of two chapters in Part III that deal with non-market risks. Chapter 11 covered credit risk, which is related to but distinct from market risk. Now in Chapter 12 we introduce several other types of non-market risks. Because there are so many non-market risks, we divide the chapter into two parts, one dealing with operational risk and the other with a very general classification of "other" risks. The risks covered in this chapter are quite different from what we have encountered before in that they are much harder to identify, quantify, and manage. Fortunately for most end users, these risks tend to be of smaller severity and lower frequency than they are for dealers, but that does not mean we can ignore them. They have the potential for causing severe damage to any entity. In addition, it is important for end users to know how banks deal with these types of risks. But before we get to the "other" risks, let us first start off with operational risk.

12.1 Operational Risk

Operational risk falls behind market and credit risk in terms of the emphasis given it by traders, regulators, and scholars. But it can be extremely costly if adverse operational risk events occur. We should also note that operational risk has on occasion been referred to as *operations risk* and also as *operating risk*. These terms are used less frequently than operational risk, but they are synonymous, so be alert for them, as they will show up sometimes in practice.

12.1.1 *Operational Risk Defined*

The Basel Committee on Banking Supervision, a consortium of banking regulators of 27 countries, is an organization whose objective is to harmonize banking regulation. In doing so, the Basel Committee has issued a number of policy documents that specify best practices. These policies primarily deal with the manner in which regulators of the member countries should require that banks manage their risks and set minimum capital requirements in the respective countries. Banks, of course, are at the forefront of the risk management world, because almost all major banks are risk management dealers and yet they are also usually commercial banks, investment banks, or both. Naturally, regulators feel a strong need to force banks to engage in sound risk management so that depositors and other customers are protected from losses that might be incurred while those banks are engaging in derivatives activities. If derivatives losses are severe, they can spill over and threaten the viability of the bank. In many countries, depositors are insured by governments, so there is yet another reason why government, through its regulatory agencies, has a strong say in how banks manage their risks.

We have devoted a great deal of space to market and credit risk. Much of the emphasis has been on quantifying these types of risks so that their impacts can be gauged and the risk managed. And yet, banks and even their end users are at considerable risk just from engaging in their day to day activities. In other words, banks face risks that are outside of market movements and potential defaults. These risks are known as operational risks.

It is not easy to define operational risk. The Basel Committee does it as follows:

> *Operational risk is the risk of loss resulting from inadequate or failed internal processes, people, and systems or from external events.*

If this definition is not clear, take heart. It is probably one of the better ones. Operational risk is essentially the risk that things can go wrong just from going about the normal business of an organization. And while the focus of these risks is typically on the banking industry, operational risk is present in all lines of business.

As consumers of financial services, we encounter operational risk in many ways. Getting your ATM card stuck in a machine is one thing, and a fairly minor one, but having your credit card comprised is another one and often quite significant. A compromised credit card usually means that the bank takes a loss. Suppose a bank processes a mortgage payment for the wrong amount, causing the loan to appear delinquent. The borrower then wires the money to the bank and the money never arrives in the bank's account, though it was charged to the customer's account at another bank. The transaction cannot be reversed, so the customer's account remains delinquent even though he has made the payment twice. Three months, innumerable phone calls, and considerable customer ill will ensue. And ultimately, the bank eats the loss and the money disappears into bankwire cyberspace.[1]

People embezzle. Computers get hacked. Terrorists destroy things. Bad things happen all the time in the financial system. The system is so large and processes so many transactions that problems occur with great frequency. Fortunately, most are easily resolved. A deposit credited to the wrong account usually gets caught quickly and cleared up. An employee makes a typo when entering a ticker symbol and the wrong security is purchased. This kind of error is easily fixed with no likely large loss. But when an accountant is found to have stolen money through a carefully designed scheme of bogus entries, there can not only be significant losses but considerable damage to the company's public image.

We can summarize this definition of operational risk by saying that it is the risk of losses from failures of processes, people, and technology and the risk of loss from events even when processes, people, and technology do not fail. Moreover, there can be multiple sources of failure. Let us now try to identify some operational risk events.

12.1.2 *Examples of Operational Risk*

Perhaps the most obvious group of operational risks in this day and age are tied to computer security. It was not too many years ago that computer

---

[1]I am not making this up. It happened to me.

security meant largely just the threat of viruses, but viruses were mostly nothing more than mischief. Virus writers often just wanted to get inside of a computer and do annoying things. They got their satisfaction simply out of being a nuisance to someone, and it did not take long before technology was able to control most viruses. But the same technology that writes and controls viruses is capable of doing severe damage that is more than just mischief. With millions of transactions occurring on computers, the amount of money that is processed today has reached staggering totals, over $300 billion of cybercommerce yearly in the U.S. alone. Moreover, cybercommerce is a repository for a tremendous amount of personal and financial information, such as bank account, social security, and credit card numbers and the passwords to access them. In addition, there is the potential that an unscrupulous person or group could take over a computer system, effectively shutting the company down, or causing havoc or blackmail. Imagine a break-in to a train system that sends two trains heading for each other. An entirely new profession called hacking has developed and has become one of the greatest perceived threats to any company's operational risks. These threats not only come from hackers isolated in front of a computer screen, but they can also come from internal sources. Employees have tremendous access to information that can be stolen for either the employee's use or sold by the employee to someone else. Computer security is almost surely the number one operational risk in this day and age, as it is now almost certainly easier to rob from a bank's computer than to physically rob from a bank.

Some companies have incurred operational risk from vandalism. Environmental protestors defacing a company's signs or violent protestors at a company's headquarters are relatively minor nuisances. But vandalism is just a small-scale form of one of the greatest threats in society today — terrorism. In 1993 a small group of terrorists planted a bomb in a basement parking lot of the World Trade Center in New York. The bomb was intended to do enough damage to bring down the tower, but it failed. Nonetheless, it killed six people and injured more than 1,000. A number of Wall Street firms learned a lesson that told them that they needed to have backup operations well away from the Wall Street area. Sadly, just eight years later, on September 11, 2001, the two towers of the World Trade Center came down in the most massive terror attack in history. The lesson that was not quite learned in 1993 was certainly learned in 2001. Besides the tremendous loss of life, terror attacks can shut a company down. Though the risk of terrorists hijacking an aircraft and crashing it into a building is probably a lot less today than it was in 2001, there remains a significant threat of a bombing similar to the 1993 attack. In addition, there are also threats of terrorists attacking an electricity grid, a subway, or a nuclear power plant. And terrorism is not just physical destruction. Cyberterrorists can break into such institutions as the Federal Reserve, the U.S. Treasury, a major bank, or Nasdaq, and disrupt the financial system.

Fraud is another important operational risk. Fraud can emanate from inside a company, such as employee embezzlement, or from being cheated by a customer or supplier. Of course, fraud is often linked to computer hacking, but it need not be. Perhaps the greatest threat from fraud lies in the trading rooms of financial institutions — the proverbial rogue trader. A rogue trader is someone authorized to engage in financial transactions who undertakes extremely risky transactions that can damage and even threaten the survival of the company. The term *rogue trader* seems to have arisen from the story of Nick Leeson, an employee of the Singapore office of Barings Bank, who in 1994–1995 engaged in a series of highly risky and fraudulent trades that eventually destroyed the entire capital of the 233-year-old bank. Leeson had been sent from London to the Singapore office to clean up a messy and backlogged amount of paperwork. Though he was very good at this back-office function, Leeson began trading. After a string of successes and a new-found reputation for trading acumen, Leeson began hiding his accumulating losses and started to take greater risks in an attempt to recoup them. The Leeson story is a classic example of poor risk management and oversight, but it is also a lesson in how there can be large enough risks in areas of a company that can take down the entire organization.

Weather is obviously a substantial operational risk. Nowhere is this problem more apparent than in the airline industry. This industry is a complex network of dozens of companies and thousands of aircraft. While obviously a weather problem at a city in which a company operates can affect its entire schedule, it is even possible for a weather problem at a city in which a company does not operate to affect its operations. For example, consider JetBlue airlines whose primary hub is in New York. It does not fly to St. Louis, but suppose a major storm hits St. Louis, causing extensive delays at Lambert-St. Louis international airport. Is that a problem for JetBlue? It could be. There are several other airlines that fly from St. Louis to New York. Their flights are scheduled into the available slots in New York by the air traffic control system at the New York airports. When those flights are delayed, they are allowed to fly in during later slots, some of which may have been allocated to JetBlue. So some of JetBlue's aircraft flying into New York could get delayed because of late arriving flights from St. Louis to New York on other airlines. Weather is also a significant factor for public utilities, creating power outages and excessive demand. And of course, weather can lead to such problems as employees unable to get to work, vehicles unable to transport merchandise, and damage from flooding, hail, or lightning.

Product defects and potential for liability is another operational risk. Companies that put their products into the hands of consumers always run the risk that not only could the products be defective, but they could also be misused and result in lawsuits. As a result, consumers get warnings such as to not use a hair dryer while sleeping, to not hold the wrong end of a chain saw, or that the coffee may be hot. Although some products certainly require warnings, in the litigious society that we live in today, especially in the U.S., the threat of litigation over simple misuse and lack of common sense is a very real possibility. But companies must also be concerned about the real risks that they themselves inject even when following standard procedures. Food processing companies do their absolute best to avoid getting bacteria in their foods, but sometimes it happens. When it does, consumers can get very sick or die. Defective brakes or airbags can lead to accidents and deaths. Drug manufacturers do their absolute best to produce safe and effective drugs, but occasionally one is found to cause an unexpected and adverse side effect.

Finally, there is the potential for simple human mistakes. An employee in an airline pricing department enters a wrong number and all of sudden, tickets from Atlanta to Paris are snapped up at $39 round trip. A launderer accidentally damages a customer's coat. A restaurant brings the food incorrectly prepared and has to throw it out. Honest mistakes occur often and are a common form of operational risk.

12.1.3 *Frequency of Operational Risk*

One of the great challenges in dealing with operational risk events is that they are not very common. Each of the examples we have given here does not occur with much frequency. Of course, that is a good thing, but it makes for considerable difficulty in managing operational risk. The less experience one has with something, the less likely one can build expertise in it. Collectively over a long period of time over many companies, operational risk events accumulate to a large number, however, and fortunately data are now being collected on an industry-wide basis.

Most operational risk data come from banking, for that is where there is the most concern about operational risk. A study by Chernobai, Jorion, and Yu (2011) of about 8,000 operational risk events in the financial industry found that almost 49% of these events are related to clients, products, and business practices, such as failing to provide what was promised, problems with disclosure, problems with fiduciary and advising responsibilities duties, improper practices, and product failures. The next highest category at about 16% was internal fraud, and the third highest category at about 10% was external fraud. The authors identify the two primary reasons for most operational risk events as lack of control and omissions. Lack of control centers on having poor risk management systems in place. We will discuss that topic more formally in Chapter 14. Omissions means that something was simply not done that should have been done. The authors conclude that losses are heavily influenced by lack of internal controls and oversight, and that losses are more frequently experienced by younger companies, more complex companies, companies with weaker corporate governance and senior level oversight, and companies with stronger incentive compensation for executives. They also find that losses tend to be firm-specific and are usually not simply cases of bad luck.

The Basel Committee on Bank Supervision has conducted surveys of operational losses.[2] Its most recent one in 2008 covered 121 banks in 17 countries. The responding banks identified over 10.6 million loss events resulting in losses of close to €60 million covering a period of at least three years for each institution. It is interesting to note that just 20 events accounted for almost about 30% of the losses, indicating that there are a small number of high impact events. Exhibit 12-1 shows the distribution of loss events by area of the bank.

The highest percentage of losses, almost 56%, comes from retail banking, which refers to the bank's checking, savings, and consumer loan transactions with its personal customers. The next highest percentage, about 10%, came from retail brokerage operations. Trading and Sales was third at just under 10%, and commercial banking was fourth at about 8%. While retail transactions tend to be the smallest in size, retail banking accounted for almost a third of all amounts lost. Corporate finance, which is the underwriting of new issues, was second at 28%, and Trading and Sales was third at just under 14%. Other areas examined were Payment and

---

[2]You can find the survey at http://www.bis.org/publ/bcbs160.htm

	Number of Losses	Euros Lost
Corporate Finance	0.7%	28.0%
Trading & Sales	9.6%	13.6%
Retail Banking	55.8%	32.0%
Commercial Banking	8.2%	7.6%
Payment & Settlement	2.2%	2.6%
Agency Services	2.7%	2.6%
Asset Management	2.2%	2.5%
Retail Brokerage	10.3%	5.1%
Unallocated	8.3%	6.0%
Total	100.0%	100.0%

Exhibit 12-1. Distribution of Loss Events from Basel Committee 2008 Operational Risk Survey

	Number of Losses	Euros Lost
Internal Fraud	4.2%	6.1%
External Fraud	26.3%	8.0%
Employment Practices & Workplace Safety	17.5%	6.1%
Clients, Products, & Business Practices	18.2%	52.4%
Damage to Physical Assets	1.2%	1.4%
Business Disruption & System Failure	2.0%	1.2%
Execution, Delivery, & Process Management	30.6%	24.9%
Total	100.0%	100.0%

Exhibit 12-2. Reasons for Losses in Basel 2008 Committee Operational Risk Survey

Settlement, Agency Services, and Asset Management, but these did not generally account for many losses or large amounts.

The survey also looked at the identified reasons for losses, which are summarized in Exhibit 12-2.

The highest category in terms of number of losses was Execution, Delivery, and Process Management, at about 31%, with the second highest being external fraud at about 26%, followed by Clients, Products & Business Practices at around 18%, and Employment Practices and Workplace Safety at around 17%. In terms of money lost, Clients, Products, & Business Practices accounted for just over half of the losses, and Execution, Delivery, & Settlement accounted for about a fourth. What is perhaps most remarkable is that Internal Fraud, Damage to Physical Assets, and Business Disruption & System Failure account for such a small number of losses and dollars lost.

Unfortunately, there have apparently not been any similar studies on operational risk in end users. The types of operational risks faced by end users can be similar to those described above for banks, but the transactions typically do not involve securities, loans, and deposits. They involve manufacturing and delivering products to customers. Nonetheless, many large non-banks engage in an extensive number of financial transactions as they manage their cash flows. The operational risks faced by non-banks are not trivial and can vary widely across different industries.

12.1.4 *Managing Operational Risk*

The process of managing operational risk has changed substantially in the last 30 years. At one time, operational risk was considered to be simply a set of events that were almost completely preventable had employees simply been more careful and vigilant. In other words, there were few if any operational risk accidents. Oftentimes employees and supervisors bore considerable blame for such events, leading to a high level of stress, burnout, and employee turnover.[3] The evolving view is that while employees can contribute to operational losses through inattention, a certain number of operational risk losses will occur regardless of employee vigilance. But of course, this more modern view does not mean that an organization accepts operational losses as part of the cost of doing business.

12.1.4.1 *Risk vs. Reward in Operational Risk Management*

The more modern view of operational risk management is that operational risks are like market and credit risks in that they must be examined in light of the risk-reward tradeoff. As we know, optimal risk management and indeed optimal financial decision-making specifics that the best decision is the one that maximizes reward for a given risk that one would take, given that person's risk tolerance. Under that criterion, no risk is taken unless there is an expected reward sufficiently large to justify taking the risk. Thus, operational risk management should be conducted the same way that any other variation of risk management is done. And yet, there are still notable

---

[3]In a previous career, the author was responsible for certain operational risks in a bank. He can attest to the stress and burnout, and he contributed to the turnover by changing careers.

differences between operational risk management and market and credit risk management.

Operational risks are not just adverse events that occur and cause losses. All losses from adverse events represent the outcomes of risks that are consciously or unconsciously taken. For example, a company that manufactures products does not inspect every product that comes off an assembly line. It may do a certain amount of quality control sampling, but it knows that it is optimal to use sampling to balance costs against prevention of losses due to defective products. An airline, and indeed the entire air transport system, that worries about terrorists getting on planes will do a certain number of inspections of luggage and passengers, but it will not physically open and inspect the detailed contents of every bag nor will it strip search every passenger. These actions, if taken, would almost surely eliminate the threat of any weapon getting on a plane, but they would be unacceptably costly and passengers would simply not agree to such a high degree of risk control. Neither companies nor society would be willing to bear that cost. Thus, some risk is always tolerated. Of courses, these are examples of conscious decisions to take risks. It is often the unconscious decisions that get an organization in trouble. For example, a small child can get into an animal cage in a zoo, but the zoo was surely not aware of the risk before the event occurred. It has never had the event happen so it has not even thought of the risk.[4]

As noted above, we usually describe financial decisions as based on a tradeoff of return versus risk. The decision maker has a certain risk tolerance. Given the risk the person is willing to accept, the decision is optimized to offer the highest level of expected return for that level of risk. Conscious operational risk management works almost that way but not quite. There is almost always no particular expected return from taking operational risks. There is, however, a cost to mitigating operational risks. By choosing to accept a degree of operational risk, the implicit return is the avoidance of the cost of risk mitigation. Thus, optimal operational risk management is a trade-off between paying for the cost of risk mitigation versus the risk accepted. Of course, there are still the unconscious risks, and they are accepted simply because no one has recognized the risk, or if someone has, it has not been taken seriously.

---

[4]There is a great deal to be said about events that have never happened but could happen. We cover this topic in Section 12.2.8.

12.1.4.2   *Where Operational Risk Management Starts*

In Chapter 14 we will learn that effective risk management starts with the senior management and the board of directors. We call this effect "good corporate governance." Nowhere is it more important than in operational risk management. Senior management and boards of directors must establish policies that recognize operational risk management as a crucial factor in the success of an organization. They must specifically institute policies and procedures that define the entity's operational risks, measure those risks, record losses, analyze the sources of losses, and establish responses. But because senior management and the board of directors cannot be involved in the minutiae of companies' day-to-day operations, they must create a culture from top to bottom that causes all employees to be operational risk managers themselves. Senior management creates the company's philosophy of operational risk management. It sets the tone and provides incentives that inspire everyone to be good operational risk managers within their domains. When all employees are aware of the operational risks and the costs of mitigating them and the personal rewards for effective risk management, the company has an effective system of dealing with operational risks.

12.1.4.3   *Challenges in Operational Risk Management*

As noted previously, these types of events do not occur frequently within a given company. Hence, the beneficial experience that one gains from repetitive exposure to complex situations is simply not there. It may even be the case that some operational risks are so infrequent that a person might not be taken seriously if he tries to make the case that something bad could happen. Imagine the Johnson & Johnson employee who in 1981 might have told senior management that the Tylenol packaging needed to be more secure for fear that someone might insert poison in them. He probably would not have been taken seriously. Yet in 1982, someone inserted cyanide in Tylenol and killed seven people.[5] And tamper-proof packaging has been with us ever since. The bounds of operational risk management are often hard to imagine.

In addition, operational risk is difficult to measure. Traditional market risk measures such as volatility simply do not apply to events that do

---

[5]That person has never been caught. *Time* magazine ranks it one of the top 10 unsolved murders of all time.

not often occur. In that sense, operational risk has something in common with credit risk, and hence, data are often pooled over a large number of companies. But it is still difficult to estimate the probability of an operational risk event. While an airline might say that it expects one emergency landing every 100 million miles flown, how does a bank say how frequently it expects an employee to steal from it? Is it one employee per 10,000, or one loss per year, or some other measure? And for a dishonest employee, how many times must the employee be exposed to temptation before he commits a dishonest act? These risks are difficult to quantify, because the total number of events in which the loss could occur can be difficult to measure. The challenges are indeed great, and the quantitative tools are not easy to use. There is a branch of mathematics called extreme value theory that builds statistical foundations for dealing with extreme but infrequent events that can be helpful in quantifying operational risks. But ultimately, no statistical tool is any better than the data to which the tool is applied. And getting reliable operational risk data is a difficult task.

12.1.4.4   *Strategies for Operational Risk Management*

Having painted what might seem a grim picture for operational risk management, let us now turn our attention to what *can* be done. We will assume that all of the foregoing recommendations have been enacted by a company. That is, the company had done the best it can to identify the operational risks to which it is exposed and at a minimum, it is attempting to formally address how to deal with these risks.

We now identify five methods of managing operational risk: insurance, capital, auditing, outsourcing, and preventive actions. Some of these methods are primarily ex ante responses and others are primarily ex post. For example, insurance is primarily an ex post response. Indeed, one buys an insurance policy before the fact, but all insurance does is compensate for losses after the fact. And while some operational losses can be insured, others cannot. For example, property and casualty losses are often insurable. An airline can hold insurance that covers plane crashes and the loss of property and compensation for liability, but the airline cannot hold insurance that compensates it for mechanical failures that cause it to delay or cancel flights. There are certain risks that the insurance industry covers and others that it does not. The choices of which risks to insure and which to not insure depend primarily on the industry's confidence in the data it has on the frequency and severity of losses and the customer's willingness to pay the necessary premium.[6]

Capital is strictly an ex post response to operational risk management. What we mean is that the company makes sure it has sufficient resources to absorb the loss. Capital is essentially self-insurance. The problem with this approach to risk management, however, is that it does nothing to prevent the loss from occurring in the future, and it basically ignores the potential ill will and loss of trust that can occur when a major operational loss is incurred. Capital is one of the primary methods used by the banking industry to manage operational risk as well as its market and credit risks. Banks must set aside a specific amount of capital for operational risk. In the past, banks could use one of three approaches to determining the required amount of capital, but new rules proposed by the Basel Committee are converging toward a single approach that is likely to increase the required level of operational risk capital.

Auditing would seem to be both an ex ante and an ex post method of operational risk management. Auditing can sometimes detect problems before they occur, but is most often oriented toward finding problems after they occur. Auditing is primarily designed to detect financial irregularities, and it cannot be used to manage very many forms of operational risk. Operational risks are simply not the kinds of risks that are overtly or subtly embedded in financial statements. Nonetheless, a company's internal and external auditors should be instructed to be vigilant for operational risks.

Outsourcing is an ex ante method of managing operational risks. Simply contracting with another entity to provide a number of services allows a company to devote its energy to other matters. But there is a subtle problem in that outsourcing one's operations also outsources one's operational risk. Unless the company providing the outsourcing service engages in effective operational risk management, the outsourcer still bears the risk. And even

---

[6]Some unusual risks are insured by private insurers such as Lloyds of London. Lloyds is a different type of entity from the usual corporate insurer. Lloyds, founded in the latter part of the 17th century, is a syndicate of corporations and individual investors who collect premiums and pledge their corporate and personal assets to cover losses. Lloyd's has specialized in insuring unusual risks such as the hands of Rolling Stones' guitarist Keith Richards, the breasts of Dolly Parton, the nose of Jimmy Durante, the voices of Whitney Houston, Celine Dion, and Bruce Springsteen, and the 69-carat diamond given by Richard Burton to Elizabeth Taylor. The list is longer, but you get the picture.

worse is the fact that the outsourcer is likely to assume that the sub-contractor is practicing effective operational risk management. On the other hand, it is quite possible that the outsourcer is more experienced and capable of providing reliable service and effective operational risk management.

Operational Risk and Hurricane Katrina — Part I: Data Protection Services, LLC

On August 25, 2005 Hurricane Katrina crossed from the Atlantic Ocean over the Florida Keys into the Gulf of Mexico, whence it began its inexorable march toward the Louisiana and Mississippi Gulf Coasts. On August 29, it made landfall in Plaquemines Parish, Louisiana, just south of New Orleans, packing 200 kilometer-per-hour winds. While the brunt of the storm passed east of New Orleans, the surge caused by its strong winds and water displacement led to the breaching of over 50 levees that protected the city from the waters of the $1,620m^2$ Lake Pontchartrain just north of the city. The resulting flooding was a landmark event in the history of worldwide natural disasters. Along the Gulf Coast, an estimated $100 billion of property was damaged, more than 1,800 people lost their lives, and New Orleans was changed forever. It is estimated that 95 billion cubic meters of water, more than 2% of the water in Lake Pontchartrain, flowed into the city of New Orleans.

Now imagine the operational risk management discussions that might have taken place prior to Hurricane Katrina. At about 10 meters below sea level at its lowest point, the potential for a major hurricane hitting the city had always been a concern. The risk, however, had been judged to be fairly low, given that the city is actually not right on the coast. And the potential flooding from Lake Pontchartrain was considered minimal due to the extensive system of levees on the north side of the city and the fact that Lake Pontchartrain is connected to the Gulf of Mexico. With regard to Hurricane Katrina, some of these views were correct in that the city did not and has never taken an extremely powerful hit from a hurricane. But with respect to the levees, the estimates were completely wrong. No one anticipated that the levees would be breached, and if so, no one expected it to occur more than 50 times in a 24-hour period.

No one, apparently, except a company called Data Protection Services (DPS), a small firm that provides off-site data backup for other companies. In fact, the services of DPS address operational risk problems of other companies. Therefore, DPS needed to have a good operational risk plan itself. And it sure did.

Located on the 10th floor of a 28-story building, DPS was confident that floodwaters would not rise to the 10th floor and indeed it would take a flood of biblical proportions to do so. But DPS was aware that flooding and power outages could literally put it out of business forever. Consequently, DPS was prepared to ride out any such events. It had generators ready and food and facilities for its employees. DPS also had a second facility in Mandeville, Louisiana, a bedroom community of about 12,000 people on the north shore of Lake Pontchartrain.

DPS was able to operate throughout the storm, but as soon as it was able to get out of the city, it planned to move its operations to its facility in Mandeville. While New Orleans was virtually uninhabitable, DPS purchased a Hummer over the Internet and arranged for its delivery the following day. It had already contracted with a fuel supplier, so it was ready to go. It then used the Hummer to move its equipment to Mandeville and also to help employees retrieve what they could from their flooded houses.

Throughout the entire time, its data storage services operated continuously.

Postscript: In 2007, DPS moved its entire operation to Hammond, Louisiana, a city of about 20,000 people about 60 miles north of New Orleans. Having learned from the Katrina experience, it decided that the risk remained too great and the cost too large to justify staying in the city.

Preventive actions encompass a variety of techniques that attempt to stop an adverse advent from occurring. Proactive maintenance, safety inspections, attention to detail, a top-to-bottom risk culture, and cross-checking work before it is submitted are good examples of preventive actions. In many respects, preventive actions are the most effective means of dealing with operational risk problems. They are proactive, and in some cases, not necessarily very costly, but as always, the benefits must be considered against the costs. For example, airlines have extensive safety checks, but the planes do not undergo complete physical examinations before every flight.

Finally, we must add that there are no operational derivatives, so one cannot simply buy an option, forward, futures, or swap on an operational problem. There has been discussion of creating operational derivatives, but no market has ever been born. The difficulties of obtaining reliable data to gauge the risks are simply too great. Some forms of weather derivatives can be used in operational hedging for companies whose services are affected by weather, but weather derivatives have not been particularly successful in attracting much trading. There simply are not enough parties that need the risk created by weather uncertainty, or at least, they are not priced high enough to compensate the sellers of weather derivatives. Of course, given that insurance is essentially a form of derivative, one could argue that insurance is a form of an operational derivative, but in the more traditional sense, there are no operational risk derivatives, and there are not likely to ever be.

Operational Risk and Hurricane Katrina — Part II: The Oreck Vacuum Cleaner Company

Founded in 1963 by David Oreck, the Oreck Vacuum Cleaner Company is a privately-owned company known for its particularly light-weight vacuum cleaners. In 2005 it employed about 1,500 people across the U.S. and had its corporate headquarters in New Orleans, and its 375,000 square-foot manufacturing plant and call center in Long Beach, Mississippi, about 100 miles away. It had disaster plans for both facilities, but it never anticipated that both the headquarters and the factory would be shut down.

CEO Tom Oreck, son of the founder, evacuated to Houston just before the storm. The company's Long Beach plant was not severely damaged, but there was no electricity and most employees had lost their homes or had incurred significant losses. Oreck then began a personal odyssey to put the company back together. Using his cell phone and credit card, he purchased generators, food, water, medical supplies, and transportation to get these items to Long Beach. He also arranged temporary housing for his 500 employees at the plant. The company then seeded $500,000 to create a disaster relief fund and arranged for counselors to help employees deal with the trauma. All employees were promised that their jobs were safe. Within just 10 days, the company was making vacuum cleaners again. It may well have been the first business to become operational following Katrina.

Postscript 1: The company and CEO Tom Oreck won many awards for its rapid and compassionate response to Katrina, but in 2007, it closed its New Orleans and Long Beach facilities and moved them to the Nashville, Tennessee area. Citing increased insurance costs and shortages of labor due to so many people moving away after the storm, Oreck said that the decision was painful but necessary.

Postscript 2: In 2013, Oreck sold the company to an Ohio-based company owned by a corporation in Hong Kong.

Thus, operational risk management will continue to be conducted as a combination of identifying and assessing the likelihood and expected costs of the risks and engaging in one or more of the various strategies discussed in this section. Much of operational risk management comes down to educated guessing about what can go wrong, how costly it could be, how likely it is to occur, what preventive actions and strategies can be done to mitigate the risk in advance, how to respond to such an event, and whether there are sufficient resources to cover any such losses.

12.2 Other Risks

There are so many types of risks we have not covered but will do so now, that we have to group them into a general category called "Other Risks." Some of them are closely related to risks we have already covered, but some are quite unique.

12.2.1 *Liquidity Risk*

We now take a look at liquidity risk. Let us start by defining it.

> *Liquidity risk is the risk that arises when there is a thin or vulnerable market for a security, resulting in an inability of a party to sell a security in a timely manner without forcing a significant decrease in the current market price.*

By a "thin market," we mean one in which there are few buyers and sellers and a low level of trading activity. A thin market might exist on securities in which there is simply not much interest in trading, unusual risk potential, unknown risks, or simply not much information. An example would be bonds of third world and emerging market countries and companies therein. A vulnerably thin market is one in which there is a modest degree of liquidity, but during turbulent times in the overall market, this particular market might dry up due to a lack of buyers in these securities when markets are stressed.

These points might prompt the question of which comes first: liquidity or trading? Investors do not like to buy and sell securities that have low liquidity. Yet, liquidity exists only if investors trade a security. If not many investors want to trade a security, it will have low liquidity. Those who are not trading the security are doing so because others are not trading it. It is the classic case of a vicious circle.

As mentioned, liquidity risk arises when the holder of a security needs to liquidate it.[7] Oftentimes, this problem occurs during stressed markets. When the holder enters the market to sell the security, it may notice that there are few if any buyers. Alternatively, there may in fact be a market, but it may be for a far less size than the size of the position that needs to be liquidated. In other words, a party may simply be holding too large of a position to be able to liquidate, given the number of participants in the market. This problem is referred to as one of market depth. Deep markets can handle large transactions without much of a price change. Liquid markets with less depth can handle smaller transactions without much of a price change, but there simply is not sufficient volume to handle larger transactions without moving the price by a large amount.

Of course, economic theory states that there is always a price at which one can sell something. If the market will not buy at the asking price, the holder can simply lower the price, but of course, that is a cost. If no one will buy at that price, it can lower the price further. Thus, the cost of selling gets higher. But again, there is always a price at which someone will buy. We know that the worst case scenario is a price of zero. The price that unloads the security is probably not zero, but it may be an unacceptable price to the seller. In some cases, the holder of the security can sell a small portion of its position at the present time, but then will need to sell the rest of it over a longer period of time. Again, this is a problem of market depth. Thus, liquidity risk is also the risk that there will be an undesirable extension of the holding period.

Liquidity risk also fuels another related risk: the risk that the company's own survival depends on its ability to generate its own liquidity to meet

---

[7]As per the above definition, liquidity risk is usually defined with respect to a seller. You may be wondering if liquidity risk can exist in purchase transactions. Indeed, it can but it probably deserves less of a risk manager's attention. If an investor wants to take a larger position in an asset or derivative than can be executed at a reasonable price, there is the risk that the trade will not be done. As such there may be lost opportunities. Generally speaking, unless the purchase is a critical coverage of a short position, there is less concern that a buy transaction cannot get executed at a reasonable price than there is for a sell transaction.

margin calls, interest or mandatory principal payments, or pay bills. Such problems can spin a company right into insolvency.[8]

12.2.1.1 *Measures of Liquidity Risk for a Security*

The primary measure of liquidity for a security is the *bid-ask spread*. We have briefly talked about the bid-ask spread for derivatives. A dealer stands ready to either buy or sell a security or derivative. Dealers quote a price at which they are willing to buy and a price at which they are willing to sell. An investor knows that there is always a dealer to take the other side of the transaction. And that is what it means to provide liquidity to the market.

As an example of a bid-ask spread, let us consider a very active stock, GE. At the time of this writing, the stock last traded at 13.90. Its bid price is 13.90 and its ask is 13.91. These bid and ask prices mean that if an investor wants to sell, the dealer is offering to buy GE for 13.90. If the investor wants to buy, the dealer is offering to sell at 13.91. The difference in the ask and bid prices, the bid-ask spread, is 0.01. There are several ways to express this number. One is by as an absolute number: 0.01. Another is as a percentage. The spread can be expressed as a percentage of the average of the bid and ask prices, called the midpoint: $0.01/((13.90+13.91)/2) = 0.0007$, or 0.07%. It can also be expressed as a percentage markup or markdown relative to the bid or ask price. As a markup, the spread is $0.01/13.90 = 0.0007$ or 0.07%. As a markdown, the spread is $0.01/13.91 = 0.0007$, or 0.07%. In today's markets, the spread on almost all very active stocks is about a penny, and therefore, one can express the spread as either a percentage of the bid, ask, or midpoint and get virtually the same percentage.

Not only is the bid-ask spread an indicator of liquidity, it is also a transaction cost. We tend to think of transaction costs as being commissions paid to brokers, but the bid-ask spread is a significant transaction cost. To see why, let us assume that you buy GE at the ask price of 13.91. You immediately realize that you made a mistake and intended to buy GM. Let us say you go back into the market to sell GE and buy GM. Barring any

---

[8]When you hear the term *liquidity risk*, you cannot always tell which risk it refers to. The first definition is the risk related to the inability to sell something without a substantial price concession, and the second is the risk that an organization will be unable to meet its obligations due to insufficient cash assets or assets that can be quickly converted to cash. You just have to figure out the meaning from the context. The first might be called *market liquidity risk*, and the second might be referred to as *corporate liquidity risk*, though those distinctions are rarely added in practice.

additional news arriving in the market to shift the bid and ask prices, you would have to sell GE at 13.90, an immediate loss 0.01. Indeed, the bid-ask spread is said to be the cost of immediacy. Given this fact, when buying a security or derivative, the price has to change by at least the bid-ask spread to generate a profit, assuming no change in the bid-ask spread. So, for example, if you bought GE at the ask price of 13.91, the bid price must move to at least 13.91 to sell it for a profit. With the bid originally at 13.90 and the bid-ask spread still at 0.01, the bid must shift up to above 13.91. Thus, there must be a general movement of the bid and ask prices upward by the spread for a buyer to profit. Likewise, there must be a general movement of the bid and ask prices downward by the spread for a seller to profit.

As noted, the average of the bid and ask prices is often called the midpoint, and it would tend to represent the dealer's assessment of the equilibrium value of the asset or derivative. In other words, say a European-style option has a Black-Scholes-Merton value of 3.25. If the dealer believes he should quote a 1.5% spread relative to the midpoint, he would set the ask price at $3.25(1.015) = 3.29875$, probably rounded to 3.30, and the bid price at $3.25(1 - 0.015) = 3.20125$, probably rounded to 3.20. So the bid and ask prices would be 3.20 and 3.30, and the spread would be 0.10 or 0.10/3.25, which is approximately 3% of the midpoint.

Let us take a look at bid and ask quotes for options on Microsoft (Symbol: MSFT). Exhibit 12-3 was constructed from the CBOE's website posted at 5:19 PM Eastern Time on 16 July, 2018.[9] At that time, Microsoft stock last traded at 104.91 and had a current quoted bid of 104.25 and an ask of 104.59. Note first that the last trade was outside the current bid and ask prices, but the bid and ask prices are generally updated, and the last trade could have occurred when the bid and ask prices were at different levels. We examine only the put and call options that expire on August 17. The volume in the later expirations is not very large. Options with exercise prices ranging from around 65 to 145 are available for trade, but this table reports only those options that traded at least one contract, and their exercise prices range from 90 to 120.

First note that the bid-ask spread on the stock is $104.59 - 104.25 = 0.34$, and the midpoint is $(104.25 + 104.59)/2 = 104.42$. So the spread relative to the midpoint is 0.3256%. Relative to the ask, the spread is 0.3251%, and

---

[9]The CBOE trading day ends at 4:15 Eastern Time for equity options. Thus, these are essentially end-of-day quotes.

| Current date | 16-Jul-2018 | | |
| Current time | 19:19 ET | | |

MSFT			
Expiration	17-Aug-2018	Midpoint	104.42
Last trade	104.91	Spread	0.34
Bid	104.25	As a percentage of	
Ask	104.59	Midpoint	0.3256%
Volume	21,778,099	Ask	0.3251%
		Bid	0.3261%

Calls	Last	Bid	Ask	Midpoint	Spread	Spread as a percentage of		Volume	Open Interest
						Midpoint	Ask		
90.00	15.40	15.15	15.55	15.350	0.40	2.61%	2.57%	8	1,069
92.50	12.54	12.45	12.85	12.650	0.40	3.16%	3.11%	9	667
95.00	10.13	10.10	10.45	10.275	0.35	3.41%	3.35%	7	1,551
97.50	7.83	8.10	8.20	8.150	0.10	1.23%	1.22%	7	1,688
100.00	6.03	6.00	6.10	6.050	0.10	1.65%	1.64%	86	13,229
105.00	2.73	2.70	2.76	2.730	0.06	2.20%	2.17%	622	23,993
110.00	0.82	0.83	0.87	0.850	0.04	4.71%	4.60%	285	10,395
115.00	0.20	0.17	0.21	0.190	0.04	21.05%	19.05%	10	2,091
120.00	0.04	0.02	0.13	0.075	0.11	146.67%	84.62%	19	668

Puts	Last	Bid	Ask	Midpoint	Spread	Spread as a percentage of		Volume	Open Interest
						Midpoint	Ask		
75.00	0.04	0.00	0.08	0.040	0.08	200.00%	100.00%	1	380
80.00	0.05	0.00	0.06	0.030	0.06	200.00%	100.00%	41	1,192
87.50	0.10	0.10	0.12	0.110	0.02	18.18%	16.67%	7	1,425
90.00	0.14	0.14	0.16	0.150	0.02	13.33%	12.50%	5	2,778
92.50	0.23	0.22	0.24	0.230	0.02	8.70%	8.33%	25	4,561
95.00	0.38	0.36	0.39	0.375	0.03	8.00%	7.69%	235	8,293
97.50	0.68	0.62	0.66	0.640	0.04	6.25%	6.06%	121	4,832
100.00	1.10	1.08	1.12	1.100	0.04	3.64%	3.57%	516	6,351
105.00	2.93	2.85	2.89	2.870	0.04	1.39%	1.38%	96	3,419
110.00	5.95	6.00	6.15	6.075	0.15	2.47%	2.44%	15	727
115.00	10.73	10.40	10.50	10.450	0.10	0.96%	0.95%	15	172

Exhibit 12-3. Bid and Ask Quotes of Microsoft Options at Chicago Board Options Exchange

relative to the bid, it is 0.3261%. These percentages represent a relatively tight spread, as would be expected. Microsoft is a highly visible stock with extremely active trading. As can be seen, more than 21 million shares have traded.

For calls, the spread ranges from 0.04 to 0.40, and the percentage spread relative to the midpoint ranges from 1.23% to 146.67%, but the very high percentages are options that have extremely low prices, which are deep out-of-the-money calls. As we see, volume and open interest are not necessarily good indicators of liquidity. The largest volume and highest open interest call does not have the lowest bid-ask spread. Generally speaking, the spreads are lowest for the options that are closest to at-the-money. For puts the results are similar. One of the most important points to note from this data is that the options have much higher percentage spreads than the stock. Indeed, there is far less trading in options than in stock. We see that at that time point, the stock had traded more than 21 million shares. The highest volume option contract had volume of 622 contracts traded, which covers 62,200 shares. Of course, there is substantial volume in the options spread out among the contracts.

The bid-ask spread reflects three factors. One is obviously the liquidity in the market, which is our primary interest at this point. Markets with high liquidity will have many active traders and will tend to have low bid-ask spreads. Many active traders will also necessitate many competing market makers. A market maker can make money only if he can generate trading. To do so, he must offer the lowest ask price and/or highest bid price. Thus, a market maker trying to draw trading from other market makers might lower his ask price or increase his bid price. Either way the spread decreases.

The second factor in the bid-ask spread price is the dealer's cost of trading. Acting as a dealer is a business with costs. The dealer must generate a reasonable return on invested capital. Based on his estimate of trading volume, he will set the spread at a size sufficient to generate his desired financial performance.

Finally, the dealer also faces a particular risk that is unique to dealers. Because a dealer is supposed to buy or sell at any time, he faces the possibility that an investor who wishes to do a trade will have information about the security or derivative that the dealer does not. This condition places the dealer at a severe disadvantage. Even though dealers typically hedge their positions with offsetting transactions with other investors or in other markets, hedging requires trading quickly at the same price at which the position was established. A fast moving market can cause the dealer to lose money, because he cannot get the hedge done before the price changes. This type of risk faced by dealers is called *adverse selection*, as it refers to the condition that a party in possession of private information sell to or buy from the dealer who is obligated to trade.

As noted, the dealer typically hedges by doing an offsetting trade in another market. A dealer will occasionally hold positions and will not be perfectly hedged. A dealer will not generally take an exposed speculative position that could result in significant losses if the market moves against it. Dealers have very low trading costs and successful ones can generally unload the risk at a better cost than the one they paid or received. Dealers also have an advantage in that they usually have a pretty good idea of the intentions of investors as indicated by the limit and stop orders that customers place. A limit order specifies a maximum price a buyer is willing to pay and a minimum price a seller is willing to accept. A stop orders specifies a price that will initiate a sale if the price is reached. The most common type of stop order is a stop order to sell, which indicates that when the price falls to a certain level, a stop order that is placed by an investor will automatically turn into a market order. The dealer typically knows the stop and limit orders that are in place. The rest of the market usually does not have access to this information, though it may see the best limit orders, meaning highest bid and lowest ask.

Of course, one might ask the obvious question of how a market can have low liquidity if there are dealers quoting bid and ask prices. Just remember that the existence of a dealer means only that there will be someone to take the opposite side of the trade. There is no guarantee that the price you get will be attractive. A dealer simply quotes prices at which he is willing to trade. He does not guarantee you will like the price.

There are several other measures of liquidity. An obvious one is volume. A high liquidity market will have high trading volume relative to other less liquid low liquidity markets. For exchange-listed derivatives, open interest is a rough measure of liquidity. Open interest represents the number of contracts created that are outstanding. There has traditionally been a belief that contracts created are contracts that will typically be reversed before expiration, but this is not true. Some contracts will be held until expiration. There is rarely any pressure for a party to unload a position before expiration. As we noted in Exhibit 12-3, volume and open interest are not perfect measures of liquidity. In particular, the quoted prices you see are as of that point in time, while the volume and open interest reflect transactions that have occurred earlier. Heavy volume and open interest could have meant tighter bid-ask spreads at that time, but by the end of the day, the bid-ask spread might be larger.[10]

The size of a company is also a measure of liquidity but mainly due to the correlation of size with trading activity. Larger companies are well-known and draw a lot of trading interest. By itself, size tells us very little with respect to trading interest. It simply tends to vary with factors that do lead to high liquidity.

Some sophisticated investors estimate the number of days it would take to liquidate an asset in an orderly manner. By orderly liquidation, we mean to sell the asset without moving the price too much. To derive such a measure, one might make an assumption that an orderly liquidation would mean that the trade would account for no more than 5% of the average daily volume. For example, suppose the average daily volume of Ford Motor Company is 50 million. Five percent of 50 million is 2.5 million. An investor holding 10 million shares might, therefore, estimate that it would take four days to sell 10 million shares without exceeding 5% of the average daily volume.

12.2.1.2 *Managing Liquidity Risk*

The first step toward managing liquidity risk is awareness of it. Most professional investors would be aware of it, but many corporate and institutional end users are not likely to be much aware of this risk. In fact, they are not likely to be aware of how dealers work. Many believe that dealers speculate on the positions they take. Understanding that the bid-ask spread is a cost of trading and that the spread measures liquidity enables a market participant to more fully understand how trading works and how its own position is affected by liquidity.

A second step toward managing liquidity risk is to quantify it. Measuring the spread and comparing it to similar alternatives provide considerable perspective on the true cost of liquidity and the potential that it will dry up.

The third method is to incorporate it into market risk measures such as volatility and *VaR*. This can be done by building bid-ask spreads into prices at which the risk manager believes he can liquidate a position. In addition, liquidity squeezes can be incorporated into scenario and sensitivity analyses.

---

[10]One example of when this situation can occur is when the underlying moves substantially during the day. The highest volume and open interest and tightest bid-ask spread tend to occur when the option is close to at-the-money. When it moves further away from at-the-money, trading will drop and the spread will widen.

12.2.2 *Model Risk*

If you have not figured it out by now, financial risk management uses a tremendous number of models. We have looked at Value-at-Risk, as well as the cost of carry models for pricing forwards, futures, and swaps, and naturally the Black-Scholes-Merton and binomial models for pricing options. These models provide us with the fair value or price of a financial instrument and/or measures of risk. Using a model entails a number of choices.

First, one must choose the model. While we have touched only on a few models in this book, in reality there are usually many models. But as you learned, *VaR* can be estimated three different ways. And of course, you have experience with two option pricing models. These choices might not always lead to the same answer. One must clearly choose the right model, or at least the best model.

Second, one must choose the right inputs that go into the model. In some cases, those inputs are easy to obtain and few would disagree on their values. For example, the current price of the underlying and the expiration of a derivative are unambiguous. The risk-free rate must be chosen from a number of candidates, such as the Treasury bill rate, LIBOR, the fed funds rate, etc. Fortunately, the variation of the impact on the price of the derivative is not great, so there is room for choosing any one from a number of reasonable candidates for the risk-free rate. There is also room for moderate disagreement in estimating dividends or other cash flows over the life of a derivative. When estimating *VaR* using either the analytical or Monte Carlo methods, one must come up with the expected return and volatility. And it almost goes without saying that the volatility input in option pricing models can easily be misestimated.

Let us now give a good definition of model risk.

Model risk is the risk that arises when one either uses the wrong model or the wrong inputs into the right model.

Model risk is, thus, quite simply the risk of misusing a model. Misusing a model does not mean being careless. It simply means making honest mistakes or having an opinion of an input value that is somewhat inaccurate.

Let us look at an example of model risk. Most experts would not make this mistake, but it is an easy one for novices to make. Consider a non-dividend paying stock priced at $150 with a volatility of 0.48. For now, we shall assume that this number is correct, but we shall introduce an error in volatility later. Now consider an American put option that expires in 90 days, so the time to expiration is 90/365. The exercise price is $160. Let the risk-free be 0.03.

Since this option is American-style, it can be exercised early. In Chapter 10, we learned that call options on non-dividend-paying stocks will not be exercised early, but put options might well be. Let us calculate the value of an American put. In Chapter 10, we learned that we would have to use the binomial model to get an accurate assessment of the effect of possible early exercise. We shall need to use many time steps, far more than we can illustrate here. So let us use the binomial model with 500 time steps, in which case we would find that the price of the option would be $19.59. Now, suppose instead we use the Black-Scholes-Merton model. We would obtain a price of $19.48. Remember that the Black-Scholes-Merton model provides the price of a European option only, so it does not incorporate the effect of early exercise. The error here is an understatement of the value by $0.11, or about 0.56%. While that does not seem like much of an error, suppose a client comes to a dealer with a request to purchase $50 million of this option. Let us say the dealer understates the price by 0.56%. This amounts to an error of almost $281,000![11]

Now let us dispense with this mistake. It is, after all, an amateurish mistake. But suppose the dealer knows what he is doing and charges the correct value of $19.59.[12] All is well and fair. But suppose another dealer believes the volatility is 0.40. Based on that number, he would calculate a price of $17.27. The end user would find that number a much better price. But suppose the second dealer has simply made a poor estimate of the volatility. If the true volatility is closer to 0.48, the dealer will sell the option for too little and will lose money because he will have to pay too much to get it hedged. This is a good example of model risk. Nowhere is it more evident than in option pricing models, where the volatility is the only input for which the user has little to no information on what the volatility should be. There is no public proclamation of what the volatility of an asset is. Historical data can be gathered and used to provide an estimate, but if the historical volatility does not come reasonably close to matching the future volatility, the user will have poor inputs and therefore poor outputs.

When estimating *VaR* using the analytical or Monte Carlo method, the volatility is a critical input. For example, suppose an investment manager has a portfolio of $10 million of a stock with an annual expected return of 0.10 and an annual estimated volatility of 0.40. We will take the expected return estimate as accurate and see what happens if the volatility is misestimated.[13]

---

[11]Of course, this is a book for end users, so they should be happy if the bank undercharges.

[12]We are ignoring the spread the dealer will add to the equilibrium price.

[13]In reality, the expected return is even more unstable than the volatility, at least based on historical data.

Based on this information a 95% annual *VaR* would be $-\$10,000,000 \times (0.10 - 1.65 \times 0.40) = \$5,600,000$. If the volatility is really 0.50, an error of 0.25%, the *VaR* would be \$7,250,000, a difference of \$1,650,000, or a 29% error.

Model risk is an important one in risk management. There is much disagreement about the right models to use in estimating *VaR* and in option pricing. There are very sophisticated models that purportedly given much better results, but they typically require far more inputs or inputs that are even harder to estimate than volatility. The only risk management strategy for model risk is to have competent people with solid knowledge of models and to engage in careful monitoring to verify that the results align with what the models predicted.

12.2.3 Settlement Risk

Settlement risk is a slight variation of credit risk. In today's markets, settlement risk is much smaller than it used to be, but there is always a fear that a problem will occur during settlement. Suppose Party A owes money to Party B, and Party B owes money to Party A. In the days prior to netting, each party would transfer the money to the other, trusting that the other was sending the money or would do so within a very reasonable period of time. But one morning in June 1974, a bank in the German city of Cologne called the Herstatt Bank declared bankruptcy shortly after it had received payments from counterparties but before it sent its payments to the counterparties. As a result of this one incident, settlement risk has come to be known as *Herstatt risk*. The problem is particularly dangerous when the counterparties are in dramatically different time zones. Imagine, a Japanese bank in Tokyo bank wiring money to a California bank in San Francisco, where there is a 16-hour time difference. Thus, at 10 AM in Tokyo, it is 6 PM the previous day in San Francisco. California banks are closed and will not send the money until around 10 AM their time the next day, which is 16 hours later. The Japanese bank may wait nervously if it thinks the California bank is on the brink of bankruptcy.

Thus, our definition of settlement risk is as follows:

Settlement risk is the risk that a party will send money or securities to another and fail to receive payment from the other party, which declares bankruptcy.

Of course, netting tends to care of this problem, but netting is not always feasible. Consider a currency swap between two parties. Party A pays Party B in dollars, while Party B pays Party A in euros. Such transactions are not typically netted, since the payments are in different currencies. The parties can reduce this risk by clearing the contract through a clearinghouse, but that is not always done.

So while settlement risk is not the problem it once was, it still remains a concern for certain types of transactions. The best defense against settlement risk is an awareness of the credit quality of the counterparty and an attempt to control that risk, as we discussed in Chapter 11. Thus, settlement risk is closely related to credit risk.

12.2.4   *Regulatory Risk*

We define regulatory risk as follows:

> *Regulatory risk is the risk that regulations are either unclear or those that are presumably clear will change, thereby putting a party at a disadvantage resulting in some potential for financial loss.*

New and different types of financial instruments are constantly being created, and it often arises that the parties may not know where the instrument falls in the regulatory system. That is, they do not know which regulatory agency has authority to regulate the instrument, and/or the regulations that exist are not clear. A common version of this problem is for an instrument that appears to fall under no particular regulator's authority. Such might arise if the instrument is quite different from anything previously appearing in the markets. An investor or dealer might engage in a transaction involving the instrument under the belief that there are no particular regulatory requirements. Later, however, the regulatory authorities may decide to write rules for the instrument, thereby making the instrument costlier to the participants, who had not factored in this possibility when they decided to do the transaction.

A similar problem arises when it is unclear where the regulatory authority lies, a common problem in the U.S., which is one of the few countries with multiple regulators. Cat-and-mouse games between regulatory agencies have occurred, leaving the parties wanting to use the instrument in a regulatory version of purgatory. Further complicating matters is that many transactions in today's markets cross borders. Hence, there are regulators in multiple countries, compounding the regulatory uncertainty.

The lack of clarity and potential for regulations to change is the driver of regulatory risk. The best way to deal with this risk is to engage with expert lawyers and regulatory consultants to seek clarity of regulations. Alternatively, a party can simply choose not to engage in transactions with regulatory uncertainty, but such actions could stifle innovation.

12.2.5 *Accounting Risk*

In Chapter 13 we shall cover the accounting of risk management products, a subject that you will see has a long and complex history. Moreover, the innovation of the financial world constantly creates new products and variations of old products that often do not fall neatly into a particular accounting prescription. In other words, there is risk than a transaction will not be properly accounted for. This risk creates the possibility that at a later time, an entity will need to make corrections that send a signal that errors were made in the past and that the company's past performance may be worse than previously thought. Of course, this might not be a mistake. It may well be the ambiguity created when financial innovation and accounting collide. Thus,

> *Accounting risk is the risk that the correct accounting for a transaction is uncertain, thereby raising the risk that financial statements will need to be corrected, leading to some potential for disclosure of weaker performance.*

In the U.S. prior to 2000, there was considerable ambiguity in the accounting for risk management products. That year, however, saw the institution of FAS (Financial Accounting Standard) 133, which provided some degree of much-needed clarity. Nonetheless, accounting rules are constantly evolving, and they are not in complete harmony across countries. Moreover, new instruments are constantly being created, and new strategies and transactions occur on an ongoing basis. Thus, while accounting risk is now far less than it was in the latter part of the 20th century, it still remains. The best defense is to employ or engage the services of the best accountants. As noted, we will cover derivatives accounting in Chapter 13.

12.2.6 *Tax Risk*

When financial decisions are made, the tax effects are always considered. These effects are based on assumptions about how income will be taxed and the rate at which it will be taxed. With that in mind,

> *Tax risk is the uncertainty that arises from the potential that tax rates and rules will change and result in the potential for financial loss due to owing more taxes than expected.*

Thus, a well-crafted long-term strategy that incorporates assumptions about tax rules and rates can deliver poor results if the rules and rates change. The taxation of risk management products depends heavily on the accounting for these products. Hence, tax risk and accounting risk are not surprisingly, interrelated. The best defense against tax risk is to employ or engage the services of the best tax accountants and attorneys.

12.2.7   *Legal Risk*

Legal risk takes on two forms. Let us start by defining legal risk.

> *Legal risk comprises two types of risks, one being that a dealer will be sued by a counterparty as a result of a loss incurred in a transaction and the other being that a court will not uphold the original terms of the transaction.*

For dealers in risk management products, legal risk is a serious threat. Dealers are typically banks and represent a storehouse of money. Hence, there is often no hesitation to sue them.[14] Fortunately, the legal risk from litigation involving risk management products has been reduced substantially in the last 20 years. The efforts of the International Swaps and Derivatives Association (ISDA) and attorneys specializing in risk management products have created standardized contracts with well-defined terms to which both parties agree. Nonetheless, there is often room for interpretation, and that, of course, is why lawyers and courts are needed.[15]

The second type of legal risk is the risk that a court will declare a contract null and void, thereby erasing the loss to one counterparty and the corresponding gain to the other. This is precisely what happened starting in 1983, when the London borough of Hammersmith & Fulham began to engage in a series of interest rate swaps. By 1989, it had nearly 600 swaps in place

---

[14]This problem should remind you of the quote by famous bank robber Willie Sutton. When asked why he robbed banks, Sutton replied, "Because that's where the money is."

[15]There is also a tremendous ignorance on the part of some end users and their attorneys on how derivatives work. The author has served as an expert witness for dealers on cases in which counterparties and their attorneys file suits when the counterparty loses money on a derivative. It was apparent that the counterparties and their attorneys were unaware that the dealer hedges the risk. They believed that if the counterparty lost money on a derivative, the dealer made money and, therefore, exploited the counterparty. The dealer did indeed make money, but because it hedged the risk, it owed that money to another counterparty on another transaction. Hedging is what dealers do to be able to provide their services of standing ready to take either side of a transaction. If dealers simply took speculative positions, betting that the outcomes would be favorable, they would eventually be bankrupted.

for a notional of more than £6 billion with an estimated net position of a loss estimated at around £300 million. An external auditor for Hammersmith & Fulham initiated an effort to get the community out of its obligation to pay the loss by challenging the authority of the community to enter into the transactions. Following a series of suits and appeals, the final ruling came in 1991 when the U.K. House of Lords, analogous to the U.S. Supreme Court, ruled that the swaps were illegal. In short, Hammersmith & Fulham had never established the legal authority to engage in swaps. The ruling declared that the dealers that did the transactions with the town had the obligation to determine if the town had the legal authority to do the transactions.

There is an incredible irony in this completely inane ruling. The town engaged in the transactions, in fact, 600 of them. So, the picture is this: over a period of six or so years, the town signed 600 swap contracts. Therefore, it certainly believed it had the legal authority to do so. It lost money, could not pay the losses, and ultimately got a court to rule as it did, wiping out the town's losses and putting the blame on the dealer for not telling the town that the town had no authority to engage in swaps.

The Hammersmith & Fulham ruling struck fear in the hears of derivatives dealers. Contracts began to contain strong language stating that the counterparty agreed that it had the legal authority to do the transactions. Also, the contracts began to state explicitly that the dealer was not the advisor to the counterparty. That is, it was not *recommending* that the counterparty do the transaction. It was simply *willing* to do the transaction with the counterparty. The counterparty had to agree that the onus was on it to obtain authority, and it had to affirm that it was not taking any advice from the dealer.

These two variations of legal risk are obviously related. The threat of lawsuits is one thing. Just being sued is costly. Losing a suit is another. The potential monetary loss and implication for possible other cases in which it might be sued tend to result in banks fighting each law suit, no matter how small tooth and nail.[16]

In spite of these improvements in the legal language, lawsuits still occur. Desperate counterparties responsible for losses often resort to desperate

---

[16]The author once served as an expert witness for a dealer in litigation involving a difference of opinion of only about $30,000. The litigation was being handled by arbitration, a much cheaper way to resolve a dispute than a full-blown trial in a federal or state court, but still expensive and far costlier than $30,000. The bank could not afford an adverse ruling for what it might have meant for other potential cases. In the end, the parties settled the matter quietly.

measures, such as lawsuits. The greater legal risk to the dealer is that a court will not uphold the terms of the contract. Such a decision can open the door for other suits. Naturally, extra care in designing contracts and legal expertise are the best measures in managing legal risk.

12.2.8   *Black Swan Risk*

We have not covered all of the risks that an end user and dealer might face, but we have hit the key ones. Or at least, the ones we know of. It is, however, the risks that we do not know of that ought to scare us, particularly, if those risks can result in large losses. Such risks have come to be known as black swan risk.

The notion of black swan risk has been popularized by trader, philosopher, and polymath Nassim Taleb, particularly in his book *The Black Swan* (2007). A black swan is something that has never happened, but just because it has never happened, it does not mean that it could not. And if it does, the damage will be great. The reason it is called black swan risk goes back to a story that all swans in Europe are white. Europeans had never seen a black swan. They began to use the term to refer to something that was impossible. But when the first European explorers landed in Australia in the 17th century, they discovered black swans. Then, the concept of a black swan came to be known as something that everyone believed could not happen but eventually did.

Black Swans in the Adirondacks

Other than in zoos, there are not likely to be any black swans in the Adirondack Mountains of upstate New York. But as your author once discovered, there is at least one hidden risk there that is frightening to say the least.

The author once attended a conference in upstate New York. It was an idyllic setting in the Adirondack Mountains. An isolated lodge on a beautiful lake. A handful of separate cabins, each with four private rooms. While the internet service was not great, everything else, combined with the crisp early September air, made for a perfect event.

I checked in, whereupon the desk clerk took my credit card information and told me which cabin and room I would be in. She pointed in the general direction of the cabin and then appeared to go on to whatever was it was that would occupy her next. I asked her if she was going to give me the key, to which she replied, "Oh, we don't lock the doors. We've never had any problems." I was stunned.

The cabin had four rooms each opening into a small common foyer in the center of the cabin with a door leading to the outside. So there were no locks on the cabins and no locks on the cabin room doors. I felt a little uneasy, and I can imagine how uneasy a woman would feel. There may have never been any crime, but the potential for crimes particularly against women is quite great. And while there was apparently only one road out the area and a perpetrator quite likely would be caught, catching the person after the criminal act does not undo the damage.

I decided not to play the role of risk management advisor. I was just hoping my laptop would not get stolen. Fortunately for me, it did not. But, just because something has not happened does not mean you should wait until it does to do something about it, particularly if what could happen is potentially quite serious and physically and permanently harmful.

Oh, and by the way, while there were no locks on the doors, the rooms did have those coat-hangers that are permanently attached to the rail in the closet. So, while you can easily break into someone's room and harm them or steal something from them, *you cannot steal the coat-hangers from this lodge.*

Go figure.

Taleb generally used the concept to refer to large market movements, but it has come to be known for any type of catastrophic event that was at one time thought impossible but could and perhaps has happened. Some examples of black swans are the 9-11 attacks, Hurricane Katrina, and the earthquake and tsunami in the Indian Ocean. And it probably would not be wrong to include the unraveling of the previously squeaky-clean Tiger Woods or Bill Cosby and what it meant for companies that used them as sponsors. Can you imagine an executive at Nike saying "Before we sign this Tiger Woods contract, has anybody stopped to think about what it would mean to us if Tiger got into a scandal? Say, cavorting with prostitutes. What would that do to our image?" "Are you serious?" the others would likely say.

So we can define black swan risk as follows:

Black Swan risk is the risk of the occurrence of extreme events with catastrophic costs in terms of financial resources and/or human life that have not been anticipated and perhaps not believed to be possible.

So how does one manage black swan risk? Can one anticipate such events? There may be some that can be anticipated. There may be futurists or experts on risk who propose that certain extreme events that have never occurred could occur. Organizations should take them seriously, hard as that is to do. For other events that are not anticipated, there is, by definition, nothing that one can do before the fact, but having a physical and financial disaster plan in place for whatever unexpected events might occur is probably the best plan.

12.3   Chapter Summary

In this chapter, we studied two general categories of risks. The first is operational risk and the second is a general category that we called *other* risks. Operational risk refers to risks that occur in the operations of an organization. These types of risks arise through accidents, negligence, and intentional damage. Operational risk is a difficult risk to manage, because the risks are often difficult to identify and to quantify. Thus, predicting how often such an event will occur and the consequences are quite challenging. Moreover, they are the first risks we have encountered for which there are no derivatives that can be used to manage them. We identified five methods of managing these risks: insurance, capital, auditing, outsourcing, and preventive actions. Some of these methods are quite limited. Insurance is not available for many types of operational risks, auditing is primarily designed to identify financial irregularities, and outsourcing may be efficient, but it outsources your risk management. Capital is merely an after-the-fact response: does the entity have the resources to absorb such losses? Preventive actions are probably the best approach, but the costs and benefits must be balanced against each other.

The second category of risks we covered in this chapter is a general collection of risks called other risks. We first looked at liquidity risk, which is the risk that arises from an inability to sell an asset or derivative without forcing a significant price decrease. We then examined model risk, which it the risk created by using an inappropriate model or bad inputs into an appropriate model. We examined settlement risk, which is a variation of credit risk that occurs when one party makes a payment expecting the other to do so, but the latter does not due to an unexpected filing of bankruptcy. Regulatory, accounting, tax, and legal risk all occur from uncertainty and potential changes in regulation, accounting rules, tax laws, and laws in general. In addition, legal risk is the risk of getting sued and having a court not upheld the terms of the contract.

Finally, we discussed black swan risk, which is the risk of a catastrophic event that is completely unanticipated, perhaps unknown, and which no one believes can happen. It is the one risk for which the best strategy is simply to prepare for the worst.

12.4 Questions and Problems

1. What are the three sources of failure in the Basel Committee definition of operational risk?
2. Consider an entity called Company A. How is it possible that the operational risk of a different company called Company B can cause an operational risk problem for Company A? Create an example.
3. Why does the relative infrequency of operational risk events make them harder to manage? What can be done about this problem?
4. Why is retail banking a source of many operational risk events but not a source of as much money lost?
5. Which type of banking activity has a disproportionately large amount of money losses in relation to the number of loss events?
6. Which form of fraud, internal or external, more commonly occurs? Why do you think one is more common than another?
7. Explain how operational risks are taken and managed in the context of the risk-reward tradeoff.
8. Why does senior management play such an important role in operational risk management, given that senior management is rarely directly connected to the activities that lead to operational risk events?
9. Identify and briefly describe the five methods of managing operational risk.
10. What is liquidity risk and what are some measures of a market's liquidity?
11. Consider a futures contract with an equilibrium price of 125.45. Determine the bid and ask prices for the following conditions:

    (a) The bid-ask spread is 1.3% of the midpoint
    (b) With the ask price at 127, the bid-ask spread is 2% relative to the ask price.

12. Explain how the bid-ask spread is a transaction cost. Provide this explanation in the context of an option with an equilibrium price of 6.50 and bid and ask prices of 6.80 and 6.20.

13. Explain how model risk poses a threat to users of option pricing models.

14. How is settlement risk related to credit risk?

15. How do governments create risk in the rules and laws they enact?

16. Why are derivatives transactions subject to accounting risk?

17. How do taxes represent a source of risk?

18. Describe the two forms of legal risk.

19. What are black swans in the context of financial markets?

Part V

Accounting, Disclosure, and Governance in Risk Management

Chapter 13

Accounting and Disclosure in Financial Risk Management

Seldom, very seldom does complete truth belong to any human disclosure;
seldom can it happen that something is not a little disguised, or a little
mistaken.

Jane Austen
Emma, Chapter 49
(1815)

Part V of this book takes a different turn. Through Part IV, we have been studying types of risks and how they are managed. In Part V, we begin to look at how companies engage in the supporting activities that are necessary for practicing good risk management. In this chapter, we look at how companies account for and disclose their risk management strategies and transactions. In Chapter 14, we examine how an entity organizes the risk management function through the process of risk management governance. These chapters are quite different from most of the preceding chapters in that they do not address specific risks, but look more at risk management from a top-down perspective.

13.1 Accounting for Financial Risk Management Activities

The financial risk management industry is a rapidly developing one. New products and strategies are constantly being created. Unfortunately, and no offense intended, the accounting profession lags behind. New products and strategies are often created almost in an instant, whereas accounting is a set of codified rules that require a great deal of time and debate to determine the best path to take. Even after policies are developed, there are often unforeseen ramifications that require revisions to existing rules or development of new ones. We alluded to this problem in Chapter 12 when we discussed accounting risk.

13.1.1 *U.S. Derivatives Accounting Standards*

In the United States, accounting standards are set by the Financial Accounting Standards Board, known as FASB, which was established in 1973 and replaced its predecessor, the Accounting Principles Board, a sub-entity within the American Institute of Certified Public Accountants.[1] FASB is a voluntary industry organization, but it is authorized by the U.S. Securities and Exchange Commission (SEC) to set accounting standards for publicly traded companies, which are regulated by the SEC. In the U.S., FASB is overseen by an organization called the Public Company Accounting Oversight Board (PCAOB), which is a private but government-authorized entity in which the board members are appointed by the SEC.[2]

As noted, FASB establishes accounting standards, which are pre-scriptions of how a business transaction should be recorded in financial statements. FASB is not a legislative body, so these standards do not have a formal legal status, but they do have near legal recognition. As noted, the SEC authorizes FASB to establish these rules, so the rules effectively apply to publicly-traded companies. Thus, a publicly-traded U.S. company would violate SEC regulations if it refused to conform to the standards set by the FASB. In addition, through the process of industry cooperation, auditing firms would refuse to give unqualified audits if a company did not comply with FASB standards.

A Quick Review of Accounting

The two primary financial statements are the balance sheet and the income statement. The balance sheet represents all of the assets of a company along with its debt and its owners' investment, called the owners' equity. The numbers that exist in balance sheets are called book values. Since all assets must be financed by either borrowing or the owners' investment, the total book value of the assets must equal the sum of the total book value of the liabilities and the total book value of the equity. The balance sheet is a snapshot of the financial position of the company.

---

[1] FASB is usually pronounced "Faz-Bee" and referred to as "FASB," not "the FASB."
[2] In the U.S., there is another entity called the Government Accounting Standards Board that establishes standards for accounting by government units.

The income statement is a summary of the changes in the financial position of the company over a period of time. It itemizes sources of income, known as revenue, and expenses. The net of income and expenses is the net profit. At the end of each period, the accounts that comprise the income statement are reduced to zero and the net profit is transferred into the owner's equity in the balance sheet. From there, the owner's equity may be reduced if the owners are paid dividends. In that case, cash is transferred out of the company's assets and the owner's equity is reduced. In receiving dividends, the owners have effectively taken some of their investment out of the firm and put it into their pockets.

The assets, liabilities, equity, revenues, and expense categories are subdivided into various accounts. Assets typically include cash, receivables, inventory, and physical assets that are often referred to as plant and equipment. Liabilities consist of such categories as short-term debt to include accounts payable and notes payable, and also long-term debt. Equity comprises common stock, preferred stock, and retained earnings, the latter being the excess of all accumulated earnings minus dividends paid since inception. The revenue accounts are divided into various sources of income such as sales and interest earned. Expenses include such categories as purchases of materials, known as cost of goods sold, interest expense, selling/general/administrative expenses, wages and salaries, and depreciation. Each of these categories is usually further sub-divided.

The process of accounting for a transaction involves making two entries into these various accounts. In fact, accounting has sometimes been referred to as "double-entry accounting," which is said to have been invented in the 15th century. Each entry consists of one debit and a matching credit. Debits are sometimes referred to as charges, though credits are always referred to as credits. Increases (decreases) in assets are debits (credits). Increases (decreases) in liabilities and equity are credits (debits). Increments to revenues are credits, while increments to expenses are debits. So, when companies sell their products or services, they record either cash received or an increase in a receivable, which represents cash to be received, and they credit sales. When they pay expenses, they increase the expense category (debit) and either reduce cash (credit) or increase a current liability (credit). If all entries are properly recorded, the total debits equal the total credits, the total assets will equal the sum of the assets and liabilities, and the assets will grow by the net profit, less dividends paid.

Well, *if only* accounting were *that* simple. Unfortunately, so many business transactions are far more complex, particularly when they involve derivatives. But even if that be the case, accounting rules for handling these complex transactions still rely on the principle that every recorded transaction consists of a debit and a credit.

These accounting standards are based on the concept of GAAP, which stands for *Generally Accepted Accounting Principles.* There is no formal definition of what constitutes GAAP, but one basic principle is that accounting is based on the concept of accrual, not cash. That is, if a business sells a product on credit, it records the sale and its profits increase, even though the money might not be collected for quite a period of time. Likewise, expenses incurred but not paid until later are recorded as expenses, even if the cash is not paid for some time. GAAP is also designed to measure profit, which is the historical accumulation of money taken in minus money paid out, taking into account the accrual effect.[3] Of course, accounting is far more complex than that, and we shall see some examples of that complexity in this chapter.

In the U.S., the specific standards were at one time referred to as Financial Accounting Standards or FAS followed by a number to identify a standard. Prior to the mid-1990s, derivatives accounting was in a state of considerable flux and confusion. This uncertainty arose, as mentioned earlier, because new products were created before FASB could determine the proper way to account for them. At one time, derivatives instruments that were in place but had not yet generated cash gains and losses were considered off-balance sheet items. Thus, the risks and uses of these powerful instruments were often hidden. Many firms were delighted with this state of confusion, because they could hide or bury deeply their derivatives activities.

Gradually over time, a number of standards were developed. By the last decade of the 20th century, there were five standards in place that covered at least one element of derivatives accounting. These were *FAS 52: Foreign Currency Translation* (issued December 1981), *FAS 80: Accounting for Futures Contracts* (issued August, 1984), *FAS 105: Disclosure of Information about Financial Instruments with Off-Balance Sheet Risk and Financial*

---

[3]In contrast, finance is based on cash flows and is forward-looking. The value of an asset is the discounted value of expected future cash flows, with the discounted rate reflecting the time value of money, expected inflation, and risk.

Instruments Concentrations of Credit Risk (issued March 1990), *FAS 107: Disclosures about Fair Value of Financial Instruments* (issued December 1991), and *FAS 119: Disclosure about Derivative Financial Instruments and Fair Value of Financial Instruments* (issued October, 1994). These statements began to progressively move accounting into the direction of requiring full disclosure of derivatives activity in the balance sheet and income statement. Nonetheless, there was still considerable confusion, as well as a rapidly expanding world of new types of derivatives. The state of accounting standards to that point was that a standard was created for each type of instrument or strategy. There was no single comprehensive general policy that would guide how to account for derivatives and risk management transactions. In other words, derivatives accounting needed a new and comprehensive set of standards that would have some staying power through its ability to explain how to account for types of transactions that had not yet been created.

FASB at least partially solved that problem with the 1998 release of its comprehensive derivatives accounting standard *FAS 133, Accounting for Derivative Instruments and Hedging Activities.* FAS 133 was amended in June, 1999 with *FAS 137: Accounting for Derivative Instruments and Hedging Activities — Deferral of the Effective Date of FASB Statement No. 133.* FAS 133 was supposed to go into effect in June, 1999, but a number of requests from members resulted in this deferral until June, 2000. And in June 2000, FASB released *FAS 138: Accounting for Certain Derivative Instruments and Certain Hedging Activities*, which provided some small adjustments and clarity to FAS 133.

Further rulings were issued in *FAS 115: Accounting for Certain Investments in Debt and Equity Securities* (issued, May 1993), which provided some edification on the distinction between bonds and stocks that are intended to be traded versus those that are intended to be held more or less permanently or until maturity. As these types of instruments are often hedged, this ruling was important. Other relevant standards were *FAS 157: Fair Value Measurement* (issued September 2006), which provided clarification on how fair value is defined and measured, and *FAS 159: The Fair Value Option for Financial Assets and Liabilities* (issued February 2007), which allows companies to measure more types of financial assets and liabilities at fair value than under previous standards.

FAS 133 was also amended in 2008 with *FAS 161, Disclosures About Derivative Instruments and Hedging Activities* (issued March 2008), which enhanced disclosure requirements, and *FAS 133-1, Disclosures about Credit Derivatives and Certain Guarantees* (issued September 2008), which brought credit derivatives under the umbrella of FAS 133.

In September 2009, FASB converted their current standards into a system called the Accounting Standards Codification or ASC. The ASC system is an attempt to re-organize the standards into a more coherent and user-friendly framework. At this time, the rules for accounting and disclosure of derivatives are in ASC 815. The rules are essentially the same as the old FAS system, but of course, they are subject to amendment at later dates.

13.1.2 *International Derivatives Accounting Standards*

Outside of the U.S., accounting standards are set by the International Accounting Standards Board (IASB), which is a voluntary consortium of 14 accounting experts headquartered in London. Its objective is to establish standards across countries. Though the U.S. is represented on the IASB, the U.S. standards are similar but not identical to those of the IASB.

International accounting standards for derivatives were first formally created with IAS (International Accounting Standard) 39, issued in 1998 and effective in 2001. It has been revised numerous times and essentially replaced with a new system called the International Financial Reporting Standard (IFRS) 9 in 2009, effective in 2010. These international accounting standards are very similar to the FASB's but with a slightly greater emphasis on measuring assets and liabilities at their fair values versus the historical cost emphasis of U.S. standards. There are also slight differences in the transactions that qualify for classification as hedges with IFRS being slightly more flexible. The additional flexibility of the international standard is, however, gained at a cost of providing somewhat less specific guidance. FASB standards are said to be more rules-based, while IASB standards are described as more principles-based. The rest of this chapter will primarily focus on U.S. standards.

13.1.3 *Hedge Accounting*

Hedge accounting is the process in which a hedge transaction is recorded in the financial statements of the hedging entity. Prior to the existence of formal guidance from accounting standards, hedging was a difficult type of transaction to record. There are two primary types of hedge transactions. One is to hedge an asset or liability that you hold or owe, respectively.

The other is to hedge an anticipated transaction.[4] Later we will refer to these transactions as fair value and cash flow hedges, respectively. The alternative to hedging is speculation. There has always been general agreement that speculation accounting is fairly straightforward. A speculative trader is a party that engages in financial trades to make a profit. Fundamentally, there is no difference in that type of work and, say, a company that manufacturers a product or provides a service for a profit. So, accounting for speculative trades results in profits and losses flowing through to earnings. Hedge accounting is different. Moreover, there is often a thin line between hedging and speculation, either realistically or through someone's biased interpretation. Prior to the formalization of accounting standards, the accounting for these types of transactions was subject to considerable abuse.

For example, suppose a company holds an asset and hedges it with a derivative, such as short a forward, short a futures contract, short a swap, short a call, or long a put. If the derivative gains in value while the asset loses value, the company augments its income by reporting the derivative gain, while leaving the asset at its book value. Losses on derivatives could be kept off the books until the derivative is settled when the company would have to report gains and losses on derivatives, as these affect its cash flow. But in the interim, it could make itself look better and push interim losses off the balance sheet. As noted, cash flow hedges are hedges of transactions that have not taken place. As such, a derivative hedge that produces a gain on a derivative would produce a loss on the transaction that has not taken place. The company could record the derivatives gain and choose not to engage in the transaction it was designed to hedge. Hence, there was plenty of room for companies to conform to accounting principles, while cosmetically improving their appearance, though in a misleading way.

13.1.4 *Fair Value Accounting*

These problems are a result of the fact that accounting theory generally relies on the principle that assets and liabilities are measured at their historical values. While the values of these assets and liabilities change on a daily basis, many of them are not very marketable, so it can be difficult to determine their values. Yet, derivatives change in value on an instantaneous basis and

---

[4]A third type of hedge transaction is an investment in a foreign subsidiary. We will cover this type of transaction later.

it is usually feasible to determine their values.[5] As such, accounting for derivatives is fair-value based, while accounting for assets is historical-value based. These approaches to accounting then collide.

The principle of historical cost is an important foundation of accounting. A traditional business purchases physical assets such as plant and equipment and depreciates them over a specified period of time according to a prescribed formula. While asset values never truly erode at these specified rates, the general idea behind this process is uniformity. Two businesses holding the same asset will depreciate the assets at the same rate, so there is uniform treatment. Nonetheless, there is room for considerable controversy. For one, the assets may not lose value at the same rate. One company may use the asset more than the other. Moreover, the asset may have a market value. Someone might pay the company money for the asset. And, what if the asset needed to be replaced? It might cost a lot more to replace it than its current depreciated value.

Replacement value and market value are forward-looking concepts that contrast with historical cost, which is obviously backward looking. With financial assets and liabilities, the notion of historical cost is somewhat problematic, though in some cases, historical costs are used. For example, consider a loan carried by a bank with a fixed rate of 5%. Now assume that a year later, the rate on comparable loans is 6%. The loan is clearly worth less, but conventional bank accounting does not mark down the value of the loan, except in the case where the loan is classified as a trading asset, meaning one that will be sold to another party. Likewise, loans are not marked up when interest rates fall. But derivatives and most tradeable securities are another matter. An option purchased at a price ¥700 will hardly retain that value for very long. Hence, the accounting profession has moved toward mark-to-market accounting for tradeable assets, while retaining historical cost with depreciation accounting for non-tradeable assets.

Determining the mark-to-market value can be a complex process for some assets. Of course, there are liquid markets for equities of well-known companies. Bonds can be problematic. There is certainly a market for bonds of well-known companies and governments, but every bond is not necessarily very liquid. Exchange-traded derivatives obviously trade in markets, but as noted in the previous chapter, the liquidity for some derivatives can be low. Where there is low liquidity, it can be a difficult process to obtain a fair value.

---

[5] And at this point in the book, you have learned how to do so for many derivatives.

Over-the-counter derivatives can also be problematic. They can be fairly standardized products for which it is easy to obtain quotes of their prices and values. Or maybe not. There are, however, companies and services that provide estimates of fair value utilizing pricing models based on whatever liquidity there is in a market, though these estimates often come down to educated guesswork.

So, in general derivatives are supposed to appear on balance sheets and income statements at fair value. But recording them as such is problematic, particularly when the instrument being hedged is an anticipated transaction.

13.1.5 *ASC 815*

Accounting Standard Codification 815, néo FAS 133, establishes seven basic principles for derivatives accounting:

1) A derivative is defined as *a contract with one or more underlyings and one or more notional amounts. Its value changes as the value of the underlying changes. Its initial value is either zero or an amount smaller than that required by other transactions to obtain the same payoff. At expiration it settles either by delivery or an equivalent cash amount.*
2) Derivatives are either assets or liabilities and should be recorded as such. They are not off-balance sheet items.
3) Fair value is the appropriate measure of a derivative.
4) There are four types of derivatives transactions:

   a. Fair value hedge
   b. Cash flow hedge
   c. Hedge of net investment in foreign operations
   d. Speculation

5) Hedge accounting is appropriate only for transactions that are clearly designated as hedges.
6) Hedge transactions can be effective, partially effective, or ineffective and must be measured as such; ineffective portions of hedges are considered speculative.
7) Derivatives that are embedded into other instruments must be separated from the instrument and accounted for as derivatives.

The second statement of the seven listed above is not technically completely true, but it is true in spirit. Earlier in this book, we noted that forwards, futures, and swaps have zero value at the start. They are neither assets nor liabilities when initiated. So it is technically not the case that all derivatives are assets or liabilities. But we did show that the values of forwards, futures, and swaps change as soon as time elapses or the price of the underlying changes. Thus, as the value of a forward, futures, or swap moves from zero to positive or zero to negative, the instrument turns very quickly into an asset or liability, respectively. We will cover most of these points in more detail as we move through examples.

ASC 815 also provides an excellent definition of a derivative. It is useful and relatively specific, even more so than the one we established in Chapter 4:

> *A derivative is a contract between two parties that provides for a payoff at a future date that will be determined by the value of an underlying asset, rate, other derivative, or risk factor.*

Let us now look at the four kinds of hedges as covered in ASC 815.

13.1.5.1 *Fair Value Hedges*

A fair value hedge is a hedge of an asset that the entity holds or a liability representing an obligation of the company. The distinguishing feature between a fair value hedge and a cash flow hedge, covered in the next section, is that the hedged instrument currently exists on the entity's balance sheet.

To qualify for fair value hedge accounting, the following requirements must be met:

1) The gain or loss on the derivative as well as that of the asset or liability being hedged must be recorded in the current period's earnings.
2) The hedge must be supported with formal documentation that indicates that the transaction is designed as a hedge and covers why the hedge is being done.
3) The entity must have a formal risk management strategy or policy.
4) The underlying asset or liability and the derivative must be clearly identified.
5) There must be a means of assessing the effectiveness of the hedge, and the effectiveness must be assessed on a regular basis.

Point 1) is simply consistent with the objective that derivatives strategies have an effect on earnings and should be recognized accordingly. Points 2) and 3) impose some administrative requirements in the sense that companies must have a formal strategy or policy in place and must have given the transaction some thought before engaging in it. When they do engage in the strategy, they must keep explicit records of why they did the strategy. Statement 4) is in place so that companies may not use hedge accounting for speculative strategies. They must clearly have an asset or liability at risk and a specific derivative designed to hedge that risk. Statement 5) forces companies to pay attention to how effective the hedge is and monitor it.

There is no prescribed method of determining hedging effectiveness, but there is an unwritten rule that states that the hedging gain or loss must be within a range of 80% to 125% of the gain or loss on the underlying. This rule has become reasonably well-accepted.

The recording of accounting entries is on a real-time basis, but balance sheets and income statements are not typically seen by the public except on a quarterly basis. We will make these assumptions throughout. Exhibit 13-1 is an example in which fair value hedging is used.

This was not a perfect hedge. Had it been one, income would not have changed at all. As we can see, over the first three months, the derivative loss was initially $220,000 and the gain in the value of the securities was $210,000, resulting in a net loss of $10,000 recorded to income. Over the month after the end of the quarter, the securities lost $3,000 and the derivative gained $4,000, a difference of $1,000, which is recorded to income. The total amount by which income is lower is $9,000. In addition, we should note that the securities are still held by the firm, but the derivative no longer exists.

We can gauge hedging effectiveness by looking at the change in the value of the securities. They gained in value by $207,000. The derivative went from a value of $0 to −$216,000, a loss of $216,000. The ratio of $216,000 to $207,000 is 104.3%, which is well within the 80% to 125% range of acceptability for an effective hedge. Had the derivatives gain or loss been outside that range, the use of hedge accounting would have been prohibited, meaning that the company would be unable to justify marking the assets to market. When so-called hedges are not able to use hedge accounting, the assets cannot be marked up or down. When you combine the gains and losses from the derivatives positions to no offsetting gains and losses from the securities, there will be substantially volatility to earnings. Thus, entities must make sure that hedges are effective.[6]

---

[6]The standards are, however, somewhat flexible. In particular, options cannot completely adhere to the 80–125 rule because their values are truncated on one side. The standards do allow for options in hedge accounting. In addition, there is some room for allowance of hedges to be partially effective. The standards, and indeed the issues, are complex and, thus, expert knowledge by accounting personnel is needed.

Scenario: Determine the accounting entries for the following situation. Suppose that at the beginning of the year, an asset management company holds a $10 million portfolio of broadly diversified large-cap stocks, resembling but not identical to the S&P 500. It hedges the portfolio by selling a four-month forward contract on the S&P 500. Three months later at the end of the quarter, the portfolio has generated a gain (on paper) of $210,000 and the derivative has generated a loss of $220,000. When the contract expires one month later, the value of the derivative has increased to −$216,000, and the portfolio has fallen in value by $3,000 since the end of the quarter. Determine the accounting entries at the beginning of the transaction, at the end of the quarter, and when the derivative expires.

Results:

No entries occur when the transaction is initiated. Had we imposed a margin requirement such that the firm had to put up some collateral, say cash or securities, the cash or securities account would be reduced by a credit and another asset account representing margin funds on deposit would be increased by a debit. We will assume away any margin requirements. Here are the entries.

End of Quarter	Debit	Credit
Income (unrealized gains/losses)	$220,000	
Derivatives (assets)		$220,000
	Records the loss generated by the derivative in income and places the derivative on the liability side of the balance sheet	
Equity Securities (assets)	$210,000	
Income (unrealized gains/losses)		$210,000
	Marks up the equity securities held as assets recognizes the gain in the value of the equity securities in income	
Net effect at end of quarter	The derivative will appear on the balance sheet as a liability of $220,000, the value of the securities will reflect an increase from $10 million to $10,210,000, and income will be lower by $10,000	

Exhibit 13-1. Accounting for a Fair Value Hedge of a Portfolio of Assets

At Expiration of Derivative	Debit	Credit
Derivatives (assets)	$4,000	
Income (unrealized gains/losses)		$4,000
	Marks up the value of the derivative by the $4,000 gain in its value since the quarter end and recognizes the $4,000 as income.	
Income (unrealized gains/losses)	$3,000	
Equity securities (assets)		$3,000
	Marks down the value of the securities by their loss of $3,000 and recognizes the loss against income.	
Derivatives (assets)	$216,000	
Cash (assets)		$216,000
	The company must pay $216,000 in cash to settle the derivative at expiration. Cash is reduced by $216,000, and the derivative is removed from the financial statements.	
Net effect at expiration	This derivative will show a value of zero on the balance sheet, income will have decreased by $9,000, cash will have decreased by $216,000, and the equity securities held as assets will have increased by $207,000.	

Exhibit 13-1. (*Continued*)

In some respects, fair value accounting for hedges is simple. An asset or liability that is current on the balance sheet is hedged. Both the asset or liability and the derivative are marked to their fair values at the end of each reporting period and when the derivative expires. What could be more difficult? Cash flow hedge accounting certainly is.

13.1.5.2 *Cash Flow Hedges*

Recall that a cash flow hedge is a hedge of an anticipated transaction in an asset or liability. Because the transaction is expected to occur in the future, there are no assets or liabilities currently on the financial statements with which to make an offsetting transaction. Hence, there is a problem right away. How can gains and losses from derivatives transactions be recorded, while the offsetting loss or gain is only an expected loss or gain in the future? The problem was solved by recording the offsetting gain or loss into a temporary equity account that does not affect earnings.

The temporary equity is called Other Comprehensive Income (OCI), which is an income statement account. FASB requires that all income be reported. OCI is added to regular income to produce a comprehensive figure, but OCI does not affect net income or earnings per share. At the end of the reporting period, OCI is reduced to zero and rolled into a balance sheet account called Accumulated Other Comprehensive Income (AOCI).

To qualify for a cash flow hedge, the following requirements must be met:

1) The transaction being hedged must be likely to occur
2) The uncertainty of the date of the transaction being hedged must be low
3) The transaction being hedged must be expected to occur within a short period of time
4) The risk must affect the entity's earnings
5) The transaction can be a single transaction or a combination of transactions, but if it is the latter, all of the transactions must have the same risk
6) The transaction must be hedged with a third party.

It is clear from the first three requirements that the transaction being hedged has to be definitive. Prior to FAS 133 (now ASC 815), an entity could designate that it *might* do a future transaction. It could then put on a hedge. If the derivative produced a profit, the entity could record the derivatives profit in its net income and then never do the transaction it was designed to hedge. If the derivative produced a loss, the company could do the future transaction and offset the derivative losses against the cost of the future transaction. The first outcome effectively gave it an opportunity to record a gain without a corresponding loss. The second would occasionally occur, but it would be just a hedge. So, the option existed for the entity to occasionally record gains without corresponding losses. But that is not possible today.

Let us now take a look at an example of cash flow hedging (Exhibit 13-2).

So here is the net effect. The company effectively paid $10 million for the gold, a resulting of paying $9.85 million to buy the gold directly from the seller and generating a $150,000 loss on the derivative. So its gold asset account is increased by $10 million and its cash account is lowered by $10 million. The AOCI balance sheet equity account held a temporary loss of $60,000 at the end of the quarter and an additional $90,000 the next

Scenario: A jewelry manufacturer is planning to buy a substantial amount of gold in four months. It is concerned about an increase in the price of gold, so it decides to hedge the transaction. The forward price of a four-month contract for the quantity of gold it plans to buy is $10 million. It goes long the forward contract. At the end of the quarter, the company is required to release its financial statements. At that time, the price of gold has fallen and the forward contract is valued at −$60,000. One month later when the contract expires, the spot price of gold is $9.85 million. Determine the accounting entries when the contract is initiated, at the end of the quarter, and when the contract expires.

Results:

There are no entries at the start of the transaction. If we had incorporated margin deposits, they would be recorded as explained in Exhibit 13-1.

End of Quarter	Debit	Credit
Other Comprehensive Income (income)	$60,000	
Derivatives (liabilities)		$60,000
Records the loss on the derivative into the OCI account, which is used for reporting purposes but does not affect earnings, and places the derivative on the balance sheet as a liability.		
Accumulated Other Comprehensive Income (equity)	$60,000	
Other Comprehensive Income (income)		$60,000
Closes out OCI and moves the balance into AOCI where it will appear on the balance sheet for the quarter end.		

By the expiration date, the derivative has lost a further $90,000 in value. It is then $150,000 in the red. The company will pay $150,000 to terminate the contract. It also pays $9.85 million to acquire the gold. So, the appropriate entries are as follows:

Exhibit 13-2. Accounting for a Cash Flow Hedge of a Future Purchase of an Asset

At Expiration of Derivative	Debit	Credit
Other Comprehensive Income (income)	$90,000	
Derivatives (liabilities)		$90,000
	Records the additional loss into AOCI and marks up the derivatives liability another $90,000 to its current value of $150,000.	
Accumulated Other Comprehensive Income (equity)	$90,000	
Other Comprehensive Income (income)		$90,000
	Closes out OCI and moves the balance into AOCI	
Gold (assets)	$9,850,000	
Cash		$9,850,000
	Records the payment of $9.85 million in cash for the acquisition of gold and records the gold as an asset.	
Derivatives (liabilities)	$150,000	
Cash		$150,000
	Records the payment of $150,000 in cash to terminate the derivatives contract and removes the derivative from liabilities	
Gold (assets)	$150,000	
Accumulated Other Comprehensive Income (equity)		$150,000
	Marks up the gold to the effective price paid of $10 million and closes out AOCI.	

Exhibit 13-2. *(Continued)*

month, but the total of $150,000 is eliminated when the transaction was settled.

The Consequences of Accounting Errors: A Slippery Slope?

Energy XXI, a young oil and gas exploration company in Houston, learned the hard way what accounting oversights can lead to. The company traditionally engaged in a number of cash flow hedges that were accounted for in the manner prescribed by ASC 815. The derivatives gains and losses were marked-to-market so that the derivatives would then appear on the balance sheet as assets or liabilities at the end of the reporting period. The corresponding losses and gains would be carried in the Accumulated

Other Comprehensive Income (AOCI) account. When the hedge was terminated and the derivative settled, the overall gain or loss would be transferred from AOCI to the asset or liability being hedged. Sounds correct, right?

Well, not completely. ASC 815 imposes some strong requirements on whether cash flow hedging can even be used. For one, each hedge must be well-documented, showing a specific need for the hedge at a specific time, as the transaction that will almost surely be done at a particular future date. The rule essentially requires that companies show evidence that they know what they are doing, that they have a specific plan, that they carry out that plan, and that they evaluate what happened after the fact.

When Energy XXI was preparing its 10-K for filing on its fiscal-year end on June 30, 2015, someone noticed that it had not backed up some of its hedges with the proper documentation. It is not known how the oversight was detected, and it may well have come from an auditor. But in any case, on September 8, 2015, it issued a press release announcing that it would be restating its earnings for fiscal years 2011–2014 and various quarterly earnings statements. It also announced that its 2015 10-K would be filed late.

Oddly enough, its 2013 earnings per share, originally stated as $1.90, was restated to $2.14, a modest improvement. Its 2015 earnings per share had originally been stated as $0.64. It was restated to $0.09, a reduction of about 86%. Its 2015 earnings per share were not re-stated, but simply delayed. When they were released, it was a bombshell: a negative $25.97! Indeed, Energy XXI had fallen on hard times during the sharp fall in oil and gas prices. On April 14, 2016, it filed for Chapter 11 bankruptcy protection.

Is there a connection between its mishandled accounting for derivatives hedges and its having to file for bankruptcy? It is not likely a direct connection. The sharp fall in energy prices put a financial vise on many energy-related companies. Evidence of poor accounting, however, can also be evidence of poor managerial oversight. Poor managerial oversight can certainly lead to bankruptcy. The documentation requirements of ASC 815 had been in place since 1999, six years before the company was created. Surely, its accountants and executives were aware of the need to comply with this rule.

So, the restatement is not likely to have led to the bankruptcy, but it is symptomatic of a plethora of internal problems and mismanagement that can certainly lead to corporate failure.

You should be able to see that the purpose of the AOCI account is to temporarily separate gains and losses on the derivative from the company's net income. Thus, while the hedge is in place, the earnings per share figure will not fluctuate due to derivatives gains and losses with no matching transaction on the asset or liability due to that transaction not having yet taken place. The OCI account temporarily holds this amount, and its entries result in changes to the AOCI account. The balance in the AOCI account is indicative of cash flow hedges that have not been completed.[7]

13.1.5.3   *Foreign Currency Hedges*

There are three types of hedges involving foreign currency risk. Two of them are the ones we have already covered. Fair value hedges involving foreign currency would occur, for example, when an entity holds a foreign currency-denominated asset, such as a stock or a bond. In that case, fair value hedges would generally be permissible. The second situation involves the anticipation of engaging in a position in a foreign currency-denominated asset or liability. In that case, a cash flow hedge would be permissible. The third situation involves a hedge of a net investment in a foreign currency subsidiary. For example, a company may own a subsidiary that operates in a foreign country with revenues and expenses in the foreign currency. When it consolidates that subsidiary's assets and liabilities into its own balance sheet, there can be significant effects from the currency translation. Thus, some companies may put on a hedge of its investment in a foreign subsidiary. In this case, the company is permitted to use cash market instruments, such as foreign currency denominated securities and bank accounts, to hedge.[8] Because a company has an investment in foreign currency-denominated assets and may be responsible for some corresponding foreign currency-denominated liabilities, it is effectively hedging its equity position. A stronger domestic currency will reduce the value of that foreign equity investment. Thus, it might go long a foreign currency asset or short a foreign currency liability on its domestic balance sheet. Given whatever change occurs in the exchange rate, it is allowed to mark up or down the asset or liability with a corresponding mark-down or mark-up to its foreign subsidiary investment.

---

[7]OCI and AOCI can reflect some non-derivatives activities as well, such as the company's pension fund and any investments in securities that it makes.

[8]Hedges involving strictly domestic assets and liabilities are not permitted to do hedge accounting using cash assets, only derivatives.

13.1.5.4 *Speculation*

The income from speculative transactions is always considered part of the entity's current income and must be recorded as such. Thus, a speculative entity is required to record income from all derivatives transactions, and there is no special accounting for such. Of course, a speculative entity may occasionally engage in a hedge, and hedge accounting is permissible in that case, provided it meets the requirements as covered above.

13.1.5.5 *A Note on Vanilla Interest Rate Swaps*

Earlier in this book, we covered how using interest rate swaps to convert floating-rate loans into fixed-rate loans is one of, if not, *the* most common transactions in derivatives. The borrower pays a floating rate of interest, but the swap enables it to receive floating payments and make fixed payments. The floating payments on the swap are tied to the same index as the floating payments on the loan. Hence, upward and downward movements in the interest rate index have offsetting effects, and the borrower effectively pays the fixed rate on the swap, plus any fixed spread over the floating rate on the loan.

Oddly enough, the accounting for interest rate swap hedges is somewhat unclear, and apparently as a result, it is more flexible. It is possible to account for this strategy as either a fair value hedge or a cash flow hedge. A fair value hedge would adjust the value of the liability in accordance with changes in the value of the swap such that there is a virtual offset. A cash flow hedge would recognize that future interest payments are being hedged by the swap so that changes in the values of these payments before they are made can be rolled into OCI and AOCI. There is also a procedure called the shortcut method that allows the entries in a transaction like an interest rate swap to be slightly simplified. Instead of recording interest on a loan and the net swap payments separately, the amounts can be pooled into a single entry. Thus, if a borrower were paying LIBOR + 200 bps and entered into a swap to pay 5.5% and receive LIBOR, the net payment would be 7.5% and could be recorded as such.

13.2 Disclosure of Financial Risk Management Practices, Policies, and Results

Accounting for risk management transactions is one thing. Disclosure is another. Just because a hedging strategy is properly recorded in the financial statements does not mean that an outsider can determine the extent to which the company is managing risk. Although most companies do have derivatives on their financial statements, these positions are snapshots taken at the financial reporting dates, which are quarterly and year-end. They do not show interim activity. It is theoretically possible that a company might have all of its derivatives completed and removed from its balance sheet on the reporting date. Outsiders would have no indication of how much hedging, or speculation, the company did.

13.2.1 *SEC Requirements*

Concerns over disclosure of derivatives activity were the subject of much debate in the 1990s. FAS 133 did not go into effect until 1999, however, and did not directly address disclosure. In 1997 the SEC took the lead on requiring publicly traded companies to disclose their derivatives positions with the issuance of a document called *Release 33-7386: Disclosure of Accounting Policies for Derivative Financial Instruments and Derivative Commodity Instruments and Disclosure of Quantitative and Qualitative Information about Market Risk Inherent in Derivative Financial Instruments, other Financial Instruments, and Derivative Commodity Instruments.* Specially, the entity was required to disclose its market risk exposures at the end of the reporting period, how it manages those exposures with respect to specific strategies and instruments, and changes in its market risk exposures or how they are managed compared to the most recent reporting period and what the entity expects for future periods. These disclosures are required in annual reports and not quarterly reports. Of course, SEC rules apply only to publicly traded companies.

The rule stipulates that disclosure of market risks must be done at least one of three ways: a tabular presentation, sensitivity analysis, and Value-at-Risk. The tabular presentation requires that the disclosures reveal fair market values and contract terms to include maturity dates. Perhaps not surprisingly, most companies do not choose this approach, as it requires the revelation of a considerable amount of information. The volume of derivatives engaged in by some companies is staggering, and having to show details on each position in place is quite onerous. Sensitivity analysis requires the company to show the effect on earnings, fair value, or cash flow from changes in interest rates, exchange rates, commodity prices, or any other relevant variables over a specific time period. Companies are, therefore, required to make assumptions about hypothetical changes in these variables. The release recommends changes of at least 10%. *VaR* disclosure can be done based on earnings, fair value, or cash flow as driven by changes in interest rates, exchange rates, commodity prices or any other relevant variables. The release recommends using a 95% confidence level, so the tail cutoff would be at 5%. The rule requires disclosure of how the Monte Carlo simulation is done, but does permit any of the three methods we studied (analytical, historical simulation, Monte Carlo) to be used. The rule also requires that a qualitative discussion be provided.

When it was first proposed, Release 33-7386 was controversial. It required the revelation of information that many would consider proprietary. Making public how a company manages risk could be considered giving its competitors information they could use. Of course, the competitors would also be required to do the same, provided they are publicly traded companies. In addition, the rule seemed to single out derivatives risk. It does not require an airline to estimate the probability and expected loss of a plane crash, or a consumer products company to estimate the probability and expected loss from injuries sustained while using the company's products. These types of risks, which we identified as operational risks not to mention the black swan risks that no one really knows about, are potentially much greater than the financial risks of derivatives. But regardless of opposition to the rule, it became effective in mid-1997.

13.2.2 *FASB Requirements*

In 2008, the FASB amended FAS 133 with FAS 161, which specified more precise requirements for the improvement of disclosure of derivatives activities. Specifically, FAS 161 requires that an entity reveal how and why it uses derivatives, how derivatives and related hedge items are accounted for, and how these items affect its financial position, financial performance, and cash flows. The statement requires qualitative disclosures about the objectives and strategies involved in using derivatives, quantitative disclosures of the fair value and gains and losses on derivatives, and factors related to credit risk in derivatives.

13.2.3 *Case Studies in Accounting and Disclosure*

To best understand these requirements, we shall study how they are used in three companies: Delta Airlines, General Mills, and a leading derivatives dealer and commercial and investment bank, JPMorgan Chase. These cases will also enable us to see how companies account for derivatives. Specifically, we will examine their 2015 10-K reports for how they report and describe their risk management and derivatives activities.[9]

13.2.3.1 *Delta Airlines*

Delta Airlines, headquartered in Atlanta, is the second largest airline in the world in terms of sales in 2017, ranking just behind American Airlines. As of December 31, 2017, its market cap was almost $40 billion, and it had about 87,000 employees. Its book value of assets is about $53 billion and in 2017 it reported revenue of almost $41 billion and a profit of $5.7 billion. Delta flies to over 325 destinations in 60 countries and has operations in all six inhabited continents. It has extensive exposures to commodity risk, particularly the price of jet fuel, and some exposure to interest rate and currency risk. Let us take a look at the language Delta uses to explain how it practices risk management, accounts for the transactions, and discloses what it does.

On p. 4 of its 2017 10-K, Delta states that

> *We purchase most of our aircraft fuel under contracts that establish the price based on various market indices and therefore do not provide material protection against price increases or assume the availability of our fuel supplies.*

Here Delta is acknowledging that the price it pays for fuel is essentially a spot price. It is acknowledging that it has considerable fuel price risk and faces the possibility of supply interruptions. It goes on to say (p. 5) that

> *We have recently managed our fuel price risk through a hedging program intended to reduce the financial impact from changes in the price of fuel as fuel prices are subject to potential volatility. We may utilize different contract and commodity types in this program and frequently test their economic effectiveness against our financial targets. We closely monitor the hedge portfolio and rebalance the portfolio based on market conditions, which may result in locking in gains or losses on hedge contracts prior to their settlement dates. In addition we enter into derivatives with third parties to hedge financial risk related to Monroe's refining margin.*

Here Delta reveals that it has an active hedging program that uses different types of instruments and underlyings and that it tests the instruments for effectiveness, occasionally making adjustments and sometimes terminating

---

[9]The 10-K is the formal annual report required by the SEC. It differs from the Annual Report released to shareholders and the public, though many companies do use their 10-Ks as their annual reports to shareholders.

positions prior to expiration. The reference to Monroe is to the refinery that
Delta operates.

On p. 12, In Item 1A: Risk Factor, Delta acknowledges a number of risks
in its business. The second risk mentioned is fuel price risk, mentioned is as
follows:

> *Fuel hedging activities are intended to manage the financial impact of the
> volatility in the price of jet fuel. The effects of rebalancing our hedge
> portfolio and mark-to-market adjustments may have a negative effect on
> our financial results.*

In effect, it is admitting that in the course of managing its fuel price risk,
it could harm earnings. It goes on to elaborate about this statement by
repeating the statement on p. 4 concerning how it manages the risk. It then
states that

> *In addition, we record mark-to-market adjustments ("MTM adjustments")
> on our fuel hedges. MTM adjustments are based on market prices at the end
> of the reporting period for contracts settling in future periods. Losses from
> rebalancing or MTM adjustments (or both) may have a negative impact on
> our financial results.*

On p. 30, Delta reports that in 2017, its fuel cost averaged $1.68/gallon
and that hedges added another $0.06/gallon to that cost. In addition, Delta
owns a refinery that generated a loss that amounted to $0.03/gallon that is
included in the $1.68 cost. So its total average price of fuel per gallon was
$1.74. The U.S. Energy Industry Administration reports that the average
price of jet fuel in 2017 was $1.63. This difference largely reflects their
hedging loss. These hedges were likely put in place well before the spot
price fell, so in 2017 Delta was paying at a slightly higher price through its
hedges. Of course, that is how hedges work. They lock in prices and rates,
and the hedger will have regrets during some periods. On p. 36, Delta reports
that fuel expenses represented 19.2% of its total expenses.

It points out (p. 12) that

> *Our fuel hedging contracts may contain margin funding requirements, which
> require us to post margin to counterparties or cause counterparties to post
> margin to us as market prices in the underlying hedged items changed. If
> fuel prices decrease significantly from the levels existing at the time we enter
> into fuel hedge contracts, we may be required to post a significant amount
> of margin, which could have a material impact on the level of unrestricted
> cash and cash equivalents and short-term investments.*

Here Delta alerts investors to how margins work in derivatives.

On p. 38, Delta discusses the termination of some of its hedge positions:

> *Fuel Hedge Restructuring: During 2016, we entered into transactions to defer settlement of a portion of our hedge portfolio until 2017. These deferral transactions, excluding market movements form the date of inception, provided $300 million in cash receipts during the second quarter of 2016 and required approximately $300 million in cash payments in 2017.*

Here it extended the maturities of some of its hedges.

On p. 47, Item 7A: Quantitative and Qualitative Disclosures About Market Risk, Delta identifies its market risks as "fuel prices, interest rates, and foreign currency exchange rates." It goes on to report a sensitivity analysis of these risks and cautions that the analysis does not incorporate the possible effects of changes in the demand for air travel or macroeconomic factors or actions it might take. The effects it analyzes are simply changes in fuel prices, interest rates, and exchange rates. It indicates that a one cent increase in the cost of jet fuel would increase full expenses by $40 million, an increase of 100 basis points in interest rates would decrease the value of its fixed-rate debt by $160 million and increase annual interest expense on variable-rate debt by $32 million, and a 10% depreciation or appreciation in the yen and Canadian dollar would change the settlement values of its hedges by $34 million and $42 million respectively. Based on its interest rate and currency exposure and what it is doing about it, the sensitivity analysis for rather large changes in the underlying demonstrate fairly low risks for a company with a market cap of $40 billion.

Page 50 contains Delta's balance sheet, and p. 67 contains further information on its derivatives balances. It carries hedged derivatives assets of $1 billion out of total assets of $53.3 billion, and hedge derivatives liabilities of $13 billion out of total liabilities of $39.3 billion. It also reports AOCI of −$7.621 billion. On p. 52, its consolidated statement of comprehensive income shows OCI related to hedges in 2017 of −$15 million. Recall that OCI is the change in AOCI from year to year.

All annual reports contain a section called Notes to the Consolidated Financial Statements, which are essentially footnotes (though not literally in the footer) explaining parts of the financial statements. Some of these notes are repetitive, but some provide new information. On p. 57, Note 1: Summary of Significant Accounting Policies, Delta explains its accounting policies for hedges. First it states that "We recognize derivative contracts at fair value on our Consolidated Balance Sheets." It then says

> *Not Designated as Accounting Hedges. We do not designate our fuel derivative contracts as accounting hedges. We recorded changes in the fair value of our fuel hedges in aircraft fuel and related taxes. These changes in fair value include settled gains and losses as well as mark-to-market adjustments ("MTM adjustments"). MTM adjustments are defined as fair value changes recorded in periods other than the settlement period. Such fair value changes are not necessarily indicative of the actual settlement value of the underlying hedge in the contract settlement period.*

We see that Delta does not do hedge accounting in its fuel hedging program. It simply records profits and losses on its derivatives in its fuel and tax account, and most of these charges are likely to go into the expense account. Thus, the gains and losses on its derivatives are not synchronized with the future purchases it has not yet made but instead are aligned with the purchases of the past period. There is obviously a bit of a timing mismatch, but that is not likely to matter much when you are purchasing the underlying on a rather continuous basis. In addition, by accounting for its fuel cash flow hedges in this manner, it avoids the onerous requirement of having to document the details of every hedge.

Delta goes on to describe its cash flow and fair value hedging.

> *Designated as Cash Flow Hedges. For derivative contracts designated as cash flow hedges (interest rate contracts and foreign currency exchange contracts), the effective portion of the gain or loss on the derivative is reported as a component of AOCI and reclassified into earnings the same period in which the hedged transaction affects earnings. The effective portion of the derivative represents the change in fair value of the hedge that offsets the change in fair value of the hedged item. To the extent the change in the fair value of the hedge does not perfectly offset the change in the fair value of the hedged item, the ineffective portion of the hedge is immediately recognized in non-operating expense.*

So it uses cash flow hedges only for its interest rate and foreign exchange risk and does the accounting in the manner in which we described earlier in this chapter.

> *Designated as Fair Value Hedges. For derivative contracts designated as fair value hedges (interest rate contracts), the gain or loss on the derivative is reported in earnings and an equivalent amount is reflected as a change in*

the carrying value of long-term debt and capital leases, with an offsetting loss or gain recognized in current earnings. We include the gain or loss on the hedged item in the same account as the offsetting loss or gain on the related derivative contract, resulting in no impact to our Consolidated Statement of Operations.

Fair value hedges are used only for interest rate risk, and they are done in the manner described earlier in the chapter.

On p. 58, Delta discusses how it evaluates the effectiveness of its hedges and what it does when a hedge is not effective.

We perform, at least quarterly, an assessment of the effectiveness of our derivative contracts designated as hedges, including assessing the possibility of counterparty default. If we determine that a derivative is no longer expected to be highly effective, we discontinue hedge accounting prospectively and recognize subsequent changes in the fair value of the hedge in earnings. We believe our derivative contracts that continue to be designated as hedges, consisting of interest rate and foreign currency exchange contracts, will continue to be highly effective in offsetting changes in fair value or cash flow, respectively, attributable to the hedged risk.

So, Delta does an assessment at least quarterly and can revoke the classification of a hedge as highly effective, though it does not anticipate doing so at present.

On p. 63, Note 2: Fair Value Measurements, it explains how it measures fair value, which it defines as "an exit price, representing the amount that would be received to sell an asset or paid to transfer a liability in an orderly transaction between market participants. Fair value is a market-based measurement that is determined based on the assumptions that market participants would use in pricing an asset or liability." It defines three levels of fair value measurement: Level 1, which is when there are observable inputs such as quoted prices, Level 2, which is when quoted prices are not available but other inputs are, and Level 3, in which there is little in the way of inputs or data and, as a result, strong assumptions have to be made. On p. 64, it states specifically how it measures the fair value of its derivatives, which it considers as Level 1 measures.

Fuel Contracts: ...[our] option contracts are valued under an income approach using option pricing models based on data either readily observable in public markets, derived from public markets or provided by counterparties who regularly trade in public markets. Volatilities used in these valuations range from 10% to 28% depending on the maturity dates, underlying commodities and strike prices of the option contracts. Swap contracts are valued under an income approach using a discounted cash flow model based on data either readily observable or provided by counterparties who regularly trade in public markets. Discount rates used in these valuations vary with the maturity dates of the respective contracts and are based on the London interbank offered rate ("LIBOR"). Futures contracts and options on futures contracts are traded on a public exchange and valued based on market prices.

Foreign Currency Exchange Contracts: Our foreign currency derivatives consist of Japanese yen and Canadian dollar forward contracts and are valued based on data readily observable in public markets.

These explanations should sound familiar, as they are consistent with what you learned in Chapters 8, 9, and 10 on how to price and value forwards, futures, swaps, and options. Incidentally, on p. 64, it indicates that it uses options, swaps, and futures in its fuel price hedging.[10]

On p. 66, Note 4: Derivatives and Risk Management, Delta provides information that is largely a repeat of what it has previously stated at various places earlier in the report. On p. 67, it mentions that it has master netting arrangements with its OTC counterparties, and it reports that its net derivatives position is -$83 million at year-end 2017, which is the net of its derivatives assets and liabilities reported on its balance sheet. On p. 68, Delta discusses its management of its credit risk.

To manage credit risk associated with our fuel price, interest rate and foreign currency hedging programs, we evaluate counterparties based on several criteria including their credit ratings and limit our exposure to any one counterparty.

It goes on to mention that there are margin requirements on its contracts that might require that it post margin or that the counterparty post margin. Its margin balance at year-end 2017 was $43 million.

Thus, we see that Delta appears to be practicing sound risk management accounting and disclosure. Somewhat unusual is the fact that Delta does not do hedge accounting for its fuel hedging, as it apparently believes that the costs are too high and that it can simply apply derivatives gains and losses

---

[10]Thus, it appears that it uses exchange-listed crude oil futures and options on futures, and OTC options and swaps on crude oil, diesel, and jet fuel. It might seem obvious that Delta should use jet fuel as the underlier, but there are no exchange-traded contracts on jet fuel. Exchange-traded crude oil contracts are, however, highly liquid, so they are appealing to use as they provide confidence of the ability to enter and exit easily at low cost. Also, OTC jet fuel contracts are not even a perfect hedge, as the payoffs are based on jet fuel price indexes, which reflect averages and are highly but not perfectly correlated with the actual jet fuel Delta purchases.

presumably offset by future purchases to purchases reported in the current period. When you are purchasing on a regular basis, that is likely to be a reasonable strategy.

13.2.3.2 *General Mills*

We now take a look at General Mills, one of the largest consumer foods companies in the world. Its iconic brands include Betty Crocker, Yoplait, Pillsbury, Bisquick, Häagen-Dazs, Green Giant, as well as Cheerios and many other popular cereals. Its fiscal year ends May 31. For fiscal year 2017, it had annual sales of about \$15.6 billion and a profit of \$2 billion. Its book assets are almost \$22 billion, and its market cap was about \$33 billion at the end of the fiscal year.

On p. 4 of its 2015 10-K, it states that it has exposure to many commodities and that

> *We often manage the risk associated with adverse price movements for some inputs using a variety of risk management strategies.*

On p. 8, Item 1A: Risk Factors, it identifies the third one as the volatility of the prices of the commodities it uses. It states that

> *We do not fully hedge against changes in commodity prices, and the risk management procedures that we use may not always work as we intend.*

It does do some hedging, as we shall see, but it clearly wishes to disavow any belief that its hedges are perfect. On p. 8, it also discusses a related risk, the market value of the derivatives it uses:

> *Volatility in the market value of derivatives we use to manage exposures to fluctuations in commodity prices will cause volatility in gross margins and net earnings.*
>
> *We utilize derivatives to manage price risk for some of our principal ingredients and energy costs, including grains (oats, wheat, and corn), oils (principally soybean), dairy products, natural gas, and diesel fuel. Changes in the values of these derivatives are recorded in earnings currently, resulting in volatility in both gross margin and net earnings. These gains and losses are reported in cost of sales in our Consolidated Statements of Earnings and in unallocated corporate items in our segment operating results until we utilize the underlying input in our manufacturing process, at which time the gains and losses are reclassified to segment operating profit. We also record our grain inventories at fair value. We may experience volatile earnings as a result of these accounting treatments.*

These statements suggest that, like Delta, it too does not use cash flow hedging for its raw inputs.

On p. 31, we learn that General Mills has a mixture of fixed- and floating-rate debt, comprised of 67% fixed-rate and 33% floating-rate. On p. 32, it reports that derivatives marked to fair value was a net liability of $24 million. This is a small amount for a company with a market cap of $33 billion.

In Item 7A, p. 46: Quantitative and Qualitative Disclosures about Market Risk, General Mills states that

> *We are exposed to market risk stemming from changes in interest and foreign exchange rates and commodity and equity prices. Changes in these factors could cause fluctuations in our earnings and cash flows. In the normal course of business, we actively manage our exposures to these market risks by entering into various hedging transactions, authorized under established policies that place clear controls on these activities. The counterparties in these transactions are generally highly rated institutions. We establish credit limits for each counterparty. Our hedging transactions include but are not limited to a variety of derivative financial instruments.*

Here the company announces that it has these sources of risks and that it manages the risks under established policies that have controls. Its counterparties are always of high credit quality, it uses a variety of derivative instruments, and that in may hedge in other ways.

On p. 46, the company discusses Value-at-Risk.

> *The estimates in the table below are intended to measure the maximum potential fair value we could lose in one day from adverse changes in market interest rates, foreign exchange rates, commodity prices, and equity prices under normal market conditions. A Monte Carlo value-at-risk (VAR) methodology was used to quantify the market risk for our exposure. The models assume normal market conditions and used a 95 percent confidence interval.*
>
> *The VAR calculation used historical interest and foreign exchange rates from the past year to estimate the potential volatility and correlation of these rates in the future. The market data were drawn from the RiskMetrics^{TM} data set. The calculations are not intended to represent actual losses in fair value that we expect to incur. Further, since the hedging instrument (the derivative) inversely correlates with the underlying exposure, we would expect that any loss or gain in the fair value of our derivatives would be generally offset by an increase or decrease in the fair value of the underlying exposure. The positions included in the calculations were: debt, interest rate swaps; foreign exchange forwards, commodity swaps, futures and options; and equity instruments. The calculations do not include the underlying*

foreign exchange and commodities or equity-related positions that are offset by these market-risk-sensitive instruments.

The table to which the first paragraphs refers shows that the *VaR* for interest rate instruments was $25.1 million for interest rate instruments, $24.6 million for foreign currency instruments, $3.2 for commodity instruments, and $1.3 million for equity instruments. These figures are fairly small amounts for a company of this size. Note that General Mills chooses to disclose this risk using *VaR*, one of the three allowable methods. It states that it uses Monte Carlo *VaR* with inputs estimated from historical data over the last year. It also notes that the assets that are being hedged with derivatives provide an offset but are not included in the *VaR* analysis.

In Note 2. Summary of Significant Accounting Policies on p. 56, the company describes its derivatives usage and accounting.

All derivatives are recognized on the Consolidated Balance Sheets at fair value based on quoted market prices or our estimate of their fair value, and are recorded in either current or noncurrent assets or liabilities based on their maturity. Changes in the fair values of derivatives are recorded in net earnings or other comprehensive income, based on whether the instrument is designated and effective as a hedge transaction and, if so, the type of hedge transaction. Gains or losses on derivative instruments reported in AOCI are reclassified to earnings in the period the hedged item affects earnings. If the underlying hedged transaction ceases to exist, any associated amounts reported in AOCI are reclassified to earnings at that time. Any ineffectiveness is recognized in earnings in the current period.

Of course, this description is consistent with common practice and allowable by FASB.

In Note 7: Financial Instruments, Risk Management Activities, and Fair Values, pp. 66, it describes its risk management activities.

As part of our ongoing operations, we are exposed to market risks such as changes in interest and foreign currency exchange rates and commodity and equity prices. To manage these risks, we may enter into various derivative transactions (e.g., futures, options, and swaps) pursuant to our established policies.

In describing its commodity price risk, p. 66, it says

Many commodities we use in production and distribution of our products are exposed to market price risks. We utilize derivatives to manage price risk for our principal ingredients and energy costs, including grains (oats, wheat, and corn), oils (principally soybean), dairy products, natural gas, and diesel fuel. Our primary objective when entering into these derivative contracts is to achieve certainty with regard to the future price of commodities purchased for use in our supply chain. We manage our exposures through a combination of purchase orders, long-term contracts with suppliers, exchange-traded futures and options, and over-the-counter options and swaps. We offset our exposures based on current and projected market conditions and generally seek to acquire the inputs at as close to our planned cost as possible.

We use derivatives to manage our exposure to changes in commodity prices. We do not perform the assessments required to achieve hedge accounting for commodity derivative positions. Accordingly, the changes in the values of these derivatives are recorded currently in cost of sales in our Consolidated Statement of Earnings.

Although we do not meet the criteria for cash flow hedge accounting, we nonetheless believe that these instruments are effective in achieving our objective of providing certainty in the future price of commodities purchased for use in our supply chain.

Here they describe the inputs they want to hedge and the instruments they use, noting their objective of eliminating the risk. The last sentence of the first paragraph, however, suggests that they may engage in a form of timing their hedges. Thus, they are speculating that they can take the hedges off and put them on at the right time, which is clearly speculating though they obviously believe it is hedging. The assertion is somewhat inconsistent with their intention of achieving certainty of the price, which can best be done by hedging in full all of the time. They go to say that they do not use cash flow hedge accounting and simply let the derivatives gains and losses flow directly into earnings. As with Delta, they buy these inputs on an ongoing basis and probably find the paperwork requirements and the inflexibility of hedge accounting too burdensome. In the third paragraph, they state, however, that they believe that the hedges are effective. At fiscal year-end 2017 (May 31), it reports that it has notional of $410 million of commodity derivatives, of which about 71% are agricultural commodity-related and the remainder energy-related.

On p. 67, it discusses interest rate risk.

We are exposed to interest rate volatility with regard to future issuances of fixed-rate debt, and existing and future issuances of floating-rate debt. Primary exposures include U.S. Treasury notes, LIBOR, Euribor, and commercial paper rates in the United States and Europe. We use interest rate swaps, forward-starting interest rate swaps, and treasury locks to hedge our exposure to interest rate changes, to reduce the volatility of our financing costs, and to achieve a desired proportion of fixed versus floating-rate debt, based on current market conditions. Generally under these swaps, we agree with a counterparty to exchange the difference between fixed-rate and floating-rate interest amounts based on an agreed upon notional principal amount.

So they describe where their interest rate risk comes from and what instruments are used. The accounting is explained in the next two paragraphs.

Floating Interest Rate Exposures — Floating-to-fixed interest rate swaps are accounted for as cash flow hedges, as are all hedges of forecasted issuances of debt. Effectiveness is assessed based on either the perfectly effective hypothetical derivative method or changes in the present value of interest payments on the underlying debt. Effective gains and losses deferred to AOCI are reclassified into earnings over the life of the associated debt. Ineffective gains and losses are recorded as net interest. The amount of hedge ineffectiveness was less than $1 million in each of fiscal 2017, 2016, and 2015.

    Fixed Interest Rate Exposures — Fixed-to-floating interest rate swaps are accounted for as fair value hedges with effectiveness assessed based on change in the fair value of the underlying debt and derivatives, using incremental borrowing rates currently available on loans with similar terms and maturities. Ineffective gains and losses on these derivatives and the underlying hedged items are recorded as net interest. The amount of hedge ineffectiveness was a $4.3 million gain in fiscal 2017 and a $1.6 million gain in fiscal 2015.

Thus, they use cash flow hedging for their swaps to convert floating to fixed. It appears that these swaps are initiated before the debt is issued. The second paragraph states that they convert some fixed-rate debt to floating-rate debt, and they use fair value hedges.

    On p. 67 there is a table that shows that the company has notional of pay-floating swaps of $1 billion at an average receive rate of 1.8% and an average pay rate of 1.6%. There is also a table showing the maturity dates of these swaps, which are 2018, and 2020.

    On p. 69, it discusses foreign exchange risk.

Foreign currency fluctuations affect our net investments in foreign subsidiaries and foreign currency cash flows related to third-party purchases, intercompany loans, product shipments, and foreign-denominated debt. We are also exposed to the translation of foreign currency earnings to the U.S. dollar. Our principal exposures are to the Australian dollar, Brazilian real, British pound sterling, Canadian dollar, Chinse renminbi, euro, Japanese yen, Mexican peso, and Swiss franc. We mainly use foreign-currency forward contracts to selectively hedge our foreign currency cash flow exposures. We also generally swap our foreign-denominated commercial paper borrowings and nonfunctional currency intercompany loans back to U.S. dollars or the functional currency of the entity with foreign exchange exposure; the gains or losses on these derivatives offset the foreign currency revaluation gains or losses recorded in earnings on the associated borrowings. We generally do not hedge more than 18 months in advance.

As of May 28, 2017, the net notional value of foreign exchange derivatives was $850.2 million. The amount of hedge ineffectiveness was less than $1 million in each of fiscal 2017, 2016, and 2015.

It discusses the risk of translating its foreign subsidiary earnings into the dollar, identifies the currencies to which it has the greatest exposure, and identifies the types of instruments it uses to hedge. It also notes that it issues foreign currency-denominated debt and swaps it back into the U.S. dollar or the currency of the subsidiary issuing the debt. Gains and losses on these derivatives flow directly into earnings, inasmuch as the hedges are more or less offset with effects that flow directly into earnings. It goes on to discuss its investments in foreign subsidiaries.

We also have many net investments in foreign subsidiaries that are denominated in euros. We previously hedged a portion of these net investments by issuing euro-denominated commercial paper and foreign exchange forward contracts. As of May 28, 2017, we hedged a portion of these net investments with €2,200 million of euro denominated bonds. As of May 28, 2017, we had deferred net foreign currency transaction losses of $39.1 million in AOCI associated with net investment hedging activity.

Note that it did some hedging by issuing foreign currency-denominated debt instead of derivatives.

On p. 70 it presents its fair value measurements. It classifies its hedge derivatives into Level 2, which is based on observable inputs, other than quoted prices, that go into pricing models. Its derivative hedge assets are valued at $17 million and its liabilities at $4 million. It also has derivatives not designated as hedges valued at $14.4 million for assets and $20.4 million for liabilities. These figures are interesting in that there are relatively large positions in non-hedge derivatives liabilities. One might wonder why these are non-hedging derivatives. Could General Mills be engaging in sheer speculation? This result may have arisen because of its decision to not to use cash flow hedge accounting in its commodity risk management program. There is no way to tell for sure, and this point is not addressed in the language used in the report.

On p. 72, the company shows the breakdown by instrument (interest rate contracts, foreign exchange contracts, equity contracts, and commodity contracts) of its cash flow hedge gains and losses that went into OCI and gains and losses in AOCI recognized as gains and losses in earnings, along with the gains and losses from fair value hedges, the results of its net investment hedges of foreign subsidiaries, and the results of transactions classified as speculation. On the speculation line (derivatives not designated as hedging instruments), we see that a loss of $9.2 million was recognized mostly from commodity contracts. This result would explain the large derivatives liability fair value balance discussed above. All other figures on this table are relatively small. Also, on this page, General Mills shows that it transferred into AOCI $12.9 million of losses from interest rate cash flow hedges and $14.4 million of gains from currency cash flow hedges, for a net transfer to $1.5 million. There were no amounts transferred from commodity hedges, which is because it does not do cash flow hedging of commodities, as noted above.

On p. 72–73, it discusses credit risk and how it manages it, which is to engage in transactions with high quality entities. It acknowledges some concentration of credit risk: not surprisingly its greatest exposure is to its number one customer, Wal-Mart, which accounts for 20 percent of net sales. Of course, this risk is from the trade credit it extends to Wal-Mart, which is unlikely to be very large. It mentions that it closely monitors its derivatives counterparties. It also uses some collateral and estimates a loss of $5.8 million from counterparty default on derivatives contracts if all counterparties fail. This is clearly a small amount for a company this size.

On p. 87, we see that is AOCI balance is −$2.2 billion, though most of that is from its pension fund and foreign currency translation adjustments. Its hedge derivatives amount to only +$1.5 million.

General Mills and Delta are end users. Now let us take a look at a dealer bank.

13.2.3.3 *JPMorgan Chase*

JP Morgan Chase (JPMC) is the largest U.S.-headquartered bank and the sixth largest bank in the world. Its total book value of assets stood at $2.4 trillion at year-end 2017. Its book equity was $248 billion, and its market cap was $366 billion. The entity as it is now known was created in 2000 when the investment bank JP Morgan, founded in 1871, merged with the commercial bank Chase Manhattan, whose origins go back to 1799.

As a dealer and a financial institution, JP Morgan Chase has considerable exposure to a variety of financial risks. As such, its 10-K is structured much differently from that of typical corporate end users. It must also pay considerable attention to its position with respect to the regulatory structure of the countries in which it operates. In fact, its first mention of derivatives occurs as early as p. 2 in a discussion of derivatives regulation, in which it talks about the extensive regulatory requirements with which it must comply in the U.S. and foreign countries. It should also be noted that while we discussed credit risk as having a potential effect on end users, the story is completely different for banks. They are exposed to credit risk across a widespread spectrum. Indeed, the core business of banks is to assume credit risk. That is the nature of lending.

In Part I, p. 8, JPMC identifies the risks it faces. Under Market Risk (pp. 11–15), it discusses its role as market-maker in many types of instruments and how that activity is subject to a number of risks, including volatility, credit, and liquidity risk. It discusses credit risk (pp. 13–15) and liquidity risk (pp. 15–16) in some detail.

On p. 47, the bank presents a condensed version of its balance sheet, where we see that of its total assets of $2.5 trillion, the fair value of derivatives comprises about $56 billion, about 2.2% of assets. Of its $2.3 trillion of liabilities, derivatives make up about $38 billion, about 1.7% of liabilities. Thus, its net derivatives position is about $18 billion, which is rather small for its market cap of about $366 billion.

On pp. 75–80, it discusses enterprise-wide risk management. We will cover this topic in more detail in Chapter 14, but basically it refers to the organization of the entire risk-management system of an entity into a comprehensive, dynamic, and effective activity. Because they have so many exposures, most large banks have to do this and they generally have an elaborate and sophisticated system. It describes and outlines its risk governance structure, a topic we will cover in Chapter 14. The bank has a Chief Risk Officer (CRO) and specifies its risk appetite, which identifies how much risk it is willing to assume and how it will take and manage that risk. It has a Risk Policy Committee within its Board of Directors that monitors the bank's risk management. It also has risk committees within each line of business. These items describe its risk governance, which we shall discuss in Chapter 14. It identifies four general types of risks: strategic, credit and investment risk (essentially credit risk), market risk, and operational risk. It also identifies 14 specific risks (p. 76) and discusses them in detail, covering how those risks are identified and managed.

On p. 114, it discusses its derivatives.

In the normal course of business, the Firm uses derivative instruments predominantly for market-making activities. Derivatives enable customers to manage exposures to fluctuations in interest rates, currencies and other markets. The Firm also uses derivative instruments to manage its own credit and other market risk exposure. The nature of the counterparty and settlement mechanism of the derivative affect the credit risk to which the Firm is exposed. For OTC derivatives the Firm is exposed to the credit risk of the derivative counterparty. For exchange-traded derivatives ("ETD"), such as futures and options and "cleared" over-the-counter ("OTC-cleared") derivatives, the Firm is generally exposed to the credit risk of the relevant CCP.[11] Where possible, the Firm seeks to mitigate the credit risk exposures arising from derivative transactions through the use of legally enforceable master netting arrangements and collateral agreements.

So here it first mentions its market-making, and then it goes on to state how it uses derivatives to manage its own credit and market risk. It mentions the risk of exchange-traded and cleared transactions and that it uses master netting and collateral for other transactions. Just below this paragraph it presents a table showing its net derivatives assets, referred to as receivables, previously mentioned as about \$56 billion, broken down into the various categories. Interest rate derivatives are largest at \$24.7 billion with foreign exchange second at \$16.2 billion. It also notes that it holds collateral of \$16.1 billion against all of these derivatives receivables.

It also discusses the credit risk it faces from its derivatives. It notes that it uses credit derivatives, which have a value at year-end of about \$17.6 billion. It also discusses how it has allowances for potential credit losses, which is standard for any entity that extends credit.

On p. 121, the bank discusses its market risk management, which it defines as

... the risk associated with the effect of changes in market factors, such as interest rates and foreign exchange rates, equity and commodity prices, and liabilities held for both the short and long term.

JPMC describes its market risk management as follows.

Market Risk Management monitors market risks throughout the Firm and defines market risk policies and procedures. The Market Risk Management function reports to the Firm's CRO.

---

[11]CCP stands for central counterparties, which means clearinghouses.

> *Market Risk seeks to manage risk, facilitate efficient risk/return deci-*
> *sions, reduce volatility in operating performance and provide transparency*
> *into the Firm's market risk profile for senior management, the Board*
> *of Directors and regulators. Market Risk is responsible for the following*
> *functions:*
>
> - *Establishment of a market risk policy framework*
> - *Independent measurement, monitoring and control of line of business*
>   *and firmwide market risk*
> - *Definition, approval and monitoring of units*
> - *Performance of stress testing and qualitative risk assessments*

These actions comprise the normal functions of market risk management in a bank and make for effective risk governance, a topic we take up in Chapter 14. The report goes on to discuss how each line of business manages its own risk, with oversight from its central risk management function. The report then identifies the tools it uses to measure risk, which are *VaR*, economic-value stress testing, nonstatistical risk measures, loss advisories, profit and loss drawdowns, and earnings at-risk.[12] It describes how the risk monitoring and control process works by the setting of limits for the various risk measures mentioned here. These limits vary by business unit. The limits are set at the firmwide level and are reviewed and changed as needed. It talks about what happens if the limits are breached, which involves notification of key personnel higher up in the bank, and possibly ultimately senior management. On p. 122, the bank identifies the factors that create market risk in its different lines of business.

Page 123 begins an extensive discussion of Value-at-Risk. It states that it uses the historical simulation method estimated over the previous 12 months with a one-day holding period and 95% confidence. The results are reported to senior management, the board of directors and the regulatory authorities. It mentions that it would expect to break the *VaR* on five days out of every 100, but that it is aware that this outcome could occur more often if volatility is higher. It also notes that it conducts *VaR* calculations for individual products and risk factors. It goes into an extensive discussion of the limitations of *VaR* and mentions that it evaluates and improves its models periodically. It also mentions that the *VaR* reported to bank regulators requires use of a 10-day holding period with 99% confidence, which is standard in global banking regulation.

---

[12]These tools are discussed in more detail further in the report and will be highlighted here.

On p. 124, it provides a table of its *VaR* figures for its various business units. The overall firm average daily *VaR* is reported as $29 million with a high of $42 million and a low of $17 million. It notes that it back-tests *VaR* to determine if the predicted results are consistent with the outcomes. This comparison is presented with a graph on p. 125. On p. 126 and 127 it discusses the other risk measures it uses: economic-value stress testing, nonstatistical risk measures, loss advisories, profit and loss drawdowns, non-dollar FX risk, and earnings-at-risk. In stress testing, the bank identifies various extreme scenarios and determines the potential losses. Nonstatistical risk measures include such factors as credit spread sensitivities, interest rate basis point sensitivities, and market values. Loss advisories and profit and loss drawdowns are used to identify unusually large losses that may have occurred during the recent period. Earnings-at-risk is a variation of *VaR* based on net interest income and interest-rate sensitive fees.

On p. 131–133, the report discusses operational risk management, which it describes as

> *... the risk of loss resulting for inadequate or failed processes, people and systems, or from external events; operational risk includes cybersecurity risk, business and technology resiliency risk, payment fraud risk, and third-party outsourcing risk. Operational risk is inherent in the Firm's activities and can manifest itself in various ways, including fraudulent acts, business interruptions, inappropriate behavior of employees, failure to comply with applicable laws and regulations or failure of vendors to perform in accordance with their arrangements.*

The bank describes that it has an Operational Risk Management Framework, which has four components: governance, risk identification and assessment, measurement, and monitoring and reporting. These topics will be discussed in Chapter 14. JPMC measures operational risk in terms of a Loss Distribution Approach that simulates operational risk based on historical data, along with various other sources of information and stress tests. There is a discussion of its use of insurance, its cybersecurity, and its resiliency in responding to operational risk events. On p. 136, it discusses its legal risk management, an especially important risk to banks.

In Note 2, pp. 155–156 of the Notes to Consolidated Financial Statements, it discusses how it measures fair value. It uses a similar hierarchy of three tiers as mentioned in the Delta and General Mills reports. Page 160 contains a financial statement of the fair values of its assets and liabilities. As previously noted, its derivative assets total $56.2 billion, with the largest two groups being interest rate and foreign exchange derivatives. Its derivative liabilities are valued at $37.8 billion with the largest two groups being foreign exchange and equity derivatives.

Note 5, p. 179, discusses its derivatives in more detail. After a brief description of what derivatives are and how they can be used, it describes how it employs derivatives in market making, which is its primary use of derivatives, and in its own risk management. It also mentions that it provides derivatives clearing services. It also discusses its accounting for derivatives. It mentions that it uses hedge accounting for some but not all of its derivatives transactions. It describes the three types of derivatives hedges (fair value, cash flow, and net foreign investment hedges) and in what manner it uses them. On p. 182 it shows the notional value of its derivatives, which amount to about $48 trillion, comprised of about $34 trillion in interest rate instruments, $11 trillion of foreign exchange instruments, about $1.4 trillion of equity instruments, $1.5 trillion of credit derivatives, and $475 billion of commodity instruments. The largest category is interest rate swaps at about $21 trillion, which is far ahead of all other categories. Recall, of course, that notional does not indicate exposure, a point mentioned just below the table. Page 183 shows the fair values of its derivatives broken down into the five classes of risks: interest rate, credit, foreign exchange, equity, and commodity. On p. 184 and 185, there is a table showing the breakdown of its derivatives into nettable derivatives and non-nettable derivatives. On p. 214 is the same information for its derivatives liabilities. Page 186 discusses liquidity risk it faces from derivatives.

On p. 187, the bank discusses the impact of its derivatives on its income. It shows that the net effect of fair value hedge gains and losses from derivatives in 2017 was a profit of $938 million. Its net effect of cash flow hedges on its profit was −$134 million, and its effect of net investment in foreign subsidiaries was −$1.3 million.[13]

On pp. 190–191 it discusses its credit derivatives, and it mentions that it uses credit default swaps and credit-related notes.[14] Its total notional of these instruments was a net of $16.9 billion purchased credit derivatives.[15]

On p. 254, the bank presents a breakdown of its AOCI. Its cash flow hedges account for about $176 million of a total OCI of about $1 billion.

---

[13]For perspective, the total net income of the bank was about $24 billion.

[14]In Chapter 11 we had called these credit-linked notes.

[15]Credit derivatives purchases refers to the acquisition of credit protection. The net figures involve not just netting credit protection purchased against credit protection sold but incorporates whether the purchase and sold protection is on the same entity.

13.3 Chapter Summary

The accounting and disclosure of risk management and derivatives trading activities is a critical element of the risk management process. Besides complying with the norms of accounting as well as securities and banking laws, proper accounting and optimal disclosure is how companies convey to the public what they are doing with regard to taking risks and managing them. It is important to present to the public and especially the financial analysts that rate and recommend investments an accurate picture of what a company is doing in the way of managing risk. A sound and comprehensive risk management program sends a positive signal that the company is aware of its risks, is monitoring them on a close basis, and is taking whatever corrective actions are necessary. But there is a downside to disclosure: your competitors know what you are doing. Unless your competitors are not publicly traded, however, they are required to do the same thing.

Accounting for risk management transactions has a long history of abuse, but FAS 133, now ASC 815, has improved the process. ASC 815 defines a derivative and provides for a classification of all derivatives transactions into either a fair value hedge, a cash flow hedge, a foreign currency hedge, or speculation. Nonetheless, there will continue to be areas of opacity, as transactions become more complex and new products and strategies are invented. Companies will always look to FASB and IASB for guidance, and those entities will always be releasing revised policies.

The material in this chapter dovetails with the material in the next chapter. There we will look at how companies organize, implement, and oversee their risk management systems.

13.4 Questions and Problems

1. In the United States, what influence does the U.S. government have on derivatives accounting rules?
2. What is hedge accounting and how can it be subject to abuse?
3. What is fair value accounting and why is it somewhat inconsistent with established accounting principles?
4. Explain how fair value hedges are accounted for and what requirements must be met for a transaction to qualify for fair value hedge accounting.
5. Consider a hedge fund that holds bonds in its inventory. It anticipates that in six months, it will sell $20 million of U.S. treasury bonds.

It is concerned about the potential for loss on the bonds, so it engages in a forward contract on a Treasury bond. No margin requirement is necessary. Answer the following questions.

(a) What type of hedge would be appropriate?
(b) What entries would be made at the start of this transaction?
(c) At the end of the current quarter, the derivative has gained $1.40 million in value, and the bonds have lost $1.6 million in value. What entries would be made?
(d) When the forward contract expires, it pays off $900,000, and the bonds have gained $850,000 since the end of the quarter.
(e) Is this transaction an effective hedge, using typical methods to assess effectiveness?

6. Explain how cash flow hedges are accounted for and what requirements have to be met for a transaction to qualify for cash flow hedge accounting.
7. A company expects to receive a lump sum of cash in the amount of $15 million in about five months. It plans to use that cash to purchase commodities it will use in its manufacturing process. The current cost of the commodities is $14.4 million. It engages in a hedge by buying a forward contract on the commodities that expires in five months. Answer the following questions.

(a) What type of hedge would be appropriate?
(b) What entries would be made at the start of this transaction?
(c) At the end of the current quarter, the derivative has gained $2.5 million in value, and the commodities are $2.2 million more expensive. What entries would be made?
(d) When the forward contract expires, it pays off $3.1 million, and the price of the commodities has increased by another $0.5 million since the quarter ended. What entries would be made?
(e) Is this transaction an effective hedge, using typical methods to assess effectiveness?

8. If a company hedges the issuance of a future liability by buying a put option, how would that transaction be accounted for?
9. What are the three types of foreign currency hedges?
10. How are speculative transactions accounted for?

11. What is the 80-125 criterion used in hedge accounting?
12. What are the three methods by which the SEC permits companies to meet its requirement that the risk associated with derivative transactions must be disclosed.
13. What is the primary argument against having to disclose how a company manages the risk associated with its derivative transactions?

Chapter 14

Organizational Structure and Corporate Governance of Financial Risk Management

True risk management is creative — there is a judgment element to it. Scenarios need to reflect economic and political factors, as well as industry-specific issues. A widely experienced board of directors can bring that kind of insight into helping risk managers ask the right kind of questions.

Lawrence Dunn
Risk Metrics
Risk magazine, July 2008, p. 27

This final chapter in our journey through the practice of financial risk management by end users is an overview of the most important organizational and governance considerations in financial risk management. The terms *organizational* and *governance* refer to the structure of an entity's risk management system and its oversight. For the first 12 chapters, we looked at how to practice financial risk management. In Chapter 13 we examined how to record and report the transactions and convey to the public what the organization is doing with respect to managing risk. None of that will matter, however, if the entity does not have an effective system to implement its risk management strategies within the organization and, most importantly, oversight by the people who are ultimately responsible.

In designing such a system and providing for oversight, it is critical that we first think about who benefits from risk management. For a profit-making company, the beneficiaries would primarily be the shareholders, as they are the ones who have placed their money at risk. But there are other stakeholders. In some countries, the primary purpose of a corporation is considered to be as a provider of jobs.[1] Hence, the employees would be

---

[1] In fact, in some countries, that is considered virtually the sole purpose of a corporation.

considered as important stakeholders. That, in itself, should get employees on board to practicing good risk management, but alas, it is not always the case. The positive incentives and negative disincentives are often not strong enough to induce the appropriate behavior. Good risk management systems are structured so that everyone has a strong reason to practice effective risk management. Nonetheless, it can be challenging to get the incentives just right: not too much and not too little.

In addition, society has a tremendous stake in the effectiveness of risk management systems. Failures are costly, particularly those that involve publicly-insured deposits at banks that are regarded as "too big to fail." When the public more or less provides a guarantee, such as with insured banks and through companies like Fannie Mae and Freddie Mac and even some non-banks like General Motors, the setting is ripe for excessive risk taking and poor risk management. The owners and high level executives receive the benefit if extreme risks work out well, but society bears the cost of adverse outcomes. Of course, companies have low incentives to satisfy regulators, who represent society. Regulators are often viewed as obstacles in the way of corporate success, and even though regulations are required, companies are known to fight them vociferously before they are enacted. So there is an uneasy give and take between regulatory requirements and a company's need to act in an optimal manner for its shareholders.

We shall assume that companies do want to practice effective risk management. They may disagree with and even resent some of the regulations they are subject to, but they do want the organization to survive and achieve its overall objectives. To enable it to do so, it must put in place a structure that facilitates the practice of risk management and a system of governance that oversees the process to ensure that the objectives are being carried out. In this chapter, we shall look at how companies should carry out their risk management programs within themselves and how they monitor the programs so that what they are doing is what they intend to do.

Before we start, it is important that we not lose sight of what risk management means and what it does not mean. Recall that we stated quite explicitly that risk management means aligning the actual risk taken with the desired risk. It is not a guarantee against losses, or even severe losses. Adverse outcomes must always be expected. They simply have an expected frequency. If the actual frequency exceeds the relative frequency, risk management has failed.

14.1 Elements of an Effective Risk Management System

An effective risk management system has three primary components. From the ground up, an organization needs a *solid front-line structure*. By this we are referring to the personnel, knowledge, and systems to measure and manage the risks on a day-to-day basis. Much of what we have covered in this book deals with the requisite knowledge. It is up to the organization to secure knowledgeable personnel and invest in the technology to use that knowledge to manage the risk effectively.

Moving up one level, the organization requires *an effective hierarchy*. Think of this concept somewhat as the idea depicted by an organization chart. Within the hierarchy of the firm, where is the risk managed? Is it at the ground level or higher up? What line and staff personnel are involved? Who reports to whom? Who is responsible for what?

Finally, at the top is *effective governance*, which refers to the senior executives and the board of directors who oversee the process. It is important to have a clear understanding of where responsibilities lie. The ultimate responsibility is with the board, but obviously the board cannot be involved in the day-to-day risk management. Where the board's responsibilities begin is a critical part of the process. Of course, the focus of this chapter is on the organization and governance, and we initially take up the subject of risk governance.

14.1.1 *Risk Governance*

The board of directors of a corporation is a group of shareholders elected by the shareholders as a whole to represent them and oversee the management of the company. Most boards consist of between five and 15 people. The board is essentially responsible for governing the company. It sets the policies, hires the senior management, monitors the performance of management and the company, and conveys information to the public about the company.

One of the principal attractions of a board of directors is that it can bring a broad perspective to an organization. Most boards are comprised of senior executives of companies and non-profits, and these individuals usually bring a vast array of diverse experiences to the entity. But a board is not capable of managing the day-to-day details of running a company. Its job is to oversee. Yet there is a critical and often blurred line between what a board should do and what it should not do and what it should know and what it would not know. Ultimately, however, the board is responsible. If the lowest level employee makes a mistake that causes the company to harm someone externally, the board bears the ultimate responsibility. It is a thin line and quite a challenge deciding how much the board should know and do itself and how much it should delegate to others.

The board of directors is led by an individual referred to as the chairman of the board. A board will also typically have a vice chairman, and its members will also sub-divide into several committees. For example, the board of directors of the Coca-Cola Company has seven sub-committees: audit, directors and corporate governance, compensation, executive, finance, management development, and public issues and diversity. These committees review issues and concerns and make recommendations to the board as a whole.

Probably the most important function of the board is to hire and oversee the senior management of the company. Senior management has a more direct responsibility in administering the operations of a company. The highest level manager at a company is typically called the chief executive officer or CEO. Other high ranking executives usually include the chief operating officer, president, chief marketing officer, chief information officer, chief financial officer, and chief legal counsel, among other titles and responsibilities.[2] It is common to refer to these officers as the C-suite.

In many companies there is an important and somewhat controversial overlap in that several members of the C-suite are often also on the board of directors. And most importantly, the CEO will sometimes be the chairman of the board. Though this fact may be troublesome, it is fairly common practice.

We have emphasized that the knowledge in this book also applies to non-profits. They are also usually governed by a volunteer board of directors, sometimes called a board of trustees. They also usually have executive officers and committees. They may have a number of volunteer workers, including some high-level committee members. Where volunteers are involved, the problems become more complex, because volunteers often have other more pressing priorities in their lives. Nonetheless, risk management remains a primary function of non-profits. While maximizing wealth is not the objective, survival and providing uninterrupted service remain critical.

---

[2]It is interesting to note how that the position of president of a corporation has become quite insignificant in recent years. The president of a corporation is often a person whose job is primarily as a figurehead. While some presidents may hold true power, the president of a company never outranks the CEO.

In the next three sub-sections, we will take a look at the three of the critical areas of responsibility for the board: adhering to regulations, setting standards and expectations, and creating a risk governance structure.

14.1.1.1 *Regulatory Requirements*

The board of directors is responsible for ensuring that a company complies with all regulatory requirements. While these regulations can vary somewhat by country and type of business, effective risk controls are generally an important element of regulatory requirements, and virtually every board of directors in the world is responsible for ensuring that the company has effective risk controls. As we learned in Chapter 13, publicly traded companies in the U.S. are required to disclose the risks they take and the ways in which they manage that risk. Indeed, we saw three examples of how companies disclose how they manage the risk of their derivatives transactions. These requirements may arise from a company's status as a publicly-traded corporation, and they may come from additional require-ments, which can include laws such as the Sarbanes-Oxley Act of 2003 (SOX), which greatly strengthens the regulations on financial reporting. The New York Stock Exchange's rules require that the audit committees of its listed companies discuss risk assessment and oversight. For banks, the Dodd-Frank Act of 2010 also tightens the requirements of risk management, mandating that all banks with over $10 billion in assets have a risk committee within their boards of directors. And the Basel bank capital regulations impose various regulatory requirements with regard to the holding of sufficient capital to cover market, credit, and operational risks. Of course, accounting and auditing standards, as discussed in Chapter 13, also imply if not require high standards of risk control. Thus, there are many layers of regulation that impose requirements that companies practice effective risk management.

In general, the objective of these regulations is to make clear that the board of directors and senior management are responsible for managing the company's risks. The regulations do not generally specify how risks are to be managed. In essence, they simply point at the board and senior management and say, "It is your job to do it right." The ultimate liabilities for failure to "do it right" can range from lawsuits, fines, and criminal liability if there is fraud.

It is not clear, however, exactly what it means when risk management is not done right. Bankruptcy of a company is not necessarily a failure of risk management. All companies must take risks. Even a well-managed company can be a victim of an exceptionally weak industry or economy. Unfortunately, it has become almost axiomatic in society that corporate failure arises from a failure to control risk. We have become accustomed to expecting board members and management to anticipate the kinds of events and changes that go on in society, the economy, and the markets that can jeopardize a company's existence. When companies fail, we usually blame it on the people at the top. Whether that is fair or not is unclear. It is usually the case that companies seldom fail over a single bad decision. It usually takes multiple bad decisions over a period of time, and for that, senior management should probably bear the blame.

Of course, many corporate failures have only limited consequences. Investors lose money, and employees lose jobs. Competitors usually pick up the demand for the product or service and often hire some of the employees. But some large companies, particularly in banking, are deemed "too big to fail" because the consequences reach far beyond the company, its owners, and its employees.[3] Thus, in some cases, the government, that is, the taxpayers, has been forced to invest public money in a company, take ownership, and absorb past and future losses until the company can turn itself around. Therefore, politicians often want a scapegoat and blame the board of directors. Since 2003, SOX has given government greater power to hold directors and management liable, and since 2010 the Dodd-Frank act has exerted similar and additional pressure on banks.

Sometimes companies incur large losses that do not threaten the survival of the company but do make for embarrassing headlines. Again, it is not clear that such losses are not just part of the extreme but rare events that will occur from time to time. When these situations happen, government is not usually involved, but there may be lawsuits, proxy battles, and pressures for resignations.[4]

---

[3]Banking is undoubtedly the most interconnected industry. Banks routinely lend to and trade with each other to the point where they become mutually dependent. A failure of one bank can cause another to fail in a giant house of cards — the systemic risk we discussed in Chapter 11. In the U.S., most bailouts have been for banks, but there have also been some bailouts of non-banks that were deemed to be critical, such as the Penn Central Railroad (1970), Lockheed (1971), Chrysler (1980), and General Motors and Chrysler (again) (2008).

[4]A proxy battle is when an outside investor attempts to gain support of the shareholders in order to acquire enough shares to take over a company and dispose of its management and/or board.

Regulatory compliance, not only in regard to risk management but also as it relates to financial reporting and physical safety, is one of the most critical functions of the board of directors. Regulatory specialists are charged with the responsibility of knowing all of the potentially thousands of laws and regulations to which a company must comply and ensuring that the organization is in compliance. Not surprisingly, these officials are usually called compliance officers, and they are usually attorneys or at least supported by attorneys. Nonetheless, the ultimate responsibility is the board's. The chairman of the board cannot simply fire a compliance officer and be absolved of blame.

Dealing with the regulatory requirements of risk management is one of the most challenging functions of a board of directors. The company must take risks or there is no reason to be in business. There are a few extreme and unlikely events that can severely damage the company, but elimination of the possibility of these events is usually too costly. The company should be able to operate with the confidence that it is in compliance with all laws and regulations, and that while adverse events will occur, it has a strong mechanism for responding to these events and keeping the company alive.

14.1.1.2 *Industry Standards and Expectations*

The concept of "industry standards" implies a generally agreed-upon set of practices. Exactly who agrees upon these practices may be unclear. There is a tendency to assume that certain practices have become commonplace among the organizations in the industry, but there may be no formal codification of these practices. Thus, it can be unclear as to exactly what industry practice means.

There are few formal industry standards of practice in the business world. Informal standards may arise from experience and the recommendations of others. Probably the most well-known source of industry standards is the International Organization for Standards (ISO), which is an independent consortium of organizations that sets standards within various countries. Its objective is to promote worldwide standards so as to improve efficiency and reduce costs. ISO standards are identified by numbers. As an example, ISO 16, established in 1975, establishes that standard tuning of a musical instrument is an A-note at 440 hertz, which is the A above middle C.[5]

---

[5]Hertz is the number of vibrations of a string per second. An A-note can sound virtually identical to a keen ear from 435 to 445 hertz. The ISO standard is set at 440 hertz.

ISO 5775 is the standard that sets the size of a bicycle tire and rim. There are literally thousands of these standards, and they are, not surprisingly, completely voluntary. A tire manufacturer can choose to make a bicycle tire of a non-ISO standard size, but if the bicycle manufacturers generally agree to use ISO, the tire will be less marketable.

In 2009, the ISO established a set of standards in risk management, designated as ISO 31000. The ISO standards are so extensive that we cannot address them here, but they cover the vocabulary, the framework, and the process. In addition, the ISO created ISO 31010, which deals with risk assessment techniques. You should be aware that ISO 31000 and 31010 are not limited to financial risk management. They also address risk management with respect to safety, operations, and engineering. ISO standards, of course, are not mandatory for any organization, though it can choose as official policy to conform to them.

In 2002 the Institute of Risk Management (IRM), in cooperation with the Association of Insurance and Risk Managers, and the National Forum for Risk Management in the Public Sector, released a report entitled "A Risk Management Standard," which provides an excellent overview of what would seem to be a reasonable set of risk management standards. We will explore these standards in some detail here.

The report defines risk management as (p. 2):

> ... *a central part of any organisation's strategic management. it is the process whereby organisations methodically address the risks attaching to their activities with the goal of achieving sustained benefit within each activity and across the portfolio of all activities.*

It characterizes risk management as (p. 2):

> ... *a continuous and developing process which runs throughout the organisation's strategy and the implementation of that strategy.*

It adds that risk management (p. 2)

> ... *must be integrated into the culture of the organisation with an effective policy and programme led by the most senior management. It must translate the strategy into tactical and operational objectives, assigning responsibility throughout the organisation with each manager and employee responsible for the management of risk as part of their job description. It supports accountability, performance measurement and reward, thus promoting operational efficiency at all levels.*

The report identifies the following benefits of risk management (p. 4):

> *Risk management protects and adds value to the organisation and its stakeholders through supporting the organisation's objectives by*
>
> - *providing a framework for an organisation that enables future activity to take place in a consistent and controlled manner*
> - *improving decision making, planning and prioritization by comprehensive and structured understanding of business activity, volatility and project opportunity/threat*
> - *contributing to more efficient use/allocation of capital and resources within the organisation*
> - *reducing volatility in the non essential areas of the business*
> - *protecting and enhancing assets and company image*
> - *developing and supporting people and the organisation's knowledge base*
> - *optimising operational efficiency*

The report goes on to discuss risk analysis, risk evaluation, risk reporting and communication, risk treatment, monitoring and review of the risk management process, and the structure and administration of risk management. The final point is of particular relevance for this chapter. The report states that (p. 12):

> *An organisation's risk management policy should set out its approach to and appetite for risk and its approach to risk management. The policy should set out responsibilities for risk management throughout the organisation.*

It notes that (p. 12):

> *To work effectively, the risk management process requires:*
>
> - *commitment from the chief executive and executive management of the organisation*
> - *assignment of responsibilities within the organisation*
> - *allocation of appropriate resources for training and the development of an enhanced risk awareness by all stakeholders.*

The report goes on to identify the role of the board of directors, which it states is (p. 12)

> *responsibility for determining the strategic direction of the organisation and for creating the environment and the structure for risk management to operate effectively.*

It goes on to discuss how each business unit should operate with respect to risk management. Finally, it discusses the risk management function, which it says includes (p. 13):

- *setting policy and strategy for risk management*
- *primary champion of risk management at strategic and operational level*
- *building a risk aware culture within the organisation including appropriate education*
- *establishing internal risk policy and structures for business units*
- *designing and reviewing processes for risk management*
- *co-ordinating the various functional activities which advise on risk management issues within the organisation*
- *developing risk response processes, including contingency and business continuity programmes*
- *preparing reports on risk for the board and its stakeholders*

As we have previously emphasized, industry standards are simply recommendations. They are not required and for all anyone knows, they may be followed very little. But having standards would seem to be a positive thing. Many companies carefully try to follow standards, in some cases because they provide a useful framework, give a concrete structure to the process, and make a great deal of sense, and in others, simply because companies are trying to engage in due diligence. If, for example, a company implements the IRM standards and still has a major loss event, it can respond that it was engaged in the industry standard practices. Of course, such a response will not make the loss go away, but many companies do look for industry practices as cover when things go wrong. This may not make it right, but it is what sometimes happens.

But of course, companies should not simply be looking for alibis. They should practice good risk management. Industry standards are often just an application of common sense, but they emphatically drive home a major point: *effective risk management starts at the top of the organization.*

Finally, we should note the term *best practices.* This expression has evolved to refer to a set of industry practices that are believed to be optimal. In that sense, following best practices is better than following industry practices. It is not clear, however, how a set of industry practices becomes "best" practices. An organization could produce what it calls a set of best practices, but whether the practices truly are optimal is unknown, and they have not been subjected to any testing. They have simply been dubbed "best practices." In short, there are no formal requirements for designating a set of procedures as best practices or even as industry practices. As such, whether to adopt any such set of practices is a judgment decision. Clearly there is an enormous element of common sense involved in deciding what industry practices or best practices to adopt.

14.1.1.3 *Creating a Risk Governance Structure*

In this sub-section we will delve into some of the details about how a board of directors creates a risk governance system. The board must begin by identifying its basic philosophy towards risk. It should do this by first defining risk, then by identifying the risks that affect the organization, and followed by specifying which risks the company should accept and which it should not. Taken together, these elements would then comprise the company's risk philosophy, as they identify the company's official policy as to what risks the company faces and which of those risks it will take.

The board then establishes a structure within which the company measures the risk it takes, monitors the risk, and takes actions to align the risk taken with the desired risk. Of course, this process is precisely what we described in Chapter 4, particularly with Exhibit 4-24. But this process does not happen unless the board and senior management make it happen. Doing so requires allocating sufficient resources, hiring the right risk management specialists, and providing the proper training for employees. In today's world, it is said that a company needs a top-to-bottom *risk culture*, by which we mean that all personnel from the CEO down to the lowest paid employee are aware of the risks and are actively engaged in monitoring and managing those risks. For some employees, this responsibility is obvious. The treasurer of an airline is keenly aware of interest rate and currency risk. The fuel purchasing manager is aware of the price volatility of the company's fuel. The mechanic is aware of potential problems that could ground or even endanger an aircraft. What about the gate agent? Let us say a check-in agent accepts a piece of luggage from the flyer, tags the luggage and starts to place it on the conveyor belt to send it off to be loaded. But at the last instant, the agent happens to turn around and notices that the bag is not closed well enough. The agent can simply let it go and think, "Not my problem." A risk-cultured agent knows, however, that if the bag comes open during transit, the airline will suffer the customer's ill will and will have to compensate the customer for the loss, even though the bag was not really up to traveling standards. Indeed, it will not be the check-in agent's problem, but it certainly is the company's problem. A company with a good risk culture has employees that recognize risks that can have harmful effects both inside and outside of their domain of responsibility and take actions to mitigate those risks. In this case, the gate agent might stop the bag, retrieve some duct tape from the back office, and wrap it around the bag, while telling the customer that he might need to replace the bag before the next trip.

A good corporate risk culture requires a considerable amount of education and motivation. Employees who simply mitigate risks without being recognized and being rewarded will eventually stop making the effort. Thus, maintaining a strong corporate risk culture requires incentives.

The management of the company would then create a system in which the relevant risks are measured and monitored. Such a system will require an investment in technology, personnel, and education. This system would feed risk information to the appropriate personnel on a timely basis. These personnel would monitor the risks and take action to align the actual risks with the desired risks. After those actions are taken, risk information would be reviewed to determine that the risks have been properly aligned.

As obvious as it would seem, it is not always the case that the system works as it should. For example, a trader responsible for hedging might be permitted to trade derivatives only where the size matches or is less than the spot market exposure. If the trader finds that he can trade a larger size without being caught, he may do so in order to potentially increase his bonus or recoup previous losses. An effective risk management system must have the ability to immediately stop someone from doing a trade beyond the permitted size. In the extreme case, the exposure taken by the trader may be sufficiently large to threaten the viability of the organization. As strange as it may seem to say, some systems do not stop traders from exceeding their limits, thereby negating the whole notion that a limit exists.

We previously mentioned that an organization must ensure that personnel are properly incentivized. Risk taking must be penalized, not because one should not necessarily take the risk but because the risk does impose a cost. Thus, a division that takes greater risks would be expected to outperform a division that takes lower risks. This is why performance evaluation must be done on a risk-adjusted basis. We will discuss this topic in more detail in Section 14.5.

A critical element of a risk governance system is effective auditing. There are both internal and external auditors. The former are employees of the organization, while the latter are employees of an accounting or auditing firm. While auditing is a process designed to review financial statements for accuracy and conformance with standards, external auditing firms are almost all engaged in general business consulting and in some cases risk management consulting. They are trained to review and provide recommendations on risk management and as noted earlier, they are required to do so. A firm's internal auditors should also be trained in what to look for in regard to weaknesses in risk management. Both internal and external auditors also generally review reports, especially those that will be sent to the public or regulators.

Reporting is one of the most important elements of risk management. Good risk decisions cannot be made without accurate and timely risk information. Thus, the system must provide this information to the decision makers on a recurring basis. It is imperative that the information be extremely accurate and current.

As mentioned above, a company will have a compliance officer whose objective is to make sure that the company obeys all laws and follows all regulations. The compliance officer must be deeply involved in the governance structure.

No system is effective forever. Times changes, and systems must change with the times. As such, the entire risk management system must be subjected to periodic review. New policies, strategies, tactics, and structure may be needed from time to time.

14.1.2 *Establishing Risk Management Systems*

The risk management systems themselves comprise the implementation and use of the models that enable companies to make risk decisions. We have covered many of these models earlier in this book. Pricing models such as the cost-of-carry model and the Black-Scholes-Merton model provide information on the prices and risk measures of various derivatives. Value-at-Risk provides information on potential losses. These models or appropriate substitutes thereof are an integral element of risk management systems. In addition, the systems must include models that measure the basic exposure. For example, a multinational company will require models that track and forecast revenues and costs in foreign currencies. Airlines must have models that provide predictions of their demand for fuel.

Dealers typically have huge risk management infrastructures and invest a great deal in models, some of which are developed by themselves and others which are purchased from external providers. End users will need to decide if the models and computer systems that implement the models will be developed in-house or purchased. Larger companies will often have the staffing and resources to develop the models and systems themselves, but many end users will buy the models rather than develop them on their own.

While risk management systems are largely quantitative systems, no computer system should have the final say in a risk management decision. People must make the final decisions. And, as we saw in Chapter 1, people are imbued with biases, so decisions should often be checked against a group consensus and of course should be consistent with the organization's risk philosophy.

People are, of course, a company's greatest resource and its most significant investment. Good risk management systems not only must be operated by competent personnel, these personnel require continuous improvement in their knowledge levels. In addition, they must be properly compensated. Risk takers must bear the burden of earning a return sufficient to cover the risk taken. Risk management can be a difficult practice to compensate. Risk managers pay a heavy price if the firm incurs significant unexpected losses, and in particular if the firm goes under. But risk managers also cannot be so incentivized that they prohibit the company from taking the risks it should take. Determining the compensation of risk managers is indeed a challenge.

Finally, risk management systems and models must be backtested. For example, let us say that a company buys a VaR software packages that says that the company should incur a loss of more than $10 million on about one day out of the month. The company should test this result against its actual experience. If, say after a year, the company finds that it loses more than $10 million an average of two days out of the month, the model is defective. Of course, a defective model is not likely a programming or conceptual error, but simply a bad input, an example of model risk that we discussed in Chapter 13. Nonetheless, backtesting models is critical.

14.1.3   *Organizational Structure*

While this book has primarily focused on end users, it is worthwhile to talk about how the risk management of dealers is organized. Dealers that are practicing effective risk management will naturally follow many of the ideas and practices described in the previous sections. They will typically have a chief risk officer (CRO) and probably a risk committee. But at a more fundamental level, dealer operations are usually divided informally into three areas: the front office, middle office, and back office. These terms do not literally refer to offices and indeed many people engaged in these activities do not have offices. They sit at desks that are usually in large rooms. These expressions are simply euphemisms.

The term "front office" usually refers to traders. They sit on desks at terminals that are connected to the market, and they engage in the transactions that buy and sell risk. The "middle office" generally refers to the risk management personnel. They monitor the trading of the front office and should have direct access to the senior management of the company. The "back office' refers to the clerical personnel who process the transactions. Using an expression somewhat loosely, the back office "processes the paperwork."[6] Back office personnel move the money and the records to the right accounts and entities. One of the challenges with a back office is the fact that back office personnel tend to be less educated and less knowledgeable and are paid less than the front and middle office personnel. Yet, the back office is an extremely important part of the process. They handle the movement of money, and if that is not done correctly, there is considerable potential for complications and losses.

The Back Office of Barings Bank

In 1994, Barings Bank, founded in 1762, was one of the oldest banks in the United Kingdom, if not the world. It had financed the Louisiana Purchase and the Napoleonic Wars and managed some of the money of Queen Elizabeth. Barings was not a tremendously large bank, but it had a global reach and was well known for its investment management services.

In 1992, the bank sent a 25-year-old clerk named Nick Leeson to its Singapore office. The records of its Singapore transactions were completely disorganized, and Leeson had acquired a reputation as an excellent back office manager, particularly in Barings' office in Jakarta, Indonesia as well as in London.

Soon, however, Leeson began trading futures contracts. Immediately there was a problem, but no one saw it. The back office and front office have distinct duties. The back office, in particular, processes the paperwork generated by the traders but operates independently, as the back office is the first line of control. If a clerk discovers an error, she is

---

[6]In this day and age, the actual amount of literal paperwork is relatively small, but the term "paperwork" will always be used to describe the electronic and physical documentation that must accompany all transactions.

responsible for correcting it and if necessary bringing it to the attention of personnel higher up.

To cover up losses, Leeson began hiding them in an account, that famously became known as the 88888 or five 8's account. The number 8 is considered lucky in East Asian culture. The five "8s" was the account number that Leeson made up to hide his losses. An account of this sort is not an uncommon arrangement and is often used to temporarily park transactions that have no offsetting transaction simply because records of the offsetting transaction have been lost in the system. Clerks are supposed to research the entries in this account, find the offsetting entries, and clear them from the account.

As head of the back office, Leeson engaged in a clever game of hide-and-seek, whereby these entries were never matched with other entries. They were simply trading losses that he managed to keep hidden from the auditors. Leeson's typical trades were spreads, whereby he went long a futures contract on the Singapore Exchange and short the identical contract on the Osaka Exchange in Japan, or vice versa. Regardless of what happens in the market, one of the transactions will make money and the other will lose. Leeson recorded the gains and hid the losses in the 88888 account.

Obviously, by hiding losses, Leeson gave the appearance of producing exceptional trading profits. Executives in London were pleased at Leeson's apparent results, even though they had never given him authority to trade. Unfortunately, no one questioned how he could produce such significant profits, perhaps because his trading was making all of the executives look good.

It soon became more challenging to keep the losses hidden. Leeson began engaging in extreme speculation mainly by selling straddles that produced considerable cash up front that he used to meet margin calls but which had the potential for producing devastating losses in the event of large market moves. And then, a black swan happened. On January 17, 1995, an earthquake struck Kobe, Japan, killing over 6,000 people, and in response, the Japanese market crashed. Leeson's straddle positions sustained significant losses, and he had finally reached the point at which he could hide them no longer.

Leeson fled the country, stopping in Kuala Lumpur, Malaysia to fax his resignation with the note, "sincere apologies for the predicament that I have left you in." The "predicament" resulted in losses of over £800 million and the consumption of the entire capital of the bank. Barings was bankrupt.

Barings was purchased for £1 by the Dutch bank ING, which began to operate it as a subsidiary called ING Barings. Subsequent spinoffs, sales, and names changes have left the only remaining Barings-named entity in the form of a company called Barings Asset Management, which is owned by the Massachusetts Mutual Life Insurance Company.

Leeson attempted to flee to London and turn himself in, preferring the British justice system to the Singaporean justice system, but he was apprehended at the Frankfurt, Germany airport. He and his attorney requested that he be extradited to the U.K., but U.K. authorities were unable to come up with a charge. He was extradited to Singapore, where he was sentenced to six and a half years for various forms of fraudulent activity including forging a document. He served about half of the sentence and was released early after developing colon cancer. Leeson recovered from the cancer, has since written two books, briefly served as the business manager of a U.K. soccer team, and works as a speaker on the dangers of poor risk controls.

Leeson is the origin of the term "rogue trader," which refers to a person within a large organization who oversteps his trading boundaries and endangers the entire company. Leeson may well have coined the phrase himself with his 1996 book *Rogue Trader: How I Brought Down Barings Bank and Shook the Financial World* (Boston: Little Brown).

The lesson learned from the Leeson story is that trading, risk management, and processing the paperwork must be completely separate functions.

In corporate end users, these front/back/middle office functions are not usually sub-divided in this manner. End users are not normally engaged in the provision of financial services. They make products or offer other services. While there are certainly clerical personnel in end users, they are usually part of the much broader accounting/bookkeeping function. The equivalent of a front office is usually a high-ranking officer of a company, such as a CFO or someone delegated by a CFO to engage in risk management transactions. And while an end user should have personnel devoted to risk management, it may have a more fragmented approach, leaving the risk management spread throughout the company, a point that leads directly to the next section.

14.1.3.1   *Completely Decentralized*

A completely decentralized risk management system would essentially result in each division or group within a company managing its own risk. There may or may not be any centralized oversight. As an example, let us say that a consumer products company has a North American division, a South American division, a European division, and an Asia-Pacific division. Each division will borrow money, buy raw materials used in manufacturing, and engage in foreign exchange transactions. Consequently, each division incurs similar risks, though viewed from different perspectives. The divisions are responsible for their own performance in the local currency.

With such an organization, risk management probably gets short shrift and may even be duplicative. One division may have long exposure to one currency, while another may have short exposure to that same currency. Yet, each division may engage in hedging that currency, resulting in considerable duplication of time, effort, and money. In addition, a decentralized system can also lead to risk management getting secondary emphasis. It is unlikely that each division will have risk management specialists. The emphasis will be on maximizing value for the division, but it is unclear the role that risk management will play in that process. The primary advantage of a decentralized system is that the decision makers of each division are probably in the best position to know what risk management actions should be taken to maximize value from their own activities, but that does not mean that they act in an optimal manner from the perspective of the company as a whole.

14.1.3.2   *Decentralized with Central Oversight*

An improvement over a purely decentralized system is to have central oversight. This framework can occur through either a risk management function at the highest level or a risk committee. The risk management function would likely include a chief risk officer, or CRO, who would be a C-suite executive. Centralized oversight would provide the ability to monitor for failure to take appropriate action at the division level and for duplicative efforts. A CRO would also be available to serve in an advisory capacity for each division. Yet, there is a problem with such an arrangement. There can easily be conflicts, whereby a CRO with no real authority over a division overrides divisional risk management decisions.[7] An alternative is to have the

---

[7] These types of conflicts are not uncommon in other functions in a company. For example, the legal department is at the highest corporate level, but may get into a conflict with a division.

CRO's decisions overlay those of the divisions but without any direct impact laid on the divisions. This is a common model in investment management companies, in which portfolio managers do no hedging, which is done in a centralized capacity overlayed with the various portfolios. It is essentially the model covered in the next sub-section.

For example, a divisional executive may choose not to hedge a particular risk. The CRO, however, believes that the risk should be hedged. The CRO is authorized to overlay a hedge and as such, he executes that transaction. The division, however, is evaluated without taking into account the hedge. Thus, the divisional executives are given free rein to make whatever risk decisions they feel they must make, but at the higher level, there may be risk-negating actions.

The risk consulting firm Protoviti describes the CRO's responsibilities as follows[8]:

- *establishes the company's risk management vision*
- *determines and implements an appropriate risk management infrastructure*
- *establishes, communicates and facilitates the use of appropriate risk management methodologies, tools and techniques*
- *facilitates enterprise-wide risk assessments and monitors the capabilities around managing the priority risks across the organization*
- *implements appropriate risk reporting to the board, audit committee and senior management.*

Protoviti states that a CRO would likely have 12–15 years of experience and would have certain other desirable characteristics. A CRO would have the ability to think strategically, understand that organizations must take some risks, have good communication and facilitation skills, have the ability to organize and motivate, be capable of working with all levels of management, have a strong presence and an ability to interact with senior management, would have experience reporting to boards and audit committees, would be concise and direct in articulating their ideas, would be good at analyzing large amounts of data and distilling the results to a few key points, and would have the ability to work with risk reports. Many CROs would have accounting and auditing experience as well.

---

[8]Protoviti (2006). Technically this bullet list refers to a slightly more integrative concept called enterprise risk management, which we shall cover in Section 14.1.3.4. We have removed the word "enterprise" here, as the points are applicable to all forms of risk management.

A Whale of a Swap

In the spring of 2012, the prestigious commercial and investment bank JPMorgan Chase (JPMC) announced that it had incurred a $2 billion trading loss that occurred out of its London Office. CEO Jamie Dimon referred to the loss as a "tempest in a teapot." After all, the bank had been earning profits of more than $5 billion a quarter. The bank had been one of the few large financial institutions that was not heavily involved in sub-prime mortgages, and hence, it was viewed as strong and with a low tolerance for risk. But over the next few months the figure widened to over $6 billion. And while the loss did not threaten the viability of the bank, it resulted in a tremendous destruction of the credibility of both Dimon and JPMC.

The bank's long run of success and its reputation for solid risk management through the Financial Crisis of 2008 ended when the stones of this loss were turned over and the troubles pointed to a single trader, a Frenchman named Bruno Iksil. Iksil, an early-fortyish trader and holder of an engineering degree from École Centrale Paris, a top tier graduate school of engineering, had joined the bank in 2003 and was part of a team of about 400 traders in its London office. Iksil, who had earned the nickname Voldemort for the antagonist in the *Harry Potter* novels, specialized in credit default swaps (CDS) and in particular, large positions in them. In fact, his positions were so large that he came to be known as the London Whale. The Whale, or rather, Iksil specialized in trading the MarkIt CDX indexes, which are measures of the combined credit risk of large corporations. In 2012, the risk had begun to breach the bank's own internal risk limits, but that did not stop Iksil or his supervisors from continuing to make the same types of trades. And it did not stop two other employees from allegedly mismarking the values of certain positions so as to appear that the losses and risks were smaller. As noted, the losses ultimately rose to over $6 billion, which ironically occurred in a rather calm time for credit markets. Had there been more turmoil, the losses would likely have been much larger.

While these losses did not threaten the viability of JPMC, they nonetheless sent chills down the backs of regulators and investors. If one of the most conservative and seemingly best-managed banks in the world could allow one trader to generate the kinds of losses that wiped out the bank's entire quarterly profit, how much additional danger was there that no one even knew about?

U.S. and U.K. regulatory authorities charged the bank with poor risk controls and ultimately fined it over \$900 million. The bank admitted that its controls were lax and in response, Dimon's pay was cut in half, costing him about \$12 million. Chief Investment Officer Ina Drew, one of the most powerful women on Wall Street and earning about \$14 million a year, was fired. Achilles Macris, Iksil's immediate supervisor, was fined about \$1.2 million and was either fired or left the bank. Iksil was fired, but U.S. and U.K. authorities chose not to file criminal charges, as Iksil cooperated with authorities. The two traders who allegedly intentionally mismarked the positions, Javier Martin-Artajo, a Spaniard, and Julian Grout, a Frenchman, were indicted in the U.S. for criminal wrongdoing, but they are living in their respective native countries and have successfully resisted extradition. Charges against them were dropped in mid-2017.

It would appear that the primary lesson to be learned from the London Whale story is that even seemingly well-managed institutions can have hidden risks. These risks can lead to huge losses, and the actions of the individuals involved may not even be illegal. Moreover, the potential for concentrated risk, which is hardly a new story, continues to rear its ugly head in the world of financial risk management.

14.1.3.3 *Completely Centralized*

A completely centralized risk management system allows divisions to make their own decisions without concern over risk mitigation. A division might be uncomfortable with a particular risk, but it cannot eliminate that risk. The divisions are asked to operate to their best of their ability within the risks they are charged with accepting. A centralized risk management function then decides on whether to eliminate or even increase those risks. As an example, a fuel purchasing manager may feel uncomfortable paying a rising price for fuel, but he cannot do anything about it. He may make his views known to the senior risk management personnel, but he is simply told to acquire the fuel at the most reasonable cost possible and not to worry about the risk. The centralized risk management function will then decide if a hedge should be overlayed.

14.1.3.4 *Enterprise Risk Management*

Since the earlier 2000s, a new and integrative concept in risk management has evolved. The idea is to take all risks of the company and bring their management under a single umbrella of responsibility. The concept has come to be known as *enterprise risk management* or *ERM*. While ERM sounds as if it is simply a variation of if, not identical to, centralized risk management, there is a distinction.

To fully appreciate this distinction, we need to step back into the history of risk management. The concept of risk management has its origins in the insurance industry. Indeed, the term *risk management* is even to this day often used synonymously with insurance. An organization might have a risk management department, which has the primary responsibility to purchase and manage the organization's insurance policies and to make all of the employees aware of the risks they face on a day-to-day basis. These risks, however, have traditionally been of the form of property and casualty risks. A risk management department would, therefore, likely be responsible for promoting safety and security so that human safety and property are preserved. Its responsibility for financial risk management would be limited to problems such as theft. While these types of risks would fall under the category of operational risk, they would not encompass all forms of operational risk, nor would they include market risk management and credit risk management.

Enterprise risk management brings the management of all risks under a single central controlling body. Of course, as with centralized risk management, such a model can pose problems. Divisional and group heads can resent the centralized oversight and control from an ERM system. That is why ERM requires a delicate balancing act. The functions of divisions and groups must be extremely well defined, and done so in such a manner that failure to manage the risk is not the responsibility of the division head but rather the responsibility of the ERM personnel. Some firms that implement ERM do allow risk management at the division levels, with oversight and assistance from the central ERM personnel.

As an example, which we similarly mentioned earlier, a fuel purchasing manager must be given a defined responsibility for acquiring the fuel and getting it delivered to the proper locations. The manager would not be held responsible for anticipating fuel price increases, or for implementing any type of hedging program. Such a program would, however, likely be implemented by an ERM group. The head of a foreign division would not be responsible for loss in the value of the currency in which it operates relative to the company's home currency. That task would be carried out by the ERM group, which might well be able to offset a risk in one division with an opposite risk in another. In other variations of ERM, risk management decisions are made at the division level with central oversight.

Of course, as mentioned, those jobs would be assigned in that manner through a centralized risk management system. An ERM system carries the process one step further. ERM would account for *all* risks, including those representing physical damage to assets or humans. By taking into account all types of risks, some economies can be generated. For example, exchange rate risk and the risk of fire to the company's assets are risks with essentially zero correlation. By recognizing that these risks are uncorrelated, the company could find that it can do less hedging or less insuring. By looking at all risks as a whole, the ERM group can make a decision on what overall level of risk it is willing to hold.

What we have described here is but a brief overview of ERM. Let us start by looking at how ERM is defined. An organization called the Committee of Sponsoring Organizations of the Treadway Commission (COSO) released a comprehensive report in 2004 on ERM.[9] It started by defining ERM as (p. 2):

> *a process, effected by an entity's board of directors, management and other personnel, applied in strategy-setting and across the enterprise, designed to identify potential events that may affect the entity, and manage risk to be within its risk appetite, to provide reasonable assurance regarding the achievement of entity objectives.*[10]

Perhaps not surprisingly, a careful reading of this definition reveals virtually nothing more than the definition of risk management, but there is no doubt that calling it *enterprise risk management* has given the process a life of its own. A risk consulting firm called Protoviti released a comprehensive study of the COSO model of ERM (2006) and argues that the advantages of ERM are as follows (pp. 3–4):

- *Reduce unacceptable performance variability*
- *Align and integrate varying views of risk management*

---

[9]The Treadway Commission was originally an organization devoted to studying fraud and internal control and consisted of five professional accounting associations. It was named after its original chairman, James Treadway. COSO was formed in 1985 out of the sponsoring entities. These entities are the American Institute of Certified Public Accountants, the Institute of Internal Auditors, the Financial Executives Institute, the Institute of Management Accountants, and the American Accounting Association.

[10]The COSO model was technically developed by the accounting and consulting firm Price Waterhouse Coopers.

  • *Build confidence of investment community and stakeholders*
  • *Enhance corporate governance*
  • *Successfully respond to a changing business environment*
  • *Align strategy and corporate culture*

Again, these advantages can simply characterize all forms of risk management. But Protoviti states that ERM is the missing link in bringing risk management to the boardroom and integrating it into the company's strategy. Prior to the development of ERM, Protiviti argues that risk management was focused almost exclusively on the protection of assets. ERM not only focuses on protection of assets, but also on enhancement of assets. In so doing, resources are better allocated, performance is better measured, products and services are more accurately priced, waste and inefficiency are reduced, communications are improved, information is more timely and accurate, and the entity is in a better position to respond to change.

It is easy to say that all of this sounds good. Indeed, it *is* good. But implementation is the trick. Many companies claim to be implementing ERM when they are far from it. Perhaps it simply sounds good to say that "We practice enterprise risk management," as though it were a seal of approval. But seals of approval, such as a statement from an auditing firm, are earned by meeting certain formal standards. There are no formal standards for ERM. No inspectors will visit a company, take notes, evaluate a report, and attest that the company is in compliance with ERM.

The COSO model identifies eight components of the ERM framework (pp. 3–4):

  • *the internal environment*
  • *objective-setting*
  • *event identification*
  • *risk assessment*
  • *risk response*
  • *control activities*
  • *information and communication*
  • *monitoring*

Implementing ERM involves a lot more than tossing around words and phrases like these. But the key characteristic is that the organization has an integrative model in which risk management begins at the top of the organization and takes into account all of the risks faced throughout the organization.

Does ERM work? Can it even be shown to be effective? When confronted with the question of whether ERM has produced positive results, most companies that claim to have implemented it would likely respond in the affirmative. When asked to provide proof, the company would generally point to its overall success following the adoption of ERM. But most of the companies were successful prior to adopting ERM. It is not possible to simply adopt ERM, point to the company's success, and imply that either the success would not have continued without ERM, or whatever success the company had, it was greater with ERM.

In short, there are simply no metrics for evaluating ERM or risk management more loosely defined. Even studies that purport to determine if ERM or risk management provides value are difficult to evaluate and have some doubt of their reliability. Moreover, as we noted earlier, a company can declare that it implements ERM, but that does not mean that it really does. Success is a compendium of many complex and interrelated activities, combined with a little positive luck or at least, the avoidance of negative luck. Exactly where ERM fits into the collective activities of a successful organization and precisely how much ERM contributes to success, over and above what the other activities contribute, is virtually impossible to assess.

But, alas, that last statement is true for almost any strategic initiative. Let us say that a highly technologically oriented company that has had remarkable success with what it perceives as little emphasis on marketing decides that it needs to place more emphasis on customer satisfaction. It brings in a marketing-oriented CEO who upsets the board and senior management by making numerous changes. Let us say that the company's success increases. Its stock price generates solid gains and its sales and profits go through the roof. Did the strategic marketing objective work? We cannot be sure. Just because A was done and B followed does not mean that A caused B to occur. Suppose during the ensuing period, other similar companies that did not implement a customer-oriented strategy also showed significantly improved performance. Perhaps the reason was simply exciting new developments in technology, strong industry performance, and robust economic activity.

Boards of directors and senior executives must often make decisions about where to devote their time and the financial resources of the company. Large donations to charities are far more than simply a warm heart. They are investments designed to lead to an improved public image. But do they? Can the company measure how much its image improved with its investment in social programs? Can the company measure the gains from the luxury box it leases at its local NFL stadium or its sponsorship of the special Olympics? Can it turn any of these estimates, if it can make them, into shareholder value?

Like these decisions, companies are often compelled to make qualitative assessments of whether ERM provides positive value. If it provides no other value, simply forcing a company to take a top-down look into its strategy, its risk tolerance, and its risk taking would seem to be a positive activity.

14.1.3.5 *Risk Budgeting*

One of the important concepts that is used to organize a risk management system is that of *risk budgeting*. The concept of a budget involves the allocation of limited resources in advance of the engagement in the activities that an entity normally undertakes. Consider a small company with a budget of $10 million in a year and two divisions that might allocate $6 million to the slightly larger division and $4 million to the slightly smaller division. But let us say that the larger division has slightly higher risk than the smaller division. In risk budgeting, the organization decides on the risk it wants to take and then allocates a portion of it to each sub-entity, which we will call a division. Thus, one division may naturally be riskier than the other, and it will be allocated more risk. Let us say a company has two equal-size divisions, one of which is twice as risky as the other. Then the riskier division will be allocated twice as much risk. Of course, the risk of the entire company will be smaller than the sum of the risks of the two divisions given that the divisions are not perfectly correlated.

Consider a company with two equally-weighted but highly correlated divisions. The correlation between those divisions is in fact 0.75. Suppose the company decides that its overall volatility should be 0.45. Consider the following equation expressing the volatility as a function of the volatilities of divisions 1 and 2 and their correlation:

$$\sigma^2 = (0.5)^2\sigma_1^2 + (0.5)^2\sigma_2^2 + 2\rho_{12}\sigma_1\sigma_2$$
$$(0.45)^2 = (0.5)^2\sigma_1^2 + (0.5)^2\sigma_2^2 + 2(0.5)(0.5)(0.75)\sigma_1\sigma_2$$

The company then needs to decide the values of σ_1 and σ_2. There are an infinite number of solutions, just as there are an infinite number of possible ways in which a company can allocate a financial budget. The company will likely be bound by some constraints. Let us say that division 1 cannot operate with less than a volatility of 0.55. Plugging in $\sigma_1 = 0.55$, we would find that the solution for σ_2 is 0.41.[11] Thus, the company would force division 2 to have a volatility of 0.41. That does not mean that the manager of division 2 would be happy with that, but that is true of a financial budget as well.

A risk budgeting system uses the overall risk of the entity as the primary metric. It then allocates risk to its sub-units based on the need to achieve that overall level of risk. Because having a precise level of risk is difficult to achieve, a risk budget might also be based on a range. Thus, the company might specify that its risk should be between 0.40 and 0.50. Its riskier division might have a risk between 0.50 and 0.60. At a maximum company risk of 0.50, with a range of risks for division 1 between 0.50 and 0.60, division 2 would be allocated risk between 0.47 and 0.66. At a minimum company risk of 0.40, with a range for division 1 between 0.50 and 0.60, the risk of division 2 would need to be between 0.24 and 0.46.

14.2 Risk Management in End Users

In Chapter 13, we took a look at the 10-Ks of three large public companies, primarily to examine the accounting and disclosure of its risk management activities. 10-Ks are an excellent source for learning how companies define and manage the risk to which they are exposed. In this chapter, we take that process a step further by examining the philosophy and structure of enterprise risk management at Johnson & Johnson, a large manufacturer of health-related products.

Johnson & Johnson (J&J) has published a document called "Framework for Enterprise Risk Management at Johnson & Johnson" that outlines how it engages in ERM.[12] It starts off by identifying its strategic framework (p. 5), which identifies its credo, its aspiration, and the factors that drive growth.[13] It is clearly heavily committed to ERM, as it states (p. 6):

> *Ultimately it is through effective risk management that we enable the enterprise to implement this Strategic Framework and grow the business*

---

[11]The solution would either be obtained using a search routine, Excel's solver, or the quadratic formula. You do not need to worry about obtaining this solution, but you should be aware that the solution can be found, given that all other terms are known.

[12]Available at https://www.jnj.com/sites/default/files/pdf/JnJ_RiskMgmt_ERMFramework_guide_v16a.pdf.

[13]The J&J Credo emphasizes its responsibility to the health care workers and consumers who use their products, their employees, the communities in which they operate, and their shareholders.

successfully in alignment with our Credo and strategic principles amidst an evolving and challenging external environment.

On p. 7, J&J goes on to identify four types of risks, which are listed below with examples:

Strategic: reduction in business vitality, loss of intellectual property and trade secrets, competition for talent, reputational risk

Operational: disruption to product supply, counterfeiting, waste and ineffi-ciency, damage to physical property, global data disruption

Compliance: violations of laws regarding environment, employee health & safety, clinical trials and patient safety, product quality, sales and promo-tion, personal data protection, local taxes and laws

Financial & reporting: foreign exchange, funding and cash flow, credit risk, financial misstatements

On p. 8, J&J presents how it implements ERM. It starts by defining ERM as:

a common framework applied by business management and other personnel to identify potential events that may affect the enterprise, manage the associated risks and opportunities and provide reasonable assurance that our Company's objectives will be achieved.

It states that ERM will enable it to:

Ensure prompt resolution of internally identified risk to compliance with laws and regulations to maintain the provision of quality products, protect patient safety and ensure appropriate relationships with customers.

Suppose "simplification" strategies to ensure effective use of resources, enable an optimized approach to auditing and identification/remediation of compliance issues and promote reporting and monitoring across compliance functions.

Enable improved decision making, planning and prioritization through a structured understanding of opportunities and threats.

Support value creation by enabling management to deal effectively with future events that create uncertainty, pose a significant risk or opportunity and to respond in a prompt, efficient and effective manner.

Support our growth drivers of creating value through innovation, extending our global reach with local focus, executing with excellence and leading with purpose.

On p. 6, J&J presents a table that identifies eleven risk management functions and marks their responsibilities within the four types of risks mentioned above. These risk management functions are Corporate Internal

Audit, Environment, Health & Safety, Global Finance, Global Medical Organization, Global Security, IT Risk Management, J&J Health Care Compliance & Privacy, J&J Human Resources — Talent Management, J&J Law Department, J&J Quality & Compliance, and J&J Supply Chain. As an example of responsibilities, its Global Finance risk management function addresses strategic risk, compliance risk, and financial & reporting risk but not operational risk. Its Global Security addresses strategic risk, operational risk, and compliance risk, but not financial & reporting risk. Its Quality & Compliance addresses operational risk and compliance risk but not strategic risk and financial & reporting risk.

On p. 10, J&J presents its ERM framework in the form of six components, which are drawn from the COSO report: event identification & risk assessment, risk response, control activities, information & communication, and monitoring. Details of these processes are provided on pp. 11–13. It concludes the report by saying that (p. 17)

> *As a leader in health care, J&J serves billions of people worldwide by bringing value, expertise and innovation in line with Our Credo. Risk is inherent in our business activities. Our strong risk management practices allow us to strengthen our organization through informed strategic and business decisions so we can continue to meet the needs of consumers, doctors, nurses, patients, mothers and fathers.*

It is obvious that J&J puts a great deal of emphasis on ERM. ERM is clearly not just a patchwork of fancy words and organization charts. It is a process woven deeply into the company's culture and strategy.

14.3 Risk Management in Asset Managers

"Asset management" is a term used to refer to the industry that manages portfolios of securities and occasionally physical property in a fiduciary manner. The asset management industry includes companies that offer their services to individual investors referred to as clients, and it also includes the mutual fund and hedge fund industries. Some major asset management companies are Blackrock, Frank Russell, and State Street Global Advisors. Some asset managers are affiliated with banks, such as JP Morgan Asset Management, and some, such as Blackrock, offer mutual funds. Of course, major mutual fund companies, such as Vanguard and Fidelity, are asset managers but are more known for their mutual funds. Some organizations, such as large private universities, have very large endowments and manage that money internally through their own asset management companies or departments.

Asset managers are end users, but they are not what we refer to as corporate end users.[14] Asset managers are something of a blend between banks and corporate end users. They are not banks in the sense of taking deposits, but, like banks, they are financial intermediaries. They take money and invest it on behalf of clients. With a few exceptions, they invest almost exclusively in the financial markets.[15]

Most asset management companies maintain strong centralized risk management systems. Because their exposures are almost exclusively in the financial markets, they have the ability to use such measures as *VaR*, volatility, and beta to capture their risks on a virtually continuous basis. They usually have a CRO or director of risk management who closely monitors the entire risk of the company and communicates that risk to the senior management as well as to the individual asset managers. If the risk is out of line, the CRO may or may not have the ability to engage in hedging transactions, but he will have the responsibility to raise the issue with senior management.

Asset management in the risk management industry may well be the easiest risk management of all to implement. There is a plethora of information, and the objectives of the company are quite clear: grow the wealth of their shareholders by investing in the financial markets. Even the relatively illiquid markets of some securities are nothing compared to the liquidity of markets for traditional corporate assets. Of course, the challenges are still quite great, as the financial markets are highly competitive, much more so than the markets for products and services.

14.4   Risk Management in Dealers

As you know, this book is for end users, not dealers. Nonetheless, we have talked a great deal about dealers. It is certainly important that end users understand what dealers do. In Chapter 13 we looked at the 10-K of

---

[14] An asset management company might technically be incorporated, but it is seldom referred to as a corporation. Of course, banks and insurance companies are also usually incorporated, but they are not commonly referred to as corporations. The term "corporation" is generally understood to refer to businesses that provide non-financial products and services.

[15] The exception is usually real estate.

JPMorgan Chase, which is not only a bank but also a dealer. We observed that the company devotes a good deal of effort to spelling out how risk management is practiced.

As we have studied in this book, derivatives dealers offer to take either side of a broad variety of derivatives transactions. They then enter into hedges with outside entities to lay off the risk, thereby maintaining a closely balanced position. These hedges could be with other dealers who happen to have the opposite risk, or they could involve exchange-listed derivatives. Because dealers engage in thousands of transactions across numerous markets and countries and involving many different employees, it is particularly important that they have effective centralized risk management, if not enterprise risk management. For dealers, an extremely organized and effective risk management system is of the highest priority. Poor risk management can quickly destroy a financial institution, as it did with Barings Bank. The risk management systems of dealers must go much further than those of corporate end users. A CRO and/or risk committee must be able at all times to obtain a view of all of the risks in the organization, in much the same way that the pilot of an aircraft gets a view of everything that is going on by looking out of the window. But in the same way in which the pilot also looks out the window, the CRO and subordinate risk managers will also draw data from a variety of sources, call on their personal experience, and use qualitative judgment to manage the overall risk.

14.5 Capital Allocation and Performance Analysis

One of the attractive features of having a formal risk management program is that it facilitates decisions about where to allocate capital and how to evaluate performance. Capital allocation refers to the process in which a company sets aside resources to back up the activities of a division. This capital protects the firm against losses generated by a division. The process of capital allocation is primarily associated with financial institutions and asset management firms. A bank, for instance, will evaluate the risks generated by its different divisions, examples of which are global banking, asset management, derivatives dealership, commercial banking, consumer banking, and investment banking. The bank would know that some divisions are naturally riskier than others, so it will set aside more capital to back one division than another. In addition, each of these divisions may have different risks within their respective sub-areas, so they too may allocate capital according to relative risks within their sub-areas.

The amount of capital to be allocated to each division is a difficult question. *VaR* is often used in capital allocation. Let us say that the bank uses a 5% *VaR* over a one-month period. It finds that the *VaR* of a division is $10 million. Recall that this means that the bank expects the division to lose at least $10 million 5% of the time, amounting to about one day in a month. Suppose the bank maintains $10 million of capital representing the *VaR* for that division. We know, of course, that the loss could exceed $10 million. We covered the fact that there is no absolute measure of the maximum loss other than the equity of the entire firm. Setting aside $10 million is clearly not an absolute cushion against adverse effects.

Another problem with capital allocation regardless of whether *VaR* is used is that the amount of capital allocated to one division versus that of another may do nothing to protect the bank unless it is willing to reallocate capital in the event of a severe loss. For example, consider a bank with two divisions, A and B, in which A is considered high risk and B is considered moderate risk. Suppose Division A performs quite well over a given period, but Division B sustains significant losses, well in excess of its allocated capital. What would the bank do? Simply let one division go out of business? Although arguably that might be an optimal choice, in all likelihood the bank would reallocate capital from its better performing division to cover the loss in the badly performing division. Or in simple terms, it would just absorb the loss knowing it has enough capital elsewhere.

One major purpose of capital allocation, however, is to facilitate performance evaluation. The profits earned by a division are a reflection of two main factors: the performance of the division and luck. The former represents the efforts made by the employees and executives. The latter represents the effects of risk. In spite of great effort and solid execution, the hand of fate can turn the performance of a division into a nightmare. For example, the currency trading group of a bank may do its best analysis and believe that the South African rand (symbol: ZAR) is highly undervalued. It believes that the South African economy is poised for a strong positive movement. It is very confident of this forecast and takes a large long position in ZAR. Soon thereafter, a highly contagious virus exerts a crippling influence on the South African population, curtails tourism, and turns around the normal level of confidence investors have in ZAR. The rand tumbles, and the currency trading group of the bank sustains huge losses. The results have been heavily influenced by sheer bad luck. Such an event, perhaps not quite on the black swan level, is definitely not normal. It is also not hard to imagine a scenario in which pure positive luck results in a substantial gain.

As a result of the effect of luck, it is become common for performance results to be adjusted for risk. For portfolio managers, one common measure is the Sharpe ratio,

$$SR_p = \frac{R_p - r}{\sigma_p}$$

where R_p is the return on the portfolio, r is the risk free rate, and σ_p is the volatility of the portfolio. The numerator is called the risk premium, representing the return earned above the risk-free rate. Dividing by the volatility penalizes for the risk. In this manner, large fluctuations reduce the performance measure. Another commonly used measure is the alpha, found as

$$\alpha_p = R_p - (r + (R_m - r)\beta_p)$$

where R_m is the return on the market portfolio and β_p is the beta of the portfolio, the measure of its systematic risk or how it covaries with the market, which we covered in Chapter 3. The term in parentheses is the benchmark return, the basis of which is the CAPM. If the portfolio had greater risk than the market, its beta will exceed one and the benchmark will be adjusted upward from the return on the market. The alpha is said to be the risk-adjusted return. We covered these points in Chapter 3.

The Sharpe ratio is widely accepted in the investment community, but it is not an absolute measure. It is only a relative measure. A Sharpe ratio of 0.3 does not mean anything by itself. Is 0.3 high enough to designate the portfolio as a strong performer? No one knows. The Sharpe ratio is only meaningful when compared to another portfolio. Alpha, however, is an absolute measure. A positive alpha is meaningful in that it implies that the portfolio produced a return over and above what it should have produced, given its risk. Trading portfolios that maintain fairly constant levels of risk are generally amenable to measures such as these. The measures do have their own set of problems, however, and they do not always agree, but they are probably the best there are to use.

But many companies, particularly banks, evaluate the performance of divisions by measuring their risk-adjusted profits. One popular measure is called *RAROC*, which stands for Risk-Adjusted Return on Capital, and it was developed at a bank called Bankers Trust[16]:

$$RAROC = \frac{Risk\text{-}adjusted\ Return}{Capital\ at\ Risk}$$

where both the numerator and denominator are in terms of money, not rate of return. The numerator is usually measured as profit minus expected losses minus costs. The denominator is sometimes called *economic capital*, and it represents the capital necessary to support the trading that produces the results in the numerator. *RAROC* is used to evaluate performance and also on an ex ante basis to determine if a risky venture, such as a loan, should be made. It is commonly used in banking.

A similar measure is called *EVA*, economic value added, developed by a company formerly called Stern Steward and now called Stern Value Management. *EVA* is a measure of a company's economic profit. Economic profit is defined as the profit over and above the return required by the investors, given the risk. In the study of corporate finance, economic profits are referred to as *positive net present values*, which occur when the net value of all cash flows, positive and negative, expected over the lifetime of an investment in an asset is positive. The value of the cash flows is done by a discounting procedure that takes into account the time value of money and the risk. Hence, *NPV* is a risk-adjusted concept. For investment portfolios, the concept of an alpha is analogous to an economic profit or positive *NPV*. In other words, economic profit, positive *NPV*, and positive alpha, are equivalent concepts reflecting the fact that the value generated is more than the amount required to pay the owners the return they expected given the risk they take.

EVA is generally calculated by determining the net after-tax operating profit minus a charge for the capital required. The capital charge is a measure of the capital invested times the rate of return required by the investors. The rate of return required by the investors is sometimes referred to as the cost of capital.

Having a risk management system in place tends to make companies more cognizant of the importance of risk-adjusted performance measurement. In addition, risk management systems generally produce a great deal of data that facilitates the implementation of risk-adjusted performance

---

[16]Bankers Trust was a U.S. bank formed in the early years of the 20th century. Following a series of controversial derivatives deals that led to major losses by clients, it was acquired by Deutsche Bank in 1998.

measurement. But most importantly, they inculcate a culture that emphasizes that risk is a part of everything an organization does. Evaluating performance without evaluating risk is like ignoring the fact that a drunken driver may have made it home safely. What did not happen is a lot more important than what did happen. Indeed, that point is critical to understanding risk management.

These performance measures are widely used in the banking industry but far less often for corporate end users. Nonetheless, they can be used in corporations and are likely to gain more adopters in the future. Measures such as *EVA*, in particular, are amenable to corporate use.

14.6 Final Thoughts

Nassim Nicholas Taleb, developer of the black swan concept in finance, Daniel G. Goldstein, and Mark W. Spitznagel (TGS) have identified what they believe are six key mistakes made in the practice of risk management. We present them here, slightly paraphrased, with reference to Taleb, Goldstein, and Spitznagel (2009):

Thinking you can manage risk by predicting extreme events. The authors argue that people have a poor record of predicting extreme events and in thinking that they are smarter than they are, they focus on some possibilities that they think could happen while ignoring others. TGS suggest that the focus should not be on predicting extreme events but on the response when such events occur.

Having faith that the past will repeat itself. TGS argue that randomness is more socioeconomic than statistical. It does not conform to the types of repeated patterns usually assumed in statistical theories.

Ignoring advice about what one should not do. TGS argue that it is far better to act on negative advice than positive advice. Not doing something, like smoking, is probably a far better piece of advice that doing something like exercising.

Assuming that risk can be measured by standard deviation. TGS argue that the concept is not well understood, often being confused with average deviation. In fact, they note that even quantitatively-oriented people are not always clear on what it means. They say that it should be never be used, but they do not say what should be used instead. Of course, one could also argue that if one does have a good understanding of standard deviation, one can use it. Hopefully this book has helped you in that regard.

Believing that what is mathematically equivalent is psychologically equivalent. Here TGS use some examples similar to those of Kahneman and Tversky mentioned in Chapter 2, which show that mathematically equivalent statements are not always interpreted the same. As an example, an investment that results in a total loss one-third of the time and a 100% gain two-thirds of the time tends to be viewed more negatively than an investment that pays an expected return of 33%, with a maximum of 100% gain and minimum of 100% loss even though the two investments are equivalent.

Thinking that redundancy is a bad thing. People tend to think that having backup systems is a good thing, but that multiple backup systems is a waste of resources. Nature is a great example of this. We have two eyes, two ears, two lungs, two kidneys, etc. when we could get by with one of each. Thus, having extra protection against financial losses is a good thing, but people tend to not tie up resources doing so.

Coach Bob Knight on Risk Management

Bob Knight was one of the most legendary basketball coaches of all time. His 42-year college coaching career at the United States Military Academy, Indiana University, and Texas Tech University produced an astounding 899 victories against 374 defeats and only two losing seasons. He won three national championships, was national coach of the year five times, coached the only undefeated team in college basketball history, and won an Olympic Gold Medal coaching the 1984 team. Moreover, his players had a near-perfect graduation rate. Always colorful and sometimes controversial, Knight was one of the most cerebral coaches in sports history. While he certainly believed in hard physical work, he also believed that games were won and lost in the minds of the players.

In 2013 Knight wrote a book called *The Power of Negative Thinking* (New York: Houghton Mifflin), the title being a takeoff on the famous book *The Power of Positive Thinking*, a classic work published in 1952 by noted theologian Dr. Norman Vincent Peale. Knight begins the book by stating that people have a positive bias. They overestimate the likelihood of success. He cites psychological research that shows that people tend to rate themselves higher than average, the so-called Lake Wobegon effect. Knight says that before each game he would ask:

What vulnerabilities do we have and what can we do to minimize them, to get around them, to survive them — and give ourselves a better chance to win.

One of his favorite slogans was *Victory favors the team making the fewest mistakes*. His coaching style was to coach his players how not to lose. He provides a list of words that he believes are most important to consider before making a decision (p. 27): prevention, hesitation, correction, suspicion, attention, recognition, reservation, anticipation, revelation, organization, dedication, education, caution, rejection, preparation, and gumption. He says that applying these words before making a decision will minimize the regret afterwards if the decision does not turn out well. Knight notes that there are significant uses of negatives in the Ten Commandments, the Gettysburg Address, presidential speeches, and Shakespeare. Knight emphasizes that his advice is not just about basketball. It applies in business and in life.

What does this have to do with risk management? Knight never says a word about the subject in his book. Well, risk management is about dealing with the potential for negative events. Risk managers have to think about the bad things that can happen. Naturally that is their job. But all decision makers must deal with risk. Whether a college student is deciding what subject to major in, or a person is deciding what job to take, whom to marry, and where to live, all decisions are fraught with risk. Knight's advice, to think of the bad things that can happen and find ways to minimize their likelihood, is as good a piece of risk management advice as one can find.

In looking at how companies have practiced risk management, we have observed a lot of talk. Whether there is action is simply a fact that we cannot verify. The banking industry was chided for practicing poor risk management, when that might not have been the case. Any company must take risks and in some cases, the events will be so extreme that it will endanger companies. The Financial Crisis of 2008–2009 involved a meltdown triggered by an unprecedented decline in house prices, wherein a great deal of the housing was financed by sub-prime loans, which are high risk loans made to low-income, low net-worth borrowers. Not surprisingly, many banks were sucked into the abyss that threatened their existence. Did this mean that the banks had poor risk management? Not necessarily. It had been official public policy that the U.S. government encouraged banks to make sub-prime mortgage loans. It did this by pressuring the banks into accepting borrowers with low income and assets and by standing ready to buy the mortgages through its implicit guarantee of Fannie Mae and Freddie Mac, two private companies that were formerly government agencies. In effect, the taxpayers stood ready to absorb losses. The banks did what everyone else would have done: they took advantage of the opportunity.

Most of the stressed banks had good risk control systems, but they never anticipated the systemic nature of the credit meltdown. Recall that in Chapter 11 we discussed how banks underestimated the credit correlation factor. Is this poor risk management? Not clearly. No risk management system will provide perfect results, with all remote contingencies anticipated. But certain banks did fail to anticipate the black swans and had no plan for dealing with them that would assure survival.

Let us recall that risk management is the process of identifying the risks that you want and the risks that you face and taking action to align the one with the other. Risk management is not a process that can eliminate extreme losses or even failures of entire entities. If risk management is practiced effectively, it results in average losses equaling expected losses. Extreme events will occur from time to time, and failures will happen. For most companies, survival is certainly an absolute mandate. But high risks must be taken from time to time, and there will always be a remote possibility of total failure. To have it otherwise would simply suggest putting the investors' funds in risk-free assets.

Let us conclude the material in this book by introducing one final risk. It seems a little late, but this risk is a special one. It is called reputational risk, the threat of losing an organization's reputation. Reputational losses involve a great deal of embarrassment, but that is only part of the picture. When customers, suppliers, employees, and investors lose confidence in a company, they refuse to buy products, sell on credit, work for such companies, and put their money at stake. A reputation lost is a difficult thing from which to recover. In this sense, it may well be the most important risk of all. But it has one important characteristic. A reputational loss is just a by-product of the other types of risks that we have covered in this book. Effective management of those risks will preserve an entity's reputation. In other words, do a good job with the other risks and reputation will take care of itself. Do a bad job, and on top of the financial losses, everyone will lose faith in you.

14.7   Chapter Summary

In this chapter we have wrapped up the book by examining how organizations practice risk management. We emphasized that the risk management process must start at the top, meaning the board of directors. An organization must have effective risk governance. But that is just the starting point. Risk management must permeate the organization with a culture that makes every employee in at least a modest way, a risk manager. There are multiple models for accomplishing this result, but generally speaking, a strong centralized risk management system is usually required. The ultimate in strong centralized risk management is enterprise risk management.

We saw some examples of how companies practice risk management. We even raised some doubts about whether companies do what they say they do. We noted that risk management is more than just avoiding losses. It is about defining risk tolerance and aligning the risk taken with the risk desired. In that sense, it is not about avoiding losses at all. It is about avoiding losses that are in excess of expected losses. In other words, bad things can and will happen to any entity that has a vision for success and a willingness to take risks to achieve its goals. Risk management is about making sure that the bad things that happen do not come as a surprise.

Finally, we noted that effective risk management facilitates the allocation of capital to divisions in an efficient manner. Those divisions whose activities are naturally riskier will require more capital. And, those divisions should be charged for that capital when their performance is measured. Generating value for the owners is all about producing a return in excess of the return the owners would expect given the risk they are accepting by investing in the company. For non-profits, the argument is virtually the same. Given the objectives of the non-profit, some risks must be accepted. The achievement of objectives when unacceptable risks have been taken is not good performance, even for a non-profit as it can lead to disastrous results in the future.

Finally, we repeat one of the most worthwhile points related to risk:

Risk is much more about what did not happen than what did happen.

The risk manager who spends more time worrying about what did not happen that what did is more likely to be a much better risk manager than one who focuses primarily on what did happen. If you do not believe this, imagine being the parent of a teenager. You go out of town and when you return, you find evidence that the teenager consumed a great deal of the alcohol you had in the house and drove the car under the influence. Nonetheless, the teenager did not wreck the car. So, there was no damage and no one got hurt. Therefore, the teenager fails to see why there is a problem. You, however, as a good parent and risk manager see what could have happened and what is likely to happen in the future if the situation arises again.

14.8 Questions and Problems

1. Why is financial risk management important for society as a whole, not just for individual companies and shareholders?
2. What are the three structures of an effective risk management system?
3. Explain the concept of risk governance.
4. Why is it difficult to establish and require industry standards or best practices in risk management?
5. What does it mean to refer to a risk culture in an organization?
6. What are the three informal organizational layers in a risk management system as typically found in banks and dealers?
7. Identify and briefly explain the three forms of risk management organizational structures.
8. What is the job of the CRO?
9. What is enterprise risk management and how does it differ from centralized risk management?
10. Why is it so difficult to evaluate the effectiveness of enterprise risk management or any form of risk management that has been implemented in an organization?
11. What is risk budgeting?
12. Why is financial risk management easier to implement in an asset management firm than in say a traditional corporation?
13. Why is risk management so important in dealers?
14. What is the process of capital allocation?
15. What are two measures of performance that adjust for risk?
16. What is RAROC?
17. What is EVA?
18. What are the five warnings on risk management offered by Taleb, Goldstein, and Spitznagel?

References

Ambrose, S. E. *D-Day: June 6, 1944: The Climactic Battle of World War II*. New York: Simon and Schuster (1995).

Aretz, K. and S. M. Bartram. "Corporate Hedging and Shareholder Value." *Journal of Financial Research* 33 (2010), 317–371.

Bachelier, L. "Théorie de la Speculation." English translation by A. J. Boness in *The Random Character of Stock Market Prices*, ed. P. H. Cootner. Cambridge, MA: MIT Press, 1967.

Bernoulli, D. "Exposition of a New Theory on the Measurement of Risk." *Econometrica* 22 (1954), 23–36. (Originally published as 'Specimen Theoriae Novae de Mensura Sortis," *Commentarii Academiae Scientiarum Imperialis Petrolitianae*, Tomus V [*Papers of the Imperial Academy of Sciences in Petersburg*, Volume 5], 1738, pp. 175–192; translated by L. Sommer).

Bernstein, P. L. *Against the Gods: The Remarkable Story of Risk*. New York: John Wiley (1996).

Bessembinder, H. "Forward Contracts and Firm Value: Investment Incentive and Contracting Effects." *Journal of Financial and Quantitative Analysis* 26 (1991), 519–532.

Bialik, C. "Deciphering a 20% Chance of Rain." *The Wall Street Journal* (December 9, 2008). Available at http://blogs.wsj.com/numbers/deciphering-a-20-chance-of-rain-470/.

Billingsley, R. S. *Understanding Arbitrage: An Intuitive Approach to Financial Analysis*. Upper Saddle River, New Jersey: Pearson Prentice-Hall (2006).

Black, F. "How We Came up with the Option Formula." *The Journal of Portfolio Management* 15 (Winter, 1989), 4–8.

Black, F. and M. Scholes. "The Pricing of Options and Corporate Liabilities." *Journal of Political Economy* 81 (1973), 637–659.

Buffett, W. E. "The Superinvestors of Graham-and-Doddsville." *Columbia Business School Magazine* (1984), 3–15.

Byrnes, J. P., D. C. Miller, and W. D. Schafer. "Gender Differences in Risk Taking: A Meta-Analysis." *Psychological Bulletin* 125 (1999), 367–383.

Carson, B. *Take the Risk: Learning to Identify, Choose, and Live with Acceptable Risk*. New York: Harper Collins (2009).

Chance, D. "Asset Swaps with Asian-Style Payoffs." *The Journal of Derivatives* 3 (Summer, 1996), 64–67.

817

Chance, D. M. and M. L. Hemler. "The Impact of Delivery Options on Futures Prices: A Survey." *The Journal of Futures Markets* 13 (1993), 127–155.

Chernobai, A., P. Jorion, and F. Yu. "The Determinants of Operational Risk in U. S. Financial Institutions." *Journal of Financial and Quantitative Analysis* 46 (2011), 1683–1725.

Center for Disease Control and Prevention. "National Vita Statistics Reoprt." (November 27, 2017).

Committee of Sponsoring Organizations of the Treadway Commission. *Enterprise Risk Management: Integrative Framework. Executive Summary* (2004). Available at http://www.coso.org/documents/coso_erm_executivesummary.pdf.

Delta Airlines 2017 10-K.

DeMarzo, P. M. and D. Duffie. Corporate Incentives for Hedging and Hedge Accounting. *The Review of Financial Studies* 3 (1995), 743–771.

Derman, E. *My Life as a Quant: Reflections on Physics and Finance.* New York: Wiley (2004).

Friedman, M. and L. J. Savage. "The Utility Analysis of Choices Involving Risk." *The Journal of Political Economy* 56 (1948), 279–304.

Froot, K., D. Scharfstein, and J. Stein. "Risk Management: Coordinating Corporate Investment and Financing Policies." *The Journal of Finance* 48 (1993), 1629–1648.

General Mills 2017 10-K.

Gigerenzer, G. *Calculated Risks: How to Know When the Numbers Deceive You.* New York: Simon % Schuster (2002).

Grable, J. "Financial Risk Tolerance and Additional Factors that Affect Risk Taking in Everyday Money Matters." *Journal of Business and Psychology* 14 (2000), 625–630.

Groopman, J. *How Doctors Think.* Boston: Mariner (2008).

Holton, G. A. "Defining Risk." *Financial Analysts Journal* 60(6) (2004), 19–25.

The Institute Risk of Management. "A Risk Management Standard." (2002). Available at http://www.theirm.org/media/886059/ARMS_2002_IRM.pdf.

Johnson and Johnson. *Framework for Enterprise Risk Management.* (2013). Available at https://www.jnj.com/sites/default/files/pdf/JnJ_RiskMgmt_ERMFramework_guide_v16a.pdf.

Jorion, P. *Big Bets Gone Bad: Derivatives and Bankruptcy in Orange County. The Largest Municipal Failure in U. S. History.* San Diego: Academic Press (1995).

JPMorgan Chase 2017 10-K.

Kahnemann, D. *Thinking, Fast and Slow.* New York: Farrar, Straus, and Giroux (2011).

Kahnemann, D. and Tversky, A. "Prospect Theory: An Analysis of Decisions Under Risk." *Econometrica* 47 (1979), 263–291.

Knight, B. *The Power of Negative Thinking: An Unconventional Approach to Achieving Positive Results* New York: Houghton Mifflin (2013).

Knight, F. *Risk, Uncertainty, and Profit.* Boston: Houghton Mifflin (1921).

Kolb, R. W. *The Financial Crisis of Our Time.* New York: Oxford University Press (2011a).

Kolb, R. W. "Risk Management and Risk Transfer: Distributive Justice in Finance." *The Journal of Alternative Investments* 13(4) (2011b), 90–98.

Lagnado, L. "The Double Mastectomy Rebellion: Defying Doctors, More Women with Breast Cancer Choose Double Mastectomies." *The Wall Street Journal* (July 10, 2015).

Leeson, N. *Rogue Trader: How I Brought Down Barings Bank and Shook the Financial World.* Boston: Little, Brown (1996).

Leland, H. "Agency Costs, Risk Management, and Capital Structure." *The Journal of Finance* 53 (1998), 1213–1243.

Levitt, S. D. and S. J. Dubner. *Freakonomics: A Rogue Economist Explores the Hidden Side of Everything.* New York: William Morrow (2005).

Lewent, J. C. and A. J. Kearney. "Identifying, Measuring, and Hedging Currency Risk at Merck," *Journal of Applied Corporate Finance* 2 (1990), 19–28.

Lewis, M. *Moneyball: The Art of Winning an Unfair Game.* New York: W. W. Norton (2004).

Lowenstein, R. *When Genius Failed: The Rise and Fall of Long-Term Capital Management.* New York: Random House (2000).

Mackay, C. *Extraordinary Popular Delusions and the Madness of Crowds.* London: Richard Bentley (1841).

Marthinsen, J. *Risk Takers: Uses and Abuses of Financial Derivatives.* Boston: Pearson Prentice Hall (2009).

Merton, R. C. "Lifetime Portfolio Selection Under Uncertainty: The Continuous-Time Case." *The Review of Economics and Statistics* 51 (1969), 247–257.

Merton, R. C. "Optimum Consumption and Portfolio Rules in a Continuous-Time Model." *Journal of Economic Theory* 3 (1971), 373–413.

Merton, R. C. "Theory of Rational Option Pricing." *Bell Journal of Economics and Management Science* 4 (1973b), 141–183.

Metrick, A. "A Natural Experiment in 'Jeopardy'" *American Economic Review* 85 (1995), 240–253.

Miller, M. and F. Modigliani. "Dividend Policy, Growth, and the Valuation of Shares." *The Journal of Business* 34 (1961), 411–433.

Modigliani, F. and M. Miller. "The Cost of Capital, Corporation Finance, and the Theory of Investment," *American Economic Review* 48 (1958), 261–297.

Modigliani, F. and M. Miller. "Corporate Income Taxes and the Cost of Capital: A Correction." *American Economic Review* 53 (1963), 433–443.

Mollenkamp, C., S. Ng, L. Pleven, and R. Smith. "Behind AIG's Fall, Risk Models Failed to Pass Real-World Test," *The Wall Street Journal* (October 31, 2008), A1.

National Cancer Institute. "Prostate-Specific Antigen (PSA) Test." National Institute of Health (2012). Available at http://www.cancer.gov/types/prostate/psa-fact-sheet.

National Collegiate Athletic Association Research. "Probability of Competing in Athletics Beyond the High School Interscholastic Level (2018).

National Highway Traffic Safety Administration. *Seat Belts* (2016). https://www.nhtsa.gov/risky-driving/seat-belts.

National Highway Traffic Safety Administration. *Traffic Safety Facts 2016.* United States Department of Transportation (2016). https://www.nhtsa.gov/press-releases/usdot-releases-2016-fatal-traffic-crash-data.

Nasar, S. *A Beautiful Mind: The Life of Mathematical Genius and Nobel Laureate John Nash.* New York: Simon and Schuster (1998).

Nelson, S. A. *The A B C of Options and Arbitrage.* New York: S. A. Nelson (1904). Available at http://books.google.com.

Norris, F. *The Pit: A Story of Chicago.* New York: Doubleday (1903).

Nusbaum, D. "Flying High, Playing Safe." *Risk: Australia and New Zealand Supplement* (August, 1996), 12–15.

Overdahl, J. and B. Schachter "Derivatives Regulation and Risk Management: Lessons from Gibson Greetings." *Financial Management* 24 (1995), 68–78.

Patterson, S. *The Quants: How a New Breed of Math Whizzes Conquered Wall Street and Nearly Destroyed it.* New York: Crown (2010).

Paulos, J. A. *Innumeracy: Mathematical Illiteracy and its Consequences.* New York: Vintage Books (1988).

Power, M. "The Risk Management of Everything." Demos (2004). Available at http://www.demos.co.uk/files/riskmanagementofeverything.pdf.

Protoviti. *Guide to Enterprise Risk Management: Frequently Asked Questions* (2006). Available at http://www.protiviti.com/en-US/Pages/Guide-to-Enterprise-Risk-Mana gement.aspx.

Reinganum, M. R. "Is Time Travel Impossible? A Financial Proof." *Journal of Portfolio Management*, 13 (Fall, 1986), 10–12.

Ropeik, D. and G. Gray. *Risk: A Practical Guide for Deciding What's Really Safe and What's Really Dangerous in the World Around You.* Boston: Houghton Mifflin (2002).

Rosenthal, J. S. *Struck by Lightning: The Curious World of Probabilities.* Toronto: Joseph Henry Press (2006).

Ross, J. F. *The Polar Bear Strategy: Reflections on Risk in Modern Life.* Reading, Mass: Perseus Books (1999).

Rumsfeld, D. News Transcript of Press Conference at NATO Headquarters, Brussels, Belgium. United States Department of Defense (June 6, 2002). Available at http://www.defense.gov/transcripts/transcript.aspx?transcriptid=3490.

Sapienza, P., L. Zingales, and Maestripieri. "Gender Differences in Financial Risk Aversion and Career Choice are Affected by Testosterone." *Proceedings of the National Academy of Sciences of the United States of America* 106 (September 8, 2009), 15268–15273.

Shafer, G. and V. Vovk. *Probability and Finance: It's Only a Game.* New York: Wiley (2001).

Sherden, W. A. *The Fortune Sellers: The Big Business of Buying and Selling Predictions.* New York: Wiley (1999).

Silver, N. *The Signal and the Noise: Why So Many Predictions Fail but Some Don't.* New York: Penguin Press (2012).

Smith, C. and R. Stulz. "The Determinants of Firms' Hedging Policies." *Journal of Financial and Quantitative Analysis* 20 (1985), 391–402.

Smith, D. *Bond Math. The Theory Behind the Formulas.* New York: Wiley (2011).

Smith, D. "Valuing Interest Rate Swaps Using Overnight Indexed Swap (OIS) Discounting." *The Journal of Derivatives* 20 (Summer, 2013), 49–59.

Stossell, J. *Give Me a Break.* New York: Harper Collins (2004).

Svenson, O. "Are We All Less Risky and More Skillful than our Fellow Drivers?" *Acta Psychologica* 47 (1981), 143–148.

Szpiro, G. G. *Pricing the Future: Finance, Physics, and the 300-Year Journey to the Black-Scholes Equation. A Story of Genius and Discovery.* New York: Basic Books (2011).

Taleb, N. N. *The Black Swan: The Impact of the Highly Improbable.* New York: Random House (2007).

Taleb, N. N. *Fooled by Randomness: The Hidden Role of Chance in the Markets and in Life.* New York: Texere (2001).

Taleb, N. N., D. G. Goldstein, and M. W. Sptiznagel. "The Six Mistakes Executives Make in Risk Management." *Harvard Business Review* 87 (October, 2009), 78–81.

Thaler, R. "Toward a Positive Theory of Consumer Choice." *Journal of Economic Behavior and Organization* 1 (1980), 39–60.

Tversky, A. and D. Kahnemann. "Extensional versus Intuitive Reasoning: The Conjunction Fallacy in Probability Judgment." *Psychological Review* 90 (1983), 293–315.

Tversky, A. and D. Kahnemann. "The Framing of Decisions and the Psychology of Choice." *Science* 211 (1981), 453–458.

United States Consumer Product Safety Commission. National Electronic Injury Surveillance System (2017). https://www.cpsc.gov/Research--Statistics/NEISS-Injury-Data.

Index